THE OLD ENGLISH HOMILY

THE OLD ENGLISH HOMILY

Precedent, Practice, and Appropriation

Edited by

Aaron J Kleist

BREPOLS

British Library Cataloguing in Publication Data

The Old English homily : precedent, practice, and appropriation. – (Studies in the early Middle Ages ; v. 17) 1. English prose literature – Old English, ca. 450–1100 – History and criticism 2. Preaching – England – History – Middle Ages, 600–1500 3. Sermons, Medieval – England – History and criticism 4. Sermons, English (Old) – History and criticism 5. Theology – History – Middle Ages, 600–1500 I. Kleist, Aaron J. 829.8'009

ISBN-13: 9782503517926

© 2007, Brepols Publishers n.v., Turnhout, Belgium

D/2007/0095/101
ISBN: 978-2-503-51792-6

Printed in the E.U. on acid-free paper

CONTENTS

Practice

Appropriation

ABBREVIATIONS

ANQ	*American Notes and Queries*
ASE	*Anglo-Saxon England*
ASMMF	Anglo-Saxon Manuscripts in Microfiche Facsimile
Assmann	*Angelsächsische Homilien und Heiligenleben*, ed. by Bruno Assmann, BaP, 3 (Kassel, 1889; repr. Darmstadt, 1964)
BaP	Bibliothek der angelsächsischen Prosa
Bazire-Cross	*Eleven Old English Rogationtide Homilies*, ed. by Joyce Bazire and J. E. Cross (Toronto, 1982; 2nd edn with a new preface, King's College London Medieval Studies, 4, London, 1989)
Belfour	*Twelfth-Century Homilies in MS. Bodley 343*, ed. by Arthur Belfour, EETS: OS, 137 (London, 1909)
Bethurum	*The Homilies of Wulfstan*, ed. by Dorothy Bethurum (Oxford, 1957)
BHL	*Bibliotheca hagiographica Latina antiquae et mediae aetatis*
Blickling	*The Blickling Homilies of the Tenth Century*, ed. by Richard Morris, EETS: OS, 58, 63, 73 (1874–80; repr. in one vol. with corrections, London, 1967)
Brotanek	Rudolf Brotanek, *Texte und Untersuchungen zur altenglischen Literatur und Kirchengeschichte* (Halle, 1913)

CCCM	Corpus Christianorum, Continuatio Mediaevalis (Turnhout, 1966–)
CCSL	Corpus Christianorum, Series Latina (Turnhout, 1953–)
CH I	*Ælfric's Catholic Homilies: The First Series, Text*, ed. by P. A. M. Clemoes, EETS: SS, 17 (Oxford, 1997)
CH II	*Ælfric's Catholic Homilies: The Second Series, Text*, ed. by M. R. Godden, EETS: SS, 5 (London, 1979)
CSASE	Cambridge Studies in Anglo Saxon England
EEMF	Early English Manuscripts in Facsimile
EETS: OS	Early English Text Society: Original Series
EETS: SS	Early English Text Society: Supplementary Series
ES	*English Studies*
Fadda	A. M. Luiselli Fadda, *Nuove omelie anglosassoni della rinascenza benedettina*, Filologia germanica, Testi e studi, 1 (Florence, 1977)
HomM	Homilies for Unspecified Occasions, Unpublished (as designated by Angus Cameron, 'A List of Old English Texts', in *A Plan for the Dictionary of Old English*, ed. by Roberta Frank and Angus Cameron (Toronto, 1973), pp. 25–306; rev. edn in the microfiche *Dictionary of Old English*, F-fascicle, ed. by Antonette DiPaolo Healey and others (Toronto, 2004))
HomS	Homilies for Specified Occasions (as designated by Cameron, 'List of Old English Texts', see HomM above)
HomU	Homilies for Unspecified Occasions, Edited (as designated by Cameron, 'List of Old English Texts', see HomM above)
Irvine	*Old English Homilies from MS Bodley 343*, ed. by Susan Irvine, EETS: OS, 302 (Oxford, 1993)
JEGP	*Journal of English and Germanic Philology*
LS	*Ælfric's Lives of Saints*, ed. by W. W. Skeat, EETS: OS, 76, 82, 94, 114 (London, 1881–1900; repr. as 2 vols, 1966)
MGH	Monumenta Germaniae Historica

MRTS   Medieval and Renaissance Texts and Studies

Napier   *Wulfstan: Sammlung der ihm zugeschriebenen Homilies nebst
                Untersuchungen über ihre Echtheit*, vol. I, *Text und Varianten*, ed.
                by Arthur Napier (1883; repr. with a bibliographical supplement
                by Klaus Ostheeren, Dublin, 1967)

NM   *Neuphilologische Mitteilungen*

NQ   *Notes & Queries*

OEN   *Old English Newsletter*

PL   *Patrologia Latina*, ed. by Jacques-Paul Migne, 221 vols (Paris,
                1844–64)

RES   *Review of English Studies*

SH   *Homilies of Ælfric: A Supplementary Collection*, ed. by John C.
                Pope, EETS: OS, 259–60 (London, 1967–68)

TCBS   *Transactions of the Cambridge Bibliographical Society*

Tristram   *Vier altenglische Predigten aus der heterodoxen Tradition mit
                Kommentar, Übersetzung und Glossar sowie drei weiteren Texten
                im Anhang*, ed. by Hildegard Tristram (Inaugural-dissertation
                Freiburg-im-Breisgau; privately printed, 1970)

Vercelli   *The Vercelli Homilies and Related Texts*, ed. by D. G. Scragg,
                EETS: OS, 300 (Oxford, 1992)

CONTRIBUTORS

CHRISTOPHER ABRAM, University College London
RACHEL ANDERSON, Grand Valley State University
AIDAN CONTI, University of Bergen
THOMAS N. HALL, University of Notre Dame
STEVEN J. HARRIS, University of Massachusetts – Amherst
JOYCE HILL, University of Leeds
AARON J KLEIST, Biola University
ANDY ORCHARD, University of Toronto
MARY P. RICHARDS, University of Delaware
MARY SWAN, University of Leeds
LOREDANA TERESI, University of Palermo
NANCY M. THOMPSON, California State University, East Bay
M. J. TOSWELL, University of Western Ontario
ROBERT K. UPCHURCH, University of North Texas
CHARLES D. WRIGHT, University of Illinois at Urbana-Champaign
SAMANTHA ZACHER, Cornell University

ACKNOWLEDGEMENTS

It is a rare privilege to find one's scholarly interests shared by colleagues of considerable and diverse gifts. When one's field is the dry and dusty domain of Anglo-Saxon homiletics, and one's colleagues move fluidly among more attractive worlds — Old English poetry, Icelandic sagas, Hiberno Latin, or what have you — it is to my mind a privilege rarer still to have them pause their varied pursuits to join an endeavour of this nature. The stage for such research was set several years ago, when under the auspices of the Society for the Study of Anglo-Saxon Homiletics I began to organize sessions at the International Congress on Medieval Studies at Western Michigan University; to such scholars as responded to my siren's call, I am gratefully indebted: Rachel Anderson, Daniel Anlezark, Martin Blake, Stewart Brookes, Aidan Conti, Gabriella Corona, Erika Corradini, Claudia Di Sciacca, Mary Dockray-Miller, Damian Fleming, Michael Fox, Dorothy Haines, Tom Hall, Stephen Harris, Joyce Hill, Tom Hill, Richard Johnson, Joyce Lionarons, Rhonda McDaniel, Jennifer Merriman, Brian Ó'Broin, Dot Porter, Mary Ramsey, Jonathan Randle, Mary Richards, Larry Swain, Mary Swan, Nancy Thompson, Hildegard Tristram, Robert Upchurch, Jonathan Wilcox, Charlie Wright, and Samantha Zacher. Of the work of such scholars I shall always be an avid fan. Of particular distinction, of course, are those who appear as contributors here, having produced new studies tailor-made for this collection; to their number, I am honored to welcome Chris Abram, Andy Orchard, Lori Teresi, and Jane Toswell. I would also express my appreciation for those whose valuable counsel advanced the project, though circumstances beyond their control prevented them from contributing to the final volume: Mary Ramsey, Bill Schipper, Paul Szarmach, Elaine Treharne, and Jonathan Wilcox. Tom Hall it was who initially directed me to Brepols Publishers, where Luc Jocqué and Simon Forde showed themselves more than patient in waiting for the project's culmination. My thanks are further due to the Editorial Board of the Studies in the Early Middle Ages series, and in particular to my gracious and gifted senior editor, Elizabeth Tyler. Patricia Taylor and Matthew Smith were indispensable proofreaders, catching many a detail which my aging eyes could not. Deborah A. Oosterhouse, true to her reputation, evinced consummate skill as our copyeditor. And finally, there is the one whose selfless efforts undergird as ever my long labours: my love and Lady, Amanda Kleist.

Opus manuum nostrarum confirma (Psalm 89. 17)
Aaron J Kleist

INTRODUCTION

The quarter century that has passed since Paul E. Szarmach and Bernard F. Huppé's groundbreaking *The Old English Homily and its Backgrounds* (Albany, 1978) has seen remarkable changes in the field of Anglo-Saxon homiletics. Primary materials, to begin with, have become accessible to scholars in unprecedented levels. Critical editions of homilies from Ælfric, Wulfstan, the Vercelli Book, and the Blickling manuscript have appeared in both traditional print and hypertext media. The *Dictionary of Old English* project at the University of Toronto has made the entire Old English corpus available in electronic form. The digitization of manuscripts at such institutions as the British Library has made it possible for scholars to recover readings previously invisible to the naked eye. The re-editing of patristic and continental writings in series such as Brepols's Corpus Christianorum Series Latina has brought a new level of linguistic and palaeographic precision to writings once available only in Jean-Paul Migne's *Patrologia Latina*, and electronic versions of these databases have had a revolutionary impact on the identification of Anglo-Saxon sources. This wealth of primary material has generated a flood of secondary scholarship. In the past two decades, hundreds of studies have been published on Ælfric alone — nearly as many studies, in fact, as were produced in the history of Ælfrician scholarship surveyed by Luke Reinsma up to 1983.[1] Homiletics, far from being a narrow avenue of inquiry, has proved a

---

[1] Reinsma, *Ælfric: An Annotated Bibliography* (New York, 1987); see now Aaron J Kleist, 'An Annotated Bibliography of Ælfrician Studies, 1983–1996', in *Old English Prose: Basic Readings*, ed. by Paul E. Szarmach, Basic Readings in Anglo-Saxon England, 5 (New York, 2000), pp. 503–52; Kleist, 'Ælfric's Corpus: A Conspectus', *Florilegium*, 18 (2001), 113–64; and for scholarship post-2001, the Prose section of the *Year's Work in Old English Studies*, ed. by Daniel Donoghue (Kalamazoo, 2004–).

wide umbrella covering a far-flung range of interests: Anglo-Saxon educational practice, Anglo-Saxon theology, the interplay of Christian and pagan practice, palaeographical and codicological concerns, Anglo-Saxon theories of translation, questions of author and authorial intent, source studies, rhetoric and style, linguistics and philology, the early role of women in scholarship, and the reuse and study of Old English homilies in post-Conquest and Elizabethan England, just to name a few. While other factors have contributed to this productivity, increased pressures regarding publication certainly being among them, the fact remains that considerable interest has been shown by scholars in this area of Anglo-Saxon literature. The time has come for a new *Old English Homily*, one that serves both as an introduction to key figures and issues in the field and as a model of studies for the next quarter century.

The entries in this volume are largely interrelated, exploring the sources of Anglo-Saxon homilies, the homilies themselves, and their impact from diverse but complementary perspectives.[2] Nonetheless, the volume has been structured along certain themes. The first five essays consider various contexts of and influences on Anglo-Saxon homilies: patristic and early medieval Latin sources, continental homiliaries and preaching practices, traditions of Old Testament interpretation and adaptation, and the liturgical setting of preaching texts. Six studies then turn our focus to the sermons themselves, examining style and rhetoric in the Vercelli homilies, the codicology of the Blickling Book, *sanctorale* and *temporale* in the works of Ælfric, and the challenges posed by Wulfstan's self-referential corpus. Finally, the last entries take us past the Conquest to discuss the reuse of homiletic material in England and its environs from the eleventh to the eighteenth centuries.

Precedent

Charles D. Wright opens the volume with a foundational introduction to the relationship of 'Old English Homilies and Latin Sources'. Few vernacular sermons, he notes, are without ties to patristic or early medieval Latin antecedents, and the past decades have seen major advances in the identification of such sources. Such exploration has limits, of course: even where borrowings can be confirmed with certainty — and only rarely is such the case — they may reveal little, for example,

---

[2] While here the terms *homily* and *sermon* are used interchangeably, certain studies below employ them in their technical sense, using *sermon* to refer to catechesis or general moral instruction while reserving *homily* for exegesis or systematic exposition of scriptural texts.

about the contexts and purposes behind their reuse. Even so, source study provides vital evidence for concerns fundamental to Old English scholarship. Taking the anonymous homilies as his focus, Wright considers general issues related to source scholarship — the importance of identifying 'compelling' verbal parallels, establishing a clear chronology for the relevant texts, considering possible intermediate stages in the transmission of ideas, and so on — before showing in detail how the study of Latin sources has furthered our understanding of the Old English homily in seven key areas: textual criticism, literary history, authorship, chronology, literacy and audience, intellectual history, and stylistic analysis. Finally, for scholars new to the field, he provides a bibliographical orientation to the surviving anonymous corpus and to major milestones in source scholarship.

Next, a consideration of the continental roots of Insular homilies comes from Joyce Hill, who offers a provisional analysis of 'Ælfric's Manuscript of Paul the Deacon's Homiliary'. In speaking of this enormously influential collection, which impacted late Anglo-Saxon England particularly through the work of Ælfric, Hill begins by reviewing scholarly efforts to reconstruct the original form of the homiliary ('PD') as against the later and heavily edited version of the compilation printed by Migne ('PDM'). Identifying the form or forms of Paul's work present in England during the Benedictine Reform likewise poses a challenge: as extant Anglo-Saxon versions of PD date only from the eleventh century and are in any case incomplete, Hill highlights the importance of source studies in determining the nature of PD as it circulated during the time of Ælfric. She also sets forth the limitations of this approach: on the one hand, the intertextuality (and thus similarity) of continental materials available to Insular writers makes it difficult to identify conclusively at any point that PD was a homilist's source. On the other hand, should an author not draw on a PD homily in his writing, one should not necessarily conclude that the homily was not available to him: other factors may well have influenced the Insular author's selection. Moving from the issue of the content to the structure of Insular version(s) of PD, Hill discusses the liturgical problem of reconciling feasts celebrated at fixed times (the *sanctorale*, based on the solar calendar) with others which were variable (the *temporale*, such as Easter, based on the lunar calendar). Early revisions to PD's system for designating liturgical dates, revisions that were likely retained in the copies of PD brought to England, would have allowed Ælfric easily to cross-reference PD with other continental homiliaries such as those of Smaragdus and Haymo. Finally, Hill reviews the surviving evidence for versions of PD written or owned in England up to 1100. Though all postdate Ælfric, Hill suggests that well-established characteristics therein may represent earlier alterations present in Ælfric's version of PD as well.

Nancy M. Thompson's study of 'The Carolingian *De festiuitatibus* and the Blickling Book' continues Hill's European focus by addressing continental traditions of preaching to laity and the possible influence of such practice on the production of Anglo-Saxon homiletic collections. Her particular concern is the capitula *De festiuitatibus*, Carolingian legislation issued by royal and episcopal authorities delineating major feasts to be celebrated through the year. Examining a range of such works from the ninth century, Thompson finds that while some appear in the context of instruction for secular clergy, most discuss ways in which feasts should be celebrated by the laity, associating these feasts, moreover, with the reading of homilies. Granted, the degree to which such prescriptions were carried out is debatable: Thompson suggests that public preaching was likely promoted in areas where the Church had long been established, while areas with poorer resources were hampered by lack of priestly education. Nonetheless, she argues that the emphasis in *De festiuitatibus* legislation on preaching to laity at major feasts would have provided a natural impetus to the creation of homiliaries for this setting. This said, the impact of such precedent on English practice is not straightforward: when copies of Carolingian *De festiuitatibus* find their way to tenth-century England in the context of the Benedictine Reform, most appear amidst texts regulating monastic life. In other words, these injunctions regarding feasts may have been studied for their implications for monks rather than for preaching to laity. Noting, however, that other Insular copies of *De festiuitatibus* appear in manuscripts with links to the secular Church, Thompson suggests that later reformers may have drawn on *De festiuitatibus* when considering the instructional needs of their lay congregations.

In addition to patristic sources and continental precedent, one of the greatest influences on Anglo-Saxon sermons was of course the Bible itself. Over three hundred years before Wycliffe and half a millennium before Luther, English writers were translating scripture and adapting the Bible to produce instructional material in the vernacular. Rachel Anderson's 'The Old Testament Homily: Ælfric as Biblical Translator' considers ways in which one of the foremost agents of such translation drew on the Old Testament for pedagogical purposes. Reviewing the state of scholarship regarding Ælfric's Old Testament sermons and his contributions to the *Hexateuch*, the first seven books of the Bible in Old English, Anderson focuses on what Milton Gatch calls Ælfric's 'non-liturgical narrative pieces', such as his translations of the biblical books Judges and Kings. Anderson shows not only how Ælfric's interpretive treatment of the material allows him to comment on social and political matters, but how Ælfric's emendations reveal his standards of storytelling and sensitivity to narrative style.

Steven J. Harris's 'The Liturgical Context of Ælfric's Homilies for Rogation' addresses a subject on which little advance in scholarship has been made since decades-old studies by Milton Gatch and Mary Clayton: the liturgical setting of preaching texts and its influence on Anglo-Saxon homilies.[3] Citing comments from Augustine, Amalarius of Metz, and Benedict of Aniane, Harris highlights the emphasis placed by such figures on the need for liturgical coherence: should the elements of liturgy for a particular occasion not complement one another theologically, it was argued, the result might not simply be discordant but endangering to the soul. Given this tradition, and Ælfric's care in his *Catholic Homilies* to expound readings for the liturgical day, Harris reasonably argues that it would be unsurprising to find the homilies reflecting themes from the liturgy proper. Focussing on Ælfric's sermons for Rogation, the feast of atonement, and then on the symbolism of the prayers and progressions of Rogation itself, he shows that subjects emphasized by the latter appear prominently in the former: the need for prayer, the value of poverty, the fundamentals of the faith, and the importance of good works, among others. While individually the topics may be commonplaces of Christian teaching in general, their convergence here in both liturgy and sermon Harris is reluctant to find coincidental. Rather, he suggests that the liturgy — whether quoted verbatim or not — may prove a more fertile ground of homiletic source-material than hitherto supposed.

Practice

Turning from contexts and influences to the homilies themselves, Samantha Zacher's 'Rereading the Style and Rhetoric of the Vercelli Homilies' calls our attention not to traditional concerns of homiletic content, sources, and manuscript context, but to the lesser-explored areas of rhetoric and form — subjects particularly elusive in the case of the Vercelli homilies, with their markedly disparate compositional styles. Following a helpful overview of the collection and introduction to scholarly work thereon, Zacher narrows her focus to stylistic analyses of the homilies, highlighting burgeoning recent interest in 'poetic' features of homiletic prose. Such features she then showcases in a detailed examination of Vercelli XVII, an exegetical homily for Candlemas. She shows that the homilist, freely adapting

---

[3] Milton McC. Gatch, *Preaching and Theology in Anglo-Saxon England: Ælfric and Wulfstan* (Toronto, 1977); Mary Clayton, 'Homiliaries and Preaching in Anglo-Saxon England', *Peritia*, 4 (1985), 207–42.

his biblical source, creates internal resonances and rhetorical power through the repetition of words and word-elements in the text, offering in the process both sophisticated typology and a straightforward message. Moreover, comparing the text to the only other surviving Old English sermon for the day, Ælfric's *CH* I.9, Zacher suggests that the texts' unusual handling of the gospel story may reflect either a common source or the influence of a shared liturgical tradition. Her study challenges the assumption, however, that all such sources must be identified before meaningful analysis of vernacular homilies can be performed: not only can inferences be drawn from a homilist's departure from such sources as are known (in this case, scripture), but valuable insights may be gained by comparing stylistic features within a homiletic collection and within the wider Old English corpus.

Another major anonymous homiletic collection comes into view in 'Blickling Unbound: The Codicology of Anglo-Saxon Homiletic Manuscripts'; here, M. J. Toswell highlights the importance of examining not only authors, themes, and sources but the individual manuscript collections in which most surviving vernacular sermons are found. Focussing on the Blickling Homilies, she notes not only the paucity of studies related to the collection but the degree to which it has suffered by comparison to homilies by Ælfric, particularly due to a perceived lack in Blickling of internal consistency. She also points, however, to scholarship arguing that certain homiliaries were compiled out of booklets, these differing markedly from one another in such features as punctuation. Outlining the irregular arrangement of the Blickling Homilies into quires and the extent to which these quires vary in their punctuation, Toswell identifies seven booklets that jointly comprise the collection. Given the striking dissimilarity among them, she concludes that they were copied over some time from different exemplars as they became available, not according to a predetermined organizational strategy. In consequence, she states, comparison with collections crafted by a single mind such as Ælfric's is unwarranted and misleading: rather than seeking for continuity between the homilies or an overarching vision behind them, scholars ought to appreciate the composite nature not just of the homilies but of the collection as a whole.

Moving from anonymous to known authors, Thomas N. Hall's 'Latin Sermons for Saints in Early English Homiliaries and Legendaries' shines light on a key question facing students of early English monasticism: what homiletic treatments of saints would monastic communities such as that of Ælfric of Eynsham have encountered in the Night Office? While considerable progress has been made in identifying hagiographic material available to the Anglo-Saxons that would have been appropriate for celebrating saints' feasts, Ælfric himself points out that sermons as well as lives or passions might be read to celebrate saints in the Night

Office. Noting that the bulk of Latin homiletic collections were likely compiled for this setting rather than for lay preaching or private devotion, Hall painstakingly sets about piecing together precisely what material was written or adapted for festal occasions, and the ways in which English writers departed from continental precedent in the process.

Another side to Ælfric's homiletic endeavour comes from Robert K. Upchurch, who provides insight into 'Homiletic Contexts for Ælfric's Hagiography' in Ælfric's *Legend of Cecilia* (*LS* II.34). Upchurch notes that while the *Legend of Cecilia* is not a sermon and may not itself have been preached, the text may better be understood in light of Ælfric's wider homiletic material and concerns. Like the sermons, the *Legend* addresses doctrinal issues Ælfric considers fundamental to Christian belief. As with the sermons, Ælfric alters aspects of his Latin sources to clarify and foreground such theological matters. Together with the sermons, Ælfric's hagiography may form part of his agenda for ecclesiastical reform. Even more than the sermons, moreover, the *Legend* may reveal an understanding of believers as 'spiritual mothers' who are called to teach the truths of the faith — whether those believers be clerical or (an astonishing proposition) lay. Through such connections, Upchurch offers a broader perspective with which to view such hagiographic works: even where stories of saints sharing their faith were not 'preached', he suggests, to the extent that they model preaching for believers, they participate in a larger homiletic tradition.

Loredana Teresi's study of 'The Making of a *Temporale* Collection in Late Anglo-Saxon England' calls scholars to reconsider Ælfric's responsibility for three manuscripts hitherto closely associated with him: Cambridge, Corpus Christi College, MS 302; London, British Library, Cotton MS Faustina A. IX; and Cambridge, University Library, MS Ii. 4. 6. Ranging from the middle of the eleventh to the first half of the twelfth century, these manuscripts represented for Peter Clemoes both the fourth phase (δ) of Ælfric's development of the First Series of *Catholic Homilies* and a major reorganization of *temporale* homilies around 1002–05 that he called TH I. Ælfric's responsibility for the ancestor(s) of these manuscripts was challenged by John Pope, who argued that errors in the collections pointed to a faulty ancestor at some remove from Ælfric. Teresi, however, suggests a third possibility: noting that the Ælfrician material in the collections, while similar, corresponds directly to the *temporale* items for the period in question from Ælfric's *Catholic Homilies* and *Lives of Saints*, she argues that the *temporale* series in CUL Ii. 4. 6 and in the ancestor of CCCC 302 and Cotton Faustina A. IX may have been compiled independently by others, perhaps at Canterbury, with access to the *Catholic Homilies* and *Lives of Saints*. Her argument challenges a major aspect of Clemoes's larger theories regarding the development, chronology, and dissemination of Ælfric's works, and as such implicitly calls for a wider re-examination of these foundational tenets of Ælfrician scholarship.

Transitioning from Ælfric to his ecclesiastical superior and counterpart, Andy Orchard offers an array of avenues for approaching the writings of Wulfstan, Archbishop of York, in his consideration of 'Wulfstan as Reader, Writer, and Re-writer'. Situating the Archbishop in the volatile political context of late tenth- and early eleventh-century England, Orchard turns to Wulfstan's homilies to illustrate not only the latter's possible frustration with his secular superiors but the manuscript complexity and challenge of dating Wulfstan's works. Even the boundaries of Wulfstan's homiletic canon, Orchard notes, are difficult to establish: on the one hand, imitation of Wulfstan's writings by contemporaries and later authors problematizes the process of establishing which are authentic, while on the other hand, Wulfstan's tendency towards exhortative catechesis regardless of genre draws into question which texts precisely should be deemed homiletic. One issue much discussed in conjunction with this problem of attribution is that of Wulfstan's style, whether in terms of specific techniques of repetition and variation or of Wulfstan's wholesale reappropriation of his own material. Additionally, scholars have focussed on particular themes that characterize Wulfstan's work, such as the need for bishops in troubled times to call the people to repentance and righteousness. Finally, students of Wulfstan's writings have found his relationship and debt to Ælfric a rewarding avenue of inquiry. While underscoring the unfairness of comparing the two in terms of style or approach to source material, Orchard examines a hitherto-unrecognized borrowing from Ælfric by the Archbishop, analysing the ways in which Wulfstan reworks Ælfric's prose using phrases characteristic to his preaching corpus. Though challenges may hinder both the identification and the appreciation of Wulfstan's writings, therefore, this study shows how analysis of style, theme, and intertextuality may help 'to capture a character who clearly dominated his age' (p. 314).

Appropriation

Building on studies in the previous section of this volume, Mary P. Richards's 'Old Wine in a New Bottle: Recycled Instructional Materials in *Seasons for Fasting*' moves from Anglo-Saxon homilists and their adapters to consider one example of late Old English poetry that echoes those homilists' concerns, sources, and compositional methods. Situating the work in the wider context of eleventh-century poetry, a body of material she describes as noteworthy for its 'prosaic' form and subject matter, Richards traces *Seasons for Fasting*'s treatment of the dating of Ember fasts, the observance of Lent, and the poor example of gluttonous priests, before examining the poem's sources. Here, in addition to previously established links between *Seasons for Fasting* and Alcuin's *De uirtutibus et uitiis*, she finds repeated connections to collections of homiletic and ecclesiastical works such as Oxford, Bodleian Library, MSS Hatton 113, Hatton 114, and Junius 121 — manuscripts all associated with eleventh-century Worcester — as well as to versions of Wulfstan's 'Commonplace Book'. While suggesting the possibility of the author's connection to Wulfstan's circle, therefore, Richards underscores the originality of the writer's achievement. By offering its message in poetry rather than prose, *Seasons for Fasting* not only parallels but extends Old English homilists' composite compositional methods.

Further insight into the lasting nature of the post-Conquest homiletic tradition is offered by Aidan Conti in 'The Circulation of the Old English Homily in the Twelfth Century'. He argues that the importance of the vernacular in twelfth-century literature is better assessed not by the (highly limited) production of new works in English, but by the 'sustained and profound interest' in English works evidenced by the ongoing reuse of Old English works. His case in point is the complex collection of material in Oxford, Bodleian Library, MS Bodley 343. The manuscript is valuable on a number of counts, particularly for preserving unique copies, major reworkings, or the sole twelfth-century witnesses to various Anglo-Saxon texts. In addition, however, in a series of little-studied Latin homilies, it reproduces a version of the Carolingian Homiliary of Angers, a work copied and translated into Old English in the eleventh-century Taunton fragments. While little analysis has been done of the homiliary's style, sources, and audience, Conti notes that the material is frequently catechetical rather than exegetical, suggests that the existing exegesis is original (if commonplace) rather than patristically derived, and argues that it was compiled as a series of notes or outlines to aid preachers delivering vernacular sermons to laity. Furthermore, pointing to yet another witness to the Homiliary of Angers, the thirteenth-century Cambridge, St John's College, MS C. 12, Conti concludes that the Bodley 343 collection reflects not antiquarian interests as much as contemporary need — a live, ongoing tradition of English preaching. Taken in conjunction with the Old English material elsewhere in the manuscript, Bodley 343 thus attests to the lasting importance of traditional homiletic works in the centuries following the Conquest.

Continuing in the thirteenth century, Mary Swan's 'Preaching Past the Conquest' examines two of the last Insular manuscripts to contain Old English homilies: London, Lambeth Palace Library, MS 487 and London, British Library, Cotton MS Vespasian A. XXII. The manuscripts present strikingly different portraits of the late treatment of vernacular homiletic material. Lambeth 487, on the one hand, modifies material from Ælfric in ways unparalleled in other copies of his works; conspicuously adds Latin quotations (or space for such quotations) to lend authority to or prompt further English exegesis; and includes a series of mistakes and inconsistencies of layout that raise questions about exactly where, by whom, and for what purpose such material was produced. Cotton Vespasian A. XXII, on the other hand, includes a series of Old English texts 'intended to be seen and valued' (p. 414). While the combination of pieces here is found in no other manuscript, and while the ruling for the quire is nearly unique for vernacular homilies, Swan draws connections both between these texts and other collections from Rochester, and between Cotton Vespasian A. XXII and Lambeth 487 as well. As a result, she highlights not only possible connections between Rochester and the West Midlands, but the possibility of a wider network in which Old English homilies were exchanged and adapted during this late post-Conquest period.

Christopher Abram's 'Anglo-Saxon Homilies in their Scandinavian Context' shifts our focus geographically as well as temporally to consider the wider reception and use of Anglo-Saxon homilies outside of England. In medieval Norway and Iceland, Abram explains, the Insular homiletic tradition directly influenced the development of vernacular preaching and devotional material in at least three ways: through the importing to Scandinavia of homiletic manuscripts, a reliance on Old English and Latin works as source material, and the incorporation of Insular rhetorical and stylistic techniques in Old Norse-Icelandic sermons. Though the surviving corpus of these sermons is small, they remain a rich field for scholarly investigation: numbers remain unedited, their influence on other genres has largely gone unexplored, and the ways in which their sources were transmitted all too often remains a mystery. Abram surveys the evidence for the export of homilies to Scandinavia, examines Latin texts of English provenance that served as sources for Scandinavian sermons, discusses rhetorical and stylistic influences of the Insular homiletic tradition, and posits potential routes of homiletic dissemination, calling for further exploration of the transmission of literary culture between these communities after the Conquest.

Finally, we come to Aaron J Kleist's consideration of 'Anglo-Saxon Homiliaries in Tudor and Stuart England', which rounds off the volume by focussing on Anglo-

Saxon studies in the early modern period. If the history of homiletic composition
and use in pre- and post-Conquest England is complex, he notes, scarcely less so is
the history of these homiliaries following Henry VIII's dissolution of the monasteries. While some of the forty-two surviving collections of sermons were associated (as one would expect) with such well-known figures as Matthew Parker and
John Joscelyn, the others passed through a remarkable panoply of hands over the
two centuries of Tudor and Stuart reign. Over three dozen figures, in fact — politicians, courtiers, archbishops, knights, jurists, heralds, historians, and antiquaries
— arguably or demonstrably held volumes of Old English homilies in their hands.
Kleist notes a number of challenges that confront those seeking to impose order on
such diversity of material and persons: the lack of consensus as to what precisely
constitutes a 'homiliary', the limits to which one can establish by whom and to
what degree homiliaries were used, and the difficulty of distinguishing between
'early' and 'later' interest in Anglo-Saxon matters when all too often figures overlap
between the Elizabethan and Jacobean ages. Such issues aside, however, Kleist's
survey offers a starting point and reference for more detailed work in future by
those interested in the early modern history of Anglo-Saxon homilies.

     As an additional aid for students of these works, an appendix, 'Anglo-Saxon
Homiliaries as Designated by Ker', begins to address the question of what may be
said to constitute the corpus of Anglo-Saxon homiliaries. In the absence of any
categorical definition of the term — the minimum number of items required to
constitute a homiletic collection, the precise qualities requisite to call a piece
'homiletic', and so on — the appendix delineates those collections of sermons
which N. R. Ker designates as homiliaries in his *Catalogue of Manuscripts Containing Anglo-Saxon*. This list provides not only a useful framework for an introductory survey of such manuscripts, but offers a method for organization: Ker
groups homiliaries into (1) ordered collections for the whole or for part of a year,
distinguishing further between (1a) *temporale* and *sanctorale*, (1b) *temporale* only,
and (1c) *sanctorale* only; (2) collections containing items of *temporale* or of *sanctorale* in disorder; and (3) collections for general occasions. Kleist acknowledges that
the categories are sometimes reductive, inasmuch as Anglo-Saxon collections are
not always known to reflect clear logical lines. He points to mixed collections of
homilies for both specified and general occasions, for which Ker's categories do not
well account, as well as other bodies of homiletic material which might arguably be
included in Ker's list. Despite such difficulties, however, the groups are conceptually helpful and therefore here retained. Forty-two homiletic collections in some
thirty-six manuscripts are listed along with date, origin, and provenance, where

known; a brief summary of contents; and a list of published descriptions.[4] Taken with the rest of the volume, such material seeks to serve in some measure as an introduction, insight, and inspiration to future scholars of the multifaceted creation that is the Old English homily.

---

[4] A fuller account of these homiliaries, noting homiletic and additional contents, their relationship to other manuscripts, and their post-dissolution use, is forthcoming by Kleist.

Precedent

OLD ENGLISH HOMILIES AND LATIN SOURCES

Charles D. Wright

Most Old English homilies draw on Latin sources, especially Latin sermons and homilies, but also biblical commentaries, doctrinal treatises, saints' lives, and other genres. The typical (though variable) structural elements of the Old English homily[1] were set by patristic, early medieval, and Carolingian models, which often supplied the Anglo-Saxon preacher with the bulk of the matter for his text as well as its organizing form.[2] In the case of 'composite' homilies that borrow from pre-existing vernacular homilies[3] the relation to Latin antecedents may be indirect, but relatively few Old English homilies are entirely independent of Latin sources, and many are direct translations of a Latin source or of multiple Latin sources. The recovery of these sources has been one of the great

---

[1] For a survey of the structure of Old English homilies, see D. R. Letson, 'The Form of the Old English Homily', *American Benedictine Review*, 30 (1979), 399–431; see also Paul E. Szarmach, 'The Vercelli Homilies: Style and Structure', in *The Old English Homily and its Backgrounds*, ed. by Szarmach and Bernard F. Huppé (Albany, 1978), pp. 241–67. Recurrent elements include quotation of the pericope (the biblical passage assigned to a given feast); an address to a congregation; an exposition of the pericope, or some combination of doctrinal exposition, moral admonition, or exemplary narration; and a concluding doxology.

[2] See Thomas N. Hall, 'The Early Medieval Sermon', in *The Sermon*, ed. by Beverly M. Kienzle, Typologie des sources du moyen âge occidental, 81–83 (Turnhout, 2000), pp. 203–69, and Hall, 'A Basic Bibliography of Medieval Sermon Studies', *Medieval Sermon Studies*, 36 (1995), 26–42.

[3] The standard guide to the anonymous homilies and to their overlapping material is D. G. Scragg, 'The Corpus of Vernacular Homilies and Prose Saints' Lives before Ælfric', *ASE*, 8 (1979), 223–77, repr. with addenda in *Old English Prose: Basic Readings*, ed. by Paul E. Szarmach, Basic Readings in Anglo-Saxon England, 5 (New York, 2000), pp. 73–150. See also Scragg's entry 'Anonymous Old English Homilies', in *Sources of Anglo-Saxon Literary Culture: A Trial Version*, ed. by Frederick M. Biggs, Thomas D. Hill, and Paul E. Szarmach (Binghamton, 1990), pp. 124–30.

undertakings — and one of the great successes — of Old English literary scholarship since the late nineteenth century, but it is still unfinished business. Even if all the written sources used by Anglo-Saxon homilists were found, or could be found, the business of understanding how the homilists used them, and for what purposes, and in what historical contexts, would not be finished. Source study (like every approach) has limitations, but it supports many fundamental concerns of Old English scholarship, including, among others, textual criticism, literary history, intellectual history, and stylistic analysis. After some general comments on the terminology and methodological assumptions of source scholarship in the first part of this essay, therefore, the second part discusses how knowledge of Latin sources has contributed to our understanding of the Old English homily in each of these areas.[4] I have chosen to focus throughout on anonymous homilies, and provide in the third part a bibliographical orientation to the surviving corpus of texts and to the pertinent source scholarship.

Sources and Source Scholarship: Definitions and Assumptions

My understanding of what the term 'source' can mean will be clarified, I hope, from the context of my discussion of source scholarship on the anonymous homilies, but a suitable working definition has been proposed by Thomas D. Hill: 'a text that provides the antecedent for some significant portion of a derivative (or if one prefers "target") text'.[5] Hill's use of the term 'antecedent' potentially

---

[4] For previous general discussions of source scholarship, see J. E. Cross, 'The Literate Anglo-Saxon – On Sources and Disseminations', *Proceedings of the British Academy*, 58 (1972), 67–100; Thomas D. Hill, 'Introduction', in *Sources of Anglo-Saxon Literary Culture*, vol. I: *Abbo of Fleury, Abbo of Saint-Germain-des-Prés, and Acta Sanctorum*, ed. by Frederick M. Biggs, Thomas D. Hill, Paul E. Szarmach, and E. Gordon Whatley (Kalamazoo, 2001), pp. xv–xxxiii; Clare Lees, 'Working with Patristic Sources: Language and Context in Old English Homilies', in *Speaking Two Languages: Traditional Disciplines and Contemporary Theory in Medieval Studies*, ed. by Allen J. Frantzen (Albany, 1991), pp. 157–80 and 264–76; Katherine O'Brien O'Keeffe, 'Source, Method, Theory, Practice: On Reading Two Old English Verse Texts', *Bulletin of the John Rylands University Library of Manchester*, 76 (1994), 51–73, repr. with addenda in *Textual and Material Culture in Anglo-Saxon England: Thomas Northcote Toller and the Toller Memorial Lectures,* ed. by Donald Scragg (Cambridge, 2003), pp. 161–81; and D. G. Scragg, 'Source Study', in *Reading Old English Texts*, ed. by Katherine O'Brien O'Keeffe (Cambridge, 1997), pp. 39–58.

[5] Hill, 'Introduction', p. xviii. Hill does not exclude orally transmitted 'sources' (see p. xx), but *Fontes Anglo-Saxonici* (see p. 65 below) specifically restricts its definition to written texts (cf. Scragg, 'Source Study', p. 40). Theoretically one could extend the concept of 'source' to include

embraces indirect or ultimate sources as well as direct or immediate ones, but since in what follows it will often be necessary to distinguish between them, I will adopt D. G. Scragg's distinction between immediate sources, 'the text[s] which the author had before him or her', and antecedent sources, the texts 'which the author of the immediate source was using, or those at an even greater distance'.[6]

The initial identification of a Latin text as a source for an Old English text is normally based on verbal correspondences that are too distinctive and extensive to be coincidental.[7] To be sure, an author might derive an idea from a source without directly translating or echoing its verbal formulation; yet without the control provided by verbal parallels, the burden of proof must be higher, since an argument based on similarity of idea alone will be more susceptible to special pleading. This is not to say that verbal parallels are 'objective', only that they are often easier to evaluate and less likely to be coincidental.

A proposed source must also demonstrably or arguably pre-date its alleged derivative. Since many texts are not securely dated it is not always easy to establish relative chronology, but the vast majority of the proposed sources of Old English homilies are Christian-Latin texts known to have been written sometime in the patristic age through the Carolingian period, so limit-cases, whether real or hypothetical, are special cases that need not detain us here.

Even when a source has been established on the basis of compelling verbal parallels and secure relative chronology, the possibility that it was transmitted through intermediaries must always be considered. Patristic texts were extensively quoted and redacted by later authors, and extracted in florilegia.[8] We know, for example, that Gregory the Great's *Homiliae in Euangelia* XVI is the source for much of Blickling III on the Temptation of Christ, yet there are indications that the Blickling homilist did not consult it as transmitted integrally in the manuscripts of Gregory's gospel homilies, or even in a standard homiliary such as Paul the Deacon's, but rather in a redacted and augmented form bundled with Hiberno-Latin commentary on the same pericope from Matthew.[9] Again, the introduction

a homilist's material culture, social milieu, and lived experience — but then it would mean everything, and nothing.

[6] Scragg, 'Source Study', p. 40.

[7] For further discussion of the role of textual parallels, see Hill, 'Introduction', pp. xvi–xvii.

[8] For medieval redactions of patristic texts, see J. Machielsen, *Clavis Patristica Pseudepigraphorum Medii Aevi*, vols I–III (Turnhout, 1990–2003).

[9] The Gregorian source was identified by Max Förster, 'Zu den Blickling Homilies', *Archiv*, 91 (1893), 179–206 (p. 180). For the Hiberno-Latin material (including some recycled patristic

to a Rogationtide homily (Bazire-Cross 7) is clearly based on Alcuin's *De uirtutibus et uitiis*, yet most of the homily is demonstrably composite. While it is possible that the homilist translated directly from a Latin source in just this one passage, Clare Lees's suggestion that he was drawing on an intermediary (indeed probably a vernacular one) is more consistent with his 'habitual method of composition'.[10] In cases such as these, the Latin text is the antecedent source, even if its original wording was transmitted with little alteration by the immediate source.

While some Latin texts, especially those by the major church fathers, had a relatively fixed original form that persisted and can readily be distinguished from non-authorial redactions, others, like many anonymous, pseudonymous, and apocryphal texts, have no standard, authoritative version. The *Apocalypse of Thomas*, for example, survives in interpolated, non-interpolated, and abbreviated recensions, with considerable textual variation even among the manuscripts of each recension. Though all four independent Old English translations seem to be based on interpolated versions, and though most of their readings are parallelled in at least one interpolated text, none follows precisely any single surviving Latin version. The Old English versions of *Thomas*, in other words, presuppose the existence of still more variant Latin texts.[11]

To paraphrase the coastguard in *Beowulf*, the prudent source-scholar who considers well must be conscious of the distinction between words and works. We may be able to identify a particular sequence of words that an Anglo-Saxon author was

---

quotations), see Charles D. Wright, 'Blickling Homily III on the Temptations in the Desert', *Anglia*, 106 (1988), 130–37. Parallels with Napier LV, Irvine V, and Ælfric, *CH* I.11 show that Gregory's homily must have circulated in a redacted form with some distinctive additions (though only Blickling III also appends the Hiberno-Latin material); see especially Susan Irvine, ed., *Old English Homilies from MS Bodley 343*, EETS: OS, 302 (Oxford, 1993), pp. 116–22, who posits as a common source a collection of materials for Lent that combined a form of Gregory's homily with verse-by-verse exegesis of Matthew 4. 1–11, the pericope for Quadragesima Sunday. On these Lenten homilies, see now Elaine Treharne, 'The Life and Times of Old English Homilies for the First Sunday in Lent', in *The Power of Words: Anglo-Saxon Studies Presented to Donald G. Scragg on his Seventieth Birthday*, ed. by Hugh Magennis and Jonathan Wilcox (Morgantown, WV, 2006), pp. 205–40.

[10] Lees, 'The Dissemination of Alcuin's *De Virtutibus et Vitiis Liber* in Old English: A Preliminary Survey', *Leeds Studies in English*, n.s., 16 (1985), 174–89 (pp. 177–78).

[11] See Charles D. Wright, '*The Apocalypse of Thomas*: Some New Latin Texts and their Significance for the Old English Versions', in *Apocryphal Texts and Traditions in Anglo-Saxon England*, ed. by Kathryn Powell and Donald Scragg (Cambridge, 2003), pp. 27–64. Hill, 'Introduction', p. xxii, refers to *Thomas* as an example of a text 'that did not circulate in a single authorized version'.

translating or adapting in a given passage without being able to identify the precise work, or the precise form of a work, that transmitted it to him. Not only might a work circulate in a variety of forms, but a particular sequence of words might occur in multiple works (what J. E. Cross termed a 'dissemination').[12] A good example is a motif found in Bazire-Cross 9 (lines 1–5), which admonishes its audience to understand that our habitation (*eard*) in this world is like that of someone who lives in another man's house and doesn't know on what day he might be told, 'Go out, because this is not your house in which you dwell; you can no longer live here' ('Gang ut, forþam þis nis þin hus þe þu on eardest. Næfst þu her leng nænige wununge'). Bazire and Cross noted parallels in two different Latin texts, a pseudo-Augustinian sermon and an anonymous text in a ninth-century florilegium.[13] The wording differs somewhat, and the Old English agrees more closely with the florilegium in introducing the eviction notice with a passive construction (*dicatur illi / him bið to gecweden*; pseudo-Augustine reads *patronus dicat*), but neither text can be called the immediate or even the antecedent 'source' for Bazire-Cross 9; rather, they are 'analogues' as defined by Scragg: 'two or more texts which draw either immediately or at greater distance upon the same source, although none is in the same line of transmission from that source as another'.[14] For a lexicographer or editor concerned with verbal correspondences as evidence for the meaning of an Old English word or for the establishment of the text, it may not matter whether the work that supplies the words is an antecedent or immediate source, or in what precise textual form it was transmitted; but it matters a great deal for anyone concerned with the transmission and influence of texts as a branch of intellectual history.

---

[12] Cross, 'Literate Anglo-Saxon', p. 70.

[13] See *Eleven Old English Rogationtide Homilies*, ed. by Joyce Bazire and J. E. Cross (Toronto, 1982), p. 114, for the parallel in pseudo-Augustine, *Sermo App.* 49 (*PL* 40.1332), and Cross's Preface to the 2nd edn, King's College London Medieval Studies, 4 (London, 1989), p. viii, for the parallel in Vatican City, Biblioteca Apostolica Vaticana, MS Pal. lat. 556. The pseudo-Augustinian sermon is translated in Michael J. B. Allen and Daniel Calder, *Sources and Analogues of Old English Poetry: The Major Latin Texts in Translation* (Cambridge, 1976), pp. 44–47. I have seen the same image in a different context in a post-Conquest English manuscript, Oxford, Bodleian Library, MS Hatton 42, part II (s. xiii^in), fol. 74ra, whose wording is close but not identical to BAV Pal. lat. 556: 'Fratres karissimi istam habitacionem quem tenet uir in hoc saeculo ita tenet si esset in domo aliena, quia nescit qua die uel qua nocte dicatur ei, Vade foras quia non est domus tua in qua es.'

[14] Scragg, 'Source Study', p. 40.

Even an 'immediate source' almost never survives in the actual manuscript used by an Anglo-Saxon author;[15] rather, in J. E. Cross's words, '*a* text (often in print in a modern edition) of the source' must by default stand in for the author's putative manuscript source.[16] One of the challenges of source scholarship, then, is to assess how closely our text approximates the Anglo-Saxon author's, since assessment of his treatment of the source at any given point depends on the degree of confidence we have that they are closely similar if not identical at that point. Source scholars try to get closer whenever possible, either by consulting new critical editions as they become available or by investigating unpublished manuscripts. Rudolph Willard's discovery of additional manuscripts of the Latin 'Three Utterances' sermon, for example, helped to clarify the relationship of the three independent Old English versions, but none translates closely any Latin text available to Willard.[17] One version in particular, that in Oxford, Bodleian Library, MS Junius 85/86, is an abbreviated redaction that differs markedly from all others.[18] My search (in collaboration with Mary F. Wack) for additional manuscripts of the Three Utterances led to the discovery of the immediate Latin source of the Junius version in a ninth-century manuscript, Munich, Bayerische Staatsbibliothek, MS Clm 28135.[19] Though not the homilist's actual manuscript source — the incipit he quotes has a few minor orthographical variants, and in any case there is no evidence that the Munich manuscript was ever in Anglo-Saxon England — it corresponds in almost

---

[15] I am aware of only two cases in which the actual manuscript used by an Old English writer has been identified. See Katherine O'Brien O'Keeffe, 'The Text of Aldhelm's *Enigma* no. c in Oxford, Bodleian Library, Rawlinson C. 697 and Exeter Riddle 40', *ASE*, 14 (1985), 61–73, and *Two Old English Apocrypha and their Manuscript Source: The Gospel of Nichodemus and The Avenging of the Saviour*, ed. by J. E. Cross and others, CSASE, 19 (Cambridge, 1996).

[16] Cross, 'Introduction', in *Two Old English Apocrypha*, ed. by Cross and others, p. 3 (Cross's emphasis); cf. Scragg's characterization of an immediate source as 'a surviving text which has, to all intents and purposes, the same form as that which the author used' ('Source Study', p. 40). The only direct evidence for this assumption of near identity is, of course, the near synonymy of the author's translation with the surviving text (which may be sense for sense rather than word for word).

[17] Willard, *Two Apocrypha in Old English Homilies*, Beiträge zur englischen Philologie, 30 (Leipzig, 1935), pp. 31–149, and Willard, 'The Latin Texts of *The Three Utterances of the Soul*', *Speculum*, 12 (1937), 147–56.

[18] HomM 5, partial edn by Willard, *Two Apocrypha*, pp. 38–57 (Text J); complete edn by A. M. Luiselli Fadda, *Nuove omelie anglosassoni della rinascenza benedettina*, Filologia germanica, Testi e studi, 1 (Florence, 1977), pp. 7–31 (no. I).

[19] Wack and Wright, 'A New Latin Source for the Old English "Three Utterances" Exemplum', *ASE*, 20 (1991), 187–202.

every significant detail to the Old English, accounting for all the substantive discrepancies that distinguish it from the other Old English, Latin, and Irish versions.
The Munich text of the Three Utterances made it possible to answer many of the
questions raised by Willard, who titled a chapter of his study 'The Problem of J'
(i.e. the Junius version). It also proved that, far from being a free adaptation, the
Junius version is a very close translation. The homilist does not even attempt to
supply a missing utterance in the Latin version, which speaks of 'three' utterances
of the damned soul but gives only two of them; instead, he simply omits the number. Another of the homilist's sources, a pseudo-Augustinian Doomsday sermon,
had previously been identified by J. E. Cross.[20] Comparison with the two texts
printed by Migne (*Sermo App.* 251; *PL* 39.2210) left a number of phrases and sentences unaccounted for, and Cross concluded that the homilist was thoroughly
conversant with Doomdsay commonplaces and added freely from memory to the
Latin sermon as he translated it. A variant text of the Doomsday sermon unknown
to Cross, however, has equivalents for most of these apparent additions, so Cross's
estimation of the homilist's mode of composition must now be qualified.[21]

   To say that a passage in a Latin source 'accounts for' one in an Old English
target text does not imply that they are precisely equivalent in meaning or implication. Translations may be sense for sense, phrase for phrase, or virtually word for
word, but any translation, however literal, invokes a new range of connotations and
associations in the target language, and the target text can be received in new
historical and cultural contexts, each of which affects how it will be understood.[22]
A homilist might even use roughly equivalent wording but say something substantively different, as the author of Fadda I seems to have done with a third source, a
pseudo-Augustinian Nativity sermon — at least as far as it is possible to judge from
the text printed by Migne. While he has equivalents for most of the words and
phrases in the Latin sermon, on several occasions the homilist alters their cumu-
lative meaning when the Latin smacks of semi-Pelagianism; and on one occasion

---

[20] Cross, 'A Doomsday Passage in an Old English Sermon for Lent', *Anglia*, 100 (1982),
103–08.

[21] See Charles D. Wright, 'An Old English Doomsday Passage Revisited' (in preparation).

[22] This point has been stressed by translation theorists, who prefer the term 'target text' to
'derivative' (see O'Brien O'Keeffe, 'Source, Method', p. 58); for recent applications to Old English
literature, see also Robert Stanton, *The Culture of Translation in Anglo-Saxon England* (Cambridge, 2002); Nicole Guenther Discenza, *The King's English: Strategies of Translation in The Old
English Boethius* (Albany, 2005); and Nancy Thompson, '*Hit Segð on Halgum Bocum*: The Logic
of Composite Old English Homilies', *Philological Quarterly*, 81 (2002), 383–419.

he actually reverses the sermon's assertion that women should no longer be held in disdain by men because Mary Magdalene had been the first witness of Christ's resurrection. The homilist, in short, may have revised substantively only when he had some concrete ideological motive for doing so.[23]

Though we can never reconstruct a homilist's source manuscript with absolute certainty, when the Old English agrees as closely with a Latin text as does Fadda I with the Three Utterances as preserved in Clm 28135, we can be confident that we have a very close approximation. Deferring for the moment the possibility of loose quotation from memory *ad res*, substantive discrepancies between the source and the target text must be due either to the homilist's revision of the source (as seems to have been the case with the pseudo-Augustinian Nativity sermon) or his use of a variant text of the source (as turns out to have been the case with the Doomsday sermon). If collation of the surviving manuscripts suggests that the text of the source was comparatively stable, and if an ample conspectus of variant readings does not account for the discrepanies, we can be more confident in regarding them as the homilist's own revisions. The purpose of such minute textual comparison, then, is not simply to amass ever closer parallels and eliminate discrepancies, but to validate as likely revisions those discrepancies that remain, and thus to enable more accurate assessment of how a homilist adapted his source — how original he was, that is, with his original.

In some cases it may be necessary to 'edit' an artificial composite text of the source, selecting variant readings based on their congruence with the Old English target text (the circularity of this process does not undermine its utility). By using the apparatus criticus of Germain Morin's edition of the sermons of Caesarius of

---

[23] See Charles D. Wright, 'A New Latin Source for Two Old English Homilies (Fadda I and Blickling I): pseudo-Augustine, *Sermo* App. 125 and the Ideology of Chastity in the Anglo-Saxon Benedictine Reform', in *Source of Wisdom: Old English and Early Medieval Latin Studies in Honour of Thomas D. Hill*, ed. by Charles D. Wright, Thomas N. Hall, and Frederick M. Biggs (Toronto, 2007), pp. 239–65. Where the source says 'Mulier enim quia [mortem] prior gustauerat, prior etiam resurrectionem uidisse monstratur, ut non perpetui reatus apud uiros opprobrium sustineret; et quae culpam nobis transfuderat, transfudit et gratiam' ('because a woman first tasted [death], a woman is likewise shown to have witnessed the resurrection first, so that she should not bear the reproach of perpetual guilt among men; and she who had dispensed guilt to us also dispensed grace'), Fadda I instead says, 'death first came to us through a woman, and therefore a woman first proclaimed and made known his resurrection to men; and the woman that first tasted death, she was henceforth suffering scorn from her husband, and the guilt which she committed there is perpetually avenged upon her, and her sins have been greatly poured out over us' (my translation of Luiselli Fadda, *Nuove omelie*, p. 13, lines 76–81, with repunctuation of the clauses).

Arles,[24] Edward B. Irving was able to reconstruct a text of Caesarius's dramatic 'Ego te, homo' speech of Christ at the Last Judgement that more closely approximates what must have been available to the authors of Vercelli VIII and the poem *Christ III* than the text cited by Willard from Migne's *Patrologia Latina*, or indeed Morin's own critical text.[25] Max Förster made use of proofsheets of Ernst von Dobschütz's unpublished edition of the *Apocalypse of Thomas* to reconstruct the Latin texts underlying Vercelli XV and the independent Old English version of *Thomas* in Cambridge, Corpus Christi College, MS 41.[26] When critical editions are not available, a source scholar may have to edit the source directly from the manuscripts, as J. E. Cross did for the sermon 'Remedia peccatorum' (a source for Napier XLIX, Vercelli X, and Ælfric's *CH* II.7).[27]

In addition to translating directly from manuscript sources, a homilist could draw on his memory of Latin and Old English texts he had previously read or heard and on commonplaces he had encountered in a variety of forms. A commonplace may have one or more identifiable ultimate sources, or none, and its formulation may admit of variation, substitution, and extension. The *ubi sunt* motif, for example, is widely attested in Old English prose and also occurs in *The Wanderer* (lines 92–96). The motif is distinctive enough to be instantly recognizable, and the formulation of many prose examples betrays an ultimate origin in Isidore's *Liber synonymorum*; yet it could also be adapted freely and circulate independently of specific written models.[28] Similarly, what Malcolm Godden has termed 'an Old

---

[24] Caesarius of Arles, *Sermones*, ed. by Germain Morin, 2 vols, CCSL, 103–04 (Turnhout, 1953).

[25] Irving, 'Latin Prose Sources for Old English Verse', *JEGP*, 56 (1957), 588–95. The Caesarian source had first been noted by Rudolph Willard, 'Vercelli Homily VIII and the Christ', *PMLA*, 42 (1927), 314–30. For other reflexes of the 'Ego te, homo' speech see below, note 114.

[26] Förster, 'A New Version of the Apocalypse of Thomas in Old English', *Anglia*, 73 (1955), 6–36; Förster had previously included a reconstructed text in the apparatus fontium of his edition of Vercelli XV: 'Der Vercelli-Codex CXVII nebst Abdruck einiger altenglischer Homilien der Handschrift', in *Festschrift für Lorenz Morsbach*, ed. by Ferdinand Holthausen and H. Spies, Studien zur englischen Philologie, 50 (Halle, 1913), pp. 20–179 (pp. 116–28).

[27] Cross, 'A *Sermo de misericordia* in Old English Prose', *Anglia*, 108 (1990), 429–40, supplementing previous studies and partial edition by Wolfgang Becker, 'The Latin Manuscript Sources of the Old English Translations of the Sermon *Remedia Peccatorum*', *Medium Ævum*, 45 (1976), 145–52, and 'The Manuscript Sources of Ælfric's Catholic Homily II 7 – A Supplementary Note', *Medium Ævum*, 48 (1979), 105–06. Becker and Cross were able to demonstrate that the English homilists had consulted a distinctive redaction of the sermon.

[28] On the *ubi sunt* motif in Old English, see J. E. Cross, '"Ubi Sunt" Passages in Old English – Sources and Relationships', *Vetenskaps-Societetens i Lund, Årsbok* (1956), 23–44; Claudia Di

English penitential motif ('it is better to be shamed for one's sins before one man [the confessor] in this life than to be shamed before God and before all angels and before all men and before all devils at the Last Judgement') has close Insular Latin analogues but no precisely definable 'sources'.[29] The motif clearly took on a life of its own in the vernacular homiletic tradition: Godden identifies two major divergent formulations, one of which may 'stem from Ælfric's rewriting' of the other, while oral dissemination and memorial citation probably account for many of the variations that characterize individual examples. 'The Men with Tongues of Iron', an inexpressibility topos attested in several Old English homilies in a variety of formulations, owes something to both the *Visio Pauli* and its source in Virgil's *Aeneid*, but no vernacular homiletic attestation is derived immediately from either Latin text; in other words, though the motif ultimately derives from Latin models it quickly became 'naturalized' and could develop with or without further immediate reliance on them.[30]

Consideration of oral transmission and memorial quotation complicates source analysis, since written sources are the only ones to which we can have direct access; yet written sources can help in assessing when a homilist was translating closely from a Latin text in front of him and when he was composing freely from memory or drawing on existing vernacular versions or oral traditions.[31] Mary Carruthers has cautioned against assuming that 'the extent of an author's reliance upon his memory can be gauged in inverse proportion to the fidelity of his quotations', since some medieval authors were capable of highly accurate memorization *ad uerba*; yet

Sciacca, 'Il topos dell'*ubi sunt* nell'omiletica anglosassone: il caso di Vercelli X', in *I Germani e gli altri, I Parte*, ed. by Vittoria Dolcetti Corazza and Renato Gendre (Alessandria, 2003), pp. 225–55; and Di Sciacca, 'The *Ubi Sunt* Motif and the Soul-and-Body Legend in Old English Homilies: Sources and Relationships', *JEGP*, 105 (2006), 366–87.

[29] Godden, 'An Old English Penitential Motif', *ASE*, 2 (1973), 221–39 (p. 237); for additional Latin analogues, see Charles D. Wright, *The Irish Tradition in Old English Literature*, CSASE, 6 (Cambridge, 1993), pp. 85–88; and Wright, 'The Irish Tradition', in *A Companion to Anglo-Saxon Literature*, ed. by Phillip Pulsiano and Elaine Treharne (Oxford, 2001), pp. 345–74 (pp. 347–48).

[30] See Wright, *Irish Tradition*, pp. 145–56; Christopher Abram, 'Anglo-Saxon Influence in the Old Norwegian Homily Book', *Mediaeval Scandinavia*, 14 (2004), 1–35 (pp. 28–33); and Loredana Teresi, 'Mnemonic Transmission of Old English Texts in the Post-Conquest Period', in *Rewriting Old English in the Twelfth Century*, ed. by Mary Swan and Elaine M. Treharne, CSASE, 30 (Cambridge, 2000), pp. 98–116.

[31] See J. E. Cross, 'Ælfric – Mainly on Memory and Creative Method in Two *Catholic Homilies*', *Studia Neophilologica*, 41 (1969), 135–55.

one of the consequences of memorization *ad res* is indeed, as Carruthers also shows, 'inaccurate' quotation or paraphrase.[32] The difficulty, it seems to me, lies in distinguishing a paraphrase due to memorization *ad res* from one due to *sensum e sensu* translation from a manuscript. When a homilist 'blends' phrasing from texts on related themes, however, it suggests the spontaneous operation of memory. A passage in Napier XLVI on the angels and demons who report the deeds of men to God and the going-out of souls is based ultimately on the *Visio Pauli*, but with several modifications including seamlessly and unobtrusively integrated echoes (without extended direct quotation) of the Three Utterances apocryphon, probably as a consequence of memorial association.[33] Again, Bazire-Cross 11, in which loose citations of scripture are woven together with brief parallels of phraseology and idea from sermons by Caesarius (including the 'Ego te, homo' speech), the pseudo-Augustinian Doomsday sermon, and the *Apocalypse of Thomas*, 'appears to have been written freely without reference to a book', as Bazire and Cross argue, but instead 'from a memory filled with ideas and phrases that were commonplace but [. . .] also read and heard in other vernacular homilies'.[34]

The intralingual context of composite homilies such as these would be more conducive to memorial transmission and composition than translation from the learned language of Latin to the native vernacular.[35] Brief paraphrase of a Latin source might also be due to memorization *ad res*, but when a homilist renders a Latin source *in extenso* he is likely to have had a manuscript copy — or perhaps extracts copied onto wax tablets, draft *schedulae*, or booklets — in front of him as he composed (though of course he might still incorporate reminiscences of related

---

[32] Mary Carruthers, *The Book of Memory: A Study of Memory in Medieval Culture* (Cambridge, 1990), pp. 87–91 (p. 88).

[33] For the homily's relation to the *Visio Pauli*, see Antonette DiPaolo Healey, *The Old English Vision of Saint Paul*, Speculum Anniversary Monographs, 2 (Cambridge, MA, 1978), p. 42, and Jonathan Wilcox, 'The Sources of Napier 46', *Fontes Anglo-Saxonici: World Wide Web Register* <http://fontes.english.ox.ac.uk/> [accessed 1 October 2006], which designates the *Visio* as SA1 ('certainly an antecedent source'); for the echoes of the Three Utterances, see Willard, *Two Apocrypha*, pp. 74–76.

[34] *Eleven Old English Rogationtide Homilies*, ed. by Bazire and Cross, pp. 136–38.

[35] For evidence of memorial transmission in the composite homilies, see Mary Swan, 'Memorialised Readings: Manuscript Evidence for Old English Homily Composition', in *Anglo-Saxon Manuscripts and their Heritage*, ed. by Phillip Pulsiano and Elaine M. Treharne (Aldershot, 1998), pp. 205–17; and Teresi, 'Mnemonic Transmission'. We should recall, however, that Ælfric explicitly envisioned the written transmission of his homilies and expressed concern about their being miscopied from an exemplar (*CH* I, Preface).

texts or commonplaces he had previously heard or read). Memorization *ad uerba* of a lengthy Latin source would rarely have been necessary, or expedient. Ælfric's memory may have been prodigious, and he may have incorporated reminiscences of related scripture and commentary as he translated his main sources from copies of the homiliaries of Paul the Deacon, Haymo of Auxerre, and Smaradgus,[36] but when he composed his *Sermo ad populum in octavis Pentecosten dicendis* (ÆHom 11), he relied on his own extracts, made some years earlier, of Julian of Toledo's *Prognosticon futuri saeculi*, and seems also to have referred back to the original text.[37] We know that the translator of the Old English *Gospel of Nicodemus* and *Vindicta Saluatoris* worked from a surviving manuscript, Saint-Omer, Bibliothèque municipale, MS 202,[38] and the fact that the survival of such a manuscript source is all but unique does not mean that manuscript sources were not the norm.

Few homilists, however, would have had access to extensive patristic libraries and been able to consult multiple copies or redactions of a given text, had it even occurred to them to do so. Moreover, instead of consulting patristic *originalia* (manuscripts of complete writings by the Fathers), they frequently had recourse to homiliaries such as the Homiliary of Saint-Père de Chartres,[39] and florilegia of

---

[36] See Cross, 'Ælfric – Mainly on Memory'. On Ælfric's use of Paul the Deacon's homiliary, see Cyril Smetana, 'Ælfric and the Early Medieval Homiliary', *Traditio*, 15 (1959), 163–204; for Haymo of Auxerre, see Smetana, 'Ælfric and the Homiliary of Haymo of Halberstadt', *Traditio*, 17 (1961), 457–69; for Smaragdus, see Joyce Hill, 'Ælfric and Smaragdus', *ASE*, 21 (1992), 203–37.

[37] Ælfric's extracts from Julian of Toledo's *Prognosticon futuri saeculi* occupy ten folios in the surviving copy in Boulogne-sur-Mer, Bibliothèque publique, MS 63, printed by Milton McC. Gatch, *Preaching and Theology in Anglo-Saxon England: Ælfric and Wulfstan* (Toronto, 1977), pp. 129–46. For Ælfric's use of both these extracts and the original text, see ibid., pp. 96–97. The manuscript is no. 800 in Helmut Gneuss, *Handlist of Anglo-Saxon Manuscripts: A List of Manuscripts and Manuscript Fragments Written or Owned in England up to 1100*, MRTS, 241 (Tempe, 2001). According to Malcolm Godden, *Ælfric's Catholic Homilies: Introduction, Commentary and Glossary*, EETS: SS, 18 (Oxford, 2000), p. xlv, 'Though some of the material [Ælfric] uses could have been drawn from a good memory of earlier reading, his close renderings of many Latin passages, especially from Gregory and Augustine at times, confirms that he had direct access to the source-texts at the time of writing'.

[38] See *Two Old English Apocrypha*, ed. by Cross and others.

[39] For a survey of these and other major early homiliaries, see Mary Clayton, 'Homiliaries and Preaching in Anglo-Saxon England', *Peritia*, 4 (1985), 207–42; repr. with corrections in *Old English Prose: Basic Readings*, ed. by Szarmach, pp. 151–98.

topically organized extracts such as Alcuin's *Liber de uirtutibus et uitiis*.[40] Identification of the Latin sources that Anglo-Saxon homilists translated, whether closely or freely, has profound implications for understanding their own words and works in their historical and social contexts, and for reconstructing the intellectual culture of Anglo-Saxon England in the tenth and eleventh centuries. In the remainder of this essay, I will focus on the contributions of source scholarship in the areas of textual criticism, literary history, intellectual history, and stylistic analysis.

Sources and Source Scholarship: Implications and Contributions

Textual Criticism

A Latin source affords an editor of an Old English homily (or indeed any text) an additional — and occasionally decisive — layer of evidence, particularly if the object is to reconstruct as closely as possible what the author wrote. If an Old English reading makes poor sense or none, the corresponding Latin may suggest an obvious emendation or tip the balance among more than one palaeographically plausible emendations. Joan Turville-Petre's reconstruction of the antecedent sources of Vercelli III, for example, suggested convincing restorations of such obvious errors as *tolysendra* (for *tohlystendra* = *auditores*),[41] and the subsequent discovery by Helen Spencer of the immediate source in the Homiliary of Saint-Père de Chartres or 'Pembroke Homiliary' enabled D. G. Scragg to improve the text further.[42] Textual criticism begins with the identification of scribal error or intervention, yet scribal readings that make sense often cannot be detected unless they diverge perceptibly from the author's dialect or *usus scribendi*. Comparison with the source is sometimes the only way to identify scribal readings that are not in themselves suspicious, or that are suspicious but can be 'defended' through resourceful albeit misguided philological arguments. As Roland Torkar has noted in his scrutiny of Max Förster's edition of Vercelli III, without benefit of the Latin

[40] See Lees, 'Dissemination'; for florilegia used by vernacular homilists, see also the essay by Turville-Petre cited in the following note.

[41] Turville-Petre, 'Translations of a Lost Penitential Homily', *Traditio*, 19 (1963), 51–78 (p. 70).

[42] Spencer, 'Vernacular and Latin Versions of a Sermon for Lent: "A Lost Penitential Homily" Found', *Mediaeval Studies*, 44 (1982), 271–305; *The Vercelli Homilies and Related Texts*, ed. by D. G. Scragg, EETS: OS, 300 (Oxford, 1992), p. 215. Subsequent quotations from the Vercelli Homilies are to Scragg's edition, by page and line numbers.

source Förster not only justified scribal corruptions (including *hapax legomena*) of well-attested words or phrases corresponding closely to the Latin, but also failed to detect felicitous scribal emendations of archetypal errors.[43] A Latin source can give us, in Torkar's words, a glimpse beyond the archetype, an 'Einblick ins stemmatische Jenseits'.[44]

The identification of a Latin source does not always yield clear-cut resolutions of textual problems. If a source gives an editor more to work with, it may also multiply the possibilities he has to consider. Where the source of Vercelli III, for example, reads *nobilitat* [scil. *ieiunium*] *mentem* ('[fasting] enobles the mind'), the Old English has *hio hylt þæs mannes mod* ('[fasting] sustains [or preserves] the mind of the man', line 46). The discrepancy has suggested more than one plausible emendation of *hylt*. Turville-Petre's restoration *hlyht* from *hligan* ('glorify') was adopted by Scragg, but Torkar proposes instead *hyht*, from *(ge)hean* ('exalt, extol'). As a rule, the emendation that best corresponds to the Latin and best accounts for the manuscript reading should be preferred. In this case not only is *hyht* preferable on palaeographical grounds, but *hean* is also a more common verb whose meaning (elsewhere it glosses *sublimare* and *exaltare*) is closer to the Latin. A conservative editor may, perhaps, wish to defend *hylt* as an authorial modification of the source that makes satisfactory sense in context. The authority of *hylt* is impeached, however, not by the mere fact of its failure to correspond to the Latin, but by the coincidence of that failure and the existence of another word palaeographically almost identical to *hylt* that does correspond to the Latin. The additional consideration that the homilist consistently translates literally (if sometimes inaccurately) is decisive in favour of *hyht*, at least for an editor attempting to restore, however imperfectly, the authorial text. For such an editor the fact that *hylt* makes satisfactory sense is not a justification of the manuscript reading, but a rationale for the scribal substitution.

---

[43] Torkar, 'Die Ohnmacht der Textkritik, am Beispiel der Ausgaben der dritten Vercelli-Homilie', in *Anglo-Saxonica: Beiträge zur Vor- und Frühgeschichte der englischen Sprache und zur altenglischen Literatur: Festschrift für Hans Schabram zum 65. Geburtstag*, ed. by Klaus Grinda and Claus-Dieter Wetzel (Munich, 1993), pp. 225–50. Förster's edition appeared in *Die Vercelli-Homilien*, vol. I: *I–VIII. Homilie*, BaP, 12 (Hamburg, 1932; repr. Darmstadt, 1966), pp. 53–71. Cross, 'Literate Anglo-Saxon', pp. 72–73, made a similar point with respect to Förster's acceptance of the phrase *soðfæstnesse sunu* ('son of justice') in all three surviving copies of Vercelli V, an archetypal error for *soðfæstnesse suna* ('sun of justice'), a commonplace epithet for Christ based on Mal. 4. 2 (*sol iustitiae*).

[44] Torkar, 'Die Ohnmacht', p. 234.

To be sure, a reading that makes sense but does not correspond to the Latin source is not necessarily scribal. It could indeed be the author's deliberate alteration of the source; it could also be his unwitting mistranslation of the source, or an accurate translation of a variant reading in his manuscript of the source. The judgement always has to be made on a case-by-case basis, taking into account the wording of both source and target texts in their immediate and larger contexts, the potential influence of other texts or traditions, and the author's *usus scribendi* to the extent it can be established from the work as a whole. Hermann G. Fiedler, who identified the main Latin source of Blickling I, chided the homilist for having mistaken *incipit* for *concepit* in the phrase 'A salutatione incipit, qui saluationem in lingua portauit' ('[Gabriel], who bore salvation in his speech, begins with a greeting') which is rendered as 'ond from þisse halettunge heo wæs geeacnod; forþon þe he hire þ[a ecean] hælo on his tungon brohte' ('and she conceived from this greeting, because he brought eternal salvation to her in his speech').[45] It seems highly unlikely that the homilist would confuse such common words as *incipio* and *concipio*, but it is entirely possible that *concepit quia* occurred as a variant of *incipit qui* in the Latin manuscript tradition. Moreover, the homilist's assertion that Mary 'conceived from this greeting' not only makes sense but accords with a distinctive early medieval understanding of the Annunciation, according to which Mary conceived *per aurem*.[46] Even if the homilist's manuscript read *incipit qui*, then, he may have rephrased the sentence in order to invoke this well-established tradition.

Latin sources do not simply help in detecting scribal readings that are otherwise unsuspicious; they may equally confirm as authorial readings that seem suspicious, or clarify the sense of authorial readings that are ambiguous. Of the four manuscripts of the popular homily Vercelli X, for example, three (including Blickling IX and Napier XLIX) agree on the reading *mildheortnesse earan ontynde* where Vercelli X (line 33) reads *mildheortnesse her ontynde*. In accordance with the majority of witnesses Scragg emends the reading of the Vercelli Book, though he still feels that 'the expression with *earan* is an odd one';[47] moreover, it is not immediately

---

[45] Fiedler, 'The Source of the First Blickling Homily', *Modern Language Quarterly*, 6 (1903), 122–24 (p. 123); *The Blickling Homilies of the Tenth Century*, ed. and trans. by Richard Morris, EETS: OS, 58, 63, 73 (1874–80; repr. with corrections in one vol., 1967), p. 3, lines 15–17.

[46] See J. E. Cross, 'The Influence of Irish Texts and Traditions on the Old English Martyrology', *Proceedings of the Royal Irish Academy*, 81C (1981), 173–92 (pp. 182–83); J. F. Kelly, 'The Virgin Birth in Hiberno-Latin Theology', in *Studia Patristica*, vol. XV.1, ed. Elizabeth A. Livingstone (Berlin, 1984), pp. 328–35 (pp. 330 and 332).

[47] *Vercelli Homilies*, ed. by Scragg, p. 215.

clear from the context whether God 'opened His ears of mercy', as in Richard Morris's translation of Blickling IX (taking *mildheortnesse* as a genitive dependent upon *earan*) or 'opened (men's) ears to His mercy', as Scragg insists (taking *mildheortnesse* as dative object of *ontynde*). No direct source has been identified for this passage, but a search of the databases of Christian-Latin texts reveals many liturgical petitions asking God to open his 'ears of mercy' (*aures misericordiae*) to the prayers of men,[48] and a search of the *Dictionary of Old English Corpus* shows that the formula occurs twice in Anglo-Latin liturgical sources with the equivalent Old English gloss.[49] So it is likely that this is what the homilist meant, whether he was translating from a written text or simply recalling the liturgical formula; and while the grammatical ambiguity remains, any reader familiar with the formula would have resolved it in this way.

Variant versions of Old English homilies are important not simply as means to reconstruct a lost archetype and the authorial original beyond it, but also as evidence of conscious or unconscious revision by scribes or preachers who adapt homilies for new contexts and audiences — whether by modifying dialect forms, substituting preferred synonyms, tinkering with the style, or abbreviating, elaborating, or otherwise modifying the content. Each witness has its own independent value, then, as a text that was produced and read or preached, and can be edited for its own sake. In an edition whose purpose is to present the text of a given manuscript in its integrity, a reading such as *hylt* in Vercelli III can be defended on the grounds that it would have made sense to those reading the manuscript or hearing it read. Source analysis, however, is relevant even to consideration of variant versions at one or more removes from the presumptive original. For it is impossible to identify revisions — or to speculate on their possible motivations — without first having determined which readings *are* original. In his analysis of the variant texts of Vercelli X, Jonathan Wilcox notes that 'Identification of the sources helps in establishing the textual relations of the manuscripts of the homily', which in turn

---

[48] *Library of Latin Texts – CLCLT 5* (Turnhout, 2002), CD-ROM; Patrologia Latina Database, <http://pld.chadwyck.co.uk/> [accessed 1 November 2005].

[49] DurRitGl 1 (Thomp-Lind), C21.1 ('*aures misericordiæ tuæ*: earo miltheart' ðines'); RegCGl (Kornexl), C27 ('*aures misericordis Domini*: earan mildheortes drihtnes'); citations from the online *DOE Corpus* <http://ets.umdl.umich.edu/o/oec/> [accessed 1 November 2005]. One will not find the example of *mildheortnesse earan* from Vercelli X in the *DOE Corpus*, which cites Scragg's edition but (for reasons that are not clear to me) retains the manuscript reading *mildheortnesse her*.

is 'crucial for the subsequent discussion of revisions to the homily'.[50] In other words, while source identification relates most immediately to the authorial original, to the extent that it enables reconstruction of that original it also contributes to the identification and understanding of later revisions by scribes and preachers who did not even have access to or knowledge of its Latin sources.

Conflicting editorial philosophies cannot be reconciled, only debated.[51] Yet both kinds of edition — the reconstructed authorial text and the individual manuscript version — are complementary, serving different but equally legitimate functions. And while editors of either persuasion may disagree on the relative weight to give known sources in establishing a text, no responsible editor can afford to ignore them.

Lest it appear that the lines of force always run from Latin to vernacular, I conclude this section by noting that an Old English translation can in turn assist in the reconstruction of a poorly transmitted Latin text. In addition to using the surviving Latin versions of the *Apocalypse of Thomas* to edit a composite source text for Vercelli XV and to suggest corrections of the homily, Max Förster used Vercelli XV (and the other three independent Old English translations of *Thomas*) to emend corrupt passages in the Latin. For example, just before a series of imprecations each beginning 'Vae illis [. . .]' the Latin reads 'In diebus illis adpropinquantem iam Antechristum hęc sunt signa illis qui habitant in terrae' ('In those days with the imminent approach of Antichrist these are the signs to those who dwell in the earth'). The corresponding sentence in Vercelli XV ('Wa ðam mannum þe in ðam dagum eardiað ofer eorðan', 'Woe to those men who in those days dwell in the earth', line 60) suggests that the word *Vae* must have dropped out, obscuring the first imprecation in the series (*Vae illis qui habitant in terrae*) and leaving *illis qui habitant in terrae* to be construed with the preceding sentence.

---

[50] Wilcox, 'Variant Texts of an Old English Homily: Vercelli X and Stylistic Readers', in *The Preservation and Transmission of Anglo-Saxon Culture*, ed. by Paul E. Szarmach and Joel T. Rosenthal, Studies in Medieval Culture, 40 (Kalamazoo, 1997), pp. 335–51 (p. 339).

[51] For a conspectus of opinion, see *The Editing of Old English: Papers from the 1990 Manchester Conference*, ed. by D. G. Scragg and Paul E. Szarmach (Cambridge, 1994). Mary Clayton has produced what she terms a 'hybrid' edition of the Old English versions of Marian apocrypha, retaining scribal substitutions but rejecting scribal additions and correcting mechanical errors in the archetype (identified by comparison with the Latin) to 'what must have been the original reading': *The Apocryphal Gospels of Mary in Anglo-Saxon England*, CSASE, 26 (Cambridge, 1998), p. 161.

Literary History

The term 'literary history' can embrace many categories of investigation, ranging from such basic issues as authorship and chronology to broader social questions such as literacy and audience. These categories are obviously not exhaustive (or mutually exclusive) but are among the most fundamental, and source study is relevant to each of them.

AUTHORSHIP

Sources can provide corroborative evidence for or against common authorship. J. E. Cross's demonstration that Vercelli XIX–XXI and Tristram III are all based on sermons transmitted in the Pembroke Homiliary was crucial to the case for these four homilies, precisely because it led Cross to reverse a previous negative judgement based on antecedent sources.[52] Paul Szarmach had tentatively broached the possibility of common authorship for the three Vercelli Homilies on the basis of shared linguistic and stylistic features, but Bazire and Cross argued that because Vercelli XIX and XX 'differ in attitude towards their definable literary sources, and in manner of composition because of this', they were probably not by the same author.[53] Comparison with the sources 'definable' at that time made it appear that the author of Vercelli XIX, unlike the author of Vercelli XX, had composed very freely, 'whether from memory or brief consultation'.[54] The subsequent discovery of the immediate source in the Pembroke Homiliary showed that he in fact translated rather closely and that all four homilies translate Pembroke-type items in a consistent way, corroborating the linguistic and stylistic evidence and enabling D. G. Scragg to make a strong circumstantial case (endorsed by Cross) that the entire set was composed by a homilist active during the Benedictine Reform period.[55] The discovery of the Pembroke Homiliary, however, not only highlighted the value of immediate sources for drawing conclusions about style and authorship, but also

---

[52] Cross, *Cambridge Pembroke College MS. 25: A Carolingian Sermonary Used by Anglo-Saxon Preachers*, Kings College London Medieval Studies, 1 (London, 1987), pp. 92–93 and 126.

[53] *Eleven Old English Rogationtide Homilies*, ed. by Bazire and Cross, p. 25, with reference to Szarmach, 'The Vercelli Homilies', p. 248.

[54] *Eleven Old English Rogationtide Homilies*, ed. by Bazire and Cross, p. 6.

[55] Scragg, 'An Old English Homilist of Archbishop Dunstan's Day', in *Words, Texts and Manuscripts: Studies in Anglo-Saxon Culture presented to Helmut Gneuss on the Occasion of his Sixty-fifth Birthday*, ed. by Michael Korhammer, Karl Reichl, and Hans Sauer (Cambridge, 1992), pp. 181–92; cf. J. E. Cross, 'Vernacular Sermons in Old English', in *The Sermon*, ed. by Kienzle, pp. 561–96 (pp. 566–67).

exposed the potential unreliability of conclusions based on antecedent sources. When multiple Latin sources have been identified we may conclude that the homilist compiled them himself, but if they are in fact antecedent sources transmitted by an intermediary, our assessment of the homilist's authorial *usus* may be based on misleading data. The use of an intermediary can sometimes be deduced from internal evidence, and in a few cases we are fortunate to have external evidence in the form of independent vernacular translations of the same materials. As Turville-Petre noted in the case of Vercelli III, however, '[t]he existence of a Latin compilation could not easily be proved, without the independent evidence' afforded by an Old Icelandic translation of the same source.[56] In default of such evidence it may not be possible to determine whether the sources in question are immediate or antecedent.

Only a few possible examples of common authorship among the anonymous homilies have been identified, but a case has also been made for Vercelli XI–XIII, rubricated for the three days of Rogationtide. Vercelli XI and XII uniquely attribute the origin of the Rogationtide processions to St Peter (instead of Mamertus of Vienne). Homily XII begins by referring to the previous day's instructions, and XIII begins by stating that it is the third day of the Rogations. All three homilies are transmitted only in the Vercelli Book, and certain features of layout and presentation suggest that they were copied from the same exemplar. Vercelli XIV shares some of the same layout features, but it is rubricated *quando uolueris* and there are no clear links with the others; moreover, as Scragg notes, although Homilies XI and XIV use the same passage from Caesarius of Arles, their translations appear to be completely independent.[57] On the other hand, the similar treatment of different sources in Homilies XI–XIII strengthens the case for the Rogationtide set. As I have shown elsewhere, each homily alters its sources so as to eliminate or qualify condemnations of wealth, suggesting a consistent motivation that corroborates the other evidence that they were composed by the same person.[58] Different homilists

---

[56] Turville-Petre, 'Translations', p. 52.

[57] For Scragg's cautious discussion of the case for common authorship, see 'The Compilation of the Vercelli Book', *ASE*, 2 (1973), 189–207 (p. 194); repr. with a new postscript in *Anglo-Saxon Manuscripts: Basic Readings*, ed. by Mary Richards, Basic Readings in Anglo-Saxon England, 2 (New York, 1994), pp. 317–43 (p. 324). In *Vercelli Homilies*, pp. xxxix–xl, Scragg states that these three homilies 'were composed as a set', but also cautions that 'there is little clear evidence of linguistic affinity between the three'.

[58] Wright, 'Vercelli Homilies XI–XIII and the Anglo-Saxon Benedictine Reform: Tailored Sources and Implied Audiences', in *Preacher, Sermon and Audience in the Middle Ages*, ed. by Carolyn Muessig (Leiden, 2002), pp. 203–27.

might have shared such a motivation, of course, and the consistent treatment of sources alone need not suggest common authorship unless it is manifested by some distinctive technique or, as in this case, corroborated by other kinds of evidence. Still, any such argument must be consistent with linguistic evidence, so the case for Vercelli XI–XIII remains inconclusive pending a full investigation of their language. The same is true for Assmann XI and XII, Belfour VI, and Brotanek II, which Karl Jost suggested on stylistic grounds may be the work of one homilist.[59] Cross was able to show that all of them adapt sermons found in the Pembroke Homiliary in a consistent way (though much more freely than Vercelli XIX–XXI and Tristram III), but in default of a thorough linguistic analysis he regarded the case as unproven.[60]

Chronology
Sources can sometimes fix the terminus post quem of a homily, or establish the relative chronology of two or more homilies. Absolute chronology is only rarely established by sources, since the great majority antedate even the earliest vernacular homilies. A vernacular homily in the mid-twelfth-century manuscript London, British Library, Cotton MS Vespasian D. XIV, however, translates a Latin sermon (copied in the same manuscript) composed *c.* 1100 and attributed to Ralph d'Escures (d. 1122). The vernacular homily is not therefore a late, linguistically updated copy of an earlier Old English homily, but must have been written in the first half of the twelfth century.[61] Sources come into play much more often in determining relative chronology. When two or more Old English homilies overlap and the verbal parallels indicate that one homilist has borrowed from the other, it may not be possible to establish the direction of borrowing on linguistic or textual grounds, and it can never simply be assumed that the relative dates of the manuscripts correspond to those of the texts. A Latin source that underlies the parallel passages, however, may reveal which of the two homilists was translating directly from it. One of the earliest published source studies, Julius Zupitza's 1898 'Zu Seele und Leib', identified the common Latin source for both Napier XXIX (HomU 26) and the 'Macarius' Homily (HomU 55) in a sermon from a Nonantola manuscript printed by Batiouchkof in his 1891 study of medieval debates of the body and

[59] Jost, *Wulfstanstudien*, Swiss Studies in English, 23 (Bern, 1950), pp. 178–82.

[60] Cross, *Cambridge Pembroke College MS. 25*, pp. 232–35.

[61] See Elaine Treharne, 'The Life of English in the Mid-Twelfth Century: Ralph D'Escures's Homily on the Virgin Mary', in *Writers of the Reign of Henry II: Twelve Essays*, ed. by Ruth Kennedy and Simon Meecham-Jones (New York, 2006), pp. 169–86 (p. 172).

soul.[62] In order to account for shared material in both homilies unparalleled in the Latin, Zupitza posited a lost common source similar to but fuller than the Nonantola manuscript. Additional manuscripts of the Latin sermon have since come to light, but without supplying any of the 'lost' material posited by Zupitza, and Karl Jost has argued that the Nonantola sermon is in fact the immediate source.[63] But are the two Old English homilies independent translations of the Latin, or is one of them a composite that borrowed from the other? There are extensive verbal parallels between them, but also substantive discrepancies. Zupitza emphasized the discrepancies, regarding the parallels as the fortuitous result of independent translation of the same source, but Jost emphasized the parallels, concluding that Napier XXIX is the composite and interpreting its discrepancies as the result of the compiler's rewriting of the Macarius Homily. However the case may be, Zupitza's identification of the Nonantola sermon remains fundamental to understanding the relation between the two Old English homilies — indeed, if Jost is correct, the Nonantola sermon is even more important than Zupitza realized, for it helps establish the priority of the Macarius Homily relative to Napier XXIX.

The Macarius Homily overlaps not only with Napier XXIX in the soul-and-body legend, but also with Vercelli IV in the introduction, and in this case the verbal parallels are so close that it is clear they cannot be independent translations. But which was the borrower, Vercelli IV or the Macarius Homily? Linguistic, textual, and stylistic evidence is inconclusive: Lars-Gunnar Hallander argued that Vercelli IV, whose text is somewhat fuller, is an expanded version of the Macarius Homily, while Malcolm Godden and D. G. Scragg argued that the Macarius

---

[62] Zupitza, 'Zu Seele und Leib', *Archiv*, 91 (1893), 369–404. The Nonantola sermon is translated in Allen and Calder, *Sources and Analogues*, pp. 41–44.

[63] Jost, *Wulfstanstudien*, pp. 206–07. Jost's chief evidence is that all the longer passages in the Latin omitted by the Macarius Homily are also omitted by Napier XXIX, and that the Macarius Homily is closer to the Latin in all but a few readings, which he would account for by assuming that Napier XXIX had access to a better copy of the Macarius Homily. Jost's argument was accepted by Hans Sauer, *Theodulfi Capitula in England*, Münchener-Universitäts-Schriften, Texte und Untersuchungen zur englischen Philologie, 8 (Munich, 1978), pp. 93–94. Moreover, Zupitza did not consider the possibility that some unparalleled material in the two Old English homilies might have been drawn, not from a lost Latin source, but from other Old English sources, as indeed has since been demonstrated (see Scragg, 'Corpus of Vernacular Homilies', pp. 102, 105, and 144, n. 162). See also Claudia Di Sciacca, 'Due note a tre omelie anglosassoni sul tema dell'anima e il corpo', in *Antichità Germaniche: II Parte*, ed. by Vittoria Dolcetti Corazza and Renato Gendre (Alessandria, 2002), pp. 223–50.

Homily is an abbreviated version of Vercelli IV.[64] The fact that the Macarius Homily survives only in a manuscript later than the Vercelli Book seemed to favour Godden's and Scragg's view, but the question was resolved in favour of Hallander's by my discovery of the Latin source, a sermon *De paenitentia* attributed (perhaps wrongly) to Ephrem the Syrian.[65] Comparison reveals that all the material shared by the two Old English homilies is parallelled in the Latin, while all the material unique to Vercelli IV (with two very minor and only apparent exceptions) is not, proving that the Vercelli homilist or his predecessor had copied and padded out the Macarius Homily (or more precisely, an earlier though now lost copy of the Macarius Homily). Were there any doubt, after the parallels with Vercelli IV cease, the Macarius Homily continues with additional material taken directly from 'Ephrem'. My conclusion about the relationship of the two homilies has been accepted by Scragg, who now regards Vercelli IV as a composite homily and argues that the original translation of the *De paenitentia* was made 'at least as early as the 960s and perhaps yet earlier in the tenth century'.[66]

The identification and analysis of common sources used by two or more Old English authors will not, of course, always be decisive in determining their relative chronology; but sources will always be relevant and must always be taken into account. A famous and famously vexed example is the relation between the descriptions of hell in Blickling XVI and of Grendel's mere in *Beowulf*. Richard Morris drew attention to the striking verbal parallels between these two texts in his edition of the Blickling Homilies, and Carleton Brown subsequently endorsed Morris's conclusion that the homilist had drawn on *Beowulf*.[67] Brown's opinion held the field until 1984, when Rowland Collins reversed it by arguing that the *Beowulf* poet had drawn on the Blickling homily.[68] The revolutionary implications for the

---

[64] Hallander, *Old English Verbs in -sian: A Semantic and Derivational Study* (Stockholm, 1966), p. 49; Malcolm Godden, review of Sauer, *Theodulfi Capitula*, *Medium Ævum*, 48 (1979), 265; *Vercelli Homilies*, ed. by Scragg, p. 87.

[65] Wright, 'The Old English "Macarius" Homily, Vercelli Homily IV, and Ephrem Latinus, *De paenitentia*', in *Via Crucis: Essays on Early Medieval Sources and Ideas in Memory of J. E. Cross*, ed. by Thomas N. Hall with assistance from Thomas D. Hill and Charles D. Wright, Medieval European Studies, 1 (Morgantown, 2002), pp. 210–34.

[66] D. G. Scragg, *Dating and Style in Old English Composite Homilies*, H. M. Chadwick Memorial Lectures, 9 (Cambridge, 1998), p. 5.

[67] *The Blickling Homilies*, ed. and trans. by Morris, p. vii; Brown, '*Beowulf* and the Blickling Homilies and Some Textual Notes', *PMLA*, 53 (1938), 905–16 (p. 909).

[68] Collins, 'Blickling Homily XVI and the Dating of *Beowulf*', in *Medieval Studies Conference Aachen 1983*, ed. by W.-D. Bald and H. Weinstock (Frankfurt am Main, 1984), pp. 61–69.

dating of *Beowulf* were not lost on Collins — though Collins may have lost his nerve when he suggested that the description of Grendel's mere could be a late 'textual modification' of the poem.[69] Kevin Kiernan has recently hailed Collins's 'convincing analysis' as evidence for a late date for *Beowulf*, though without mentioning Collins's escape clause or my extended re-examination of the entire question in 1993.[70] A fundamental weakness in both Brown's and Collins's arguments was their failure to compare the two Old English texts closely to their possible common source, the *Visio Pauli*. In 1935 Theodore Silverstein had argued that 'the main foundation' of the Blickling homilist's description was the 'Hanging Sinners' scene in the redactions of the apocryphal *Visio Pauli*, while *Beowulf* had 'furnished merely a transforming suggestion' to the homilist.[71] Yet even Silverstein did not investigate in detail the relation between the *Visio* and the homily or *Beowulf*. My analysis of the parallels drew on all the surviving Latin versions of the *Visio*, including the more recently discovered Redaction XI, which provided crucial new evidence for the form of the *Visio* that must have been available to the Blickling homilist. *Beowulf* and Blickling XVI, however, each has significant independent parallels with the *Visio* that are most economically accounted for by positing their common use of an Old English translation of the *Visio Pauli*, which would also account for the striking verbal parallels.[72] Although sufficient to 'save the appearances', this hypothesis does not foreclose the possibility that the homilist also drew on the poem, or indeed the poet on the homily. The question remains open, yet no hypothesis that purports to explain the relation between *Beowulf* and Blickling XVI can ignore their common relation to the *Visio Pauli*.

LITERACY AND AUDIENCE

The very existence of an extensive corpus of vernacular homilies based upon Latin sources has significant implications for our estimation of Anglo-Saxon literacy.[73] At least a generation before Ælfric and Wulfstan there must have been Anglo-Saxon preachers with sufficient command of Latin to read and translate these

---

[69] Collins, 'Blickling Homily XVI and the Dating of *Beowulf*', p. 69.

[70] Kiernan, *Beowulf and the 'Beowulf' Manuscript*, rev. edn (Ann Arbor, 1996), p. xix.

[71] Silverstein, *Visio Sancti Pauli: The History of the Apocalypse in Latin together with Nine Texts*, Studies and Documents, 1 (London, 1935), p. 11.

[72] Wright, *Irish Tradition*, pp. 116–36.

[73] For a convenient recent discussion of Anglo-Saxon literacy with references to earlier literature, see Hugh Magennis, 'Audience(s), Reception, Literacy', in *Companion to Anglo-Saxon Literature*, ed. by Pulsiano and Treharne, pp. 84–101.

sources for an audience with small Latin or none. The range of competence varies widely: some homilists, such as the author of Vercelli X, translate accurately (though often freely) and idiomatically, while others, such as the author of Blickling XIII, who seems barely to have understood his sources (two recensions of the apocryphal *Transitus Mariae*), translate inaccurately and unidiomatically.[74] Unfortunately, we have little firm evidence for dating and localizing these homilies other than the dates of the manuscripts (the internal dating of Blickling XI to the year 971 being a unique case), so it is difficult to draw conclusions from them about the latinity of the clergy at particular times or places; but to whatever extent the more competent performances are pre-Reform, they must impact our evaluation of the reformers' representations of the pastoral conditions that obtained in the non-monastic churches they attempted to regularize, and of the learning of the secular clergy whose expulsions they justified in part by characterizing them as ignorant and negligent. A batch of homilies competently translated from Latin sources and dating before Edgar's reign would be a powerful counterweight to Ælfric's complaint about the 'unlearned priests' of his youth, who thought themselves great teachers if they knew any Latin at all.[75] No doubt there were such ill-trained priests (at all times), but there may have been others of respectable attainments (by the standards of the time), and it is by no means clear that the common run of monks during Ælfric's maturity were very much more learned.[76]

The fact that these homilies are in the vernacular presupposes that their intended audiences, whether laypersons or clerics, would not readily have understood homilies in Latin; most, perhaps, were *illitterati* in the medieval sense of the term (i.e. not literate in Latin). We know that Ælfric and Wulfstan urged bishops to preach to their clergy in the vernacular, and notwithstanding exceptional cases of (semi-)latinate laypersons such as Ælfric's patrons Æthelweard and Æthelmær, we can assume that lay audiences who heard sermons either heard them in English or

---

[74] For Vercelli X, see Samantha Zacher, 'Sin, Syntax, and Synonyms: Rhetorical Style and Structure in Vercelli Homily X', *JEGP*, 103 (2004), 53–76; on the poor latinity of Blickling XIII, see Mary Clayton, *The Cult of the Virgin Mary in Anglo-Saxon England*, CSASE, 2 (Cambridge, 1990), pp. 232–35, and *Apocryphal Gospels of Mary*, pp. 239–45, with a new edition of the homily (based on another manuscript) at pp. 246–314.

[75] Preface to Genesis, ed. by Jonathan Wilcox in *Ælfric's Prefaces*, Durham Medieval Texts, 9 (Durham, 1994), p. 117.

[76] C. E. Hohler, 'Some Service-Books of the Later Saxon Church', in *Tenth-Century Studies: Essays in Commemoration of the Millennium of the Council of Winchester and Regularis Concordia*, ed. by David Parsons (London, 1975), pp. 60–83 and 217–27, esp. pp. 71–74, rates very low the latinity of both clergy and monks during the Reform period.

heard them in Latin without understanding them.[77] Since vernacular homilies could serve both clergy and laity, however, and since audiences could be mixed, it is that much harder to specify the audience for which any particular surviving homily was composed, unless the preacher addresses them more concretely than *men þa leofestan* — which is rarely the case. Homilies could be composed for devotional reading as well as for oral delivery (whether to a congregation in the context of the Mass, or at the Night Office), so we may not even be able to say whether a particular homily was meant to be preached at all.[78] We will probably never be able to say that a particular homily was preached to the congregation of a particular Anglo-Saxon church — unless we are lucky enough to identify a precisely localized actual source manuscript used by the homilist. Failing that, the highest level of specificity we can hope to achieve is whether a particular homily's intended audience was monastic or non-monastic, or lay, or mixed, and in many cases the only recoverable 'audience' will be an implied one, and perhaps no more specific than a generalized Christian 'subject position'.[79] In the Blickling Homilies the paucity of direct and exclusive addresses to specific groups or estates, as well as the frequency of simultaneous discussion of both lay and clerical obligations, led Milton McC. Gatch to conclude that their audience is 'unknowable'.[80]

[77] For Ælfric's charge to bishops, see *Councils and Synods with Other Documents Relating to the English Church*, vol. I: *A.D. 871–1204*, Part 1: *871–1066*, ed. and trans. by Dorothy Whitelock and others (Oxford, 1981), pp. 26–61. Thomas N. Hall has noted cases in which Latin sermons were preached to laypersons during the Middle Ages, and argues that a group of four late tenth-century Latin sermons from Canterbury were preached to an audience that included laypersons: 'Latin Sermons and Lay Preaching: Four Latin Sermons from Post-Reform Canterbury', in *The Power of Words*, ed. by Magennis and Wilcox, pp. 132–70. On performance in relation to identity and community, see Mary Swan, '*Men ða leofestan*: Genre, the Canon, and the Old English Homiletic Tradition', in *The Christian Tradition in Anglo-Saxon England: Approaches to Current Scholarship and Teaching*, ed. by Paul Cavill (Cambridge, 2004), pp. 185–92 (pp. 189–91).

[78] For the various contexts of preaching in Ælfric's time, see *Ælfric's Prefaces*, ed. by Wilcox, pp. 11–12 and 20–21, and Wilcox, 'Ælfric in Dorset and the Landscape of Pastoral Care', in *Pastoral Care in Late Anglo-Saxon England*, ed. by Francesca Tinti (Cambridge, 2005), pp. 52–62.

[79] For a concise discussion of the various kinds of audience, see Paul Strohm, 'Chaucer's Audience(s): Fictional, Implied, Intended, Actual', *Chaucer Review*, 18 (1983), 137–45. The 'implied audience' is defined by Strohm as 'a hypothetical construct, the sum of all the author's assumptions about the person he or she is addressing'. On the formation and 'interpellation' of the Christian subject in the vernacular homilies, see Clare A. Lees, *Tradition and Belief: Religious Writing in Late Anglo-Saxon England* (Minneapolis, 1999), pp. 120 and 130–34.

[80] Gatch, 'The Unknowable Audience of the Blickling Homilies', *ASE*, 18 (1989), 99–115; the following quotations are from pp. 115 and 114.

Gatch does, however, hold out the hope for progress through the identification of the homilies' Latin sources: 'We need to know as much as can be learned about how Latin, ecclesiastical — often, indeed, monastic — conventional materials were prepared and transmitted to serve the needs of Anglo-Saxon Christians.' Gatch rightly cautions that 'it is not necessarily the case that authors will tailor their materials to the special needs and conditions of those who will read their writings or hear them read'; still, we may be able to venture reasonable hypotheses based on the kinds of sources used and especially the ways they have been tailored if they are tailored at all. Substantive changes that can be attributed to the homilist (as opposed to an intermediary) must have been purposeful — though the purpose may not always relate immediately to the needs or conditions of his intended audience. Any hypothesis must take into account not just what sources were used but also in what form they were transmitted and how they were used. The use of a passage on the fear of God from Cassian's monastic treatise *De institutis coenobiorum* in Vercelli XII, for example, might seem to suggest that its author was a monk. Yet two other considerations urge against this conclusion. First, the context of the passage within a sequence of unsourced motifs on the same virtue suggests that the homilist did not draw directly on Cassian, but on a florilegium of extracts *De timore Dei* (or on a Latin homily that had incorporated such extracts). Second, in adapting the passage the homilist (or conceivably his predecessor) systematically eliminated all the distinctively monastic virtues relating to the renunciation of possessions. He may have been a monk tailoring his source for an audience of laypersons, but he is more likely to have been a member of the secular clergy, and this hypothesis is also more consistent with the references to the teaching functions of bishops and masspriests in Vercelli XI, which is probably by the same author.[81]

If systematic omission of material specifically appropriate to monks points to a non-monastic audience, systematic omission of material not appropriate or relevant to monks, by the same token, points to a monastic audience. Elaine Treharne has shown this to be the case with the homilies in Cotton Vespasian D. XIV, including the translation of the sermon by Ralph d'Escures. Treharne makes the important qualification, however, that a monastic audience could include not just 'monks' in the strict sense but also *conuersi* (lay brothers) and confraternity members.[82] The

---

[81] See Wright, 'Vercelli Homilies XI–XIII', and pp. 33–34 above.

[82] Treharne, 'Life of English', pp. 171–72. For evidence from Bede for monastic preaching to an augmented audience at special occasions, see Alan Thacker, 'Monks, Preaching and Pastoral Care in Early Anglo-Saxon England', in *Pastoral Care before the Parish*, ed. by John Blair and Richard Sharpe (Leicester, 1992), pp. 137–70 (pp. 140–41).

dichotomies of lay and clerical or monastic and non-monastic, then, can be complicated by circumstances and occasions that brought together more than one kind of audience; and we have to allow not only for homilists who envisioned 'mixed' audiences but also for those who anticipated different audiences on different occasions. A bishop, for example, might compose model sermons *ad clerum* with the expectation that they would subsequently be preached in some form *ad populum*. Precisely this context has been invoked by Gatch as a way to account for certain of the Blickling Homilies that seem to address clergy principally yet also admonish laypersons.[83]

The very conventionality of homiletic discourse also complicates efforts to identify a homily's intended audience or institutional contexts. Just as practices condemned in a penitential may not reflect contemporary conditions, so admonitions in a homily may be generic and taken over from sources composed centuries earlier and in another part of the Christian world.[84] Nonetheless, a homilist's treatment of patristic or Carolingian sources may well involve some modification for an Anglo-Saxon audience — if nothing more than omission or explanation of references to concepts or things that may be unfamiliar to them. At times a homilist may intervene more decisively, even tendentiously, to control the ideological thrust of his source: not simply adopting the source's authority, but diverting it in order to address beliefs and behaviours he wishes to commend or condemn, or social and institutional groups he wishes to admonish, defend, or reform. Close attention to omissions, additions, and alterations may thus yield insight into a homilist's assumptions about his audience — what he thought needed to be

---

[83] Gatch, 'Unknowable Audience', pp. 104–05.

[84] On the 'atemporality' of homiletic discourse, see Lees, *Tradition and Belief.* As Lees acknowledges, Wulfstan's *Sermo Lupi ad Anglos* is a striking exception to the general rule, but she is reluctant to allow others, including the complaint in Vercelli XI (ed. by Scragg, lines 90–99) against the plundering of churches and holy orders by kings, bishops, and ealdormen (cf. Lees, p. 85). I have argued that this passage may be a secular cleric's protestation against the state-sponsored expulsions of the clerks by the reforming bishops ('Vercelli Homilies XI–XIII', pp. 222–26). Elsewhere, moreover, I have suggested that a prophecy added by the author of Vercelli XV to the *Apocalypse of Thomas*, attributing the corruption of the Last Days to 'young kings, young popes, young bishops, and young ealdormen' (ed. by Scragg, lines 6–8) is an example of politically motivated *uaticinia ex euentu* directed against the Benedictine reformers, who acted with the approval of King Edgar and Pope John XII, both then still in their twenties: 'Vercelli Homily XV and the *Apocalypse of Thomas*', forthcoming in *New Readings on the Vercelli Book*, ed. by Samantha Zacher and Andy Orchard (Toronto).

simplified, elaborated, or qualified in order to accommodate the source to their needs and conditions.

Intellectual History

Source identification tells us something about the texts consulted by an Anglo-Saxon author, and hence what texts were available in at least one Anglo-Saxon library — though for reasons discussed above, it may not always tell us in precisely what form a text was transmitted. Knowing what kinds of texts were available in turn tells us something about the intellectual life and spirituality of the ecclesiastical centres (or peripheries) within which the homilists worked. Even if a homilist does not 'tailor' his sources, he has already interposed his own authority by virtue of selecting those sources rather than others (presumably neither at random nor by default).[85] Invention, in the rhetorical sense of 'finding' the appropriate materials, is an integral part of composition, and the choices a homilist makes may tell us a good deal not just about his library, but also about his ideology.

It goes without saying that the Bible was the single most pervasive source for Old English homilists; biblical citations and allusions are a special case, however, that I must set aside here.[86] Yet to speak of the influence of the Bible begs a crucial question (aside from the question of variant versions such as Vulgate or Vetus Latina), for in the early Middle Ages there was considerable uncertainty, or at any

---

[85] Cross, *Cambridge Pembroke College MS. 25*, p. 175, notes that the author of Tristram III had two Latin Ascension sermons in the Pembroke Homiliary from which to choose: one that 'concentrates mainly on the apostles [...] with applications to the priestly offices of the present', and one that 'is directed more pointedly to the ordinary Christian'. 'By choosing the second Latin sermon as the basis for his own,' Cross concludes, 'the Anglo-Saxon composer indicated his purpose and audience, but he takes from the first [material] which is made applicable to all Christians.' Moreover, when the homilist adapts a Latin sequence for Ascension, he expands the source to explain that the apostles were Christ's followers, that Jerusalem was a city, that Samaria was a nation, and that the first man's name was Adam. For the Latin source, see Jane Moores, '*Rex omnipotens*: A Sequence Used in an Old English Ascension Day Homily', *Anglia*, 106 (1988), 138–44; the corresponding passage is edited by Hildegard Tristram, *Vier altenglische Predigten aus der heterodoxen Tradition mit Kommentar, Übersetzung und Glossar sowie drei weiteren Texten im Anhang* (Inaugural-dissertation Freiburg-im-Breisgau; privately printed, 1970), pp. 162–63.

[86] For an incomplete inventory of biblical citations, see A. S. Cook, *Biblical Quotations in Old English Prose Writers [First Series]* (London, 1898), and Cook, *Biblical Quotations in Old English Prose Writers: Second Series* (New York, 1903). For a survey of the influence of the Bible in Old English literature, see Thomas N. Hall, 'Biblical and Patristic Learning', in *Companion to Anglo-Saxon Literature*, ed. by Pulsiano and Treharne, pp. 327–44.

rate flexibility, as to what constituted 'scripture'. As Nancy Thompson has noted, vernacular homilists often conflate biblical citations with non-biblical material as if they were of comparable authority, sometimes casually identifying the source of a non-biblical dictum as 'se godspellere' (literally, 'the evangelist').[87] The author of Fadda I even introduces the Latin incipit of the pseudo-Augustinian Doomsday sermon as the words of 'the Lord himself' (*Drihten selfa*), despite its address to 'fratres dilectissimi' and third-person reference to 'Dominus'.[88] There was, in addition, a vast body of apocryphal and pseudepigraphal literature whose relation to canonical scripture was ill defined, at least for those who did not have access to the pseudo-Gelasian decree (or chose to ignore it).[89] Apocryphal narratives satisfied curious minds wanting to know about pivotal moments in Salvation history which the Bible treats cursorily or not at all: the childhood of Jesus, the Harrowing of Hell, the Assumption of Mary, the acts and martyrdoms of the apostles, and the revelations and visions accorded to Christ's favoured disciples. The recently revised and updated *SASLC* entries for the Apocrypha show just how liberally Anglo-Saxon authors availed themselves of these non-canonical writings.[90] In the anonymous homilies alone we find material taken from, inter alia, the pseudo-Matthew Infancy Gospel (Vercelli VI and Assmann X), the Gospel of Nicodemus (HomS 29, NicC), the *Transitus Mariae* (Blickling XIII and Tristram I),[91] the *Visio Pauli* (HomM 1, Blickling IV and XVI, Napier XLVI, etc.),[92] and the *Apocalypse of Thomas* (Blickling VII, Vercelli XV, Bazire-Cross 8, and HomU 12),[93] not

---

[87] Thompson, '*Hit Segð on Halgum Bocum*', pp. 393–99. For examples of the 'fusion' of scriptural echo with elaborations on scripture from sermon and exegesis, see the commentary on Bazire-Cross 10, *Eleven Old English Rogationtide Homilies*, pp. 126–27.

[88] Luiselli Fadda, *Nuove omelie*, p. 27, lines 262–65. The homilist also refers to the Three Utterances exemplum as *godspel* (p. 19, line 171).

[89] On the fluid boundary between canonical and apocryphal writings, see Frederick M. Biggs, 'Ælfric's Andrew and the Apocrypha', *JEGP*, 104 (2005), 473–94, and for a survey of Anglo-Saxon understandings of what constituted 'apocrypha', see Biggs, 'An Introduction and Overview of Recent Work', in *Apocryphal Texts*, ed. by Powell and Scragg, pp. 1–25. For the pseudo-Gelasian decree, see *Das Decretum Gelasianum de libris recipiendis et non recipiendis*, ed. by Ernst von Dobschütz, Texte und Untersuchungen, 38.4 (Leipzig, 1912).

[90] *Apocrypha in Anglo-Saxon England*, ed. by Frederick M. Biggs (Kalamazoo, forthcoming), with entries on all the apocryphal texts next mentioned.

[91] See especially Clayton, *Apocryphal Gospels of Mary*.

[92] See Healey, *Old English Vision of Saint Paul*; Wright, *Irish Tradition*, chap. 3.

[93] See Förster, 'New Version of the Apocalypse of Thomas'; Wright, '*The Apocalypse of Thomas*'.

to mention more loosely defined apocryphal traditions such as the Harrowing of Hell (Blickling VII, HomS 27, HomS 28, NicD, and NicE), 'Delivering the Damned' (Vercelli XV, Fadda III, HomS 6, and HomS 29),[94] the Sunday Letter (Napier XLIII, XLIV, and LVII, HomS 33, HomS 44, HomU 53, HomU 54, and HomM 6),[95] the Seven Heavens (HomU 12.2), and the Three Utterances (Fadda I, Bazire-Cross 9, and HomS 5).[96]

The acceptance or rejection of apocrypha has often been regarded as a defining contrast between the homilies of Ælfric and a pre-Reform homiletic tradition. The classic statement of this dichotomy is Malcolm Godden's essay 'Ælfric and the Vernacular Prose Tradition', which noted that Ælfric condemned three apocryphal narratives found in anonymous homilies: the Assumption of Mary, the Vision of Paul, and 'Delivering the Damned'.[97] Godden concluded that 'what Ælfric objected to in these earlier homilies was not primarily their theological ideas or their views on religious practices, but rather their use of sensational narratives which were clearly fictitious and in some cases of dubious morality'. More recently Mary Clayton has argued that Ælfric objected to the *Transitus Mariae* and *Visio Pauli* not because of their sensational narratives (since he does translate other sensational narratives) but rather because these particular texts had already been impugned by Carolingian authorities, and that he objected to the story of the delivery of the damned on moral rather than theological grounds.[98] Clayton also challenges the assumptions that the anonymous homilies are pre-Reform (since most of the manuscripts date from the second half of the tenth or the eleventh centuries) and that Ælfric's views on apocrypha were in any way representative of the Reform (since monks of the Reform period actively disseminated the very kinds of writings that Ælfric condemned, often in conjunction with his own writings). For Clayton, the 'distinguishing factor' is Ælfric's access to Carolingian sources that may have been unavailable to the anonymous homilists.

---

[94] See Mary Clayton, 'Delivering the Damned: A Motif in Old English Homiletic Prose', *Medium Ævum*, 55 (1986), 92–102; Thomas D. Hill, 'Delivering the Damned in Old English Anonymous Homilies and Jón Arason's *Ljómur*', *Medium Ævum*, 61 (1992), 75–82; Sarah Cutforth, 'Delivering the Damned in Old English Homilies: An Additional Note', *NQ*, n.s., 40 (1993), 435–37.

[95] See Clare Lees, 'The "Sunday Letter" and the "Sunday Lists"', *ASE*, 14 (1985), 129–51.

[96] See Willard, *Two Apocrypha*.

[97] Godden, 'Ælfric and the Vernacular Prose Tradition', in *Old English Homily*, ed. by Szarmach and Huppé, pp. 99–117; the quotation following is from p. 102.

[98] Clayton, *Cult of the Virgin Mary*, pp. 260–65.

I am more inclined than is Clayton to accept the consensus that the anonymous homilies (excluding manifestly late composites) are broadly representative of pre-Reform preaching traditions, and to interpret Ælfric's aversion towards certain apocryphal narratives as evidence of his own judgement as to what constituted *gedwyld*.[99] At the same time, I think that it is problematic to characterize the anonymous homilies as 'heterodox', since 'orthodoxy' in matters relating to the particular and final judgement of souls was not as clearly and unambiguously defined as (for example) Trinitarian doctrine.[100] Of course, anonymous homilies do not always draw on apocrypha relating to Last Things — though the relative frequency with which they do is in striking contrast to Ælfric's restraint, or for that matter Wulfstan's.[101] As Ananya Kabir has shown, anonymous homilists drew on apocryphal sources such as the *Transitus Mariae* and the *Visio Pauli* that distinguished between an interim repose of souls in heaven or in a paradise distinct from heaven, whereas Ælfric followed Augustine in equating paradise typologically with heaven.[102] The fact that four anonymous homilies draw independently on the *Apocalypse of Thomas* and another three on the Three Utterances, while Ælfric and Wulfstan both studiously avoid these manifestly popular sources, likewise indexes

[99] Thomas N. Hall, 'Ælfric and the Epistle to the Laodicians', in *Apocryphal Texts*, ed. by Powell and Scragg, pp. 65–83, has argued that Ælfric accepted this work as canonical (despite its rejection by Augustine, Gregory, and Jerome) on the basis of 'his own individual experience as a reader' (p. 81).

[100] On the inherent difficulty of defining orthodoxy in the context of early medieval eschatological traditions, see Thomas N. Hall, 'The Psychedelic Transmogrification of the Soul in Vercelli Homily IV', in *Time and Eternity: The Medieval Discourse*, ed. by Gerhard Jaritz and Gerson Moreno-Riaño, International Medieval Research, 9 (Turnhout, 2003), pp. 309–22 (pp. 310–11). I have elsewhere argued against characterizing Irish traditions that draw on apocryphal sources as 'heterodox' (*Irish Tradition*, pp. 38–41 and 228–29, n. 65). See also Nancy M. Thompson, 'Anglo-Saxon Orthodoxy', in *Old English Literature in its Manuscript Context*, ed. by Joyce Tally Lionarons (Morgantown, 2004), pp. 37–66.

[101] As Aideen O'Leary and Frederick Biggs have noted, the *passiones* of the apostles were a special case of writings that we now regard as 'apocryphal' but that Ælfric was more than willing to use, unless he objected to some particular doctrinal point — and even then he might simply excise the offending passage. See O'Leary, 'An Orthodox Old English Homiliary? Ælfric's Views on the Apocryphal Acts of the Apostles', *NM*, 100 (1999), 15–26; Biggs, 'Ælfric's Andrew', and 'Ælfric's Comments about the *Passio Thomae*', *NQ*, n.s., 52 (2005), 5–8.

[102] Kabir, *Paradise, Death and Doomsday in Anglo-Saxon Literature*, CSASE, 32 (Cambridge, 2001), esp. p. 36.

a radical difference not just of eschatological doctrine but of intellectual culture, whether or not it was a function of the Reform movement.[103]

After the Bible and the apocrypha, one might expect the most influential writings to have been patristic texts;[104] but manuscript evidence and source analysis converge to show that the major Fathers of the Church had comparatively little direct influence on the anonymous homilists. Of the four major Fathers as defined by Bede, only Gregory the Great was a significant source. Max Förster demonstrated that Gregory's gospel homilies were used in both the Blickling and Vercelli Homilies, and subsequent research has identified a number of additional borrowings.[105] In stunning contrast, not a single direct borrowing from a genuine work by Jerome or Ambrose has been identified in the entire corpus of anonymous homilies, and only one or two slight ones from works by Augustine; even indirect borrowings are rare.[106] Gregory's special position was no doubt due to his reputation

---

[103] Overviews of apocryphal eschatological traditions in the anonymous homilies include Willard, *Two Apocrypha*; Milton McC. Gatch, 'Two Uses of Apocrypha in Old English Homilies', *Church History*, 33 (1964), 379–91; Gatch, 'Eschatology in the Anonymous Old English Homilies', *Traditio*, 21 (1965), 117–65; Hildegard L. C. Tristram, 'Stock Descriptions of Heaven and Hell in Old English Prose and Poetry', *NM*, 79 (1978), 102–13; Wright, *Irish Tradition*, esp. chap. 3, 'The Insular Vision of Hell'; and Thomas N. Hall, 'Old English Religious Prose: Rhetorics of Salvation and Damnation', in *Reading Medieval Literature: Interpretations of Old and Middle English Texts*, ed. by Elaine M. Treharne and David F. Johnson (Oxford, 2005), pp. 137–48.

[104] The authoritative guide to Latin patristic texts (through Bede) is E. Dekkers, *Clavis Patrum Latinorum*, 3rd edn (Turnhout, 1995). For a survey of the influence of the major Fathers in Anglo-Saxon England, see Hall, 'Biblical and Patristic Learning'.

[105] See Thomas N. Hall, 'The Early English Manuscripts of Gregory the Great's *Homilies on the Gospel* and *Homilies on Ezechiel*: A Preliminary Survey', in *Rome and the North: The Early Reception of Gregory the Great in Germanic Europe*, ed. by Rolf H. Bremmer, Jr, Kees Dekker, and David F. Johnson, Mediaevalia Groningana, 4 (Paris, 2001), pp. 115–36, with a partial list of anonymous homilies that use Gregory's gospel homilies at p. 116 and n. 8, including Blickling II and III, Vercelli V, VIII, and XVI, and HomS 48. Gregory's homilies are critically edited by Raymond Étaix: Gregory the Great, *Homiliae in euangelia*, CCSL, 141 (Turnhout, 1999); for an English translation, see David Hurst, *Gregory the Great: Forty Gospel Homilies*, Cistercian Studies Series, 123 (Kalamazoo, 1990).

[106] I base this statement on the inventory of source discoveries by Adam Dunbar McCoy, 'The Use of Writings of English Authors in Old English Homiletic Literature' (unpublished doctoral dissertation, Cornell University, 1973), pp. 176–238 (Appendix, 'The Homilies and their Sources'), my own survey of more recent published source scholarship, and searches of the *Fontes Anglo-Saxonici* database. The only direct borrowing from Augustine hitherto identified, to the best of my knowledge, is in Blickling XVI, which makes brief use of an Augustinian sermon

as the Pope who sent Augustine of Canterbury to evangelize the English (and the fact that his gospel homilies were frequently anthologized in homiliaries such as Paul the Deacon's);[107] but this does not really explain why homilists failed to use the voluminous writings of the other Augustine. The answer is that they did — only the other Augustine was not Augustine of Hippo, but the equally prolific pseudo-Augustine of Hippo. The relative dearth of patristic originalia in Anglo-Saxon England prior to the eleventh century was offset by a wealth of pseudony-mous writings, and homilists did not, as a rule, have the resources or acumen to distinguish the authentic from the spurious. Moreover, many pseudo-Augustinian sermons were legitimated by their inclusion in early homiliaries such as Alan of Farfa's.[108] In such conditions, even a text so patently un-Augustinian as the Doomsday sermon could pass for the real thing. But vernacular homilists were no mere dupes of medieval forgeries, for they found in them something they wanted, something they also found in the apocrypha and could not have found in the Bible or the genuine works of Augustine: vivid, indeed lurid, narratives of the afterlife. As Rudolph Willard noted,[109] the pseudonymous sermons in the Augustinian appendix in volumes 39 and 40 of the *Patrologia Latina* (notably the sermons *Ad fratres in eremo*[110]) are 'a rich treasury' of the sort of extra-biblical eschatological

---

identified by Max Förster, 'Altenglische Predigtquellen II,' *Archiv*, 122 (1909), 246–56 (pp. 255–56). Förster thought the homilist used another Augustinian sermon as well, but Cross considered this doubtful; see J. E. Cross, 'Blickling Homily XIV and the Old English Martyrology on John the Baptist', *Anglia*, 93 (1975), 145–60 (p. 146); Cross argued that the first Augustinian parallel is 'less than Förster suggested', but accepted it as a source for one sentence. Cross elsewhere suggested that the author of Blickling XI derived a 'hint' for part of one sentence from a sermon by Augustine: 'On the Blickling Homily for Ascension Day (No. XI)', *NM*, 70 (1969), 228–40 (p. 235). For a few indirect borrowings from Jerome and Ambrose, see my 'Blickling Homily III'.

[107] For a survey of the manuscript transmission of Gregory's homilies, see Hall, 'Early English Manuscripts'.

[108] Gatch, *Preaching and Theology*, p. 243, n. 13, points out that Alan's homiliary contains a much higher concentration of pseudo-Augustinian (and Caesarian) items than does Paul the Deacon's, upon which Ælfric relied.

[109] Willard, 'The Address of the Soul to the Body', *PMLA*, 50 (1935), 957–83 (pp. 960–61). Compare Gatch's comments, *Preaching and Theology*, p. 102. Three of the sermons *Ad fratres in eremo* (nos 49, 58, and 68) are translated in Allen and Calder, *Sources and Analogues*, pp. 44–50 and 146–49.

[110] See Richard Sharpe, *A Handlist of the Latin Writers of Great Britain and Ireland before 1540*, Publications of the Journal of Medieval Latin, 1 (Turnhout, 1997), with *Additions and Corrections, 1997–2001* (Turnhout, 2001), no. 388; Machielsen, *Clavis Patristica*, I, no. 1127.

lore retailed by Anglo-Saxon homilists: here we find descriptions of the struggle of angels and demons over the soul as it exits the body, the addresses of good and bad souls to their bodies (*Sermo App.* 59, a version of the Nonantola sermon translated by the Macarius Homily), and the signs and events of Doomsday (*Sermo App.* 251, translated by Fadda I, echoed in Bazire-Cross 11). Such tales from the crypt would keep a congregation on the edge of their pews and motivate even the cynical to repent — the most immediate goal of the preacher's 'design for terror'.[111]

If the sermons *Ad fratres in eremo* were the B-movies of the 'pastoral scare' genre, the art films were the sermons of Caesarius of Arles (which likewise often circulated under Augustine's name). Joseph Trahern has inventoried the many Old English texts, especially homilies, that draw directly or indirectly on Caesarius, whose sermons must have been among the most widely circulated in Anglo-Saxon England, whether in the form of complete collections, or — as the surviving manuscript evidence again suggests — anthologized in small groups within multiple-author compilations.[112] As Trahern has suggested, the popularity of Caesarius's sermons with Anglo-Saxon homilists was a function of their original purpose as models for parish clergy to instruct the laity by means of simple but vivid and memorable images.[113] It is hardly accidental that the most influential passages were dramatic admonitory speeches from the beyond — Christ's 'Ego te, homo' address at Doomsday[114] and the 'Dry Bones Speak' exemplum — though to ensure that their audiences were not misled by Caesarius's literary conceits, some homilists

---

[111] I am not the first to transfer this formulation of Arthur Brodeur's from *Beowulf* to the vernacular homilies: see Szarmach, 'The Vercelli Homilies', p. 245.

[112] See Joseph B. Trahern, 'Caesarius of Arles and Old English Literature: Some Contributions and a Recapitulation', *ASE*, 5 (1976), 105–19; and Trahern's entry on Caesarius in the forthcoming C-volume of *Sources of Anglo-Saxon Literary Culture*, ed. by Thomas N. Hall. Of the twelve manuscripts of Caesarius's sermons listed by Helmut Gneuss, *Handlist*, only nos 574 and 808.2 contain more than one or two sermons. For Morin's critical edition see above, note 24; for a recent edition with French translation and commentary, see Marie-José Delage, Cyrille Lambot, and Germain Morin, *Césaire d'Arles: Sermons au peuple*, 3 vols, Sources Chrétiennes, 175, 243, and 330 (Paris, 1971–86); Joël Courreau and Germain Morin, *Césaire d'Arles: Sermons sur l'Écriture*, vol. I, Sources Chrétiennes, 447 (Paris, 2000). Three sermons by Caesarius (nos 57, 58, and 151) are translated in Allen and Calder, *Sources and Analogues*, pp. 101–06 and 149–53. All the surviving sermons are translated in *Caesarius of Arles: Sermons*, trans. by Mary Magdeleine Mueller, 3 vols, Fathers of the Church, 31, 47, 66 (Washington, D.C., 1956–73).

[113] Trahern, 'Caesarius of Arles', pp. 118–19.

[114] Other reflexes of the 'Ego te, homo' speech in Old English occur in HomS 29, Bazire-Cross 10 and 11, and Assmann XIV. See *Vercelli Homilies*, ed. by Scragg, p. 141.

went out of their way to explain that in addressing a singular 'homo' Christ was really speaking to all mankind, and that the dry bones didn't really speak at all![115] Not that Caesarius was valued only for his powerful warnings of the transience of life and the fate of the soul after death; though not as subtle a psychologist as Gregory, like Gregory he had a bishop's practical skill in linking personal salvation in the next world to concrete ethical and social obligations in this world: another of his popular dramatic speeches (used in Blickling IV, Napier XLIX, and Ælfric's *CH* II.7) was God's stern rebuke of 'man' for his reluctance to tithe.[116]

After Gregory and Caesarius, the next most influential source was Isidore of Seville; but for vernacular homilists the favourite Isidorean text was not the *Etymologiae* but the *Liber synonymorum de lamentatione animae peccatoris*, a dialogue between Man and Reason about the transitoriness of the world and immortality of the soul that survives in eight Anglo-Saxon manuscripts, many with vernacular glosses.[117] I have already noted that the *Synonyma* is the direct or ultimate source of several *ubi sunt* passages in Old English. It is the main source for Vercelli XXII, HomU 16, and one of the main sources of Vercelli X (and its variant Napier XLIX, as well as Irvine VII, both composite homilies that borrow from Vercelli X). Like Caesarius's dramatic speech of the dry bones, Isidore's notoriously bombastic *contemptus mundi* profoundly impacted the way Anglo-Saxon homilists gave verbal expression to 'perceptions of transience'.[118]

---

[115] See Willard, 'Vercelli Homily VIII', p. 327 (who compares Vercelli VIII, line 46, 'emne þon gelicost þe he to anum men sprece', with *Christ III*, lines 1376–77, 'Onginneð sylf cweðan, | swa he to anum sprece, ond hwæðre ealle mæneð'); and J. E. Cross, 'The Dry Bones Speak: A Theme in Some Old English Homilies', *JEGP*, 56 (1957), 434–49 (p. 437: 'Both the Old English homilies independently insert "if the bones speak" and the Bodley sermon feels it necessary to conclude with "Then dear men, though the dead bones *cannot* speak from the tomb yet we can teach ourselves by this"').

[116] See Rudolph Willard, 'The Blickling-Junius Tithing Homily and Caesarius of Arles', in *Philologica: The Malone Anniversary Studies*, ed. by Thomas A. Kirby and Henry B. Woolf (Baltimore, 1949), pp. 65–78 (p. 68).

[117] See Claudia Di Sciacca, 'The *Synonyma* by Isidore of Seville as a Source in Anglo-Saxon England' (unpublished doctoral thesis, University of Cambridge, 2002). For the manuscripts, see the index to Gneuss, *Handlist*. For the use of the *Synonyma* in Vercelli XXII, see *Vercelli Homilies*, ed. by Scragg, pp. 366–67; for HomU 16, see Friedrich Kluge, 'Zu altenglischen Dichtungen', *Englische Studien*, 8 (1885), 472–79, and Cross, '"Ubi Sunt" Passages', pp. 27–29; for Vercelli X, Zacher, 'Sin, Syntax, and Synonyms', pp. 67–75; and for Irvine VII, *Old English Homilies*, ed. by Irvine, pp. 192–95.

[118] Christine Fell, 'Perceptions of Transience', in *The Cambridge Companion to Old English Literature*, ed. by Malcolm Godden and Michael Lapidge (Cambridge, 1991), pp. 172–89.

Source scholarship has contributed to our understanding of the anonymous homilists and their cultural milieu not only by documenting the pervasive influence of such standard Christian-Latin authorities as Gregory, Caesarius, and Isidore (and, as a by-product, the pervasive absence of such standard authorities as Augustine, Jerome, and Ambrose), but also by confirming the availability of certain texts by rarer ones, including some non-western Fathers. Recent discoveries have shown, for example, that vernacular homilists drew upon Latin versions of sermons attributed to Ephrem the Syrian and John Chrysostom. The use of a highly wrought admonition to tears and penance from the sermon *De paenitentia* in the so-called Macarius Homily (and indirectly in Vercelli IV) provides the most concrete and extensive evidence to date for the influence of 'Ephremic' writings in Anglo-Saxon England, which has been the subject of intensive (but often inconclusive) research. Again, prior to Samantha Zacher's recent discovery that Vercelli VII translates a Latin version of a homily of Chrysostom on the weakness and indulgence of women, there had been no documented use of a genuine work by Chrysostom in any Old English text, and only sporadic borrowings in Anglo-Latin sources ranging from the Canterbury Glosses to a treatise by Alcuin (written after he left England).[119] Nor are these sources merely rarities to add to the list of 'books known to the English'; the respective contributions of Ephrem's lachrymose spirituality and Chryosotom's arch misogyny[120] to the rhetoric of the Anglo-Saxon pulpit underscore the diversity of intellectual influences that informed English books and Anglo-Saxon ideologies.

The striking differences in style and substance manifested by the authors and texts I have discussed serve to remind us that the Christian-Latin sources of Anglo-Saxon literature were far from homogenous or univocal. Even 'commonplaces' circulated in variant forms, just as international folktales with Aarne-Thompson numbers have their regional oecotypes.[121] While sometimes crudely equated with Robertsonian 'patristics' or *Toposforschung*, source study counters the levelling tendency of these approaches by revealing the range and diversity of literary influences and identifying the textual bases of ideological conflicts within medieval

---

[119] Wright, 'The Old English "Macarius Homily"'; Zacher, 'The Source of Vercelli VII: An Address to Women', forthcoming in *New Readings on the Vercelli Book*, ed. by Zacher and Orchard.

[120] Compare J. E. Cross's comment on Vercelli VII: 'Such a comment on the life of women is a unique passage in Old English homiletic literature and we may suspect that this derives from a foreign source' ('Vernacular Sermons', p. 582).

[121] Antti Aarne and Stith Thompson, *The Types of the Folktale: A Classification and Bibliography*, Folklore Fellows Communications, 184 (Helsinki, 1961).

culture. I have argued, for example, that the Anglo-Saxons received from the Irish missions and from Hiberno-Latin writings certain distinctive stylistic preferences, doctrinal emphases, and devotional practices.[122] Within the corpus of anonymous homilies, material of Irish inspiration or background includes, for example, redactions of apocrypha (the 'Niall' version of the Sunday Letter homilies in Napier XLIII and XLIV), eschatological narratives ('the Pledge of the Soul', a Doomsday dialogue in Bazire-Cross 3), exegetical motifs (the pinnacle of the temple as a *lareowsetl* (*sedes doctorum*) in Irvine V), and rhetorical features such as the 'enumerative style' and numerical *gradatio* (notably in Vercelli IX). To identify specific sources or characteristics as an index of the Irish contribution to Anglo-Saxon culture is not to suggest that these anonymous homilies are somehow less 'English', or that Old English literature is a hybrid of starkly opposed 'Celtic' and 'Roman' elements. It is, rather, to argue that Irish Christian culture had an identity of its own, not indeed outside but within the mainstream of European Christian culture, and that the Anglo-Saxons assimilated certain literary and devotional traditions from the Irish as a consequence of their early and extensive interactions. This moderate claim is opposed both to the now-discredited Romantic image of the medieval Irish as saints and scholars who saved civilization as well as to the still-fashionable revisionist impulse to deny them any character or contribution of their own (a lingering manifestation of the 'fallacy of homogeneity' in medieval studies).[123] No one would deny that early Irish handwriting was distinctive, even though it was ultimately modelled on Late Antique continental scripts, or that Anglo-Saxon pointed minuscule was in turn based on the Irish form of the script, even though it was thoroughly assimilated by English scribes. It would be remarkable if Irish Christian culture was otherwise indistinguishable, or if Anglo-Saxons managed not to borrow anything distinctive from the Irish except their handwriting. The challenge for literary scholars is to define what they did borrow and how they adapted it. Without the kind of visual evidence that palaeographers and

---

[122] See Wright, 'Hiberno-Latin and Irish-Influenced Commentaries, Florilegia, and Homily Collections', in *Sources of Anglo-Saxon Literary Culture: A Trial Version*, ed. by Biggs, Hill, and Szarmach, pp. 87–123; *Irish Tradition*; and 'Irish Tradition'. J. E. Cross's work on the influence of Hiberno-Latin texts was groundbreaking; see his survey, 'On Hiberno-Latin Texts and Anglo-Saxon Writings', in *The Scriptures and Early Medieval Ireland*, ed. by Thomas O'Loughlin, Instrumenta Patristica, 31 (Turnhout, 1999), pp. 69–79.

[123] This fallacy was invoked in a somewhat different context by Stanley B. Greenfield, *The Interpretation of Old English Poems* (London, 1972), p. 9.

art historians can appeal to, we must appeal instead to textual evidence, including sources.

Ideological debates motivated by doctrinal or institutional differences are sometimes submerged beneath the surface of texts by the very process of selection, omission, and adaptation of sources, surfacing only when such operations are revealed by source identification and analysis. As Rudolph Willard, Mary Clayton, and Ananya Kabir have shown, Anglo-Saxon clerics contested not just whether Mary was corporeally assumed, but if so whether she was assumed into the earthly paradise or heaven, and they did so by selecting and tailoring sources, ranging from multiple recensions of the apocryphal *Transitus Mariae* to a tract by Paschasius Radbertus that purported to be by Jerome.[124] In his conflation of *Transitus C* and *Transitus B²*, the author of Blickling XIII deliberately altered a crucial detail by referring to the translation not of Mary's body (*corpus*) but of her soul (*sawol*) in order to minimize the contradiction between the two accounts (a strategy that generated other contradictions which the homilist failed to resolve).[125] Again, the author of Vercelli XI–XIII — if I am right in ascribing these homilies to a secular cleric — subtly manipulated both Cassian and Caesarius so as to contest the monastic appropriation of the virtue *timor Dei* as an exclusively Benedictine virtue tied to observance of the Rule and renunciation of material possessions.[126] Such ministrations bear witness to Anglo-Saxon writers' active, but sometimes covert, manipulation of what Clare Lees has called 'the politics of belief'.[127] Tradition was not an inert consensus of unchanging and uncontested doctrine, but a dynamic, even polemical process in which choosing sources could also mean choosing sides; as Lees notes, the 'impression of sameness' is a function of that very selectivity.[128] Susan Irvine's close analysis of three anonymous homilies in Bodley 343 in relation to both their Latin sources and vernacular parallels reveals how the homilists negotiated a wide range of opinion and attitude on pastoral, exegetical, and theological questions, whether by moderating the severity of a Gregorian admonition so as to imply that 'tithing was not even morally, let alone legally, binding if it

---

[124] Willard, 'The Two Accounts of the Assumption in Blickling Homily XIII', *RES*, 14 (1938), 1–19; Clayton, *Cult of the Virgin Mary*, and *Apocryphal Gospels of Mary*; and Kabir, *Paradise, Death and Doomsday*, esp. pp. 31–37.

[125] Willard, 'Two Accounts of the Assumption', pp. 6–7; Clayton, *Apocryphal Gospels of Mary*, pp. 301–02.

[126] Wright, 'Vercelli Homilies XI–XIII'.

[127] Lees, *Tradition and Belief*, p. 1.

[128] Lees, *Tradition and Belief*, p. 28.

entailed undue personal hardship', or by resolving several mutually exclusive interpretations of I Thessalonians 4. 16–17 in favour of 'a universal aerial resurrection
for judgement, after which only the righteous will be led to heaven'.[129]

It is possible, of course, to exaggerate the polemical burden of homilists' selection and handling of Latin sources. They were preachers, not controversialists, and
no doubt many compiled sources for their paraenetic value without perceiving,
much less adjudicating or reconciling, their contradictions.[130] Many fundamental
tenets of faith and morality, moreover, were uncontested, and homilists directed
their energies towards inculcating norms of belief and behaviour — the dominant
ideology — more often than debating partisan ideologies.[131] Yet dominant ideologies seek to suppress evidence of internal conflict, while partisan ideologies seek
to identify themselves as tradition. Source analysis is a critical tool that can help us,
as modern readers, understand how both are constructed, and how to tell the
difference.

Stylistic Analysis

Critical assessment of a homily's prose style, imagery, and structure (and how well
these elements are coordinated) can be conducted without reference to Latin
sources, and sometimes has to be. Indeed, one could argue that Latin sources are
irrelevant insofar as stylistics is concerned with rhetorical effects of the vernacular
target text that are specific to its language and are, in any case, the only ones its
audience can perceive. Yet it is easy to forget that a homilist who translates a Latin
source is himself a reader, one who actively seeks to mediate his audience's access
and responses to the content of the source — and whose own responses to it are
conditioned by that intention. If it is appropriate to extrapolate a hypothetical
audience's responses to rhetorical effects in an Old English homily solely on the
basis of assumptions about universal human affective and cognitive behaviour or

---

[129] *Old English Homilies*, ed. by Irvine, pp. 134 and 161.

[130] In *Preaching and Theology*, p. 7, Gatch characterized the Blickling and Vercelli collections
as 'conservative' and 'uncritical', borrowing indiscriminately from both authoritative and un-
authoritative sources incompatible doctrines on such fundamental questions as the fate of the soul
between death and Judgement. Thompson, '*Hit Segð on Halgum Bocum*', argues that anonymous
homilists' reverence for Latin sources led them to regard all as equally authoritative and to
disregard their contradictions.

[131] Lees, *Tradition and Belief*.

medieval mentalities and Anglo-Saxon attitudes, it is surely appropriate to speculate about an Anglo-Saxon homilist's responses to rhetorical effects in his Latin
source on the basis of his actual treatment of it. The dichotomy between production and reception should not obscure the dynamic interrelation among sources,
authors, target texts, and audiences.

Approaching a homily's style and structure from the perspective of its sources
does risk treating it not as an independent work with its own aims and contexts but
instead as secondary (or roughly equivalent) to the Latin source, and hence basing
aesthetic judgements on an external standard that is neither appropriate nor fair.
At the same time, sources reveal what a homilist was working with and thus afford
some insight into his purposes and methods, enabling us to assess the fit between
intention and execution more appropriately and fairly. Certain pitfalls remain.
One by-product of source analysis, the segmentation of a homily into discrete passages borrowed from diverse sources (as in the *Fontes Anglo-Saxonici* database and
the apparatus fontium of critical editions such as Scragg's of the *Vercelli Homilies*),
can be a useful tool in analysing its structure; but as Paul Szarmach has cautioned,
'What source or textual critics might see as a pastiche could very well have a unity
obscured by a critic's overconcern with the antecedent parts of the whole'.[132] A
related occupational hazard of source scholarship is the tendency to isolate from
its larger context any passage for which a new source has been identified.

Such pitfalls are avoidable so long as the source scholar is conscious of them.
Nor is it inevitable that a 'derivative' text will be compared unfavourably to its
source, though this was often the case in early scholarship on the anonymous
homilies. The first scholar to read many Old English homilies alongside their Latin
sources was Max Förster, who in 1898 followed up his ground-breaking investiga-
tions of the sources of Ælfric's homilies with an essay identifying the major sources
of no fewer than eight of the Blickling Homilies. Förster's discoveries revealed that,
so far from being original compositions, or even free adaptations of Latin models,
the Blickling Homilies were for the most part close translations, sometimes nearly
word-for-word. The impact must have been revelatory, and it led Förster to form
a rather low estimation of the homilies as literature. Whereas scholars such as
Richard Morris and Bernhard Ten Brink had praised the Blickling Homilies for
certain literary qualities of style and structure, Förster felt compelled to transfer
most of whatever credit was due to their Latin sources. The further and inevitably
invidious comparison with Ælfric, already broached by Morris, was facilitated by

---

[132] Szarmach, 'The Vercelli Homilies', p. 252.

the Blickling homilists' translations of some of the same Latin texts that Ælfric later translated both more competently and more freely. Thus the Blickling Homilies suffered by comparison not only with the more polished style of their Latin sources but also with the more supple, idiomatic, and independent translations of Ælfric. In Förster's essay one sees the emergence of an evaluative hierarchy of Old English homilies based on their degree of dependence on their Latin sources, ranging from slavish to free, and a concomitant hardening of the distinction between the homilies of Ælfric and the anonymous homilies, almost invariably to the detriment of the latter.

Förster's conclusions regarding the Blickling Homilies set the tone for source scholarship in the early decades of the twentieth century. Fiedler, who in 1904 identified a pseudo-Augustinian sermon *In Natale Domini* as the source for the bulk of Blickling I, was harsh in his estimation of the homilist's latinity and Old English prose style: 'His style, by the side of the Latin original, seems crude and clumsy', Fiedler remarked, and he explicitly endorsed Förster's view that Ten Brink's praise of the Blickling Homilies' literary qualities had been misapplied, if not misguided.[133] Fiedler concluded that the homily is 'nothing but a literal translation of the Latin' and that — to make matters worse — the homilist 'frequently misunderstood his original'.[134] Fiedler's initial impression of the homily led him to assume that it would not repay close reading. To see how much this assumption caused him to miss, one need only compare Mary Clayton's detailed analysis of the homilist's treatment of his Latin source. While conceding that Blickling I is 'a fairly close translation' of *Sermo App.* 120, Clayton finds that the homilist shows 'a critical spirit' and 'independence', and she suggests compelling rationales for various omissions, additions, and modifications.[135] Fiedler also failed to appreciate that even a close translation may produce rhetorical effects that are independent of the Latin. To cite just one example, the homilist's rendering of the clauses 'Expandat nunc fides splendentis uteri pulchra tentoria, obumbret virtus, Spiritus sibilet' ('Let faith now unfold the beautiful tabernacles of her noble womb, let the power overshadow, let the Spirit inspire') combines a crisp alliterative phrase with an elegant *figura etymologica* ('Openige nu þin se *fægresta fæþm* [. . .] sy þæt geteld aþened þines innoþes, ond seo onblawnes þære heofonlican *onfæþmnesse* sy

---

[133] Fiedler, 'The Source', p. 123. Quotations from the Blickling Homilies are from Morris's edition (note 45 above) by page and line number.

[134] Fiedler, 'The Source', pp. 123 and 124.

[135] Clayton, *Cult of the Virgin Mary*, pp. 222–30 (p. 223).

gewindwod on þe', p. 7, lines 24–27; 'Open now your most beautiful womb [...] let the tabernacles of your womb be expanded, and let the inspiration of the heavenly embrace be wafted through you').

In comparison to the long stretches of (apparently) verbatim translation, such liberties as the homilists permitted themselves must have appeared trivial to scholars such as Förster and Fiedler; but within a couple of decades, when their dependence upon Latin models was no longer a revelation but a given, the liberties they took were appreciated as cumulatively more impressive and interesting. Rudolph Willard's characterization in 1927 of Anglo-Saxon homilists' treatment of their sources contrasts with Förster's verdict that most of the translations in the Blickling Homilies were almost verbatim ('fast wörtlich'): 'In fact,' Willard argued, 'we find that the redactors and translators took liberties with their sources, here following closely, there translating freely, now condensing and omitting, and again, expanding and introducing new material.'[136]

The impact of New Critical methods of close reading in the 1960s and 1970s encouraged even more favourable estimations of at least some anonymous homilies as unified and artful adaptations of their Latin models. In a 1978 essay on the style and structure of the Vercelli Homilies, Paul Szarmach adopted an avowedly 'formalist' approach in order to urge 'a salutary reevaluation of the anonymous tradition'.[137] In extended close readings of several homilies, Szarmach argued that rhetorical structure, thematic material, and narrative tension worked in unison to further the homilists' 'moral design' and evoke emotional responses in their audience. Szarmach supported his close readings with comparative source analysis, showing how the homilists' local adaptations of Latin texts by Caesarius and Alcuin were explicable as choices that contributed to the larger rhetorical design. The unity and craftsmanship that Szarmach recuperated by close reading varied considerably from one homily to another, however, and even the most accomplished still fell short of the high standards that were later set by the homilies of Ælfric. In a subsequent essay Szarmach compared Vercelli I with Ælfric's handling

---

[136] Willard, 'Vercelli Homily VIII', p. 319. Förster ('Zu den Blickling Homilies', p. 180) conceded that the translation in Blickling IV was not quite so literal as that in Blickling II, but stressed that both were far closer than Ælfric's translation of the same sources. Willard's estimation of the method of Blickling IV is more appreciative and unqualified by comparison with Ælfric: 'The Old English translator has handled his materials freely, usually giving meaning for meaning, after Jerome's phrase, rather than word for word, generously adding such materials as he finds appropriate to his needs and manner' ('Blickling-Junius Tithing Homily', p. 67).

[137] Szarmach, 'The Vercelli Homilies', pp. 241 and 252.

of the Passion narrative, acknowledging his superior skill but repositioning the anonymous writers as forerunners whose 'skill and homiletic craftsmanship anticipate Ælfric's achievement and explain how they are possible'.[138] If source scholarship tended, in Szarmach's words, 'to reward the freer, more independent author',[139] the formalist approach, it seems, could only narrow the gap that separated Ælfric from the anonymous homilists, not cut the Gordian knot that defined their achievement in relation to his.

To be sure, positive assessments of a homilist's originality, competence, and craftsmanship are not always more just or accurate than negative ones, and Latin sources sometimes serve to backlight infelicities in the Old English. Thus in Blickling I the homilist's curious statement that 'Eve bore tears in her womb' (p. 3, line 6) was revealed by Fielding's discovery as an inept misreading and compression of an elegant syllepsis in the Latin source: 'illa lacrymas, ista gaudium in ventre portavit' ('That woman [Eve] bore tears, this one [Mary] bore joy in her womb'). To characterize the result of this misprision as a bold image would, I think, be too charitable; but any assessment of the homilist's achievement, favourable or unfavourable, will be indebted to Fiedler's discovery of its Latin source. Knowledge of any homilist's source allows us to determine whether he set out to translate it closely or freely, and thus to judge how successful he was by his own standards. Zacher's discovery of the main source of Vercelli VII in a sermon by Chrysostom, for example, made it possible to define the characteristic features of this homilist's 'idiosyncratic style' in relation to his specific responses to the figures and metaphors in the Latin.[140]

Source discoveries also facilitate stylistic comparison of homilies that draw on common sources, whether independently or not. D. G. Scragg, for example, has pursued the stylistic implications of my discovery of the Latin source of the overlapping introductions to the Macarius Homily and Vercelli IV. I suggested that the Vercelli homilist's translation reveals his prolix style;[141] Scragg focuses particularly on his 'insistent use of pairs of near synonyms', a feature that anticipates one of Wulfstan's characteristic stylistic preferences.[142] Now, this feature might have been

---

[138] Szarmach, 'The Earlier Homily: *De Parasceve*', in *Studies in Earlier Old English Prose*, ed. by Szarmach (Albany, 1986), pp. 381–99 (pp. 390–94; quotation from pp. 381–82).

[139] Szarmach, 'The Vercelli Homilies', p. 260.

[140] Zacher, 'Source of Vercelli VII'.

[141] Wright, 'Old English "Macarius" Homily', p. 234.

[142] Scragg, *Dating and Style*, pp. 5–7 (with reference to a prepublication conference version of my paper).

observed even without knowledge of the antecedent Latin source; but comparison
with the source threw it into relief, and also proved that the Vercelli homilist's
doublets are expansions of the Macarius Homily and hence characteristic of his
style, not merely imitations of a specific Latin or Old English model. At the same
time, it highlighted the contrasting style of the author of the Macarius Homily,
who translated Ephrem directly with relatively little embellishment — and
whether a particular phrase or sentence is an embellishment or not obviously
depends on the extent to which it corresponds to something in the source.

The compositional strategies and stylistic preferences of homilists who translate
the same source independently are accentuated as well. J. E. Cross's study of three
independent Old English versions of 'The Dry Bones Speak' exemplum showed
that each homilist handles it differently: the author of Vercelli XIII translates
closely for substantial stretches, taking over the speech of the dry bones with little
alteration; the author of Belfour XII (= Irvine VII) uses selected sentences from
Caesarius within 'a patchwork of borrowings' from other sources, to which he adds
material apparently of his own composition; and the author of Blickling X fashions
a 'radical' and 'distinctive' adaptation of the exemplum, treating it with such freedom that only the 'basic similarity of pattern' and scattered 'echoes of phrases and
ideas' remain to betray the relation.[143] The use of a common Latin source, then,
does not in itself impose a common approach or style, but provides the raw
material that homilists use to suit their own purposes and audiences.

A recent and exemplary stylistic analysis of an Old English homily that takes
full advantage of Latin sources is Samantha Zacher's study of Vercelli X.[144] Zacher
shows how the Vercelli homilist artfully adapts his sources by adding, deleting, and
reorganizing material and by employing many figures of repetition — some of
which were prompted by the Latin, but many of which were entirely independent
(as only comparison with the Latin could reveal). A subsequent discovery may yet
reveal these multiple sources to have been antecedent rather than immediate, but
will not likely affect Zacher's assessment of the local stylistic effects the homilist has
crafted from the Latin wording. Focussing on the homilist's treatment of three
main sources, Zacher identifies recurrent patterns of revision and embellishment
that suggest that the homily is a unified composition by a single author, not simply

---

[143] Cross, 'The Dry Bones Speak', pp. 438–39. See also Irvine's discussion, *Old English
Homilies*, pp. 183–86.

[144] Zacher, 'Sin, Syntax, and Synonyms'. See also Andy Orchard's stylistic analysis of the Old
English translations of the *Gospel of Nicodemus* and *Vindicta Salvatoris* apocrypha, in *Two Old
English Apocrypha*, ed. by Cross and others, ch. 5.

a composite, even if the homilist used some pre-existing vernacular materials in addition to preparing his own translations of multiple Latin sources. Although Zacher's reading of the homily follows the structural divisions determined by its sources, this does not prevent her from perceiving how the homilist's rhetorical strategies cut across these divisions and unify his composition. Finally, Zacher draws an illuminating contrast with another vernacular homilist's far less adroit translation of one of the same passages from Isidore's *Synonyma*. Access to their common starting point thus facilitates a more precise description and aesthetic evaluation of the compositional technique of each homilist.

If source scholarship on the Old English homily has its origins in the nineteenth century, source identification has its origins in the homilies themselves. There does not seem to be an Old English equivalent of the word 'source' in the abstract sense modern scholars use this term — that is, as 'a particular mode of textual relationship'.[145] Anglo-Saxon homilists who refer to what we would call sources tend to define them in material, generic, or personal terms. Most often they simply speak of 'books' or 'writings', typically qualified as 'holy' (*halige bec*, *gewreotu*). If they wish to specify a particular kind of book, they may refer to a 'gospel' (*godspel*, but potentially embracing any authoritative religious text) or a 'commentary' or 'treatise' (*trahtnung*), or more broadly a 'composition' (*gesetnys*), or 'story', 'narrative' (*spel*, *racu*, *gerecednys*). If they wish to specify a particular human authority, they may refer to an 'evangelist' (*godspellere*, but again with a broader range than the modern equivalent) or a 'teacher' (*lareow*), or they may specify one by name (*cwæþ Agustinus*). While some homilists choose to appropriate these sources silently, suppressing their difference and their distance from them, this is a rhetorical strategy. Even when a homilist translates a first-person singular verb from a Latin source, there may be slippage, as in Blickling XIV, in which the homilist first adopts the voice of his source as if it were his own ('ic secge' = *dicam*; p. 163, line 24), but subsequently feels compelled to acknowledge that it is not ('Hwæt sceal ic þonne ma secgan [...] cwæþ se þe þas boc worhte [...]?' ('What more should I say [...] said he who made this book [...]?') = *Quid dicam* [...]?; p. 169, lines 21–24).

Source identification resolves the discrete voices, words, and works that a homilist has compiled and appropriated (whether overtly or covertly), enabling us to observe how they have been transformed in the process, and helping us to assess what the homilist wrote (textual criticism), when he wrote it and for whom

---

[145] Hill, 'Introduction', p. xvi; for reflections on the nature of that relationship, see also O'Brien O'Keeffe, 'Source, Method'.

(literary history), what kind of intellectual milieu, library, and ideological position he wrote from (intellectual history), and how he rewrote the rhetorical and verbal fabric of a Latin text in his own language (stylistic analysis). If it is harder now, after more than a century of intensive source-scholarship, to identify new sources, there are better tools available to search for them,[146] and also for accessing the discoveries that have already been made (see the bibliographical orientation below). The business of interpreting and contextualizing these discoveries, moreover, is not merely unfinished; it has hardly begun, and new approaches and new questions will undoubtedly enable Anglo-Saxonists to exploit them in new ways. I would not predict what directions source study will take, but I do predict that sources will continue to be central to our understanding of the Old English homily.

Anonymous Homilies and Latin Sources: A Bibliographical Orientation

The surviving Old English homilies are listed in N. R. Ker, *Catalogue of Manuscripts Containing Anglo-Saxon* (Oxford, 1957; repr. with a Supplement, Oxford, 1990), pp. 527–36. The standard inventory of anonymous homilies is D. G. Scragg, 'The Corpus of Vernacular Homilies and Prose Saints' Lives before Ælfric', *ASE*, 8 (1979), 223–77, reprinted with Addenda in *Old English Prose: Basic Readings*, ed. by Paul E. Szarmach (New York, 2000), pp. 73–150 (subsequent references are to the reprint). The prose saints' lives, many of which take the form of homilies, have also been surveyed by Alex Nicholls, 'The Corpus of Prose Saints' Lives and Hagiographic Pieces in Old English and its Manuscript Distribution', *Reading Medieval Studies*, 19 (1993), 73–96; 20 (1994), 51–87. See also J. E. Cross, 'English Vernacular Saints' Lives Before 1000 A.D.', in *Hagiographies*, ed. by G. Philippart, 2 vols (Turnhout, 1996), II, 413–27, and *Holy Men and Holy Women: Old English Prose Saints' Lives and their Contexts*, ed. by Paul E. Szarmach (Albany, 1996). A comprehensive *Handlist of Old English Sermons and Homilies* is in preparation by Thomas N. Hall.

Scragg's inventory is organized by manuscript, with those affording 'primary evidence of early homilies' assigned the sigla A–Z, excepting X, which is reserved for eleven manuscripts (X^a–X^k) affording 'secondary evidence', usually in the form of late composite homilies or 'translations related to the homiletic tradition but not themselves homilies' (p. 74). Those manuscripts whose homiletic items are

---

[146] See Thomas D. Hill, 'CETEDOC and the Transformation of Anglo-Saxon Studies', *OEN*, 26.1 (Fall 1992), 46–48, and Scragg, 'Source Study'.

fragmentary are assigned the sigla fᵃ–fᵒ. Scragg's primary focus is on the relation between the manuscripts and the degree to which individual homilies overlap, but he also provides references to major source scholarship. An Appendix (pp. 117–28) provides a 'Tabular Summary of Anonymous Homilies', listed in the order established by Angus Cameron's comprehensive numbering system for Old English texts, 'A List of Old English Texts', in *A Plan for the Dictionary of Old English*, ed. by Roberta Frank and Angus Cameron (Toronto, 1973), pp. 25–306, most recently updated in the F-fascicle of the microfiche *Dictionary of Old English*, ed. by Antonette DiPaolo Healey and others (Toronto, 2004). Cameron numbers 3.2.1–50 designate homilies for specified occasions in the *temporale*, beginning with Christmas; 3.3.1–35 homilies for the *sanctorale*, listed alphabetically by saint; 3.4.1–59 homilies for unspecified occasions, listed alphabetically by first editor; and 3.5.1–15 unpublished (in 1973) homilies for unspecified occasions, listed alphabetically by first word (ignoring salutations such as 'Leofan men' and 'Men þa leofestan'). The 'List' also assigns a standard Short Title for each homily (HomS = Homilies for Specified Occasions; HomU = Homilies for Unspecified Occasions, edited; HomM = unpublished Homilies for Unspecified Occasions), but many homilies are conventionally referred to in the scholarship by manuscript or edited collection (e.g. Vercelli Homily IX (= HomU 11); Napier Homily XLIX (= HomS 40)).

The two most extensive manuscript collections are the Vercelli Homilies (twenty-three homilies, with six poems interspersed among them) and the Blickling Homilies (eighteen homilies).[147] Both have been edited integrally: *The Vercelli Homilies and Related Texts*, ed. by D. G. Scragg, EETS: OS, 300 (Oxford, 1992), superseding earlier partial editions by Max Förster and Paul E. Szarmach;[148] and *The Blickling Homilies of the Tenth Century*, ed. and trans. by Richard Morris, EETS: OS, 58, 63, 73 (1874–80; repr. in one vol. with corrections, London, 1967).[149] A recent edition

---

[147] Morris has nineteen, but his Homily 'XVI' is actually a misplaced leaf from Homily IV. For a facsimile, see *The Blickling Homilies: The John H. Scheide Library, Titusville, Pennsylvania*, ed. by Rudoph Willard, EEMF, 10 (Copenhagen, 1960).

[148] Förster, 'Der Vercelli-Codex CXVII nebst Abruck einiger altenglischer Homilien der Handschrift'; Förster, *Die Vercelli-Homilien*; Paul E. Szarmach, *Vercelli Homilies IX–XXIII*, Toronto Old English Series, 5 (Toronto, 1981). For a facsimile, see *The Vercelli Book: A Late Tenth-Century Manuscript Containing Prose and Verse (Vercelli Biblioteca Capitolare CXVII)*, ed. by Celia Sisam, EEMF, 19 (Copenhagen, 1976).

[149] A useful motif-index to the Blickling and Vercelli Homilies as well as to the homilies of Ælfric is Robert DiNapoli, *An Index of Theme and Image to the Homilies of the Anglo-Saxon*

of the Blickling Homilies by Richard J. Kelly (New York, 2003) is unsatisfactory
(see the reviews by Jonathan Wilcox in *Speculum*, 80 (2005), 604–08, and D. G.
Scragg in *Medieval Sermon Studies*, 49 (2005), 71–73). Late homilies from Bodley
343, including Ælfrician as well as anonymous items, were edited with facing-page
translation by Arthur Belfour, *Twelfth-Century Homilies in MS. Bodley 343*, EETS:
OS, 137 (London, 1909); three of the anonymous homilies have been re-edited by
Susan Irvine, *Old English Homilies from MS Bodley 343*, EETS: OS, 302 (Oxford,
1993). Another edition of homilies from a single manuscript is Raymond J. S.
Grant, *Three Homilies from Cambridge, Corpus Christi College 41* (Ottawa, 1982).

Important collective editions drawn from multiple manuscript sources rather
than a single manuscript include *Wulfstan: Sammlung der ihm zugeschriebenen
Homilien nebst Untersuchungen über ihre Echtheit*, vol. I: *Text und Varianten*, ed.
by Arthur Napier (1883; repr. with a bibliographical supplement by Klaus
Ostheeren, Dublin, 1967) (sixty-two homilies, including thirty-five that are falsely
attributed to Wulfstan); *Nuove omelie anglosassoni della rinascenza benedettina*, ed.
by A. M. Luiselli Fadda, Filologia germanica, Testi e studi, 1 (Florence, 1977); *Vier
altenglische Predigten aus der heterodoxen Tradition mit Kommentar, Übersetzung
und Glossar sowie drei weiteren Texten im Anhang*, ed. by Hildegard Tristram
(Inaugural-dissertation Freiburg-im-Breisgau; privately printed, 1970); and *Eleven
Old English Rogationtide Homilies*, ed. by Joyce Bazire and J. E. Cross (Toronto,
1982; 2nd edn with a new preface, King's College London Medieval Studies, 4,
London, 1989).[150] Homilies from these editions are conventionally cited by the
editors' name and number (e.g. 'Napier XXX', 'Bazire-Cross 8'). Editions of
smaller groups of anonymous homilies include *Angelsächsische Homilien und
Heiligenleben*, ed. by Bruno Assmann, BaP, 3 (Kassel, 1889; repr. Darmstadt, 1964)
(four anonymous homilies together with a group of Ælfrician items); R. Brotanek,
Texte und Untersuchungen zur altenglischen Literatur und Kirchengeschichte (Halle,
1913) (two anonymous homilies, also with Ælfrician items); and Rudolph Willard,
Two Apocrypha in Old English Homilies, Beiträge zur englischen Philologie, 30
(Leipzig, 1935) (partial edition of the Three Utterances and Seven Heavens homi-
lies).[151] Editions of post-Conquest collections that transmit items which may

Church: Comprising the Homilies of Ælfric, Wulfstan, and the Blickling and Vercelli Codices
(Hockwold cum Wilton, 1995).

[150] A convenient table concording the homilies in Bazire and Cross with previous editions is
provided in Hans Sauer's review, *Anglia*, 104 (1986), 184–88 (p. 185).

[151] Complete editions of two of the sermons in Willard's *Two Apocrypha* have been published
since Willard's study, by Luiselli Fadda, *Nuove omelie* (no. I) and by Loredana Teresi, 'Be

originally have been composed in the Anglo-Saxon period include the Vespasian Homilies, edited by Rubie D.-N. Warner, *Early English Homilies from the Twelfth-Century MS. Vesp. D. XIV*, EETS: OS, 152 (London, 1917),[152] and the Lambeth Homilies and Trinity Homilies, both edited by Richard Morris, *Old English Homilies and Homiletic Treatises [. . .] of the Twelfth and Thirteenth Centuries, First Series*, EETS: OS, 29 and 34 (London, 1867–68; repr. as one volume, 1988), and *Old English Homilies of the Twelfth Century: Series II*, EETS: OS, 53 (London, 1873).[153] A number of anonymous homilies have been edited separately in journals and unpublished dissertations. Those edited in North American dissertations through 1986 are conveniently listed in an appendix to Phillip Pulsiano, *An Annotated Bibliography of North American Doctoral Dissertations on Old English Language and Literature* (East Lansing, 1988), pp. 287–88; others can be located in Ker's *Catalogue*, the Dictionary of Old English 'List of Texts', and especially in Janet Bately, *Anonymous Old English Homilies: A Preliminary Bibliography of Source Studies* (Binghamton, 1993), pp. 1–3 (2nd electronic edn (1996) at <http://www.wmich.edu/medieval/research/rawl/homilies/home.htm>; as of August 2007 this site was 'temporarily unavailable').

The secondary literature to 1990 relating to the Latin sources of Old English anonymous homilies (excluding those for the *sanctorale*) is covered in Bately's bibliography. Section D lists individual homilies in Cameron order, with relevant secondary references for each. Appendices list homilies by manuscript collection and concord the homily numbers in major edited collections with Cameron numbers, and there is an index of authors. Editions and secondary literature to 1972 are also included in Fred C. Robinson and Stanley B. Greenfield, *Bibliography of Publications on Old English Literature to 1972* (Toronto, 1980; see 'Homilies', pp. 356–61) and in Karen J. Quinn and Kenneth P. Quinn, *A Manual*

Heofonwarum 7 be Helwarum: A Complete Edition', in *Early Medieval English Texts and Interpretations: Studies Presented to Donald G. Scragg*, ed. by Elaine Treharne and Susan Rosser, MRTS, 252 (Tempe, 2002), pp. 211–44.

[152] Two of the Vespasian Homilies adapt texts by Ælfric, but Mary Richards judges that the remainder cannot be much earlier than 1200: 'MS Cotton Vespasian A. XXII: The Vespasian Homilies', *Manuscripta*, 22 (1978), 97–103.

[153] According to R. M. Wilson, 'The Provenance of the Lambeth Homilies with a New Collation', *Leeds Studies in English*, 4 (1935), 24–43, '[a]t least two of them — Nos. 9 and 10 — are Middle English adaptations of extant Old English material and it is probable that most are of pre-Conquest origin' (p. 24). See now Mary Swan, 'Old English Textual Activity in the Reign of Henry II', in *Writers of the Reign of Henry II*, ed. Kennedy and Meecham-Jones, pp. 151–68 (pp. 161–64).

of Old English Prose (New York, 1990), which excludes the works of Ælfric and Wulfstan.[154] Bately's bibliography is indispensable and for most purposes the best resource, though the Robinson and Greenfield bibliography is more convenient for surveying the secondary literature (to 1972) chronologically. Current scholarship can be located in the annual bibliographies published in *Anglo-Saxon England* (1972–present) and *Old English Newsletter* (1967–present); the *OEN* bibliographies (from 1972 onward) are now accessible online at <http://www.oenews letter.org/OENDB/index.php>.

Bately's bibliography of secondary scholarship is not annotated, so one will not find in it a list of the Latin sources that have been discovered for each homily. The brief annotations in the Quinns' *Manual* occasionally specify the source discoveries, but often simply state that an essay identifies a source.[155] Editions such as Scragg's of the Vercelli Homilies naturally survey the Latin sources of the homilies they include, and some, like Scragg's, also print the sources of each homily. An older resource that conveniently summarizes the major source discoveries for Old English homilies to 1972 is Adam Dunbar McCoy, 'The Use of Writings of English Authors in Old English Homiletic Literature' (unpublished doctoral dissertation, Cornell University, 1973). The Appendix, 'The Homilies and their Sources' (pp. 176–238), includes Latin as well as Old English sources; the Blickling and the Vercelli Homilies are listed separately, then 'Early Anonymous Published Homilies', 'Early Anonymous Unpublished Homilies', and (following sections devoted to the homilies of Ælfric and Wulfstan) 'Anonymous Homilies Later than Ælfric'. This valuable if skeletal survey is now being superseded by *Fontes Anglo-Saxonici*, but is still useful for homilies that have not yet been included in the database, and remains the only comprehensive listing of source discoveries for Old English homilies.

---

[154] The *Manual* lists anonymous homilies first: A001–50 are the homilies for the *temporale*, A201–35 those for the *sanctorale*, A401–70 miscellaneous homilies, A501–02 Homily Collections (Blickling and Vercelli), and A600 lists general criticism not tied to single homilies. Each entry gives the manuscript title (if any) and first line, the Cameron number, manuscript (foliation is not specified), a one- or two-sentence description of the topic or contents, and references to the relevant items in the *Manual*'s bibliographies of editions and criticism. The *Manual* includes indices of manuscript titles and first lines; homilies are listed by feast or topic in the Modern Title Index, pp. 419–20.

[155] The annotations can be misleading, as when Förster's essay 'Zu den Blickling Homilies' (no. 0287) is described as 'Textual notes for some of the homilies, chiefly on points of interpretation, mostly grammatical', with no indication that the essay identified for the first time the Latin sources for eight of the homilies.

The two major source projects, *Fontes Anglo-Saxonici* and *Sources of Anglo-Saxon Literary Culture*, concern themselves with both words and works, but their approaches are complementary. *Fontes* entries source Anglo-Saxon texts line by line, thus emphasizing words in the form of discrete verbal correspondences in database 'segments' (with annotations identifying the work in which the wording is transmitted and sigla denoting whether it is an immediate or antecedent source or an analogue). *SASLC* entries are based on sources (not just of Anglo-Saxon texts but of Anglo-Saxon 'literary culture' broadly conceived) that circulated as discrete works (including their variant textual forms), documenting their transmission in Anglo-Saxon England through surviving Anglo-Saxon manuscripts, entries in Anglo-Saxon booklists, and references by Anglo-Saxon authors, but also through any use of their words in translations, quotations, or citations in Anglo-Saxon texts.

Fontes Anglo-Saxonici can be accessed online <http://fontes.english.ox.ac.uk/> or in a stand-alone CD-ROM. To access a list of sources for a given Old English homily, search by 'Anglo-Saxon Author', then choose 'Anon. (OE)'. Anonymous texts are listed alphabetically by conventional title (e.g. 'Blickling homily 14'). For a list of sources by line number in the standard edition of a selected Old English text, click on 'Show Records'; for an alphabetical list of sources by author or title, click on 'Show Sources'. Clicking on the name of the Old English text leads to the field 'A-S text title details', including the edition of the Old English text, its Cameron number, the author of the *Fontes* entry, and a bibliography of secondary scholarship. The *Fontes* bibliographies <http://fontes.english.ox.ac.uk/data/content/biblio/> can also be browsed by Primary (i.e. source) text, Anglo-Saxon text, and secondary scholarship. The 'A-S text title details' field also includes a general note on 'Text and Transmission' that can be an important aid to interpreting the sigla and comments in the individual source records. To date (November 2005) there are *Fontes* entries for six of the Blickling Homilies, twenty-one of the Vercelli Homilies, nine Napier Homilies, five Bazire-Cross Homilies, and a number of other homilies from various edited collections, including those by Assmann, Belfour, Irvine, Tristram, and Grant. New *Fontes* entries are listed each year in the bibliography in *Anglo-Saxon England*. Further information on the *Fontes* database is found on the Web site pages 'How to use the *Fontes* database' <http://fontes.english.ox.ac.uk/howtousedb.html> and 'Tips for using the resources available on the *Fontes* web site' <http://fontes.english.ox.ac.uk/tips.html>.

Scholarship on the use of specific Latin (as well as Old English) texts and authors in Anglo-Saxon writings, including the anonymous homilies, is being summarized in *Sources of Anglo-Saxon Literary Culture* <http://www.wmich.edu/

medieval/research/saslc/>. Two volumes have appeared to date: *SASLC: A Trial Version*, ed. by Frederick M. Biggs, Thomas D. Hill, and Paul E. Szarmach (Bing-hamton, 1990), with sample entries (including one for 'Anonymous Old English Homilies' as sources for other texts); and *SASLC*, vol. I: *Abbo of Fleury, Abbo of St. Germain-des-Prés, and Acta Sanctorum*, ed. by Biggs, Hill, Szarmach, and E. Gor-don Whatley (Kalamazoo, 2002). The headnotes to *SASLC* entries distinguish kinds of evidence for the knowledge of a given source text in Anglo-Saxon England: Anglo-Saxon manuscripts of the text (*MSS*); Anglo-Saxon booklists that include the text (*Lists*); Anglo-Saxon versions or translations of the text (*A-S Vers*); quo-tations or citations from the text in Anglo-Saxon texts (*Quots/Cits*); and references to the text by Anglo-Saxon authors (*Refs*). If one wishes to know whether a given Latin author or text was a source for any Old English homily, or for a particular anonymous homily, the relevant entry in *SASLC* will (eventually!) supply that information, and projected entries such as '(pseudo-)Augustine' and 'Paul the Deacon' will be of special significance for Old English homilies. (One can also search the source records of *Fontes* to determine whether a particular Latin author or text was used in any of the homilies that have been sourced to date.)[156]

---

[156] I am grateful to Frederick M. Biggs, Thomas N. Hall, Thomas D. Hill, and Aaron J Kleist for their comments on this paper.

ÆLFRIC'S MANUSCRIPT OF PAUL THE DEACON'S HOMILIARY: A PROVISIONAL ANALYSIS

Joyce Hill

Introduction

In his study of liturgical books in Anglo-Saxon England, published in 1985, Helmut Gneuss presented a challenge for modern scholars:

> It should be one of the foremost tasks of future research to establish the version or versions of Paul's Homiliary employed in the late Anglo-Saxon period, taking into account not only the evidence of the homiliary manuscripts, but also of other liturgical manuscripts like F.1 and of Ælfric's Homilies, which are largely based on Paul's collection.[1]

'F.1', a textual designation in Gneuss's study, was Cambridge, Corpus Christi College, MS 391, known to us as *The Portiforium of Saint Wulstan*. The challenge of exploiting liturgical texts of this kind in the search for the version or versions of Paul the Deacon's homiliary known in Anglo-Saxon England has not yet been taken up.[2] Where further work has been done, however, is with the homiletic tradition, with Ælfric as the chief point of entry. The purpose of the present article is to assess the progress that has been made to date, and to draw attention to the complexity of the research that still needs to be done. The quest is thus for the particular form of Paul the Deacon's homiliary known to Ælfric and used by him in his collection of *Catholic Homilies*, in connection with which we should also take account of his

---

[1] Helmut Gneuss, 'Liturgical Books in Anglo-Saxon England and their Old English Termi-nology', in *Learning and Literature in Anglo-Saxon England: Studies Presented to Peter Clemoes on the Occasion of his Sixty-fifth Birthday*, ed. by Michael Lapidge and Helmut Gneuss (Cambridge, 1985), pp. 91–141 (p. 123).

[2] On the origins of Paul the Deacon's homiliary, see below, p. 71.

own subsequent supplementation. Whether we can ever arrive at a definitive description of his copy of the homiliary is, I think, a matter for debate, for reasons that will become clear, particularly in the section below concerned with the source-study approach, but there is certainly room for further progress to be made.

When Gneuss was writing in 1985 it was already little short of one hundred years since Förster, in his study of the sources of the *Catholic Homilies*, had surmised that Ælfric may have known much of his source material, not as discrete works (as they are available to modern scholars), but in sundry collections, including homiliaries.[3] Förster's speculations have been confirmed, with Smetana's demonstration that Ælfric used the homiliary of Paul the Deacon being the pioneer work, published in 1959.[4] His schedule of the homilies was drawn from Wiegand's 1897 study of the collection in its original form, insofar as this could be ascertained from the complex manuscript tradition as then understood.[5]

Smetana's analysis would have been impossible without Wiegand's schedule since the only version of Paul's homiliary that was known prior to this was that printed by Migne in *Patrologia Latina*.[6] This, however, reproduces an edition published in Cologne in 1539 and presents a much later development of the homiliary than is appropriate for the later Anglo-Saxon period. Instead of the 244 items that made up the original, this version contains 299 (discounting one that is included twice), although it is not a simple matter of the accretion of 55 texts because 125 of the original items are not included. Thus, the 'new' items actually total 180, being replacements as well as additions.[7] Apparent correspondences with Ælfric which are in the Migne version and not in the original schedule therefore need to be examined with extreme care.[8]

---

[3] Max Förster, 'Über die Quellen von Ælfrics exegetischen *Homiliae Catholicae*', *Anglia*, 16 (1894), 1–61 (pp. 58–59). Förster here was expressing agreement with a suggestion made ten years earlier by John Earle, *The Dawn of European Literature: Anglo Saxon Literature* (London, 1884), p. 215.

[4] Cyril L. Smetana, 'Ælfric and the Early Medieval Homiliary', *Traditio*, 15 (1959), 163–204.

[5] F. Wiegand, *Das Homiliarium Karls des Grossen auf seine ursprüngliche Gestalt hin untersucht* (Leipzig, 1897).

[6] *PL* 95.1159–66.

[7] The nature of the enlarged homiliary as printed by Migne is briefly discussed by Cyril L. Smetana, 'Paul the Deacon's Patristic Anthology', in *The Old English Homily and its Backgrounds*, ed. by Paul E. Szarmach and Bernard F. Huppé (Albany, 1978), pp. 75–97 (pp. 88–89).

[8] Where appropriate in the following discussion, PD will be used to indicate the homiliary of Paul the Deacon in its original form or a form relatively close to the original (such as it might have

In working towards a characterization of Ælfric's copy of this homiliary, the starting point must necessarily be the PD original. As we shall see below, it is highly likely that his copy had some augmentations, but we should only conclude that this is so when the Ælfrician text has been closely examined alongside the full range of options available to him through his array of intertextual sources. It is also important to use, as the PD reference point, not Smetana's contents list — which in any case has a number of errors and which, as we have noted, derives from Wiegand's nineteenth-century analysis — but the much more accurate account published by Grégoire in 1980, superseding his earlier but less detailed analysis of 1966.[9] Because no single complete manuscript of the original version survives from the last years of the eighth century or as a copy from the early ninth, Grégoire reconstructs the homiliary using seven manuscripts, of which five are from the ninth century (with two of these being from the earlier part of the century) and two from the earlier part of the eleventh century, although most of his information is derived from the ninth-century manuscripts. All seven manuscripts are continental, from Reichenau, Benediktbeueren, and Tours.

Because it was comparative analysis of subject matter that first led to the identification of Paul the Deacon's homiliary as one of Ælfric's authoritative Latin texts, and because it is through this form of source study that further work needs to be done, I begin below with an examination of this approach. It is followed by a section which looks at the important issue of the homiliary's form and organization as it may have been known to Ælfric, on which some progress has been made. The fourth section, preceding the short conclusion, describes the chief features of the more substantial manuscripts based on Paul the Deacon's homiliary which are included in Gneuss's list of manuscripts and manuscript fragments written or owned in England up to 1100.[10]

been known in the tenth century), and PDM will be used to indicate the much augmented and considerably later version published by Migne.

[9] Réginald Grégoire, *Homéliaires liturgiques médiévaux: Analyse des manuscrits* (Spoleto, 1980). The homiliary of Paul the Deacon is analysed in chapter eight, pp. 423–79. This supersedes Réginald Grégoire, *Les homéliaires du moyen âge: inventaire et analyse des manuscrits* (Rome, 1966).

[10] Helmut Gneuss, *Handlist of Anglo-Saxon Manuscripts: A List of Manuscripts and Manuscript Fragments Written or Owned in England up to 1100*, MRTS, 241 (Tempe, 2001).

The Source-Study Approach

Paul the Deacon's homiliary, which came to England with the Benedictine Reform, or possibly a little earlier,[11] gave Ælfric exactly the kind of material he needed for the *Catholic Homilies*: a liturgically organized selection of homilies covering the whole year, firmly located in the orthodox exegetical tradition which Ælfric wanted to promote within the Anglo-Saxon secular Church, and with authoritative attributions in each rubric. These attributions, the majority of which were patristic, confirmed for him the validity of the texts and allowed him to cite key names in the body of the homilies themselves as verifying signs of the respectability and high authority of the tradition in which his own homilies stood. In building his collection of vernacular homilies on this clearly advertised bedrock of orthodoxy, Ælfric was extending to the secular Church the standards of homiletic writing that he knew in Latin within the reformed monastic context. In so doing, he placed himself firmly within the Frankish traditions to which the Anglo-Saxon Benedictine Reform was heir. As he explained to Archbishop Sigeric of Canterbury, in order to combat fallacy and error, his intention was to 'translate' into English works by writers whose authority was 'ab omnibus catholicis libentissime susciptur' ('most willingly acknowledged by all the orthodox').[12] The names he lists in this letter are the great Fathers — Augustine of Hippo, Jerome, Bede, and Gregory — together with two Frankish authorities, Smaragdus and Haymo, this last being singled out as used 'aliquando' ('sometimes'), thus making an implied contrast with the others.[13] Paul the Deacon is not named, but even if Ælfric knew that

---

[11] The suggestion that the homiliary of Paul the Deacon might have reached England before the Benedictine Reform is made by J. E. Cross, 'The Literate Anglo-Saxon – On Sources and Disseminations', *Proceedings of the British Academy*, 58 (1972), 67–100 (pp. 84–85).

[12] *Ælfric's Catholic Homilies: The First Series, Text*, ed. by Peter Clemoes, EETS: SS, 17 (Oxford, 1997), p. 173. The translation is my own. For a discussion of what Ælfric means by 'translation' in this context, see Joyce Hill, 'Translating the Tradition: Manuscripts, Models and Methodologies in the Composition of Ælfric's *Catholic Homilies*', *Bulletin of the John Rylands University Library of Manchester*, 179 (1997), 43–65 [the Toller Lecture for 1996]; reissued with corrections in *Textual and Material Culture in Anglo-Saxon England: Thomas Northcote Toller and the Toller Memorial Lectures*, ed. by D. Scragg (Cambridge, 2001), pp. 241–59.

[13] The only editions of the homiliaries of Smaragdus and Haymo are those by J. P. Migne in *Patrologia Latina*: Smaragdus, *Collectiones in epistolas et evangelia*, PL 102.13–552 (a more common name for the work being *Expositio libri comitis*); and Haymo, *Homiliae de Tempore*, PL 118.11–746 (where it is incorrectly attributed to Haymo of Halberstadt, rather than Haymo of Auxerre, as more modern scholarship has determined).

he was the compiler of one of his major source-homiliaries (which is a matter of considerable doubt, as discussed below),[14] there would have been no need to name him, since the homiliary was an anthology of discrete items from various authors, with the original authors' names still preserved at the head of each piece. It was precisely to give this ready access to such authoritative material that Paul had been commissioned by Charlemagne to produce a homiliary near the end of the eighth century, the brief being to collect certain flowers from the far-flung fields of the catholic Fathers.[15] In this context, it was their names that mattered; Paul's was of little account.

In demonstrating that Ælfric made considerable use of this homiliary rather than drawing upon a wide range of discrete works by the patristic authorities, Smetana repeatedly points out the identity between the liturgical lection in PD and that in Ælfric for a notably high proportion of the days covered in the *Catholic Homilies* and is able to show, above all, that the orthodox interpretation present in Paul the Deacon is closely reflected in Ælfric's corresponding homily. Nevertheless, this was not Ælfric's only available source for a significant proportion of the *Catholic Homily* material, since the homiliary of Smaragdus, which Ælfric cites as a source authority in the *Letter to Sigeric*, has a wealth of marginal letter-abbreviations — over five hundred in the earliest manuscripts — which indicate the source authorities of the extracts that he brings together.[16] As in the homiliary of Paul the Deacon, these are mainly patristic, although there is a fundamental difference between the two collections in that, whereas Paul the Deacon created an anthology of discrete items, Smaragdus created a collection in which each homily was a *catena* of verbatim extracts. Thus, for some homilies there were several marginal attributions indicating various authorities, which changed as the exegesis of the lection proceeded, whereas in Paul the Deacon there was only one attribution for each item, contained within the rubric. Despite this structural difference, however, they were potentially useful for Ælfric in exactly the same way, since each provided textual validation by means of authors' names, which Ælfric could take over, and each was demonstrably orthodox in precisely the same way. Furthermore, the two source homiliaries and Ælfric were working to a lectionary which,

---

[14] See pp. 80–82.

[15] *Capitularia Regum Francorum*, ed. by A. Boretius, MGH, Capitularia Regum Francorum, 1 (Hannover, 1883), p. 81.

[16] For information about the manuscripts, see Joyce Hill, 'Ælfric and Smaragdus', *ASE*, 21 (1992), 203–37 (pp. 234–37).

although not absolutely fixed, was nevertheless fairly stable.[17] This correlation eased Ælfric's reading across from one to the other, and gave him access to frequent and sometimes substantial textual overlap, since the material used in a given homily by Smaragdus often embodied, verbatim, some element or elements of the material for that day in Paul the Deacon — hardly surprising given the highly influential nature of Paul's homiliary when Smaragdus was writing in the earlier part of the ninth century.

Other Frankish exegetes, in homilies and commentaries, display the same degree of textual derivation, giving us, in consequence, a corpus of writing that is densely intertextual. Indeed, intertextuality is also a hallmark of the patristic period itself, and was a compositional technique much used by Bede who, in his commentaries on Mark and Luke, provided the model of marginal attribution which was used by some, though not all, of the Frankish authorities.[18] It was this model that Smaragdus followed, and it was in this tradition of explicit authority-recognition that Paul the Deacon stood. Ælfric follows them, but in so doing obliges us to confront the nature of the material with which he is working. Given that the whole Latin tradition is so profoundly intertextual, with shared liturgical order, common biblical lections, and often some measure of agreement in text and attribution, it is not possible to say that Ælfric used the homiliary of Paul the Deacon at a given point simply because of demonstrable common ground. Other options may be in play.

In the 2004 Gollancz Lecture at the British Academy, I discussed in detail the problems presented to modern source-study by the richly intertextual and highly derivative traditions of biblical exegesis to which, among many others, Paul the Deacon and Ælfric belonged, and on which they self-consciously drew.[19] One inevitable conclusion was that we may sometimes be able to do no more than identify a range of possible sources for a given Ælfrician passage, rather than assume that,

---

[17] See pp. 74–79 below for some examples of variations in the tradition within which Ælfric was working. These are, however, relatively rare.

[18] For a discussion of this tradition, with a particular focus on its use by Bede and his influence on others, see Joyce Hill, *Bede and the Benedictine Reform* (Jarrow, 1998) [the Jarrow Lecture]. As noted here (p. 5), Claudius of Turin used this practice, citing Bede as his model, and it was probably Bede who was the ultimate model for Hrabanus Maurus, although he claims to have learnt the practice from his teacher Alcuin. The acknowledgement of the source authority (though not of the source itself) became common practice in the Carolingian period, since it confirmed the exegetes' participation in the orthodox tradition, which the Carolingian *renovatio* sought to re-establish.

[19] Joyce Hill, 'Authority and Intertextuality in the Works of Ælfric', *Proceedings of the British Academy*, 131 (2005), 157–81.

because something is available in Paul the Deacon's homiliary, this must be what Ælfric used. On other occasions, despite the inclusion of appropriate material in Paul the Deacon, it might be possible to show that Ælfric actually consulted a text other than Paul's, because he reflected modifications, textual juxtapositions, or other details not in fact present in the PD text, but available to him in a text that was ostensibly the same, though in fact only superficially so. On yet other occasions, close textual analysis can show that Ælfric moved between PD and other sources, although always, of course, remaining within the acceptable range of validated orthodoxy.[20] As a basis for future source-study in this complex area, I proposed four guiding principles for conducting the necessary comparative textual analysis: those of accessibility, contiguity, abridgement, and indicative detail.[21] I provided several examples of how each worked in practice, and was able to demonstrate repeatedly that it is often not safe to make too ready an assumption that Ælfric accessed material through Paul the Deacon. The examples are unavoidably detailed, and there is no need to repeat them here, but I refer to them because it is necessary in the present context to emphasize that the evidence for Ælfric's use of PD at a given point is more complex than the broad-based correspondences indicated by Smetana might suggest, and that in consequence, conclusions about the content of Ælfric's version of PD, even with reference to the original schedule, can be reached only if the source evidence is examined within a broader frame of reference and with closer attention to detail than it has previously been given. When speculating about augmentations and omissions, care is required in even greater measure.

I have already commented on the caution that needs to be used in the case of augmentations present in Migne's *Patrologia Latina* edition. Amongst the 180 'new' items there are additions by Haymo and Hericus, homilists from the mid-ninth-century school of Auxerre. Ælfric would have had no theological objection to either of these since both are steeped in the patristic tradition. Neither, however, provides patristic authority-attributions, which was a disadvantage from Ælfric's point of view, and neither proceeds with quite the same verse-by-verse method that Ælfric favours and to which he had extensive access through PD and in Smaragdus, whose *catenae*, where they go beyond Bede and Gregory, Ælfric's preferred authors, still maintain the systematic, predominantly lection-based approach that Ælfric

---

[20] Examples illustrative of these conclusions are also to be found in Joyce Hill, 'Ælfric and Smaragdus', and 'Ælfric's Sources Reconsidered: Some Case Studies from the *Catholic Homilies*', in *Studies in English Language and Literature. 'Doubt Wisely': Papers in Honour of E. G. Stanley*, ed. by M. J. Toswell and E. M. Tyler (London, 1996), pp. 362–86.

[21] 'Authority and Intertextuality in the Works of Ælfric', pp. 170–80.

found congenial.[22] Indeed, it is likely that Haymo was used by Ælfric only 'some-times', as Ælfric himself admits, because he provided a resource which, from a textual point of view, was not quite as compatible with Ælfric's compositional aims as PD and Smaragdus were.[23] Yet the fact that Haymo is named as a discrete source in the *Letter to Sigeric*, albeit with a caveat about frequency of use, suggests that Ælfric had access to an independent copy of his homiliary. In any case, although Ælfric's use of Haymo is relatively modest, it is more wide-ranging than PDM would allow for and is firmly focussed on Haymo's *temporale* collection whereas, apart from one instance, the PDM additions are drawn from Haymo's *sanctorale*.[24] By contrast, Ælfric's use of Hericus has not been subjected to an independent study, although Godden proposes a number of instances where he may have been exploited.[25] The problem with these examples, however, is that not all of them are even in PDM, the examples themselves are very brief, often amounting to no more than a sentence of textual comparison, of a kind readily available throughout this intertextual tradition, and two of these — the etymology of Nain in *CH* I.33, and the meanings of the names of the four disciples in *CH* I.38 — are in any case better accounted for through Smaragdus.[26]

Nevertheless, augmentations to PD were undoubtedly introduced from an early date, and we should not imagine that Ælfric's copy was entirely free of these. For example, Paul the Deacon originally included thirty-two out of Gregory the Great's

---

[22] Malcolm Godden, *Ælfric's Catholic Homilies: Introduction, Commentary, and Glossary*, EETS: SS, 18 (Oxford, 2000), p. xxxviii, draws attention to the fact that when Ælfric lists his sources when writing to Archbishop Sigeric, he names Augustine first (see above p. 70). Godden takes the view that Augustine 'was clearly the authority that he [sc. Ælfric] respected most (though he is also the one he differed from most)'. It would be surprising if Augustine were not to have pride of place in an acknowledgement of authority, but this does not, of course, mean that, in practice, Ælfric used him most, as Godden's following source-analyses amply confirm.

[23] In the *Letter to Sigeric*: see above, p. 70 and note 12. For the distinctive resource provided by Haymo, which sets him apart from Paul the Deacon and Smaragdus, see Hill, 'Translating the Tradition', pp. 56–62.

[24] The initial study of Ælfric's use of Haymo was undertaken by Cyril L. Smetana, 'Ælfric and the Homiliary of Haymo of Halberstadt', *Traditio*, 17 (1961), 457–69. The fact that we now know that the author of the homiliary was Haymo of Auxerre does not invalidate Smetana's work. Godden, *Introduction, Commentary, and Glossary*, pp. liv–lv, adds to the list of possible uses by Haymo. Ælfric's use of Haymo is, however, a topic that needs further investigation.

[25] Godden, *Introduction, Commentary, and Glossary*, p. lv.

[26] *CH* I.33, p. 458, and I.38, pp. 512–13. Both are discussed in 'Authority and Intertextuality in the Works of Ælfric', pp. 178–80.

forty homilies on the Gospels, but PDM includes a further seven. On the evidence of the major manuscripts available in England before 1100 (all of which post-date Ælfric, however) we can see that at least some of these Gregorian additions were introduced fairly early on, since Gregory's Homilies 22, 28, 33, 38, 39, and 40 all occur in Cambridge, Pembroke College, MS 23, Cambridge, University Library, MS Ii. 2. 19, and Worcester, Cathedral Library, MS F 93, and in Durham, Cathedral Library, MS A. III. 29, with the exception of Homily 33.[27] Although none of these homilies was in the original PD, their rubric is identical in each of these eleventh-century manuscripts, despite the fact that the manuscripts differ in various ways. One can therefore safely argue that these augmentations were already a well-established feature by this date and it is thus likely that they were added relatively early. Furthermore, since Ælfric used material from Homilies 22, 38, 39, and 40, it is reasonable to suppose that his manuscript of PD already had these Gregorian additions. That said, it is worth probing these instances more closely, in order to illustrate the kinds of considerations that have to be taken into account in arguing backwards from Ælfric to Ælfric's version of Paul the Deacon.

In the first place, the fact that Ælfric does not use Gregory's Homily 33 does not necessarily mean that it was not in his copy. The consistency between three of the four manuscripts noted above suggests that it was present in an early tradition of Gregorian augmentation on exactly the same basis as the additional Gregorian homilies that Ælfric did use. But Gregory's Homily 33 is the one instance out of all these additions that is for a weekday (feria VI); all of the others are for Sundays. Since Ælfric's purpose was to provide for Sundays and special days, his failure to use this homily may thus indicate not that it was absent from his copy, but simply that it was not liturgically relevant for his immediate purpose; the *Catholic Homilies*, even in Ælfric's later supplemented form, are far less comprehensive in their coverage of the year than the original PD, and markedly less so than PD as it went through the process of augmentation, when there was often greater choice of items for days that had always been provided for, together with a more extensive coverage of days, including greater provision for ferias.

Different reasons account for Ælfric's failure to use Gregory's Homily 28, even though, prima facie, it was likely to have been in his copy along with the other Gregorian augmentations — and was in any case a Sunday item. In these

[27] For further information about these manuscripts, see below pp. 90–92. For permission to consult them, I am indebted respectively to the Master and Fellows of Pembroke College Cambridge, the Librarian of Cambridge University Library, the Dean and Chapter of Worcester Cathedral, and the Dean and Chapter of Durham Cathedral.

manuscripts the homily is for the Twenty-First Sunday after Pentecost, with the lection being John 4. 46–53, the story of the healing of the nobleman's son at Capernaum. Although Ælfric's provision of homilies for the Sundays after Pentecost is far from complete, he did cover the Twenty-First Sunday in the First Series, but for this he used one of the other augmenting homilies of Gregory referred to above: Homily 38, which dealt with Matthew 22. 1–14, the parable of the Marriage of the King's Son.[28] Matthew 22. 1–14 is also the lection for the Twenty-First Sunday after Pentecost in the homiliary of Smaragdus, which could thus have influenced Ælfric's choice of lection for this day. More interestingly still, Smaragdus's homiliary would have shown, through the marginal letter G, that Gregory provided useful exegesis for the Matthean lection, since Smaragdus made substantial use of Gregory's Homily 38.[29] By contrast, in the PD manuscripts known in England from before 1100, the lection of Matthew 22. 1–4, for which the augmenting Gregorian Homily 38 provides the exegesis, is rubricated for the Twentieth Sunday after Pentecost. Since, however, Ælfric did not provide for the Twentieth Sunday in the First Series, he was free to use this material for the Twenty-First Sunday, if he so wished. His augmented PD would have given him the whole of Homily 38, and it seems clear that Ælfric made use of it, since his Old English homily incorporates more of Gregory's exegesis than is extracted by Smaragdus. Homily 28, based on John 4. 46–53, would then simply not be needed, and it was not needed later, since he did not subsequently write a second homily for the Twenty-First Sunday in the Second Series, and did not provide for the Twentieth Sunday either. Again, then, the evidence from source study, *ex silentio*, needs to be handled with care. On the other hand, we should not assume that, simply because Ælfric seems to have drawn upon Gregory's Homily 38 in the fuller form probably available to him in his augmented copy of PD, it there appeared for the Twenty-First Sunday, as Godden seems to imply.[30] It could well have been present for the Twentieth

---

[28] *CH* I.35, pp. 476–85. The identification of Gregory's Homily 38 as Ælfric's source was made by Förster, 'Über die Quellen', pp. 5–6, §51. Smetana, 'Ælfric and the Early Medieval Homiliary', p. 194, notes that this Gregorian homily is one of the additions to the original PD, and he cites two continental manuscripts and the *PL* version of PD, but he does not refer to the manuscripts known in England before 1100 in which it also occurs, as noted above, p. 75.

[29] For an analysis of Smaragdus's sources, see Fidel Rädle, *Studien zu Smaragd von Saint-Mihiel* (Munich, 1974), p. 210.

[30] Godden, *Introduction, Commentary, and Glossary*, p. 290, rather oddly states that Gregory's Homily 38 is 'the only item provided for this occasion in Paul the Deacon's homiliary', but Smetana (who is footnoted in support) does not say this. In any case, as we shall see below, the

Sunday, as in the augmented manuscripts here under discussion, with Ælfric drawing upon it for his Twenty-First Sunday homily under the prompting of the homiliary of Smaragdus, where he would have seen that Gregory was used to explicate Ælfric's preferred lection for that day, a preference which he shared with Smaragdus and not with PD.

By contrast, there is positive evidence for the use of four of the additional Gregorian items. The use of Homily 38 has just been dealt with. Homily 22, though rubricated in the pre-1100 manuscripts for the Saturday after Easter, provided Ælfric with his Second Series Homily for Easter Day (*CH*. II.15),[31] alongside the First Series Easter Day homily (*CH* I.15), for which he had already used Gregory's Homily 21, given in the original PD for the Vigil of Easter,[32] so that in this instance the augmentation for the Easter period gave him a useful alternative. In this case, by contrast with the instance of the use of Gregory's Homily 38, Ælfric probably came to it in his augmented PD directly, rather than being prompted by Smaragdus, since the lection in question, John 20. 1–9, occurs in Smaragdus's homiliary for the Saturday in the Octave of Easter. Smaragdus made use of Gregory's Homily 22 in elucidating this Johannine lection, but only in extracted form, and Ælfric demonstrably used more of the homily than Smaragdus provided.[33] It

original PD has a completely different way of rubricating the Sundays after Pentecost, so it is difficult to see what Godden means here by 'this occasion'. Further, while noting that Gregory's Homily 38 is an augmenting item, Smetana does not specify what its rubric is in the various places where he has noted it and, as is noted in the present discussion, it is used for the Twentieth Sunday after Pentecost, not the Twenty-First in the manuscripts written or owned in England up to 1100.

[31] For Ælfric's Second Series Easter Day homily, see *Ælfric's Catholic Homilies: The Second Series, Text*, ed. by M. R. Godden, EETS: SS, 5 (London, 1979), pp. 150–60. Ælfric's use of Gregory's Homily 22 was identified by Förster, 'Über die Quellen', p. 12–13, §62. Smetana, 'Ælfric and the Early Medieval Homiliary', p. 197, notes that this is an augmenting homily, not in the original. Godden, *Introduction, Commentary, and Glossary*, p. 488, in noting Förster's identification of the Gregory's Homily 22, remarks 'it is assigned for Easter Day in Paul the Deacon's homiliary'. But this is not true in either respect: it is not in the original at all, contrary to what one might suppose from Godden's unqualified statement; and when it first occurs as an augmenting item, it is not assigned to Easter Day — at least as far as one can judge from the manuscripts known in England from before 1100.

[32] *CH* I, pp. 299–306. The source identification was originally made by Förster, 'Über die Quellen', pp. 2–3, §42. See also Smetana, 'Ælfric and the Early Medieval Homiliary', p. 189.

[33] This is clear if one examines the extent of Ælfric's use of Gregory in Godden, *Introduction, Commentary, and Glossary*, pp. 487–500, with the use of Gregory by Smaragdus, as detailed by Rädle, *Studien zu Smaragd*, p. 218.

is therefore all the more likely that he drew upon the whole homily as he would have found it in his augmented PD.

Finally, for the Second Sunday after Pentecost in the First Series (*CH* I.23) Ælfric created a new *catena* by using Gregory's Homily 40 for the exposition of the lection (Luke 16. 19–31, the story of Dives and Lazarus), and Gregory's Homily 39 for the exemplum (the story of Martyrius, a monk who carried a leper, who turned out to be Christ).[34] In the manuscripts under consideration here, Homily 40 is for the Second Sunday after Pentecost, and Homily 39 for the Tenth Sunday. For the Second Sunday after Pentecost, the original version of Paul the Deacon's homiliary has Luke 14. 16–24 as the lection (the parable of the Great Supper), for which the exegesis is Gregory's Homily 36. In choosing to write instead on Luke 16. 19–31, Ælfric was not only following what seems to have been the revised and augmented model of Paul the Deacon for the Second Sunday, but also the model — at least from the point of view of the lection — of Haymo and Smaragdus, who both use the Luke 16 text.[35] This may be an instance where, for certain days of the year, the lections were in flux in the Carolingian period, and that the tradition which comes through for Ælfric to follow is the post-PD tradition, as witnessed in Smaragdus and Haymo, and probably also in the revised PD to which Ælfric had access.[36] Subsequently, in the Second Series homily for the Common of the

---

[34] *CH* I, pp. 365–70. There are several instances where Ælfric creates a new *catena* by bringing together exposition and exemplum from two different Gregorian homilies. For a discussion of these, including the example cited here, see Joyce Hill, 'Ælfric, Gregory and the Carolingians', in *Roma, Magistra Mundi: Itineraria Culturae Medievalis. Mélanges Offerts au Père L. E. Boyle à l'Occasion de son 75e Anniversaire*, ed. by Jacqueline Hamesse (Louvain-la-Neuve, 1998), pp. 409–23. The source identification was originally made by Förster, 'Über die Quellen', pp. 3–4, §45. See also Smetana, 'Ælfric and the Early Medieval Homiliary', p. 190.

[35] Godden, *Introduction, Commentary, and Glossary*, p. 184, notes that Haymo and Smaragdus make use of Gregory's Homily 40, although in the case of Smaragdus, as Rädle shows, *Studien zu Smaragd*, p. 215, Smaragdus's immediate source is in fact Bede's Commentary on Luke. Since Bede habitually draws on Gregory, however, one can easily account for the textual similarity, and thus also recognize that Ælfric would readily develop a sense of confidence in working within an obviously intertextual and thus mutually reinforcing tradition as he looked across from one homiliary manuscript to another. For Bede's use of Gregory when commenting on Luke 16. 19–31, and the signalling of this by a marginal letter G, see *In Lucae evangelium expositio*, in *Opera Exegetica*, ed. by D. Hurst, CCSL, 120 (Turnhout, 1960), pp. 302–06.

[36] Ælfric's PD may thus be more like the homiliaries of Smaragdus and Haymo than an original version would have been. This would have made movement between them, as his main source-texts, all the easier. For further examples of the way in which cross-referencing was facilitated by the 'modernization' of PD, see the section below on form and organization.

Martyrs (*CH* II.37), Homily 40 was used again, this time for the exemplum, in conjunction with Gregory's Homily 35, which was one of the items in the original PD for this occasion (the others being by Ambrose and Maximus, whose work Ælfric never chose).[37] The only reasonable explanation for all of these uses of Gregory is that Ælfric had full-text copies of the homilies readily available, and this was most likely to be in an augmented PD. Such a conclusion is supported by evidence from the manuscripts written or owned in England up to 1100, and by the fact that there is no alternative source in the homiliary of Smaragdus, which was the other manuscript that would have given him authoritative attributions, since Smaragdus made no use of the exempla from Homily 39 or 40, while Ælfric used the exempla from both.

This discussion of early Gregorian additions to PD, which we can demonstrate were in all probability in Ælfric's own version of the homiliary, draws attention to the tendency, even from an early date, to enlarge the collection. At the other end of the scale are omissions, which certainly occurred — by comparison with the original — as the modifications grew. PDM provides ample testimony to this since its extensive augmentation brought with it the loss of a substantial number of the items included by Paul.[38] Caution is nevertheless needed when considering what might not have been in Ælfric's manuscript version. For example, it is notable that Ælfric makes no use whatever of the thirty-five homilies attributed to Leo and the fifty-three attributed to Maximus in Paul the Deacon's original, and this led Smetana to suppose that they were simply not in Ælfric's copy. In support of this *argumentum ex silentio* he refers to a tenth-century manuscript, believed by Wiegand to be for monastic use, which omits Leo and Maximus, but Smetana then admits that Durham A. III. 29 has some homilies by Leo and Maximus, and at the same time includes the Gregorian modifications to the post-Pentecost Sundays that Ælfric demonstrably exploited.[39] These modifications are the ones that have just been discussed and, as noted, they are present in other PD manuscripts also, pointing to a stable tradition of relatively early augmentation. What Smetana identifies, however, with his reference to the Durham version, is a PD manuscript tradition that may be closer to Ælfric's original than the supposed monastic

---

[37] *CH* II, pp. 310–17. This is also discussed in Hill, 'Ælfric, Gregory and the Carolingians'. The source identification was originally made by Förster, 'Über die Quellen', pp. 4–5, §48. See also Smetana, 'Ælfric and the Early Medieval Homiliary', p. 201.

[38] See above, p. 68.

[39] Smetana, 'Ælfric and the Early Medieval Homiliary', pp. 203–04.

manuscript identified by Wiegand.[40] In any case, while it is true that there are already fewer homilies by Maximus and Leo in the pre-1100 manuscripts known in England in comparison with the PD original, Ælfric's failure to use their homilies may not be a matter of what was omitted from his manuscript, but a matter of choosing what suited his purpose and ignoring the rest. Neither Leo's homilies, which are brief and doctrinal, nor those of Maximus, which make much use of the natural world in order to draw out spiritual analogies and moral lessons, are in harmony with Ælfric's patristically validated, lection-based exegetical approach, nor are they in harmony with the similarly lection-based exegetical approach used in the homiliaries of Smaragdus or Haymo, the two Frankish homiliaries that he cites by name as authorities. Thus, although an argument from silence might be tempting, it is yet another instance of where we need to be cautious in drawing conclusions from source study.

Form and Organization

Turning now from the content of Ælfric's version of PD, on which much detailed work still needs to be done, to consideration of the form and organization of Ælfric's copy, we might first ask whether it included the prefatory material. Since it was only here that Paul was identified as the compiler, we can begin by considering whether Ælfric associated the collection with any single person, or whether he simply saw it as an authoritative collection in which each item was authorially validated in the rubric. Of course, Ælfric did not *need* to refer to Paul the Deacon by name, even if he had had this information, since the nature of the collection — discrete items by individual authors, whose names carried far greater weight than Paul's — meant that he could, and did, cite the authorities directly. The same held true for the homiliary of Smaragdus, whose authority-identifications recorded in the margins gave him access to the same kind of validating information, which Ælfric then cited in the body of the homilies. But it is notable that, in the *Letter to Sigeric*, when referring to this manuscript as a whole, Smaragdus's name is used, as also is Haymo's as a further source,[41] whereas Paul the Deacon's is not. There is more than one possible explanation for this. Each individual homily of Smaragdus and Haymo is the author's own; however derivative they are, they are essentially individual compositions. Thus the only way that one can refer to the overall

---

[40] See further below, pp. 90–91.

[41] For the *Letter to Sigeric*, see p. 70 and note 12 above.

homiliary in each case is to say that it is the homiliary of Smaragdus or of Haymo. This was not so necessary for the collection of Paul the Deacon, however, since it could be referred to as a patristic anthology, or indicative names could be given, much as we often refer to anthologies by some indicative title rather than citing the name of the editor (compiler, in medieval terms). Thus, the listing of Augustine, Jerome, Bede, and Gregory in the *Letter to Sigeric*, while certainly reflecting information in the Smaragdus homiliary, may primarily be Ælfric's way of referring to the PD anthology. One could argue that he chose to refer to it in this way, while still assuming that his copy included the prefatory material with its identification of the author. However, judging from the surviving manuscripts, there is a strong likelihood that the anthology circulated without its collection of prefatory material, and that could well be how it came to Ælfric. Paul's name is referred to within the prefatory material, but rather inconspicuously, hidden within running text, and since the items which originally formed the prefatory matter were about how and why Charlemagne had asked Paul to draw up the compilation, the prefatory matter, tied to a particular historical moment, rapidly became redundant and was dropped.[42] It is not uncommon for this to happen, as we see from Ælfric's own works, which soon lost their circumstantial prefaces. Furthermore, since PD was soon modified, taking on a life of its own through augmentation and even undergoing major structural reordering, as will be demonstrated in this section, it is easy to see why the supplementary matter at the beginning would disappear. Once this happened, even if only in some of the evolving versions, manuscripts of PD will have circulated without its compiler's name. In this respect, it contrasted with the homiliaries of Haymo and Smaragdus (and other similarly 'personal' homiliaries). Clearly, as the *Letter to Sigeric* shows, Ælfric's manuscripts of Haymo and Smaragdus bore their names as identifiers; by contrast, it is highly likely that his version of PD was simply an anthology, with no prefaces, and thus with no identification of the compiler.

If this is so, Godden's proposition that Ælfric modelled the *Catholic Homilies* on what the PD prefatory matter said is unsustainable.[43] He starts with the untested assumption that Ælfric had access to the prefatory matter and supports his case with the false analogy that the two books of the *Catholic Homilies* are modelled on the two books of PD. Paul's collection was initially arranged in liturgical order for two halves of the year, the *pars hiemalis* (Advent to Holy Saturday) and

---

[42] The prefatory material is given by Wiegand, *Das Homiliarium Karls des Grossen*, pp. 14–17. See also Grégoire, *Homéliaires liturgiques médiévaux*, pp. 423–24.

[43] Godden, *Introduction, Commentary, and Glossary*, pp. 3–4.

the *pars aestiva* (the Vigil of Easter to the end of the post-Pentecost period, followed by homilies for the Common observances).[44] Subsequent reordering of PD produced something significantly different, as we shall see below. Each of Ælfric's First and Second Series, by contrast, ranged across the full year, and they were produced in sequence, over a period of time, to provide variety, with the possibility of either combining them as a more comprehensive composite for the whole year, or leaving them as two series that could be alternated.[45] It was, of course, the case that PD provided a model of liturgically ordered, systematic, patristically based interpretation, and its influence on and usefulness to Ælfric on that account was of paramount importance, but even if we consider this dimension, PD was not the only model he had, since he was demonstrably working within a rich and well-established tradition which gave him several textual witnesses of equal validity.

In fact, the structure of the original compilation put together by Paul the Deacon made it difficult to use, not because it was divided into the *pars hiemalis* and the *pars aestiva*, which were straightforwardly consecutive, but because, throughout these two parts, it combined in one temporal sequence feasts within the lunar and solar cycles, whose relationship, one to another, varied from year to year. It was the pressing need to overcome this awkwardness and so make the collection an easy reference work for all time, together with developments in how parts of the liturgical year were designated, that provided the chief impetus for the early reordering of the collection. We see in Ælfric's *Catholic Homilies* evidence that he was generally working to the more modern practices, and given that he undoubtedly made heavy use of his copy of PD, exploiting it alongside his homiliaries of Haymo and Smaragdus, cross-referring from one to the other even in the midst of writing one homily, we can safely assume that his PD manuscript was also of the reordered variety. As a means of explaining this further, however, it is necessary to comment on the coexistence of the solar and lunar cycles within the Church's year.[46]

---

[44] See note 60 below for the scope of the Common material in the original homiliary of Paul the Deacon.

[45] When Ælfric sent the First Series to Archbishop Sigeric, he noted that he was already working on the Second Series, and so, already in the Latin letter accompanying the First Series, he explained the possibility that this would open up of combining the two sets or using them separately in alternate years: *CH* I, pp. 173–74.

[46] For the following summary of the evolution of the Church's year, see the greater detail in G. G. Willis, *A History of the Early Roman Liturgy to the Death of Pope Gregory the Great*, Henry Bradshaw Society, Subsidia 1 (London, 1994), particularly chap. III, pp. 78–115, and Cyrille Vogel, *Medieval Liturgy: An Introduction to the Sources*, rev. and trans. by William G. Storey and Niels Krogh Rasmussen (Washington, D.C., 1986). See also, with particular reference to the

Within Christianized western Europe, it was the Roman tradition that provided the fixed system of days and months, and it was on specified dates within this framework that the commemoration of the saints (the *sanctorale*) was observed. But this ran in parallel with the lunar cycle, which determined many of the major feasts of the Church, so that, in any given year, the precise relationship between a lunar-based and a solar-based feast would vary until, after a period of years, the two cycles returned (for one year) to their previous relative position. So, for example, a particular saint's day, falling on a fixed date in early April, might be before or after Easter, depending on the changing date of Easter year by year.

It was Easter, universally established as a historical commemoration from the second century onwards, that was the focal point around which the lunar-based feasts, the *temporale*, grew up. Suggestions were made in the third and fourth centuries that the date should be fixed, with various dates in March and April being proposed, but the association with the Jewish Passover, enshrined in the gospel narrative, prevailed, and the Good Friday, Holy Saturday, Easter Sunday sequence remained tied to the old Jewish chronology, resulting in a movable feast because the date of the Passover was calculated in relation to the lunar cycle. In consequence, other gospel-derived feasts such as Ascension (forty days after Easter) and Pentecost (fifty days after) were also movable, and so too was the period of preparation leading up to Easter, calculated backwards from whenever Easter occurred. Holy Week was well established by the fifth century, and was preceded by a period of fasting of variable length, settling down finally to being Lent or Quadragesima, beginning with Ash Wednesday, by the sixth century. Quinquagesima is first referred to in the first half of the sixth century; Sexagesima is from a little later in the sixth century; and Septuagesima is a seventh-century addition.

However, a complication had by then developed with the introduction into the *temporale* of the commemoration of Christ's birth and other gospel events associated with it, since these commemorations placed within a movable (lunar-based) annual cycle a certain number of fixed dates. December 25 as the Feast of the Nativity is first mentioned in 336; the Feast of the Annunciation thus logically comes to be March 25, nine months earlier; and there is a further fixed date of January 6 for the Feast of the Epiphany.[47] The result was that there were now two

Anglo-Saxons, Joyce Hill, 'Coping with Conflict: Lunar and Solar Cycles in the Liturgical Calendars', in *Time and Eternity: The Medieval Discourse,* ed. by Gerhard Jaritz and Gerson Moreno-Riaño, International Medieval Research, 9 (Turnhout, 2003), pp. 99–108.

[47] The most likely reason for choosing 25 December for the Nativity is that, since it could not be celebrated in spring anywhere near Easter, the Church seized upon the old Roman Feast of

pivotal points within the *temporale*: Christmas using fixed dates within the solar
calendar; and Easter using movable dates within the lunar. The conflict between
them was accommodated by two buffer-zones which could be of variable length
according to need: the Sundays after Epiphany, which carried one up to Lent (or
to the pre-Lent countdown of Septuagesima, Sexagesima, and Quinquagesima);
and the much longer run of Sundays after Pentecost, which filled up the rest of the
year until Advent. But this second buffer zone, known as the Sundays in Ordinary
Time, which takes up about half of the year, and so figures prominently in whole-
year homiliaries, was rather awkwardly configured in the early centuries. It was
evidently thought sensible to break it up into manageable units, but this was done
by tying groups of Sundays to certain fixed dates of hagiographical commemoration. The pivotal saints' days were the Feast of the Apostles Peter and Paul (June
29), the Feast of St Laurence (August 10), and the Feast of the Holy Angel (i.e. the
Archangel Michael, September 29), with the Feast of St Cyprian (September 14)
sometimes being used in addition. Sundays were counted as Sundays *after* Pentecost, Sundays *after* the Feast of the Apostles, and so on.[48] The problem with this
arrangement, however, is that the Sunday lections, particularly as they stabilized
over the course of the years, ran in sequence from the movable (*temporale*) feast of
Pentecost and, thus, from one year to the next had different relative positions to
the *sanctorale* anchor-points. To look at it the other way round, the lection for,
shall we say, the second Sunday after the feast of St Laurence (which is how the
Sunday itself was identified) was not the same year on year, since the lection was
determined not by the designation of the Sunday in relation to St Laurence, as the
rubric indicated, but by the number of Sundays one had had since Pentecost,
whenever that had occurred in the particular year in question.

   Paul the Deacon's original homiliary caters for saints' days throughout the year,
interspersed among the many lunar-based feasts, and also, for Ordinary Time, uses
the old designations for the Sundays after Pentecost by anchoring them to the
Feasts of Saints Peter and Paul, St Laurence, and the Holy Angel.[49] He has a homily

Natalis Solis Inuicti on 25 December, conveniently placed within the calendar, and metaphorically
apt for celebrating the birthday of the Sun/Son of Righteousness, whom death and darkness could
not conquer.

[48] This system is clearly set out in tabular form by Vogel, *Medieval Liturgy*, p. 409.

[49] This original form of rubrication is evident in Grégoire, *Homéliaires liturgiques médiévaux*
and in Smetana's summary account of the contents of PD following Wiegand, 'Ælfric and the
Early Medieval Homiliary'. It should be noted, however, that Smetana uses Ælfric's rubrics in his
ensuing discussion. Since Ælfric used the more modern system of counting the Sundays in a con-

for the Feast of St Cyprian, but he does not use this feast as part of his post-Pentecost counting system. The difficulty is that, in effect, it is a system that is actually year-specific. Not long after Paul's collection entered circulation, however, the Carolingian reformers came up with a much better solution: they abandoned this anchoring by saints' days, and instead simply designated the Sundays in an unbroken sequence, counting always from Pentecost or sometimes from the Octave of Pentecost.[50] Thus, major homily collections such as those of Hrabanus Maurus, Smaragdus, and Haymo all use this new system, which was devised by Benedict of Aniane in the early ninth century. By this method, there was a maximum of twenty-four Sundays after Pentecost. This could be cut short according to the position of Easter: if Easter was late, the number of Sundays after Pentecost could be cut by ignoring the appropriate number at the end, while more of the potentially available Sundays after Epiphany could be used to cover the correspondingly longer period to the somewhat later onset of Lent — with the reverse being done if Easter was early. Nothing more complicated than this was needed to accommodate the movable nature of this part of the liturgical cycle. Lections were constant within this numbering system, and any manuscript which set out the full sequence (i.e. including the maximum number of Sundays after Epiphany and Pentecost) could be used easily in any year. Furthermore, cross-reference could be made from one homily collection to another without any difficulty, since the organization was not year-specific.

Ælfric, writing and revising his *temporale* sequence, the *Catholic Homilies*, invariably uses the new, continuous counting method. But when I first began to examine in detail how he made use of his principal source-collections, the homiliaries of Paul the Deacon, Smaragdus, and Haymo, I was puzzled by how, for the second half of the year, he could so easily move between them. Smaragdus and Haymo were not a problem, since they both use continuous counting; it was Paul that presented the difficulty. The answer to the problem lies in manuscript copies,

---

tinuous numerical sequence from Pentecost, this disguises somewhat the difficulty that Ælfric would have faced if he had had before him a copy of PD as originally rubricated. As will be seen from the ensuing argument, however, it is probable that Ælfric's version of PD had already replaced this old method of counting the Sundays in Ordinary Time with the easier system of counting continuously from Pentecost, thus facilitating cross-reference between his various source homiliaries.

[50] In essence, this is the system still in use today. The variation of counting from the Octave of Pentecost (now Trinity Sunday, but not by then established) makes no difference to the clarity and simplicity of the new scheme, although it presents obvious opportunities for scribal error.

which show that the homiliary was also rapidly updated in being given the new and more flexible rubrics for the post-Pentecost period. Examples include Worcester F 93, CUL Ii. 2. 19, Pembroke 23, and Durham A. III. 29, which have already been cited as manuscripts known in England before 1100. While these manuscripts post-date Ælfric, it is difficult not to believe — as I argued in the Toller lecture — that they are indicative of the form of his own manuscript of Paul the Deacon: updated in the rubrics for the Sundays of Ordinary Time, providing the same kind of model for his own practice in dealing with this half of the Church's year as did his copies of Smaragdus and Haymo, and facilitating what was clearly a very easy movement between these principal source-homiliaries.[51]

Another Carolingian tendency was to separate out *temporale* and *sanctorale* by assembling preaching and reading materials for these two differently organized cycles in separate sets. This is how Haymo orders his work and, more interestingly, it is how Paul the Deacon's homiliary was soon reordered as it was successively recopied, separating *temporale* and *sanctorale* material into companion collections, rather than leaving them as an entangled combined collection, where the relative sequence would not necessarily work year on year.[52] This is what happens, for example, in the augmented collections of Pembroke 23 (*temporale*) and Pembroke 24 (*sanctorale*); and Worcester F 92 and F 93 (two-volume *temporale*) and F 94 (*sanctorale*). Ælfric does not quite adhere to this, since the *Catholic Homilies* do include some of the more popular saints' lives (certainly there from the start), whilst his *Lives of Saints* collection includes some homiletic material (although we cannot be sure whether these items are later additions). There is a degree of specialization between *temporale* and *sanctorale* in these collections, however, and in any case, where the collection does not provide exhaustive coverage for the year, as Ælfric's *Catholic Homilies* do not, the conflicts between lunar and solar cycles, between movable feasts and fixed dates, are not necessarily in evidence: when there are 'unused' Sundays and relatively few saints' days, there is simply not a tight enough sequence for the changing relativities to be apparent. Even so, given the speed with which the separation of *temporale* and *sanctorale* occurred throughout the year, and the way that the Sundays of Ordinary Time were provided with a more flexible designation (which Ælfric himself employed), it is probable that Ælfric's PD had these separations too. Reordering on this scale would, of course, increase the

---

[51] Hill, 'Translating the Tradition', pp. 54–56.

[52] Smaragdus's homiliary, by contrast, was a *temporale* from the outset, providing material for the epistle and gospel lections.

likelihood of the prefatory matter being lost, almost regardless of its historical relevance, which in any case rapidly diminished.

Another structural change that may well have been present in Ælfric's PD is the relocation of the homilies for the Major Litany.[53] This observance, in the Roman traditions with which Paul the Deacon would have been familiar, was on the fixed date of 25 April. But the dominant tradition in Francia was the Gallican observance on the Monday, Tuesday, and Wednesday before the movable feast of the Ascension (a feast within the lunar cycle because it always occurred forty days after Easter). Confusingly, this three-day observance was also known as the Major Litany. In the original PD, nothing was provided for this observance; there is only material rubricated for the Vigil of the Ascension in accordance with the homiliary's practice throughout of catering for the Vigil of significant feasts. Paul did, however, provide three homilies for 25 April, designated in the rubric as the Major Litany. There was nothing unusual in that, since many days within the original collection had several items from which to choose, but having three available was an opportunity that copyists could not resist, and in Pembroke 23, CUL Ii. 2. 19, Durham A. III. 29, and Worcester F 93, we find these three homilies deployed instead for the three days before Ascension, with textual evidence in the rubrics that this was recognized as the Litany period. In none of these manuscripts is there anything for 25 April; as far as the evidence of the manuscripts indicates, the Litany observance of 25 April simply does not exist. The homily collections of Smaragdus, Haymo, and also Hrabanus Maurus provide for this same three-day observance rather than that of 25 April, in response to what was for them the dominant tradition, and so does Ælfric, writing in a country where this Gallican (Frankish) tradition of a three-day, pre-Ascension Major Litany was also strong. In this instance, despite the very broad correspondence arising through the shared moral message and some common threads in biblical reference, there is no evidence that Ælfric used PD's Major Litany material, two items of which, in any case, were by Maximus, whose homilies he always avoided. That being so, it might be thought that this discussion of the differing Roman and Gallican observances of the Major Litany and their respective treatment in the original PD and its derivations is little to the point. But if the reordering was already in Ælfric's copy, as it is in the eleventh-century manuscripts of PD written or owned in England, it would be a

---

[53] For a detailed examination of this issue, which is here summarized in brief, see Joyce Hill, 'The *Litaniae maiores* and *minores* in Rome, Francia, and Anglo-Saxon England: Terminology, Texts, and Traditions', *Early Medieval Europe*, 9 (2000), 211–46. As I demonstrate in this analysis, the relocation creates no awkwardness in respect of subject matter.

further example of how Ælfric's PD was closer in form and organization to the homiliaries of Haymo and Smaragdus than the original PD would have been, and so it provides a further indication of how much easier it was for him to move from one homiliary to another without being faced by contradictions or incompatibilities. To that extent, it is a detail which contributes to the characterization of Ælfric's version of Paul the Deacon's anthology and to our understanding of the circumstances under which he was working.

Relevant also to the question of the organization of Ælfric's source-homiliaries is when the Church's year actually begins. The four Sundays in Advent, leading up to Christmas, mark the start in the modern period, but in the early Middle Ages it was not so clear-cut. The original PD, judging from the reconstructions of Wiegand and Grégoire, started the year with Advent, as is the practice now. The homiliaries of Haymo and of Hericus of Auxerre, from mid-ninth-century Francia, are similarly arranged to begin with Advent. By contrast, Smaragdus, writing a generation earlier than Haymo and Hericus, but later than Paul, keeps to the older tradition in putting the Sundays of Advent at the end of the year, and Ælfric follows Smaragdus. This is also the preferred arrangement in subsequent Old English homily collections where the contents are liturgically arranged.[54] The West Saxon lectionary likewise starts with Christmas and ends with Advent.[55] What Ælfric actually had in his copy of PD is impossible to say, but the variability in the start of the year is a reminder that we are dealing with a liturgical system that was, in some respects, still subject to change — a situation which further complicates the characterization of Ælfric's copy of PD.[56]

---

[54] The one exception is Cambridge, Corpus Christi College, MS 302 in which, as noted by N. R. Ker, *Catalogue of Manuscripts Containing Anglo-Saxon* (Oxford, 1957), article 56, pp. 95–99 (p. 96), the four Sundays in Advent come at the beginning. Since this manuscript is from the late eleventh/early twelfth century, the more modern arrangement may simply be a reflection of gradual change over time.

[55] Ursula Lenker, *Die westsächsische Evangelienversion und die Perikopenordnungen im angelsächsischen England*, Texte und Untersuchungen zur englischen Philologie, 20 (Munich, 1997).

[56] Another variable was the number of Sundays in Advent. Paul the Deacon's original homiliary, as reconstructed by both Wiegand and Grégoire, has five Sundays, whereas the homiliaries of Smaragdus and Haymo have four. Since it is positioning rather than number that affects the structure of the homiliary, the question of how many Advent Sundays there might have been in Ælfric's PD is not explored here, but the gradual establishment of four Sundays in Advent rather than five (or even six in some contexts) draws attention to another point at which successive copies of PD might have been modified to satisfy local expectation and practice. On the number of Sundays in Advent, see Willis, *History of the Early Roman Liturgy*, p. 94.

Manuscripts within the PD Tradition Written or Owned in England up to 1100

Durham, Cathedral Library, MS B. II. 2

Gneuss no. 226.[57] Provenance: Durham. Date: s. xi[ex], before 1096. This manuscript has not been cited in the preceding discussion because it is in fact a very faithful copy of the original PD, at least insofar as one can judge from the surviving part. It is of great interest on these grounds, because it shows that, as on the Continent, there were reasonably faithful copies of the original being made up to at least the end of the eleventh century. However, as far as one can tell, such manuscripts were far less common than the modified ones, and in the light of the foregoing discussion, it seems clear that Ælfric was working with a version of PD that had undergone some modifications. The manuscript as it now survives covers Sundays and feastdays from Christmas to Good Friday. There are occasional lacunae, not noted in Rud's 1825 catalogue, so that it is not quite complete, even for the period that it now covers.[58] Gneuss describes it as a 'companion volume' to Durham A. III. 29, and so it may have been in practice. But it is not a companion volume within the PD manuscript tradition since, by contrast with B. II. 2, A. III. 29 shows modifications and augmentations, as noted in the course of the discussions above. Since the original material in Durham B. II. 2 now begins part way through PD 15, one of the homilies for the vigil of Christmas, and then follows the original PD order, we must presume that the preceding homilies were once present, so that the homiliary started with Advent, as did Paul the Deacon's original. Some of the homilies are numbered in roman numerals (e.g. up to the equivalent of PD 23, again from the equivalent of PD 34 to PD 38 inclusive, and PD 40, with PD 39 omitted entirely), but the numbering is not carried through consistently. What is remarkable, however, is that when numbers are given, even when they are resumed after a break or after a homily from PD has been omitted (as occurs very occasionally), the numbers at the point of resumption are always correct in relation to the PD original, which only serves to emphasize its use of a good quality copy-text which preserved even these details from a PD manuscript which had little or no modification.

---

[57] In each of the following accounts of manuscripts, reference is made to Gneuss, *Handlist*, from where details of provenance and date are also taken.

[58] Thomas Rud, *Codicum manuscriptorum Ecclesiae Cathedralis Dunelmensis: catalogus classicus* (Durham, 1825).

Durham, Cathedral Library, MS A. III. 29

Gneuss no. 222. Provenance: Durham. Date: s. xi[ex], before 1096. This is said by
Gneuss to be a 'companion volume' to Durham B. II. 2, although this is a faithful
copy of a PD original,[59] whereas Durham A. III. 29 has Gregorian augmentations,
as noted in the foregoing discussion. It is remarkably close to the *pars aestiva* of the
original PD, nonetheless, taking the materials in order, and covering the whole
period of the *pars aestiva* from Easter to the end of Ordinary Time. It is noteworthy, however, that items relating to the *sanctorale* are omitted, and that there
are fewer homilies by Maximus and Leo than in this part of the original, thus giving
homilies by Gregory and Bede greater relative prominence. That these changes are
present in a manuscript that is in other respects quite close to the original suggests
that changes of this kind were made early on. On the other hand, the fact that
sanctorale items were not omitted from the *pars hiemalis* material extant in Durham B. II. 2 indicates that, while these two manuscripts may have been copied out
and used as companion volumes, they do not in fact derive from the same manuscript tradition. In addition to the Gregorian augmentations, Durham A. III. 29
uses the modern designations for the Sundays after Pentecost, counting them, as
Ælfric, Smaragdus, and Haymo did, in an unbroken numerical sequence, rather
than retaining the old method used in the PD original. Again, given that these augmentations and new liturgical designations occur in a context so faithful to PD, the
supposition must be that these were modifications made fairly early in the
homiliary's transmission. The same conclusion may be drawn in respect of this
manuscript's relocation of the PD material for the Major Litany from its original
position of 25 April to the three days before Ascension. The *pars aestiva* represented in Durham A. III. 29 is not followed by the material for the *commune
sanctorum* even though this is what comes next in the original PD.[60] This omission
is no doubt because Durham A. III. 29 is a *temporale* collection, to which the items
for the Common observances do not really belong. The Common items fit well

---

[59] See above, p. 89.

[60] In the original PD, the *commune sanctorum* is a substantial body of texts which makes
general provision for apostles, priests, confessors, martyrs, and virgins not expressly catered for by
name in the liturgically organized part of the homiliary. This is followed by material for the dedication of a church, for a litany observance, for the anniversary of the burial of one of the faithful,
and for the December Ember Week. These further items, which are likewise open to being used
as needed, should also be regarded as part of the Common observances. As is customary in PD,
there is a choice of homilies under most rubrics, giving a total of thirty-four items for this section
of the homiliary.

enough at the end of the PD original, which is a mixed collection of *temporale* and *sanctorale* items, but once these have been separated out, the items for the Common observances fit more naturally at the end of the resulting *sanctorale* volume (as with Pembroke 24 and Worcester F 24 below).

Cambridge, Pembroke College, MSS 23 and 24

Two companion volumes, Gneuss nos 129 and 130 respectively. They originate in France, perhaps Saint-Denis (s. xi^2), but had reached England by s. xi/xii, their provenance being Bury St Edmunds. Pembroke 23 is a *temporale* collection, covering Easter to Advent (Paul the Deacon's *pars aestiva*). Pembroke 24 is a *sanctorale*, which now runs from 3 May (St Philip) to 30 November (St Andrew); it concludes with material for the *commune sanctorum*, drawn from PD. Although both are very obviously based on Paul the Deacon and retain much of his material, they are augmented, in the case of Pembroke 23 chiefly with further homilies of Gregory, some extracts from Bede's commentary on Luke, which are presented as homilies, and some further extracts which, though not attributed in the rubrics, appear to be from Augustine's *Tractates on John*, although these may have come via an intermediary rather than directly. Augmentation provides for ferias (with which Ælfric was generally not concerned) and some of the Sundays after Pentecost (i.e. the Gregorian homilies, as previously discussed).[61] In Pembroke 23, the Sundays after Pentecost use the continuous numerical sequence, not the old method originally employed by Paul the Deacon, and the Major Litany material is transposed to the three days before Ascension.

Cambridge, University Library, MSS Ii. 2. 19 and Kk. 4. 13

Two companion volumes, Gneuss nos 16 and 24 respectively. Their provenance is Norwich, with a date of s. xi/xii. Ii. 2. 19 is a *temporale* sequence covering the Vigil of Easter to the Fourth Sunday after Epiphany. CUL Kk. 4. 13 continues straight on, as a *temporale*, from Septuagesima to the Easter Vigil, after which it is an ordered *sanctorale*. We see here separation of the PD *temporale* and *sanctorale*, augmentation in CUL Ii. 2. 19 very similar to that in Pembroke 23, a transposition of the material from the Roman Major Litany date of 25 April to the three days

---

[61] See above, pp. 74–79.

before Ascension, and use of the continuous numerical sequence for the Sundays after Pentecost. The whole year is covered, beginning with Easter, but the division of the *temporale* between manuscripts does not correspond to the *pars hiemalis / pars aestiva* division of Paul the Deacon's original; instead, the year is treated as a continuous whole.

Worcester, Cathedral Library, MSS F 92, F 93, and F 94

These are companion volumes, Genuss nos 763, 763.1, and 763.2 respectively. Provenance: Worcester. Date: s. xi/xii or xii[in]. They are all based on Paul the Deacon but show separation of *temporale* and *sanctorale* items. Worcester F 92 is a *temporale* from Advent to Easter (corresponding to the period covered by the *pars hiemalis* of the PD original, although without the *sanctorale* items); Worcester F 93 is a *temporale* from Easter to the end of Ordinary Time (corresponding to the period covered by the *pars aestiva* of the PD original, although without the *sanctorale* items); and Worcester F 94 is a *sanctorale*, from St Philip (3 May) to St Andrew (30 November), followed by the PD material for the *commune sanctorum*. The order of PD is observed for the most part in Worcester F 92 and F 93, although there are several augmentations that are interspersed, there are some omissions from PD (in addition to those that are a necessary result of separating out the *sanctorale* material), and the earlier part of Worcester F 92 has more PD items not quite in numerical sequence than one might expect. In common with the other version of PD known in England before 1100, this set displays the Gregorian augmentations discussed earlier, the transposition of Major Litany material to the three days before Ascension, and rubrication for the Sundays after Pentecost using the system of continuous numbering.

Other Manuscripts

Some of the other surviving manuscripts written or owned in England before 1100 which show a relationship to Paul the Deacon's homiliary are valuable in providing further evidence of the practice of radically reorganizing the homiliary into separate *temporale* and *sanctorale* sequences. In many cases, however, their fragmentary state means that they offer little evidence for the organization of the *temporale*, on which the investigation of Ælfric's PD must principally rest. They would nevertheless need to be studied in more detail, along with the manuscripts described above and the continental manuscripts used by Grégoire,[62] if the investigation of Ælfric's PD were to be taken further.

The manuscripts are briefly described by Mary Clayton in her study of homiliaries and preaching in Anglo-Saxon England[63] and are listed by Gneuss.[64]

Canterbury, Cathedral Library, MS Add 127/1

Gneuss no. 209. A fragmentary copy of the *pars aestiva* of PD, with some other texts. It includes homilies for the Decollation of St John the Baptist, the Nativity of the Virgin, the Feasts of Matthew, Michael, All Saints, and A Confessor, and three texts for the Dedication of a Church, but nothing from the *temporale*, unless the two leaves in Kent County Archives, Maidstone PRC 49/2 are from the same manuscript. If they are, we would have evidence of homilies for the Fifth Sunday after Easter and for Rogationtide, although in fact these are not from PD, but from the homiliary of Haymo of Auxerre, and both Gneuss and Clayton regard this fragment as an independent item.[65]

Lincoln, Cathedral Library, MS 158

Gneuss no. 273. This is very restricted in scope, covering only from the beginning of Lent to the Saturday of Holy Week, plus saints' days from the Conversion of Paul (25 January) to the Feast of St Andrew (30 November), followed by a *commune sanctorum*.

London, British Library, MS Harley 652

Gneuss no. 424. This is a manuscript which is based on PD but with many additions and departures. It covers the *temporale* from Easter Saturday to the Fourth

---

[62] See above, p. 69.

[63] Mary Clayton, 'Homiliaries and Preaching in Anglo-Saxon England', *Peritia*, 4 (1985), 207–42 (pp. 218–20).

[64] Gneuss, *Handlist*.

[65] The suggestion that Maidstone PRC 49/2 belongs to Canterbury, Cathedral Library, MS Add 127/1 is made by N. R. Ker, *Medieval Manuscripts in British libraries*, vol. II: *Abbotsford to Keele* (Oxford, 1977), pp. 315–16. By contrast, see Gneuss, *Handlist*, no. 546.6, and Clayton, 'Homiliaries and Preaching', p. 218.

Sunday after Epiphany, followed by some material for saints' days and the Arch-bishops of Canterbury.

London, British Library, MS Royal 2. C. iii

Gneuss no. 452. This manuscript has little from the *temporale*, covering only the period from Septuagesima to Easter. However, this is followed by an extensive part of the *sanctorale* (Stephen, 26 December, to Andrew, 30 November), followed by a *commune sanctorum*.

Salisbury, Cathedral Library, MS 179

Gneuss no. 753. This manuscript covers the *temporale* from Easter to the Sunday after Ascension, followed by a *commune sanctorum* and homilies for the period from Rogationtide to All Saints.

Conclusion

In the quotation with which this article began, Helmut Gneuss described the establishment of the version or versions of Paul the Deacon's homiliary known in late Anglo-Saxon England as 'one of the foremost tasks of future research'.[66] That research remains to be done. The purpose of the present article has been something much more modest: to demonstrate that we are at least a little closer than we were then to characterizing Ælfric's version of Paul the Deacon's homiliary. Given the current state of scholarship, this approach through Ælfric may well be the most productive line to pursue in the immediate future although, as Gneuss recognized, we must always bear in mind that the version used by Ælfric is not likely to have been the only version available in late Anglo-Saxon England. Further examination of the manuscript tradition will cast at least some light on this broader picture, at the same time as it provides more evidence about what Ælfric is likely to have had before him. More work is needed on both form and content, and for this source study will be an additional and indispensable tool. Nevertheless, as the present study repeatedly demonstrates, source study is a complex undertaking when applied to an intertextual tradition, particularly when, within that tradition, we

---

[66] See above, p. 67 and note 1.

seek to identify immediate rather than ultimate sources. In using source study as an element in the recovery of Ælfric's manuscript of PD, or as a tool in the wider question of what versions of PD were available in late Anglo-Saxon England, we must always check whether some or all of the same material was available to him elsewhere, consider practicality of usage at the point of composition, and admit the possibility that we may not be able finally to decide which source was used at a given point. The positivist approach to broad textual correlation, which characterizes Smetana's pioneering study, is not a sound enough foundation on which to build this more precisely focussed work.

If manuscript evidence is drawn upon, however, if the practicalities of composition and compilation are taken into account, and if careful attention is paid to the detail of source usage within an intertextual tradition, there are some characteristics of Ælfric's version of PD about which we can now be reasonably confident. In terms of organization, it may well have had *temporale* and *sanctorale* material separated out, and in all probability it had 'modern' rubrics for the Sundays following Pentecost, thus facilitating Ælfric's cross-referral between his manuscript of PD (which in its original form had an older and more complicated system for designating these Sundays) and the homiliaries of Smaragdus and Haymo (which always employed the 'modern' method of counting continuously from Pentecost). It is also likely that Ælfric's version, somewhat reorganized as it was, did not have the prefatory material, so that, in common with the extant manuscripts to which reference has been made in this article, knowledge that the collection owed anything to a certain Paul the Deacon was not available to him: this is privileged knowledge that is available to us only through the scholarship of modern times, and we should be careful to recognize this. As far as the homilies themselves are concerned, we cannot tell whether Ælfric's version began with Christmas or with Advent, although an examination of this as yet unresolved question has the benefit of reminding us, as does consideration of lections, that there was much about liturgical organization that was still in flux in the ninth and tenth centuries. We can be reasonably confident, however, that Ælfric's copy differed from the PD original in having material for the Frankish three-day Major Litany preceding Ascension, and nothing at all for the Roman Major Litany observance of 25 April. Instances of straightforward omission, by contrast, are hard to identify, since Ælfric's failure to use an item may either be because it was superfluous to requirements, given that he was far less comprehensive in his coverage than even the PD original, or that an individual homily or a series of homilies by particular authors that were present in PD took an approach that was not consistent with Ælfric's own and was consequently ignored. Augmentations are easier to deal with, since textual correspondences can be analysed. The evidence has to be handled with care, however, and although it has been possible to demonstrate in this article that Ælfric's PD was almost certainly augmented by a number of Gregory's Homilies on the Gospels that were not included in the PD original, the detailed arguments that are presented show how complicated the source evidence is, and how deeply it needs to be probed. If this article identifies some of the means by which further advances can be made, it does, I hope, also draw attention to the complexity of what needs to be done.

THE CAROLINGIAN *DE FESTIUITATIBUS*
AND THE BLICKLING BOOK

Nancy M. Thompson

There was a time when scholars assumed they knew the intended audience of the Blickling Book. Its homilies were written in the vernacular; they employ a mode of address (*men þa leofestan*, 'dearly beloved') that suggests oral delivery; and they tend to stress moral exhortation over exegesis, reiterating such basic themes as good works, repentance, and judgement. The presumed audience therefore was neither familiar with Latin nor theologically sophisticated — most probably a lay congregation who heard these homilies preached in the course of the Mass. From this perspective, the Blickling Book, as one of our earliest Old English homiletic manuscripts, seemed a rare and valuable witness to an early stage of preaching in the Anglo-Saxon Church, perhaps reflecting religious attitudes that predated the Benedictine Reform. Marcia Dalbey, for example, compared the Blickling Homilies with their Latin sources and suggested that they reflect accommodations made for an Anglo-Saxon audience.[1]

The picture changed with the publication of Milton McC. Gatch's *Preaching and Theology in Anglo-Saxon England: Ælfric and Wulfstan* and his subsequent

---

[1] Marcia A. Dalbey, 'Hortatory Tone in the Blickling Homiliaries: Two Adaptations of Caesarius', *NM*, 70 (1969), 641–58, and Dalbey, 'Patterns of Preaching in the Blickling Easter Homily', *American Benedictine Review*, 24 (1973), 478–92. Stanley B. Greenfield and Daniel G. Calder cite Dalbey and speak of Blickling's 'liturgical purpose': *A New Critical History of Old English Literature* (New York, 1986), pp. 73–74. The assumption of a popular audience underlies J. Elizabeth Jeffrey's *Blickling Spirituality and the Old English Vernacular Homily: A Textual Analysis*, Studies in Mediaeval Literature, 1 (Lewiston, 1989), pp. 20–21.

article on the 'unknown audience' of the Blickling Book.[2] In these he argued that without dedications or prefaces, the purpose of Blickling Book could not be determined.[3] In his view, there was no established context for public preaching: during the centuries preceding the compilation of the Blickling Book, preaching 'fell into disuse'. Even in the Carolingian period, with its emphasis on ecclesiastical reform, the evidence for preaching *ad populum* ('to the people') is weak, Gatch suggested, pointing to ambiguities in Carolingian exhortations to teach the people. Less convincingly, he suggested that if preaching to lay people occurred, it did so in the context of a newly developing 'office' distinct from the Mass that was later called the prone.[4]

Gatch's arguments were challenged by other scholars who turned to Carolingian precedents to show an established tradition of preaching *ad populum* into which Anglo-Saxon homilies, including the Blickling Book, could fit. Their arguments depended on two types of evidence: first, the existence of continental homiletic collections that might have served for preaching to the people, and second, Carolingian legislation, which seemed to promote lay religious education as part of the overall Carolingian program of Church reform. In the same year that Gatch published *Preaching and Theology*, Rosamond McKitterick's impressive study of Carolingian legislation appeared, making a strong case for a vigorous program of public preaching that reached down to the local level through the efforts of parish priests and strove to instill not only Christian ritual but theological understanding in the populace.

It seems reasonable to look for evidence of the context for the Blickling Homilies on the Continent, for Carolingian ideas about right order in the Church inspired and influenced the Anglo-Saxon reform programme that was beginning to take shape at about the time the Blickling manuscript was written.[5] Yet the fact

---

[2] Gatch, *Preaching and Theology in Anglo-Saxon England: Ælfric and Wulfstan* (Toronto, 1977), and 'The Unknowable Audience of the Blickling Homilies', *ASE*, 18 (1989), 99–115.

[3] Gatch, *Preaching and Theology*, p. 58.

[4] Gatch, *Preaching and Theology*, pp. 35–38, 45–46, and 53–58.

[5] On the date of the Blickling manuscript, see N. R. Ker, *Catalogue of Manuscripts Containing Anglo-Saxon* (Oxford, 1957), p. 451; Mary Clayton, 'Homiliaries and Preaching in Anglo-Saxon England', *Peritia*, 4 (1985), 207–42; repr. with corrections in *Old English Prose: Basic Readings*, ed. by Paul E. Szarmach, Basic Readings in Anglo-Saxon England, 5 (New York, 2000), pp. 151–98 (p. 167); Greenfield and Calder, *New Critical History*, p. 71; Peter Clemoes, review of *Blickling Homilies*, ed. by Rudolph Willard, *Medium Ævum*, 31 (1962), 60–63 (pp. 60–61). On continental influences in the English Benedictine Reform, see e.g. Patrick Wormald, 'Æthelwold

that careful scholars, consulting the same body of evidence, have reached such different conclusions indicates a need for further investigation; the state of Carolingian preaching remains an issue not yet resolved.

In this paper I shall consider a set of Carolingian texts that has received somewhat limited attention in connection with the issue of preaching and homiliaries: the capitula *De festiuitatibus*, which set out the special feasts of the year.[6] Their provisions shed additional light on Carolingian aspirations for lay religious practice. They may also help to illuminate the place of homilies in the Anglo-Saxon Church; at minimum they suggest possible avenues for further study.

We should note at the outset the inherent difficulties in making statements about the condition of the Carolingian Church, for it spanned a vast and diverse territory. In some areas — northern Italy or the south of France — the Church had put down roots during the Roman Empire and Christian culture was well established. There it is not improbable that the tradition of preaching as handed down by Caesarius of Arles, Leo the Great, and Gregory the Great survived. In other areas the process of conversion was ongoing: one thinks of the labours of Willibrord and Boniface among the Frisians and Thuringians, or Charlemagne's forcible Christianization of the Saxons. In the lands of the newly converted, instilling a very basic catechism could have been the only realistic goal. Even finding sufficient numbers of priests to carry out the ministry to the laity must have presented a challenge to ecclesiastical authorities.[7]

But even where conditions were ideal, the evidence for the state of Carolingian preaching is not clear. Of the homiletic collections adduced to support a tradition of popular preaching, only Hrabanus Maurus's seems unquestionably intended for that purpose for its preface, addressed to Archbishop Aistulf of Mainz, plainly states that it was meant *ad praedicandum populo* ('for preaching to the people').[8]

---

and his Continental Counterparts: Contact, Comparison, Contrast', in *Bishop Æthelwold: His Career and Influence*, ed. by Barbara Yorke (Woodbridge, 1988; repr. 1997), pp. 13–42; Mechthild Gretsch, 'Cambridge, Corpus Christi College 57: A Witness to the Early Stages of the Benedictine Reform', *ASE*, 32 (2003), 111–46 (p. 146).

[6] J. E. Cross, '*De festivitatibus anni* and Ansegisus, *Capitularum Collectio* (827) in Anglo-Saxon Manuscripts', *Liverpool Classical Monthly*, 17 (1992), 119–20; Gretsch, 'Cambridge, Corpus Christi College 57', pp. 116–18.

[7] On the fundamental differences in ecclesiastical organization between the Romanized South and Frankish territories, see John Blair, *The Church in Anglo-Saxon Society* (Oxford, 2005), pp. 34–43.

[8] Hrabanus Maurus, 'Praefatio', *Homiliae de festis praecipuis, item de uirtutibus*, *PL* 110.9.

The intended audience of other collections is more difficult to determine. The homiliary of Landpertus of Mondsee may have been compiled with lay people in mind, for it too was dedicated to an archbishop; yet as Clayton notes, it provides readings for days when lay people would not normally be present in church.[9] The sermons attributed to St Boniface have been also proposed as possible candidates.[10] Only one of them, however, seems definitely composed for a lay audience; two seem more probably directed to the clergy, and the audience for the rest is uncertain.[11] The homilies of Saint-Père de Chartres have been suggested as another possibility, especially since they deal with 'popular' themes — moral exhortation, apocrypha, and saints' lives. Written in Latin (as are all discussed here) they would have needed translation, but Barré thinks they could have served as models for priests.[12] Even if all these were certainly intended for delivery to the people, however, it is still a rather short list to supply an active program of preaching. That other collections originally compiled for the monastic Night Office (for instance, that of Paul the Deacon) might have also been pressed into *ad populum* service is certainly possible, but possibility does not constitute proof.[13]

---

[9] Henri Barré, *Les homéliaires carolingien de l'école d'Auxerre: authenticité, inventaire, tableaux comparitifs, initia*, Studi e Testi, 225 (Vatican City, 1962), p. 25, says it has 'une orientation pastorale très marquée'. See also H. Barré, 'L'homéliaire carolingiens de Mondsee', *Revue Bénédictine*, 71 (1961), 17–107; Clayton, 'Homiliaries and Preaching', pp. 157–58.

[10] Thomas L. Amos, 'Preaching and the Sermon in the Carolingian World', in *De Ore Domini: Preacher and the Word in the Middle Ages*, ed. by Thomas L. Amos, Eugene Green, and Beverly Mayne Kienzle (Kalamazoo, 1989), pp. 41–60 (p. 48).

[11] In Boniface, *Sermo 5*, *PL* 89.852–55, auditors are told (albeit in Latin) to keep faith with their spouses, teach their children, memorize the Lord's Prayer and creed, and not accept baptism more than once. By contrast, Boniface, *Sermo 1*, *PL* 89.844, addresses the clergy explicitly: it begins with the admonition that preachers must learn proper doctrine, for 'what kind of shepherd will he be, if he does not know how to give the bread of life to the flock committed to him?' ('uel qualiter pastor esse poterit, si pane uitae gregem sibi commissum pascere ignorat?'). *Sermo 3*, *PL* 89.849 reminds priests to live blameless lives in the presence of lay people (*coram saecularibus*). Admittedly content is not an infallible guide to audience; few sermons have an explicit address and some might have been intended for a mixed audience of laymen and clergy.

[12] Barré, *Les homéliaires carolingien*, pp. 17–24; Clayton, 'Homiliaries and Preaching', p. 157; also James E. Cross, *Cambridge Pembroke College MS. 25: A Carolingian Sermonary Used by Anglo-Saxon Preachers*, Kings College London Medieval Studies, 1 (London, 1987), pp. ix and 45–60.

[13] Thomas Martin Buck, *Admonition und Praedication: Zur religiös-pastoralen Dimension von Kapitularien und kapitulariennahen Texten (507–814)*, ed. by Hubert Morek, Frieburger Beiträge zu mittlealterlichen Geschichte, 9 (Frankfurt am Main, 1997), p. 130; Rosamond McKitterick,

Carolingian legislation also presents interpretive difficulties. The capitula are often abbreviated, intended more as an aide-memoire than a complete set of instructions for carrying out pastoral duties. The terms they use are open to varying interpretations: Does *parrochia* mean bishopric or parish? Is *praedicare* to preach or simply to make known? Does *docere* imply instruction via a sermon or in some less formal setting?[14] And even if there were complete agreement on the definition of terms, there remains the issue of whether the mandated policies could be fully implemented.

The evidence of the capitula *De festiutatibus* cannot resolve all the difficulties, but they do supply an additional kind of evidence for Carolingian goals. Issued by both royal and episcopal authorities, they circulated with legislation governing priestly duties or lay religious obligations, providing a convenient list of the most solemn occasions of the Church year. Although monks of course included the same days among their obligations,[15] the *De festiuitatibus* texts usually targeted lay people, requiring them to refrain from work and to attend Mass. As we will see, some of the capitula also associated the special feasts with the reading of homilies — indeed, one might expect that if the clergy used homilies at all, they would most likely mark special occasions with readings that explained the significance of the day.

From the capitula *De festiuitatibus* we turn to the Blickling Book, which provides homilies more or less *per circulum anni* for the principle feasts of the year.[16]

The Frankish Church and the Carolingian Reforms, 789–895 (London, 1977), p. 102; Clayton, 'Homiliaries and Preaching', p. 159.

[14] McKitterick, *Frankish Church*, p. 6n, comments that *parrochia* can mean parish, but the capitula often use the term for an episcopal diocese; a priest (*presbyter*) has an *ecclesia*. See, for example, Alfred Boretius, *Capitularia regum Francorum*, MGH, Capitularia regum Francorum, 1 (Hannover, 1883), pp. 403, 407. Since bishops traditionally held the office of preaching, the distinction is important: at issue is to what extent these duties were extended to priests. *Praedicare*, as Gatch notes (*Preaching and Theology*, p. 35), may not always mean to preach; see, e.g., *Capitularia Regum Francorum*, ed. by Boretius, p. 413, where priests are to order women to prepare altar cloths ('ut presbyteri [...] praedicent feminis, ut linteamina altaribus praeparent').

[15] Carolingian monastic customaries generally include additional occasions for special observance by monks, whose religious lives would naturally incorporate what we might call occasions of a second tier — saints, fasts, and festivals important enough to the life of the Church to be celebrated by those who had dedicated their lives to God's service, but not sufficiently important to draw any but the most devout lay people away from their work.

[16] The homiliary is described by Ker, *Catalogue*, pp. 451–55; *The Blickling Homilies of the Tenth Century*, ed. by Richard Morris, EETS: OS, 58, 63, 73 (London, 1874–80; repr. as one volume 1967); *The Blickling Homilies: The John H. Scheide Library, Titusville, Pennsylvania*, ed.

The occasions provided for are reminiscent of the lists of festivals in the Carolingian *De festiuitatibus*, and it seems worthwhile to consider the possibility that the Blickling Book was assembled in response to a similar list. Both offer abbreviated liturgical calendars. They include the most important dominical feasts — Christmas, Easter, Ascension Day, and Pentecost.[17] They also specify a limited number of saints' days for veneration. Blickling has sermons for six: Mary's Assumption, and the feasts of John the Baptist, Peter and Paul, Michael, Martin, and Andrew. The *De festiuitatibus* texts differ in the particular saints' days they specify, but most include the saints that Blickling does, sometimes omitting Michael.[18] They also generally specify the observance of Rogationtide; Blickling's fragmentary Homilies VIII, XI, and X were apparently meant for that occasion, for they are penitential in content and appear in the manuscript just before the sermon for Ascension Day.[19]

There are some differences. The *De festiuitatibus* do not mention Lent, for which Blickling provides readings; and most list several occasions around Christmas time (not only Christmas and Epiphany, but their octaves, and perhaps also the feasts of St Stephen, St John the Evangelist, the Innocents, or the Purification of Mary). These occasions are absent from the Blickling Book, although readings for some of them may have been present originally. The manuscript now lacks four quires at the beginning, starting the first homily mid-sentence, and it is missing a number of leaves in the middle.[20] But even when it was complete, Blickling's list of occasions must have been, like the various *De festiuitatibus* texts, relatively short.[21] This suggests that, if not directly inspired by one of the Carolingian *De festiuitatibus*, the collection may well have been a response to the same impulse that

---

by Rudolph Willard, EEMF, 10 (Copenhagen, 1960), X; new edition *The Blickling Homilies: Edition and Translation*, ed. and trans. by Richard J. Kelly (London, 2003).

[17] Morris identified the first Blickling Homily with the Annunciation (March 25); as Clemoes (review of Willard, p. 62) and Kelly (*Blickling Homilies*, pp. xxxi and 164–65) observe, it may well have served for Christmas.

[18] See, for example, the *Capitularium* of Ansegisis, *Capitularia regum Francorum*, ed. by Boretius, p. 413.

[19] *Blickling Homilies*, ed. by Kelly, p. xxxi.

[20] On the missing leaves, see Ker, *Catalogue*, p. 451. On Homily I for Christmas, see Clemoes, review of Willard, p. 62; *Blickling Homilies*, ed. by Kelly, pp. xxxi and 164–65. The assumption of the Virgin (15 August) is out of order, perhaps, as Willard (*Blickling Homilies*, p. 26) suggests, to reflect the relative importance of Mary over other saints.

[21] Compare the more numerous occasions that Paul the Deacon supplied, *PL* 95.1159–1566; also Ælfric's *Lives of Saints*, which was compiled expressly for monks.

encouraged secular and ecclesiastical authorities to publish such lists for their clergy. To be more precise, the Carolingian capitula suggest an inspiration for the Blickling Book, without necessarily revealing its intended audience.

As it happens, at least one version of the *De festiuitatibus* reached Anglo-Saxon England. When it did, however, it came bearing robe and cowl — that is, it had lost its *ad populum* character and circulated as part of what Mechthild Gretsch has called a 'monastic dossier', a set of texts intended to regulate the life and conduct of monks.[22] The shift is surprising, for a survey of the original Carolingian *De festiuitatibus* shows that monastic life was not their original focus. They were intended to regulate lay religious observance, circulating as part of the Carolingian attempts to bring lay people into church, to familiarize them with such fundamentals as the paternoster and the creed, and to convince them to refrain from Sunday labor.

The Carolingian De festiuitatibus

Lists of the principle feasts of the year circulated widely in the Carolingian era. Although they often differed in form and in the specific festivals named for commemoration, they may well have been influenced by one another — legislation of this type often was.[23] In general, however, they were not taken over word for word, and they were accompanied by different sets of capitula. That these regulations exist in a number of versions suggests the authorities reconsidered the need both to establish in writing an annual calendar for lay people and, at least to some extent, to rethink the festivals included on it, whenever the lists were reissued.

One of the earliest versions illustrates the type of lists we are considering. According to Alfred Boretius, who revised G. H. Pertz's edition of the capitula for the Monumenta Germaniae Historica, it dates to somewhere between 810 and 813. It is one of twenty capitula that address various matters pertaining to the obligations of local priests, including the distribution of tithes, the preparation of altar cloths, the preparation of the Eucharist, and the use of the chrism. The text reads:

> Hae sunt festiuitates in anno quae per omnia uenerari debent: natalis Domini, sancti Stephani, sancti Iohannis euangelistae, innocentum, octobas Domini, epiphania, octabas epiphaniae, purificatio sanctae Mariae, pascha dies octo, letania maior, ascensa Domini,

---

[22] Gretsch, 'Cambridge, Corpus Christi College 57', p. 138.

[23] See, for example, the extensive notes provided by the editors of MGH *Capitula episcoporum* (Hannover, 1984–95) on the source and reception of the documents they print.

pentecosten, sancti Iohannis baptistae, sancti Petri et Pauli, sancti Martini, sancti
Andreae. De adsumptione sanctae Mariae interrogandum relinquimus.[24]

[These are the feasts in the year which should be venerated in all respects: Christmas, St
Stephen, John the Evangelist, the Innocents, the octave of Christmas, Epiphany, the
octave of Epiphany, the purification of St Mary, eight days of Easter, the Greater Litany,
Ascension, Pentecost, St John the Baptist, Saints Peter and Paul, St Martin, St Andrew.
The assumption of St Mary we leave for further investigation.]

The capitula in this collection, including the provision *De festiuitatibus*, circulated widely, for Ansegisus, Abbot of Fontanelle, included them in his *Quatuor
libri capitularium regum Francorum*, a collection of legislation from the reigns of
Charlemagne and Louis the Pious that became an authoritative source of canon
and civil law for the ninth century.[25] I shall refer to this version of the *De festiuitatibus* as Ansegisus I. Although Ansegisus attributed the capitula to Charlemagne,
Boretius reasonably suggested that they originated in a minor council held some
time before 813: a major council called by the Emperor would not have left the
question of the Assumption unresolved.[26]

Ansegisus attributed a similar capitulum — hereafter referred to as Ansegisus II
— to Louis the Pious (although it seems to date to the reign of Charlemagne), and
this is the version that ultimately reached Anglo-Saxon England.[27] It is introduced
differently than the *De festiuitatibus* we have just considered and starts with Easter
rather than Christmas, but it was promulgated with the same intent: to establish
a calendar of the most important days for the Christian Church.

Festos dies in anno celebrare sanximus [var. sancimus]: hoc est diem dominicum paschae
cum omni honore et sobrietate uenerari, simili modo totam ebdomadam illam obseruare
decreuimus.[28]

---

[24] *Capitularia regum Francorum*, ed. by Boretius, p. 179.

[25] *Capitularia regum Francorum*, ed. by Boretius, p. 413; also *Die Kapitulariensammlung des
Ansegis*, ed. by Gerhard Schmitz (Hannover, 1996), pp. 514–15.

[26] *Capitularia regum Francorum*, ed. by Boretius, p. 178.

[27] Albert Werminghoff, *Concilia Aevi Karolini*, MGH Concilia, 2 (Hannover, 1906), I.1,
269–70, lists it as canon 36 of the Council of Mainz (813); Cross, 'De festivitatibus anni and
Ansegisus', p. 120. *Capitularia regum Francorum*, ed. by Boretius, pp. 311–12, suggested that
Louis the Pious later (*c.* 826) reconfirmed the provision, which would explain why Ansegisus
attributed it to the later Emperor.

[28] *Capitularia regum Francorum*, ed. by Boretius, p. 422 (Ansegisus) and p. 312, the fragmentary *Capitula e conciliis excerpta* (dated 826 or 827).

[We have established the holy days in the year to celebrate: that is the Sunday of Easter to be celebrated with every honour and sobriety; we have commanded to observe that whole week likewise.]

The list of holy days is not quite the same as in the earlier version: the Feast of the Assumption, all doubts now resolved, appears in its proper place *per circulum anni* after the nativity of John the Baptist. Ansegisus II specifies a four-day Christmas observance and adds to the calendar the dedication of Michael and the natal day of St Remigius, but omits the feasts of Stephen, the Evangelist John, and the Innocents, as well as the octave of Epiphany and the Greater Litany (*letania maior*). It also provides for local variation, concluding, 'Et illas festiuitates martyrum uel confessorum obseruare decreuimus, quorum in unaquaque parrochia sancta corpora requiescunt'[29] ('We have commanded to observe those feasts of the martyrs and confessors in each district where their holy bodies lie').

As we will see, Ansegisus II circulated in Anglo-Saxon England with monastic texts and hence seems to have been directed towards the religious observance of monks. Both of Ansegisus's original texts, by contrast, addressed lay conduct, as is evident from their placement in his collection. Ansegisus carefully organized his material, dividing the capitula into four books by subject (ecclesiastical or secular matters) and imperial reign (Charlemagne or Louis the Pious with Lothair as co-emperor).[30] Within each book the capitula are likewise arranged systematically: Ansegisus I appears in Book I (Charlemagne's Church legislation) with a series of instructions for local priests; Ansegisus II appears in Book II (Louis's Church legislation) and comes in between protections for paupers and provisions dealing with tithes of ancient churches, the instruction of godchildren, and the conduct of secular clergy. In these contexts, we must suppose that monks are not the primary target of the capitula (though one would expect them to observe the same holy days); the target was the ordinary faithful.

Other Carolingian legislation besides *De festiuitatibus* likewise addressed lay practice. The *Capitula ecclesiastica* of Haito, Bishop of Basle from 807 to 823, prescribed the celebration of holy days in a list clearly directed to lay people, who were cautioned to keep Sundays 'from dawn until evening on account of veneration of the resurrection of the Lord' and to work Saturdays 'lest one be taken in Judaism'. Haito's particular holy days are yet another variation on the theme: along with the usual list, he ordered the commemoration of the twelve apostles, 'but especially Peter and Paul, who illuminated Europe with their teaching', and he included 'the dedication

---

[29] *Capitularia regum Francorum*, ed. by Boretius, p. 422.

[30] *Capitularia regum Francorum*, ed. by Boretius, p. 394.

of whatever oratory or of whatever saint in whose honor that same church is founded, which is enjoined only on those dwelling nearby and not everyone in general'.[31] The people were to observe publicly ordained fasts, but, he added, 'the rest of the feasts of the year, such as Remedius, Mauritius, and Martin are not to be celebrated as holy days, but are not prohibited if the people chastely and with zeal for God wish to do this'.[32] A similar list, from the canons once attributed to St Boniface, but probably dating from nearly a century after his day, ordered priests to announce on Sundays the days to be 'sabbatized in the highest manner'.[33] Sabbatize — that is, to abstain from work — again suggests that the directive was aimed specifically at the labouring classes.[34] In fact, getting the people to abstain from working on holy days was a regularly expressed concern of Carolingian legislation.[35]

There are a number of other lists *De festiuitatibus*, perhaps inspired by the example in Ansegisus, but differing in word or form. Often issued by bishops, they address, with few exceptions, lay practice: they either refer explicitly to the people,

---

[31] *Capitularia regum Francorum*, ed. by Boretius, p. 363; printed also in MGH *Capitula episcoporum*, vol. I, ed. by Peter Brommer (Hannover, 1984), p. 212: 'Octauo pronuntiandum est, ut sciant tempora feriandi per annum, id est omnem dominicam a mane usque ad uesperam ob ueneratione dominicae resurrectionis. Sabbatum uero operandum a mane usque ad uesperam, ne in iudaismo capiantur. Feriandi uero per annum isti sunt dies [the list of feasts follows] [. . .], duodecim apostolorum, maxime tamen sanctorum Petri et Pauli, qui Europam sua predicatione inluminauerunt [. . .] dedicatio cuiuscumque oratorii seu cuiuslibet sancti, in cuius honore eadem ecclesia fundata est, quod uicinis tantum circum commorantibus indicendum est, non generaliter omnibus.'

[32] *Capitularia regum Francorum*, ed. by Boretius, p. 363; *Capitula episcoporum*, vol. I, ed. by Brommer, p. 212: 'Reliquae uero festiuitates per annum, sicut sancti Remedii, sancti Mauricii, sancti Martini non sunt cogendae ad feriandum nec tamen prohibendum, si plebes hoc caste et zelo dei cupiunt exercere.'

[33] MGH, *Capitula episcoporum*, vol. III, ed. by Rudolph Pokorny (Hannover, 1995), p. 366: 'Adnuntient presbyteri diebus Dominicis per annum sabbatizandum. PRIMO MODO [*sic*]: In natale domini [list follows] [. . .].' On the date of these capitula, see p. 357.

[34] Benedictus Levita picked up his version from pseudo-Boniface; see Emil Seckel, 'Studien zu Benedictus Levita VII. (Studie VII, Teil II)', <http://www.benedictus.mgh.de/studien/seckel/studie_7-2.htm>, p. 144 [accessed 1 April 2005]: 'Has quidem praecipuas festiuitates annuntient presbiteri ut diebus dominicis sabbatizare, id est natale [list follows] [. . .]' ('Let priests announce the special feast days to be sabbatized as Sundays, that is Christmas' etc.).

[35] To cite a few of many examples, see *Concilium Dingolfingense* (770), in *Concilia Aevi Karolini*, ed. by Werminghoff, I.1, 94, and *Concilium Arlatense* (813), in ibid., I.1, 252; *Capitula episcoporum*, vol. I, ed. by Brommer, p. 28 (Bishop Ghaerbald of Liège); *Capitularia regum Francorum*, ed. by Boretius, p. 55 (*Admonitio generalis*).

as in the capitula of Walter of Orléans (d. after 891)[36] or they appear with other capitula governing the duties of local priests.[37] Even when a list includes feasts that one might expect to be venerated only by monks, lay practice seems to be the focus. For example, Radulf, Archbishop of Bourges, perhaps influenced by his earlier life as a Benedictine, repeated the *De festiuitatibus* of Ansegisus for his flock, but he included among the listed holidays the feasts of Saints Ursinus, Austregisilus, and Sulpicius. These, he said, were to be celebrated by a respite from work, and he added that other festivals of saints, martyrs, and confessors should be observed with the appropriate honour.[38]

These capitula are clearly distinct from lists governing the celebrations of the clergy, who had to honour those same principle feasts, but who had additional obligations. Monastic *consuetudines*, for example, provided the regular clergy with lists that included more holidays (e.g. the feast of St Benedict) and/or that specified particularly monastic concerns such as the recitation of offices and the number of meals.[39]

---

[36] *Capitula episcoporum*, vol. I, ed. by Brommer, p. 191.

[37] MGH, *Capitula espiscoporum*, vol. II, ed. by Rudolph Pokorny and Martina Stratmann (Hannover, 1995), p. 141. The list of Herard of Tours seems inspired by Ansegisus, but not copied, for it begins '*De festiuitatibus* anni quae feriari debeant' ('on the feasts of the year which ought to be celebrated') and ends with the feasts 'eorum, quorum corpora ac debite uenerationes in locis singulis peraguntur' ('of those the veneration of whose bodies are fittingly performed in individual locations'). The *Capitula Neustrica prime* (*Capitula episcoporum*, vol. III, ed. by Pokorny, p. 56) begins as Ansegisus II, but adds to the list 'similiter etiam dedicationes templi' ('likewise the dedications of the temple'). The *Capitula Ottoboniane* (ibid., p. 131) specifies that Christmas is to be celebrated to mid-week and includes the dates of specific festivals — e.g. 'IIII Nonis Februariis purificationem sanctę Marię' ('the purification of St Mary, February 2'); it also adds the feasts of St Germanus and St Remigius and All Saints to the list.

[38] *Capitula episcoporum*, vol. I, ed. by Brommer, p. 254 'His praedictis diebus ab operibus quiescendum esse duximus. Ceteras festitiuates sanctorum, martyrum, confessorm atque uirginum congruo honore celebrandos censimus' ('We consider that one should desist from labour on these days. We hold that other festivals of the saints, martyrs, and virgins should be celebrated with appropriate honour'). The previous capitulum, ibid., p. 253, set out the kind of work to be avoided: servile work, agricultural tasks, building, hunting, attendance at court, and for women, weaving. The provision is derived from Ansegisus, Book 1, cap. 75. Walter of Orléans also lists monastic feasts (Benedict and Benedict of Aniane); see ibid., p. 191.

[39] Examples are in Kassius Hallinger, *Corpus Consuetudinum Monasticarum* (Siegburg, 1963), I, 113–14, 122 (*Ordo Casinensis*, ed. by Tommaso Leccisotti), 132–33 (*Theodmari abbatis Casinensis epistula*, ed. by Jacques Winandy), 163–65 (*Theodmari abbatis Casinensis epistola ad Karolem regem*, ed. by Kassius Hallinger), 370, 419 (*Consuetudines Corbeienses*, ed. by Joseph Semmler). See also *Capitulare monasticum*, in *Capitularia regum Francorum*, ed. by Boretius, pp. 346–47; the prologue, p. 343, attributes the legislation to Louis the Pious (817), undertaken with

The *Statuta Rhispacensia Frisingensia Salisbugensia* (799/800), which was directed towards all the clergy, names the special occasions when they were excused from their twice-weekly fast from wine and meat. Even in this case, however, there was a nod towards lay observance: the council wished the clergy to try to persuade the people likewise to adopt the salutary practice of fasting.[40]

We have seen that a number of versions of capitula *De festiuitatibus* circulated during the Carolingian period. They offered relatively short lists of days to be observed, specifying major holy days of the Christian calendar, with some variation in the additional feasts to be commemorated. Their *ad populum* character is evident: either they charged priests directly with the duty of proclaiming the feast days, or they accompanied other capitula that dealt with lay religious observances. The *De festiuitatibus* were meant to ensure that the Christian faithful observed all the listed days with appropriate 'honour and sobriety' by attending religious services and abstaining from labour. Thus they reflected the Carolingian concern with establishing a well-ordered Church at every level of society.

De festiuitatibus, *Homilies, and Preaching*

This brings us back to the controversy over the state of *ad populum* preaching in the Carolingian Church, for it is one thing to enforce the religious observance of holy days and quite another to demand regular moral or theological instruction. The evidence in fact supports both McKitterick's optimism and Gatch's pessimism about the state of Carolingian preaching. In some parts of the Carolingian domains, vigorous bishops promoted public preaching. At times, they issued capitula associating the reading of homilies with the principle feasts of the year. Such legislation increases the likelihood that homiliaries were compiled to provide readings for special occasions and suggests a possible inspiration for a manuscript like the

---

abbots for the regular clergy. The enlarged Rule of Chrodegang took over this provision, with Benedict's feast omitted and in company with such secular matters as blessing marriages and dividing tithes; see *The Old English Version, with the Latin Original, of the Enlarged Rule of Chrodegang*, ed. by Arthur S. Napier, EETS: OS, 150 (London, 1916), p. 81. Chrodegang's original rule also listed special feasts with instructions for the clergy; ibid., p. 44.

[40] *Capitularia regum Francorum*, ed. by Boretius, p. 227: 'Et hoc admonemus, ut praedicetur in populis, ut per exortationem et persuasionem uel per quamlibet occasionem hoc populis persuadere possimus, cum omni studio fideliter et devote faciamus' ('And we advise that it be announced among the people, so we may encourage the people to do this through exhortation and persuasion or whatever opportunity, let us do it with all zeal, faithfully and devoutly').

Blickling Book. Yet other capitula seem to require only minimal religious education for lay people: the rote recitation of the paternoster and the creed. More could hardly be demanded where, as some capitula frankly acknowledge, local churches had few resources: a tiny library and minimally educated priests.[41]

Perhaps the most optimistic statement of a program of Christian education is the *Admonitio generalis* of 789, which prescribed instruction in the nature of the Trinity, Christ's Incarnation and Second Coming, and the basic precepts of Christian life and conduct.[42] The stated goals support McKitterick's assertion that the Carolingians wanted 'above all to ensure that the people *understood* their religion'.[43] But however ambitious the plan to educate the faithful in all aspects of their professed belief, it cannot have been fully implemented, as is demonstrated by other capitula that, in addressing the necessary level of knowledge for lay people, set out far more modest goals.

The most common requirement is that the secular clergy instill the paternoster and creed *memoriter* ('by memory') in the faithful.[44] This is repeated so often, it seems fair to assume that it was the universal minimum standard, which could be met without regular liturgical preaching, but through some less formal kind of instruction.[45] Indeed, we have one admittedly unusual set of episcopal instructions

---

[41] See, for example, *Capitula episcoporum*, vol. III, ed. by Pokorny, p. 362; *Capitularia regum Francorum*, ed. by Boretius, pp. 143 and 372; *Capitula espiscoporum*, vol. II, ed. by Pokorny and Stratmann, pp. 45 and 103. These capitula are discussed more fully below.

[42] *Capitularia regum Francorum*, ed. by Boretius, p. 61. On the structure and unusual nature of this capitulum, see Buck, *Admonition und Praedication*, pp. 123–29.

[43] McKitterick, *Frankish Church*, p. 6.

[44] *Capitularia regum Francorum*, ed. by Boretius, p. 241. Similar provisions are found in ibid., p. 110, *Capitula de examinandis ecclesiasticis*; *Capitula episcoporum*, vol. I, ed. by Brommer, p. 55 (*Capitula Treverensia*), p. 68 (Ruotger of Trier), p. 222 (*Capitula Florentina*), pp. 119 and 250 (Theodulf of Orléans and repeated by Radulf of Bourges); *Capitula espiscoporum*, vol. II, ed. by Pokorny and Statmann, p. 93 (Willebert of Chalons); *Capitula episcoporum*, vol. III, ed. by Pokorny, pp. 80–81 (*Capitula Siluanectensia prima*), p. 97 (*Capitula Cordesiana*): 'tam uiros et feminas quamque pueros' ('men and women as well as children'); p. 123 (*Capitula Ottoboniane*), p. 179 (*Capitula Moguntiacensia*), p. 186 (*Capitula Helmstad*), p. 204 (*Capitula Frisingesia prima*), p. 301 (Atto of Vercelli).

[45] The Council of Mainz (813), *Concilia Aevi Karolini*, ed. by Werminghoff, I.1, 271–72, indicated that instruction would take place in various venues: 'Propterea dignum est, ut filios suos donent ad scolam siue ad monesteria siue foras presbyteris, ut fidem catholicam recte discant et orationem dominicam, ut domi alios edocere ualeant. Qui uero aliter non potuerit uel in sua lingua discat' ('It is therefore fitting that they give their sons to a school or a monastery or outside

of uncertain date that compels the faithful either to learn or to face the penalty of beatings or fasts.

> Symbolum et orationem dominicam uel signaculum omnes discere constringantur. Et si quis ea nunc non teneat, aut uapulet aut ieiunet de omni potu excepto aqua, usque dum haec pleniter ualeat; et qui ista consentire noluerit, ad nostram praesentiam dirigatur. Feminae uero aut flagellis aut ieiuniis constringantur. Quod missi nostri cum episcopis praeuideant ut ita perficiatur; et comites similiter adiuuant episcopis, si gratiam nostram uelint habere, ad hoc constringere populum ut ista discant.[46]

> [All should be made to learn the creed and paternoster and the sign of the cross. And if someone does not now know these things, let him either be beaten or fast from all drink except water until he is thoroughly able; and if someone does not wish to comply, let him be sent to our presence. Women should be made to comply by whips or fasts. Our envoys, with the bishops, should see that it is thus carried out, and similarly counts, if they wish to have our favour, should assist the bishops to make the people do this, so that they learn these things.]

More gently persuasive are the numerous capitula that require godparents to memorize paternoster and creed before receiving the newly baptized from the font.[47] Since god-relationships (as also marriages or fostering children) were an important means of forging the links that bound one person to another in early medieval society, this should have served as a significant incentive to learn. Nevertheless there were more than a few adult Christians who had failed to master the formulae. A letter of rebuke from Charlemagne to Bishop Ghaerbald of Liège reminded the Bishop of his obligation to teach

> Primum omnium de fide catholica, ut et qui amplius capere non ualuisset tantummodo orationem dominicam et simbolum fidei catholicae, sicut apostoli docuerunt, tenere et

to the priests, in order that they properly learn the creed and paternoster, so that they will be able to teach others at home. Whoever cannot do otherwise, let him learn them in his own language').

[46] *Capitularia regum Francorum*, ed. by Boretius, p. 257. The severity of the threats, in his view, make it unlikely that this capitulum originated with Charlemagne. Yet his Council of Mainz, *Concilia Aevi Karolini*, ed. by Werminghoff, I.1, 271, provided for disciplinary action: 'disciplinam condignam habeant, qui haec discere neglegunt, siue in ieunio siue in alia castigatione' ('let those who neglect to learn these things have suitable correction, either in fasting or in other punishment').

[47] Examples include *Capitularia regum Francorum*, ed. by Boretius, p. 110 (*Capitula de examinandis ecclesiasticis*); *Capitula episcoporum*, vol. I, ed. by Brommer, p. 68 (Ruotger of Trier), pp. 250–51 (Radulf of Bourges); *Capitula espiscoporum*, vol. II, ed. by Pokorny and Stratmann, p. 140 (Herard of Tours) requires that god parents know these *iuxta linguam suam et intellectum*; *Capitula episcoporum*, vol. III, ed. by Pokorny, pp. 80–81 (*Capitula Siluanectensia*), p. 301 (Atto of Vercelli).

memoriter recitare potuisset; et nullus de sacro fonte baptismatis aliquem suscipere praesumeret, antequam in uestra aut in ministrorum uestrorum sacri ordinis praesentia orationem dominicam et simbolum recitaret.[48]

[First of all about the catholic faith, so that even someone who could not grasp more would at least be able to hold and recite from memory the paternoster and the catholic creed as the apostles taught it; and that no one should presume to receive another from the sacred font of baptism before he had recited the paternoster and creed either in your [Ghaerbald's] presence or in the presence of your ministers in holy orders.]

Apparently Charlemagne had recently discovered from his own inquiry that many (*multi*) potential sponsors lacked this basic qualification; he therefore sent them away from the font until they learned what they needed, and ordered the Bishop to rectify the negligence of his clergy.

The insistence on the basic formulae of the Christian faith for lay people circulated with demands for a basic level of competence for their priests. Annual episcopal examinations were supposed to ensure that the priests could 'make their signs' or perform a baptism. One capitulum ordained:

Unusquisque episcopus in sua parrochia diligenter discutiat suos presbiteros, et faciat, ut illorum signacula et baptisteria bene faciant; et doceant presbiteros, quid in illo baptisterio unumquodque uerbum uel sententia per se significet.[49]

[Let each bishop in his diocese diligently send out his priests, and make sure that they can make their signs and baptismal rites well, and let them teach the priests what in that baptismal rite each word and sentence in itself signifies.]

The proper performance of ritual, rather than the ability to instruct the people, seems the major issue here. A similar capitulum, also concerned mainly with ritual, provided that each priest 'show and repeat to the bishop himself every Lent the rationale and order of his ministry, whether in regard to baptism or to the catholic faith, or to the prayers and order of the Mass' ('semper in quadragesima rationem et ordinem ministerii sui, siue de baptismo, siue de fide catholica, siue de precibus et ordine missarum, episcopo reddat et ostendat').[50] Again, in the *Capitula siluanectensia secunda*, priests were required to recite and explain (*tradere atque exponere*) the paternoster and creed to the bishop (*coram nobis*).[51] These capitula do not set out especially demanding standards; the authorities seem most anxious

---

[48] *Capitularia regum Francorum*, ed. by Boretius, p. 241; Ghaerbald's letter to his clergy follows.

[49] *Capitula episcoporum*, vol. III, ed. by Pokorny, p. 362.

[50] *Capitularia regum Francorum*, ed. by Boretius, p. 25.

[51] *Capitula episcoporum*, vol. III, ed. by Pokorny, p. 88.

to ensure that priests had some basic catechetical knowledge and could carry out the ritual functions of their office.

In many villages the basics may have been all the authorities could expect, and perhaps more than they could expect in some cases, for we also find legislation on how to handle the problem of illiterate priests. A Roman council ordered them suspended from their ministry until they could be taught to take up their obligations (*ad debitum ministerium advenire*), or handed over to the bishop if they proved unable to learn.[52] Such priests seem unlikely candidates to have been charged with the task of preaching to the laity.

There are, however, capitula that demand more comprehensive religious instruction.[53] We sometimes find the comment (which harks back to *Sermo* I of Caesarius of Arles) that those unable to expound on theology should at least warn sinners of their sins.[54] Bishop Haito of Basel clearly wanted more than rote repetition of the formulae when he required that his priests know 'primo omnium [...] qualiter credant et alios credere doceant; ubi et exempla proponenda sunt, quatenus a creatura quantulumcumque possit intellegi'[55] ('first of all [...] what to believe and how to teach others, whence examples ought to be posed, at least insofar as the creator can be understood by the created'). His priests were to know the Lord's prayer and creed *tam latine tam barbarice* ('in Latin as well as the vernacular'), presumably so they could explain them to the faithful. Priests were also to recite the *fides Athanansii* (Athanasian creed) regularly, and to know Christ's body and blood as a visible mystery.[56] He did not expressly require the clergy to communicate these matters to the laity, although he may have felt that the people would benefit from their pastor's deeper understanding of the liturgy. In any case, he wanted

---

[52] *Capitularia regum Francorum*, ed. by Boretius, p. 372, Eugenius II (Pope from 824 to 827), *Concilium Romanum de indoctis sacerdotibus*: 'Si autem non potuerint edoceri, in potestate episcopi sit.'

[53] See e.g. *Capitularia regum Francorum*, ed. by Boretius, pp. 109–10 and 234–35, *Capitula de examinandis ecclesiasticis* (802); *Interrogationes examinationis*; *Quae a presbyteris discenda sunt*. These place more specific demands on priests, including the ability to teach, to assess penance, or simply to write letters and charters.

[54] Caesarius of Arles, *Sermones*, ed. by Germain Morin, 2 vols, CCSL, 103–04 (Turnhout, 1953), I, 8; e.g. *Capitula episcoporum*, vol. I, ed. by Brommer, p. 66 (Ruotger of Trier), p. 125 (Theodulf of Orléans). Of course, the capitula can be taken not only as an indication of the bishops' desire for lay education, but also priests' reluctance to supply it.

[55] *Capitularia regum Francorum*, ed. by Boretius, p. 363.

[56] *Capitularia regum Francorum*, ed. by Boretius, p. 363.

everyone — *non solum clerci* [...] *sed omnis plebs* ('not only the clergy, [...] but all the people') — to participate vocally in Masses by learning the responses.

Just as the capitula show greater or lesser demands of people and clergy, so they also reveal differences in the kinds of resources available to individual churches. Gatch quite rightly argued that homiliaries do not always make the list of required books. Very poor churches would have only the minimum. Ghaerbald of Liège asked of his priests,

> Ut unusquisque secundum possibilitatem suam certare faciat de ornatu ecclesiae suae, scilicet in patena et calice, planeta et alba, missale, lectionario, martyrologio, poenitentiale, psalterio uel aliis libris quos potuerit, cruce, capsa, uelud diximus iuxta possibilitatem suam.[57]

> [That each according to his ability should strive for the equipment of his church, that is in the paten and chalice, chasuble and alb, missal, lectionary, martyrology, penitential, psalter, or other books that he may have, cross, pyx [or reliquary] just as we have said, according to his ability.]

The *Capitula siluanectensia* repeated his provision in much the same words.[58] The desired 'other books' could of course include homiliaries, but the point here is episcopal recognition that even the items on this relatively short list might not always be available.[59]

In churches with plenty of books, the authorities expressed the desire to see homilies read to the people, and some capitula identify feast days as a particularly appropriate time. According to the *Capitula de examinandis ecclesiasticis* of 802, priests should learn not only the canons and the *Cura pastoralis* (*Pastoral Care*) of Gregory the Great, but also homilies suitable for the instruction of the people for

---

[57] *Capitularia regum Francorum*, ed. by Boretius, p. 243: Ghaerbaldi Leodiensis (802–10), *Episcopi capitula*.

[58] *Capitula episcoporum*, vol. III, ed. by Pokorny, pp. 87–88: it adds 'antifonario, uel in alios libros [*sic*], sicut diximus, iuxta possibilitem suam' ('[in] an antiphonary, and in other books, as we have stated, according to his ability'); *Capitula episcoporum*, vol. I, ed. by Brommer, p. 198, Hildegar of Meaux, who repeated a provision from Radulf of Bourges, p. 237; see also *Capitularia regum Francorum*, ed. by Boretius, p. 279 and the shorter list of the *Capitulare ecclesiasticum* (818–19): 'missalem et lecitionarium siue ceteros libellos [. . .] bene correctos' ('a missal and lectionary or other well-corrected little books').

[59] The unequal distribution of books is also reflected in the capitula of Hincmar of Rheims; *Capitula espiscoporum*, vol. II, ed. by Pokorny and Stratmann, p. 45. Along with extensive examination of their life and conduct, priests in every church or chapel of his diocese (*per singulas matrices ecclesias et per capellas parocchi[a]e nostr[a]e*) were to report the number of books they had and what they were.

each of the feast days.[60] The *Capitula frisingesia secunda* offers an abbreviated form of the same requirement.[61] We might also note in this connection that the certainly *ad populum* homiliary of Hrabanus Maurus and the possibly *ad populum* homiliary of Landpertus of Mondsee have titles indicating that they are meant for the principle feasts.[62]

Other capitula add Sundays to the main festivals. Waltcaud of Liège required examination of his priests for 'exhortatory words for the people, how each understands and admonishes [them], homilies about Sundays and the solemnities of the saints for preaching' ('uerba exortatoria ad plebem, quomodo unusquisque admonet uel intellegit, omelias de dominicis diebus et sollemnitatibus sanctorum ad praedicandum').[63] Haito of Basel listed among the books his clergy needed 'homilies for the cycle of the year suitable for Sundays and individual feasts' ('homeliae per circulum anni dominicis diebus et singulis festiuatibus aptae'). He added,

> Ex quibus omnibus si unum defuerit, sacerdotis nomen uix in eo constabit: quia ualde periculose sunt euangeliae minae quibus dicitur; 'si c[a]ecus caeco ducatum praestet, ambo in foueam cadunt'.[64]

> [If one out of all these things is lacking, he can hardly be called by the name of priest; for the evangelical threats are very perilous to those to whom it is said: 'if the blind leads the blind, both fall into a pit'.]

These requirements are in addition to capitula that required homilies without specifying when they were to be read. Walter of Orléans listed homiliaries among

---

[60] *Capitularia regum Francorum*, ed. by Boretius, p. 110: 'Ut canones et librum pastoralem necnon et homelias ad eruditionem populi diebus singulis festiuitatum congruentiam discant' ('that they learn the canons and the pastoral book and also homilies for the instruction of the people suitable for each of the feast days').

[61] *Capitula episcoporum*, vol. III, ed. by Pokorny, p. 211: 'et omelias diebus singulis festiuitatum discant' ('and let them learn homilies for each of the feast days').

[62] Hrabanus Maurus, *PL* 110.9; Cross, *Cambridge Pembroke College MS 25*, p. 62.

[63] *Capitula episcoporum*, vol. I, ed. by Brommer, p. 47. In this same capitulary, p. 49, Waltcaud also expressed concern for the proper celebration of the principle feasts; the priests must know 'de praecipuis festis atque sollemnitatibus anni circuli, quomodo adnuntiantur uel qualiter celebrantur et quomodo plebs obseruatur [*sic*]' ('about the principle festivals and solemn occasions in the course of the year, how they should be announced, and how celebrated and how the people should observe them').

[64] *Capitularia regum Francorum*, ed. by Boretius, p. 363; ibid., p. 235, *Quae a presbyteris discenda sunt*, abbreviates the requirement to 'omelias dominicis diebus et sollemnitatibus dierum ad praedicandum canonem' ('homilies for Sundays and for the liturgies of the days for preaching the canon').

a priest's required books.[65] The *Capitula sangallensia* named various accessories and books for Mass, 'including also a little book of preaching, since without these it seems completely impossible to carry out the holy office' ('nec non et libello praedicationis, quoniam sine his fungi sacro officio pleniter nequaquam posse uidetur').[66] Similarly the *Capitula moguntiacensia* desired priests to own 'homilies for preaching to the people' ('omelias ad populum praedicandum').[67]

Some capitula even specified the kinds of homiliaries priests should have. The capitula of pseudo-Boniface seem to allow for commentaries from any devout and learned man — a provision that would permit the composition of homilies by contemporaries.[68] More commonly, however, the authorities prescribed patristic works,[69] specifically the homilies of Augustine or, more often, Gregory.[70] (Significantly perhaps, both authors are represented in the Blickling Book, although its 'Augustine' is in fact pseudo-Augustine and Caesarius of Arles.) Their works, originally composed *ad populum*, no doubt seemed especially appropriate for

---

[65] *Capitula episcoporum*, vol. I, ed. by Brommer, p. 189.

[66] *Capitula episcoporum*, vol. III, ed. by Pokorny, p. 117.

[67] *Capitula episcoporum*, vol. III, ed. by Pokorny, p. 179.

[68] *Capitula episcoporum*, vol. III, ed. by Pokorny, p. 366: 'Si uero ipse uerbis manifeste explicare non potuerit, petat sibi ea a doctiore alio transscribi, qualiter aperte legat quod, qui audiunt, intellegant' ('If indeed he himself cannot clearly expound in [his own] words, let him seek to have [expositions] transcribed for him by someone more learned, so that he may read aloud something that those who hear may understand').

[69] According to the *Interrogatione examinationis*, in *Capitularia regum Francorum*, ed. by Boretius, p. 234, an examiner should inquire into a priest's understanding of the orthodox Fathers and his ability to teach them to others: 'Homelias orthodoxorum patrum quomodo intellegetis uel alios instruere sciatis.' Similar provisions are in *Concilia Aevi Karolini*, ed. by Werminghoff, I.1, 288 and 298 (*Concilia* 813 and appendices to the Councils).

[70] *Capitula episcoporum*, vol. I, ed. by Brommer, p. 223, *Capitula florentina*, requires 'omelia beati Augustini uel sancti Gregorii'. *Capitula espiscoporum*, vol. II, ed. by Pokorny and Stratmann, p. 38, Hincmar of Rheims names Gregory, although it is for the edification of his priests rather than delivery to the people. Yet he certainly implies that they should preach: 'et, ut [presbyter] cognoscat se ad formam LXX duorum discipulorum in ministerio ecclesiastico esse promotum, sermonem praedicti doctoris [Gregorii] de LXX discipulis a domino ad praedicandum missis plenissime discat ac memoriȩ tradat' ('And so that the priest recognize himself to be advanced in ecclesiastical ministry in the form of the seventy-two disciples, let him most fully learn and commit to memory the sermon of the aforementioned teacher about the seventy disciples sent by the Lord to preach').

instructing a lay congregation,[71] at least if the priest had the means. Since not all did, the *Capitula Ottoboniane* ended its list of necessary items with the comment that the priest should possess, 'if he can, the forty homilies of Gregory. If someone is able to have [the book of] Genesis or other holy histories, we urge that he have them' ('Uel si potest, quadraginta homelias Gregorii. Si quis autem Genesim uel ceteras diuinas historias habere potuerit, ut habeat, exortamur').[72] Riculf of Orléans also wanted his priests to have copies of Gregory's homilies; he too seems to have recognized the consequences of clerical poverty, for he sternly warned his priests to keep the books and not to part with them.[73]

From Riculf's potentially venal priests to the ambitious program of the *Admonitio generalis*, what we have found in the capitula suggests great diversity in the Carolingian Church. At best the authorities laboured to impart theological understanding along with moral instruction; at worst they had to deal with illiterate local priests. As a result of the diverse conditions, much Carolingian legislation was concerned with fundamentals, ensuring that priests could function in their office and that the faithful learned the paternoster and the creed. But in places with greater goals for lay education, the authorities advocated the reading of homilies, either on Sundays or as part of the celebration of the principle feasts.

The capitula thus suggest a possible context for the compilation of the Blickling Book. Its limited offerings coincide to a large extent with the holy days specified in Carolingian *De festiuitatibus* texts; it stands therefore in contrast to the larger collections of Hrabanus Maurus or Landpertus. The person who put together the Blickling Book showed no commitment to regular public preaching; instead he wished to explain or enhance the observance of the holiest days of the year.

---

[71] It may be relevant here that Gregory's forty homilies were written for the principle feasts of the Roman church, if Raymond Étaix has correctly identified the occasions; see Gregory the Great, *Homiliae in euangelia*, ed. by Raymond Étaix (Turnhout, 1999), pp. lix–lxx. The saints' days differ from those listed in the Carolingian capitula *De festiuitatibus*, but since Gregory's homilies do not always make internal reference to the particular day for which they were intended (they are expositions of the pericope), Carolingian clergy could have employed them on various occasions. As noted at the beginning of this essay, one of the problems associated with the issue of Carolingian preaching is the limited number of suitable texts. A potentially fruitful area of investigation would involve examination of the manuscripts of these authors to see if they provide actual evidence of *ad populum* use.

[72] *Capitula episcoporum*, vol. III, ed. by Pokorny, pp. 124–25.

[73] *Capitula espiscoporum*, vol. II, ed. by Pokorny and Stratmann, p. 103.

The De festiuitatibus *in Anglo-Saxon England*

I have argued that the Carolingian *De festiuitatibus* targeted the laity; I have also shown that lay instruction by means of homilies sometimes formed part of the celebration of the principle feasts. Unfortunately, however, we are still no nearer to conclusions about the Blickling Book's intended audience, for when a version of the Carolingian *De festiuitatibus* reached Anglo-Saxon England, its intended target seems to have changed. No longer directed towards the religious observance of lay people, the capitulum now circulated as part of a collection of texts governing the religious observance of monks in manuscripts associated with the English Benedictine Reform.

The particular version of the *De festiuitatibus* that we find in English manuscripts is Ansegisus II. It appears in a collection of legal texts in Oxford, Bodleian Library, MS Hatton 42 (s. ix²; Brittany), with the rest of Ansegisus's *Capitularium*; there Ansegisus I is lacking, but Ansegisus II has been copied in its place.[74] It also appears separately in several manuscripts of the later tenth and eleventh centuries: Cambridge, Corpus Christi College, MS 57 (s. x/xi, Abingdon or Canterbury), and two London, British Library manuscripts, Cotton MS Titus A. IV (s. xi med., Winchester or Canterbury), and Cotton MS Tiberius A. III (s. xi med., Canterbury). In addition, it was copied into London, British Library, Harley MS 5431 (variously dated to s. x/xi or earlier, probably Canterbury) and later erased; only the heading now remains.[75] In these latter cases, it is accompanied by the Benedictine Rule, along with the *Memoriale qualiter* and a *Collectio capitularis*, two texts that supplement the Rule with additional precepts for monastic life.[76] Although Gretsch raises the possibility that the collection may have arrived in England as

---

[74] Cross, '*De festivitatibus anni* and Ansegisus', p. 120. According to Cross, Hatton 42 originated in Brittany, but came to England in the tenth century.

[75] On the manuscripts, see Ker, *Catalogue*, p. 46 (no. 34), p. 241 (no. 146), and p. 263 (no. 200); Gretsch, 'Cambridge, Corpus Christi College 57', pp. 111–18; Cross, '*De festivitatibus anni* and Ansegisus', p. 119; Helmut Gneuss, 'Origin and Provenance of Anglo-Saxon Manuscripts: The Case of Cotton Tiberius A. III', in *Of the Making of Books: Medieval Manuscripts, their Scribes and Readers: Essays Presented to M. B. Parkes*, ed. by P. R. Robinson and Rivkah Zim (Aldershot, 1997), pp. 13–48; Timothy Graham, 'Cambridge, Corpus Christi College 57', in *Anglo-Saxon Manuscripts and their Heritage*, ed. by Phillip Pulsiano and Elaine M. Treharne (Aldershot, 1998), pp. 21–69. Cotton Titus A. IV may be a copy of Harley 5431; see Ker, *Catalogue*, p. 263, Gretsch, 'Cambridge, Corpus Christi College 57', p. 119n.

[76] In Hallinger, *Corpus Consuetudinem Monasticarum*, I, 177–282 (*Memoriale qualiter*, ed. by Claude Morgand) and 501–36 (*Collectio capitularis*, ed. by Joseph Semmler).

early as the reign of Alfred, perhaps with other materials intended to revitalize the secular Church, she firmly links this 'monastic dossier' with an early period in the Benedictine Reform.[77] Since the *De festiuitatibus* is thus associated with other monastic texts, we can reasonably conclude that it was likewise considered a directive for monks.

Three manuscripts have an entirely monastic focus (CCCC 57, Cotton Titus A. IV, and Harley 5431); however, the case of Cotton Tiberius A. III is somewhat more complicated. For the most part, it too seems intended for monastic use:[78] in its original state, the Benedictine Rule was the first item, followed by other texts of the 'monastic dossier', including the *De festiuitatibus*. But at some point, other sections were added, including a few leaves relevant to the administration of the secular Church. The additions provide a number of short homiletic pieces which, although not intended for oral delivery, were addressed *To eallan folce* ('to all the people').[79] They are followed by various admonitions to priests (*maessepreostas*) and confessors and a set of questions for the examination of a bishop-elect.[80] This last item, which cites the archbishop's authority and the consent of monks, clergy, and people to the bishop's ordination, places the manuscript at Christ Church, Canterbury, and suggests that it was meant for an archbishop responsible for both a monastic community and pastoral care.[81] Hatton 42 also has links to the secular Church: it too was at Christ Church, Canterbury, during the tenth century, before settling in Worcester, where Wulfstan read and annotated it.[82]

Neither the Hatton nor the Tiberius manuscript seems likely to have been directly employed for pastoral care of the laity, but perhaps that is not surprising: in its early stages the Anglo-Saxon reform movement was concerned with regular

---

[77] Gretsch, 'Cambridge, Corpus Christi College 57', pp. 138–39. Her chief interest is the *Memoriale qualiter* and the *Collectio capitularis* and their association with the Benedictine Rule, rather than the *De festiuitatibus*.

[78] I wish to express my appreciation to Donald Scragg for his helpful comments on this point.

[79] They appear on fols 88ᵛ–93; they are brief and copied closely one after the other, which makes them unlikely candidates for reading aloud to a congregation.

[80] Fols 93–97, 106. Ælfric's letter to Wulfstan is on fol. 106; see Ker, *Catalogue*, p. 247.

[81] Gneuss (citing Humfrey Wanley), 'Origin and Provenance', pp. 34–36, notes that most other copies of the *Examinatio episcopi* mention only clergy and laymen, not monks.

[82] Cross, '*De festivitatibus anni* and Ansegisus', p. 120; Neil Ker, 'The Handwriting of Archbishop Wulfstan', in *England before the Conquest: Studies in Primary Sources Presented to Dorothy Whitelock*, ed. by Peter Clemoes and Kathleen Hughes (Cambridge, 1971), pp. 315–31 (pp. 315–16).

life, reviving monasteries and replacing secular cathedral canons with communities of monks, a practice at odds with continental custom.[83] It seems that the *De festiuitatibus* underwent a parallel kind of transformation when imported into England: what began as a text for the secular Church became instead a monastic directive. But it is possible that the reforming clergy who read the *De festiuitatibus* in Cotton Tiberius A. III and Hatton 42 thought beyond their household of monks to the lay people in their care — a broadening of scope that would parallel the second stage of the reform, when the homilists Wulfstan and Ælfric took on the religious education of the laity.

We are left with the vexed problem of the Blickling Book, for which we have a likely context, but not an identifiable audience. The Carolingian *De festiuitatibus* suggest an inspiration for the manuscript's compilation and an explanation for its somewhat limited scope. Certainly a Blickling-like homiliary seems a better fit with the terms of the capitula than most of the Carolingian candidates for *ad populum* preaching — for instance, the longer homiliary of Landpertus or the short and unfocused collection of pseudo-Boniface. We also have a link between the Anglo-Saxon Church and continental practice in the reception of a *De festiuitatibus* text. But we cannot take the evidence much further at present. To those who see the Blickling Book as evidence for popular preaching, Gretsch's hypothesis of an Alfredian 'secular dossier' of Carolingian texts may be attractive, for we could then reasonably associate the *De festiuitatibus* with concern for the secular Church. The manuscript context as we presently have it, however, is monastic; and if we assume there is a connection with the order and compilation of the Blickling Book, we should perhaps also conclude that it was also put together with monks in mind. We would need solid evidence that the *De festiuitatibus* circulated in a broader milieu before we could say that it encouraged lay preaching in England.

Whether such evidence exists is a question worth investigating. As we have seen, the Carolingians promulgated *De festiuitatibus* legislation in a number of variants; however all were closely connected with a more general effort to promote Christian habits in the laity, teaching them (at minimum) the fundamentals of their faith and ensuring that they kept with due reverence Sundays and the holiest feasts of the year. Given that precedent, it is strange to find that the essence of the legislation was lost when one of the *De festiuitatibus* texts crossed the Channel.

---

[83] Wormald, 'Æthelwold and his Continental Counterparts', pp. 32 and 37–41. Blair, *Church in Anglo-Saxon Society*, pp. 349–52, observes that Æthelwold, in desiring a purely monastic Church, held stricter views than his fellow reformers.

THE OLD TESTAMENT HOMILY:
ÆLFRIC AS BIBLICAL TRANSLATOR

Rachel Anderson

The Anglo-Saxon contribution to Old Testament translation is rarely noted in overviews of medieval biblical scholarship. For example, leading biblical scholars like Bruce Metzger, F. F. Bruce, and Beryl Smalley neglect to even mention most of these contributions.[1] Metzger refers only in passing to the Lindisfarne Gospels; none mention Ælfric's extensive translation work. Smalley goes so far as to call this period in biblical scholarship a 'dramatic pause'.[2] However, it cannot be denied that there was a strong tradition of Old Testament translation and commentary in Anglo-Saxon England, most specifically in the works of Ælfric, a late tenth-century monk known primarily for his homiletic compilations and hagiographic translations. In a groundbreaking article, Milton McC. Gatch both outlined the corpus of Ælfric's Old Testament homiletic writings and translations and stipulated a liturgical context for them.[3] His analysis divided them into three major groupings: the Old Testament homilies in the Second Series of *Sermones catholici* plus another sermon on Job; his translation of parts of the Old English Hexateuch; and, in a less well-defined category, the remainder of his 'non-liturgical narrative pieces', or 'reading pieces'. Gatch spends significantly less time on this last

---

[1] See Bruce Metzger, *The Bible in Translation: Ancient and English Versions* (Grand Rapids, MI, 2001); F. F. Bruce, *The English Bible: A History of Translations from the Earliest English Versions to the New English Bible* (New York, 1970); and Beryl Smalley, *The Study of the Bible in the Middle Ages*, 3rd edn (Oxford, 1952; repr. 1983), pp. 37–52.

[2] Smalley, *Study of the Bible*, p. 44.

[3] Milton McC. Gatch, 'The Office in Late Anglo-Saxon Monasticism', in *Learning and Literature in Anglo-Saxon England: Studies Presented to Peter Clemoes on the Occasion of his Sixty-fifth Birthday*, ed. by Michael Lapidge and Helmut Gneuss (Cambridge, 1985), pp. 341–62.

set of texts, presumably because of their relatively 'non-liturgical' character. His
categories provide a useful framework for examining this rather overlooked genre
of Old English literature; this article will primarily consider the 'non-liturgical
narrative pieces' to which Gatch pays less attention. These pieces point to a strong
interpretive tradition in Old Testament translation that allows an author such as
Ælfric to comment on such topics as kingly responsibility and the role of women
in government. By examining his methodology in detail, we can also see that he
places a strong emphasis on coherent storytelling and the balance of a narrative,
even to the point of eliding characters and elements of his biblical text in order to
make his larger points unambiguous to his readers.

The Old Testament clearly functioned as a rich source for both Anglo-Saxon
homilists and poets. While the evidence of Latin versions of the Old Testament in
Anglo-Saxon England is somewhat scant,[4] it cannot be denied that Anglo-Saxon
writers obviously had access to the text and found it compelling enough to use
frequently as a source text. Malcolm Godden, in an analysis of this topic, sums up
the feelings of the tenth century towards this portion of the Bible:

> For Anglo-Saxons the Old Testament was a veiled way of talking about their own
> situation [...]. Most often the Old Testament offered them a means of considering and
> articulating the ways in which kingship, politics and warfare related to the rule of God.
> Despite Ælfric's insistence that the old law had been replaced by the new, at least in its
> literal sense, in many ways the old retained its power for the Anglo-Saxons, and gave them
> a way of thinking about themselves as nations.[5]

In addition to his homilies based on Old Testament material,[6] Ælfric undertook a series of relatively precise Old Testament translations. He translated the
book of Genesis at the request of his patron, Æthelweard — but only until
Abraham's servant's encounter with Rebekah (Genesis 24. 22), as Æthelweard

---

[4] Richard Marsden, 'The Old Testament in Late Anglo-Saxon England: Preliminary Observations on the Textual Evidence', in *The Early Medieval Bible: Its Production, Decoration and Use*,
ed. by Richard Gameson (Cambridge, 1994), pp. 101–24. Stewart Brookes, in his analysis of
Ælfric's source texts for his translation of Esther, finds indications of the use of both Old Latin
and Vulgate biblical texts. See Stewart Brookes, 'Ælfric's Adaptation of the Book of Esther: A
Source of Some Confusion', in *Essays on Anglo-Saxon and Related Themes*, ed. by Jane Roberts
and Janet Nelson (London, 2000), pp. 37–64.

[5] Michael Godden, 'Biblical Literature: Old Testament', in *The Cambridge Companion to Old
English Literature*, ed. by Malcolm Godden and Michael Lapidge (Cambridge, 1991), pp. 206–25
(p. 225).

[6] See Gatch, 'The Office', pp. 356–60, for an excellent overview of these homilies.

already had a translation of the rest of the book in his possession. This other translation was perhaps the one used by the compiler of what is currently known as the 'Old English Hexateuch'. This work, which contains an Old English translation of the first six books of the Hebrew Bible (Genesis, Exodus, Leviticus, Deuteronomy, Numbers, and Joshua) was only partially written by Ælfric. In fact, Ælfric's authorship may be assigned only to the initial portion of Genesis, the second half of Numbers, and the entirety of Joshua.[7] The authorship of the remaining portion had been previously assigned to Byrhtferth of Ramsey,[8] but more recent work by Richard Marsden has shown that a committee of at least three authors created the non-Ælfrician portions of the Hexateuch.[9] Generally characterized as a 'direct, literal translation of Jerome's Vulgate',[10] the Hexateuch translation nevertheless contains subtle variations on the original and perhaps even incorporates Alcuinian and Old Latin versions of the Old Testament.[11] For example, most commentators on the Hexateuch have noted that both Ælfric and the anonymous translators 'downplay or eliminate references to patriarchs' deception, trickery, and embarrassing sexual or marital practices'.[12] These alterations, as Melinda Menzer has noted, reflect Ælfric's desire to translate the text accurately, while, at the same time, not miseducate his readers about acceptable social practices.[13]

The relationship of the Old Testament to Anglo-Saxon life is a key theme in much recent work on the Hexateuch. For example, Catherine E. Karkov, in her

---

[7] Rebecca Barnhouse and Benjamin C. Withers, 'Introduction: Aspects and Approaches', in *The Old English Hexateuch: Aspects and Approaches*, ed. by Rebecca Barnhouse and Benjamin C. Withers (Kalamazoo, 2000), pp. 1–13 (p. 3).

[8] Peter Clemoes, 'Introduction', in *The Old English Illustrated Hexateuch*, ed. by C. R. Dodwell and Peter Clemoes (Copenhagen, 1974), pp. 47–52.

[9] Richard Marsden, 'Translation by Committee? The "Anonymous" Text of the Old English Hexateuch', in *Old English Hexateuch*, ed. by Barnhouse and Withers, pp. 41–89. For a brief discussion of this development, see Robert D. Fulk and Christopher Cain, *A History of Old English Literature* (Oxford, 2003), p. 108.

[10] Fulk and Cain, *History of Old English Literature*, p. 108.

[11] See Richard Marsden, 'Ælfric as Translator: The Old English Prose *Genesis*', *Anglia*, 109 (1991), 319–58, and the discussion above. See also Marsden, 'Old Testament' for a discussion of the lack of contemporary evidence for Latin Bibles in general during this period. Fulk and Cain, *History of Old English Literature*, also note the various possibilities of source material.

[12] Barnhouse and Withers, 'Introduction', p. 8.

[13] Melinda J. Menzer, 'The Preface as Admonition: Ælfric's Preface to Genesis', in *Old English Hexateuch*, ed. by Barnhouse and Withers, pp. 15–39.

examination of the genealogies of Genesis, points out that the West Saxon regnal
lists contain Old Testament patriarchs. She suggests that, using Bede's formulations as a model, the Anglo-Saxon kings moulded themselves after the Old Testament patriarchs, and even saw themselves as their direct descendants.[14] She cites
specifically the Chronicle list included in the year 855,[15] and the list found in
London, British Library, Cotton MS Tiberius B. V, which continues the West
Saxon pedigree to include Edgar and his sons, Edward, Edmund, and Ælfric's king,
Æthelred. Thus, these lists, which allow kings like Æthelred to 'gaze down the
length of their pedigree to God's creation of cosmic order [. . .] and the source of
their own political authority',[16] serve as proof that the Old Testament was more
than a remote story for the Anglo-Saxon kings. This relationship between patriarch
and king was also reinforced visually, especially in the illustration program for the
narrative Old Testament poems in Oxford, Bodleian Library, MS Junius 11.[17] The
line drawings accompanying the text consistently show the early patriarchs as
seated on a throne. Occasionally, some are crowned, and some, like Cainain, are
not only crowned but holding a sword as regalia.[18] Relationships like this, which
placed the Old Testament into a contemporary context, served to make the models
given in the text useful to contemporary readers. Thus both the Genesis patriarchs,
who are specifically mentioned in Saxon regnal lists, and the later illustrations of
kings and rulers in Ælfric's translations of Judges and Kings can be seen as a 'mirror
for princes' that illustrates both positive and negative portraits of kings that the
Anglo-Saxon kings saw as their ancestors.

One of the more intriguing — and neglected — facets of Old Testament work
in the Anglo-Saxon period, however, can be found in Ælfric's non-Hexateuch
translation-homilies, Gatch's 'non-liturgical narrative pieces'. The biblical summary in his *Letter to Sigeweard* and his translations of the minor or historical works
of the Hebrew Bible (Kings, Esther, Judith, and Maccabees) freely mix the elements of strict translation and homiletic interpretation. These texts, as scholars

---

[14] Catherine E. Karkov, 'The Anglo-Saxon Genesis: Text, Illustration, and Audience', in *Old English Hexateuch*, ed. by Barnhouse and Withers, pp. 201–37 (pp. 210–11).

[15] *The Anglo Saxon Chronicle: A Collaborative Edition*, vol. III: *MS A*, ed. by Janet M. Bately (Cambridge, 1983), pp. 45–46.

[16] Craig R. Davis, 'Cultural Assimilation in the Anglo-Saxon Royal Genealogies', *ASE*, 21 (1992), 23–26; cited by Karkov, 'Anglo-Saxon Genesis', p. 212.

[17] For a facsimile, see *The Caedmon Manuscript of Anglo-Saxon Biblical Poetry: Junius XI in the Bodleian Library*, ed. by I. Gollancz (London, 1927).

[18] Oxford, Bodleian Library, MS Junius 11, p. 57.

such as David Daniell have noted, showcase Ælfric's ability to employ biblical material within a framework of exegetical instruction, including suppressing, expanding, or altering the source text to suit his needs.[19] Ælfric's commentary on his earlier biblical translations, such as his Genesis work for his patron Æthelweard, shows great anxiety about how his translations might be interpreted. For example, in his preface to Genesis, Ælfric states that:

> Nu þincð me, leof, þæt þæt weorc is swiðe pleolic me oððe ænigum men to underbegin-nenne, for þan þe ic ondræde, gif sum dysig man ðas boc ræt oððe rædan g[e]hyrþ, þæt he will wenan þæt he mote lybban nu on þære niw[an] æ, swa swa þa ealdan fæderas leofodon þa on þære tide ær þan þe seo ealde æ gesett wære, oþþe swa swa men leofodon under Moyses æ.[20]

> [Now it seems to me, sir, that this work is very dangerous for me or another person to undertake, because I fear, if some foolish man would read this book, or hear it read, that he would believe that he might live now under the new law, just as the patriarchs lived in their time before the old laws were set, or just as men lived under the law of Moses.]

However, as has been noted, Ælfric proceeded with his relatively faithful transla-tion of the book of Genesis, 'buton to Isaace, Abrahames suna, for þam þe sum oðer man þe hæfde awend fram Isaace [þa] boc oþ ende'[21] ('up to Isaac, Abraham's son, because another man has translated the book from Isaac until the end'). Recent scholarship has shown that Ælfric's translation process in Genesis is not as word-for-word as many earlier analyses have indicated;[22] it cannot be denied that Ælfric's translation methodology is not even close to word-for-word by the time he translates the non-Hexateuch books of the Old Testament, some of which feature wholesale elimination of characters and chapters. Paradoxically, perhaps, it is the looseness of his translations which enables a more nuanced understanding of

---

[19] David Daniell, *The Bible in English: Its History and Influence* (New Haven, 2003), p. 50.

[20] Ælfric, 'Old English Preface to the Translation of *Genesis*', in *Ælfric's Prefaces*, ed. by Jonathan Wilcox, Durham Medieval Texts, 9 (Durham, 1994), p. 116. (Translations throughout are my own.)

[21] Ælfric, 'Old English Preface', p. 116.

[22] For earlier opinions on this topic, see Stanley Greenfield, Daniel G. Calder, and Michael Lapidge, *A New Critical History of Old English Literature* (New York, 1986), p. 85; and H. Minkoff, 'Some Stylistic Consequences of Ælfric's Theory Translation', *Studies in Philology*, 73 (1976), 29–41; for a re-evaluation of these scholars' assumptions, see Marsden, 'Ælfric as Translator'; in this article Marsden challenges the perception of Ælfric's prose translation of Genesis as 'literal' to the point of occasional nonsense. Instead, he asserts that Ælfric's method, while faithful, nevertheless indicates an awareness of Old English clarity and a willingness to expand or clarify the text when necessary.

Ælfric's perception of his role as translator-author. Indeed, the homilies on Kings, Judith, Maccabees, and the rest are all constructed not so much as to faithfully re-create the biblical text, but more to use the story to showcase a particular moral lesson or highlight a current political relevance. For example, as both Mary Clayton and Hugh Magennis have noted, Ælfric's translation of the apocryphal book of Judith and its emphasis on chastity is particularly directed towards his audience of nuns.[23] Similarly, his meditation on just war that concludes his translation of the book of Maccabees clearly relates his narrative to the continuing and increasing Danish attacks on English shores. In fact, Ælfric's methodology often seems to prioritize the clarity and consistency of his text over the details of his source.

Not only by examining Ælfric's broad emphases in these 'non-liturgical' translations, but also by peering intently at the smaller choices he makes when constructing his narratives, we can recover, in part, a master-translator's narrative methodology at work. This work will first provide an overview of Ælfric's 'non-liturgical' homilies, and then more closely demonstrate how a detailed look at his translations of Kings and Judges shows his clear concern for narrative harmony and balanced storytelling, even if it means omitting major biblical figures like Solomon and Deborah.

Ælfric's Old Testament translations are not well studied.[24] Recent critical interest, however, seems to indicate that these works are working towards a well-deserved popularity. Stuart Lee's recent electronic edition of Ælfric's homilies on *Judith*, *Esther*, and the *Maccabees* provides the scholarly world with much-needed updated editions of these texts.[25] These three homilies also have received the most

---

[23] Mary Clayton 'Ælfric's *Judith*: Manipulative or Manipulated?', *ASE*, 23 (1994), 215–27; Hugh Magennis, 'Contrasting Narrative Emphases in the Old English Poem *Judith* and Ælfric's Paraphrase of the Book of Judith', *NM*, 96 (1995), 61–67.

[24] See Luke M. Reinsma, *Ælfric: An Annotated Bibliography* (New York, 1987) and Aaron J Kleist 'An Annotated Bibliography of Ælfrician Studies: 1983–1996', in *Old English Prose: Basic Readings*, ed. by Paul E. Szarmach, Basic Readings in Anglo-Saxon England, 5 (New York, 2000), pp. 503–52. Between 1900 and 1996, only three articles focus on Ælfric's non-Genesis biblical translations; Genesis itself garnered five, and Ælfric's translation of Maccabbees shows evidence of recent interest with two listed articles in Kleist's update of Reinsma's bibliography. Ælfric's biblical translations have been most often analysed in the context of a survey of his work, but even then, only seven listed in these works discuss Ælfric's Old Testament translations.

[25] Stuart D. Lee, *Ælfric's Homilies on 'Judith', 'Esther', and the 'Maccabees'* <http://users.ox.ac.uk/~stuart/kings/main.htm>, 1999. The standard printed editions of both *Judith* and *Esther* are found in *Angelsächsische Homilen und Heiligenleben*, ed. by Bruno Assmann, BaP, 3 (Kassel, 1889), pp. 92–101, 102–16. A printed edition of *Maccabees* may be found in *LS* II.25,

critical attention in recent years. Ian Pringle, Mary Clayton, Hugh Magennis, as well as Lee in his new edition, have all written on Ælfric's translation of *Judith*.[26] This biblical text, popular among Anglo-Saxonists because of the existence of a poetic version in the *Beowulf* manuscript, features the story of Judith, a widow from Bethulia, who saves her city from the Assyrian army by first seducing and then beheading their leader, Holofernes. Ælfric's views of this text actually exist in two places in his recorded works. He briefly characterizes the work in his *Letter to Sigeweard*; there he states that the story of Judith is particularly applicable to a nation facing foreign invasion.[27] This interpretation is contrasted, however, in his homiletic treatment and commentary, which dwells on Judith's chastity. Ian Pringle's 1975 article attempts to harmonize these two apparently divergent views of the biblical text.[28] He argues that an exhortation to national (armed) defiance and a call to a chaste life both function similarly in Ælfric's mind; they are both methods of resistance to the Danish invasions properly suited to those who fight (the *bellatores*) and those who pray (the *oratores*).[29]

Clayton's and Magennis's more recent work resists the desire to unify Ælfric's purpose in his *Judith* translations, and instead focuses on his narrative technique with respect to audience. In her work, Clayton contrasts the 'defence of the homeland' characterization of the text Ælfric presents in his *Letter to Sigeweard* to the typological interpretation in the translation itself. In this concluding section, Ælfric emphasizes Judith's chastity, and notes that it should serve as an example for contemporary nuns who might be tempted to break their own vows.[30] Clayton questions the two interpretive strategies and concludes that Ælfric's awareness of

---

Ælfric's Lives of Saints, ed. by W. W. Skeat, EETS: OS, 76, 82, 94, 114 (London, 1881–1900; repr. as 2 vols, 1966), pp. 66–120.

[26] Ian Pringle, '"Judith": The Homily and the Poem', *Traditio*, 31 (1975), 83–97; Clayton, 'Ælfric's *Judith*'; Magennis, 'Contrasting Narrative Emphases'; Stuart D. Lee, 'A Study of the Themes in *Judith*, *Esther*, and *Maccabees*', in Lee, *Ælfric's Homilies*, pp. 11–17 <http://users.ox.ac.uk/~stuart/kings/VIII.htm>.

[27] Ælfric, 'Treatise on the Old and New Testament', in *The Old English Version of the Heptateuch: Ælfric's Treatise on the Old and New Testament, and his Preface to Genesis*, ed. by S. J. Crawford, EETS: OS, 160 (London, 1922; repr. 1969), pp. 15–75 (p. 48).

[28] Pringle, '"Judith"'.

[29] Pringle, in creating this reconciliation, relies on Ælfric's own conception of the orders of society as put forth in his addendum to his translation of *Maccabees*; see Ælfric, 'The Maccabees', in *LS*, pp. 120–24.

[30] *Angelsächsische Homilien*, ed. by Assmann, pp. 434–37.

audience was subtle, showing that he was not reluctant to put forth a reading and interpretation of his text suitable to a specific audience. She states that

> The two meanings which Ælfric imposes on the text, therefore, seem oddly incongruous with the text itself, even though both had been sanctioned by tradition. Instead of reflecting the narrative, they reflect a desire to make safe that text, to contain and defuse it.[31]

The 'warlike' connotation for the ealdorman Sigeweard and the 'chaste' overtones for the nuns addressed in Ælfric's epilogue[32] both have meaning for their respective audiences — and both use Old Testament material to comment on present-day concerns. Furthermore, Ælfric's epilogue to this text indicates that he had, at least once, a predominately female audience for his translation work. Magennis concurs with Clayton's general conclusions in a brief article that compares the poetic version to Ælfric's homiletic one. He emphasizes that Ælfric understood his source text from within the scheme of history, and that he tailors his translated text to suit his audience.[33] Furthermore, Magennis argues that Ælfric not only broadly translated his text, but was aware of his power as a narrator; the aptness of this assertion will only be further apparent when we come to analyze his translations of Kings and Judges.

Ælfric's homily on another Old Testament woman, Esther, has also received current critical attention. Like *Judith*, *Esther* dates to rather late in Ælfric's career; Clemoes places the composition for both of them after 1002 and before his death in 1006.[34] Also, like *Judith*, Ælfric both expands and condenses his text to help his audience understand the text; passages which may be defined as 'close translation' are very rare.[35] These translations, as Clayton has noted, can be seen as dealing directly with issues of contemporary relevance and politics; like *Judith*'s relevance for national defence (or chastity) she suggests that his translation of Esther was perhaps a *speculum reginae* ('mirror for queens') for Æthelred's new queen, Emma of Normandy. Clayton opens her analysis of the piece by noting Lee's dismissive attitude towards it; she then goes on to suggest that the meaning of the piece lies

---

[31] Clayton, 'Ælfric's *Judith*', p. 225.

[32] For a brief discussion of 'min swustor' in line 442 of *Judith*, see Clayton's Appendix to her article, 'Ælfric's *Judith*', pp. 225–27.

[33] Magennis, 'Contrasting Narrative Emphases', pp. 63, 64.

[34] Peter Clemoes, 'The Chronology of Ælfric's Works', in *Old English Prose*, ed. by Szarmach, pp. 29–72 (p. 56).

[35] S. D. Lee, 'Sources for *Judith*, *Esther* and the *Maccabees*', in Lee, *Ælfric's Homilies*, p. 1 <http://users.ox.ac.uk/~stuart/kings/VII.htm>.

not in the standard 'resistance to the Vikings' theme that explicitly characterizes much of Ælfric's later work, but on the role of counsel in government.[36] Clayton notes that the focus of the text, what Ælfric chooses to translate, is meaningful. He

> concentrates on the events leading up to the command to kill the Jews, especially on Hanan's role as evil counsellor and on Mordecai's as that of the good man, on their rescue 'þurh þære cwene þingunge' ('through the intercession of the queen', line 313) and on her [Esther's] role as intercessor, as 'forespræcan' ('mediator', line 317). He almost completely omits the aftermath, drawing on chapters 9 to 16 of the Vulgate for a few details only. Had Ælfric's primary intention in translating the Book of Esther been to inspire armed resistance to the Vikings, then one would certainly expect some mention of the Jews successfully taking up arms against their enemies.[37]

Rather than on military action, Ælfric's focus is on the role of Esther. She becomes an example of 'what a good wife can do for a king' and an example of a good counsellor.[38] Clayton suggests that Ælfric's motivations behind this translation are twofold. On the one hand, she relates the 13 November 1002 order of Æthelred to kill all Danes in England (commonly called the St Brice's Day massacre) to the predicament of the Jews in the book of Esther. Furthermore, she relates the translation to another significant event in 1002: the marriage of Æthelred to Emma. Clayton suggests that this text may have been written for the new queen, illustrating how she should have acted (or how she could have acted) in this situation. Clayton argues that Ælfric 'resignifys' the Jews as Danes,[39] thus supporting her assertion that the text does not follow the standard reading of Viking resistance. The text becomes a mirror for a queen, contrasting how a queen should not behave (by the example of Esther's predecessor, Vashti) with how she can and should serve as a king's counsellor for good reasons.

The relationship between Old Testament narratives and contemporary politics has also occupied the scholarship on Ælfric's translation of the apocryphal book of Maccabees. This translation, which appears in his *Lives of Saints* collection along with his translation of the books of Kings, is a longer work that opens with a very hagiographic portrait of the martyrdom of the seven sons and their mother, and quickly moves on to repetitive descriptions of battles and warfare. The text

---

[36] See Lee, 'Study of the Themes', pp. 17–18.

[37] Mary Clayton, 'Ælfric's *Esther*: A *Speculum Reginae*?', in *Text and Gloss: Studies in Insular Learning and Literature Presented to Joseph Donovan Pheifer*, ed. by Helen Conrad O'Brian, Anne Marie D'Arcy, and John Scattergood (Dublin, 1999), pp. 89–101 (p. 91).

[38] Clayton, 'Ælfric's *Esther*', p. 93.

[39] Clayton, 'Ælfric's *Esther*', p. 99.

concludes with an 'item alia' which spells out, for the first time in the vernacular, the 'three orders' of medieval society: those who work, those who pray, and those who fight.[40] Ælfric, in his *Letter to Sigeweard*, states specifically that this work, like Judith, may be seen in a contemporary context:

> Ac uton wyrcean mighte on þone mihtigan God, and he to nahte gedeð urne deriendlican fynd. Machabeus þa gefylde ðas forsædan word mid stranglicum weorcum, and oferwann his fynd, and sint for ði gesette his sigefæstan dæda on þam twam bocum on bibliothecan Gode to wurðmynte, and ic awende hig on Englisc and rædon gif ge wyllað eow sylfum to ræde.[41]

> [But let us rely on the might of Almighty God, and he will bring the dreadful enemy who afflicts us to nothing. Machabeus then performed what he had said with great valor, and overcame his enemy, and therefore his glorious deeds are recorded in these two books of the Bible, to the glory of God. I have translated them into English and you may read them if you want counsel for yourself.]

Yet the text is not without its own idiosyncrasies. As Jonathan Wilcox has noted, Ælfric's translation skips around within his source and adds commentary condemning the Jews. Finally 'he [Ælfric] condemns (or, at least, radically delimits) the use of violence even as he describes glorious military exploits'.[42] Another analysis by Stuart Lee asserts that this homily, instead, 'seeks to explain and justify the violence of war [...] as well as engaging in a clearly related examination of the order of society'.[43] This end meditation on the idea of a 'just war' and the places and orders of society in its context is apparently without source. Lee cites Wulfstan's *Institutes of Polity* and Alfred's version of the *Consolation of Philosophy* as possible analogues to the topic;[44] neither, however, can be seen as a direct source. This additional rumination again ties the concerns of Old Testament narrative to current questions in political policy.

---

[40] A good overview of this topic may be found in George Duby, *The Three Orders: Feudal Society Imagined*, trans. by Arthur Goldhammer (Chicago, 1980). Additionally, Wulfstan does use this formulation in his later 'Institutes of Polity'. See Wulfstan, 'Institutes of Polity', in *Die 'Institutes of Polity, Civil and Ecclesiastical'*, ed. by Karl Jost, Swiss Studies in English, 47 (Bern, 1959).

[41] Ælfric, 'Treatise on the Old and New Testament', pp. 50–51.

[42] *Ælfric's Prefaces*, ed. by Wilcox, p. 44. See also his 'A Reluctant Translator in Late Anglo-Saxon England: Ælfric and Maccabees', *Proceedings of the Medieval Association of the Midwest*, 2 (1994), 1–18.

[43] Stuart Lee, 'Ælfric's Treatment of Source Material in his Homily on the Books of the Maccabees', *Bulletin of the John Rylands University Library of Manchester*, 77 (1995), 165–76 (p. 165).

[44] Lee, 'Ælfric's Treatment', p. 171. See also Wulfstan, 'Institutes of Polity', lines 24–29, 55–56.

Not all scholars, it should be noted, are interested in the political ramifications of these texts. Ælfric's translation of *Esther* proved a fertile text for Stewart Brookes's recent analysis of Ælfric's use of both the Vulgate and Old Latin Bibles in his translation work.[45] He notes that most previous scholars (including Lee, Clayton, and Magennis) have assumed Ælfric's use of the Vulgate. By examining *Esther* in conjunction with the Old Latin Bible, Brookes shows that several of Ælfric's 'deviations' from his source could, in fact, be seen to be uses of an Old Latin rather than Vulgate source. However, he notes that on several occasions Ælfric seems consciously to choose a Vulgate reading over an Old Latin one. Therefore, Brookes concludes, Ælfric may have been aware of both sources, and deliberately combined them. This view of Ælfric's role as translator-author clearly follows the trajectory that the scholarship has been tracing in recent years. From Pringle's insistence on harmonizing divergent views, to Wilcox's and Marsden's analysis of Ælfric's translation methods in detail,[46] the work of recent scholars has clearly been to acknowledge Ælfric's agency and skill as a translator, and to see his choices in translation as conscious, meditated, and directed towards a particular audience and/or political situation.

One particular place in which this narrative agency can clearly be seen is in Ælfric's translation of the books of Kings, a text currently collated within his *Lives of Saints*.[47] The whole work is a selective translation of the four books of Kings (I and II Samuel and I and II Kings in modern biblical versions). In this translation, Ælfric's translation choices actively work against the narrative structure of successive stories about kings that make up the bulk of his source. By only selecting the narratives that fit in with his theme, namely examples of laudable versus wicked kings, he creates a commentary on the features of rulership inherent in such figures. The narrative moves back and forth, continually contrasting the strong king with the weak king, and concentrating in particular on the deficiencies of Ahab before moving on to the more positive portraits of such kings as Hezekiah and Josiah. In the process, however, Ælfric conspicuously omits large sections of his biblical source: he fails to make any mention of the kingship of Solomon and devotes relatively little attention to the figures of Saul and David. This narrative construction can be explained, however, by a close analysis of the text. Through the following examination, we can see that Ælfric's choices reflect his desire to make the

---

[45] Brookes, 'Ælfric's Adaptation'.

[46] See Pringle, '"Judith"'; Marsden, 'Ælfric as Translator'; and Wilcox, 'Reluctant Translator'.

[47] Ælfric, 'Sermo excerptus de libro regum', in *LS* I.18, pp. 384–412.

dichotomy between good and bad kings clear (not an easy thing to do with a king like Solomon) and his brief treatment of Saul and David forms a concise preface to this narrative construction. Therefore, the first thirty-six lines of Ælfric's translation serve as an introduction to the major theme of his translation of the book of Kings: namely, what constitutes a good king. Unlike his biblical source, Ælfric focuses his reader's attention on the guiding contrast that he will continue to emphasize over the entire narrative: how *godes ræd* ('God's counsel') is imperative when selecting a king to rule a people.

Ælfric does not waste any time getting to this theme. The second sentence of his translation lays it out plainly:

> Saul hatte se forma cyning þe ofer godes folc rixode
> Se wæs to cynicge ahafen swyðor for folces gecorennysse
> þonne ðurh godes ræd. (*LS* I.18, lines 1–3)

[Saul was the name of the first king who ruled over God's people. He was raised to kingship more by the people's choice than through the counsel of God.]

Ælfric chooses to relate the second version of Saul's accession; he does not mention the first, in which Samuel finds and anoints Saul, or the third, in which Saul's kingship is verified and solidified by his military prowess.[48] To construct his vision of Saul's rise to power, Ælfric chooses the strongest negative view of kingship available to him. His choice of this particular narrative strand perhaps indicates an opening view of kingship that is quite negative. Unlike the anointing of Saul by an acquiescent Samuel who seems more a local holy man than a powerful judge, this version of the tale features an angry Samuel who first chastises the people of Israel. In the biblical text, he says, 'Vos autem hodie proiecistis Deum uestrum, qui solus saluauit uos de universes malis et tribulationibus uestis, et dixistis nequaquam sed regem constitue super nos' ('but today you have rejected your God, who saves you from all your calamities and your distresses; and you have said, "No! but set a king over us"', I Samuel 10. 19). This passage emphasizes the rituals of folk-belief (choice by lot, choice by exceptional physical attribute) rather than divine counsel; however, even this biblical passage makes it clear that the Lord is not absent from the choice and Samuel attributes the choice of Saul to divine power, however far removed from the actual process of selection.

---

[48] I Samuel 10. 17–25. Saul's rise to kingship is detailed in three discrete series of events, which may be viewed as three versions of the same story integrated by the later Deuteronomistic redactors; these may be found in I Samuel 9. 1–10. 16 (Saul chosen by prophecy); I Samuel 10. 17–25 (Saul chosen by lot); and I Samuel 11. 1–14 (Saul chosen by success in battle).

Ælfric ignores this distinction, and instead paints a clearer contrast: Saul was made king solely by the 'people's choice'. God's counsel — or even subsequent approval — had nothing to do with the process of kingmaking in Ælfric's narrative. This contrast is further emphasized by the next sentence in the passage:

> Fela oðre cynincgas
> rixodon ær geond ealne middan-eard ofer hæðenum leodum
> ac ofer israhela folc þe on god belyfde
> næs nan eorðlice cynincg ærðan þe saul
> swa swa hi sylfe gecuron ofer hy cynerice under-fencg. (*LS* I.18, lines 3–7)

[Before, many other kings throughout the whole world had ruled over heathen nations; but over the Israelites, who believed in God, there had never been an earthly king before Saul, as they themselves had chosen, received the rule over them.]

Ælfric not only re-emphasizes the idea of popular election ('swa swa hi sylfe gecuron'), but also recasts the contrast in terms of nationality and belief. Kings were something 'hæðene leode' ('heathen people') had, not the 'folc þe on god belyfde' ('people who believed in God'). This anti-regnal feeling can be found in I Samuel 8. 4–22. When the Israelites first request a king, they ask Samuel to 'constitue nobis regem ut iudicet nos sicut uniuersae habent nationes' ('appoint for us, then, a king to govern us, like other nations', I Samuel 8. 5). In response, God warns them, through Samuel, that a king is a plague upon a people. Among other ravages, he will 'agros quoque uestros et uineas [. . .] sed et segetes uestras et uinearum reditus addicimabit [. . .] seruos etiam uestros et ancillas et iuuenes optimos' ('take the best of your fields and vineyards [. . .] one-tenth of your grain and of your vineyards [. . .] your male and female slaves, and the best of your cattle', I Samuel 8. 14–16). The people refuse to listen, and repeat that they wish to have a king 'sicut omnes gentes' ('like other nations', I Samuel 8. 20). Ælfric's translation selects particularly negative statements about kingship in I Samuel and concisely works these elements into a clear contrast that aligns kings with those who are not the people of God — and that the election of a king over the Israelites at this juncture was a function not of God, but of the people's will.

The wrongness of the people's choice is not left long in doubt. Ælfric immediately tells his reader that Saul 'beah hrædlice from þæs ælmihtigan godes willan' and that he 'nolde be his willunge and be his witegan lare faran' (*LS* I.18, lines 8–9; 'turned quickly from the will of the Almighty God'; 'would not go by his will or by the teaching of the prophets'). Not only was the election of Saul a negative act, the entire reign was an example of bad rulership. Saul's inability to listen to or obey the will of God, or to attend to the 'witegan lare' precipitated a descent into madness that eventually caused him, according to Ælfric's translation, to be cast out in favour of David. This extraordinarily truncated version of Saul's reign is obviously not intended to give the reader a synopsis of the biblical course of events. All references to Saul's victories in battle and his good deeds for his country are elided. Instead, Ælfric is setting up the first half of the guiding contrast of his translation: Saul is what a king should not be, and David, Saul's successor, is the exemplar of what a king should be.

Like Saul, David has several legends associated with his rise to power. I Samuel 16. 1–13 describes a private anointing of David by Samuel, and I Samuel 16. 14–23 describes a young David who pleases Saul by his comforting lyre-playing. However, Ælfric chooses the third introduction of David, the well-known description of his battle with the giant Goliath. While this passage emphasizes David's power, even when faced with overwhelming odds, it gains narrative strength by contrasting his eventual victory with his unprepossessing appearance. In Ælfric's source, David's youth, lack of battle experience (his job is cheese-bearer and messenger boy), and inability to even lift Saul's shield all contribute to his appearance as an unlikely champion of the Israelites. When questioned, however, he gives his credentials:

> 'et Veniebat leo uel ursus, tollebatque arietem de medio gregis et sequebar eos et percutiebam eruebamque de ore eorum; et illi consurgebant aduersum me et adprehendebam mentum eorum et suffocabam interficiebamque eos. Nam et leonem et ursum interfeci ego seruus tuus.'

> ['Whenever a lion or bear came, and took a lamb from the middle of the flock I went after it and struck it down, rescuing the lamb from its mouth; and if it turned against me, I would catch it by the jaw, strike it down, and kill it. I, your servant, have killed both lions and bears.'] (I Samuel 17. 34–36)

Ælfric seizes on this speech to introduce David to the reader of his translation; he presents David's protection of the lambs as a parallel to his defeat of Goliath. Unlike the biblical passage, which tends to contrast David's youth and inexperience in battle with his belief in the power of God, Ælfric uses David's description of his own power to create a portrait of a confident king who was chosen by God to defeat the enemy: he 'hæfde ða gewunnen sige his leode' (*LS* I.18, line 27; 'had so won the victory for his people'). In this respect, David is not unlike the judges who rescued the Hebrew people in eras past.

This element of choice is key. Unlike Saul, who was chosen by the people, David was chosen by God. While Ælfric primarily focuses on David's power and prowess in battle, this element of choice is emphasized at the end of this brief passage:

> Be þysum dauide cwæð se ælmihtia wealdend
> þæt he hine gecure þus sweðende
> Ic afunde me dauid æfter mine heortan
> þæt he ealne mine willan mid worcum gefremme. (*LS* I.18, lines 28–31)

[About this David the Almighty Ruler said that he had chosen him, saying: 'I have found for myself David after my own heart; he will perform all that is my will with his works'.]

Ælfric makes a rare translation choice in this passage. Instead of reproducing the text of I Samuel, he draws the last two lines from Acts 13. 22: 'Inueni Dauid filium Kese uirum secundum cor meum qui faciet omnes uoluntates meas' ('I have found David, son of Jesse, to be a man after my heart, who will carry out all my wishes'). While Ælfric often condenses and omits large portions of the books of Kings in this translation, he rarely adds to the text at hand. In this case, he substitutes this passage from Acts for a passage he might have chosen from I Samuel: 'sed nequaquam regnum tuum ultra consurget; quaesiuit sibi Dominus uirum iuxta cor suum; et praecepit ei Dominus ut esset dux super populum suum, eo quod no seruaueris quae praecepit Dominus' ('But now your kingdom will not continue; the Lord has sought out a man after his own heart; and the Lord has appointed him to be ruler over his people, because you have not kept what the Lord commanded you', I Samuel 13. 14). This passage, spoken by Samuel to Saul, precedes any introduction of David into the text; it is a vague threat rather than a concrete comparison. Furthermore, the Acts passage highlights David's obedience to God's will rather than Saul's disobedience. Ælfric's substitution at this precise point indicates the importance of this theme to his translation. The obedience of David and his willingness to listen to God's counsel are what separate him from Saul, a king who turned away from God. This Acts passage makes this distinction clear in a way the Samuel passage does not; therefore Ælfric chose to use a New Testament quotation in an Old Testament translation — a rare choice in the context of this translation.[49]

Finally, Ælfric's summation of the Saul/David comparison makes this theme almost painfully clear. David 'gode gelicode oð his lifes ende' (*LS* I.18, line 33; 'pleased God until his life's end') because he 'mid ealre heortan him gehyrsumode a' (*LS* I.18, line 34; 'always obeyed him with all his heart'). Again, this summation is not a very accurate rendition of the biblical text; Ælfric conveniently ignores the Bathsheba incident and David's all-too-human disobedience and fall into sin. In this text, both Saul and David serve as kingly exemplars rather than historical, albeit biblical, personages. In this introductory summation, Ælfric signals to his readers or listeners that this text will not be a synopsis of the whole, or a simple word-for-word translation. Instead, it is a discourse on what constitutes a good or a bad king, and how important it was for a king to be counselled wisely.

---

[49] For an analogue in which Ælfric substitutes Deuteronomy 5. 21 for Exodus 20. 17, see Aaron J Kleist, 'The Division of the Ten Commandments in Anglo-Saxon England', *NM*, 103 (2002), 227–40.

Ælfric's power over his narrative mode does not showcase itself only in his translation of the books of Kings. A similar process of selection and deletion is also at work in his homiletic translation of the book of Judges. Like Kings, it is a historical book that focuses on the deeds of Old Testament leaders and rulers. In addition, like his translation choices in Kings, Ælfric's work in Judges also highlights his desire to create a didactic text that showcases his narrative desire to create clear oppositions and repetitions. In the case of Kings, he showed how the cycle of good and bad rulers highlights the importance of good counsel. In his translation of Judges, he concentrates on the cycle of judgeship and battle, ending up with a treatment of Samson as a type of Christ — and a side discourse on the role of women in government.

Ælfric's translation of Judges[50] is a text that has usually been considered part of the Old English 'Heptateuch', a spurious term for the first seven books of the Hebrew Bible — specifically Genesis, Exodus, Leviticus, Deuteronomy, Numbers, Joshua, and Judges. However, his Homily on Judges (as some scholars refer to it) is more properly considered as a separate work. This separateness has been part of the homily's characteristic from the beginning; for example, in the most complete manuscript of these biblical translations, Oxford, Bodleian Library, MS Laud Misc. 509, Judges was separated from the other translations. As Crawford notes in his edition's introduction, 'That Judges, though included, was not regarded by the scribe as an integral part of the translation of the Bible, is suggested by the fact that he leaves a blank page, fol. 107^v, at the end of the Book of Joshua, and begins the Book of Judges, or rather Ælfric's Homily on the Book of Judges, on fol. 108^r'.[51] Crawford continues to support the view of Judges as a separate work by referring to its inclusion in Oxford, Bodleian Library, MS Hatton 115 on folios 108^r–116^r with the title 'Sermo excerptus de libro Iudicum' (Ælfric, *Judges*, pp. 6–7). The composition and style of the text have more in common with a homily than with a strict translation. Ælfric concentrates on only a few episodes from the book, and interjects his translations of biblical verses with homiletic exegetical prose passages that introduce, conclude, and explain particularly puzzling aspects of the text, like how Samson was able to kill a thousand men with a jawbone of an ass. Like his biblical exemplar, he keeps and concentrates the bulk of his narrative within the cyclical pattern of apostasy and repentance. His translation quickly sets the pattern

---

[50] The standard edition is in *Old English Version of the Heptateuch*, ed. by Crawford, pp. 401–17.

[51] Ælfric, *Judges*, in *Old English Version of the Heptateuch*, ed. by Crawford, p. 3. (Further citations to page numbers in this edition are in the text.)

with a faithful translation of Judges 3. 5–11, omitting only the specific detail that Othniel (OE Othoniel), the appointed judge, was the younger brother of Caleb, a character whose earlier exploits Ælfric had elided (Judges 3. 9). However, Ælfric's faithfulness to the text is severely tested by his translation choices later in the text, specifically his complete omission of the figure of Deborah. This significant omission, combined with the text's concentration on the Samson/Delilah narrative, indicates that Ælfric's translation motives must have gone beyond a simple truncating and streamlining of the narrative.

Ælfric's omission of Deborah from his translation of the fourth chapter of Judges has gone curiously unremarked. Deborah has the distinction of being both a woman and holding a ruling position within Hebrew society. Unlike her predecessors, she is presented to the biblical reader as already in possession of her leadership role (Judges 4. 4). Also unlike the purely military roles assigned Othniel and Ehud (OE Aoth), 'et sedebat sub palma quae nominee illius [Debbora] uocabatur inter Rama et Bethel in monte Ephraim; ascendebantque ad eam filii Israhel in omni iudicum' ('[s]he used to sit under the palm of Deborah between Ramah and Bethel in the hill country of Ephraim; and the people of Israel came up to her for judgment', Judges 4. 5). Deborah functions as a prophetess, a leader in peace rather than in war. The narrative begins by her summoning Barak (OE Barac) and commanding him to assemble an army to fight off Israel's oppressor, Jabin, and his warleader, Sisera. Barak is loath to go, saying that he will only lead them if she will accompany him. Deborah agrees, warning Barak 'sed in hac uice tibi uictoria non reputabitur, quia in manu mulieris tradetur Sisara' ('nevertheless, the road on which you are going will not lead to your glory, for the Lord will sell Sisera into the hand of a woman', Judges 4. 9). This victory, however, lies not in Deborah's agency, but in another woman's. After the battle, in which the enemy's troops are defeated and scattered by Barak, Sisera, the enemy war-leader, takes refuge in the tent of Jael. Jael is a Kenite, a member of an outside tribe not strictly affiliated with either the Hebrews or Sisera's army. In both the biblical account and Ælfric's text Jael, like Judith, uses her position as a woman to lure Sisera into her tent. He asks her for water, she gives him milk; to Sisera, this is an indication that he could trust her loyalty to his side. However, once he falls asleep, Jael takes up a tent peg and hammer and drives the peg into Sisera's temple, killing him (Judges 4. 18–22). Thus Deborah's prophecy that Sisera would be killed at the hand of a woman is fulfilled.

Ælfric's omission of Deborah from this narrative, while including Barak, Jael, and almost every other aspect of the story, is significant. Only Micheline Larès has dealt with this odd omission. In her discussion of women in Ælfric's translations, she notes that:

Le role de la femme n'est pas systématiquement réduit, au contraire. Il arrive précisément qu'on l'escamote lorsqu'elle tient le beau rôle et qu'on y insiste au contraire lorsqu'elle est incitation au péché (Dalila contre Deborah). Or, dans les adaptations d'Ælfric, Deborah n'est même pas mentionée dans le récit de la victoire qui se trouve alors attribuée à Baraq![52]

[The female role is not systematically minimized; quite the opposite. It is repressed when she holds centre stage but, on the contrary, is emphasized when she incites someone to sin (Delilah versus Deborah). Indeed, in Ælfric's adaptations, Deborah is not mentioned at all in the narrative of the victory, which is instead attributed to Barak!]

She goes on to contrast Deborah's elision to Delilah's starring role in other portions of Ælfric's text, suggesting mildly that Ælfric was more interested in a sinning rather than a ruling woman. However, Larès fails to note that while Ælfric omitted Deborah, he did include a positive portrait of a woman in that section: Jael, Judith's prototype of violent enticement. Before examining his elimination of Deborah in favour of Delilah, one needs to examine his elimination in favour of Jael.

One reason Ælfric might have eliminated Deborah was to keep the cyclical narrative pattern more intact. As previously noted, Deborah's judgeship is presented in a slightly different way than that of her predecessors. In terms of the basic narrative, the relationship between her and Barak constitutes what might be seen as a double judgeship, or at least a strong political relationship that prior judges did not have. In any case, this situation may constitute a complication that Ælfric would have wanted to eliminate. The construction of his narrative indicates that a reduction of complications or breaks in structure might have been one aspect of his translation process. For example, he opens this cycle of judgeship by citing the Israelites' backsliding and God's imposition of an oppressive ruler:

Æfter Aothes forðsiðe hi geeacnodon eft heora unrightwisnysse ond heora yfel ongean God. Ond he hig betæhte sumum gramlican cininge, Iabin gehaten. And he hæfde heora geweald ealles twentig geara, ond hig yfele ofsette; ond hig þa clipodon on hira earforð-nisse to þam mildheortan Gode, his mildsunge biddende. Ða asende him God sumne heretogan to, Barac gehaten, ond he þa ferde mid tyn þusend mannum to þære burnan Cison, ond se cining Iabin send im togeanes anne ealdorman him swiðe getreowe, Sisarra gehaten, mid nigonhund crætum ond mid ealre his fyrde to gefeohte gearowe. (Ælfric, *Judges*, pp. 403–04)

[After the death of Aoth, they again expanded upon their unrighteousness and their evil against God. He [God] then appointed a cruel king named Iabin. He held dominion over

[52] Micheline-Maurice Larès, 'Types et Optiques de Traductions et Adaptations de l'Ancien Testament en Anglais du Haut Moyen Âge', in *The Bible and Medieval Culture*, ed. by W. Lourdaux and D. Verhalst (Leuven, 1979), pp. 70–88 (p. 79).

them for twenty years, and afflicted them with evil; then they cried out about their troubles to the mild-hearted God, praying for his mercy. Then God sent a certain war-leader, named Barac, to them. He then went to the Cison river with ten thousand men, and the king Iabin sent an ealdorman, a man named Sisara who was very faithful to him, to oppose them with nine hundred chariots and with all his army to fight as prepared.]

His vocabulary and phrasing echo his presentation of the previous two judges, Othoniel and Ehud. By eliminating Deborah's role in the narrative, and Barak's deference to her, Ælfric manages to construct a narrative that follows the set cyclical pattern almost exactly. However, he does not elide Jael's role in the narrative. Unlike Deborah, Jael's messy dispatch of Sisera is retained in all detail; in fact, Ælfric adds an extra detail to his narrative — namely, a last kick from Sisera as he dies from Jael's tent peg through his head (Ælfric, *Judges*, p. 405).

Ælfric's role as translator/storyteller is equally evident in his treatment of the Samson and Delilah narrative; in fact, this story is the narrative goal of the homily as the final portion of the homily is a typological exegesis of Samson as a Christ-figure. This portion of *Judges* has a similar level of detail to the Jael/Sisera encounter, and Ælfric obviously constructs them as parallel events, thus inviting a reader to see the similarities and differences between them. Like Jael and Sisera, the encounter between Samson and Delilah is private and seductive; the difference lies in the relative political and moral allegiances of the participants. In his translation, Ælfric encapsulates the happenings of Judges 13–16 into approximately one quarter of his homily, ending in the aforementioned typological exegesis of Samson. Ælfric's omissions eliminate tangential narratives and essentially whitewash Samson's character, as one might expect. Like the rest of the judgement cycles, this section begins with the provocation of God and his deliverance of the Israelites into the power of oppressors, in this case the Philistines. However, instead of a judge simply appearing, the narrative presents the reader with a childless couple. In the biblical text, an angel appears first to Samson's (future) mother, and tells her she will have a child. When she tells her husband, Manue, he refuses to believe her and insists that the angel come back and tell him specifically — and then only believes after the angel provides him with further divine signs (Judges 13. 1–23). Instead of giving his reader this detailed account, Ælfric truncates this long narrative into a simple line: 'Him com þa gangende to Godes engel, ond ceæð ðæt hi sceoldon habban sunu him gemæne' (Ælfric, *Judges*, p. 410; 'Then an angel of God came up to him, and said that they [he and his wife] should have a son together'). He then specifies the restrictions on Samson: that he should never cut his hair nor shave, nor drink ale, nor eat anything unclean 'for þam þe he onginð to alysenne his folc, Israhela þeode, of Philistea þeowte' (Ælfric, *Judges*, p. 410; 'because he will begin to free his people, the Israelites, from the Philistine bondage'). This truncation manages to convey the core of the narrative and has the added benefit of relating more clearly to a parallel New Testament passage: the angelic annunciation of John the Baptist to Zechariah and Elizabeth (Luke 1. 5–25). In this episode, Zechariah receives the heavenly good news about his son, John, before his wife Elizabeth. By eliminating the angel's first visit to Samson's mother, Ælfric both condenses the narrative considerably and strengthens his eventual typological argument.

As a type of Christ, Samson's blatant, enthusiastic sexuality poses a challenge to Ælfric's needs for the character. In the biblical text, Samson's major downfall is his attraction to inappropriate women — especially Philistine women. Ælfric eliminates the entire narrative relating to his first almost-marriage to a Philistine woman, including only his encounter with a lion on the way to the bridal celebration (Ælfric, *Judges*, p. 410). Furthermore, in his description of Samson's victory over the Philistines in Gaza, Ælfric eliminates the prostitute with whom Samson was spending the night (Judges 16. 1–3; Ælfric, *Judges*, p. 410). In both situations, Ælfric retains details that would highlight the theme of Samson's heroic strength and eliminates the inappropriate women whose influence caused the situations in which Samson exhibited his unusual strength. In this respect, Ælfric takes away much of the moral ambiguity that surrounds Samson in the biblical text. However, the figure of Delilah, unlike Samson's other lovers, was not excised from Ælfric's version of the text. Why?

Delilah, like Jezebel, is one of the iconic 'bad women' of the Old Testament. An unrepentant temptress, she seduces Samson for the money the Philistines give her to find out the secret of his strength, and orders the haircut that eventually removes that strength from him. As Carol Smith has noted, the figure of Delilah has prompted differing interpretations of both Judges 13–16 and the role of women in the book in general.[53] Delilah's portrayal has been viewed as 'reprehensively stereotypical' and 'appropriated by an androcentric agenda to serve male interests'.[54] On the other hand, another scholar has argued that the whole book of Judges is a satire in its depiction of men — and the book might have even been written by a woman.[55] In any case, many of these scholars, feminist or otherwise,

---

[53] Carol Smith, 'Samson and Delilah: A Parable of Power?', *Journal for the Study of the Old Testament*, 76 (1997), 45–57.

[54] Smith, 'Samson and Delilah', p. 47; J. C. Exum, *Fragmented Women: Feminist (Sub)versions of Biblical Narratives* (Sheffield, 1993), p. 89.

[55] A. J. Bledstein, 'Is Judges a Woman's Satire of Men who Play God?', in *A Feminist Companion to Judges*, ed. by A. Brenner (Sheffield, 1993), pp. 55–71 (p. 66).

have noted that women, especially in the story of Samson, play a dominant role. As Cheryl Exum has noted, 'the story of Samson is a story about women. Just try to imagine it without them'.[56] Yet this is almost exactly what Ælfric does. By eliminating all but Delilah from the Samson narrative, Ælfric downplays the text's implicit criticism of its hero. Furthermore, by adjusting small details of the text, Ælfric manages to make Delilah even more of a figure of blatant betrayal than the biblical text does.

Ælfric's first alteration to the biblical text is to clearly align Delilah with the Philistines. The Vulgate text reads: 'post haec amavit mulierem quae habitabat in valle Sorech et vocabatur Dalila' ('After this he loved a woman in the valley of Sorek, whose name was Delilah', Judges 16. 4). In this introduction, Delilah is not positively associated with the Philistines. Delilah, in fact, is a Hebrew name, and the valley of Sorech is a borderland between the Philistines and the Israelites.[57] However, Ælfric does what generations of commentators both before and after him have done — he assumes that Delilah is a heathen, and identifies her as such: 'Hine beswac swa þeah siððan an wif, Dalila gehaten, of þam hæðenan folce' (Ælfric, Judges, p. 412; 'He then afterward took a wife named Delilah, one of the heathen folk'). Delilah's allegiances, while never long in question in the biblical text, are even less nebulous in Ælfric's version.

In Ælfric's text, Delilah is referred to consistently as a betrayer, seductress, and deceiver. She is characterized with the adjective 'swicol' several times; Ælfric never lets the reader doubt her evil intentions. While he truncates the repetitiveness of her seductions and Samson's lies to her about the source of his strength, Ælfric retains the back-and-forth rhythm of seduction, binding attempt, and release that characterizes the biblical narrative (see Judges 16. 5–14). When she finally learns that the true secret to his strength lies in his hair, Ælfric depicts her as the one willing to act:

> Heo þa on sumum dæge, þa þa he on slæpe læg, forcearf his seofan loccas ond awrehte hine siðþan; ða wæs he swa unmihtig swa swa oðre men. (Ælfric, Judges, p. 413)

> [Then, on a certain day, when he was sleeping, she shaved his seven locks [of hair] and then woke him up afterwards; he was then as weak as other men.]

Delilah's agency in this episode is Ælfric's addition. The Vulgate text reads:

---

[56] Exum, *Fragmented Women*, p. 61.

[57] Foster R. McCurley, 'Sorek', in *The HarperCollins Bible Dictionary*, ed. by Paul J. Achtmeier (New York, 1985), p. 1055.

At illa dormire eum fecit super genua sua et in sinu suo reclinare caput vocavitque tonsorem et rasit septem crines eius et coepit abicere eum et a se repellere statim enim ab eo fortitudo discessit.

[She made him sleep upon her knees; and she called a man, and had him shave off the seven locks of his head. Then she began to torment him, and his strength left him.] (Judges 16. 19)

Ælfric elides the sexual innuendo in the above verse (Samson sleeping in Delilah's lap) and eliminates the man she calls in to do the actual shaving. Instead, Delilah herself acts. The most compelling reason for this deception, within the context of Ælfric's translation, is to more closely align her actions with those of Jael. Both use their seductive powers (but not too overtly for the rather prudish Ælfric) to lure a man into their private realms. Both act violently upon a sleeping man, causing him either death or severe injury. Yet only Delilah is considered the 'betrayer'. The only difference between them, in Ælfric's version, is the side of their loyalty. This particularly female act — allurement leading to violence — can be used both to aid and work against the Israelites, much as male rulership and violence (as depicted by the series of hero-judges and their heathen opponent-kings) can be used by God to both rescue and punish his people.

Therefore, within this narrow view of women's roles in the context of one of Ælfric's main themes of his translation, it is not surprising that Deborah falls out of the picture. As a woman who leads, but does not fight, she has no role in Ælfric's drama of the active nature of heroic repentance. Her elimination, while disturbing, enables Ælfric to streamline his narrative and create the striking parallel of Jael and Delilah for his readers and listeners. While one's actions are lauded by the text, and the other's vilified, both show a great amount of anxiety about the power women have when they get men with ruling power into their private chambers: in both cases, the man so allured gets the worse end of the deal.

THE LITURGICAL CONTEXT
OF ÆLFRIC'S HOMILIES FOR ROGATION

Stephen J. Harris

Time does not pass capriciously in the Church, but cyclically. Time to a Christian is pregnant with memory and celebration. The ecclesiastical structure of time determines in part the liturgical content of human devotion, and monastic time is therefore ordered accordingly.[1] Monks are strictly regulated in the times of their prayers, and in their oblations and obligations. The *Regularis concordia*, for example, requires that the seven Penitential Psalms be sung during the winter at Prime.[2] But why these psalms, and why at Prime? Why a particular verse and not another? The order of prayer in a monastic office or a liturgy is neither haphazard nor accidental. The pericope, lection, gospel, collects, tropes, psalms, hymns, and homily of a Mass all fit together to fulfill the symbolic mandate of a particular moment in time. Examining how a given homily relates to that

---

[1] E. H. van Olst notes that the Christian liturgy is premised on the 'datum that prayer does not arise from human desire but from God's desire': *The Bible and Liturgy* (Grand Rapids, MI, 1991). See also Stephan Borgehammar, 'A Monastic Conception of the Liturgical Year', in *The Liturgy of the Medieval Church*, ed. by Thomas Heffernan and E. Ann Matter (Kalamazoo, 2001), pp. 13–14 (p. 13): 'We learn to experience not a ceaseless progression of days and nights but a pattern of meanings.' I would like to thank Sarah Keefer for her guidance and encouragement, Drew Jones for his help and generosity, and Jen Adams and Joe Black for their many helpful suggestions. Any errors are my own.

[2] *Regularis concordia*, ed. by Dom Thomas Symons (London, 1953), p. xliii. The first three Penitential Psalms (6, 31, and 37) are said during the *Trina oratio*, said out loud when a brother first reaches the oratory after waking. The order of prayer was taken very seriously, and it was an offence to ignore it. The Northumbrian Priests' Law fines a priest if he sings the hours at an inappropriate time (no. 36), or if he fetches the chrism at an improper time (no. 8); *English Historical Documents, c. 500–1042*, ed. by Dorothy Whitelock (London, 1955), vol. I, §53, pp. 434–39.

symbolic mandate may allow us a fuller appreciation of Old English homilies. By reading homilies in their liturgical context, we can observe how homilists dealt with broader liturgical themes. First, we can determine, even if vaguely, how the prayers of a Christian feast are interconnected thematically or symbolically. Then, we can inquire into how the liturgy could have affected compositions prepared for that day's feast. Homilies for Rogationtide, the Christian feast of atonement, by Ælfric of Eynsham, Anglo-Saxon England's greatest prose stylist, provide a particularly interesting place to consider how liturgy affects homilies.[3] Liturgical texts are not considered fertile sources for Ælfric's homilies for Rogationtide, yet his homilies contain elements for which no other sources are known. I will argue that the liturgy of Rogationtide provides some of the themes that guided Ælfric as he composed.

To search out Ælfric's sources is also to inquire into his method of composition, to guess at the principles that guided him to some sources and away from others. Malcolm Godden has provided a remarkably full list of Ælfric's sources and suggests that Ælfric relied on relatively few volumes to compose his homilies.[4] Another source, one that Godden calls 'liturgical texts', may be more fertile than we currently suppose. 'Liturgical texts' is a category under which Godden lists the Psalms, a 'line from an Office for the Assumption [. . .] and some words from a hymn for the Annunciation'.[5] I would like to explore that category, and to propose a closer association of Ælfric's homilies to their liturgical context. A homily, as part of a liturgy, is bound by the peculiarities of ecclesiastical time. It arises out of a particular festival, out of a scriptural reading for the day, or sometimes out of liturgical texts such as antiphons.[6] In an annual cycle of liturgy, homilies will often

---

[3] I do not distinguish between homilies and sermons here. Milton McCormick Gatch defines a sermon as 'a general address on a religious theme', and a homily as 'an exegetical address on a passage of Scripture'. Ælfric often does both in the same work. Gatch, 'The Achievement of Ælfric and his Colleagues in European Perspective', in *The Old English Homily and its Backgrounds*, ed. by Paul E. Szarmach and Bernard F. Huppé (Albany, 1978), pp. 43–73 (p. 45).

[4] Malcolm Godden, *Ælfric's Catholic Homilies: Introduction, Commentary and Glossary*, EETS: SS, 18 (Oxford, 2002), p. xlv.

[5] Godden, *Introduction, Commentary, and Glossary*, p. lxii. Defining a source is no easy thing, and I refer the reader to Allen Frantzen's discussion of sources as they pertain to Anglo-Saxon studies: *Desire for Origins: New Language, Old English, and Teaching the Tradition* (New Brunswick, 1990), pp. 62–95; and to Donald G. Scragg, 'Source Study', in *Reading Old English Texts*, ed. by Katherine O'Brien O'Keeffe (Cambridge, 1997), pp. 39–58. The liturgical texts that I discuss might better be described as influences, rather than sources.

[6] One thinks, for example, of certain sermons by the twelfth-century Cistercian monk Aelred of Rievaulx. See *Aelred of Rievaulx: The Liturgical Sermons*, trans. by Theodore Berkeley and M. Basil Pennington (Kalamazoo, 2001), p. 26.

reflect on readings and themes proper (that is, specific) to a day or a season.[7] A Christmas homily might reflect on the promise of salvation; a homily at Easter, on the fulfilment of that promise. Topics that are proper to a day or a season, themes that are relevant to a point in time, are expressed throughout a liturgy. It is not too much to expect that a homily designed for a feast like Rogationtide echoes the liturgy of that feast. In fact, one of Ælfric's resources was a homiliary that was, as Father Cyril Smetana writes, 'designed specifically for the liturgy'.[8]

It was (and is) important that a liturgy for any given day be thematically consistent. One can imagine that consistency is difficult to achieve simply because there are so many parts to a liturgy. Notwithstanding some variation, Anglo-Saxon liturgy was largely the liturgy of Rome. Some parts of the liturgy were common to every Mass; some parts were proper to a Mass on a particular day. The former is known as the *Ordinary* of the Mass. The latter is known as the *Proper* of the Mass and was understood after the fourth century to be consistent with the larger theme(s) of the day.[9] Augustine, Bishop of Hippo and perhaps the most influential Christian thinker for the Middle Ages, offers an exposition of Psalm 56 during his sermon on the Gospel of John. (Augustine was also author of the Middle Ages's most influential commentary on the Psalms.) The psalm and the Gospel were both proper to the Mass during which Augustine read his sermon.[10] 'Most opportunely,' he comments, 'and by the Lord's disposition, it happens that the gospel chimes in

---

[7] *Ælfric's Letter to the Monks of Eynsham*, ed. and trans. by Christopher A. Jones, CSASE, 24 (Cambridge, 1998), pp. 144–49, §§70–80. See Jones's notes on pp. 217–28.

[8] Paul the Deacon's homiliary is described by Cyril L. Smetana, 'Paul the Deacon's Patristic Anthology', in *Old English Homily*, ed. by Szarmach and Huppé, pp. 75–97. Ælfric's version was possibly 'a shortened form adapted for monastic use' (p. 86).

[9] Until the Council of Carthage in AD 397, liturgical prayers were the uncensored inventions of local prelates. After Carthage, 'liturgical prayers would require official approval of some sort, and in 407 another synod of Carthage insisted that a collection (*collectio*) of *preces, praefationes, commendationes*, and *impositiones manuum*, composed under the supervision of the hierarchy, should become obligatory': Cyrille Vogel, *Medieval Liturgy: An Introduction to the Sources*, rev. and trans. by William Storey and Neils Rasmussen (Washington, D.C., 1986), pp. 34–35. One is reminded of Bede's story of Caedmon, who also required doctrinal supervision before composing his poetry. See *Bede's Ecclesiastical History of the English People*, ed. and trans. by Bertram Colgrave and R. A. B. Mynors (Oxford, 1969; repr. 1992), IV, 24, pp. 414–15. Current Catholic catechesis is described in Chapter Two of the *Catechism of the Catholic Church* (Ottawa, 1992); section 1206 warns against liturgical diversity that threatens to damage ecclesiastical unity.

[10] Psalms are numbered according to the Catholic distribution, which follows the Greek and Vulgate Bibles.

with the psalm.'[11] Augustine suggests that both coincidence and the Lord's disposition are at work in the coherence of the liturgy. More explicit about the inherent
consistency or coherence of the liturgy is Amalarius of Metz (*c.* 775 – *c.* 850) in his
preface to his *Liber officialis*, a work consulted by Ælfric while he composed his
Rogationtide homilies.[12] In an eleventh-century manuscript, Salisbury, Cathedral
Library, MS 154, one reads, 'Scimus enim nichil agere in aecclesia imitando patres
nostros secundum constitutionem illorum nisi omnia ordinate et rationem
habentia' ('For we know that no things are done in church by imitation of our
fathers and by their ordinance save that they all have a reason and are done by
design').[13] Amalarius calls the liturgy a 'manifestatio domini' ('manifestation of the
Lord'). The order and reason of ritual are not capricious, in other words, but
cohere by design.

A conviction in a rational and ordered liturgy is not peculiar to a few commentators, nor was it treated lightly. The Gregorian sacramentary commissioned by
Charlemagne and known as the *Hadrianum* was an important witness to early
medieval liturgical practice. Benedict of Aniane corrected and updated it in the
early ninth century and wrote in his preface that those who refuse to use a Gregorian sacramentary are 'endangering their souls'.[14] Such danger was possible only
if the coherence of the liturgy were considered integral to redemption. Benedict's
warning is dire enough to suggest that the thematic or symbolic coherence of the
liturgy for any given day was a serious matter. One wonders whether a sermon
writer ran the risk of compromising the coherence of the liturgy with a poor sermon awkwardly wedged into an otherwise coherent liturgical experience. A more
secular analogy is a jazz composition in, say, the key of b-flat. A trumpeter taking

---

[11] The lection is John 15. 12. St Augustine, *Enarrationes in psalmos*, ed. by E. Dekkers and
J. Fraipont, 3 vols, CCSL, 38, 39, 40 (Turnhout, 1956), CCSL, 39, p. 694, lines 25–26: 'oppor-
tune namque accidit, et illo procurante, ut ei consonaret euangelium'; trans. by Maria Boulding,
'Exposition of Psalm 56', in *Expositions of the Psalms*, 6 vols (Hyde Park, NY, 2001), III, 103–19
(p. 103). Augustine did not believe that liturgy was purely symbolic; see Pier Franco Beatrice,
'Christian Worship', in *Augustine through the Ages: An Encyclopedia*, ed. by Allan D. Fitzgerald
(Grand Rapids, MI, 1999), pp. 156–64 (p. 158). But see D. R. Letson's assessment that homiletic
digressions cohere through a general thematic unity, 'The Poetic Content of the Revival Homily',
in *Old English Homily*, ed. by Szarmach and Huppé, pp. 139–56 (p. 147).

[12] For example, in his sermon for the Monday of Rogationtide in the First Series, *CH* I.18.
See Godden, *Introduction, Commentary, and Glossary*, p. 145.

[13] *A Lost Work by Amalarius of Metz*, ed. and trans. by Christopher A. Jones (London, 2001),
pp. 183 and 230, his translation. This is an abridgment of the *Liber officialis* with interpolations.

[14] Vogel, *Medieval Liturgy*, pp. 80–92 (p. 88).

a solo runs the risk of compromising the coherence of the composition by improvising in an inharmonious key. The coherence of a jazz song depends upon soloists submitting their improvisational urges to a governing key. This secular analogy notwithstanding, it is likely that Ælfric, in composing or selecting elements for his sermons, paid attention to the governing liturgy, which set the tone for the Mass in which his sermons partook.

There is evidence to suggest that a liturgy was thought to cohere not only symbolically or thematically, but also supernaturally. Benedict claimed that an improperly executed liturgy could imperil the soul. Furthermore, a properly executed liturgy could positively affect earthly and heavenly reality. Augustine held that the sacraments were a vehicle of grace: 'The use of material things, elevated to the level of sacrament, has the ability to work spiritual realities.'[15] Accordingly, sacramental words have a supernatural effect, like an intercession for the soul of a dead relative. The spiritual effect of sacraments and liturgies in the economy of salvation cannot be physically measured or sensed — they are literally operating beyond nature. Christian Anglo-Saxons endowed the liturgy with a supernatural effect, with a power to change terrestrial reality. Certainly Rogationtide liturgy, as described below, sought to assuage terrestrial suffering by removing the spiritual causes of that suffering. Such confidence in the affective power of liturgy is not inconsistent with more remarkable instances of affective prayer, for example. The affective power of liturgy is not categorically distinct from the affective power of prayer, since liturgies are comprised in part of prayers. An invocation of the cross, according to a prayer in London, British Library, Cotton MS Tiberius A. III, will protect from enemies. St Tibertius was considered so holy that when he incanted his prayers of invocation over a sick man, the man was healed. Psalm verses incanted over a mixture of herbs and butter made the salve holy.[16] Ælfric speaks to liturgy's affective ability during the Rogationtide festival. In his Rogationtide 'Hortatory Sermon on the Efficacy of the Holy Mass', a variant of the Tuesday sermon, he describes how the Mass-prayers of the priest Tunna burst the fetters of his enslaved

---

[15] Emmanuel J. Cutrone, 'Sacraments', in *Augustine through the Ages*, ed. by Fitzgerald, pp. 741–47 (p. 745). This view is longstanding: see J. Rivière, 'Sacrement', in *Dictionnaire pratique des connaissances religieuses*, ed. by J. Bricout, 6 vols (Paris: Librairie Letouzey et Ané, 1926), VI, 114. On Ælfric's view of grace with respect to the sacraments, see Lynne Grundy, *Books and Grace: Ælfric's Theology* (London, 1991), chap. 3.

[16] Phillip Pulsiano, 'Prayers, Glosses and Glossaries', in *A Companion to Anglo-Saxon Literature*, ed. by Phillip Pulsiano and Elaine Treharne (Oxford, 2001), pp. 209–30 (pp. 211–12).

brother Ymma.[17] Again, in his second Monday sermon, Ælfric reminds his audience that Elijah brought on a drought by prayer, and ended it by prayer (*CH* II.21, pp. 330–31). The point to be taken is that more depended upon the coherence of a liturgy than symbolic or thematic consistency. One wonders whether the spiritual and sometimes terrestrial efficacy of a Mass depended upon a degree of liturgical coherence.

To return to the example of a jazz song, one wonders how detrimental to the efficacy of a Mass an inharmonious sermon would have been. In other words, was Ælfric obliged by the inherent coherence of the liturgy to compose a sermon in harmony with liturgical themes? One could argue that the Mass was efficacious not because of its coherent liturgy, but because of the singular potency of its prayers. It is, after all, the effective *Mass-prayers* of Tunna that Ælfric emphasizes. Psalms comprise a large part of the liturgy. And, along with the paternoster and the creed, psalms were considered potent prayers and integral to the ritual of monastic life. Each psalm and many psalm verses have particular associations by which they were classed. Some psalms prompted God's clemency; the Rogationtide liturgy was also thought to prompt God's clemency. Alcuin of York (*c.* 735–804) wrote in his *De laude psalmorum* that he who sings the five Penitential Psalms 'will find that God's immediate clemency will illuminate [his] entire mind with spiritual joy and gladness [...] and promise you great hope of God's indulgence'.[18] These five psalms

---

[17] *CH* II.20, in *Ælfric's Catholic Homilies: The Second Series, Text*, ed. by M. R. Godden, EETS: SS, 5 (London, 1979), pp. 190–98. References to the First Series are to *Ælfric's Catholic Homilies: The First Series, Text*, ed. by P. A. M. Clemoes, EETS: SS, 17 (Oxford, 1997). See Paul E. Szarmach, 'The Vercelli Homilies: Style and Structure', in *Old English Homily*, ed. by Szarmach and Huppé, pp. 241–67 (p. 249), concerning the 'efficacy of Christian worship'. See also the especially clear explanation by Janet Nelson, 'Ritual and Reality in the Early Medieval *Ordines*', in *The Materials, Sources and Methods of Ecclesiastical History*, ed. by Derek Brewer (Oxford, 1975), pp. 41–51.

[18] Jonathan Black, 'Psalm Uses in Carolingian Prayerbooks: Alcuin and the Preface to *De psalmorum usu*', *Mediaeval Studies*, 64 (2002), 1–60 (p. 15), his translation. This derives from an Augustinian idea that those who pray should come to understand what they say and in this understanding achieve blessedness. See Augustine's second exposition of Psalm 18. 1, in Augustine, *Enarrationes*, CCSL, 38, pp. 105–13; trans. by Boulding, *Expositions of the Psalms*, II, 204–14 (p. 204). Alcuin makes this clear in the preface to his *Enchiridion siue Expositio in Psalmos poenitentiales*: monks sing psalms in order to learn diligently from the senses 'ut sciant et intelligant corde quid ore et lingua resonent' (*PL* 100.574B; 'in order that they know and understand by means of the heart what resonates by means of the mouth and tongue'). The consequence is a contrite and humble heart prepared to beseech God. Alcuin says that the ablution of one's penitential tears as one reads is cleansing, and is God's medicine (*PL* 100.575A).

are employed, like tools, for a specific spiritual effect. One doesn't say them so much as *use* them. In fact, Carolingian prayer books speak about the eight uses of the psalms.[19] The efficacy of psalms was sufficiently established as a Christian tenet that Anglo-Saxon ecclesiastical councils feared that psalms could be abused. The Council of Clofeshoe in 747 dedicated its twenty-sixth and twenty-seventh canons to remedy the misuse of psalms — they were being used to secure divine forgiveness for wrongdoing in lieu of penance.[20] Some of these same psalms are found in the Rogationtide liturgy.

Medieval Christians needed guidance in the proper use of these potent prayers, and they were helped by writers like John Cassian, a fourth-century Gaulish monk, Amalarius, and Hrabanus Maurus, Archbishop of Mainz in the ninth century. The guidance these writers offered found its way into the liturgy. Psalms and other prayers were coming to be explicated during the tenth century in the liturgy itself in a practice known as *troping*. As Mary Berry explains,

> [T]his is the art by which the traditional chants of the Proper and Ordinary of the Mass were introduced, followed by, or interlaced with newly-composed passages, expanding and interpreting the meaning of the texts.[21]

A trope *explains* what a prayer *does*. The offertory prayer for Ascension Day, for example, is taken from Psalm 46. 6, 'Ascendit Deus in iubilatione, et Dominus in uoce tubae, alleluia' ('The Lord ascends amid shouting, and God amid the blast of

---

[19] Black, 'Psalm Uses', p. 2: '(1) to do penance, (2) to pray, or (3) to praise God; in times of (4) temptation, (5) world-weariness, (6) tribulation, or (7) regained prosperity; and (8) when one wishes to contemplate divine laws'. The same is true of prayer. See John Cassian, 'Ninth Conference: On Prayer', in *The Conferences*, trans. by Boniface Ramsey (Mahwah, NJ, 1997), 9.8.1–3, pp. 335–36.

[20] Catherine Cubitt remarks that psalms were being used to buy 'spiritual relief in order, not to atone for the burden of sin, but to obtain greater freedom in wrongdoing': *Anglo-Saxon Church Councils, c. 650–850* (London, 1995), p. 101.

[21] Mary Berry, 'What the Saxon Monks Sang: Music in Winchester in the Late Tenth Century', in *Bishop Æthelwold: His Career and Influence*, ed. by Barbara Yorke (Woodbridge, 1988; repr. 1997), pp. 149–60 (p. 150). On tropers in Anglo-Saxon England, see E. C. Teviotdale, 'Tropers', in *The Liturgical Books of Anglo-Saxon England*, ed. by Richard W. Pfaff, OEN, Subsidia, 23 (Kalamazoo, 1995), pp. 39–44. Three Anglo-Saxon tropers are extant. For hymns newly introduced from the second half of the tenth century through the later Anglo-Saxon period, see Helmut Gneuss, *Hymnar und Hymnen in Englischen Mittelalter* (Tübingen, 1968), pp. 55–74. The dramatic element of the liturgy is explored by M. Bradford Bedingfield, *The Dramatic Liturgy of Anglo-Saxon England* (Woodbridge, 2002); I am indebted to him for his intriguing chapter on Rogationtide, pp. 191–209.

a trumpet, alleluia'). The tenth- or eleventh-century Winchester Troper adds, 'Eleuatus est rex fortis in nubibus' ('The mighty king is elevated into the heavens').[22] The Winchester trope keeps to the same theme, but complicates slightly the theological implications of the psalm. A careful reader might wonder whether the trope's passive form, *eleuatus est*, implies Christ's passivity, while the psalm's active *ascendit* implies Christ's active participation in the Ascension. If Christ were elevated (in the passive), one might be inclined to ask, 'Elevated by Whom?'. Tropes, along with hymns and collects, appear in a liturgical context, and in that context threaten to have real-world effect, such as offering incorrect teaching. In explaining the psalm's active verb with a passive form, is the Winchester trope deepening our understanding of the Ascension or is it teaching incorrect doctrine? Ælfric warns, 'Over the teachers is God's ire most excited'.[23] And so one might infer that homilies and tropes were composed with careful attention to the liturgical context in which they were slated to appear. Whether the liturgy was thought effective on account of its coherence, or on account of the potency of its component prayers, Anglo-Saxon clerics had a pedagogical obligation to guide the faithful through the liturgical experience. For that reason, the harmony of a sermon with its liturgical context is as much a matter of correct teaching as it is a matter of liturgical coherence.

So what attention did Ælfric give to the liturgical context of his Rogationtide sermons? We can begin to answer this question by establishing the liturgical distinctives for Rogation days, and then to evaluate the extent to which Ælfric picks up on them in his Rogationtide homilies. Ælfric wrote two homilies entitled *In Letania maiore* to be preached on the Monday of Rogationtide. Seven more Rogationtide homilies by Ælfric are extant, nine in total. The Monday is part of a three-day feast of Gallic origin celebrated on the Monday, Tuesday, and Wednesday

---

[22] Walter Howard Frere, *The Winchester Troper* (London, 1894), p. 149. Early dating is by Frere, p. xxvii, for Oxford, Bodleian Library, MS Bodley 775, 'The Bodleian Troper' or 'Æthelred Troper'. But see Teviotdale, 'Tropers', pp. 43–44.

[23] 'On the Greater Litany: Tuesday', *CH* II.20, lines 183–84 (p. 195). Speaking of the Old Testament, Ælfric writes, 'ða lareowas, þe nellað heora lare nyman of þisum halgum bocum, ne heora gebysnunga, þa beod swilce lareowas, swa swa crist sylf sæde: *Cecus si ceco ducatum prestet, ambo in foueam cadent*' ('Teachers who do not want to take their teachings [doctrine] or examples from these holy books are the same teachers of whom Christ said, *If the blind lead the blind, both fall into the pit*'): *The Old English Version of the Heptateuch: Ælfric's Treatise on the Old and New Testament, and his Preface to Genesis*, ed. by S. J. Crawford, EETS: OS 160 (London, 1922), p. 69, lines 1164–67. Ælfric's emphasis on teaching is explored by Frederick M. Biggs, 'Ælfric's Andrew and the Apocrypha', *JEGP*, 104 (2005), 475–96.

before Ascension (which always falls on a Thursday). Its Roman counterpart, one day rather than three in length, falls on April 25.[24] Ælfric wrote two series of homilies, and he provides sermons for each of the three days in both series, along with variants. The feast, also called Rogationtide (after the Latin *rogatio*, a request or entreaty), has a penitential character — something it shares with the Ember days, for example. During Ember days, which are three days of prayer and fasting during each season of the year, the liturgy is modified to accommodate a penitential theme.[25] For example, the joyous *alleluia* is omitted from the Mass during Ember days since it is unsuitable to a penitential theme. During Rogationtide, only one *alleluia* of two is omitted, perhaps to imply that Rogationtide is a time for penance but also a time for hope.[26] Rogationtide liturgy is celebrated in anticipation that it will act as a supplication to God, that it will appease him, and that so appeased, he will lessen the burdens of the prayerful community.[27] The prayers of the feast

---

[24] Joyce Hill, 'The *Litania maiores* and *minores* in Rome, Francia, and Anglo-Saxon England: Terminology, Texts, and Traditions', *Early Medieval Europe*, 9 (2000), 211–46. Amalarius points this out in his *De ecclesiasticis officiis*, *Praefatio* and 1.37 (*PL* 105.985C and 1067C).

[25] Andrew Hughes, *Medieval Manuscripts for Mass and Office* (Toronto, 1982), p. 85. On the coherence of the liturgy of Ember days, see van Olst, *The Bible and Liturgy*, pp. 79–80. The Roman liturgy is given by M. Andrieu, *Les Ordines Romani du haut moyen âge*, 5 vols (Leuven, 1931–61), III, 248; cited by *Anglo-Saxon Litanies of the Saints*, ed. by Michael Lapidge, Henry Bradshaw Society Publications, 106 (London, 1991), p. 40. It is taken from a ninth-century ordinal of St Amand, Paris, Bibliothèque nationale de France, fonds latin 974. Another litany can be found in the Romano-German Pontifical, a tenth-century work from Mainz, edited by C. Vogel and R. Elze, *Le Pontificale romano-germanique*, 3 vols (Vatican City, 1963–72). Very helpful in sorting out Rogationtide traditions is Gordon B. Sellers, 'The Old English Rogationtide Corpus: A Literary History' (unpublished doctoral dissertation, Loyola University Chicago, 1996). On the significance of parts of the Mass, Ælfric seems to have relied on Amalarius of Metz, *Liber officialis*, ed. by J. Hanssens in *Amalarii Episcopi Opera Liturgica Omnia* (Vatican City, 1948); Haymo of Auxerre; and possibly an anonymous *expositio missae* described by David Dumville, *Liturgy and the Ecclesiastical History of Late Anglo-Saxon England*, Studies in Anglo-Saxon History, 5 (Woodbridge, 1992), pp. 116–17.

[26] Adrian Fortescue writes that during Rogation days, 'It is not allowed to sing joyful chants'. He adds, 'Since it is Eastertide, *Alleluia* is added to the antiphon, versicle and response': *The Ceremonies of the Roman Rite Described* (London, 1934), p. 369.

[27] Ælfric makes the point again in his sermon for Lent, *De oratione Moysi*, 'ac we ne scelon swaðeah geswican þære bene | oðþæt se mild-heorta god us mildelice ahredde' ('but nevertheless we should not desist from prayer | until the compassionate God mercifully saves us'): *LS* I.13, lines 36–37, *Ælfric's Lives of Saints*, ed. by W. W. Skeat, EETS: OS, 76, 82, 94, 114 (London, 1881–1900; repr. as 2 vols, 1966), p. 286.

were carefully enumerated. In the Benedictine *regula* governing Ælfric's monastic life, Mondays have a specific order of prayers, although there are variants. Variation during Rogationtide Monday is introduced early in the day during the Mass.[28] This Mass, as best as I can reconstruct it, may have comprised the following prayers (the items in italics are the *Proper*, the others are the Ordinary): Prayer at Altar, *Introit*, Kyrie Eleison, Gloria (omitted), *Prayer*, *Commemoration* (if any), *Epistle*, *Gospel*, Creed (omitted), *Offertory*, Oblation prayers, Lavabo, *Secret*, Preface, Sanctus, Canon of the Mass, *Communion*, *Postcommunion*, and the last Gospel. The Proper in the current Roman use (as well as in the Leofric Missal) declares the Introit to be Psalm 17. 7 (also verses 2 and 3);[29] the Prayer (or Collect) is 'Praesta quaesumus';[30] there is no Commemoration prayer; the Epistle is James 5. 16–20; prior to the Gospel, an Alleluia and Psalm 17. 1[31] are sung; the Gospel is Luke 11. 5–13; the Offertory is Psalm 108. 30–31;[32] the Secret, 'Haec munera';[33] the

[28] The Proper of *Letania maiore* on VII Kalends Mai. I have recreated ninth-century observance, with reservations, from *The Leofric Missal*, ed. by F. E. Warren (Oxford, 1883), p. 107 (fols 126ᵃ–27ᵇ); and *The Missal of Robert of Jumiège*, ed. by H. A. Wilson (London, 1896), pp. 111–13 (fols 79ʳ–80ᵛ). I have underlined phrases from the Jumiège Missal that differ from Leofric.

[29] 'Exaudiuit de templo sancto suo uocem meam et clamor meus in conspectu eius introibit in aures eius' ('He heard my voice from his holy temple, and my shout went before his sight, even into his ears'). The verb *introire* of this verse echoes against the first utterances of a priest during the Ordinary: 'Introibo ad altare Dei' ('I will go in to the altar of God'). Verse 2, 'Diligam te Domine fortitudo mea' ('I will love thee, O Lord, my strength'); and verse 3: 'Dominus firmamentum meum et refugium meum et liberator meus Deus meus adiutor meus et sperabo in eum protector meus et cornu salutis meae et susceptor meus' ('The Lord is my foundation and my refuge and my deliverer, my God, my support, in whom I will trust, my guardian, and the horn of my salvation and my harbor').

[30] Amalarius, *De ecclesiasticis officiis*, 1.37, notes the prayers proper to the day. This prayer he calls the 'Prima oratio ad missam' ('the first prayer of the Mass') and quotes, 'Praesta, quaesumus, omnipotens Deus, ut qui in afflictione nostra de tua pietate confidemus, contra aduersa omnia, tua semper protectione muniamur' (*PL* 105.1067C; 'Grant, we beseech thee, omnipotent God, that we who in our affliction trust in thy mercy, may always be sheltered by your protection from all adversaries').

[31] 'Diligam te Domine fortitudo mea' ('I will love thee, O Lord, my strength').

[32] 'Confitebor Domino nimis in ore meo: et in medio multorum laudabo eum, quia astitit a dextris pauperis: ut saluam faceret a persequentibus animam meam, alleluia' ('I will confess beyond measure to God with my mouth, and in the midst of multitudes I will praise him, who shall stand at the right hand of the poor: he will save me from those who persecute my soul, alleluia').

[33] 'Haec munera, *quaesumus, domine* [*domine quaesumus*] et uincula nostrae prauitatis absoluant, et tuae nobis misericordiae dona concilient. Per dominum nostrum' ('May these

Communion prayer is Luke 11. 9–10;[34] and the Postcommunion prayer, 'Vota nostra'.[35]

The prayers of the Proper may have influenced portions of Ælfric's sermons for the Monday of Rogationtide. Ælfric adopted some of the images and phrases in his sermons from homiletic sources that addressed penitential themes. These sources can be found listed and cited in Godden's commentary, and include Augustine, Caesarius of Arles, Gregory the Great, Amalarius, and Paul the Deacon.[36] Other portions of Ælfric's sermons appear to come out of the Proper of Rogationtide Monday. The most obvious example of Ælfric's attention to the Proper is his extended discussion of the day's Gospel in both of his sermons for the Monday. Other examples are not so obvious, and include the theme of poverty, a need for prayer, fundamentals of the Christian faith, and an emphasis on good works. These are topics common to Christian sermons and homilies, but their coincidence in Ælfric's Rogationtide sermons suggests that he may have been taking direction from the liturgy. Joyce Bazire and James Cross suggest a number of themes for Rogationtide: penance, care of the soul, catechism, learning, and right behaviour.[37] Importantly, they do not include prayer, poverty, or good works.

Prayer is exceptionally important to Ælfric in these sermons. He begins his Monday sermon in the First Series (*CH* I.18) by explaining that the feast requires Christians to pray, and that they should pray for wealth, health, peace, and forgiveness of sins. The fact is that *all* feasts require Christians to pray. That Ælfric places special emphasis on prayer during Rogationtide must be accounted a likely effect of the thematic mandates of this particular feast. Following Amalarius, Ælfric

---

offerings, we beseech thee, O Lord, loose our chains of depravity, and win for us the gifts of your mercy. Through our Lord').

[34] 'Petite et accipietis: quaerite, et inveietis: pulsate, et aperietur uobis: omnis enim qui petit, accipit: et qui quaerit, invenit: et pulsanti aperietur, alleluia' ('Ask, and you shall be given: seek, and you shall find: knock, and it shall be opened to you: indeed, everyone who asks, receives: and who seeks, finds: and to whomever knocks, it is opened, alleluia').

[35] 'Vota nostra, quesumus, domine, pio fauore prosequere, ut dum *tua dona* [*dona tua*] in tribulatione perce[i]pimus, de consolatione nostra in tuo amore crescamus. Per' ('May thy kind favour, we beseech thee, O Lord, follow our prayers, that when we receive thy gifts in [our] tribulation, we may increase through our consolation in thy love'). Compare *The New Roman Missal* (Chicago, 1937), pp. 578–81.

[36] Godden, *Introduction, Commentary, and Glossary*, pp. 145–53 and pp. 519–29.

[37] *Eleven Old English Rogationtide Homilies*, ed. by Joyce Bazire and James E. Cross (Toronto, 1982), p. xxiv; and Bedingfield, *Dramatic Liturgy*, p. 191.

relates the origin of the feast in Vienna where Bishop Mamertus commanded his people to fast, and thus stopped an earthquake, fire, and attacks by wolves and bears. This fast, Ælfric explains, was suggested to Mamertus by the story of Jonah.[38] Jonah saved Nineveh from destruction by exhorting the Ninevites to fast and pray, Ælfric says, unlike Sodom and Gomorrah, which God destroyed 'for heora leahtum' ('on account of their crimes').[39] Like Jonah, Ælfric exhorts his audience to pray that they might be saved from God's anger. By enacting Jonah's exhortation during his own sermon, Ælfric implicitly asks the congregants to consider their association to Ninevites. Ælfric thus restages the historical moment of Nineveh's salvation, and implies the recurrence of that moment first in Vienna, and then potentially, if the congregants fulfill their role as penitent Ninevites, in Anglo-Saxon England. In words and by implication, Ælfric assures his listeners that their prayers will be answered. Perhaps to allay doubt about God the Father's forgiveness, he explains Luke 11, asking what father would give his son a stone if asked for bread?[40]

Poverty is another important theme in these sermons. From prayer, Ælfric shifts suddenly to poverty. A sudden shift in theme is startling, and seems inconsonant with his discussion of the economy of prayer and suffering so far. Ælfric asks the rich to share with the poor since 'ealle we sind godes þearfan' ('We are all God's poor').[41] If the rich act well towards the poor, he explains, then God will act well towards the rich. Then, Ælfric argues that there is an existential need for both rich and poor, concluding that each is made for the other. The rich man offers sustenance to the poor; the poor man offers prayers for the rich. Even in his discussion of poverty, Ælfric is emphasizing prayer, but surely he is not suggesting that only the poor need pray. Instead, Ælfric is describing how prayer can act on behalf of others. In the analogy that informs this shift in theme, as the rich sustain the prayerful poor, so will God sustain the prayerful Anglo-Saxons. Ælfric takes much of this sermon from other sources, especially Amalarius. But unlike Amalarius,

---

[38] Paul Szarmach discusses Ælfric's modifications to the Jonah story in his 'Three Versions of the Jonah Story: An Investigation of Narrative Technique in Old English Homilies', *ASE*, 1 (1972), 183–92. Chief among these modifications is Ælfric's omission of the three days and nights that Jonah spent in the belly of the fish.

[39] *CH* I.18, line 39 (p. 318).

[40] The significance of each object in this passage is explained. Godden attributes these explanations to Augustine, Bede, and Haymo of Auxerre, although Amalarius makes the same points. Godden, *Introduction, Commentary, and Glossary*, p. 150; Amalarius, *De ecclesiasticis officiis*, *PL* 105.1068A.

[41] *CH* I.18, line 179 (p. 323).

Ælfric equates the Vienna story with Nineveh, as does an anonymous Rogationtide homily found in the Vercelli Book (Homily XL), and as does Maximus of Turin in his Sermon 80, 'De ieiuniis Niniuitarum'.[42] Like Ælfric, Maximus writes that the Ninevites fasted 'ut iram diuinitatis, quam luxuriando prouocauerant, abstinendo lenirent' ('so that the anger of God which they had provoked through extravagance, they would soften through abstinence'). Ælfric is not following Maximus too closely here, since Maximus's *luxuria* is not Ælfric's wealth, but lasciviousness and excess. Ælfric's discussion of wealth and poverty in this sermon is unlikely to have arisen out of the fallacious implication that wealth brings on the ire of God. Nor is Ælfric's declared interest here in *luxuria*.

Two other seemingly anomalous themes are an emphasis on works and defining who is and is not a Christian. The latter theme is to be distinguished from catechizing those who are already considered Christians. In his Second Series, Ælfric begins his Monday sermon (*CH* II.19) by explaining that Christians need to be taught, especially to love God. One is commanded to love thy neighbour. Ælfric limits neighbours to 'þa ðe þurh geleafan us gelenge beoð, and ðurh cristendom us cyððe to habbað' ('those who through belief are related to us, and through [Christendom] are allied to us').[43] The definition of who is and who is not a Christian is therefore very important to the salvation of the community. Ælfric is emphasizing the need for Christians to understand the fundamentals of their faith, for it is faith and often faith alone that distinguishes them from their neighbours.[44] Yet any liturgical catechesis presupposes that those gathered before Ælfric are Christians who nevertheless fail to understand or barely understand the fundamentals of their own faith. Perhaps this tension between understanding and faith compels Ælfric to emphasize a need for good works, to say that the love of God manifests itself in good works. Few sources have been proposed for this sermon, and Ælfric's emphasis on defining the Christian and on his good works seems, like Ælfric's emphasis on

---

[42] *Eleven Old English Rogationtide Homilies*, ed. by Bazire and Cross, p. 10. The sermon of Maximus is edited by Almut Mutzenbecher in *Sermonum collectio antiqua, nonnullis sermonibus extravagantibus adiectis*, CCSL, 23 (Turnhout, 1962), pp. 332–34.

[43] *CH* II.19, lines 11–12 (p. 180).

[44] One thinks here of the anonymous second-century letter to Diognetus, long thought to be by Justin Martyr. The author writes, 'The difference between Christians and the rest of mankind is not a matter of nationality, or language, or customs. Christians do not live apart in separate cities of their own, speak any special dialect, nor practice any eccentric way of life [. . .]. [They] conform to ordinary local usage in their clothing, diet, and other habits': *Early Christian Writings: The Apostolic Fathers*, trans. by Maxwell Staniforth and Andrew Louth (London, 1987), pp. 139–51 (p. 144).

poverty, somewhat capricious. If we look away from the liturgy to Ælfric's book-shelves, one possible source for Ælfric's emphasis on the importance of works is Jerome. Jerome's commentary on Jonah is significant to Ælfric's understanding of Rogationtide. In his commentary, Jerome remarks on 4. 10, 'Et uidet Deus opera eorum' ('and God looked on their works'). God, says Jerome, looked on their works, but did not hear their words.[45] Perhaps accordingly, Ælfric lays a similar stress on works, although he is much more hopeful than Jerome about the efficacy of prayer. Jerome, too, makes a connection between the pleading of Nineveh and that of Sodom and Gomorrah, a connection Ælfric also makes in his first sermon.[46] Incidentally, in the midst of Ælfric's second Monday sermon, he uses the figure of a bird with wings of love to describe the soul; Jerome says that Jonah is a *columba*, dove.[47]

But we need not look exclusively to Jerome, since Ælfric's emphasis on prayer, poverty, good works, and Christian doctrine might also be explained by looking to the liturgy. For example, Ælfric speaks of a need for prayer; the pericope of the Mass, Luke 11. 5–13, also deals with prayer. Perhaps the most productive influence on Ælfric's Rogationtide sermons is the procession of Rogationtide, during which penitents march with holy relics between the hours of Terce and None, from one station to another.[48] The Leofric Missal and the Missal of Robert of Jumièges direct that the Roman stations be followed. These stations would likely have been built for the feast in Anglo-Saxon England. Beginning at a station for St Laurence, penitents would have moved to stations portraying St Valentine, the Milvian Bridge, and the Holy Cross, then finally to the atrium of a church before entering and celebrating Mass.[49] This procession takes its liturgical order from the physical geography of Rome. The Roman procession of 25 April begins at the church of St Laurence in Lucina, and moves along the Flaminian Way past the celebrated

---

[45] Jerome, *Commentaria in Ionam*, 3.10 (*PL* 25.1144C).

[46] *CH* II.19, pp. 182–83, and Jerome, *In Ionam*, 1.1 (*PL* 25.1120D).

[47] Jerome, *In Ionam*, 1.1 (*PL* 25.1120D). This connection between a bird and the soul is not noted in Robert DiNapoli's useful *An Index of Theme and Image to the Homilies of the Anglo-Saxon Church: Comprising the Homilies of Ælfric, Wulfstan, and the Blickling and Vercelli Codices* (Hockwold cum Wilton, 1995), s.v. 'Birds' and 'Dove'.

[48] Each station in the procession houses a relic, making it a spiritual place, a 'gastlice gemotstowe'. Bazire-Cross 5: 'our ghostly meeting place is in the area around our relics, as much in the church as outside as in any place in which they are set' (p. 73, line 123). See also Bedingfield, *Dramatic Liturgy*, p. 201.

[49] Another word commonly used for the atrium of a church is *Paradisum*, Paradise, used in Latin in Ælfric's translation of *Genesis*. Intriguingly, Ælfric describes a vision of paradise in one of his Rogationtide sermons.

fourth-century church of St Valentine's, the first stop for pilgrims on that road. Then, over the Milvian Bridge and along the Claudian Way, the pilgrims walk alongside the Tiber to the *Campus Neronis*, and raise a cross — this is where pagans once processed to sacrifice to the god Robigus, preserver of grain.[50] The processing pilgrims end up in the church of St Peter, to whom special prayers are offered.[51] In Rome, the focus of the festival is on the power of prayer, not on works or fasting. After Pope Leo III (795–816) adopted the Gallic three-day feast, he abolished the fasting which forms so central a part of the Anglo-Saxon rite.[52]

The theme of poverty is raised early on during the procession. In the Sarum Processional, which is convenient (if late) for reconstructing the Anglo-Saxon procession, congregants are directed to begin at None with the antiphon 'Exurge, Domine'.[53] The psalm is 43 in the Vulgate numbering, 'We have heard with our ears, O God, Our fathers have told us'. In keeping with the theme of the day, this psalm asks God to awake, and to stop the suffering he brings on his people.[54] (The psalm also speaks of the importance of fathers, a topic Ælfric also addresses at length.) Augustine remarks that this psalm reminds us that God 'chose to turn away from his people, or so it seemed, with the result that his holy ones were mowed down in widespread slaughter'.[55] After an invocation of the suffering of the people, a prayer for St Laurence follows:

---

[50] *Dictionnaire pratique*, s.v. 'Litanie majeure'. Lat. *robigo* means 'blight'. Vogel, *Medieval Liturgy*, calls these 'stational churches', p. 84.

[51] In the prayer preceding Mass in the Leofric Missal, Mary is substituted for Peter, who appears in the Missal of Robert of Jumièges. This may be because, as in the Sarum Missal, a high Mass for Mary is said on Rogationtide Tuesday. *The Sarum Missal in English*, trans. by Frederick E. Warren (London, 1911), s.v. There was a belief that Christ, during the forthcoming Ascension, exalts Mary in heaven above the angels. See *CH* I.30, p. 431; and Mary Clayton, *The Cult of the Virgin Mary in Anglo-Saxon England*, CSASE, 2 (Cambridge, 1990), p. 237. Assumption seems to be an important theme: Elias (whom Ælfric equates with Elijah) also figures in Rogationtide sermons, and he, too, was assumed. See Bazire-Cross 2.

[52] *New Roman Missal*, pp. 1668–69.

[53] *Processionale ad usum insignis praeclarae ecclesiae Sarum* (Leeds, 1882), pp. 103–21. Also, the *Liber usualis*, p. 835.

[54] Samuel Terrien, *The Psalms: Strophic Structure and Theological Commentary* (Grand Rapids, MI, 2003), p. 362. See King Alfred's *tituli* to the relevant Old English psalms; Patrick O'Neill, *King Alfred's Old English Prose Translation of the First Fifty Psalms* (Cambridge, MA, 2001).

[55] Augustine, *Enarrationes*, CCSL, 38, p. 482, lines 10–12: 'quasi auerterit faciem suam a gemitibus eorum, quasi oblitus sit eos, quasi ipse non sit Deus' (trans. by Boulding, *Expositions of the Psalms*, II, 265).

Ad sanctam laurentium. Mentem familiae tuae, qu*a*esumus, domine, intercedente beato laurentio martyre tuo, et munere conpunctionis aperi, et largitate tuae pietatis exaudi. Per dominum nostrum.

[*To St Laurence.* 'We beseech you Lord, with blessed Laurence, your martyr, interceding, reveal your mind to your servants, and through the offering of remorse, and through the gift of your mercy, hear us. Through Christ our Lord.']⁵⁶

St Laurence (*Laurentius*) suffered martyrdom for presenting the poor and the sick to the Prefect of Rome as the treasures of the Church. This was commemorated in a famous hymn by the poet Prudentius, and in *De officiis* by Ambrose of Milan, who reports the saint's words: 'Hi [pauperes] sunt thesauri ecclesiae' ('These are the treasures of the Church').⁵⁷ The prayer to St Laurence reminds us that those who pray on Rogationtide also suffer impoverishment and affliction. With this prayer, they become the gifts of the Church offered by the intercessing spirit of St Laurence. Ælfric makes reference to the poor and the sick in both his Monday sermons. In one he writes, 'Gif hwa ðearfan forsihð. he tælð his scyppend; Be untrumum mannum. se ælmihtiga cwæð. Ic ðreage and swinge. Þa ðe ic lufige' ('If any one despises the poor, he calumniates his creator. Of sick men the Almighty said, "I chastise and scourge those whom I love"').⁵⁸ And, in another Rogationtide sermon, 'ealle we sind godes þearfan' ('We are all God's poor').⁵⁹ By invoking poverty in liturgical proximity to this prayer to St Laurence, Ælfric is able to imply a connection between the suffering of his people, the place of the poor in Anglo-Saxon society, and the intercessory role of St Laurence.

Ælfric speaks about poverty in the context of the Rogationtide liturgy, and of Laurence's donation of the poor in his sermon on Laurence (*CH* I.29, p. 422). Ælfric apparently takes that sermon on Laurence largely from the Cotton-Corpus Legendary, which in turn is based on an anonymous passion.⁶⁰ There, Ælfric reports that Laurence gave the treasures of the Church to the poor, and said of the

---

⁵⁶ Culled from the *Leofric Missal* and the *Missal of Robert of Jumiège*; see above, note 28.

⁵⁷ H. Leclercq, 'Saint Laurent', in *Dictionnaire d'archéologie chrétienne et de liturgie*, ed. by F. Labrod and H. Leclercq, 15 vols (Paris, 1929), VIII, 2. See also Ambrose, *De officiis*, 2.28 (*PL* 16.139C–42A).

⁵⁸ *CH* II.19, lines 245–47 (pp. 187–88).

⁵⁹ See note 41 above.

⁶⁰ See Godden, *Introduction, Commentary, and Glossary*, pp. 238–47. The Cotton-Corpus Legendary may not have been Ælfric's chief source for such *vitae*. See Biggs, 'Ælfric's Andrew', pp. 477–78.

poor, 'hi sind þa ecan maðmas' ('they are the eternal treasures').[61] In Bede's *De temporum ratione liber*, which relates a history of the world, under the entry for the year 4472 *anno mundi*, Bede writes that Pope Symmachus built a house dedicated to Saints Peter, Paul, and Laurence, a house for the poor.[62] Ælfric likely knew this text, as well as Prudentius's poem celebrating Laurence, which discusses Laurence's relation to the poor of Rome (it is the second song of the *Peristephanon*). Eight manuscripts that contained all or part of the poem are extant from Anglo-Saxon England.[63] Whether Ælfric took a connection between Laurence and the poor directly or indirectly, or whether he or a source is responsible for that connection, his mention of poverty in the midst of a liturgy that includes a prayer to Laurence is more than coincidental. More importantly, whether his discourse on poverty is Ælfric's invention or not, his sermon is tied thematically through Laurence to prayers of the Rogationtide liturgy.

After Psalm 43 and a prayer to Laurence, the liturgy continues to evoke its penitential theme. In the modern liturgy, the antiphon is followed by a *Kyrie eleison* and a litany of saints. The litany itself evokes penance. As Michael Lapidge comments, 'From its very beginning, litanic prayer was used for penitential

---

[61] *CH* I.29, lines 113–14 (p. 422).

[62] *De temporum ratione liber*, ed. by C. W. Jones, CCSL, 123B (Turnhout, 1977), cap. 66, line 1686.

[63] Godden does not include Prudentius in his 'Summary List of Sources', *Introduction, Commentary, and Glossary*, pp. xlvi–lxii. The extant manuscripts are Cambridge, Corpus Christi College, MSS 231 (Gneuss no. 38, s. x^ex, prov. southern England), 223 (Gneuss no. 70, s. ix^3/4, prov. Arras, Saint-Vaast), and 448 (prologue only, Gneuss no. 114, s. xi/xii, prov. southern England); Durham, Cathedral Library, MS B. IV. 9 (Gneuss no. 246, s. x^med, prov. Durham); Oxford, Bodleian Library, MS Auct. F. 3. 6 (Gneuss no. 537, s. xi^1, prov. Exeter); Oxford, Oriel College, MS 3 (Gneuss no. 680, s. x^ex, prov. Christ Church, Canterbury); Boulogne-sur-Mer, Bibliothèque municipale, MS 189 (Gneuss no. 805, s. x/xi, prov. Christ Church Canterbury, and its Old English gloss: s. xi^in, prov. Saint-Bertin); and Paris, Bibliothèque nationale de France, fonds latin 8085 (Gneuss no. 889.5, s. ix^med, prov. France). Helmut Gneuss, *Handlist of Anglo-Saxon Manuscripts: A List of Manuscripts and Manuscript Fragments Written or Owned in England up to 1100*, MRTS, 241 (Tempe, 2001). The fifth item is also found on the donation list of Bishop Leofric of Exeter. At his death in 1072, Leofric donated his personal library to Exeter Cathedral. One of those books was listed as 'liber Prudentii de martyribus', identified by Michael Lapidge as the *Peristephanon*. Michael Lapidge, 'Surviving Booklists From Anglo-Saxon England', in *Anglo-Saxon Manuscripts: Basic Readings*, ed. by Mary P. Richards, Basic Readings in Anglo-Saxon England, 2 (New York, 1994), pp. 87–167, item X.37, p. 135. (Another item on this list is Amalarius's *Liber officialis*, now Cambridge, Trinity College, MS B. 2. 2 of the second half of the tenth century.)

purposes'.[64] Early medieval liturgical practice is illustrated by two continental exemplars. They are the primary witnesses to the Roman liturgy of Rogationtide. A ninth-century ordinal of St Amand (Paris, Bibliothèque nationale de France, fonds latin 974), directs the poor to leave the almshouse, process with a cross, sing the *Kyrie eleison*, and then ask for the prayers of Christ and Mary. A litany follows. In order, the celestial powers invoked are Christ, Mary, St Peter, St Paul, St Andrew, St John, St Stephen, St Laurence, the saint who is patron to the church in which the Mass is celebrated, and all the saints.[65] A second continental example, the eleventh-century Romano-German pontifical, contains this same litany. Unfortunately, we do not know at what point during the Anglo-Saxon procession a litany was recited. The Sarum use puts the litany after the seven Penitential Psalms and before a series of prayers uttered prior to entering the church.

The procession that follows these prayers has symbolic relevance to Ælfric's sermons, especially as concerns his catechetical theme. The procession is meant to demonstrate the coordinated and directed advance of the Church (that is, of believers). In part, the procession is also a means of demonstrating the limits of the Church — who is and who is not a member. According to the Sarum use, an antiphon begins the procession: 'Surgite sancti de mansionibus uestris; loca sanctificate, plebum benedicite, et nos humiles peccatores in pace custodite, alleluia' ('Rise, Holy One, from your dwellings; sanctify these places, bless the people, and watch over us humble sinners in peace. Alleluia'). The procession then moves out singing Psalm 66: 'May God be merciful unto us, and bless us, and cause his face to shine upon us.'[66] Patristic commentators say that the psalm's 'us' indicates that this psalm is a benediction called for by the whole people, rather than one given by a priest.[67] Augustine concludes of this psalm that what gives us joy is 'the devotion

---

[64] *Anglo-Saxon Litanies*, ed. by Lapidge, p. 46.

[65] *Anglo-Saxon Litanies*, ed. by Lapidge, p. 40.

[66] Alternative antiphons include Psalm 131, 'Lord, remember for David all his affliction'; Psalm 121, 'I was glad when they said unto me, Let us go unto the house of the Lord'; Psalm 67, 'Let God arise, let his enemies be scattered; let them also that hate him flee before him'; and Psalm 68, 'Save me, O God; for the waters are come in unto my soul'.

[67] A benediction given by a priest is illustrated in Numbers 6. 24–27, a blessing by Aaron; Terrien, *Psalms*, p. 483. Augustine likens God in this blessing of 66. 2 to a farmer 'compluenti nos et colenti', Augustine, *Enarrationes*, CCSL, 39, p. 856, lines 14–15 ('who sends rain on us and cultivates us', trans. by Boulding, *Expositions of the Psalms*, III, 307). Perhaps coincidentally, Rogation processions include the blessing of fields and cattle.

of those who confess and the deeds of those whose lives are upright'.[68] Like the procession itself, the psalm is thought to emphasize the body of believers, those who confess Christianity. As we have seen, Ælfric spends a good deal of time in his Rogationtide sermons discussing who is and who is not a Christian. Moreover, the activity of the procession — its movement — is significant of a need for an active life in faith. Similarly, Ælfric writes that Christians earn the consolation of heaven by doing good: 'we geearnian þæt ece lif mid gode' ('we earn eternal life with good deeds').[69] Cassiodorus comments on this psalm that a Christian cannot earn God's blessing by merit alone, but needs prayer and confession.[70] Again, Ælfric says of God, 'He commanded us also to be watchful in prayers, repeatedly praying with bold faith, that we may escape from future harm'.[71] Ælfric emphasizes, like this liturgy's Psalm 66, the blessings possible through prayer. After Psalm 66, two psalm antiphons follow: 131. 1, 'memento Domine David et omnis mansuetudinis eius' ('O Lord, remember David, and all his meekness'), and 121. 1, 'laetatus sum in his quae dicta sunt mihi in domum Domini ibimus' ('I rejoiced in the things that were said to me: we shall go into the house of the Lord'). These antiphons are also steeped in patristic commentary. Cassiodorus notes that 131. 1 implies God's patience, and Augustine remarks that the psalm calls for our humility and, further-more, is not the voice of one man singing but of all who are in the body of Christ.[72] Like Psalm 66, this last antiphon stresses the body of the Church, and perhaps makes necessary Ælfric's explicit delineation in his sermons on Rogationtide of who precisely belongs to Christ's Body.

---

[68] 'Et quam non delectemur nisi profectibus uestris, in istis autem laudibus quam periclitemur, ille nouerit', Augustine, *Enarrationes*, CCSL, 39, p. 868, lines 53–55 ('God knows that it is your progress, and nothing else, that delights us', trans. by Boulding, *Expositions of the Psalms*, III, 323).

[69] *CH* II.19, line 298 (p. 189). See also *CH* I.19, lines 174–75 (p. 331): 'geearnian þæt ece rice ond þa ecan blisse mid gode'.

[70] Cassiodorus, *Explanation of the Psalms*, trans. by P. G. Walsh, 3 vols (New York, 1991), II, 117.

[71] *CH* II.19, lines 271–73 (p. 188): 'He het us eac beon on gebedum wacole gelomlice us biddende mid bealdum geleafan þæt we moton forfleon ða toweardan frecednysse.'

[72] Cassiodorus, *Psalms*, III, 322; Augustine, *Enarrationes*, CCSL, 40, p. 1898, lines 1–3: 'In isto psalmo commendatur nobis humilitas serui Dei et fidelis, cuius uoce cantatur, quod est uniuersum corpus Christi.' Verse four, which refers to tribes, speaks to the delineation of the faithful, as Ælfric has done.

The role of prayer in securing peace is now stressed once more. The processing church comes to its next station, which requires a prayer to St Valentine and a request for grace in return for penance:

Ad s. ualentinum. Deus, qui culpas delinquentium districte, feriendo percutis, fletus quoque lugentium non recuses, ut qui pondus tuae animaduersione[-*is*] cognouimus, etiam pietatis gratiam sentiamus.

[*To St Valentine.* 'God, you who firmly strike down the sins of offenders, do not refuse the tears of the mourners, as we who recognize the weight of your reproach, let us also know the grace of your mercy.']73

The reference to tears and to the reciprocity implicit in their offering recalls Psalm 6. 9–10, 'exaudiuit Dominus uocem fletus mei | exaudiuit Dominus deprecationem meam | Dominus orationem meam suscepit' ('The Lord hath heard the voice of my weeping. The Lord hath heard my supplication: the Lord hath received my prayer'). This psalm is the first of the Penitential Psalms mentioned above. Cassiodorus comments in respect of these verses that persistent prayer 'appeases [God] by its insistence'.74 Similarly, in his first Monday sermon, Ælfric writes that even though there might be some delay in God's response, 'ne sceole we for ði þære bene geswican' ('we should not on that account desist from prayer').75 And further, 'Ælc þæra þe geornlice bitt, *and* þære bene ne geswicð, þam getiðað god þæs ecan lifes' ('To everyone who eagerly asks, and does not cease from prayer, God will grant everlasting life').76 The tradition of patristic commentary on Psalm 6, represented by Cassiodorus, seems to inform Ælfric's understanding of insistent prayer found in his sermons.

At this point in the procession, participants have considered several themes: an amelioration of suffering, the body of the Church, and a need for prayer. These themes are reiterated in the next antiphon, which sets the faithful if suffering Church against the enemies of God. The Sarum use directs that an antiphon from Psalm 67. 2 be sung: 'Exsurgat Deus, et dissipentur inmici eius et fugiant qui oderunt eum a facie eius' ('Let God arise, and let His enemies be scattered, and let them that hate Him flee before His face'). This antiphon recalls *surgite* from the

---

73 See note 53 above.

74 Cassiodorus, *Psalms*, I, 97.

75 Ælfric, *Sermones catholici*, ed. by Benjamin Thorpe, 2 vols (Hildesheim, 1983), I, 248. This phrase does not seem to be in Clemoes's *CH* I.18, pp. 319–20, where Thorpe's p. 248 is presumably collated. I cannot explain Clemoes's apparent omission.

76 *CH* I.18, lines 94–96 (p. 320).

opening prayer of the procession, and thereby compels the prayerful to compare them. The first prayer calls directly on God to rise; this antiphon asks indirectly that God arise. The difference in mood may point to another difference: the first is a call by all the people; the second is a benediction by a priest. Symbolically, and as a recollection of the appointment of Aaron as high priest in the desert, this benediction suggests that the body of faithful now speaks through one sanctified voice. As to the second phrase in this antiphon, Cassiodorus comments that the psalmist 'appropriately proclaims what is to befall the Lord's enemies, and what is to happen to the faithful at the judgement to come'.[77] In one Monday sermon, Ælfric says that Christians will not rise from ignorance or darkness to eternal life if they do not believe in the Trinity.[78] We see here a rationale for Ælfric's emphasis on fundamental Christian doctrine — by their faith will Christians be identified at the judgement to come. As to the third phrase in this antiphon, to remind the faithful of the enemies of God, Ælfric describes in his Tuesday sermon the demons that appear to Fursa; and, to reinforce the reality of the heavenly realm, Ælfric describes paradise as seen by men who are 'of þissum life gelædde' ('led out of this [earthly] life').[79] In a physical analogy, the processors will be heading back to their church, whose entrance is called the *Paradisum*, and which will soon house the repentant body of processing Christians. The antiphon thus reminds Christian participants literally and figuratively that their suffering has a larger purpose and a distant goal.

Speaking to the theme of suffering's larger purpose, Psalm 68. 1 and 68. 17 follow. This psalm is traditionally seen as prophetic of Christ's suffering and passion. Cassiodorus remarks that the first portion of the psalm is spoken in the voice of Christ who 'begs the Father to grant Him safety, since He has suffered many hardships and attacks undeservedly'.[80] The verses read, 'Save me, O God; for the waters are come in unto my soul', and 'Answer me, O Lord; for thy mercy is good: according to the multitude of thy tender mercies turn thou unto me'. Ælfric consoles his audience in his second Monday sermon with the story of Job, whom God forgave (*CH* II.19, p. 188). He tells them to forbear, as Job did, through many harms that come to middle earth over the children of men. In another Rogationtide sermon, Ælfric describes how Christ prayed to his father and asked for forgiveness (*CH* II.22, p. 206). The waters of Psalm 68 are reflected in the next

---

[77] Cassiodorus, *Psalms*, II, 121.

[78] *CH* I.18, lines 63–65 (p. 319).

[79] *CH* II.21, line 113 (p. 203). The dream of Fursa is described in *CH* II.20, pp. 190–98.

[80] Cassiodorus, *Psalms*, II, 141.

prayer over the Milvian Bridge, which echoes Joel's call to repentance (2. 17, *parce populus tuo*, 'spare your people'). It asks for the redemption offered by God, specifically in the form of Christ: 'Parce, domine, qu*æ*sumus, parce populo tuo, et nullis iam patiaris aduersitatibus fatigari, quos precioso filii tui sanguine redemisti' ('Spare, O Lord, we beseech thee, spare your people, and now permit them to be worn down by no adversity, whom you have redeemed by the precious blood of your son'). Ælfric, too, reminds his audience that it is through Christ alone that redemption comes (*CH* II.22, p. 207 and p. 209). The next station, the cross, requires a prayer that speaks to themes already familiar to participants in the procession: redemption had through suffering and a need for mercy and consolation: 'Deus, qui culpas nostras piis uerberibus percutis, ut a nostris iniquitatibus emundes, da nobis et de uerbere tuo proficere, et de tua citius consolatione gaudere' ('O God, you who strike down our sins with righteous blows in order to cleanse us of our iniquities, grant to us that we benefit on account of your blows, and rejoice swiftly in your consolation'). Although this prayer echoes the themes surrounding the liturgical psalms, punishment was a pedagogic technique, as illustrated at the beginning of Ælfric's *Colloquy*. Punishment can be retributive, but it can also indicate that the recipient has done wrong. To punish a man is also to demand that he admit his wrongdoing. Augustine comments that Psalm 68 (which is sung near the end of the Rogationtide procession) calls for penance since 'the sinner who has lost the ability to confess is truly dead'.[81] Ælfric emphasizes the importance of confession and prayer in the process of redemption, apparently even in the life of Christ. He writes, 'Nu forgeaf se almihtiga fæder his ancennedan suna' ('Now the almighty Father forgave his only-begotten son').[82]

God's mercy is a topic stressed in both the procession and in Ælfric's sermons. At the next station, the processors have approached their church. The prayer *In atrio* reads, 'Adesto, domine, supplicationibus nostris, et sperantes in tua misericordia, intercedente beato petro apostolo tuo, caelesti protege benignus auxilio' ('Be at hand, gracious Lord, for our supplications, protect us who are hopeful on account of your mercy and through the intercession of the blessed apostle Peter with heavenly aid'). *Adesto* recalls Psalm 144. 18, 'Prope est Dominus omnibus inuocantibus eum' ('The Lord is near to all who call upon him'), something Ælfric will also claim in his sermons for the day. Psalm 68 closes with a promise to sing a

---

[81] Augustine, *Enarrationes*, CCSL, 39, p. 916, lines 22–23: 'Perditit enim confessionem; uere mortuus est'; trans. by Boulding, *Expositions of the Psalms*, III, 382. To Augustine, the waters represent the crowds who persecute Christ.

[82] *CH* II.22, lines 44–45 (p. 207).

song to the Lord, and an expectation that all of creation will sing praise as well. Then, as a ward against mortality in time of war, an antiphon follows, 'Free, O Lord, your people from the hand of death, and defend this people by your right hand, that living we may bless thee, Lord, our God', followed by Psalm 8, 'O Lord, our God, how excellent is thy name in all the earth'. This beseeching antiphon, followed by the psalmic praise of God, is reminiscent of the movement of the previous psalm, as well as of Psalms 55 and 56, both of which are Proper to this procession. Both ask God to pity men in return for their praise. Ælfric in his sermons for these days will continually stress God's mercy as well as a need to pray. Psalm 8 picks up on the last strophe of Psalm 68, witnessing the marvel of creation as itself praise of the Lord. At the same time, Psalm 8 illustrates the relative smallness of man, echoing the answer God gives Job after intense suffering, alluded to in Ælfric's second Monday sermon.[83] The psalm also speaks about the glory of the Lord's ascension above the heavens, also appropriate for a feast that ends at Ascension.

The themes of the procession are now gathered together during the Mass, when they will be reiterated in part by the Proper and in part by Ælfric. Once the processors have passed through the *Paradisum* and back into the church, Mass begins. As described above, the prayer following the introit beseeches God for his protection and trusts that his mercy will follow upon the congregants' affliction. Following the Gospel and Offertory, the prayer known as the Secret asks again for God's mercy. The Prefatory prayer speaks about the logic of this service: 'Aeterne deus. Et te auctorem et sanctificatorem ieiunii conlaudare, per quod nos liberas a nostrorum *debitis* peccatorum. Ergo suscipe ieiunantium pr[a]eces, atque ut nos a malis omnibus propitiatus eripias, iniquitates nostras, quibus merito affligimur, placatus absolue' ('Eternal God, both Father and sanctifier of fasting, we praise you on account of which you free us from the debts of our sins. Therefore receive the prayers of those fasting, so that you, having been placated, take us away from all our sins, absolve us of our iniquities, by which we are deservedly afflicted'). At this point, the various themes of the procession and its prayers have been comprehended in the Prefatory prayer.

The exchange of prayerful fasting for release from suffering is central to the Rogationtide liturgy. Since God will undoubtedly fulfill His portion of the bargain, a successful exchange depends upon the promises of men, on the vows made in

---

[83] The psalm's title speaks of winepresses, which Augustine says indicate churches: 'Torcularia ergo possemus accipere ecclesias' (Augustine, *Enarratione*, CCSL, 38, p. 49, lines 5–19). Churches separate the good from the evil according to the intentions of one's heart.

their prayers. Cassian calls prayer a kind of oath or vow.[84] In this vein, we might consider the benediction of the Mass:

> Omnipotens deus deuotionem uestram dignanter intendat, et suae uobis benedictionis dona concedat. Amen. Indulgeat uobis mala omnia, quae gessistis, et tribuat ueniam quam ab eo deposcitis. Amen. Sicque ieiunii uestri, et precum uota suscipiat, ut a uobis adversa omnia, quae peccatorum retributione meremini, auertat, et donum in uobis spiritus paraclyti infundat. Amen.

> [May the Omnipotent God kindly hear your devotions, may He grant you the gifts of his blessings. Amen. May He pardon all your evils, which you have borne, and may He grant forgiveness which you ask of Him. Amen. And then may He receive the vows [or petitions or oaths] of your fasting and prayers, so that he may turn away all adversities from you, which you earn as retribution for your sins, and may He pour forth upon you the gifts of the consoling Spirit. Amen.][85]

Here we see some of the implicit assumptions that govern parts of this liturgy made more explicit. Fasting and repentance please the Lord, and He in return (but not solely on that account) offers grace and consolation.[86] In that consolation, each person may grow in the love of God towards eternal salvation. As we have seen, Ælfric stresses the need for love above and beyond good works. These themes are also the substance of the postcommunion prayer, as described above. Even clearer is the prayer over the people, 'Pretende nobis, domine, misericordiam tuam, ut quae uotis expetimus, conuersatione tibi placita consequamur' ('Extend to us, Lord, your mercy, so that through our repentance [*conuersatione*], which is pleasing to you, we may attain what we seek through our petitions [or vows or oaths]').

---

[84] Cassian, *Conferences*, 9.12.1, 'Prayers are those acts by which we offer or vow something to God, which is called [*euxi*] in Greek — that is, a vow' (trans. by Boniface Ramsey (New York: Newman Press, 1997)). And Isidore, *Etymologiae*, 6.19.59, 'orare est petere' (*PL* 82.257B; 'to pray is to entreat'). And Tertullian, *De ieiunio aduersus psychicos*, ed. by A. Reifferscheid and G. Wissowa, Corpus scriptorum ecclesiasticorum latinorum, 20 (Vienna, 1890), p. 289, line 11: 'Tamen et uotum, cum a deo acceptatum est, legem in posterum facit per auctoritatem acceptatoris' ('Even a vow, when it has been accepted by God, constitutes a law for posterity, on account of the authority of the acceptor').

[85] See note 53 above.

[86] Thus St Augustine, *Enchiridion*, in *Nicene and Post-Nicene Fathers*, 1st series, 14 vols (Peabody, MA, 1994), vol. III, ch. 19: 'For the passing and trivial sins of every day, from which no life is free, the everyday prayer of the faithful makes satisfaction. For they can say, "Our Father who art in heaven", who have already been reborn to such a Father "by water and the Spirit". This prayer completely blots out our minor and everyday sins. It also blots out those sins which once made the life of the faithful wicked, but from which, now that they have changed for the better by repentance, they have departed.'

Much the same sentiment is found in the Gospel for the day, at Luke 11. 10: 'Ask, and you will receive.'[87] The point that Bede and Ælfric both make in their homilies on Rogationtide, and one implicit in the procession itself, is that one must actively seek, one must ask.

Ælfric emphasizes in his sermons that Rogationtide's exchange of prayer for relief from suffering depends not only upon vows, but also upon the unity of the Christian community. Ælfric calls *Litaniae* 'gebeddagas', or prayer days, as the Roman feast emphasizes. Other homilies, Vercelli among them, also call these *gangdaegas*, or procession days.[88] This going out of the church, turning, and coming back to the church is central to the messages of the feast. The faithful call out to the Lord from the church at the outset of the feast. Thus, the introit from Psalm 17. 7 reads, 'Exaudiuit de templo sancto suo uocem meam' ('He heard from afar my voice from your holy temple'). Voices in prayer call out to the Lord from a temple. The *temple* — the Latin word is also used in vernacular texts (as in Vercelli XX) — is not equivalent to the Old English term *cirice*, which usually glosses *ecclesia*.[89] The temple is the sacred altar of the Lord, and its ministers are priests and monks. But, in his first sermon for Rogation Tuesday, Ælfric says that 'the good man is a temple [*templ*] of the Holy Ghost'.[90] So, when Ælfric says in his first Monday sermon that we 'offer up *our* prayers, and follow *our* relics out and in', he presumably means the prayers of both clerics and Christian laymen.[91] This invocation of a Christian community accords with the benediction of the procession from Psalm 66, described above, in which the whole people calls for God's mercy. The unity of the people in Christian fellowship accords with and explains Ælfric's discussion of who is and who is not one's neighbour. That the introit and processional benediction are spoken by a priest suggests that the progress of the people, as in a procession, depends upon the proper direction of clergy and teachers. Again, the liturgy evokes themes found in Ælfric's Rogationtide sermons.

---

[87] Bede points this out in his own homilies on Rogationtide: the promise is made by God in Matthew 7. 21; Bede, *Homilies on the Gospels*, trans. by Lawrence T. Martin and David Hurst, 2 vols (Kalamazoo, 1991), II, 124. The pericope for Bede is Luke 11. 9–13.

[88] Vercelli XI, XII, and XIII; see *Eleven Old English Rogationtide Homilies*, ed. by Bazire and Cross, p. xviii.

[89] Bazire-Cross 2, p. 31, line 11. For glosses, see Mattie Harris, *A Glossary of the West Saxon Gospels* in *Word-Indices to Old English Non-Poetic Texts* (Hamden, 1974), pp. 1–115, s.v.

[90] *CH* I.19, line 67 (p. 327): 'se goda man bið þæs halgan gastes templ'.

[91] *CH* I.18, lines 40–41 (p. 318): 'began ure gebedu ond fylian urum haligdomum ut ond in'.

Ælfric echoes the liturgy most significantly in his emphasis on *conuersatione*. In the prayer over the people *conuersatio*, literally 'a turning', also means conduct or behaviour. Turning to God, as enacted at the cross during the procession, pleases him. The processors come to the cross, pray, and then convert to the Church, through which they will find salvation. In his first sermon for Monday, Ælfric relates that Bishop Mamertus of Vienna instituted a fast in order to stop God's scourging the city. The king's palace, says Ælfric, 'was burnt with heavenly fire [*heofonlicum fyre*]'. So, king, people, children, and animals all fasted for three days, and 'through that conversion [*gecyrrednysse*] [...] God had mercy on them'.[92] This same fire had earlier burnt Sodom and Gomorrah. It is God's righteous anger.[93] It is the purging fire of the apocalyptic visions of Fursa and Drihthelm that fill Ælfric's sermons for the second Tuesday of Rogationtide. The *conuersatio* is pivotal to the exchange that is made during this feast, as Paul Szarmach has pointed out in his study of the Jonah story, and is equally essential to Ælfric's Monday homilies.[94] God exchanges his mercy for penitence, and for prayers withdraws his anger.[95] This exchange of prayer for terrestrial bounty is also found in social relations. As described above, Ælfric speaks in his first Monday sermon about the relation of poor to rich: 'The rich man is made for the poor man, and the poor man for the rich one. It is incumbent on the affluent, that he scatter and distribute; on the indigent it is incumbent that he pray for the distributor'.[96] As the rich man gives sustenance to the poor man, so does the poor man 'give to the rich everlasting life'.[97] Prayers are

---

[92] *CH* I.18, lines 34–39 (p. 318): 'mid heofenlicum fyre forbærnde'; 'þa ðurh ða gecyrrednysse [...] him gemiltsode god'.

[93] Thus, in the 'Second Commentary on the Gospels' of the Canterbury biblical commentaries, we find that someone who *saepe cadit in ignem* ('falleth often into the fire') is 'someone whom anger overcomes'. See Matthew 17. 4. In Bernhard Bischoff and Michael Lapidge, *Biblical Commentaries from the Canterbury School of Theodore and Hadrian*, CSASE, 10 (Cambridge, 1994), pp. 404–05. See also Vercelli XIX, and Alcuin, *Enchiridon*, who comments on Psalm 6. 2 that *furor* (anger) signifies 'ignem purgatorium' (*PL* 100.575AB; 'a purgative fire').

[94] Szarmach, 'Three Versions of the Jonah Story', p. 185: 'a change of heart during Rogationtide will result in divine forgiveness'.

[95] See more explicitly, Maximus of Turin, *Sermo LXXXI: De Ieiuniis Niniuitarum*, CCSL, 23, pp. 332–34, especially p. 334.

[96] *CH* I.18, lines 205–07 (p. 324): 'Se welega is geworht for ðan þearfan. ond se þearfa for ðam welegan. Ðam spedigum gedafenaþ þæt he spende ond dæle. ðam wædlan gedafenað þæt he gebidde for ðam dælere.'

[97] *CH* I.18, line 210 (p. 324): 'sylð þam rican þæt ece lif'.

part and parcel of the world's exchanges. One commentator has perhaps misproposed this exchange as the 'prayers of the poor *to* the rich'.[98]

When we ask why Ælfric's Rogationtide homilies discuss the poor, explain the Apostles' Creed, stress prayer and grace, relate dream visions of heaven, and stress good works, we ask why Ælfric chose to emphasize these particular themes and not others. Of all the topics and themes Ælfric might have addressed, he chose to compose or to select passages which fulfilled the mandate of the Rogationtide liturgy. This mandate is to encourage blessings and bounty, to stop war, to heal the sick, and to abate the fiery anger of God.[99] Rogationtide coheres in its progression and reiteration of themes, themes distinct from those of, for example, the Easter liturgy. During the Rogationtide Mass, the Christian seeks blessedness through progressive and varied striving. This striving (for penance, forgiveness, understanding, and mercy) is re-enacted physically during the Rogationtide services. Rogationtide liturgy serially invokes suffering, resignation, wisdom, and joy. A celebrant moves from place to place, moment to moment, prayer to prayer, in a constant ritual peregrination. The themes of Rogationtide are manifested in the liturgy, specifically in those elements proper to the feast. Ælfric's sermons, *qua* sermons, contribute generally to the efficacy of the Rogationtide Mass, and therefore find their principle of coherence within a liturgical ordo. But Ælfric's method of composition, his principles of selection and invention, required him to look beyond his library to the symbolism and thematic coherence of the Rogationtide liturgy.

---

[98] Godden, *Introduction, Commentary, and Glossary*, p. 145.

[99] Thus, Cassian, 'Ninth Conference: On Prayer', 9.3.3, pp. 330–31.

Practice

REREADING THE STYLE AND RHETORIC
OF THE VERCELLI HOMILIES

Samantha Zacher

Aesthetic and literary criteria have, in general, not been high on the list for evaluating Old English homiletic prose. Though the considerable work of several scholars has taught us better to tune our ears to hear the 'lyrical' stress-patterns and the artful use of formulas cultivated especially in the homilies of Ælfric and Wulfstan,[1] many of us nevertheless still need to be reminded to listen for the (albeit less predictable and habitual) skilled use of rhythms, stylistic flourishes, and complex rhetorical patternings of those anonymous homilies that comprise the wider homiletic corpus. But even where the often scrutinized prose works of Ælfric and Wulfstan are concerned, the critical attention to manuscript context and source study has, overall, continued to play formidable king to the seemingly secondary analysis of form and rhetoric.[2] This criticism has been especially true of the anonymous homilies contained in the Vercelli Book, where

---

[1] One of the most important discussions of Wulfstan's two-stress style remains that by Angus McIntosh, 'Wulfstan's Prose', *Publications of the British Academy*, 35 (1949), 109–42; for further analysis, see Andy Orchard, 'Re-editing Wulfstan: Where's the Point?', in *Wulfstan, Archbishop of York: The Proceedings of the Second Alcuin Conference*, ed. by Matthew Townend, Studies in the Early Middle Ages, 10 (Turnhout, 2004), pp. 63–92. For studies of Ælfric's alliterative prose, see *Homilies of Ælfric: A Supplementary Collection*, ed. by John C. Pope, EETS: OS, 259–60 (London, 1967–68), I, 105–36. Also see Anne Middleton, 'Ælfric's Answerable Style: The Rhetoric of the Alliterative Prose', *Studies in Medieval Culture*, 4 (1973), 83–91.

[2] For an early analysis of Old English prose styles using Latin rhetorical devices, see J. W. Tupper, *Tropes and Figures in Anglo-Saxon Prose* (Baltimore, 1897). On the study of prose style specifically in relation to Old English homilies, see especially the collection of essays in *The Old English Homily and its Background*, ed. by Paul E. Szarmach and Bernard F. Huppé (Albany, 1978).

the collection's variety of authorship, subject matter, and form has been notoriously difficult to pin down with any formalizing consistency.[3] As late as 1978, in what is now widely regarded as one of the formative essays on the style and structure of the Vercelli homilies, Paul Szarmach had this to lament about the scholarly treatment of the Vercelli Book: 'This historically important collection has [. . .] received very little attention for its strictly literary characteristics.'[4] Though several partial editions and facsimiles had been available since the manuscript's first transcription in 1834,[5] a considerable milestone in the study and appreciation of the homilies can be traced to the publication of Donald Scragg's edition of all twenty-three homilies, which came equipped with a weighty critical apparatus highlighting some of the variants and known sources, so providing scholars with an invaluable point of reference.[6] In addition to a wellspring of recent articles on the subject of the homilies, the past few years have seen the emergence of several book-length studies devoted to either the prose texts alone or the wider manuscript context.[7]

---

[3] Primarily for these reasons Milton Mc C. Gatch called the Vercelli Book a sui generis collection, in his *Preaching and Theology in Anglo-Saxon England: Ælfric and Wulfstan* (Toronto, 1977), p. 57.

[4] Paul E. Szarmach, 'The Vercelli Homilies: Style and Structure', in *Old English Homily*, ed. by Szarmach and Huppé, pp. 241–67 (p. 242).

[5] The Vercelli Homilies have also been edited in whole or in part in the following published editions (in reverse chronological order): Paul E. Szarmach, *Vercelli Homilies IX–XXIII*, Toronto Old English Series, 5 (Toronto, 1981); M. Förster, *Die Vercelli-Homilien*, vol. I: *I–VIII. Homilie*, BaP, 12 (Hamburg, 1932; repr. Darmstadt, 1964) and also 'Der Vercelli-Codex CXVII nebst Abdruck einiger altenglischer Homilien der Handschrift', in *Festschrift für Lorenz Morsbach*, ed. by Ferdinand Holthausen and H. Spies, Studien zur englischen Philologie, 50 (Halle, 1913), pp. 20–179 (also published separately, Halle, 1913). Unpublished editions by different authors include Sr M. Corfilia Pinski, 'Six Unpublished Homilies in the Vercelli Manuscript' (unpublished doctoral dissertation, University of Ottawa, 1966); Paul Peterson, 'The Unpublished Homilies of the Old English Vercelli Book' (unpublished doctoral dissertation, New York University, 1951); Rudolph Willard, 'The Vercelli Homilies: An Edition of Seven Homilies from the Old English Vercelli Codex' (unpublished doctoral dissertation, Yale University, 1925). Two facsimiles have likewise been published: *The Vercelli Book: A Late Tenth-Century Manuscript Containing Prose and Verse (Vercelli Biblioteca Capitolare CXVII)*, ed. by Celia Sisam, EEMF, 19 (Copenhagen, 1976); and Max Förster, *Il Codice Vercellese con Omelie e Poesie in Lingua Anglo-sassone* (Rome, 1913).

[6] *The Vercelli Homilies and Related Texts*, ed. by Donald G. Scragg, EETS: OS, 300 (Oxford, 1992); all quotations from the Vercelli Book are from this edition; translations are my own.

[7] See *Vercelli tra oriente ed occidente tra tarda antichità e medioevo*, ed. by Vittoria Docetti Corazza, Bibliotecha Germanica: studi e testi, 6 (Alessandria, 1998); also see the impending volumes by Andy Orchard and Samantha Zacher, *New Readings on the Vercelli Book* (Toronto,

In the following discussion, I hope to present a general (and obviously highly selective) introduction to some of the major studies of the Vercelli homilies, paying special attention to those that take a 'literary' approach to the prose texts. In addition, the essay will attempt to outline some of the current (and also decidedly traditional) methodologies that have been used to undertake stylistic and rhetorical analysis of these texts, offered partially with the transparent hope of enticing newcomers to pour as lovingly over the prose contents of the manuscript as they have done with the poetic portions. Finally, a rhetorical and stylistic analysis of just one of the Vercelli homilies will be presented, in order to 'put into practice' some of the approaches explored or referenced in the essay. Though it is impossible finally for such a small sampling to speak for its whole, especially in the case of the Vercelli Book, where there is such a diversity of authorship and styles, it is hoped that this brief examination will be able to provide a taste of the richness of the prose texts in the Vercelli Book.

The Vercelli Manuscript

The so-called Vercelli Book (Vercelli, Biblioteca Capitolare, MS CXVII) has long been recognized as one of the most important surviving collections of Old English prose and poetry.[8] Dated paleographically to the last quarter of the tenth century, the codex takes its familiar title from its current location in Northern Italy.[9]

---

forthcoming), and Samantha Zacher, *Preaching the Converted: Anglo-Saxon Rhetoric and Style in the Vercelli Book Homilies* (Toronto, forthcoming); since this book is forthcoming, references will henceforth correspond to Samantha Zacher, 'The Style and Rhetoric of the Vercelli Homilies' (unpublished doctoral dissertation, University of Toronto, 2003; abstract in *Dissertation Abstracts International – A*, 64 (2003), 1249).

[8] Though the manuscript survives in this unique copy, it is clear that the Vercelli scribe was working from prefabricated collections of homilies that circulated independently of the Vercelli manuscript; some of the tell-tale signs include marks in the manuscript of independent numeration (as in homilies VI–X, where the numbers ii–v are attached to the final four of these homilies), rubrication (as in Vercelli XI–XIV, where the first three homilies are designated for Rogationtide and the last for 'whatever time one wishes'), and sometimes even titles linked sequentially across several of the Vercelli homilies in a row (as in Vercelli XI–XIV and XV–XVIII). For a fuller discussion of these exemplars, see Donald Scragg, 'The Compilation of the Vercelli Book', *ASE*, 2 (1973), 189–207, repr. in *Anglo-Saxon Manuscripts: Basic Readings*, ed. by Mary P. Richards, Basic Readings in Anglo-Saxon England, 2 (New York, 1994), pp. 317–43.

[9] The collection of Vercelli poems as a whole is regarded on paleographical grounds as one of the earliest of the four extant major poetic codices; however, a recent redating of the Junius

Though the manuscript was likely already in Italy before 1100 (the main evidence being an inscription in a twelfth-century Italian hand of a portion of the Latin Psalter), it is unknown how the manuscript ended up in its present location; it has been suggested that it was left there (wittingly or unwittingly) by an Anglo-Saxon pilgrim headed to or returning from Rome, or perhaps even intending specifically to go to Vercelli.[10] The manuscript itself was compiled and written in England, apparently by a single scribe, and perhaps over an extended period of time.[11]

The Vercelli Book contains a unique combination and arrangement of poetry and prose. The six poems contained in the manuscript are as follows: *Andreas* (fols 29ᵛ–52ᵛ), *Fates of the Apostles* (fols 52ᵛ–54ʳ), *Soul and Body I* (fols 101ᵛ–103ᵛ), *Homiletic Fragment I* (fol. 104ʳ⁻ᵛ), *Dream of the Rood* (fols 104ᵛ–106ʳ), and *Elene* (fols 121ʳ–133ᵛ). As can be seen from these folio numbers, the poems appear interspersed between the prose texts, an arrangement which has perhaps been veiled by the tendency to edit separately the poetry and verse.[12] The poetry in the manuscript needs little commentary here, as many of these texts will be recognizable even to the beginning student of Old English, but it is perhaps worth mentioning that the increased attention given to homiletic styles in the Vercelli Book has served to cast new light on what have been seen to be 'homiletic' features in each of these poems. Particularly noteworthy in this regard have been the thematic and verbal

---

manuscript to 960–90 by Leslie Lockett ('An Integrated Re-examination of the Dating of Oxford, Bodleian Library, Junius 11', *ASE*, 31 (2002), 141–73) would place this codex earlier than the Vercelli Book.

[10] For a consideration of the manuscript's date (and cause) of arrival in Vercelli, see most recently Éamonn Ó Carragáin, 'Rome, Ruthwell, Vercelli: *The Dream of the Rood* and the Italian Connection', in *Vercelli tra oriente ed occidente*, ed. by Corazza, pp. 59–100 (pp. 93–97); Ó Carragáin highlights in particular the attractiveness of the shrine of St Eusebius (located in Vercelli) for secular clerics in the period leading up to Edgar's reform. Also see *Vercelli Homilies*, ed. by Scragg, p. xxiv; *The Dream of the Rood*, ed. by Michael Swanton (Exeter, 1987), pp. 2–4; and Kenneth Sisam, *Studies in the History of Old English Literature* (Oxford, 1953; repr. 1998), pp. 113–15.

[11] Scragg's argument for an extended period of compilation is based on the general haphazardness with which he views the arrangement of texts in the Vercelli Book. For an opposing view of this organization, see Zacher, 'Style and Rhetoric', especially pp. 32–67. Also see Ó Carragáin, 'Rome, Ruthwell, Vercelli', pp. 91–92, who discusses the scribe's recopying of portions of the *Dream of the Rood* in order to splice it into the manuscript's booklet B; Ó Carragáin reads this as reflecting the compiler's intention of creating special continuity with regard to themes expressed in this portion of the manuscript.

[12] The standard edition of the Vercelli poems remains *The Vercelli Book*, ed. by Philip Krapp, Anglo-Saxon Poetic Records, 2 (New York, 1932; repr. 1969).

correspondences noted between the poem *Soul and Body I* and Vercelli IV and XXII (on the fate of the 'wicked' and 'good' soul), the 'homiletic' close to *The Dream of the Rood*, the sermon-like and exegetical speeches in *Elene*, and, as the title would suggest, the structure and theme of *Homiletic Fragment I*.[13] Certainly, the consideration of the poems within their manuscript context, and alongside of the prose, has proved mutually illuminating.

However, by far the majority of the Vercelli manuscript is comprised of prose texts. These are generally classified according to two main varieties: homilies and hagiographical prose, though as we shall see these terms are often misleading and insufficiently descriptive. Although prose texts XVIII and XXIII, dedicated to the lives of St Martin and St Guthlac respectively, are broadly hagiographic in focus and correspond in terms of theme, language, and style to both Latin sources and Old English analogues, certain stylistic criteria link them with homiletic discourse.[14] For example, not only does the Vercelli text on Guthlac introduce a series of stylistic modifications that seem consistent with that of homiletic prose, but it also appears to offer a new 'homiletic' ending, allowing Guthlac to be translated to heaven without first performing miracles. Likewise, Vercelli XVIII on St Martin telescopes the details of Martin's secular life to focus on his role as a soldier of Christ, all the while making elaborate use of exhortation, homiletic address, and conclusion.[15] An even stranger model, as we shall see, is Vercelli XVII, dedicated

---

[13] Jonathan T. Randle examines this generic overlap of poetry and prose in 'The Homiletic Context of the Vercelli Book Poems' (unpublished doctoral dissertation, University of Cambridge, 1999). For studies of the homiletic content of individual poems in the manuscript, see, for example, Éamonn Ó Carragáin, *Ritual and the Rood: Liturgical Images and the Old English Poems of the 'Dream of the Rood' Tradition* (Toronto, 2005); Gordon Whatley, 'Bread and Stone: Cynewulf's *Elene* 611–618', *NM*, 76 (1975), 550–60; and Charles D. Wright, 'The Pledge of the Soul: A Judgment Theme in Old English Homiletic Literature and Cynewulf's *Elene*', *NM*, 91 (1990), 23–30.

[14] Among the Old English treatments of these lives, there are two anonymous homilies found in Blickling and Oxford, Bodleian Library, MS Junius 86 (fols 62ʳ–81ʳ) (drawn from the same Latin exemplar as the text in Vercelli), as well as a life of St Martin in Ælfric's *CH* II.39 and in his *LS* II.31; while for Guthlac there are the two poems *Guthlac A* and *B* in the Exeter manuscript, there is also a fuller translation of the Latin *Vita* in London, British Library, Cotton MS Vespasian D. XXI (fols 18–40).

[15] The feast of St Martin is celebrated on November 11, while the feast of St Guthlac falls on April 11. For a list of conventional feast days celebrated in the Anglo-Saxon period, see Michael Lapidge, 'Ælfric's *Sanctorale*', in *Holy Men and Holy Women: Old English Prose Saints' Lives and their Contexts*, ed. by Paul E. Szarmach (Albany, 1996), pp. 115–29. See now Juliet Hewish, 'Living on the Edge: A Study of the Translations of the Life of St Martin into Old English,

to the Purification of the Virgin Mary. Though the text has at times been classified
as a saint's life, the piece only tangentially relates to the life of Mary herself (a phenomenon which owes in part to the newness of the celebration of the feast day),
and instead makes extensive use of recognizable biblical exegesis based primarily
upon its Gospel pericope in Luke 2. 22–32.

The eighteen remaining homilies likewise resist easy classification. Some of the
items clearly correspond to portions of the temporal cycle: Homily I is ostensibly
set for Good Friday; III for Lent; V and VI for Christmas; XI, XII, and XIII for
Rogationtide; XVI for the Epiphany; and XIX, XX, and XXI also for Rogationtide. But even where a liturgical function and order can be detected for these items,
such a broad characterization does not provide a clear index to the style of any
individual piece. To add to this confusion, although the blanket term 'homily' is
generally employed by its critics and editors for all the prose works in the Vercelli
Book, this term traditionally (and I suppose still properly) refers to exegetical texts,
while 'sermon' is conventionally employed for works whose primary focus is exhortation. The seven remaining homilies, by contrast, are usually described as being
either catechetical (in their emphasis upon points of general Christian doctrine)
or eschatological (in their emphasis upon Judgement Day) or both, and it is only
recently that more subtle distinctions have been formulated for describing this type
of homily.[16] These homilies tend to present some of the most iconographically
provocative and memorable passages in all of Old English literature. To choose one
example, the following response of the devil to the anchorite in Vercelli IX as he
explains the future punishment of the sinner offers a sense of the heightened
rhetoric found in the Vercelli texts:[17]

Middle Irish, and Old Norse–Icelandic' (unpublished doctoral dissertation, University College,
Dublin, 2005), especially pp. 116–87.

[16] Paul Szarmach skilfully addresses this problem in his 'The Vercelli Prose and Anglo-Saxon
Literary History', forthcoming in *New Readings on the Vercelli Book*, ed. by Orchard and Zacher.
I am grateful to Professor Szarmach for allowing me to cite from his work before its publication.

[17] For a discussion of the devil's speeches in Vercelli IX, see especially Charles D. Wright, 'The
Literary Mileu of Vercelli IX and the Irish Tradition', in *The Irish Tradition in Old English
Literature*, CSASE, 6 (Cambridge, 1993), pp. 215–71. Also see *Vercelli Homilies*, ed. by Scragg,
pp. 151–90, and his 'The Devil's Account of the Next World Revisited', *ANQ*, 24 (1986),
107–10. Scragg's article responds in part to Fred Robinson, 'The Devil's Account of the Next
World: An Anecdote from Old English Homiletic Literature', *NM*, 73 (1972), 362–71, repr. in
The Editing of Old English: Papers from the 1990 Manchester Conference, ed. by D. G. Scragg and
Paul E. Szarmach (Cambridge, 1994), pp. 196–205. This passage is supplied by Scragg from
Oxford, Bodleian Library, Hatton 113, fol. 76ʳ; a leaf is lost from the Vercelli Book at this point.

And he, se deofol, þa gyt cwæð to þam ancran: 'Gyf ænig mann wære ane niht on helle 7 he eft wære æfter þam ofalædd, 7 ðeah man þone garsecg mid isene utan ymbtynde, 7 þonne ealne gefylde mid fyres lige up oþ ðone heofonas hrof, 7 utan emsette hine þonne ealne mid byligeon 7 heora æghwylc oðres æthrinan mihte, 7 to æghwylcum þæra byligea wære man geset 7 se hæfde Samsones strengðe (se wæs ealra eorðwarena strengest þe ær oððe syððan æfre gewurde) 7 þeah man þonne gesette an brad isen þell ofer þæs fyres hrof, 7 þeah hit wære eall mid mannum afylled 7 ðæra æghwylc hæfde ænne hamor on handa, 7 þeah man bleowe mid eallum þam byligeon 7 mid þam hameron beote on þæt isene þell and se lig brastlode, ne awacode he næfre for eallum þisum, to ðam werig he wære for þære anre nihthwile.'

[And he, the devil, again said to the anchorite: 'if any man were one night in hell, and he afterwards were again led away, and though one surrounded the ocean about with iron, and then filled it completely with the fire's flame up to the roof of heaven, and surrounded it entirely with bellows, and each of them might touch one another, and a man were placed at each bellows, and he had the strength of Samson (he was the strongest of all earth-dwellers that ever might exist either before or after) and though one might set a broad iron plate over the roof of the fire, and though it were all filled with men, and though each had a hammer in hand, and though one might blow with all the bellows, and with the hammer beat on that iron plate and cause the fire to crackle, he would (nevertheless) never awake on account of all of this, because he would be weary on account of the duration of that single night.']

Though metaphor and simile are generally presumed by modern scholars to be the province of Old English poetry (so diverging from patristic treatments of figurative language as being essential to exegetical writing), this elaborate conceit dazzles both the ear and the imagination.[18] In the above passage, it is evident that as the homilist fashions his image of hellfire, he generates a parallel crescendo effect through his constant deferral of comparisons to known 'human' experiences that ultimately fall short of an imaginable hell-torment.[19] Though the conceits in Vercelli IX are particularly indulgent, the use of such figurative language and imaginings of both hell and heaven are nevertheless characteristic of many Vercelli homilies.[20]

---

[18] For a discussion of figurative language in the Vercelli Homilies, see Zacher, 'Style and Rhetoric', pp. 139–80. For the use of these figures elsewhere in prose, see Tupper, *Tropes and Figures*.

[19] For a discussion of related formulas in Old English literature, see especially Hildegard L. C. Tristram, 'Stock Descriptions of Heaven and Hell in Old English Prose and Poetry', *NM*, 79 (1978), 102–13.

[20] For visions in Vercelli Homilies of the joys of heaven, see especially Vercelli II.112–19, V.197–204, VIII.90–94, IX.168–209, X.263–75, XIV.141–47, XV.200–06, XIX.170–78, XX.197–203, XXI.238–55; for images of the horrors of hell, see especially Vercelli II.60,

But it is not just the admixture of form and style that makes the Vercelli collection appear to be so diversified in its content. It is also the choice and organization of the homilies as a unit. Whereas the traditional homiliary follows the order of the liturgical calendar, by contrast the Vercelli collection follows no parallel systematic calendrical program.[21] Instead, the manuscript offers what may (anachronistically) be described as a 'greatest hits' anthology of homilies for very specific feast days, probably grouped in this manner precisely for their emphasis upon such themes as sin, punishment, doomsday, and the corresponding reward for good works.[22] Indeed, the collection has all the earmarks of being (in the words of Ó Carragáin) 'one man's book', arranged and compiled to reflect the personal tastes of the compiler, or perhaps (being slightly more cautious) that of the close-knit community in which he lived.[23] The inclusion of poetry in the collection undoubtedly complicates how we view its particular arrangement, as the combination of homiletic and poetic genres is relatively rare both in Old English and Latin manuscripts.[24]

IV.51–56, VIII.75–87, IX.20–31 and 84–143, XXI.211–18, XXII.37–46 and 56–66 (all references here are from Robert DiNapoli, *An Index of Theme and Image to the Homilies of the Anglo-Saxon Church: Comprising the Homilies of Ælfric, Wulfstan, and the Blickling and Vercelli Codices* (Hockwold cum Wilton, 1995)).

[21] By contrast, the so-called Old English Blickling Book (Princeton, Princeton University Library, W. H. Scheide Collection, MS 71), with its partial *temporale* and *sanctorale*, can be considered a 'homiliary' proper. For editions, see *The Blickling Homilies of the Tenth Century*, ed. by Richard Morris, EETS: OS, 58, 63, 73 (London, 1874–80; repr. as one volume, 1967); the former edition should be consulted over *The Blickling Homilies: Edition and Translation*, ed. and trans. by Richard J. Kelly (London, 2003).

[22] Joyce Hill takes this view in 'Reform and Resistance: Preaching Styles in Late Anglo-Saxon England', in *De l'homélie au sermon: histoire de la prédication medievale, Actes du Colloque international de Louvain-la-Neuve*, ed. by Jaqueline Hamesse and Xavier Hermand (Louvain-la-Neuve, 1993), pp. 15–46 (p. 21); in Hill's words, these recurring themes include 'penitence, judgment, eschatology, and instruction on vices and virtues and on such basic Christian practices as prayer, fasting, and tithing'.

[23] Ó Carragáin, 'Rome, Ruthwell, Vercelli', p. 94.

[24] One of the better parallels for this intermixture remains the later eleventh-century Cambridge, Corpus Christi College, MS 201, which contains a miscellany of homilies and poetry in addition to law codes, liturgical items, lists, and the sui generis 'prose romance' *Apolonius of Tyre*. A discussion of the various genres in CCCC 201 can be found in *The Old English Poem Judgment Day II: A Critical Edition*, ed. by Graham D. Caie (Cambridge, 2000), pp. 1–24. For treatments specifically of the intersection between the poetry and prose texts in the manuscript, see for example Fred C. Robinson, 'The Rewards of Piety: Two Old English Poems in their Manuscript Context', in *Hermeneutics and Medieval Culture*, ed. by P. J. Gallacher and

Yet the inability to find a clear model to which we can compare the Vercelli collection is only a 'problem' insofar as it prompts questions relating to its audience and purpose. Since the variety and arrangement of the items in the manuscript have been argued to preclude its primary use in a preaching context, the alternative suggestion that the collection was intended to serve as a reading book for private devotion has garnered particular favour. Proponents of this theory have further attempted to posit a target audience for the manuscript. Milton Gatch (building on the work of Sisam) suggested the design of an ascetic florilegium, intended for monastic readers.[25] Others, more recently, have questioned the fitness of some of the homilies for a monastic audience and have proposed instead that the collection may have served as a canon's private book.[26] Arguing this perspective, Éamonn Ó Carragáin, for one, has suggested that 'there is no sign in the book that its compiler lived the full community life enjoined in the *Regularis Concordia*'. Charles D. Wright arrives independently at the same conclusion by focussing provocatively on the numerous references in homilies to private ownership and wealth, which seem incongruent with the belt-tightening spirit of the Benedictine Reform.[27] Recent surveys focussing on the Vercelli Book's apparent interest in female spirituality (for example, in Vercelli VII's lavish address to women, and in the poem *Elene*, which focuses on her contribution to the finding of the 'true cross')

H. Damico (Albany, 1989), pp. 193–200; and Samantha Zacher 'The Rewards of Poetry: "Homiletic" Verse in Cambridge, Corpus Christi College 201', *SELIM* [*La Sociedad Española de Lengua y Literatura Inglesa Medieval*], 12 (2003–04), 83–108.

[25] See Milton McC. Gatch, 'Eschatology in the Anonymous Old English Homilies', *Traditio*, 21 (1965), 117–65 (p. 144), and also *Preaching and Theology*, p. 103; Sisam, 'Marginalia in the Vercelli Book', in his *Studies in the History of Old English Literature*, p. 118; Éamonn Ó Carragáin, 'How Did the Vercelli Collector Interpret *The Dream of the Rood*?', in *Studies in English Language and Early Literature in Honour of Paul Christophersen*, ed. by P. M. Tilling, Occasional Papers in Language and Language Learning, 8 (Coleraine, 1981), pp. 66–67; and Mary Clayton, 'Homiliaries and Preaching in Anglo-Saxon England', *Peritia*, 4 (1985), 207–42, repr. with corrections in *Old English Prose: Basic Readings*, ed. by Paul E. Szarmach, Basic Readings in Anglo-Saxon England, 5 (New York, 2000), pp. 151–98.

[26] Ó Carragáin, 'Rome, Ruthwell, Vercelli', pp. 93–97.

[27] Charles D. Wright, 'Vercelli Homilies XI–XIII and the Anglo-Saxon Benedictine Reform: Tailored Sources and Implied Audiences', in *Preacher, Sermon, and Audience in the Middle Ages*, ed. by Carolyn Meussig (Leiden, 2002), pp. 203–27. It is perhaps worth pointing out that while Ó Carragáin ('Rome, Ruthwell, Vercelli', p. 95) views the compilation of the Vercelli Book as belonging just prior to the Benedictine Reform, Wright regards individual homilies as posing a reactionary response to it.

certainly seem to point to the possibility of a less stringently monastic audience, if not possibly a fully mixed audience.[28]

Though a single target readership (if such an ideal ever existed) for the Vercelli collection remains to be identified, it is important to qualify that the theory of the 'reading book' does not exclude the possibility that individual homilies were at some point performed in a 'live' setting, a dimension which is too often ignored in the context of manuscript study in general, and especially in the context of the Vercelli book, where the emphasis has always been upon its role as a 'readerly' text. Though the specific conditions under which a homily is performed obviously cannot be recovered, textual 'keys to performance' can perhaps be used as an index for its preaching context.[29] Dorothy Haines, for one, has taken a novel approach in examining the use of direct speeches in the Vercelli homilies, showing that the addresses delivered by the soul to the body in Vercelli IV, between Christ and the 'dry bones' in Vercelli VIII, and between God, Satan, and the Sinner in Vercelli X are perhaps best seen as precursors to the more modern 'dramatic monologue'.[30] This approach finds a powerful analogue in those so-called elegies rendered in the voice of the first-person speaker, and one might be tempted to look even further at examples of prosopopoeia in the Exeter Book riddles and (within the Vercelli Book itself) in *The Dream of the Rood*.[31] Several other studies investigating the

---

[28] For a detailed discussion of the address to women in Vercelli VII, see Samantha Zacher, 'The Source of Vercelli VII: An Address to Women', forthcoming in *New Readings on the Vercelli Book*, ed. by Orchard and Zacher. Also see *The Vercelli Book*, ed. by Sisam, p. 44, who argued that the compiler of the Vercelli manuscript may have been a nun; also see now Mary Dockray-Miller, 'The *eadgiþ* Erasure: A Gloss on the Old English *Andreas*', *ANQ*, 18 (2005), 3–7, who has explored the possibility of a female readership, largely on the basis of an erased reference to *eadgyþ* on the last line of fol. 41[v] (in the *Andreas* portion of the manuscript), which she takes as a direct reference to St Edith of Wilton.

[29] John Miles Foley (in his *The Singer of Tales in Performance* (Bloomington, 1995), especially p. 83) uses the term to denote 'the rhetorical persistence of traditional forms' in written texts. In the case of the Vercelli homilies, the performance event is, of course, not the singing of a traditional tale, but rather the delivery of a sermon drawn from various textual and (ostensibly) oral traditions.

[30] Dorothy Haines, 'Courtroom Drama and the Homiletic Monologues of the Vercelli Book', in *Verbal Encounters: Anglo-Saxon and Old Norse Studies for Roberta Frank*, ed. by Antonina Harbus and Russell Poole, Toronto Old English Series, 8 (Toronto, 2005), pp. 105–23.

[31] For the use of personification and the speaking object in the riddles, see for example Marie Nelson, 'The Paradox of Silent Speech in the Exeter Book Riddles', *Neophilologus*, 62 (1978), 609–15; Bruce Karl Braswell, '*The Dream of the Rood* and Aldhelm on Sacred Prosopopoeia', *Mediaeval Studies*, 40 (1978), 461–67; Peter Orton, 'The Technique of Object-Personification

various forms of address (to both lay and clerical audiences) embedded within individual homilies remind us that, although the homilies of the Vercelli Book reach us (and some of their Anglo-Saxon audiences) in a purely textual medium, there is evidently a rich oral dimension to these texts.[32]

Style and Rhetoric

Perhaps one of the greatest obstacles to the study of style and rhetoric in homilies is the perception that there is no available descriptive vocabulary for this kind of analysis. With regard to poetry, there is now in place a vibrant vocabulary for analysing the repetition of words and phrases, and other rhetorical flourishes. Many of these terms have become essential in the context of oral theory (as it relates to Old English poetry and in a wider cross-cultural context); no student can read *Beowulf* without coming across vocabulary for describing verbal repetition, such as 'variation', 'formulae', 'appositive style',[33] or types of structural repetition, such as 'envelope patterning', 'interlace structure', and 'ring composition'.[34] Other terms

in *The Dream of the Rood* and a Comparison with the Old English Riddles', *Leeds Studies in English*, n.s., 11 (1980), 1–18.

[32] See especially Clayton, 'Homiliaries and Preaching', pp. 228–29, and Zacher, 'Style and Rhetoric', pp. 9–10.

[33] For some of the formative discussions of these terms (in the above order), see Arthur G. Brodeur, *The Art of Beowulf* (Berkeley, 1959), pp. 39–70; Katherine O'Brien O'Keeffe, 'Diction, Variation, the Formula', in *A Beowulf Handbook*, ed. by Robert E. Bjork and John D. Niles (Lincoln, 1997), pp. 85–104; John D. Niles, 'Formula and Formulaic System in *Beowulf*', in *Oral Traditional Literature: A Festschrift for Albert Bates Lord*, ed. by John Miles Foley (Columbus, 1981), pp. 394–415; Alain Renoir, 'Oral-Formulaic Rhetoric: An Approach to Image and Message in Medieval Poetry', in *Medieval Texts and Contemporary Readers*, ed. by Laurie A. Finke and Martin B. Schichtman (Ithaca, 1987), pp. 234–53; Mark Amodio, 'Anglo-Saxon Oral Poetics', in *Writing the Oral Tradition: Oral Poetics and Literate Culture in Medieval England* (Notre Dame, 2004), pp. 33–78; and Fred C. Robinson, *Beowulf and the Appositive Style*, John C. Hodges Lectures Series (Knoxville, 1985).

[34] Select studies include (in the order presented above), Constance B. Hieatt, 'On Envelope Patterns (Ancient and Relatively Modern) and Nonce Formulas', in *Comparative Research on Oral Traditions: A Memorial for Milman Parry*, ed. by John Miles Foley and Albert B. Lord (Columbus, 1987), pp. 245–58; A. C. Bartlett, *The Larger Rhetorical Patterns in Anglo-Saxon Poetry*, Columbia University Studies in English and Comparative Literature, 12 (New York, 1935), especially p. 9; Lewis E. Nicholson, 'The Art of Interlace in *Beowulf*', *Studia Neophilologica*, 52 (1980), 237–49; Morton W. Bloomfield, '"Interlace" as a Medieval Narrative Technique,

are drawn from classical rhetorical devices; often cited rhetorical figures (which the Venerable Bede himself defines as 'the artificial arrangement of words'; 'the way that language is so to speak clothed or adorned') include 'anaphora' ('the repetition of the same word or phrase'; particularly in a catalogue structure), 'paronomasia' ('wordplay'; 'the name of the figure in which two very similar words differing only by a letter or syllable are used in different senses'), and 'homoeoteleuton' (the use of 'like endings'; a major cause of scribal error through eye-skip), to name a few.[35] These classically derived devices have in turn been supplemented by custom-tailored terminology designed to pinpoint features in Old English poetry. Examples include 'ornamental alliteration' (the use of extra and non-metrical alliteration), 'incremental repetition' (the repetition of successive phrases to highlight the development in the argument or narrative), and 'echo words' (the repetition of the same simplex either independently or as part of different compound structures).[36]

with Special Reference to *Beowulf*', in *Magister Regis: Studies in Honor of Robert Earl Kaske*, ed. by Arthur Groos and others (New York, 1986), pp. 49–59; Albert B. Lord, 'Ring Composition in *Maldon*: or, a Possible Case of Chiasmus in a Late Anglo-Saxon Poem', in *The Ballad and Oral Literature*, ed. by Joseph Harris (Cambridge, MA, 1991), pp. 233–42; John D. Niles, 'Ring Composition and the Structure of *Beowulf*', *PMLA*, 94 (1979), 924–35, as well as *Beowulf: The Poem and its Tradition* (Cambridge, MA, 1983), pp. 152–62.

[35] For Bede's definitions of these terms, see *Libri II De arte metrica et De schematibus et tropis, The Art of Poetry and Rhetoric: The Latin Text With an English Translation*, ed. and trans. by Calvin B. Kendall, Bibliotheca Germanica, n.s., 2 (Saarbrücken, 1991). For a survey of the use of some of these rhetorical devices in Old English poetry, see Jackson J. Campbell, 'Rhetoric in Old English Literature: Adaptation of Classical Rhetoric in Old English Literature', in *Medieval Eloquence: Studies in the Theory and Practice of Medieval Rhetoric*, ed. by James J. Murphy (Berkeley, 1978), pp. 173–97; and Janie Steen, 'Latin Rhetoric and Old English Poetic Style' (unpublished doctoral dissertation, University of Cambridge, 2002), forthcoming as a monograph, *Verse and Virtuosity: The Adaptation of Latin Rhetoric in Old English Poetry* (Toronto). For discussions particularly of the use of paronomasia, see Roberta Frank, 'Some Uses of Paronomasia in Old English Scriptural Verse', *Speculum*, 47 (1972), 207–26, repr. in *The Poems of MS Junius 11: Basic Readings*, ed. by R. M. Liuzza (New York, 2002), pp. 69–98; and Samantha Zacher, 'Cynewulf at the Interface of Literacy and Orality: The Evidence of the Puns in *Elene*', *Oral Tradition*, 17 (2002), 346–87.

[36] On the use of ornamental alliteration in Old English poetry, see Andy Orchard, 'Artful Alliteration in Anglo-Saxon Song and Story', *Anglia*, 113 (1995), 429–63. For the device of incremental repetition, see Andy Orchard, 'Oral Tradition', in *Reading Old English Texts*, ed. by Katherine O'Brien O'Keeffe (Cambridge, 1997), pp. 101–23. On the use of the echo word in Old English poetry, see John O. Beaty, 'The Echo-Word in *Beowulf* with a Note on the *Finnsburg Fragment*', *PMLA*, 49 (1934), 365–73; James L. Rosier, 'Generative Composition in *Beowulf*', *ES*, 58 (1977), 193–203; and Paul H. R. Battles, 'The Art of the Scop: Traditional Poetics in the

Whether in point of fact these devices are inherited from the Graeco-Latin tradition or from a native tradition that developed (semi-)independently matters little strictly in terms of classification itself, though clearly the question of influence continues to form a hotbed of discussion within scholarly circles.[37] Given the considerable interpenetration of Latin and the vernacular throughout the Anglo-Saxon period, we can only assume that an Anglo-Saxon author was potentially influenced by both traditions.[38]

Much more central questions include whether and how a similar stylistics can be applied to prose. With specific reference to the Vercelli Book, a variety of approaches to the style and rhetoric of these texts have come to light. For example, there has been a continued focus on the phenomenon of 'prosimetrum' (or the combination of verse and prose) not only within the broader scope of the manuscript itself, but also within individual homilies. Angus McIntosh and Charles D. Wright have both detected examples of embedded verse within Vercelli XXI, some of which has been linked to portions of poems known through other manuscripts.[39] Importantly, the device is not limited to Vercelli XXI, but has also been established for a portion of Vercelli X (and its variant texts in Cambridge, Corpus Christi College, MSS 302 and 421), where Christ speaks in poetry to Satan in the moment that he casts the angel from heaven into his hellish exile.[40]

Old English *Genesis A'* (unpublished doctoral dissertation, University of Illinois, Urbana-Champaign, 1998; abstract in *Dissertation Abstracts International – A*, 59 (1999), 2996), pp. 168–240.

[37] Janie Steen lays out some of these arguments in the introduction to her 'Latin Rhetoric and Old English Poetic Style'.

[38] The weighty two-volume *Latin Learning and English Lore: Studies in Anglo-Saxon Literature for Michael Lapidge*, ed. by Katherine O'Brien O'Keeffe and Andy Orchard (Toronto, 2005) surely endorses this view.

[39] For example, McIntosh ('Wulfstan's Prose', p. 141) demonstrates that Vercelli XXI.149–55 corresponds roughly to a portion of the poem *An Exhortation to Christian Living* in CCCC 201; he also identifies a run of alliterative prose in Vercelli XXI.128–41. Charles D. Wright ('More Old English Poetry in Vercelli Homily XXI', in *Early Medieval English Texts and Interpretations: Studies Presented to Donald G. Scragg*, ed. by Elaine Treharne and Susan Rosser, MRTS, 252 (Tempe, 2003), pp. 245–62) has since argued that lines 141–49 (discussing the expulsion of the angels from heaven) also constitutes verse.

[40] See especially Joseph B. Trahern, Jr, 'An Old English Verse Paraphrase of Matthew 25.41', *Mediaevalia*, 1 (1977), 109–14; and Samantha Zacher, 'Sin, Syntax, and Synonyms: Rhetorical Style and Structure in Vercelli Homily X', *JEGP*, 103 (2004), 53–76. While Trahern demonstrates the poetic arrangement for the variants found in Cambridge, Corpus Christi College, MSS 302 and 421, Zacher shows the alliterative structure of Vercelli X.105–08.

A more globalized approach to the styles of the Vercelli Book is exemplified by Paul Szarmach, who has indexed a host of techniques used by the various Vercelli homilists, such as extensive lists, antithesis, and enumeration;[41] Szarmach, recently revisiting this topic, has likewise shown that through the use of these sophisticated devices, the Vercelli Book offers 'a summary of the options for prose style' acting as a '*fons et origo* not precisely in a source relation but rather as a set of potential directions and paths for later prose writers'.[42] And lest the prospect of locating themes seem an overly daunting task in relation to this massive collection of homilies, it is worth mentioning that Robert DiNapoli has undertaken an immensely useful survey of themes across several of the main homiletic corpora, and in so doing presents a log of the astounding variety of topics witnessed in the Vercelli Book.[43] A somewhat different approach can be found in Donald Scragg's study of the 'compilation of the Vercelli Book', which uses codicological evidence to shed light on the various groupings of homilies according to exemplar.[44] This study has been particularly helpful in bringing to light themes across individual homilies that are linked through a previous manuscript context.[45] Though each of these examinations focus on just part of the manuscript, by providing snapshots of the style and rhetoric of the Vercelli Homilies, they provocatively highlight the artistry of individual authors, as well as the sensitivity of the compiler of the collection as a whole.[46]

[41] Szarmach, 'The Vercelli Homilies'.

[42] Szarmach, 'Vercelli Prose'.

[43] DiNapoli, *Index of Theme*.

[44] Scragg, 'Compilation of the Vercelli Book'.

[45] To cite just one recent example, Michael Fox has recently argued that Vercelli XIX–XXI, which are linked in their exemplar, are likewise connected formally and thematically through their use of classical *narratio*; in 'Vercelli XIX–XXI, the Ascension Day Homily in Cambridge, Corpus Christi College 162 and the Catechetical Tradition from Augustine to Wulfstan', forthcoming in *New Readings on the Vercelli Book*, ed. by Orchard and Zacher. I am grateful to Professor Fox for allowing me to cite his paper before its publication.

[46] For a study devoted entirely to the analysis of style and rhetoric in the Vercelli Book, see in general Zacher, 'Style and Rhetoric', which examines features such as the repetition of passages within the Vercelli collection, the adaptation of Latin sources, recurring themes, connected metaphors, and mixed genres. The study advances the idea that so far from being the anomalous compilation of an eccentric individual, the Vercelli Book significantly demonstrates close connections with prevailing literary trends in both Latin and vernacular poetry and prose.

Style and Rhetoric: The Case of Vercelli XVII

Having reviewed some of the available methodologies for analysing the style and rhetoric of prose homilies, we turn to an analysis of Vercelli XVII, selected both because this homily has received little critical attention and because of its intricate use of the various types of rhetorical devices discussed above. Vercelli XVII, as its manuscript rubric indicates, is set for the 2 February feast of the Purification of the Virgin Mary, also known as Candlemas in the English liturgy (named for the customary procession with candles) and *Hypapante* in the Greek (or 'meeting'; referring to the biblical gathering between Mary, Simeon, and Anna).[47] The homily marks one of only two surviving Old English homilies for the feast day, with the other located in Ælfric's *CH* I.9. The paucity of Old English homilies for the feast day is likely connected to the lack of patristic models for the subject; Mary Clayton has shown that the celebration of the four feasts of Mary (namely the Purification, Annunciation, Assumption, and Nativity) was a relatively new phenomenon in Church history, popularized only as late as the eighth century.[48] As Ó Carragáin has shown, the feasts themselves, originally Eastern in origin, reached Rome over a period of time between 620 and 680, where they were organized into a formal series by Pope Sergius; the celebration of Candlemas itself 'was recorded as early as the reign of Pope Honorius'.[49] The relative newness of the celebration of the feast day, particularly in England, certainly accounts in part for the allusive manner in which Mary is treated in Vercelli XVII: as we shall see, the role of Mary herself is largely contained to the brief opening, which describes her righteousness in adhering to the law. This brief focus upon Mary seems particularly pronounced when set aside such Old English texts as Blickling I, set for the feast of the Assumption, in which Mary receives obvious and full attention: not only is she glorified for giving

---

[47] For Anglo-Saxon liturgy and practices relating to Candlemas, see Bradford Bedingfield, 'Reinventing the Gospel: Ælfric and the Liturgy', *Medium Ævum*, 68 (1999), 13–31 (pp. 15–23). Bedingfield draws upon such primary texts as Ælfric's *Second Letter for Wulfstan* (in *Die Hirtenbriefe Ælfrics in altenglischer und lateinischer Fassung*, ed. by Bernhard Fehr, BaP, 9 (Hamburg, 1914), p. 216) and the *Regularis concordia* (ed. by Dom Thomas Symons (London, 1953), pp. 30–31). Also see now Ó Carragáin, *Ritual and the Rood*, pp. 98, 107, and 237–40, who provides both an account of the origins of the feast day in Rome and England and also a discussion of the liturgy associated with the feast day.

[48] Mary Clayton, 'The Virgin in Old English Prose', in *The Cult of the Virgin Mary in Anglo-Saxon England*, CSASE, 2 (Cambridge, 1990), pp. 210–66 (pp. 210–12).

[49] On the celebration of the feast in Rome, and on the influence of Pope Sergius, see Ó Carragáin, *Ritual and the Rood*, pp. 237–40.

birth to Christ, and the object of prayer, but she herself is a speaking subject. But where the homily for the Assumption can so plausibly celebrate the role of Mary as a conduit for Christ, the feast of the Purification, focussing on the cleansing and perfection of the Virgin herself, was demonstrably slower to develop the same kind of focus.[50]

If Vercelli XVII stands out as being nearly unique within the Old English corpus, the homily likewise presents something of a rarity within the Vercelli collection itself, offering as it does one of the few texts in the collection (another is Vercelli I) that contains both a full gospel pericope (from Luke 2. 22–32) and sustained formal exegesis.[51] Though in strictly stylistic terms, Vercelli XVII cannot boast some of the embellishing whistles and bells characteristically become associated with the homilies of the Vercelli Book (in their ornate speeches, lavish figures, extensive lists, and embedded poetry),[52] at least one persistent rhetorical schema has been detected by its most recent editor. Donald Scragg writes the following (albeit somewhat dismissively) about the homily's use of sustained patterns of repetition:

> Though its intellectual content is slight, it is a relatively well-ordered piece with a straight-forward message rendered forcefully by repetition. The iterative effect of the message is paralleled — perhaps even reinforced — by a repetition of words or word-elements within the sentence, sometimes even the recurrence of phrases, and by verbal echoes.[53]

Such determined repetition is all the more intriguing in the light of the observation by Mary Clayton concerning the homily's relationship to its known sources:

> Vercelli XVII appears to be freely composed, probably using a variety of sources: most of its points can be paralleled in Latin homilies or commentaries (for example, by Ambrose, Bede, Ambrosius Autpertus and Haymo), but no precise source has yet been identified. No one Latin text includes all the points made by the vernacular homilist and the Latin texts are, rather, the kind of works with which the homilist would have been acquainted and from which he would have derived his interpretation of the pericope.[54]

---

[50] On the slow shift from the focus on Christ during these Marian feast days to a more coherent focus on the Virgin herself, see Ó Carragáin, *Ritual and the Rood*, especially pp. 93–109.

[51] Though the term 'homily' is used for Vercelli XVII throughout this essay, the *Dictionary of Old English* surprisingly still classifies Vercelli XVII as a saints' life (Cameron number: B3.3.19) (after Peterson, 'Unpublished Homilies'). Following suit, the homily has been left out of Janet Bately's *Anonymous Old English Homilies: A Preliminary Bibliography of Source Studies Compiled for Fontes Anglo-Saxonici and Sources of Anglo-Saxon Literary Culture* (Binghamton, 1993).

[52] See Szarmach, 'The Vercelli Homilies'.

[53] *Vercelli Homilies*, ed. by Scragg, pp. 279–80 (as well as the examples he provides on p. 280, nn. 1 and 2).

[54] Clayton, *Cult of the Virgin Mary*, p. 218.

Clayton's notion of 'free composition' lends itself well to an examination of the style of Vercelli XVII, as the following investigation of the various additions, omissions, and changes to the few known biblical and Latin sources for the homily will indicate. Furthermore, as we will see, the author's use of verbatim parallels between the gospel portions of the text and the rest of the homily seek likewise to indicate considerable extemporization upon the biblical material. The following table shows the various correspondences between the vernacular and Latin treatments of the pericope (Luke 2. 22–32). The units below are organized according to the structure of the Vulgate rather than according to the sense in the Old English, so as to present a clearer gauge of where and how the vernacular author departs from the Latin. The Old English text below (and throughout) is drawn from Scragg's edition, though portions in angle brackets represent readings reinstated from the manuscript where Scragg has emended them out of his edition.[55]

Table 1: Comparison of the Vulgate and Vercelli XVII

	Luke 2. 22–32 (ed. Vulgate; trans. Douay-Rheims)	Vercelli XVII.1–27 (ed. Scragg)
1		1–4: Men ða leofastan, sægeð us 7 myngaþ þis halige godspel be þysse arwyrðan tide þe we nu todæge gode ælmihtigum to lofe 7 to are wyrðiaþ, þæt is se feowertiga dæg nu todæg ures Dryhtnes Hælendes Cristes acennesse, [Dearest men, this holy gospel says and reminds us about the honourable time which we now today honour God Almighty for praise and for grace. That is the fortieth day now today of the birth of our Lord Saviour Christ,]
2	2. 22: et postquam impleti sunt dies purgationis eius secundum legem Mosi tulerunt illum in Hierusalem ut sisterent eum Domino [And after the days of her purification, according to the law of Moses, were accomplished, they carried him to Jerusalem, to present him to the Lord:]	4–6: 7 þy dæge þæt his aldoras hine brohton in Hierusalem in þa mæran burg, þæt hie hine gode agefon, [and on that day that His elders brought Him into Jerusalem into the famous city, so that they gave Him to God,]

---

[55] *Vercelli Homilies*, ed. by Scragg, pp. 281–86.

Luke 2. 22–32 (ed. Vulgate; trans. Douay-Rheims)

Vercelli XVII.1–27 (ed. Scragg)

3 2. 23: sicut scriptum est in lege Domini quia omne masculinum adaperiens uuluam sanctum Domino uocabitur [As it is written in the law of the Lord: Every male opening the womb shall be called holy to the Lord:]

6–7: swa swa hit awriten is in Dryhtnes naman þæt æghwylc wæpnedcild bearn þe wif ærest acynde sceolde be[o]n ærest gode gehalgod. [just as it is written in the name of the Lord, that each male child which a woman first brought forth should first be sanctified to God.]

4 2. 24: et ut darent hostiam secundum quod dictum est in lege Domini par turturum aut duos pullos columbarum [And to offer a sacrifice, according as it is written in the law of the Lord, a pair of turtledoves or two young pigeons:]

7–12: 7 þa cwomon dryhtnes aldoras to ðam Godes temple 7 hie ðær gode ælmihtigum asægdnesse brohton, swa hit be þan awriten is in Dryhtnes naman þæt hie sceoldon þær bringan to þam temple twegen turturas oððe twegen culfran briddas, gode ælmihtigum to lofe 7 to wyrðunge, to ðam godes temple. [And then the parents of the Lord came to God's Temple, and they brought there a sacrifice to God Almighty, just as it is written about that in the name of the Lord that they should bring there to the temple two turtle-doves or two pigeons to God Almighty for praise and for honour to the temple of God.]

5 2. 25: et ecce homo erat in Hierusalem cui nomen Symeon et homo iste iustus et timoratus expectans consolationem Israhel et Spiritus Sanctus erat in eo [And behold there was a man in Jerusalem named Simeon: and this man was just and devout, waiting for the consolation of Israel. And the Holy Ghost was in him.]

12–15: Ðær wæs þa sum eald man in Hierusalem in þære byrig in þa ilcan tid se wæs haten Simeon. He wæs soðfæst 7 rihtwis, 7 he bead þære fr[o]fre þære þe he wiste þæt he his folce gehaten hæfde. 7 se halga gast wæs mid þone Simeon. [There was then a certain old man in Jerusalem in the city at that time who was called Simeon. He was truthful and righteous, and he prayed for the consolation which he knew had been promised to his people. And the Holy Ghost was with that Simeon,]

6 2. 26: et responsum acceperat ab Spiritu Sancto non uisurum se mortem nisi prius uideret Christum Domini

15–17: 7 he þære andsware onfeng fram þam halgan gaste, 7 he him cydde 7 sægde þæt he ne moste deaðes byrigan, ær he mid his eagum dryhten gesege.

Luke 2. 22–32 (ed. Vulgate; trans. Douay-Rheims)	Vercelli XVII.1–27 (ed. Scragg)
[And he had received an answer from the Holy Ghost, that he should not see death before he had seen the Christ of the Lord.]	[and he received an answer from the Holy Ghost, and he made known and said that he might not taste death, before he should see the Lord with his eyes.]

	Luke 2. 22–32	Vercelli XVII.1–27
7	2. 27: et uenit in Spiritu in templum et cum inducerent puerum Iesum parentes eius ut facerent secundum consuetudinem legis pro eo [And he came by the Spirit into the temple. And when his parents brought in the child Jesus, to do for him according to the custom of the law,]	17–20: He ða cwom þurh haliges gastes gife in þæt godes templ on þa ilcan tid þe Cristes aldoras hine þyder brohton. 7 he þa þæt dyde beforan him þone ilcan gewunan þe he ær dyde in þære ealdan æ. [He then came through the gift of the Holy Ghost into that temple of God, on that same time which Christ's parents brought him there. And he did that before them that same custom which he before did in the old law.]
8	2. 28: et ipse accepit eum in ulnas suas et benedixit Deum et dixit [He also took him into his arms and blessed God and said]	20–23: 7 þa genam se halga Simeon þone Hælend on his earmas, 7 he hine mid bam handum beclypte, 7 he [hine] mid eallre modlufan sette to his breostum, 7 he bledsode 7 wuldrade God fæder ælmihtigne, 7 he ðus cwæð: [And then St Simeon seized the Savior in his arms, and he clasped him with both hands, and he with all love set (him) to his breast. And he blessed and honoured God the father almighty, and he thus said:]
9	2. 29: nunc dimittis seruum tuum Domine secundum uerbum tuum in pace ['Now thou dost dismiss thy servant, O Lord, according to thy word in peace:]	23–25: 'Min dryhten, forlæt þinne þegen in sybbe faran þa, æfter þinum wordum swa ðu him ær gehehtest, ['My Lord, let thy servant go then in peace, according to thy word, just as you promised him before]
10	2. 30: quia uiderunt oculi mei salutare tuum [Because my eyes have seen thy salvation,]	25–26: for ðan, dryhten, mine eagan gesegon þa hælo [Because, Lord, my eyes have seen the salvation]
11	2. 31: quod parasti ante faciem omnium populorum [Which thou hast prepared before the face of all peoples:]	26: þe ðu gearwadest to onsyne eallra folca, [which thou hast prepared before the face of all peoples]

Luke 2. 22–32 (ed. Vulgate; trans. Douay-Rheims)	Vercelli XVII.1–27 (ed. Scragg)
12 2. 32: lumen ad reuelationem gentium et gloriam plebis tuae Israhel [A light to the revelation of the Gentiles and the glory of thy people Israel.']	26–27: 7 to frofre eallum þeodum 7 to wuldre þines folces, Israhela <bearnum>.' [and as a comfort for all peoples and as the glory of your people, the <children> of Israel.']

Some of the repetitions within the vernacular pericope seem deliberately aimed at creating internal resonances where there are none in the Latin. For example, the phrase *gode ælmihtigum to lofe 7 to are wyrðiaþ* ('[to] God Almighty for praise and for grace'), located in the opening homiletic address to Vercelli XVII (in section 1), occurs almost verbatim in section 4 (*gode ælmihtigum to lofe 7 to wyrðunge*), where both of these passages are clearly added to the Latin account. Another example can be found in the phrase *in Dryhtnes naman* ('in the name of the Lord'), which twice replaces the Latin *in lege Domini* ('in the law of the Lord'; sections 3 and 4); though the substitution is minor, the exchange of *nama* for *lex* echoes Vercelli XXVII.47–63, where the homilist links the *nama* ('name') of Jerusalem (in Vercelli XVII.47–48), together with that of God (line 55) and also that of the *bearn Godes* ('children of God'; line 63), highlighting the importance of this triad for devotional purposes.

Perhaps even more striking is the high degree of repetition between the vernacular pericope itself and the remainder of the homily. Scragg points out the repetition of the phrase *to þam (Godes) temple* ('to God's temple') three times in passage 4 (none of which are found in the Latin), as well as five more times at lines 29, 34, 44, 52, and 68, together with the variant phrase *in þæt Godes templ* ('into that temple of God') in passage 7 (also in the Latin) and line 31.[56] The presence of the phrase *in templum* only once in the Latin pericope seems to indicate that it was converted into a formula by the vernacular author, perhaps in order to keep the focus on the temple as the centre of the purification ritual. This type of 'filler' line appears again in the phrase *in þære ealdan æ* ('in the old law'), which in passage 7 substitutes for the phrase *secundum consuetudinem legis* ('according to the custom of the law'), and which appears again in the vernacular at line 65. Taken together with the double iteration of the phrase *Godes æ* ('God's law'; lines 30 and 45), these references emphasize Mary's adherence to the Old Testament laws of purification, a point which is essential for highlighting her righteousness in undergoing this voluntary act of unnecessary purification.

---

[56] *Vercelli Homilies*, ed. by Scragg, p. 280, n. 1

A number of the gospel quotations likewise repeat in later portions of the homily: Scragg, for one, has highlighted the repetition of the Old English translation of Luke 2. 29–30 in passages 9–12 and again in lines 109–20, where it is expanded considerably through commentary.[57] But while this type of repetition of biblical quotations is common in exegetical homilies, and serves as a way of bringing attention back to the pericope, other examples in Vercelli XVII are clearly used solely for hortatory purposes; for example, the doublet *bledsode 7 wuldrade* ('blessed and glorified'; in section 8), which highlights Simeon's piety as he praises God, is picked up in a chiastic structure in line 108, where the homilist remarks that, like Simeon, his audience ought to *wuldrian 7 bletsian* ('glorify and bless') God.

The homily's 'free composition' is nevertheless best exemplified by those passages in which there are identifiable word-clusters of the same term. For example, the root *clæn-* ('pure') occurs no fewer than eighteen times in the space of this 155-line homily and is, remarkably, confined to three identifiable clusters: lines 29–43 (at lines 33, 37, 38, 39, 40, 41, and 42); lines 78–85 (at lines 78, 79, 81, 82, 84, and 85); lines 131–41 (at lines 131, 137 (twice), and 141 (twice)). Some of these elements demonstrate further parallelism: for example, in lines 78 and 79 successively, the cluster *lif-* [...] *clæn-* [...] *unsceþ-* ('life [...] pure [...] innocent') appears twice. Synonymic doublets also occur in the pairs *unmælu* [...] *clæne* ('unmarred [...] pure'; line 40) and *clænlice* [...] *haliglice* ('purely [...] in holy fashion'; line 131). Of the three aforementioned clusters, only lines 29–43 have been linked to a possible source in Ambrosius Autpertus's purification homily, and as previous scholarship has concluded, the borrowing is both indirect and tenuous. Even here the heavy-handed manipulation of the vernacular author is detectable in the dense repetition of language: examples within these fourteen lines include the reiteration of the phrase *feowertigan dæge* ('forty days') four times (at lines 29, 32, 33, and 37), *Godes templ* twice (at lines 31 and 34), as well as the more complex constellation *clænnesse* [...] *mægðhad* [...] *ðurhwunode* ('purity [...] maidenhood [...] persevered') twice (at lines 41 and 42, though in the latter case the two final items are reversed). The remaining two clusters at lines 78–85 and 131–41 also 'echo' the term *clæn-* in order to build the same kind of thought–word–deed triad found

---

[57] One might also point to the similar reiteration of the phrase *folca* [...] *frofre* [...] *eallum* [...] *þeodum* [...] *folces* in passages 11 and 12, which recurs with different emphases at different points in the homily: for example at line 91 (where *folce* [...] *frofre* is paired with *hælo*), line 95 (*ealles* [...] *folce* [...] *hælo* [...] *frofre*), and again at 115 (with the variation *to leohte* [...] *to frofre* [...] *manigum* [...] *þeodum*).

widely elsewhere in Old English literature, notably in *Beowulf*.[58] In the case of lines 85–86, the passage 'soðlice he hæfde lifes clænnesse gehealden, ge in wordum ge in dædum ge in geðohtum 7 eac in gesiehðe' ('truly he had held the purity of life, in words, in deeds, in thoughts, and also in sight') evidently adds to the formula the emphasis upon 'sight', which becomes a leitmotif in Vercelli XVII. The triad is then picked up again in passage 140–41, this time for the purpose of exhortation, with the phrase: 'herian we urne Dryhten Hælende Crist, 7 hine wuldrian 7 wyrðian in halgum wordum 7 in clænum geþohtum 7 in clænum dædum' ('let us praise our Lord Saviour Christ and glorify him and honour [him] in holy words, and in pure thoughts and in pure deeds').

A far more complex use of echo words can be seen in the repetition of phrases linked to sight. Consider the following passage (Vercelli XVII.47–67) delineating the traditional etymology of Jerusalem as *uisio pacis* ('vision of peace'); the elements in bold repeat parts of the stated etymology:[59]

> Men þa leofestan, us is nu eac to witanne þære burge naman þe is genemned Hierusalem, þæt is þonne on ure geþeode gereht '**sybbe gesyhðe**'. Swa þonne bið symble þam soðfæstum 7 þam godfyrhtum mannum in **sybbe**, him bið gegearwad ece lean 7 ece hælo 7 ece gefea 7 ece blis, 7 þam mannum þe mid **sybbe** 7 mid geleafan 7 mid god[um] willan cumað oft to godes temple, þæt is þonne to þære halgan godes cirican. 7 hie sylfe þær gode ælmihtigum 7 his ðam halgan him sylfum bebeodaþ mid halgum gebedum, 7 hie godes naman heriað 7 wuldriaþ, 7 hie to him mildheortnesse 7 forgifnesse biddaþ 7 ece reste æfter þysse worulde 7 eac þysse anweardra **gesyhðe**. 7 hie þurh þæt geearniaþ æt gode ælmihtigum, þæt hie moton becuman to þære soðan **sybbe gesyhðe**, ðæt is þonne to ures Dryhtnes Hælendes Cristes. For þan, men þa leofestan, us gedafenað þæt we symble in

---

[58] For the use of this trope in *Beowulf*, see Andy Orchard, *A Critical Companion to Beowulf* (Cambridge, 2003), pp. 55, 146, and 218 (for example); for appearance of this triad in Celtic literature, see Patrick Sims-Williams, 'Thought, Word, and Deed: An Irish Triad', *Ériu*, 29 (1978), 78–111. In Vercelli XVII, the word *dæd*- repeats independently nine times (at lines 76, 86, 98, 104, 106, 107, 133, 135, 141), with five of these examples including the formula *mid/ in godum dædum*.

[59] It is perhaps noteworthy that Ambrosius Autpertus uses the same etymology and association in his homily on the purification, and to my knowledge this usage is unique among the extant Latin homilies for the Purification. Ambrosius Autpertus, *Sermo in Purificatione sanctae Mariae*, ed. by R. Weber, CCCM 27B (Turnhout, 1979), 4.20–21: 'Ipsa enim Ecclesia non solum ex gentibus, uerum etiam ex Iudaeis, Hierusalem, id est uisio pacis, recte uocatur, de qua per Psalmistam dicitur: Hierusalem, quae aedificatur ut ciuitas, cuius participatio eius in id ipsum' ('the Church itself is not only from the gentiles, but indeed from the Jews; Jerusalem, that is rightly called "vision of peace", concerning which is said through the Psalmist: "Jerusalem, which is built as a city, which is compact together"').

ealle tid rihte lufan 7 **sybbe** betweonan us sylfum hæbben we 7 healden þæt in us, þurh þæt sy gefylled þæt dryhten sylf cwæð be þam **gesybsumum** mannum: 'Eadige beoð þa **gesybsuman** men, for þan þe hie beoð godes bearn genemde'.

[Dearest men, it is also now for us to know the name of the city which is named Jerusalem, that in our language is interpreted **'vision of peace'**. So then, it will always be for the righteous and the god-fearing men in **peace**, for them will be prepared eternal reward and eternal salvation and eternal rejoicing and eternal bliss, and [also] for the men who with **peace** and love and good will come often to God's temple, which is, then, to holy God's Church. And they themselves there will offer themselves to the almighty God and to them his saints with him with holy prayers, and they will praise and glorify God's name, and they pray to him for mercy and forgiveness and eternal rest after this world, and also in this **vision** of things (or times) present. And they through that will earn from God Almighty that they must come to the true **vision of peace**, that is, then, to that of our Lord Saviour Christ. Therefore, dearest men, it is fitting for us that we always in every occasion love rightly and we have for ourselves **peace** between us, and hold that in us, through that will be fulfilled what the Lord himself says about the **peace**-bringing men: 'blessed are the **peace**-bringing men, because they are named the sons of God'.]

This passage presents a sophisticated and intricate typology that reinterprets the temple as a figure for both Christ himself and by extension those who 'sylfum bebeodaþ mid halgum gebedum' ('offer themselves to the almighty God [...]with holy prayers'), in imitation of the earlier dedication of Christ by Mary to God (Vercelli XVII.7). The repetition of -*sybb*- (seven times) and *gesyhð*- (three times) in the passage links the temple, described as the *sybbe gesyhðe*, with the figure of Christ who is cast as the *soð sybbe gesyhðe* ('the true vision of peace'). This association probably originates with a passage like that found in John 2. 19–22, where the destruction and rebuilding of the temple is linked with Christ's death and resurrection. However, the homilist takes this commonplace further by connecting Christ and his *ciric* ('church'; a term used only here in the homily) with those 'gesybsum menn' ('peace-bringing men') 'þe mid sybbe 7 mid geleafan 7 mid god[um] willan cumað oft to godes temple' ('who with peace and love and good will come often to God's temple') so that they become part of this true vision of peace that is Christ. Such an extended typology emphasizes the displacement of Old Testament ritual purification through the Jewish Temple with New Testament faith, which serves as the new prerequisite for salvation, as expressed through the symmetrical list of rewards for those peace-bearing men: 'him bið gegearwad ece lean 7 ece hælo 7 ece gefea 7 ece blis' ('for them will be prepared eternal reward and eternal salvation and eternal rejoicing and eternal bliss'). This string of echo words is capped off by the idea that prayer to Christ 'for mercy and forgiveness and eternal rest' brings about reward both 'æfter þysse worulde' ('after this world') and also 'þysse anweardra gesyhðe' ('in this vision of things (or times) present'). While these repetitions serve to carry the typology created in this passage, the homilist likewise uses structural repetition to mark the passages cited above as a discrete unit, a technique which can sometimes be compared to the modern paragraph.[60] The repetition of the salutation, *men þa leofestan*, in both the first and last statements of this passage performs this function, an effect which is highlighted further through the use of an envelope-pattern in the first line concerning the naming of Jerusalem (*genem-*) and in the final line to the naming (again *genem-*) of *godes bearn*, 'the children of God'.

The repetition of the elements *-sybb-* (mentioned five further times outside of this passage at lines 24, 111, 125, 126, and 152) and *-syhð-* (used again at lines 17, 25, 82, 86, 88, 118 (twice), and 127) further fleshes out the passage's typological potential. For example, the idea of 'vision' becomes especially potent in the context of a discussion about the purity of those who believe in Christ, linking it back to the theme of *clænnesse* mentioned above. So, for example, in line 82 the homilist quotes from Matthew 5. 8, offering the following loose translation: 'Eadige bioð þa <clænan mildheortan> men for þan þe god gesyhð heora heortan clænnesse' ('blessed are the <clean, mildhearted> men, because God will see the cleanness of their heart'). Scragg emends the awkward double adjective *clænan mildheortan* to *clænheortan* to bring it closer to the Vulgate 'beati mundo corde quoniam ipsi Deum uidebunt' ('blessed are the clean of heart: they shall see God'). It might be better to suppose that the homilist originally wrote 'clænan mildheortan men' ('clean and mildhearted men'), so emphasizing the chiastic structure formed through the repetition of *clænan* [. . .] *mildheortan* [. . .] *heortan* [. . .] *clænnesse* through a doublet, as the homilist does elsewhere in relation to his expansion of the passage from Matthew 5. 9 (in Vercelli XVII.62–63).[61] The switch in the Vercelli translation of God as the object of the vision to its subject is, however, less easily explained, though the point may be to stress God's judgement of *clænnesse* ('cleanness' or 'purification') as set against the perfect example of Mary.[62] Importantly, the passage from Matthew 5. 8 shows that Simeon fits into the typological nexus that

---

[60] Andy Orchard discusses Alfred's use of incremental repetition in this manner in his 'Oral Tradition', p. 102.

[61] See further the discussion of this passage below, p. 205.

[62] Scragg too allows for that the possibility that 'the homilist has deliberately altered the Gospel reading for homiletic effect, but in light of his misunderstanding of the Latin elsewhere it is more likely that this is an error'; however, for Scragg the more likely scenario is that the 'manuscript reading *þa clænan mildheortan men* is presumably corruption introduced during transmission' (*Vercelli Homilies*, ed. by Scragg, p. 287).

links the Temple in Jerusalem, Christ, and his believers (as above, Vercelli XVII.47–62).

The freedoms taken by the author with respect to the pericope seem to show signs of the incorporation of patristic exegetical materials; Scragg in particular cites the homilist's inclusion of the epithet *eald* for Simeon, where there is no such designation in the Vulgate itself.[63] A clearer case could be made for passage 3 above, where what looks like a serious misconstruction of the Vulgate Latin may instead present a sophisticated exegetical splicing in of materials from Exodus 13. 12–13, which describe the Jewish laws for purification. Indeed, the tautologous phrasing of the Old English *wæpnedcild bearn* seems to gloss more than the Lucan *masculinum*, and correlates better with the Exodus phrase *primitiuum [. . .] masculini sexus*.[64] Indeed, just such a conflation of these New and Old Testament passages occurs both in Bede's Homily I.18 for the Purification of Mary, and in his commentary on Luke 2. 22,[65] which has been established elsewhere as a possible source for Vercelli XVII.64–78.[66] The term *bearn* may also have held particular exegetical significance for the Vercelli homilist, as he uses it several more times to refer both to the first-born male mentioned in the laws of purification (lines 30 and 34) and typologically to designate those who follow in the laws of God, in Vercelli XVII.27

[63] The epithet for Simeon is extremely common, and examples in Old English can be found in Ælfric's *CH* I.9 as discussed below.

[64] Peterson ('Unpublished Homilies') parses the compound as *wæpned cildbearn*. Though the compound *cildbearn* forms a hapax legomenon in Old English, the compounds *wæpnedcild* and *wæpnedbearn* are attested elsewhere: the former can be found in St Machutus 7v.10, *Medicina de quadrupedibus* 1.1.5.12 and 1.1.5.13; while the latter can be found in Bede's *Ecclesiastical History* I.16.76.6.

[65] In Bede, *Opera homiletica. Opera rhythmica*, ed. by D. Hurst and J. Fraipont, CCSL, 122 (Turnhout, 1955), pp. 128–33 (p. 128, lines 17–18), and *Opera Exegetica*, ed. by D. Hurst, CCSL, 120 (Turnhout, 1960), pp. 5–425 (pp. 61–62, lines 17–20), respectively.

[66] The online *Fontes Anglo-Saxonici* database (<http://fontes.english.ox.ac.uk> (accessed 1 November 2005)), lists CCSL, 120, p. 63, lines 1739–40 as a possible direct source for these lines. The closer parallel for the Vercelli passage in Bede's Homily I.18 is as follows: 'Postquam impleti sunt dies purgationis ejus (uidelicet matris illius) secundum legem Moysi, tulerunt illum in Jerusalem, ut sisterent eum Domino, sicut scriptum est in lege Domini, quia omne masculinum adaperiens uuluam, sanctum Domino uocabitur [...] primogenitum autem omnis masculini sexus sanctum Domino uocari, atque ideo munda quaeque offerri Deo' ('After the days of his/her purification were fulfilled according to the laws of Moses, they took him to Jerusalem to present him to the Lord, as is written in the law of the lord: every male that opens the womb shall be called holy to the Lord [...] the firstborn of all of the male sex was to be called holy to the lord, and for that reason all clean beasts were to be offered to the Lord').

(where the homilist squeezes in the phrase *Israhela bearnum* ('children of Israel'), though it is grammatically unwieldy) and again in lines 81–82.

A more extensive departure from the Latin pericope can be found in those portions of text describing Simeon's role in the purification ceremony, detailed in the Table above. In section 8, the Vercelli author greatly elaborates upon the actions and emotions of Simeon as he accepts the infant Jesus. The Latin phrase *et ipse accepit eum in ulnas suas* is expanded into three parallel clauses that emphasize Simeon's receipt of Christ and his embrace: '7 þa genam se halga Simeon þone Hælend on his earmas. 7 he hine mid bam handum beclypte, 7 he mid eallre modlufan sette to his breostum' ('And then St Simeon seized the Saviour in his arms, and he clasped him with both hands, and he with all love set (him) to his breast'). The homilist also expands the Latin *benedixit* and *Deum* into two doublets, using *bledsode* [...] *wuldrade* for the former and *god* [...] *fæder ælmihtigne* for the latter. The expansions seem especially geared to emphasize the zeal of Simeon.

These additions appear all the more significant when set beside a crux noted by Scragg in passage 1 above. There seems to be a puzzling shift from the Latin where it is clearly Christ's parents who both bring (*inducerent*) the infant Jesus to the temple and also act for him (*facerent*) according to the law. In the Old English, while Christ's parents are responsible for having brought (*brohton*) Christ to the temple, by contrast, the one performing the custom according to the law is Simeon, who acts *beforan him*, a line which has a number of potential meanings including 'before them/him' or even 'on account of them/him'. Scragg reads this alteration as a 'misunderstanding of scripture, where the subject is Christ's parents. The translator seems to believe the subject is Simeon'.[67] But what appears to be a sloppy interpretation of the Vulgate pericope may perhaps be illuminated through a series of vernacular parallels. Both Malcolm Godden and Bradford Bedingfield have pointed out expansions of a precisely similar nature in Ælfric's *CH* I.9 for the Purification of Mary (though without consideration of Vercelli XVII).[68] Significantly, as in the Vercelli Homily, Bedingfield notes the uncharacteristic freedom with which Ælfric handles the same pericope from Luke 2.22–32 and argues that these expansions are directed deliberately to enhance the role of Simeon in the purification ritual. We can see these departures in the following passage explicating Luke in I.9.28–37 (the portions in bold signify additions to the Vulgate):

[67] *Vercelli Homilies*, ed. by Scragg, p. 287, nn. 19–20.

[68] See Malcolm Godden's commentary on Ælfric's *CH* I.9 in *Ælfric's Catholic Homilies: Introduction, Commentary, and Glossary*, ed. by Godden, EETS: SS, 18 (Oxford, 2000), pp. 68–77 (p. 69), and also Bedingfield, 'Reinventing the Gospel', pp. 15–23.

And **seo halige maria** com þa to ðam temple mid þam cylde: and **se ealda man symeon**. eode togenes þam cylde and geseah þone hælend and hine **georne gecneow. þæt he wæs godes sunu: alysend ealles middaneardes;** He hine genam ða on his earmum **mid micelre onbryrdnesse: and hine geber into ðam temple and þancode georne gode. þæt he hine geseon moste**; He cwæð þa min drihten þu forlætst me nu mid sybbe of þysum life æfter þinum worde: for ðon þe mine eagan gesawon þinne halwendan: þone þu gearcodest ætforan ansyne ealles folces: leoht to onwrigenysse þeoda. and wuldor þinum folce israhel.

[And **the holy Mary** came then to the temple with the child, and the **old man Simeon** went towards the child and saw the saviour and **eagerly knew him that he was God's son, the saviour of all the middle earth**. He seized him in his arms **with great ardour and bore him into the Temple and eagerly** thanked **God that he might see him.** He spoke then 'My Lord, Now thou dost dismiss me with peace, O Lord, according to thy word in peace: Because my eyes have seen thy salvation which thou hast prepared before the face of all peoples, a light to the revelation of the Gentiles and glory to thy people Israel.']

Ælfric twice adds the intensifying adverb *georne* ('eagerly'), as well as the phrase *mid micelre onbryrdnesse* ('with great ardour') apparently in order to stress Simeon's zeal. Furthermore, there is a similar emphasis upon Simeon's active participation in the ritual at least once more in his homily, in lines 45–49, with the added weight of a rhetorical question: 'Hu bær þæt cild hine? ðone bær se ealda simeon on his earmum. þe ealle þincg hylt and gewylt' ('who bore that child to him? The old Simeon bore in his arms him who all things holds and wields'). With respect to these unsourced interpolations, Bedingfield and Godden have argued that they represent Ælfric's incorporation of contemporary liturgical practice for the celebration of Candlemas, where the priest (following in the role of Simeon) meets the candle-bearers at the gate and then proceeds alone with the candle into the church. As Bedingfield writes:

> Throughout the Candlemas liturgy we see something of a deposition of Mary in favor of Simeon, as he who received and held Christ as the liturgical participants receive and hold the candle, comes to dominate the processional highlights, especially the entrance into the church. This usurpation is reflected in Ælfric's innovative rendering of the Gospel story.[69]

Yet, given the similarity of these expansions of the gospel text in Ælfric's homily to those found in Vercelli XVII, it is worth testing whether further verbal parallels are detectable.

Compare, for example, the interpretation in both Old English texts of the Latin Luke 2. 26 'et responsum acceperat ab Spiritu Sancto non uisurum se mortem nisi

---

[69] Bedingfield, 'Ælfric and the Liturgy', p. 201.

prius uideret Christum Domini' ('and he had received an answer from the Holy Ghost, that he should not see death before he had seen the Christ of the Lord'). In Vercelli XVII.16–17, the line is rendered '7 he him cydde 7 sægde þæt he ne moste deaðes byrigan, ær he mid his eagum dryhten gesege' ('and he said and made known to him that he must not taste death, before he sees the Lord with his eyes'), with the reference to 'tasting death' repeated two more times in Vercelli XVII.86–87 and 117–18. Significantly, the reference to 'tasting death' is likewise echoed twice in Ælfric's homily at lines 23–24 and again in 25–27, with the latter stating that Simeon 'ne sceolde deaðes onbyrian ær þan þe he crist gesawe' ('must not taste death before he sees Christ'). Though the phrase *deaþes (on)byrigan* is a relatively familiar phrase in Old English, and presents a good translation of the (also relatively widespread) Latin *gustare mortem*, it is nevertheless notable that both texts uniquely share the same aberration from the Vulgate passage. The phrase itself likely has its ultimate source in the synoptic Gospels (in Mark 9. 1, Matthew 16. 28, Luke 9. 27) concerning those who will not 'taste death' until the Son of Man comes. Though the parallels between Vercelli XVII and Ælfric's homily are perhaps not secure enough to argue a direct connection, these similarities may show a common influence whether from a particular source or, following Bedingfield and Godden, a shared liturgical tradition.

Though I cannot propose a more direct source for these particular passages in Ælfric and Vercelli XVII, I can perhaps offer a closer origin of influence than what has been previously conjectured. An intriguing analogue can be found among the large and variegated corpus of writings devoted to the miracle of the transubstantiation. The genre in general affords interesting comparison in its focus upon the tactile presence of the body of the Christ-child, a detail often used to emphasize the literalness of the conversion of Christ's body into the bread and wine. Among these texts, the eighth-century *Carmen Nyniae* offers an especially poignant comparison, as it likens the ecstatic supplicant (in the figure of the priest below) to Simeon in the temple, focussing especially upon the embrace that binds these figures in imitation of the biblical event as reported in the Lucan pericope:[70]

---

[70] My inspiration for connecting this poem with Vercelli XVII is twofold: the first is a recent paper given by Thomas N. Hall (entitled 'The Study of Eucharistic Theology at Salisbury Under Bishop Osmund (1078–99)', delivered at Kalamazoo in May 2006), in which Hall discussed a homily found in London, British Library, Cotton MS Tiberius C. I (on fols 173ᵛ–176ᵛ) featuring a similar account of the Eucharistic miracle. The second comes from a subsequent discovery by Andy Orchard in which he found the poetic source for just this passage in the *Carmen Nyniae*. Orchard treats this poem in his 'Wish You Were Here: Alcuin's Courtly Poetry and the Boys

425 Presbiter at pauidus prostratus uultibus herbas
Liquerat et stupidus sacrae super ardua mensae
Cernere promeruit patris uenerabile pignus:
Conspicit in disco puerum sedisse beatum,
Quem senex Simeon ueteris sub culmine templi
430 **Infantem uenerans palmis portare sacratis**
Promeruit letus. Nitidus tum nuncius infit:
'Terrore discusso Christum si cernere uelis,
Quem prius absconsum nitidi sub tegmine panis
Mystica uerba canens semper sacrare solebas,
435 Nunc oculis spectans manibus tractare memento.'
Presbiter inde pius celesti munere fretus,
Quod mirum dictu est, puerum trementibus ulnis
Accepit et pectus uenerandum pectori iunxit,
Fusus in amplexum dat uultibus oscula sanctis,
440 **Attingens labris pulcherrima labia Christi.**
His demum exactis fulgentia corporis almi
Membra restituit praeclare in uertice mensae;
Rursus sub pauido compressit pectore terram
Obsecrans dominum caeli, dignetur ut ipse
445 In panem uerti naturam corporis album.
Post haec exsurgens nitidam super ardua lancis
Inuenit oblatam in formam remeasse priorem.

[But the fearful priest, prostrate on his face, had left the lawn and, amazed, was deemed worthy to see the venerable child of the Father above the top of the sacred altar. **He saw, sitting in the dish, that holy boy whom the old man Simeon happily was deemed worthy to carry and venerate as an infant in his blessed hands under the roof of the old temple**. Then a shining messenger spoke: 'if, having put aside your fear, you wish to see Christ who formerly has been hidden under the covering of the shining bread, whom, singing mystical words, you always used to worship, now looking with your eyes remember to touch him with your hands.' **Then that pious priest endowed with a heavenly gift took up the boy with trembling arms (a thing marvelous to tell) and he touched the venerable breast to his own breast, and, locked in an embrace, he kissed the sacred face, touching most beautiful lips to the lips of Christ.** Finally, once this was done, he put back the brilliant limbs of the fine body on the top of the bright altar; and once again he pressed the ground under his fearful breast, praying to the Lord of heaven that he might deign to change the nature of His body into white bread. Rising up after this, he found on the top of the paten that the shining form had returned to the earlier one presented.]

Back Home', in *Courts and Regions in Medieval Europe*, ed. by Sarah Rees Jones, Richard Marks, and A. J. Minnis (New York, 2000), pp. 21–43. Though the comparison of this passage to the Old English homilies for the Purification is new, I am indebted to both sources.

The focus on the ecstatic embrace is certainly suggestive of the kind of gesture seen in both Old English homilies, and it is easy to see why these authors, in search of an appropriate commemorative model, may have looked beyond the still slim canon of writings about the Purification. One wonders too whether the Eucharistic context itself may have served to suggest the idiomatic 'tasting of death' in both texts, already noted as an aberration from the pericope text, and perhaps also the particular emphasis in Vercelli XVII upon sight and spectacle. Though the influence here cannot be but tentative, it is nevertheless evident that both Old English authors culled their materials from a variety of texts, and often with notable freedom.

But if the Vercelli homilist takes such liberties with the Vulgate material, perhaps a similar independence can be expected with regard to other source materials. For example, previous scholarship has linked the following passage in Vercelli XVII.121–28 to both Gregory the Great's Homily viii on the Gospels[71] and also John 1. 9 and Luke 2. 14. Here, the elements in bold designate verbal repetitions:

> **Soðlice** ure Hælend is ðæt **soðe leoht** 7 þæt **soðe** ece, se ðe **inlihteð** ælcne mannan, ðe in middangeard cymeð. 7 eall mancynn he gebyrhteð 7 **inlihteð** mid his þrymmes mihte 7 mid his **wuldre**, for þan englas hine heredon 7 **wuldredon** 7 him lof sægdon æt his acennesse 7 ðus cwædon: '**Wuldor** si ðe gode in heannesse 7 in earðan 7 **sib** þam mannum þe <synd> godes willan <wyrcende>.' þa **cyrdon** þa englas to ure **sybbe** 7 to ure lufan þa hie gesegon 7 ongeaton ðæt Dryhten Crist wæs **gecyrred** 7 ymbesald mid mennissce lichoman.

> [**Truly** our Saviour is the **true light** and the **true** eternity, he who **enlightens** each man who comes into middle-earth. And all mankind he brightens and **enlightens** with his might of magnificence and with his **glory**. Therefore angels praised him and **glorified** him and spoke praise to him at his birth and thus spoke: '**Glory** be to you, God, in the highest part and on earth, and **peace** to the men who <are working> the will of god.' Then **turned** the angels to our **peace** and to our love when they saw and perceived that the lord Christ was **turned** and was surrounded with a human body.]

As can be seen from the rhetorical flourishes above, the passage demonstrates exceptional verbal artistry. A particularly notable effect is the homilist's use of dense repetitions of discrete word elements in *wuldor-*, *soð-*, *inliht-*, *sib-* (*syb-*), and *gecyr-*. Though Scragg has argued elsewhere that such repetitions betray the paucity of the homilist's vocabulary, I would argue by contrast that they reveal his formal artistry. The effect is enhanced by the use of parallel structures throughout: I note in particular the construction of two examples of a *tricolon abundans*, or a statement containing three elements that grows longer in the final clause. The first of these

---

[71] *PL* 76.1077A.

occurs in the phrase *heredon 7 wuldredon 7 him lof sægdon æt his acennesse*, and the second in the phrase *in heannesse 7 in earðan 7 sib þam mannum þe <synd> godes willan <wyrcende>*. The effect is compounded by the presence of pervasive doublets, including *soðe leoht 7 þæt soðe ece* ('true light and the true eternity'), *gebyrhteð 7 inlihteð* ('brightens and enlightens'), *mid his þrymmes mihte 7 mid his wuldre* ('with his might of magnificence and with his glory'), *to ure sybbe 7 to ure lufan* ('to our peace and to our love'), *gesegon 7 ongeaton* ('saw and perceived'), and *gecyrred 7 ymbesald* ('was turned and was surrounded').

The detection of this highly symmetrical structure reveals probable interference to the few sources that have been identified. For example, the first sentence, linked to John 1. 9 ('erat lux uera quae inluminat omnem hominem uenientem in mundum'; 'That was the true light, which enlighteneth every man that cometh into this world'), shows the homilist picking up on the semantic parallel between *lux* and *inluminat*, but expanding *lux uera* to a doublet *soðe leoht 7 þæt soðe ece*. The Vercelli passage 'wuldor si ðe gode in heannesse 7 in earðan 7 sib þam mannum þe <synd> godes willan < wyrcende>' ('Glory be to you, God, in the highest part and on earth, and peace to the men who are working the will of god') likewise roughly parallels Luke 2. 14, 'gloria in altissimis Deo et in terra pax in hominibus bonae uoluntatis' ('Glory to God in the highest: and on earth peace to men of good will'). As can be seen from the above notation, Scragg emends the final clause to *syn godes willan* ('are of good will') to make it conform more readily to the source passage, arguing that the mistake in the passage results from the scribal confusion of the Old English stresses in *god* ('God') and *gōd* ('good'). However, a comparison of this passage with several parallel lines in Vercelli V (likewise drawn from Gregory's Homilies viii and v) may serve better to illumine the source of this error. It is perhaps significant that a similar mistranslation of Luke 2. 14 occurs twice in Vercelli V (drawn from the same Gregory Homily viii):[72]

> Vercelli V.36–37: 'Wuldor sie Gode on heannesse 7 sybb on eorþan þam
>   mannum þe godes willan sien <wyrcende>' [Scragg omits *wyrcende*]
> Vercelli V.167–68: 'Wuldor sie on heanessum Gode 7 sibb on eorðan þam
>   mannum, þe <god willað habban>' [Scragg: *godne willan habbað*]
> ('Glory be to God in the highest part and peace on earth to the men who will
> have God' [Scragg: 'who have good will'])

---

[72] There are likewise two variant texts for Vercelli V, in Oxford, Bodleian Library, MS Bodley 340 (fols 1ʳ–5ᵛ) and in Cambridge, Corpus Christi College, MS 198 (fols 1ʳ–7ʳ); however, for the passages being discussed above, the variant texts are close enough to avoid their specific mention.

In both examples the Vercelli V homilist has 'god's will' as the object, rather than the Vulgate 'good will', and in the first example we find the addition of the word *wyrcende* as in Vercelli XVII, to help make better sense of the rogue syntax. Indeed, a close inspection of the first example in Vercelli V shows that the only significant departure from the line in Vercelli XVII is the position of the word *sien* and the addition of a paratactic *and*; however, as we have already seen, the parataxis seems to have been added as a stylistic flourish by the homilist in order to create a second *tricolon abundans*. Interestingly, the misreading of *gōd* for *god* in Vercelli V is later corrected in Vercelli V.178–79, which states 'sibb sie mid mannum, þe <godes> willan hæbben' ('peace be with men, who have God's will'), though it requires the undoing of Scragg's emendation of *godne* back to the MS *godes* to see this correspondence. Significantly, this latter quotation in Vercelli V is derived not from Gregory's Homily viii, but rather from his Homily v,[73] so perhaps accounting for the disparate translation. Rather than hiding such discrepancies in the translation, the Vercelli V homilist makes a virtue of these homophones by punning continually on the connection between 'good will' and 'God's will', as in Vercelli V.181–83: 'Hæbben we forþam godne willan on ure heortan, for þan þe we ne bioð æfre idele godra weorca for Godes eagum gif usse heortan bioð gefyllede mid <Godes> willan' ('let us have therefore good will in our hearts, because we will not ever idle of good works before God's eyes, if our hearts are filled with God's will'; note Scragg's emendation to *god[um]*).

While Scragg points out the correspondence between these shared passages in Vercelli V and XVII, he does not push the point beyond coincidence.[74] It seems possible, however, that either both homilies are drawing from the same (and likely Old English) version of Gregory's Homily viii, or that Vercelli XVII is borrowing directly from Vercelli V or a close variant (since Vercelli V draws heavily from Gregory's homily throughout). Several other verbal parallels with regard to these two homilies may add weight to this theory.[75] For example, the above Vercelli XVII.126 'þa cyrdon þa englas to ure sybbe 7 to ure lufan, for þan þe hie gesegon' ('then turned the angels to our peace and to our love, because they saw') presents a nearly verbatim match for Vercelli V.174–75: 'ac hie sona cyrdon to ure sibbe 7 ure lufan, þa he gesegon'.[76] Furthermore, a comparison of both texts with the

---

[73] For the identification, see *Vercelli Homilies*, ed. by Scragg, p. 120, *ap. crit.* 177–83.

[74] *Vercelli Homilies*, ed. by Scragg, p. 279, n. 1, and p. 288, nn. 125–26.

[75] Scragg cites these in *Fontes Anglo-Saxonici*, but not in his edition.

[76] The parallelism is noted broadly by Scragg in *Vercelli Homilies*, p. 279, n. 1.

relevant Gregorian passage reveals unique similarities between Vercelli XVII and V (and its variants):

> Quia enim coeli Rex terram nostrae carnis assumpsit, infirmitatem nostram illa jam angelica celsitudo non despicit. <u>Ad pacem nostram angeli redeunt</u>, intentionem prioris discordiae postponunt; et quos prius infirmos abjectosque despexerant, jam socios venerantur.

> [For because the King of Heaven has taken up the earth of our flesh, that angelic loftiness does not now despise our weakness. <u>Angels return to our peace</u>, they put back the intention of our earlier quarrel, and those whom they had despised previously as weak and lowly, they now honour as companions.]

The doublet *to ure sybbe 7 to ure lufan* found in the two vernacular quotations is not represented in the Latin. Though it would perhaps be premature to suggest a connection beyond the Gregorian material, it is noteworthy that, elsewhere, Vercelli XVII and V share verbal correspondences which have not yet been traced to a Latin source:[77]

> Vercelli XVII.70–71: 'and he for ure lufan astah of heofonum on eorðan'
> Vercelli V.184–85: 'and he for ure lufan astah of heofonum to eorðan'.
> ('for our love he descended from heaven to earth'.)

I also note the particular closeness of the two Vercelli renderings of Matthew 5. 9 ('beati pacifici quoniam filii Dei uocabuntur'; 'Blessed are the peacemakers: for they shall be called the children of God'):[78]

> Vercelli XVII.62–63: 'Eadige beoð þa gesybsuman men, for þan þe hie beoð Godes bearn genemde.'
> Vercelli V.85–86: 'Eadige bioð þa sybsuman men, for þan þe hie bioð Godes bearn genemnde.'
> ('blessed are the peace-making men, because they are named the sons of God'.)

Though the Old English in both cases is too close to the gospel passage to show any unique sharings between Vercelli XVII and V, comparison with other translations of this passage in Old English are nevertheless illuminating:[79]

---

[77] Scragg identifies the parallelism in his *Fontes Anglo-Saxonici* entry for Vercelli V.184–85, but not in his entry for Vercelli XVII.70–71, nor in his textual edition of the homilies.

[78] This time Scragg notes the connection in his *Fontes Anglo-Saxonici* entry for Vercelli XVII.62–63, but not in his entry for Vercelli V.85–86, nor in his textual edition.

[79] These passages are cited from the online *Dictionary of Old English* (<http://www.doe.utoronto.ca/> [accessed December 2005]).

C8.2.1 (Rushworth) Matthew: 'þa sibsume vel friðsume forþon þe hie beoþ godes bearn genemde'.

C8.1.1 (Lindisfarne) Matthew: 'eadge biðon sibsume vel friðgeorne forðon ða suna godes geceigd biðon vel genemned'.

C15 Defensor, *Liber scintillarum*: 'drihten segð on godspelle eadige gesibsume forþi bearn godes hi byð gecigede'.

Here again, the comparison shows how close the two Vercelli homilies are to each other, by comparison with other extant Old English renderings.

What the evidence of the comparison between Vercelli XVII and both Ælfric's *CH* I.9 and Vercelli V demonstrates is that the author (or given the likehood that Vercelli XVII is a copy, several authors) was likely using both Latin and Old English sources as a mediating step in the composition of this homily. These influences can be measured not only by the negative evidence of the absence of a source text, but also through the use of such intricate rhetorical devices as verbal repetition, echo words, wordplay, and doublets, all of which go beyond those sources we have on record for the homily, and which showcase the potential of vernacular prose as a medium of effective, flexible, and artistic expression. In the case of Vercelli XVII, the use of sustained repetition seems to offer more than just an adorning feature. Through the use of repeating words and gestures, the homilist is able provocatively to create a complicated model of mimesis through which Mary's 'cleanness' becomes imitated and repeated in the subsequent purification of Christ himself, Simeon, and even (so the homilist hopes) the audience. Though according to the linear structure of the homily, Mary seems at first to disappear as the focus of veneration shifts to Christ and Simeon, it is precisely through the author's use of mimesis that Mary, offered here as our exemplar, is powerfully reinserted into the text.

Though it seems in recent years that it has become something of a taboo to take to task the discussion of the style and rhetoric of Old English prose without first having in place a firm set of sources for textual comparison (and again the bias with respect to Old English poetry is notable), it should be clear from the foregoing analysis that this step need not present an absolute prerequisite. Indeed, in the case of Vercelli XVII, it seems likely thatm should a governing Latin source be detected for this homily, the same kind of free 'prosaic license' would be evident in the homilist's handling of the source material as he exemplified in his relaxed adaptation of the gospel pericope. What this immediate comparison calls for, then, is a closer attention in general to the parallels between vernacular texts both within single-manuscript compilation and, indeed, across those more densely perceived barriers with respect to authorship and chronology. And if this small sampling can offer any larger paradigm, it is perhaps the notion that it is time to treat Old English prose, even anonymous and unsourced Old English prose, not as the poor relation of Latin, but rather as a remarkable and characteristically Anglo-Saxon vehicle for the artful expression of specifically Anglo-Saxon concerns.[80]

[80] I would like to thank Andy Orchard in particular for his helpful comments with regard to this essay.

The Codicology of Anglo-Saxon Homiletic Manuscripts, Especially the Blickling Homilies

M. J. Toswell

Some fifty manuscripts from Anglo-Saxon England contain homilies written in the vernacular. A few are single occurrences, often added texts at the end of other collections; others are part of mixed-text manuscripts, according to modern notions of genre, such as the penitential works in prose and poetry of the Vercelli Book, or the range of liturgical and pedagogic texts found in Cambridge, Corpus Christi College, MS 201. Most of the surviving Old English homilies, however, occur in collections in a single manuscript. Until quite recently, research completed on these homiletic materials has addressed individual authors or themes or sources. Ælfric has been particularly well served on the first count, themes of biblical or popular significance (dry bones speaking, apocalypse, catechetical *narratio*) on the second, and Paul the Deacon's homiliary and the many patristic sources for ideas in the homilies on the third. The manuscripts qua manuscripts, however, worth investigating for what they might reveal about the intellectual and spiritual concerns of Anglo-Saxon England, have only begun to come into their own in the past decade.[1] Elaine Treharne considers the post-Conquest reception

---

[1] The trend towards 'turning to the manuscript' happening across medieval studies is difficult to date and place. Some will argue that manuscript studies, or codicology as was, has always been going on, that scholars have always learned some of its aspects, and that as a specialist field it is better left to specialists. Others will suggest that the return to the manuscript and to thinking about the manuscript origins of the medieval texts which we see sanitized and organized and generally altered in ways both large and small is a major shift in thinking that is only partly complete. For Anglo-Saxonists, the principal signposts along to the way might be Fred C. Robinson's articles on editing and the manuscript context of Old English texts, now collected in his *The Editing of Old English* (Oxford, 1994), but starting with his 'Old English Literature in its Most Immediate

of Anglo-Saxon texts, as evidenced in the many twelfth-century copies — particularly of homilies — made and obviously used in the early Norman period.[2] Christine Franzen studies the glosses and commentaries of the so-called 'tremulous hand' for what they suggest about post-Conquest reception of a range of texts which correspond very closely with the sermons and homilies which interest Treharne.[3] Mary Swan examines the multiple manuscript copies of individual homilies in order to ascertain what principles of arrangement and revision were at work in the scribe's or compiler's head.[4] Swan's work lies closest to my concerns here, which are the manuscripts themselves for what they reveal about the Anglo-Saxon creation, dissemination, and reception of these homiletic works. In particular, my focus is the compilation and layout of these manuscripts, and the evidence provided by the quiring, wear on particular folia of the manuscript, copying process as best we can deduce it, and especially the punctuation used by the scribes in producing these texts. More specifically, I will consider how the copying of many of the homiletic manuscripts as collections of booklets might alter our sense of the homogeneity of homily collections from Anglo-Saxon England. The principal focus by which to address these issues will be the manuscript of the Blickling Homilies, one of the most well known but nonetheless the least-analysed collection of homiletic texts

Context', in *Old English Literature in Context*, ed. by J. D. Niles (Cambridge, 1980), pp. 11–29 and 157–56; more recent signposts include Katherine O'Brien O'Keeffe, *Visible Song: Transitional Literacy in Old English Verse* (Cambridge, 1990), and collections since then which have focussed on editing (e.g. *The Editing of Old English: Papers from the 1990 Manchester Conference*, ed. by D. G. Scragg and Paul E. Szarmach (Cambridge, 1994), and *New Approaches to Editing Old English Verse*, ed. by Sarah Larratt Keefer and Katherine O'Brien O'Keeffe (Woodbridge, 1998)), and on manuscripts (e.g. *The Poems of MS Junius 11: Basic Readings*, ed. by R. M. Liuzza (New York, 2002)).

[2] See, for example, Elaine M. Treharne, 'The Dates and Origins of Three Twelfth-Century Old English Manuscripts', in *Anglo-Saxon Manuscripts and their Heritage*, ed. by Phillip Pulsiano and Elaine M. Treharne (Aldershot, 1998), pp. 227–53.

[3] Christine Franzen, *The Tremulous Hand of Worcester: A Study of Old English in the Thirteenth Century* (Oxford, 1991).

[4] See, for example, Mary Swan, 'Ælfric's *Catholic Homilies* in the Twelfth Century', in *Rewriting Old English in the Twelfth Century*, ed. by Mary Swan and Elaine M. Treharne, CSASE, 30 (Cambridge, 2000), pp. 62–82. Note also the joint project directed by Mary Swan and Elaine Treharne on 'The Production and Use of English Manuscripts 1060 to 1200' at the University of Leicester in conjunction with the University of Leeds, details of which can be found at <http://www.le.ac.uk/ee/em1060to1220/index.htm>.

available from Anglo-Saxon England.[5] More careful study of its codicological features, beginning with a reminder about the booklets which are a feature of many of these manuscripts, may lead to a reconsideration of our usual treatment of homiletic manuscripts as coherent wholes, the product of a compiler's careful intent.

Pamela Robinson's famous article 'Self-Contained Units in Composite Manuscripts of the Anglo-Saxon Period' addresses the question of booklets or *libelli* added to or included in manuscripts compiled in early medieval England. She starts by pointing out two examples, both of vernacular homilies, in which the booklet so clearly circulated separately that it was folded down the middle.[6] She gives examples of booklets in manuscripts of poetry (Cambridge, University Library, MS Gg. 5. 35, the 'Cambridge Songs' manuscript, which is a schoolbook made up of four booklets of poetry), medical material (London, British Library, Harley MS 585 consists of two booklets, a *lacnunga* and a herbal), and a Wulfstan manuscript. However, her principal concern is, in her own words, 'those booklets which were

---

[5] The Blickling Homilies is MS 71 of the Scheide Library, now housed at Princeton University. See Helmut Gneuss, *Handlist of Anglo-Saxon Manuscripts: A List of Manuscripts and Manuscript Fragments Written or Owned in England up to 1100*, MRTS, 241 (Tempe, 2001), no. 905, in which the manuscript is dated s. x/xi. The first edition is *The Blickling Homilies of the Tenth Century*, ed. by Richard Morris, EETS: OS, 58, 63, 73 (London, 1874–80; repr. as one volume, 1997). A useful edition is R. MacG. Dawson, 'An Edition of the Blickling Homilies' (unpublished doctoral thesis, Oxford University, 1969), in four volumes with text, translation, notes, and glossary. More recently, see *The Blickling Homilies: Edition and Translation*, ed. and trans. by Richard J. Kelly (London, 2003), which is not a significant advance on Morris. Kelly's facing translation is insufficiently unlike the one appearing in Morris; Kelly himself in the preface states that it 'updates the Modern English translations' (p. vii). Some problems in Morris's edition, long known to scholars acquainted with the compilation of the manuscript, are corrected, and Kelly provides a short overview of preaching in the early medieval church, as well as a more extensive discussion of the later medieval use (in Lincoln as an oath book) and recent history of the manuscript. The textual notes provide helpful explanations of the liturgical and biblical backgrounds of each homily, and bring together some of the scholarship on each text. Kelly's stated interest, however, is primarily palaeographical, and he has a table of punctuation by sermon, and detailed study of the capitals and the scribal hands of the manuscript. He unfortunately depends for his analysis of the quires on a microfilm made in 1955 when the manuscript was unbound and rearranged into its proper order in New York. His description of the quiring (p. xxxii) is nonetheless useful, although Kelly does not reach the conclusions posited here.

[6] See Pamela Robinson, 'Self-Contained Units in Composite Manuscripts of the Anglo-Saxon Period', *ASE*, 7 (1978), 231–38, repr. in *Anglo-Saxon Manuscripts: Basic Readings*, ed. by Mary P. Richards, Basic Readings in Anglo-Saxon England, 2 (New York, 1994), pp. 25–35. See also her '"The Booklet": A Self-Contained Unit in Composite Manuscripts', in *Codicologica 3: Essais typologiques*, ed. by A. Gruys and J. P. Gumbert (Leiden, 1980), pp. 46–69.

assembled to form collections of vernacular homilies'. Later in the article, Robinson goes so far as to propose that '[i]t may have been the practice to keep a collection of homiletic booklets loose in a wrapper rather than sewn into a binding'.[7] These are bold and far-reaching claims, and Robinson provides detailed examples to prove each one. She considers in some detail Cambridge, Corpus Christi College, MS 198, which includes two booklets incorporated into the existing collection (itself already a collection of booklets), and Cambridge, Corpus Christi College, MS 421, which has two booklets of homilies (one of which is from Exeter) added to two earlier booklets written elsewhere. Oxford, Bodleian Library, MS Junius 85 includes several small and portable booklets of homilies, as do several other eleventh-century manuscripts.[8] The booklets can easily be carried about and used as necessary, perhaps in parish churches. Homiliaries themselves, on the other hand, tended to be large manuscripts for use on a lectern, since they required the support of a desk. However, a booklet was portable. Robinson notes that transmission in booklet exemplars means that individual sections of a homiletic collection may have very different textual relations. What she does not do, because it is not her concern, is to speculate on what her argument means for those of us who think about the compilation of Anglo-Saxon homiletic manuscripts in the context of the intellectual, religious, and popular culture of early medieval England.

Robinson's argument is an important one, and she adduces a great deal of evidence in support of her thesis. Her work, implicitly or explicitly, has been picked up by several scholars working on the poetry manuscripts of Old English. Thus, Patrick Conner contends, with a very great deal of evidence, that the Exeter Manu-

---

[7] Robinson, 'Self-Contained Units', pp. 30 and 31.

[8] Jean Vezin provides a wider consideration of the role of the booklet, *libellus*, or *cahier* in his '"*Quaderni simul ligati*": Recherches sur les manuscripts en cahiers', in *Of the Making of Books: Medieval Manuscripts, their Scribes and Readers: Essays Presented to M. B. Parkes*, ed. by P. R. Robinson and Rivkah Zim (Aldershot, 1997), pp. 64–70. He argues that the Book of Mulling from the second quarter of the eighth century in Ireland consists of four booklets and was kept in a small leather box to keep the booklets safe. Some twenty such collections survive from the Carolingian era, about half of them from Fulda, and others come from the twelfth century including Durham, Cathedral Library, MS A. IV. 34, a very small codex of notes on the *Cantica canticorum*. Elsewhere in the same volume, Helmut Gneuss intriguingly points out that save for fols 174–79, London, British Library, Cotton MS Tiberius A. III is a composite but single volume and not a collection of booklets; see 'Origin and Provenance of Anglo-Saxon Manuscripts: The Case of Cotton Tiberius A. III', pp. 13–48. Gneuss here almost seems to imply that we should think of Anglo-Saxon manuscripts as potentially collections of booklets unless other interpretations intervene.

script is a collection of booklets.[9] Similarly, Kevin Kiernan argues that the Nowell Codex is a collection of four booklets, with the most important of those booklets being the one that contains the poem *Beowulf*.[10] Don Scragg has also proposed that the Vercelli manuscript is a collection of booklets, though interestingly he does not extend his careful codicological analysis of the Vercelli manuscript to the Blickling Homilies.[11] Given that Robinson's argument has had currency among scholars of Old English poetry (and the mixed collection of poetry and prose that is the Vercelli manuscript), it seems worth reconsidering Robinson's much more extensive argument that homiletic manuscripts in particular were collections of booklets, perhaps kept in the medieval equivalent of a filing cabinet and looking rather like our favourite lectures, available at a moment's notice. In particular, her argument may be worth considering in tandem with a consideration of how the copying of punctuation (or lack thereof) might reflect organization into booklets.

More specifically, if punctuation features were to change from homily to homily, or from section to section (or even, if booklets had otherwise been identified, from booklet to booklet) in a given homiletic manuscript, this might well suggest that we should look more carefully at the texts. Few scholars have hitherto been closely interested in punctuation, especially in homiletic manuscripts. Two that have are Peter Clemoes and Malcolm Parkes. Clemoes is very much concerned with questions of performance and audience when he discusses punctuation, either with respect to a specific manuscript of Ælfric's *Catholic Homilies* or in more general terms with respect to Anglo-Saxon practice. His was the proposal that liturgical punctuation was to be found in Anglo-Saxon manuscripts.[12] Succeeding him in a concern for the close analysis of punctuation of the manuscript is

---

[9] Patrick Conner argues that the Exeter Book consists of three booklets, proposing that although one scribe wrote the manuscript, the work was done at several different times; see his 'The Structure of the Exeter Book Codex (Exeter, Cathedral Library, MS. 3501)', *Scriptorium*, 40 (1986), 233–42 (p. 309), repr. in *Anglo-Saxon Manuscripts*, ed. by Richards, pp. 301–15, and also the further analysis in his *Anglo-Saxon Exeter: A Tenth-Century Cultural History* (Woodbridge, 1993).

[10] See Kevin Kiernan, *Beowulf and the 'Beowulf' Manuscript* (New Brunswick, 1981; rev. edn Ann Arbor, 1996).

[11] See D. Scragg, 'The Compilation of the Vercelli Book', *ASE*, 2 (1973), 189–207, repr. in *Anglo-Saxon Manuscripts*, ed. by Richards, pp. 317–43. Also useful for the comparative study of the Blickling and Vercelli collections is his 'The Corpus of Vernacular Homilies and Prose Saints' Lives before Ælfric', *ASE*, 8 (1979), 223–77.

[12] See Peter Clemoes, *Liturgical Influence on Punctuation in Late Old English and Early Middle English Manuscripts* (Cambridge, 1952; repr. Kalamazoo, 1980).

Malcolm Parkes, whose *Pause and Effect* indirectly suggests another approach to Anglo-Saxon homiletic manuscripts. Parkes argues for the 'sense of decorum which Anglo-Saxon scribes brought to the production of books',[13] citing their introduction of word-separation, their development of a disciplined and improved insular minuscule, and their sophisticated approach to *ordinatio* or the layout of the page. They developed a hierarchy of scripts and imitated features of punctuation found in a range of manuscripts. They made use, for example, of 'the ancient system of *distinctiones* by means of single points placed at three different heights',[14] a system they probably derived from Irish practice. From the same source came the tendency to add extra punctuation marks in order to delineate the importance of a given pause, so that the end of a segment or of a sermon might have a triangle, or even a double triangle, of dots or punctuation marks. Parkes argues, in short, that Anglo-Saxon scribes brought intelligent and careful thought to bear on the layout and punctuation of their texts, whether vernacular or sacred. Manuscripts of homilies, which might have been intended for oral delivery and which certainly were intended for careful reading, perhaps even meditation, would bear scrutiny from the point of view of punctuation. Should a given manuscript written by one, or perhaps two, scribes evince great differences in its approach to punctuation, differences which correspond to the booklet divisions elucidated by Robinson, then more analysis would obviously be necessary. Since Parkes's assessment of the Anglo-Saxon attitude to the text might preclude carelessness as an explanation for differences in approach within the same manuscript, other explanations are worth exploring. Several are possibilities: the different booklets had different provenances, or the manuscript itself was a more haphazard collection than has been suggested, or the scribes were reworking some texts into matched sets and did not have time for similar care with other texts.

Thus, both the punctuation copied from a source text or applied by an individual copyist and the organization of a manuscript into booklets provide information that will allow for further reflection as to the compilation of particular Anglo-Saxon manuscripts. Since Robinson highlights homiletic manuscripts in particular as partaking of the booklet format, it becomes important that we closely examine these manuscripts for possible evidence of this codicological feature. At the same time, it must be noted at the outset that punctuation evidence by itself

---

[13] Malcolm Parkes, *Pause and Effect: A History of Punctuation in the West* (Berkeley, 1993), p. 26.

[14] Parkes, *Pause and Effect*, p. 27.

will not be sufficient since punctuation is particularly tricky evidence to assess. Only a combination of pieces of evidence (including quiring, wear, and evidence of the copying process) can lead to any conclusions about the compilation of Anglo-Saxon homiletic manuscripts. To test these ideas in a very preliminary way, therefore, the Blickling Homilies manuscript may prove useful.

The Blickling Homilies as a manuscript and as a collection of texts have a chequered past and a chequered present.[15] Once seen as a prickly pear of a manuscript and the creation of an eschatologically obsessed monk, MS 71 of the Scheide Collection held today in the Princeton University Library is nowadays generally considered to be a not entirely successful early attempt at a *temporale*, with six texts at the end providing a sketchy *sanctorale*.[16] Until the middle of the twentieth century, the manuscript had many leaves bound out of order; when it was rebound, however, the binding was too tight, the glue extremely thick, and it is now very difficult to work with.[17] One of the two pre–Benedictine Reform vernacular collections of anonymous homilies in Anglo-Saxon England, the Blickling Homilies gets overshadowed, and stands in need of rehabilitation, because the other such collection is the Vercelli Book. In his collection of essays *On Old English*, Bruce Mitchell listed the Blickling Homilies as one of the texts in most desperate need of being properly re-edited.[18] That was many years ago. More recently, Scragg has called for a good edition of the homilies with their sources, and (though he does not say it) with a full glossary and textual notes. On the other hand, the homilies are at least garnering some good thematic studies and steadily better assessments

---

[15] The facsimile edition of the manuscript is edited by Rudolph Willard, *The Blickling Homilies: The John H. Scheide Library, Titusville, Pennsylvania*, EEMF, 10 (Copenhagen, 1960). For descriptions of the manuscript see also Rowland Collins, *Anglo-Saxon Vernacular Manuscripts in America: Exhibited at the Pierpont Morgan Library, 1 April – 9 May 1976* (New York, 1976), §8, pp. 52–57; Neil Ker, *Catalogue of Manuscripts Containing Anglo-Saxon* (Oxford, 1957; repr. with suppl. 1990), §382, and Gneuss, *Handlist*, no. 905.

[16] The most important discussion of the manuscript is D. G. Scragg, 'The Homilies of the Blickling Manuscript', in *Learning and Literature in Anglo-Saxon England: Studies Presented to Peter Clemoes on the Occasion of his Sixty-fifth Birthday*, ed. by Michael Lapidge and Helmut Gneuss (Cambridge, 1985), pp. 299–316. Kelly's discussion in *The Blickling Homilies* neither subtracts from nor adds to Scragg's conclusions.

[17] I am very grateful to Paul Needham, Scheide Librarian at Princeton University, for permitting me to examine the manuscript in some detail in April 2003, and to the staff in the Rare Book Room at the Princeton Library for their consideration.

[18] Bruce Mitchell, *On Old English: Selected Papers* (Oxford, 1988), p. 332.

in the general studies of Old English literature.[19] For example, the 1986 *New Critical History* by Greenfield and Calder has the following:

> Both theological and literary criticism have often characterized all the anonymous homilies as crude; but although they draw heavily upon fragments of Latin originals, they do create coherent orations. And while the Blickling collection may not be entirely consistent in its theology, particularly in its explanations of what happens to the soul between death and the Last Judgment, it nevertheless reveals an informed idea of confession and penance. As Dalbey has shown, the compiler had a special interest in gathering homilies that stress gentleness and compassion: they are parenetic (that is, hortatory) in tone, rather than stern and didactic. While their emphasis is on repentance, it is also on the possibility of living a virtuous Christian life and achieving redemption. To this end the various authors in the Blickling group devote considerable attention to stylistic effects which will make their pleadings psychologically effective. These homilies may be theologically conservative, but they are not without some intelligent awareness of the human predicament seen from a benevolent Christian perspective.[20]

Greenfield and Calder, then, note the inconsistencies among the homilies while nonetheless arguing for a compiler with a plan for a homogeneous collection, and a compiler with compassion and 'intelligent awareness' of the early medieval world in which the audience for these homilies strove to maintain their faith. The last serious study of the role of that compiler, that gentle and sympathetic individual, was Scragg's 1985 analysis in the Clemoes festschrift. Scragg revisited the vexed question of the quiring of the manuscript, following Clemoes in correcting Rudolph Willard's introduction to the facsimile edition on a number of points, and noting that Neil Ker had been obliged to work from photographs and thereby was unable to provide a detailed analysis of the manuscript. Scragg divides it into

---

[19] See Milton McC. Gatch, *Preaching and Theology in Anglo-Saxon England: Ælfric and Wulfstan* (Toronto, 1977), and especially the essays collected in his *Eschatology and Christian Nurture* (Aldershot, 2000), which are the best introduction to this field. The only monograph on these texts is J. Elizabeth Jeffrey, *Blickling Spirituality and the Old English Vernacular Homily: A Textual Analysis*, Studies in Mediaeval Literature, 1 (Lewiston, 1989). Jeffrey takes the Blickling manuscript as a coherent whole and moves back and forth in her analysis through all the sermons as if they were a monolithic block in service to early Christian dogma. There are many good points in the details, but her approach does not correspond with that taken here.

[20] Stanley B. Greenfield and Daniel G. Calder with Michael Lapidge, *A New Critical History of Old English Literature* (New York, 1986), p. 72. Robert D. Fulk and Christopher M. Cain in *A History of Old English Literature* (Oxford, 2003) make very similar remarks, noting a focus in the texts on charity to the poor and kindness, but also the eschatological elements in these sermons to be preached to the laity during Mass. In particular, they note the love of 'colourful narrative' in the material in the hagiographical homilies at the end of the collection (p. 75).

three blocks of homilies, the opening seven which start a *temporale*, homilies eight through fifteen which include five more *temporale* pieces and three homilies which follow the order of a *sanctorale*, and homilies sixteen through eighteen, a continuation of the *sanctorale*. He considers in some detail the relationships of the homily texts with other Old English homiletic manuscripts, adducing and explicating all the overlaps and assessing their relative importance. He finds the closest relationship to be that with Cambridge, Corpus Christi College, MS 198, partly a Canterbury-influenced homiliary of the early eleventh century, largely based on Ælfric's *Catholic Homilies*, and partly an extended series of additions in several hands of the second half of the eleventh century. The manuscript was later at Worcester. Scragg proposes that the Blickling Homilies manuscript, with its language of Mercian origin, might have close connections to CCCC 198 by way of provenance.

Scragg's argument with respect to the compilation of the Blickling manuscript in many ways resembles the general statements, as previously noted, of Pamela Robinson. It has connections with several other Old English manuscripts and extensive overlap with one. Scragg considers in some detail whether individual pieces in the Blickling manuscript were copies, or copies of copies, of other extant Old English manuscripts. The manuscript was clearly unfinished. Robinson similarly adduces extensive evidence for Old English homiletic manuscripts as being always in a state of construction and reconstruction. She further proposes that they were perhaps not even bound but kept as a collection of booklets in the monastery. She argues that the booklets which make up part or all of these manuscripts were likely available for borrowing by monks of the house or by local parish priests who needed to deliver sermons. Mary Clayton also considers these questions, although her principal concern is a slightly different aspect of the same issue: preachers and preaching in Anglo-Saxon England. Clayton concludes with respect to the Blickling Homilies that the closest analogues are collections specifically designed for the laity, or for the lay congregation.[21] She concludes their usage as preaching texts, and possibly for devotional reading, and argues that the Blickling manuscript was for preaching during Mass. As such a preaching text, it stands in contrast to the ascetic florilegium that is the Vercelli Book. Not a homiliary, the Vercelli Book is the other principal collection of homiletic material available in Anglo-Saxon England before Ælfric prepared the *Catholic Homilies* sequences in the 990s. Clayton, while acknowledging the links (three points of overlap) between the

---

[21] Mary Clayton, 'Homiliaries and Preaching in Anglo-Saxon England', *Peritia*, 4 (1985), 207–42 (pp. 223–36).

Vercelli Book and the Blickling Homilies, suggests that the stronger parallels for the Blickling manuscript are the Latin homiliaries of this type, including the collection known as the Homiliary of Saint-Père de Chartres and that of Hrabanus Maurus. She seems to value the Blickling material more highly than does Scragg, who considers the Vercelli Book the 'earliest and most important collection of anonymous homilies extant', assessing the Blickling Homilies as 'the second largest collection of anonymous homilies, which, despite the loss of five quires at the beginning and further material at the end, remains very significant in the study of the tenth-century tradition. Eighteen homilies survive, following the order of the church year'.[22]

Scragg, then, appears simply to consider the Blickling manuscript as a large collection which is significant. Clayton appears to find it of more interest, partly because it is the earliest homiliary and thereby more readily connected to Latin models for such collections, but also partly because it provides a clear set of examples of material collected and prepared for preaching. Thus, Clayton rightly concludes that, although the Vercelli Book includes twenty-three homilies and in sheer numbers is more imposing, the Blickling Homilies repays study. The Vercelli Book is nowadays generally seen as a Canterbury manuscript; Blickling is very definitely not, and has Mercian linguistic elements. Blickling, despite its meagre surviving eighteen homilies, is organized as a *temporale* with hints of a *sanctorale*, a significant step in the development of a coherent homiletic tradition. Much as Ælfric might have been horrified to learn it, his natural predecessors were the Blickling homilists, despite the use of apocryphal material, exciting narratives for no particular exegetical purpose, and saints' lives within what should properly have been a cycle of homilies set up as an early version of a *temporale*. The Vercelli Book, with its organization purely by theme — penitence, asceticism, confession, and repentance — was not generally useful for preaching. Blickling, however, was. Vercelli has been generally recognized as having been a set of booklets, but Blickling has not. The quiring of Blickling may offer some clues as to its organization as a manuscript. It would, after all, make sense if a manuscript used for preaching were a collection of booklets (to return to Robinson's argument). Thus, the quiring of the manuscript and any evidence of wear in places other than at the beginning and end of the manuscript (and particularly on the last pages of quires or the ends of homilies) will constitute the first detailed set of evidence studied here.

---

[22] Scragg, 'Corpus of Vernacular Homilies', p. 225 (re Vercelli) and p. 233 (re Blickling).

Rowland Collins in his catalogue comments on the highly irregular arrangement of sheets into quires in the Blickling Homilies and proposes that the homilist's dating of his composition in the year 971 is also an accurate date for the manuscript itself.[23] At least by implication, Collins seems to be suggesting that the compiler also wrote, or in some cases copied and revised, the texts in the manuscript. He does not mention the division into booklets. Scragg revises the collation by Willard, arguing that rather than being quires of eight with added singletons, several of the structures were quires of ten with one leaf cut back upon completion of the homily. Scragg divides the manuscript into three blocks, suggesting that the first part, with seven homilies, was pieced together over time from a number of sources. Though Scragg does not mention the implications of the point, four of these seven homilies end at the end of a quire, or within a few blank lines of the quire's end. In the second section, the outer bifolium is lost from quire 9, and a quire is lost in the middle. Most of the quires are of eight folios, and a surprising number of quire ends correspond to the end of homilies.

Another relevant issue in the quiring is wear, something not previously discussed by scholars with respect to Blickling. Wear on the last page of several homilies suggests individual circulation, if the homilies correspond to the ends of quires which could be booklets. The size of the manuscript is very small indeed, currently about the size of an A5 page (approximately the size of a child's first school notebook). Even with the cut pieces from the top, bottom, and outside edge taken into account, the manuscript would have originally been about 7.5 x 11 inches — small enough that it probably did not need folding in order to be carried about outside the scriptorium. Considerable wear does affect the end of each quire, at times rubbing off an entire section of text.

Other elements of the manuscript also support Robinson's proposition: each quire is a slightly different size, so that the whole manuscript does not quite seem to match; words rarely break at the end of a line and there are very few abbreviations in the manuscript, which would make it significantly easier to read the pieces aloud; the manuscript is left justified only, except for a few rather interesting sections, especially at the end of some sermons; the manuscript itself is very small, the writing by comparison often disproportionately large; and the parchment used for the manuscript is extremely supple (possibly easy to roll up?). Even the fact that the manuscript has traditionally been out of order tends to suggest that it was less a coherent whole than a package of pieces. The amount of wear at the end and

---

[23] Collins, *Anglo-Saxon Vernacular Manuscripts in America*, p. 53.

beginning of some quires is extreme. Table 1 below provides the details of the division of the manuscript into booklets: some booklets have but one quire, others several.

Table 1: The Booklets of the Blickling Homilies Manuscript

Homily	Occasion	Folios	Booklet
Temporale			
I	Annunciation	fols 1ʳ – 6ᵛ line 12 [fol. 1ʳ very worn]	1
II	Quinquagesima	fols 6ᵛ line 13 – 14ʳ line 7	1
III	First Sunday in Lent	fols 14ʳ line 8 – 21ᵛ line 16	1
IV	Third Sunday in Lent	fols 22ʳ line 1 – 31ᵛ line 21 [fol. 31ᵛ very worn]	2
V	Fifth Sunday in Lent	fols 32ʳ line 1 – 40ʳ line 9 [fol. 32ʳ very worn]	3
VI	Palm Sunday	fols 40ʳ line 10 – 49ᵛ line 17 [fol. 49ᵛ quite worn]	3
VII	Easter Day	fols 50ʳ line 1 – 58ᵛ line 20 [fols 50ʳ and 58ᵛ very worn]	4
VIII	Post Easter (*Sauwle þearf*)	missing leaf [fol. 59ʳ line 1] – fol. 63ᵛ line 16	5
IX	Post Easter (*Crist se goldbloma*)	fols 63ᵛ line 17 – 65ʳ line 3	5
X	Post Easter (*Þisses mid-dangeardes ende neah is*)	fols 65ʳ line 4 – 70ʳ line 21	5
XI	Holy Thursday	fols 70ᵛ line 2 – 80ʳ line 4	5
XII	Pentecost	fols 80ᵛ line 1 – 84ᵛ line 6	5
Sanctorale			
XIII	Assumption of Mary	fols 84ᵛ line 7 – 98ᵛ line 9	5
XIV	John the Baptist	fols 98ᵛ line 10 – 104ʳ line 16	5
XV	Peter and Paul	fols 104ʳ line 17 – 119ᵛ line 21	5
XVI	St Michael	fols 120ʳ line 1 – 127ʳ line 12	6
XVII	St Martin	fols 127ʳ line 13 – 133ᵛ line 21	6
XVIII	St Andrew	fols 134ʳ (one leaf missing) line 1 – 139ᵛ line 2	7

As the table demonstrates, the Blickling manuscript divides cleanly into seven booklets, three of them corresponding to individual homilies, two of them including two homilies, and one each with three and eight homilies. The last of these overlaps the end of the *temporale* and the beginning of the *sanctorale*, which is a striking feature of the manuscript's compilation. The fourth quire shows heavy wear at both the beginning and end of the booklet, the beginnings of both the first and third quires show heavy wear, and the end of the second quire shows heavy wear. The central booklet, the extended booklet five with eight homilies, is missing its first leaf, which itself may suggest that this booklet too circulated separately. Thus, the quiring and wear suggest that the manuscript was not a coherent and organized compilation of texts (except for the central section).

The second complex of evidence for consideration is the manuscript punctuation of the Blickling Homilies. Malcolm Parkes notes that the role of punctuation in a manuscript is not restricted to the basic function of disambiguation (which is essential to comprehension of both the written and the spoken languages), but can 'become a feature of the pragmatics of the written medium'.[24] The punctuation and layout of the text can therefore help to determine both the coherence of the creation of the manuscript as a single whole and the extent to which the texts used in the manuscript are reconstructed and reworked to fit into this codex. As a working thesis, it seems possible, based on the division of the manuscript into booklets, that the punctuation and layout will also reveal differences in presentation significant enough to raise questions about the fundamental coherence of the manuscript. The codex, or one of its constituent booklets, would have fit very neatly into the hand. The writing, similarly, is large enough to be easily read aloud, and the manuscript pointing and the use of accents to mark long vowels not otherwise immediately recognizable also suggest oral delivery.[25] More intriguingly, the punctuation varies by the quire, or sometimes by the booklet. Thus, for example, folio 1^r is very heavily worn, even torn at the top left edge, and uses only the mid-point dot, and that only for final punctuation. At the foot of folio 5^v the scribe takes the opportunity for a decorative touch, and writes very long descenders for all the appropriate letters. At the end of folio 6^v, on line 12, a very neat hand spreads out the last line of the homily, even stretching the 'Amen'. The homily almost looks to have been copied line for line.

The second homily starts on line 13 and also uses mid-point dots and long descenders on folios 6^v and 7^v. The mid-point dots are somewhat more frequent, and there is a slightly greater number of abbreviations in the text. Again, at the end of the homily the scribe stretches the text in order to get to the end of the line, using large spaces between the words, and an elaborate capital 'A' for Amen, with

---

[24] Parkes, *Pause and Effect*, p. 72.

[25] The manuscript does also contain several line drawings. Its concerns are not entirely aural.

a closing triangle of points to mark the end of the homily. By contrast, the next homily starts on folio 14^r, line 8 and has for its punctuation both the punctus versus and the mid-point dot. The homily continues through the end of the second quire and to the end of the shortened third quire. Interestingly, however, the punctuation changes at the start of the third quire, so that rather than using primarily mid-point dots, the scribe uses primarily the punctus versus and also adds the punctus elevatus. At the end of the homily, the scribe slightly miscalculates on line 16, stretching out the final words so much that the abstract noun suffix *-nesse* and 'Amen' have to move forward, rather awkwardly, to the next line. There are several explanations for the change in scribal behaviour here. One, obviously, is that the scribe simply copies what is there in the original. Another is that the second part of the homily comes from another source with different punctuation habits, so that this homily might be a composite of two yet earlier texts. A third possibility is that so much time passed between the scribe's copying of the first part of the homily and the copying of the rest into the next (or another) quire that the scribe's habits had changed and a different mark of punctuation had replaced the mid-point dot in the scribe's personal usage. In any case, the end of the homily coincides with the end of the quire, making this a potential booklet including the first three homilies and the first three quires, and demonstrating a range of approaches to the punctuation of the homilies as they were copied into the manuscript.

Homily IV runs from the beginning of quire four to the end of quire five, squashing onto the last few lines of the last folio to fit. The punctuation is a mixture of mid-point dots and punctus versus. One homily occupies two quires, perhaps one booklet. Homily V, like the latter part of Homily III, uses all three pieces of punctuation, but ends plainly, with 'a buton ende on ecnesse. Amen' ('[world] without end, forever, Amen') rather than an elaborate decorative balancing of the text. This is the only homily to use the punctus elevatus freely and consistently; elsewhere it appears only about once in each homily, and may well be a mistake in the scribal copying of those homilies (that is, having decided to transcribe this mark as a mid-point dot, occasionally the scribe forgot and wrote what was in the exemplar).[26] In Homily VI, the versals sometimes appear in the margins,

---

[26] Kelly's edition does include a count of punctuation, and in this homily the punctus elevatus appears ninety-nine times, according to his table (p. 198). It otherwise occurs, according to Kelly, four times in Homily III and once each in Homilies VI, XIII, and XV. Kelly does not draw any conclusions from this. The distribution of points is erratic through the manuscript, as is the distribution of the punctus versus according to his table, which also, oddly, includes a total of numbers of punctuation marks per homily.

sometimes flush with the text; generally, they are in the margins when a structural opportunity arises in the copying of the text so that the scribe will not break at the mid-line and put the following versal in the margin, but will do so if the end of the segment falls towards the end of the line. The homily uses only the mid-point dot and the punctus versus, and like the first homily it has long descenders stretching down from the last line on several folios. The homily ends with the final line stretched out to produce justification, and a three-point punctuation mark. Homilies V and VI occupy quires six to nine and have extensive wear on the folios at beginning and end, though they do not correspond with each other in terms of layout and punctuation.

Homily VII corresponds with quire ten and my proposed booklet four, and also has a lot of wear on the lower part of the recto of folio 50, so that the text is almost indecipherable. The punctuation is very sparse throughout the homily, including mostly mid-point dots, with very occasional use of the punctus versus. The homily's end is missing, but there is a lot of wear on the last available folio, the end of the quire. Homily VIII, which starts at the beginning of quire eleven and booklet five, ends very plainly midway through folio 63ᵛ, and Homily IX begins on the next line. Punctuation here is the mid-point dot only, and the ending of this text is similarly plain, though the homily does begin with a rubricated title and a capital with some colour-washing. Homily X has space left for a rubric but it is not provided; the punctuation is almost all mid-point dots, but some use of the punctus versus does occur. The opening capital is an unattractive 'M' with some inept colour-washing; this may be a later addition. However, the last line is extremely elaborate, with frills and trills in the text and an elongated 'n' for the final 'Amen'. The start of Homily XI is particularly interesting, since the first line is blank and the second line has, written in ink in a different and later hand, the title which has become standard: 'on þa halga þunres dei' ('Holy Thursday'). A capital 'M' occupies three lines in the margin, a splashier planned opening than for many of the other homilies. The punctuation in the text is extremely sparse, and all that does occur is the mid-point dot. The ending is very plain, though it uses the three-part •ᴗ• for the first time in the manuscript to emphasize the end. Once, long descenders occur at the foot of a page.

Homily XII has what appears to be a post-medieval capital and a title also added in a later hand. The punctuation is very sparse and only includes the mid-point dot. Nor is there any special treatment at the end of the homily, save a single punctus versus to mark the Amen. Homily XIII, on the other hand, while it also has no rubrics, does have a poorly written title and a three-line capital with rust-coloured colour-wash. More importantly, the opening line is written in capitals with diminuendo, so there is here a serious attempt at marking off the homily. The punctuation throughout is a mid-point dot only, which is very infrequent. Twice, however, the •,• appears, once after the Latin *benedictionem* and after the Hebrew 'amen' in the text. Moreover, the scribe has one versal to mark a major shift in the text, uses long descenders to ornament at least one page, and spreads the last line of the homily so that it approximates a justified line, with the more elaborate •,• at its end.

The next text, Homily XIV, also has no rubric, long descenders in places, sparse punctuation which is only a mid-point dot, and one versal to mark a new section of the text. At its end, perhaps as a demonstration of inexperience, the scribe severely squashes line 15 of the page to fit, then realizes not enough words are left to make line 16 look even. The scribe stretches out the words in that line greatly, producing especially a very elongated 'amen' followed by •.•. Homily XV did not originally have rubrics, although another hand adds them in light ink; it uses the mid-point dot and also the punctus elevatus. The homily has numerous abbreviations, and also accents, for its first sections, which then disappear. This also suggests a scribe smoothing out and revising the elements of a text copied from another exemplar with a different layout and presentation of the text. The scribe does seem to be copying page for page, since folio 117ᵛ starts to spread out the lines, to the point that on folio 118ᵛ the text is down to four words per line. The ending also extends and elongates. From folio 111ʳ, the scribe includes versals throughout, so that this homily is widely spaced and carefully presented. The homily ends at the end of quire sixteen, and ends booklet five, the longest of the booklets; it includes eight sermons and corresponds exactly to Scragg's second block of homilies.

The next homily, Homily XVI, by a new scribe, starts a new quire and booklet and has the title in ink touched with a rust-coloured wash, a two-line initial M, and a very different approach to the text, with versals in the left margins, some serious attempt at right justification, a mid-point dot for punctuation but with a space before and after it, and elongation of the last line of the text so that the whole piece is carefully and neatly presented. Homily XVII, in the same hand, has exactly the same layout, including an even greater use of space before and after the medial *distinctio* when a new idea is to be introduced in the homily. These two homilies, so similar in presentation, occupy two quires and one booklet. Homily XVIII adds another feature to the versals, justification, and careful layout in that it uses the punctus versus to mark references to God. It occupies one short quire and is the seventh, though truncated, booklet in the manuscript.

What all this detail suggests is that there was not a coherent plan for the layout and presentation of the texts in the manuscript. The practice of the two scribes with respect to punctuation, both in the kinds of symbol used and the frequency thereof, varied greatly from homily to homily. The *ordinatio* of the texts similarly varied, so that some have a rubric, some have ordinary titles in ink, some have capitals (rustic or square) beginning the homily, some have elegant endings or beginnings, some ornament the top or bottom lines of specific pages, yet others have different aspects of the above, or none of the above. Anglo-Saxon manuscripts were certainly not a homogeneous lot, yet they do not vary as much as this unless they are combining texts copied at different times and for different purposes.

My conclusion from this complex of evidence (quiring, wear, patterns of copying, and punctuation) is that the texts of the Blickling Homilies were copied from different exemplars, and were clearly not composed by the scribe or compiler. Scragg suggests that the texts in the first manuscript segment were collected and organized over a period of time and were compiled into the first part of a *temporale* slowly and methodically. This certainly seems likely, and may also apply to the last section of the manuscript, with only the large central booklet five being copied all at one time. If the compilation of the manuscript took place over a period of time, as the evidence suggests, then one conclusion might be that the manuscript was put together in a scriptorium which did not have instant access to sermon materials — perhaps one of the smaller, less well-known scriptoria of Anglo-Saxon England. Clearly, not a lot of sermons were available, and of those available, it seems likely that not all would have fit into the proposed structure of the *temporale*. Thus, what became available, if it was in any way appropriate, is what was copied. The scribe did not revise the layout and textual details of the homilies as they were copied, which suggests perhaps that the need to get these texts written overwrote any urge towards uniformity in layout and presentation. Given the differences from homily to homily, the direct sources seem likely to have been whatever was available to the scribe or compiler.

Work on the Blickling Homilies tends, whether explicitly or not, to perceive the homilist as an individual coordinating a careful codex aimed specifically at producing a particular set of effects in the audience for the homilies. Careful study of the manuscript suggests that this mythical being needs to be wholly discarded from the critical approach, in favour of considered study of individual homilies for their composition and content. Though the manuscript exists for us as an apparently complete whole, it did not for its Anglo-Saxon scribe and in its Anglo-Saxon environment; it will repay further study less concerned to find a unifying thread and more concerned to treat these texts as individual expressions of homilies for important days in the liturgical year.[27]

---

[27] This project began as an undergraduate assignment, requiring students to choose one of the Blickling Homilies from the Dictionary of Old English Corpus on the internet, and to translate

A conflict, even a paradox, exists in approaches to the Blickling homiliary. Scholars who pick single homilies and analyse them, often in comparison to other homilies on the same subject and/or using the same sources, tend to expect some kind of coherent approach and be disappointed when they do not find it. Scholars who consider the collection as a whole tend to place it in a chain of progress, a link on the way to the glories that were Ælfric and Wulfstan, and to see it more charitably but also as a unified whole, often leaping into the trap of thinking of the compiler as a single homilist. A compilation providing preaching material, the manuscript is not a coherent whole (perhaps its compiler or compilers would have said 'not yet' as they continued to collect homilies to fit into the set). Scholars nowadays recognize many of the homilies of late Anglo-Saxon England as composite homilies, formed of segments taken from other homilies and other homiletic texts and combined to form a new whole; perhaps we need now to proceed to considering the manuscripts in which these texts appear as also having a composite nature.

and write a commentary on fifty lines. This was a largely unplagiarizable assignment since the only library copy in the area of Morris's EETS edition with translation was safely stowed in my office, and because it took surprisingly little time to check the scholarship on the Blickling homiliary. In the same year a graduate class decided to prepare Web sites of texts related to the apocalypse, and Steve Voyce prepared and posted a very impressive consideration of the Blickling Homilies. In the course of marking these two sets of research, it became clear to me that a reconsideration of the manuscript and its codicology would be worthwhile. A student from the undergraduate class went on to complete a translation and glossary of three of the Blickling Homilies as her undergraduate thesis and an M. A. on the Easter Sunday homily; for the latter, see Emira Bouhafna, 'An Old English Homily for Easter and its Source Reconsidered' (unpublished masters thesis, University of Western Ontario, London, Canada, 2004). Bouhafna prints the account of the Harrowing of Hell derived from the pseudo-Augustine *Sermo 160* with the adaptation into Old English of that material found in the Easter Sermon, Blickling VII. Her analysis is far-reaching and important.

LATIN SERMONS FOR SAINTS
IN EARLY ENGLISH HOMILIARIES AND LEGENDARIES

Thomas N. Hall

The large number of Latin sermons that have come down to us in English manuscripts of the tenth, eleventh, and twelfth centuries are for the most part not sermons intended for lay preaching or private devotion but for communal reading in the monastic Night Office. The sixth-century *Rule* of St Benedict states that when the monks rise shortly after midnight to perform their nightly round of prayers, recitations, and readings, they should read together not only from the inspired books of the Old and New Testament but from 'explanations of scripture by reputable and orthodox catholic Fathers'.[1] Efforts to put this directive into practice in monastic communities throughout western Christendom eventually gave rise to the more precise custom of distinguishing twelve readings or lections in the Office of Nocturns (later known as Matins) every Sunday, feast day, and octave, with either one or three lections at the same hour on less important weekdays. On Sundays, feasts days, and their octaves, the Nocturns were divided into three, and the readings for the first Nocturn were taken from scripture, the readings for the second Nocturn were taken from patristic commentaries and sermons, and the readings for the third Nocturn were taken from a homily on the Gospel.[2] On feasts of saints, when it was desirable to recall a particular saint's

---

[1] *RB 1980: The Rule of St. Benedict in Latin and English with Notes*, ed. and trans. by Timothy Fry (Collegeville, 1981), pp. 204–05 (§9.8): 'expositiones earum, quae a nominatis et orthodoxis catholicis patribus factae sunt'. I am grateful to Aaron J Kleist, E. Gordon Whatley, and Charles D. Wright for their generous and insightful comments on a draft of this essay.

[2] On patristic readings in the monastic Night Office, see J. B. L. Tolhurst, *Introduction to the English Monastic Breviaries* (*The Monastic Breviary of Hyde Abbey* VI), Henry Bradshaw Society, 80 (London, 1942; repr. Woodbridge, 1993), pp. 178–95; Pierre Salmon, *L'Office divin au Moyen*

virtues and accomplishments, readings on the life of that saint were often substituted for the readings from scripture at the first Nocturn and also for the readings from a patristic sermon at the second Nocturn, yielding a total of eight lections from a hagiographic text. This set of requirements for a full annual cycle of patristic sermons, gospel homilies, and saints' legends for readings in the monastic Night Office was the original impetus for gathering sermons and homilies into books known as homiliaries, and a great many examples of such homiliaries survive from the early Middle Ages to illustrate the formative stages of the development of this important class of monastic literature.[3]

The structure and contents of the readings for the Night Office as they were meant to be conducted in England in the late Anglo-Saxon period are nowhere more clearly articulated than in Ælfric's *Letter to the Monks of Eynsham*, a customary for the Eynsham community which Ælfric composed at some point between the refoundation of Eynsham abbey in 1005 and his death in about 1010, relying in large part on the *Regularis concordia* drawn up at Winchester in the early 970s.[4] Ælfric devotes several chapters towards the end of his *Letter* to an overview of what is to be read and sung during the Night Office throughout the entire year according to ecclesiastical ordinance and local custom. Different feasts and different seasons call for their own traditional readings, most often taken from the Bible or a homily by one of the church fathers, with sung responses dictated by an antiphoner. This is the pattern that obtains for most of the year, but as Ælfric

---

Age: Histoire de la formation du bréviaire du IXe au XVIe siècle, Lex Orandi, 43 (Paris, 1967), pp. 108–10; Aimé Georges Martimort, 'La lecture patristique dans la liturgie des heures', in *Traditio et Progressio: Studi liturgici in onore del Prof. Adrien Nocent, OSB*, ed. by Giustino Farnedi, Studia Anselmiana, 95, Analecta Liturgica, 12 (Rome, 1988), pp. 311–31; and Martimort, *Les lectures liturgiques et leurs livres*, Typologie des sources du Moyen Âge occidental, 64 (Turnhout, 1992), pp. 77–96.

[3] The major milestones in the early history of the homiliary are inventoried by Réginald Grégoire, *Homéliaires liturgiques médiévaux: Analyse de manuscrits*, Biblioteca degli 'Studi Medievali', 12 (Spoleto, 1980); and Raymond Étaix, *Homéliaires patristiques latins: Recueil d'études de manuscrits médiévaux* (Paris, 1994).

[4] On the date and sources of Ælfric's letter, see *Ælfric's Letter to the Monks of Eynsham*, ed. and trans. by Christopher A. Jones, CSASE, 24 (Cambridge, 1998), pp. 5–70; and Aaron J Kleist, 'Ælfric's Corpus: A Conspectus', *Florilegium*, 18 (2001), 113–64 (pp. 135–36). The materials available for the study of the monastic Night Office in Anglo-Saxon England are concisely surveyed by Milton Mc. Gatch, 'The Office in Late Anglo-Saxon Monasticism', in *Learning and Literature in Anglo-Saxon England: Studies Presented to Peter Clemoes on the Occasion of his Sixty-fifth Birthday*, ed. by Michael Lapidge and Helmut Gneuss (Cambridge, 1985), pp. 341–62.

explains, the content of the Office lections is modified on saints' feasts to allow for the inclusion of readings from a saint's life or from a sermon on the saint:

> But on all feasts of the saints, throughout the entire year, we read lives or passions of the saints themselves, or sermons appropriate to the given solemnity, and [we sing] proper responsories, if these are to be had; if not, we sing other appropriate ones and adopt for the third position [readings] from a homily on the gospel, as we do always and everywhere.[5]

The detail I wish to focus on in this passage is Ælfric's remark that at least one of the three sets of lections for the Night Office on a saint's feast can be taken from a *sermon* appropriate to the given solemnity. The saints' lives that Ælfric knew and that he no doubt employed for some of these readings are by now well known thanks to the prodigious scholarship that has been directed at the study of saints' lives in Anglo-Saxon England, including the many dozens of legends incorporated into the *Old English Martyrology*, the 'Cotton-Corpus Legendary', and Ælfric's own collection of *Lives of Saints* in Old English, to name just three of the most prominent collections of hagiographic texts from pre-Conquest England that have been carefully investigated.[6] But what sermons for saints did Ælfric and his colleagues read in the Night Office at Eynsham? And for that matter, what sermons for saints were available in England in general at the time, and how did they circulate? Ælfric does not tell us exactly which texts he has in mind, but a partial sense of the ones he was familiar with can be had through the voluminous studies of Ælfric's hagiographic sources, including the masterful set of entries on the 'Acta Sanctorum' published by E. Gordon Whatley in the inaugural A volume of *Sources of Anglo-Saxon Literary Culture*.[7] Generations of source studies by Max Förster and

---

[5] *Ælfric's Letter to the Monks of Eynsham*, ed. and trans. by Jones, pp. 146–47 (§73): 'Omnibus uero festiuitatibus sanctorum in toto anno legimus uitas aut passiones ipsorum sanctorum siue sermones congruentes ipsi sollempnitati et responsoria propria, si habeantur. Sin alias, alia congruentia canimus tertiam sedem de tractu euuangelii sicut et ubique semper sumimus.'

[6] For surveys of this territory supported by abundant bibliography, see E. G. Whatley, 'Late Old English Hagiography, ca. 950–1150', in *Hagiographies: International History of the Latin and Vernacular Hagiographical Literature in the West from its Origins to 1550*, ed. by Guy Philippart, 3 vols to date (Turnhout, 1994–), II, 429–99; and M. Lapidge and R. C. Love, 'The Latin Hagiography of England and Wales (600–1550)', in *Hagiographies*, ed. by Philippart, III, 203–325. The sources and contents of the *Old English Martyrology* are most recently examined by Michael Lapidge, 'Acca of Hexham and the Origin of the *Old English Martyrology*', *Analecta Bollandiana*, 123 (2005), 29–78.

[7] E. Gordon Whatley, 'Acta Sanctorum', in *Sources of Anglo-Saxon Literary Culture*, vol. I: *Abbo of Fleury, Abbo of Saint-Germain-des-Prés, and Acta Sanctorum*, ed. by Frederick M. Biggs, Thomas D. Hill, Paul E. Szarmach, and E. Gordon Whatley (Kalamazoo, 2001), pp. 22–486.

his successors have made use of Ælfric's own writings to identify the sermons and saints' lives at his disposal, and Whatley's encyclopedic 'Acta Sanctorum' entries have built upon that information and have extended it significantly by adding to it the corroborating testimony of booklists and Old English translations and other evidence for the wider transmission histories of hundreds of hagiographic texts throughout the Anglo-Saxon period, including sermons for saints. But as valuable as these studies are, they still do not tell us which sermons were read in the Night Office at Eynsham on the feasts of saints. To get at this question from a different angle, I have therefore drawn up the following set of notes on Latin sermons for saints in early English manuscripts under the assumption that surely at least some of these surviving texts reflect the actual reading habits of Anglo-Saxon monks. As will soon become apparent, the only question this scattering of texts allows us to answer satisfactorily is what manuscript evidence there is for the circulation of hagiographic sermon literature in England through the first quarter of the twelfth century.[8] I have taken the evidence up through the early twelfth century because the bulk of the surviving manuscripts are from the early post-Conquest period, and I should emphasize that the chief determining factor for including a text in this casual inventory is that the text in question must either be labelled by its author or by an established transmission history as a *sermo* or *homilia*, or it must be rubricated in the manuscript as a *sermo* or *homilia*.[9] Saints' lives are excluded unless they are identified in the manuscript as a *sermo* or *homilia*. These criteria for acceptance have led me to omit from discussion the many dozens of saints' *vitae* and *passiones* in the Salisbury and Worcester recensions of the 'Cotton-Corpus Legendary' and other manuscripts from the period. What we are left with is a group of about two dozen manuscripts from England written through the first quarter of the twelfth

---

[8] I am unaware of any general overviews of the hagiographic sermon literature of the early Middle Ages, but for discussion of some later medieval sermons for saints, see Carlo Delcorno, 'Il racconto agiografico nella predicazione dei secoli XIII–XIV', in *Agiografia nell'Occidente cristiano secoli XIII–XIV (Roma, 1–2 marzo 1979)*, Atti dei Convegni Lincei, 48 (Rome, 1980), pp. 79–114; George Ferzoco, 'Sermon Literatures Concerning Late Medieval Saints', in *Models of Holiness in Medieval Sermons: Proceedings of the International Symposium (Kalamazoo, 4–7 May 1995)*, ed. by Beverly Mayne Kienzle and others (Louvain-la-Neuve, 1996), pp. 103–25; and Ferzoco, 'The Context of Medieval Sermon Collections on Saints', in *Preacher, Sermon, and Audience in the Middle Ages*, ed. by Carolyn Muessig (Leiden, 2002), pp. 279–91.

[9] I resist entering into a prolonged discussion of the meaning of these terms, but for an attempt at definition, see Thomas N. Hall, 'The Early Medieval Sermon', in *The Sermon*, ed. by Beverly Mayne Kienzle, Typologie des sources du moyen âge occidental, 81–83 (Turnhout, 2000), pp. 203–69.

century containing sermons and homilies — as well as texts that are claimed to be sermons and homilies — that are concerned with saints or that have been adapted for saints' feasts. This is an unwieldy assortment of texts, but for reasons that should become clear as I identify and comment on them, I do think they are important for showing us how a particular kind of text came to be defined and constituted for liturgical usage in the late Anglo-Saxon period. I begin with sermons for saints in homiliaries and then proceed to sermons in legendaries and other hagiographic manuscripts.

Sermons for Saints in Homiliaries

The earliest collection of patristic homilies for monastic reading in the Night Office was compiled in Rome in the seventh century for use at monasteries in the service of St Peter's basilica.[10] The saints' feasts represented in this collection, which is often simply referred to as the Roman Homiliary, are all reflective of the sanctoral cycle of the Roman Church as it came to be enshrined in the ninth-century sacramentary known as the *Hadrianum*, which gives particular emphasis to some of the oldest saints of Roman tradition.[11] There are no surviving copies of the seventh-century homiliary that first brought these sermons for saints together, but its contents can be reconstructed on the basis of several eighth-century collections that developed directly from it, including the Office homiliary compiled in the early eighth century by the Roman priest Agimundus, which contains sermons for the Office celebration of the feasts of John the Baptist, James and Philip, Peter

---

[10] The following account of the rise of the Office homiliary is vastly simplified and sidesteps many of the developments most thoroughly examined by Grégoire, *Homéliaires liturgiques médiévaux*, and Étaix, *Homéliaires patristiques latins*.

[11] Grégoire, *Homéliaires liturgiques médiévaux*, p. 127; E. Bourque, *Étude sur les sacramentaires romains*, vol. II: *Les textes remaniés*, part 2: *Le sacramentaire d'Hadrien, le supplément d'Alcuin et les Grégoriens mixtes*, Studi di antichità cristiana, 25 (Vatican City, 1958). On the cult of saints in early medieval Rome, see Walter Howard Frere, *Studies in Early Roman Liturgy*, vol. I: *The Kalendar*, Alcuin Club Collections, 28 (London, 1930); V. L. Kennedy, *The Saints of the Canon of the Mass*, 2nd edn, Studi di antichità cristiana, 14 (Vatican City, 1963), pp. 97–204; G. G. Willis, *A History of Early Roman Liturgy to the Death of Pope Gregory the Great*, Henry Bradshaw Society, Subsidia 1 (London, 1994), pp. 105–11; and Alan Thacker, 'In Search of Saints: The English Church and the Cult of Roman Apostles and Martyrs in the Seventh and Eighth Centuries', in *Early Medieval Rome and the Christian West: Essays in Honour of Donald A. Bullough*, ed. by Julia M. H. Smith, Medieval Mediterranean, 28 (Leiden, 2000), pp. 247–77 (pp. 248–55).

and Paul, the Macchabees, Xystus (Pope Sixtus II), Laurence, the Assumption of
the Virgin Mary, Andrew, Cyprian, Cosmas and Damian, Vincent, Perpetua and
Felicitas, Victoria, Genesius of Arles, Felix and Adauctus, and Pope Leo the Great
(in that order).[12] These are all either popes or biblical or apostolic figures or martyrs who perished during the third- and fourth-century persecutions in Italy, Spain,
or Africa. All were widely venerated in seventh- and eighth-century Rome and its
environs, and all are commemorated in the Homiliary of Agimundus through sermons authored by Augustine, Caesarius of Arles, John Chrysostom, Leo the Great,
Maximus of Turin, and other writers whose identities are now lost to us. In the
same tradition, the eighth-century homiliary compiled by Alan of Farfa (d. 769 or
770) is a parallel but incomplete witness to the seventh-century Roman Homiliary
which includes sermons for the feasts of Stephen, John the Evangelist, the Purification of the Virgin, John the Baptist, Peter and Paul, Peter, Laurence, the Nativity
of the Virgin, Martin, and Andrew.[13] A major step in the development of the
Office homiliary at the end of the eighth century was the collection compiled by
Paul the Deacon around 790 at the request of Charlemagne, who wanted an up-to-
date and comprehensive collection of sermons for reading in monasteries throughout Carolingian territories.[14] In fulfilling this commission, Paul relied heavily on
the homiliaries that had grown out of the Roman tradition and adopted many of
the sermons that were circulating in the homiliaries of Agimundus and Alan of
Farfa, but when it came to feasts for saints, he passed over martyrs and popes whose
cults had never taken hold in Carolingian Francia, and in a small number of cases
he introduced new texts for feasts that had resulted from more recent liturgical
developments. Thus Paul the Deacon's Homiliary includes no sermons for the
feasts of Popes Leo the Great and Xystus, and none for the martyrs Cosmas and
Damian, Felix and Adauctus, Genesius of Arles, Perpetua and Felicitas, Victoria,
and Vincent, who all figure in the Homiliary of Agimundus. However, Paul added

---

[12] Grégoire, *Homéliaires liturgiques médiévaux*, pp. 343–92. One of the three volumes of the
Homiliary of Agimundus is lost, so this list is no doubt incomplete. On the sources of this
collection and its ties to the seventh-century Roman Homiliary, see Antoine Chavasse, 'Le sermonnaire des Saints-Philippe-et-Jacques et le sermonnaire de Saint-Pierre', *Ephemerides Liturgicae*, 69 (1955), 17–24; and Chavasse, 'Le sermonnaire d'Agimond: Ses sources immédiates', in
Kyriakon: Festschrift Johannes Quasten, ed. by Patrick Granfield and Josef A. Jungmann, 2 vols
(Münster, 1970), II, 800–10.

[13] Edoardo Hosp, 'Il sermonario di Alano di Farfa', *Ephemerides Liturgicae*, 50 (1936),
375–83, and 51 (1937), 210–41; Grégoire, *Homéliaires liturgiques médiévaux*, pp. 127–221.

[14] Grégoire, *Homéliaires liturgiques médiévaux*, pp. 423–86.

texts for the feasts of the decollation of John the Baptist (29 August) and for the Nativity of the Virgin Mary (9 September), which were both relatively new feasts in seventh-century Rome and are not recorded in the earliest Roman homiliaries although they were regularly observed in Francia by the end of the eighth century.[15] Thanks to the Carolingian legislation that ensured its proliferation, Paul the Deacon's Homiliary rapidly became the dominant collection of texts for monastic reading in the Night Office throughout western Europe and remained so for centuries, and the reading habits of English monks in the late Anglo-Saxon period were profoundly shaped by its contents, which, however, continued to undergo modification in response to evolving local traditions.[16] As we shall see, several of the earliest English versions of Paul the Deacon's Homiliary follow Paul's move towards innovation by introducing even more sermons for recently established feasts, especially those honouring the Virgin Mary.

[15] On the feast of the Nativity of the Virgin, which was first introduced into Rome in the second half of the seventh century, see Mary Clayton, *The Cult of the Virgin Mary in Anglo-Saxon England*, CSASE, 2 (Cambridge, 1990), p. 29; and Margot Fassler, 'Mary's Nativity, Fulbert of Chartres, and the *Stirps Jesse*: Liturgical Innovation circa 1000 and its Afterlife', *Speculum,* 75 (2000), 389–434 (pp. 392–99). On the feast of the decollation of John the Baptist, which was likewise unknown in Rome before the seventh century, see René Marichal, 'Jean le Baptiste dans la tradition', in *Dictionnaire de spiritualité ascétique et mystique, doctrine et histoire*, ed. by Marcel Viller, Charles Baumgartner, and André Rayez, 16 vols in 22 and *Tables générales* (Paris, 1937–95), VIII, cols 184–92 (col. 187); Veronica Ortenberg, *The English Church and the Continent in the Tenth and Eleventh Centuries: Cultural, Spiritual, and Artistic Exchanges* (Oxford, 1992), p. 205; and Hansjörg Auf der Maur, 'Feste und Gedenktage der Heiligen', in *Feiern im Rhythmus der Zeit II/1*, Gottesdienst der Kirche: Handbuch der Liturgiewissenschaft, 6.1 (Regensburg, 1994), pp. 65–357 (p. 119).

[16] On the reception and influence of Paul the Deacon's Homiliary in Anglo-Saxon England, see Cyril L. Smetana, 'Aelfric and the Early Medieval Homiliary', *Traditio*, 15 (1959), 163–204; J. E. Cross, 'The Literate Anglo-Saxon – On Sources and Disseminations', *Proceedings of the British Academy*, 58 (1972), 67–100 (pp. 84–85); Cyril L. Smetana, 'Paul the Deacon's Patristic Anthology', in *The Old English Homily and its Backgrounds*, ed. by Paul E. Szarmach and Bernard F. Huppé (Albany, 1978), pp. 75–97; Mary Clayton, 'Homiliaries and Preaching in Anglo-Saxon England', *Peritia*, 4 (1985), 207–42 (pp. 210–12 and 216–20), repr. in *Old English Prose: Basic Readings*, ed. by Paul E. Szarmach, Basic Readings in Anglo-Saxon England, 5 (New York, 2000), pp. 151–98 (pp. 154–56 and 160–65); Thomas N. Hall, 'The Bibliography of Anglo-Saxon Sermon Manuscripts', in *Old English Scholarship and Bibliography: Essays in Honor of Carl T. Berkhout*, ed. by Jonathan Wilcox (Kalamazoo, 2004), pp. 83–104; Hall, 'The Development of the Common of Saints in the Early English Versions of Paul the Deacon's Homiliary', in *Anglo-Saxon Books and their Readers*, ed. by Thomas N. Hall and Donald Scragg (Kalamazoo, forthcoming); and Joyce Hill, 'Ælfric's Manuscript of Paul the Deacon's Homiliary: A Provisional Analysis' in this volume.

There are eight surviving English homiliaries from the first quarter of the twelfth century and earlier containing texts for the *sanctorale*, and all eight are homiliaries based on the eighth-century collection of Paul the Deacon.[17] The earliest of these is Canterbury, Cathedral Library, Additional MS 127/1, a set of four fragments totalling eight folios from a version of the summer part of Paul the Deacon's Homiliary copied in the first half of the eleventh century.[18] Of the four sermons for saints among these fragments, the first is a sermon for the decollation of John the Baptist by Hrabanus Maurus on folio 1[r], a text lifted from Bede's commentary on Mark, as are a number of Hrabanus's sermons.[19] This sermon occurs as a standard text for the decollation of John the Baptist in four other eleventh-century English homiliaries.[20] Second is a sermon for the Nativity of Mary at folio 1[r-v] (inc. 'Prefatio totius operis'), an incomplete copy of a rare unpublished composite text that occurs complete in only one pre-twelfth-century English manuscript: Oxford, Bodleian Library, MS Barlow 4, from eleventh-century Worcester.[21] The complete homily as preserved in Barlow 4 (pp. 1–6) is pieced

---

[17] Surviving homiliaries from Anglo-Saxon and early Norman England are discussed by Clayton, 'Homiliaries and Preaching'; and Helmut Gneuss, 'Liturgical Books in Anglo-Saxon England and their Old English Terminology', in *Learning and Literature in Anglo-Saxon England*, ed. by Lapidge and Gneuss, pp. 91–141 (pp. 122–25).

[18] On Canterbury Add. 127/1, see N. R. Ker, *Medieval Manuscripts in British Libraries*, 4 vols (Oxford, 1969–92; vol. IV with A. J. Piper), II, 315–16; J. E. Cross and Thomas N. Hall, 'The Fragments of Homiliaries in Canterbury Cathedral Library MS. Addit. 127/1 and in Kent, County Archives Office, Maidstone, MS. PRC 49/2', *Scriptorium*, 47 (1993), 186–92; Helmut Gneuss, *Handlist of Anglo-Saxon Manuscripts: A List of Manuscripts and Manuscript Fragments Written or Owned in England up to 1100*, MRTS, 241 (Tempe, 2001), no. 209.

[19] Hrabanus Maurus, *Hom.* 157, *In passione s. Iohannis Baptistae* (*PL* 110.444–46) = Bede, *In Marci evangelium expositio* VI.28–29, ed. by D. Hurst, CCSL, 120 (Turnhout, 1960), pp. 509–10, lines 803–24.

[20] Other copies of Hrabanus's *Hom.* 157 appear in Cambridge, University Library, MS Kk. 4. 13, fols 95[v]–96[r]; Cambridge, Pembroke College, MS 23 (s. xi[2], N. France; provenance Bury St Edmunds by s. xi/xii), fols 126[v]–129[r]; Lincoln, Cathedral Library, MS 158 (s. xi[ex], Normandy or England), fols 88[v]–89[v]; and London, British Library, Harley MS 652 (s. xi/xii, Canterbury, St Augustine's Abbey), fols 104[r]–105[r], all for the decollation of John the Baptist (29 August).

[21] On Barlow 4, see Heinrich Schenkl, *Bibliotheca Patrum Latinorum Britannica*, 3 vols in 1 (Vienna, 1891–1908; repr. Hildesheim, 1969), no. 243; F. Madan, H. H. E. Craster, and N. Denholm-Young, *A Summary Catalogue of Western Manuscripts in the Bodleian Library at Oxford*, 7 vols in 8 [vol. II in 2 parts] (Oxford, 1895–1953; repr. with corrections in vols I and VII, Munich, 1980), II.2, 1044–45 (no. 6416); Richard Gameson, *The Manuscripts of Early Norman England (c. 1066–1130)* (Oxford, 1999), no. 628; Gneuss, *Handlist*, no. 539. This homily seems

together from two separate texts, the first of which is used for the seventh and eighth lections of the third Nocturn for the feast of the Nativity of the Virgin in the *Sarum Breviary*, which shows that at least a portion of this homily continued to play a role within the English tradition of Marian devotion for some time.[22] In the *Sarum Breviary* the Marian homily from which these readings are taken is attributed to Bede ('Omelia uenerabilis Bedae presbyteri'), but it is certainly not by Bede, and I have not been able to trace it back earlier than its appearance in Barlow 4 and the Canterbury fragments. The second part of the Barlow 4 sermon for the Nativity of Mary is identical to a pseudo-Alcuin text known as the *Interpretationes nominum Hebraicorum*, a work probably of the tenth century not to be confused with Jerome's treatise on Hebrew names.[23] This is one of at least a dozen unpublished composite homilies in eleventh-century English homiliaries, a text structurally comparable to many of the composite homilies that occur in Old English, Old Norse, and Middle High German.[24] The third sermon for a saint among the Canterbury fragments is an incomplete copy of *BHL* 5948 at folio 2ᵛ, the well-known legend of St Michael's appearance atop Mount Gargano.[25] And fourth is the sermon for All Saints at folio 4ʳ⁻ᵛ beginning 'Legimus in ecclesiasticis

to have been added to the front of the manuscript in about the third quarter of the eleventh century. Possibly misled by the assignment of this sermon to the feast of the Nativity of Mary (8 September), Ker, *Medieval Manuscripts in British Libraries*, II, 316, incorrectly identifies its source as pseudo-Bede, *Sermo* 55, *In natale divae Mariae virginis* (*PL* 94.413–14).

[22] *Breviarium ad usum insignis ecclesiae Sarum*, ed. by Francis Procter and Christopher Wordsworth, 3 vols (Cambridge, 1886), III, cols 777–79.

[23] See Marie-Hélène Jullien and Françoise Perelman, *Clavis Scriptorum Latinorum Medii Aevi. Auctores Galliae 735–987*, vol. II: *Alcuin* (Turnhout, 1999), pp. 468–69.

[24] On the nature of these composite texts, see Malcolm R. Godden, 'Old English Composite Homilies from Winchester', *ASE*, 4 (1975), 57–65; Hall, 'Early Medieval Sermon', pp. 213–16; and Nancy M. Thompson, '*Hit Segð on Halgum Bocum*: The Logic of Composite Old English Homilies', *Philological Quarterly*, 81 (2002), 383–419.

[25] *Apparitio sancti Michaelis in Monte Gargano*, in *Scriptores rerum Langobardicarum et Italicarum saec. VI–IX*, ed. by G. Waitz, MGH (Hannover, 1878), pp. 541–43; also printed as Hrabanus Maurus, *Hom.* 32 (*PL* 110.60–63) and as *Hom.* 56, *In festo s. Michaelis Archangeli* within the expanded version of Paul the Deacon's Homiliary edited by Eucharius Cervicornus (*PL* 95.1522–25). The sermon is indexed by Jan Machielsen, *Clavis Patristica Pseudepigraphorum Medii Aevi. 1A–1B: Opera Homiletica*, 2 vols (Turnhout, 1990) (hereafter *CPPM* I), no. 5316. On the knowledge of *BHL* 5948 in Anglo-Saxon England, see Richard F. Johnson, *Saint Michael the Archangel in Medieval English Legend* (Woodbridge, 2005), pp. 50–63, who reprints and translates Waitz's text at pp. 110–15.

historiis', which was the standard reading for All Saints in Anglo-Saxon England.[26] Too little of this Canterbury homiliary has survived to enable one to make an informed judgement about its relationship to other Paul the Deacon manuscripts, but it is worth noting that all four of these sermons for saints are supplements to the texts originally chosen by Paul the Deacon, and three of them (all but the sermon for the Nativity of Mary) occur in other versions of Paul the Deacon's Homiliary from the eleventh and early twelfth centuries.

A more complete witness to a version of Paul the Deacon's Homiliary produced in England during this period is the two-volume homiliary in Cambridge, University Library, MSS Ii. 2. 19 and Kk. 4. 13, from late eleventh-century Norwich.[27] The second volume, CUL Kk. 4. 13, includes readings for the *sanctorale* from the feast of St Stephen (26 December) through the feast of St Andrew (30 November). There are 118 sermons and homilies in all in this manuscript, most of which are for saints' feasts. In most cases these are sermons that occur with some regularity in other copies of Paul the Deacon's Homiliary circulating in England in the late eleventh and early twelfth centuries. The few remarkable additions are an apparently unique sermon for All Saints (a feast that gained wide recognition beginning in the early ninth century *after* Paul the Deacon had compiled his Homiliary[28]) at folio

---

[26] J. E. Cross, '"Legimus in ecclesiasticis historiis" – A Sermon for All Saints, and its Use in Old English Prose', *Traditio*, 33 (1977), 105–21; see *CPPM* I, nos. 4046 and 6074. On readings for the feast of All Saints, see Hall, 'Development of the Common of Saints'.

[27] On CUL Ii. 2. 19 and Kk. 4. 13, see Charles Hardwick and Henry Richards Luard, *A Catalogue of the Manuscripts Preserved in the Library of the University of Cambridge*, 6 vols (Cambridge, 1856–67), III, 388–93 and 658–63 (nos 1752 and 2028); M. R. James, 'List of Manuscripts from the Cathedral Priory of Norwich Now Existing in English Libraries', *Norfolk Archaeology*, 19 (1917), 93–116 (p. 98, no. 61); N. R. Ker, 'Medieval Manuscripts from Norwich Cathedral Priory', in his *Books, Collectors and Libraries: Studies in the Medieval Heritage*, ed. by Andrew G. Watson (London, 1985), pp. 243–72 (pp. 255–56); Mary P. Richards, *Texts and their Traditions in the Medieval Library of Rochester Cathedral Priory*, Transactions of the American Philosophical Society, 78.3 (Philadelphia, 1988), pp. 104–08; Gameson, *Manuscripts*, nos 31 and 42; Gneuss, *Handlist*, nos 16 and 24.

[28] The origin and early history of the feast of All Saints are still subject to debate. Against the prevailing view that it came into being in Northumbria during the eighth century, when it is first explicitly attested in the *Metrical Calendar of York*, composed probably in the third quarter of that century, Carl I. Hammer, '"For All the Saints": Bishop Vivolo of Passau and the Eighth-Century Origins of the Feast', *Revue Mabillon*, n.s., 15 (2004), 5–26, has recently put forward the claim that the 1 November feast of All Saints was first formally observed at Enknach in Bavaria in the 730s through a church dedication by Bishop Vivolo, a native Irishman (so Hammer speculates) ordained in Rome who sought to combine the liturgical observance he had witnessed in Rome

151^{r-v},[29] a sermon for the Assumption of Mary at folios 152^r–158^r excerpted from Paschasius Radbertus's *De assumptione sanctae Mariae Virginis*,[30] a copy of Fulbert of Chartres's *Sermo* 4 for the Nativity of Mary at folios 158^r–159^v,[31] and an abridged version of the pseudo-Gennadius life of St Jerome (*BHL* 3869) divided for eight lections at folios 159^v–160^v.[32]

Another two-volume homiliary derivative of Paul the Deacon is Cambridge, Pembroke College, MSS 23 and 24, written in the late eleventh century not in England but in northern France, probably at Saint-Germain-des-Prés or Saint-Denis, whence it travelled to Bury St Edmunds shortly before the end of the eleventh century, very likely through contacts established by Abbot Baldwin of Bury St Edmunds (1065–97/98), who was a monk at Saint-Denis before coming to England in the 1050s.[33] The second volume of this two-volume set, Pembroke 24,

at Pope Gregory III's oratory dedicated to All Saints with an Irish festival he recalled from his youth that was celebrated on 1 November. Independently, Michael Lapidge, 'Acca of Hexham', has revived the argument that the feast of All Saints was an Insular innovation, suggesting that it was celebrated in Northumbria as early as the 730s before it was transplanted to the Continent. In any case, the feast is unacknowledged in Paul the Deacon's original Homiliary, although subsequent versions of the collection from the ninth century and later often supply one or more sermons for All Saints; for details, see Hall, 'Development of the Common of Saints'.

[29] This sermon appears to have been added to the manuscript in the first quarter of the twelfth century by an English-trained scribe writing a late form of Style IV Anglo-Caroline minuscule; for an edition and translation, see Hall, 'Development of the Common of Saints'.

[30] Paschasius Radbertus, *De assumptione sanctae Mariae Virginis*, ed. by A. Ripberger, CCCM 56C (Turnhout, 1985), pp. 109–62, this excerpt corresponding to lines 1–488 and 739–944 (pp. 109–36, 149–59), also printed as pseudo-Jerome, *Epist.* 9, *Ad Paulam et Eustochium* (*PL* 30.122–42), this excerpt corresponding to §§1–9 and 14–17 (cols 122–132B, 137C–142B); see E. Dekkers, *Clavis Patrum Latinorum*, 3rd edn (Turnhout, 1995), no. 633 (*epist.* 9). The complete text appears in two other English homiliaries of roughly this date: Durham, Cathedral Library, MS A. III. 29 (s. xi^{ex}, Durham), fols 236^v–249^v; and Worcester, Cathedral Library, MS F. 94 (s. xi/xii or xii^{in}, Worcester), fols 59^r–69^v.

[31] Fulbert of Chartres, *Sermo* 4, *De nativitate beatissimae Mariae Virginis* (*PL* 141.320–24). On this and other Marian sermons by Fulbert that circulated in early English manuscripts, see the comments below on London, British Library, Additional MS 19835.

[32] *Vita s. Hieronymi perperam adscripta Gennadio* (*PL* 22.175–84); see *CPL* 623, and Whatley, 'Acta Sanctorum', p. 250.

[33] On Pembroke 23 and 24, see Schenkl, *Bibliotheca*, nos 2561–62; Montague Rhodes James, *A Descriptive Catalogue of the Manuscripts in the Library of Pembroke College, Cambridge* (Cambridge, 1905), pp. 20–25; Gameson, *Manuscripts*, nos 110–11; Gneuss, *Handlist*, nos 129–30. For Baldwin's career and his connections to English books, see Antonia Gransden, 'Baldwin, Abbot of Bury St Edmunds, 1065–1097', *Proceedings of the Battle Conference on Anglo-Norman*

contains texts for the *sanctorale* from the feast of St Philip (1 May) to the feast of
St Andrew (30 November), followed by a Common of Saints, for a total of ninety-
nine sermons. Twenty-eight of these sermons are supplements to the texts originally chosen by Paul the Deacon. Seven are excerpts from Bede's commentary on
Luke.[34] Five are added sermons for Mary,[35] including a sermon for the feast of the
Assumption at the very end of the manuscript (fols 374ᵛ–375ʳ) that was copied by
a scribe known to have been active at Bury St Edmunds at the end of the eleventh
century.[36] The latest datable item in the manuscript is the copy of Haymo of Saint-
Denis's sermon for the anniversary of the viewing of the relics of St Denis at the

---

Studies, 4 (1981), 65–76 and 187–95; Gransden, 'The Cult of St Mary at *Beodericisworth* and
then in Bury St Edmunds Abbey to *c.* 1150', *Journal of Ecclesiastical History*, 55 (2004), 627–53
(pp. 638–44); and Rebecca Jane Rushforth, 'The Eleventh- and Early Twelfth-Century Manuscripts of Bury St Edmunds Abbey' (unpublished doctoral dissertation, University of Cambridge,
2002) pp. 66–68, 100–01, 103.

[34] Bede, *In Lucae evangelium expositio* XII.1–9, ed. by Hurst, CCSL, 120, pp. 245–48, lines
594–699, for the feast of the martyrs Basilides, Cyrinus, and Nabor (fols 43ʳ–45ᵛ); Bede, *In Lucae
evangelium expositio* XIII.1–2 (CCSL, 120, pp. 595–97, lines 5–105), for the feast of the martyrs
Gervase and Protase (fols 45ᵛ–47ᵛ); Bede, *In Lucae evangelium expositio* XIX.12–26 (CCSL, 120,
pp. 336–41, lines 1636–1821) for the feast of St Stephen (fols 103ᵛ–108ʳ); Bede, *In Lucae evangelium expositio* X.38–42 (CCSL, 120, pp. 225–26, lines 2316–77) = pseudo-Bede, *Hom.* III.57
(*PL* 94.420–21), for the feast of the Assumption (fols 118ᵛ–120ᵛ); Bede, *In Lucae evangelium
expositio* XXII.24–30 (CCSL, 120, pp. 380–82, lines 682–782) = pseudo-Bede, *Hom.* III.60 (*PL*
94.423–25), for the feast of St Bartholomew (fols 120ᵛ–123ʳ); Bede, *In Lucae evangelium expositio*
XI.47–53 (CCSL, 120, pp. 244–45, lines 528–93), not rubricated for a particular feast (fols
148ʳ–149ᵛ); and Bede, *In Lucae evangelium expositio* XI.47–53 (CCSL, 120, pp. 244–45, lines
527–93), for the feast of St Martin (fols 267ʳ–268ᵛ).

[35] Pseudo-Hildefonsus, *Sermo* 7 (*PL* 96.267–69), for the feast of the Assumption (fols
116ᵛ–118ᵛ); the copy of pseudo-Bede, *Hom.* III.57 mentioned in the previous note, for the feast
of the Assumption (fols 118ᵛ–120ᵛ); pseudo-Augustine, *Sermo* 194 (*PL* 39.2104–07) = pseudo-
Fulbert, *Sermo* 9 (*PL* 141.336–42), for the Nativity of the Virgin (fols 137ʳ–140ʳ); Fulbert of
Chartres, *Sermo* 4 (*PL* 141.320–24), for the Nativity of the Virgin (fols 140ʳ–145ᵛ); and the
sermon identified in the next note.

[36] This added sermon for the Assumption (inc. 'Haec nimirum est') is an excerpt from Augus-
tine, *In Iohannis evangelium tractatus* CXIX.1 line 10 – 3 line 23, ed. by R. Willems, CCSL, 36
(Turnhout, 1954), pp. 658–59. On the scribe, see Antonia Gransden, 'Some Manuscripts in
Cambridge from Bury St Edmunds Abbey: Exhibition Catalogue', in *Bury St Edmunds: Medieval
Art, Architecture, Archaeology, and Economy*, ed. by Gransden, British Archaeological Association
Conference Transactions 20 (Leeds, 1998), pp. 228–85 (p. 254); Teresa Webber, 'The Provision
of Books for Bury St Edmunds Abbey in the Eleventh and Twelfth Centuries', in ibid., pp.
186–93 (p. 188); and Rushforth, 'Eleventh- and Early Twelfth-Century Manuscripts', pp. 67–68.

abbey of Saint-Denis in Paris (fols 361ʳ–374ᵛ), a sermon composed about the middle of the eleventh century (see *BHL* 2198, which dates it *c.* 1050).[37] The manuscript's French origin of course means that its selection of texts reflects French monastic reading practices rather than English ones, but the final sermon for the Assumption added by a scribe working at Bury St Edmunds is an important witness to the vitality of the Marian cult at Bury in the early post-Conquest period.[38]

Another amplified Paul the Deacon manuscript roughly contemporary with CUL Ii. 2. 19 + Kk. 4. 13 and Pembroke 23 + 24 is Durham, Cathedral Library, MS A. III. 29, from late eleventh-century Durham, containing homilies from Easter to the twenty-fifth Sunday after Pentecost followed by a robust cycle of eighty-one sermons for the *sanctorale* and Common of Saints beginning 1 May (for Phillip and James) and extending through 21 December (for Thomas and multiple martyrs).[39] Most of these eighty-one sermons for saints occur with some regularity in other homiliaries of the eleventh and twelfth centuries, but six can be singled out as texts that have been adapted unusually if not uniquely for the feasts of English saints who were vigorously culted in the late tenth and eleventh centuries, an unmistakable sign that the collection has been modified for English use. The first is a sermon at folios 172ᵛ–173ᵛ taken from Bede's commentary on Luke, a text originally chosen by Paul the Deacon as a reading for the common of a confessor and thus one suitably adaptable for any number of saints' feasts; here it is rubricated for the 26 May feast of St Augustine of Canterbury ('In natale Augustini Anglorum archiepiscopi').[40] Second is a sermon by Augustine of Hippo at folios 181ʳ–184ᵛ on the parable of the ten wise and foolish virgins which has been tailored for the 23 June feast of the East Anglian virgin saint Æthelthryth ('.x. kl.

---

[37] Gransden, 'Some Manuscripts in Cambridge', p. 254; Webber, 'Provision of Books for Bury St Edmunds', p. 188.

[38] The growth of the Marian cult at Bury during this period is discussed by Thomas N. Hall, 'The Earliest Anglo-Latin Text of the *Trinubium Annae* (*BHL* 505zl)', in *Via Crucis: Essays on Early Medieval Sources and Ideas in Memory of J. E. Cross*, ed. by Thomas N. Hall with assistance from Thomas D. Hill and Charles D. Wright, Medieval European Studies, 1 (Morgantown, 2002), pp. 104–37 (pp. 117–24); and Gransden, 'Cult of St Mary at *Beodericisworth*'.

[39] On Durham A. III. 29, see Thomas Rud, *Codicum manuscriptorum Ecclesiae Cathedralis Dunelmensis catalogus classicus* (Durham, 1825), pp. 45–56; Schenkl, *Bibliotheca*, no. 4380; R. A. B. Mynors, *Durham Cathedral Manuscripts to the End of the Twelfth Century* (Oxford, 1939), p. 43 (no. 49); Gameson, *Manuscripts*, no. 211; Gneuss, *Handlist*, no. 222.

[40] Pseudo-Bede, *Hom*. III.77 (*PL* 94.463) = Bede, *In Lucae evangelium expositio* XI.33–36 (CCSL, 120, pp. 239–40, lines 322–74). See Grégoire, *Homéliaires liturgiques médiévaux*, pp. 473–74 (PD II.107).

Iulii. Natale sancte Atheldrythe uirginis').[41] Devotion to St Æthelthryth (or Etheldreda or Audrey) was promoted during the Anglo-Saxon period through an influential account of her life by Bede as well as by two martyrology entries, an Old English life by Ælfric, several miracle stories (now lost), and at least one hymn, but this is the only sermon assigned to her feast in a pre-twelfth-century manuscript.[42] Next is a sermon at folios 208^r–210^v ascribed to Maximus of Turin which in its original form was meant to serve as a reading for the feast of St Eusebius of Vercelli.[43] In Paul the Deacon it functions as another common sermon for confessors;[44] in Durham A. III. 29 it is rubricated for the 2 July feast of the nativity or deposition of St Swithun ('.vi. non. Iulii. Natale sancti Suuithuni episcopi et confessoris'), the ninth-century Bishop of Winchester whose cult became especially active in the late tenth century and following, after his relics were translated into the new Winchester cathedral in 971 by Bishop Æthelwold, a cardinal event of the Winchester-based reforms.[45] Fourth is a copy of Gregory the Great's ninth gospel homily at folios 227^r–229^v, which has been designated for the 15 July feast of the translation of St Swithun ('Id. Iulii. Translatione sancti Suuithuni episcopi et confessoris').[46] The fifth and sixth sermons for English saints in this manuscript are texts by Bede and Alcuin that have been adapted for the feast of St Birinus of Wessex, the first bishop of the West Saxons.[47] The sermon at folios 332^v–333^v

---

[41] Augustine, *Sermo* 93, *De verbis evangelii secundum Matthaei* XXV.1–13 (*PL* 38.573–80), omitting the opening sentence and ending incomplete within §17 (col. 580, line 5) due to the loss of leaves after fol. 184.

[42] On the Anglo-Saxon cult of St Æthelthryth, see Whatley, 'Acta Sanctorum', pp. 47–49; John Blair, 'A Handlist of Anglo-Saxon Saints', in *Local Saints and Local Churches in the Early Medieval West*, ed. by Alan Thacker and Richard Sharpe (Oxford, 2002), pp. 495–565 (pp. 507–08); *Goscelin of Saint-Bertin: The Hagiography of the Female Saints of Ely*, ed. and trans. by Rosalind C. Love, Oxford Medieval Texts (Oxford, 2004), pp. xxiii–xlviii; and Virginia Blanton, *Signs of Devotion: The Cult of St. Æthelthryth in Medieval England, 695–1615* (University Park, PA, 2007).

[43] Pseudo-Maximus, *Hom.* 78, *De natali s. Eusebii Vercellensi* 2 (*PL* 57.417–22); *CPPM* I, no. 5810.

[44] Grégoire, *Homéliaires liturgiques médiévaux*, p. 473 (PD II.106).

[45] The sermon for St Swithun at fols 208^r–210^v is ed., trans., and discussed by Michael Lapidge, *The Cult of St Swithun*, Winchester Studies, 4.2 (Oxford, 2003), pp. 116–22.

[46] Gregory the Great, *Hom. 9 in Evangelia*, ed. by Raymond Étaix, CCSL, 141 (Turnhout, 1999), pp. 57–64.

[47] These two sermons adapted from Bede and Alcuin also occur in Oxford, Bodleian Library, MS Digby 39 (s. xi^2–xii^{in}, Abingdon), fols 50^r–52^r and 52^r–56^r respectively, noted further below.

entitled 'De sancto Byrino Occidentalium Saxonum apostolo' is taken wholesale from Bede's *Historia ecclesiastica* III.7, which tells the story of the conversion of the West Saxons during the reign of King Cynegils in the 630s by Birinus, whose episcopal see was located at Dorchester.[48] The text immediately after that at folios 333ᵛ–335ʳ is a sermon by Alcuin (*BHL* 8509) originally written for the feast of the Flemish saint Vedast but repackaged here as a sermon for Birinus.[49] Because Birinus's relics were taken from Dorchester and placed in a new shrine in Winchester in 980 by Bishop Æthelwold, who evidently sought to adopt Birinus as a Winchester saint, the promotion of Birinus's cult in the late Anglo-Saxon period runs parallel to that of the cult of St Swithun, and the appearance of these four sermons for the feasts of Swithun and Birinus in Durham A. III. 29 shows that the *sanctorale* of this manuscript embodies a set of hagiographic concerns that can be traced back to reform-era Winchester under Æthelwold.[50] It is not unreasonable to suppose, in fact, that these four sermons may have been initially developed for readings in the Night Office at Winchester in the 970s or 980s when Ælfric was a young novice there.

Another Paul the Deacon Homiliary that has been outfitted with a rare group of sermons for English saints — and in this case *all* the sermons for saints in the manuscript are for English saints — is London, British Library, Harley MS 652, written at St Augustine's Abbey, Canterbury, towards the very end of the eleventh

---

[48] *Bede's Ecclesiastical History of the English People*, ed. and trans. by Bertram Colgrave and R. A. B. Mynors (Oxford, 1969), pp. 232–36.

[49] Alcuin, *Adhortatio ad imitandas uirtutes s. Vedasti* (*AASS* Februarii, I, 800; *PL* 101.678–81). On the text, see Jullien and Perelman, *Clavis Scriptorum Latinorum Medii Aevi*, II, 8–9.

[50] A Winchester exemplar for Durham A. III. 29 has been posited on similar grounds by Clayton, 'Homiliaries and Preaching', p. 163, and by Lapidge, *Cult of St Swithun*, p. 117. In addition to the sermons just mentioned, there is also an entry in Durham A. III. 29, fol. 181ʳ, for the 22 June feast of the British protomartyr St Alban ('.x. kl. Iulii. Natale sancti Albani martyris'). No sermon accompanies that entry, however, and the reader is instead directed to make use of the sermon provided elsewhere in the homiliary for the feast of St Cyriacus ('Huius expositionem euangelii in antea requirens in natale sancti Ciriaci martyri descriptam inuenies'). Several such internal cross-references occur in Durham A. III. 29, which in at least eleven instances uses a single sermon for more than one saint's feast. Further suggestive of Winchester ties to Durham A. III. 29 is the copy of Gregory the Great's thirty-seventh gospel homily at fols 292ᵛ–296ʳ, which is designated for the 18 October feast of St Justus of Beauvais ('.xv. kl. Nouembris. Natale sancti Iusti martyris'), the third-century boy-martyr whose relics were enshrined at the New Minster, Winchester, in the eleventh century: on the English cult of St Justus, see Whatley, 'Acta Sanctorum', pp. 282–83, and Blair, 'Handlist', p. 542.

century.[51] This is an amplified Paul the Deacon Homiliary containing 180 sermons for the Vigil of Easter Sunday (PD II.2) through the fourth Sunday after Epiphany (PD I.64), followed by six sermons at the end of the manuscript (fols 209ᵛ–216ᵛ) that are all abridged versions of saints' lives by Goscelin. These are Goscelin's *Translatio s. Mildrethae virginis cum miraculorum attestatione* (*BHL* 5961 and 5964) divided for eight lections, his *Libellus de adventu beati Hadriani in Angliam eiusque virtutibus* (*BHL* 3740) and *Translatio et miracula s. Hadriani* (*BHL* 3742) together divided for twelve lections, his *Vita s. Laurentii* (*BHL* 4741) divided for twelve lections, his *Vita s. Iusti* (*BHL* 4601) divided for eight lections, his *Elogium s. Honorii* (*BHL* 3986) divided for eight lections, and his *Adventus s. Theodori in Angliam* (*BHL* 8083) divided for at least eight lections but ending incomplete within the eighth lection at the bottom of the final folio of the manuscript.[52] All six sermons are for Kentish saints (Mildreth) or for Bishops and Archbishops of Canterbury (Hadrian, Laurence, Iustus, Honorius, and Theodore). The sermons for Mildreth and Hadrian are explicitly rubricated for the feasts of these two saints ('In translatione sanctae Myldrithe uirginis', fol. 209ᵛ, and 'In festiuitate sancti Adriani abbatis', fol. 210ʳ), and the fact that all six sermons are accompanied by *lectio* numbers reveals that they were read in the Night Office at St Augustine's Abbey as part of the local commemoration of these Canterbury dignitaries.

Lincoln, Cathedral Library, MS 158 is a version of Paul the Deacon's Homiliary compiled at Lincoln towards the end of the eleventh century containing just under thirty sermons for Lent and Easter week, followed by a more extensive programme of readings for the *sanctorale* and the Common of Saints, for a total of 116 texts.[53] The *sanctorale* of this manuscript consists of sixty-three sermons and scriptural readings for the feast of St Stephen (26 December) through the feast of St Andrew

---

[51] On Harley 652, see *A Catalogue of the Harleian Manuscripts in the British Museum*, 4 vols (London, 1808–12), I, 398; Richards, *Texts and their Traditions*, pp. 104–09; Gameson, *Manuscripts*, no. 438; Gneuss, *Handlist*, no. 424; Hall, 'Bibliography of Anglo-Saxon Sermon Manuscripts'.

[52] For details, see J. E. Cross and Thomas N. Hall, 'Fragments of Alanus of Farfa's Roman Homiliary and Abridgments of Saints' Lives by Goscelin in London, British Library, Harley 652', in *Bright is the Ring of Words: Festschrift für Horst Weinstock zum 65. Geburtstag*, ed. by Clausdirk Pollner, Helmut Rohlfing, and Frank-Rutger Hausmann, Abhandlungen zur Sprache und Literatur, 85 (Bonn, 1996), pp. 49–61 (pp. 49–52).

[53] On Lincoln 158, see Schenkl, *Bibliotheca*, no. 4022; R. M. Woolley, *Catalogue of the Manuscripts of Lincoln Cathedral Chapter Library* (Oxford, 1927), pp. 119–23; R. M. Thomson, *Catalogue of the Manuscripts of Lincoln Cathedral Chapter Library* (Cambridge, 1989), pp. 124–27; Gneuss, *Handlist*, no. 273.

(30 November). Twenty-six of these sixty-three sermons for saints' feasts are texts chosen by Paul the Deacon; the rest are routine supplements to Paul's collection that occur frequently in other homiliaries of the ninth century and later. Many of these sermons are divided to accommodate the requirement for multiple readings in the Night Office, so that, for example, the copy of Caesarius's *Sermo* 216 for the nativity of John the Baptist at folios 60ᵛ–61ᵛ is divided for eight lections (for reading at Nocturns 1 and 2), and the text immediately following, Bede's *Homilia* II.20 *in Evangelia* at folios 61ᵛ–63ᵛ, is divided for lections 9–12 (for Nocturn 3), yielding a complete set of twelve lections for the Office celebration of the nativity of John the Baptist. In his *Letter to the Monks of Eynsham*, Ælfric explains that the readings for Nocturns on a saint's feast can be taken from a sermon appropriate to the given solemnity followed by a homily on the Gospel at the third position, and this is precisely the arrangement we find in Lincoln 158 for the feast of John the Baptist (and for other saints' feasts as well).

Salisbury, Cathedral Library, MS 179 is an expanded version of the summer part of the Homiliary of Paul the Deacon produced at Salisbury in the final quarter of the eleventh century.[54] This is a physically compromised manuscript that has suffered from the loss of several quires, so that the full original contents are now impossible to reconstruct. What remains are 114 sermons and homilies and fragments thereof, eighteen of which are for saints' feasts that take place in the summer and early autumn, from the nativity of John the Baptist (24 June) through the feast of St Michael (29 September), plus a copy of Gregory the Great's thirteenth gospel homily at folios 37ᵛ–38ʳ rubricated for the feast of St Felix the confessor ('Beati Felicis confessoris'), which is a bit of a problem since there are numerous saintly Felixes in Roman and medieval tradition to whom this rubric might conceivably refer; quite possibly the one intended here is St Felix of Nola, the subject of several poems by Paulinus of Nola that were well known in Anglo-Saxon England, especially to Alcuin, Aldhelm, and Bede.[55] Also well represented in this manuscript are texts for the feast of Saints Peter and Paul (29 June), for which eight sermons are

---

[54] On Salisbury 179, see E. M. Thompson, 'Catalogue of the Manuscripts in the Cathedral Library of Salisbury', in *A Catalogue of the Library of the Cathedral Church of Salisbury* (London, 1880), pp. 3–36 (p. 35); Schenkl, *Bibliotheca*, no. 3771; Teresa Webber, *Scribes and Scholars at Salisbury Cathedral c. 1075–c. 1125* (Oxford, 1992), p. 154; Thomas N. Hall, review of Webber's *Scribes and Scholars*, *Analytical and Enumerative Bibliography*, n.s. 8 (1994), 133–40 (p. 138); Gameson, *Manuscripts*, no. 893; Gneuss, *Handlist*, no. 753.

[55] On this and other sainted Felixes known to the Anglo-Saxons, see Whatley, 'Acta Sanctorum', pp. 211–16.

provided on folios 77ᵛ–82ʳ, all taken from the original contents of Paul the Deacon's Homiliary.[56]

The largest English homiliary of the period is the impressive three-volume homiliary in Worcester, Cathedral Library, MSS F. 92, 93, and 94, which was compiled at Worcester at the beginning of the twelfth century.[57] The final volume, Worcester F. 94, contains just over a hundred sermons for the *sanctorale* for May through December followed by a Common of Saints and then after that an additional batch of fourteen sermons for the Assumption and Nativity of the Virgin Mary.[58] This pronounced emphasis on Marian feasts makes Worcester F. 94 one of the richest repositories of Marian sermons from early Norman England and a key witness to the Marian cult that was flourishing in England in the late eleventh and early twelfth centuries. The very first item in the manuscript is a sermon for the Assumption of the Virgin at folios 1ʳ–2ᵛ by Ralph d'Escures, who was to become Bishop of Rochester (1108–14) and later Archbishop of Canterbury (1114–22), although this sermon was probably written while Ralph was still Abbot of Saint Martin of Séez in Brittany (1089–1108), since the sermon is addressed jointly to William, Abbot of Fécamp (*c.* 1078–1107), and Arnulf, Abbot of Saint Martin of Troarn (*c.* 1088–1112), who are both identified in the sermon's prefatory address as abbots.[59] In the preface Ralph tells us that he first delivered this sermon in

---

[56] See Grégoire, *Homéliaires liturgiques médiévaux*, pp. 461–62 (PD II.45–51, 53).

[57] On Worcester F. 92, 93, and 94, see Schenkl, *Bibliotheca*, nos 4320–22; Gameson, *Manuscripts*, nos 921–23; Gneuss, *Handlist*, nos 763–763.2; and R. M. Thomson, *A Descriptive Catalogue of the Medieval Manuscripts in Worcester Cathedral Library* (Cambridge, 2001), pp. 58–68.

[58] The contents are itemized by Thomson, *Descriptive Catalogue*, pp. 65–68.

[59] The sermon is printed (under false attribution) as Anselm, *Hom.* 9 (*PL* 158.644–49) and as *Hom.* 48 in the expanded version of Paul the Deacon's Homiliary edited by Eucherius Cervicornus and reprinted by Migne (*PL* 95.1505–08), which omits the prologue. On the sermon's authorship and transmission, see André Wilmart, 'Les homélies attribuées à s. Anselme', *Archives d'histoire doctrinale et littéraire du moyen âge*, 2 (1927), 5–29 and 339–41 (pp. 20–23 and 27–29); J. E. Cross, 'Ralph D'Escures', in *Sources of Anglo-Saxon Literary Culture: A Trial Version*, ed. by Frederick M. Biggs, Thomas D. Hill, and Paul E. Szarmach, MRTS, 74 (Binghamton, 1990), p. 157; and Beverly Mayne Kienzle, 'Exegesis on Luke 10: 38 around 1100: Worcester MS F.94, ff. 1r–2r, a Tribute to James E. Cross', *Medieval Sermon Studies*, 40 (1997), 22–28. An Old English translation of Ralph's sermon survives in London, British Library, Cotton MS Vespasian D. XIV (s. xiiᵐᵉᵈ, Canterbury or Rochester), fols 151ᵛ–157ᵛ, ed. by Rubie D.-N. Warner, *Early English Homilies from the Twelfth Century MS. Vesp. D. XIV*, EETS: OS, 152 (London, 1917), pp. 134–39; see the discussion by Elaine Treharne, 'The Life of English in the Mid-Twelfth Century: Ralph D'Escures's Homily on the Virgin Mary', in *Writers of the Reign of Henry II: Twelve Essays*, ed. by Ruth Kennedy and Simon Meecham-Jones (New York, 2006), pp. 169–86.

French (*uulgariter*) to his fellow-monks in chapter (*in conuentu fratrum*) and that he has now translated it into Latin at the request of Abbots William and Arnulf. Ralph's sermon is followed at folio 2ᵛ by a twenty-line Marian poem by the sixth-century Roman poet Andreas Orator which seems to have been copied as a companion piece to the sermon.[60] The other sermons for saints in this manuscript supplementary to Paul the Deacon's original collection are too numerous to mention, but they include dozens of texts by Augustine, Bede, Caesarius, Gregory the Great, and others that serve as extra sermons for feasts already represented in Paul the Deacon.

Seven of these eight English versions of Paul the Deacon's Homiliary (all but Harley 652) have sermons for saints that did not appear in Paul's original collection but that occur with some consistency in the eleventh- and twelfth-century derivatives of his collection. In spite of their many differences, these English homiliaries evidently rest upon a common set of supplements to Paul the Deacon, although it would take a far more detailed study of their contents to work out the nature and sequence and origins of these accretions. Most interesting perhaps are the rarities and inconsistencies in these manuscripts: the unpublished sermon for the Nativity of Mary in Canterbury Add. 127/1, the unique sermon for All Saints in CUL Kk. 4. 13, the sermon for the viewing of the relics of St Denis in Pembroke 24, the sermons for English saints in Durham A. III. 29 and Harley 652, and the Assumption sermon by Ralph d'Escures in Worcester F. 94. These less common additions and adaptations help demonstrate how Paul the Deacon's Homiliary, far from being a static collection whose contents were fixed in the eighth century,

Ralph's career is usefully summarized by Martin Brett, 'Escures, Ralph d' (*c*.1068–1122)', in *Oxford Dictionary of National Biography*, ed. by H. C. G. Matthew and Brian Harrison, 60 vols (Oxford, 2004), XVIII, 592–95, and is more fully examined by Mary Amanda Clark, 'Ralph d'Escures: Anglo-Norman Abbot and Archbishop' (unpublished doctoral dissertation, University of California at Santa Barbara, 1975), who discusses the sermon at pp. 252–54.

[60] Andreas Orator, 'De Maria uirgine ad Rusticianum carmen', ed. by Alexander Riese, *Anthologia Latina sive Poesis Latinae Supplementum. Pars Prior: Carmina in Codicibus Scripta*, 2nd edn, 2 vols, Bibliotheca Scriptorum Graecorum et Romanorum Teubneriana (Leipzig, 1894–1906; repr. Amsterdam, 1964), I.2, 57–58 (repr. *PL* Suppl. 3.1429–30). The poem (inc. 'Virgo parens') is indexed by Ulysse Chevalier, *Repertorium Hymnologicum: Catalogue des chants, hymnes, proses, séquences, tropes en usage dans l'église latine depuis les origines jusqu'à nos jours*, 6 vols (Brussels, 1892–1920), no. 34625; and Dietrich Schaller and Ewald Könsgen, *Initia Carminum Latinorum Saeculo Undecimo Antiquiorum* (Göttingen, 1977), no. 17345. On the poem and its author, see Pietro M. Lustrissimi, 'Andreas Orator, poeta cristiano del secolo VI, in un dimenticado carme di lode alla Madre di Dio', in *De cultu mariano saeculis VI–XI: Acta Congressus Mariologici-Mariani Internationalis in Croatia anno 1971 celebrati*, ed. by Joseph Lécuyer and others, 5 vols (Rome, 1972), III, 35–48.

underwent multiple transformations to meet the liturgical needs of individual monastic communities in Anglo-Saxon and early Norman England. Comparable innovations and accretions are also to be found in legendaries and other hagiographic manuscripts of the period.

Sermons for Saints in Legendaries and Other Hagiographic Manuscripts

Although manuscripts containing *passiones* and *vitae* of multiple saints were produced in small numbers as early as the eighth century, it was not until the ninth century that such collections began to be organized systematically around the Church calendar, with the texts copied sequentially according to the date of each saint's feast.[61] These calendrically ordered collections of saints' legends, known in their earliest manifestations as passionals and later on as legendaries (when they came to be designed specifically for reading in the Night Office), multiplied rapidly over the course of the ninth, tenth, and eleventh centuries, reaching the height of their production in the twelfth century, with a modest decline thereafter.[62] Unlike the homiliaries in the tradition of Paul the Deacon, which were designed exclusively for monastic liturgical usage, the earliest passionals and legendaries were created and employed for several different purposes — some for private devotional reading, some for reading at Mass, others for monastic reading in the refectory or at collations in the evening.[63] However, a good many possess *lectio* numbers in the

---

[61] Guy Philippart, *Les légendiers latins et autres manuscrits hagiographiques*, Typologie des sources du moyen âge occidental, 24–25 (Turnhout, 1977), pp. 30–39.

[62] Philippart, *Les légendiers latins*, pp. 37–39.

[63] The texts and manuscripts that were used for these various purposes are abundantly documented by C. A., 'Les lectures de table des moines de Marchiennes au XIIIᵉ siècle', *Revue Bénédictine*, 11 (1894), 27–35; Ph. Schmitz, 'Les lectures de table à l'abbaye de Saint-Denis vers la fin du moyen-âge', *Revue Bénédictine*, 42 (1930), 163–67; Baudouin de Gaiffier d'Hestroy, 'L'hagiographie et son public au XIᵉ siècle', in *Miscellanea Historica in honorem Leonis van der Essen Universitatis Catholicae in oppido Lovaniensi iam annos XXXV professoris* (Brussels, 1947), pp. 135–66, repr. in de Gaiffier's *Études critiques d'hagiographie et d'iconologie*, Subsidia Hagiographica, 43 (Brussels, 1967), pp. 475–507; de Gaiffier, 'La lecture des actes des martyrs dans la prière liturgique en Occident: à propos du passionnaire hispanique', *Analecta Bollandiana*, 72 (1954), 134–66; de Gaiffier, 'La lecture des passions des martyrs à Rome avant le IXᵉ siècle', *Analecta Bollandiana*, 87 (1969), 63–78; H. Moretus, 'De l'usage des légendiers au moyen-âge', in Henri Rochais, *Un légendier cistercien de la fin du XIIᵉ siècle: Le 'Liber de natalitiis' et de quelques grands légendiers des XIIᵉ et XIIIᵉ s.*, 2 vols, La Documentation Cistercienne 15 (Rochefort, 1975), II, 151–55; Philippart, *Les légendiers latins*, pp. 112–18; François Dolbeau, 'Typologie et formation

margins which show that the individual texts were divided for reading in the monastic Night Office, just as sermons in homiliaries were.[64] Not all legendaries contain sermons, but the natural drive towards accumulating more and more texts representative of more and more saints inevitably drew some sermons for saints into their compass. The few sermons for saints in the very few extant early English legendaries are all prime candidates for the type of hagiographic sermon Ælfric would have consulted for reading in the Night Office at Eynsham, as are the somewhat more plentiful sermons for saints in a variety of other hagiographic manuscripts which are harder to classify owing to their miscellaneous nature. In what follows, I comment first on sermons in legendaries, then on some of these more miscellaneous manuscripts, including *libelli* of works devoted to a single saint as well as manuscripts in which the principle for ordering and selecting texts (if there is one) is difficult to make out.

The largest and best-known legendary from the pre-Conquest period is the 'Cotton-Corpus Legendary', so called because it now exists in the form of two large manuscripts (London, British Library, Cotton MS Nero E. I and Cambridge, Corpus Christi College, MS 9) divided between the Cotton collection of the British Library and the library of Corpus Christi College, Cambridge.[65] Both

des collections hagiographiques d'après les recueils de l'abbaye de Saint-Thierry', in *Saint-Thierry, une abbaye du VIᵉ au XXᵉ siècle: Actes du Colloque international d'Histoire monastique Reims-Saint-Thierry, 11 au 14 octobre 1976*, ed. by Michel Bur (Saint-Thierry, 1979), pp. 159–82 (pp. 174–75); Donatella Nebbiai-Della Guarda, 'Les listes médiévales de lectures monastiques: Contribution à la connaissance des anciennes bibliothèques Bénédictines', *Revue Bénédictine*, 96 (1986), 271–326, who identifies the saints' lives prescribed for reading in the refectory or at collations in nine French and English monasteries of the twelfth, thirteenth, and fourteenth centuries, including Reading and Bury St Edmunds; Katrien Heene, '*Audire, legere, vulgo*: An Attempt to Define Public Use and Comprehensibility of Carolingian Hagiography', in *Latin and the Romance Languages in the Early Middle Ages*, ed. by Roger Wright (London, 1991), pp. 146–63 (pp. 147–49); and Wolfert S. Van Egmond, 'The Audience of Early Medieval Hagiographical Texts: Some Questions Revisited', in *New Approaches to Medieval Communication*, ed. by Marco Mostert, Utrecht Studies in Medieval Literacy (Turnhout, 1999), pp. 41–67.

[64] Several examples from eleventh-century Fleury are analysed by Élisabeth Pellegrin, 'Notes sur quelques recueils de vies de saints utilisés pour la liturgie à Fleury-sur-Loire au XIᵉ siècle', *Bulletin d'information de l'Institut de Recherches et d'Histoire des Textes*, 12 (1963), 7–30, repr. in Pellegrin, *Bibliothèques retrouvées: Manuscrits, bibliothèques, et bibliophiles du Moyen Age et de la Renaissance* (Paris, 1988), pp. 233–56.

[65] Important introductions to the collection include Peter Jackson and Michael Lapidge, 'The Contents of the Cotton-Corpus Legendary', in *Holy Men and Holy Women: Old English Prose Saints' Lives and their Contexts*, ed. by Paul E. Szarmach (Albany, 1996), pp. 131–46; *Three*

manuscripts were produced at Worcester in the third quarter of the eleventh century, although several dozen more texts were added to the beginning and end of each volume between the late eleventh and thirteenth centuries. The original eleventh-century core contains texts for about 150 saints, most deriving ultimately from some form of Roman passional that had been fleshed out with a substantial number of texts concerning saints associated with cult centres in Flanders and northern France, leading some scholars to suspect that the exemplar for the 'Cotton-Corpus Legendary' was produced somewhere in that region.[66] That exemplar has never been found, however, and a number of problems remain in sorting out the relationship between the 'Cotton-Corpus Legendary' and continental hagiographic traditions generally. It is also significant that while the exemplar for the 'Cotton-Corpus Legendary' must have been continental, its transmission history is entirely English since all of the known recensions of this collection were made in England in the eleventh and twelfth centuries.

Together, Cotton Nero E. I and CCCC 9 contain eight sermons for saints. All but one of these sermons have parallels in continental manuscripts, although not too surprisingly the parallels are better represented in continental homiliaries than in legendaries. Seven of the eight sermons appear in Cotton Nero E. I, which is such a large manuscript that at some point it was split into two volumes or 'parts', so that three sermons appear in what is now Part 1 and the remaining four appear in Part 2. The three sermons in Cotton Nero E. I Part 1 are all sermons for the Purification of the Virgin Mary: one by Augustine (fol. 142[r-v]),[67] one taken from

---

Eleventh-Century Anglo-Latin Saints' Lives: Vita S. Birini, Vita et Miracula S. Kenelmi, and Vita S. Rumwoldi, ed. and trans. by Rosalind C. Love, Oxford Medieval Texts (Oxford, 1996), pp. xiii–xxix; and E. Gordon Whatley, 'Cotton-Corpus Legendary', in *Sources of Anglo-Saxon Literary Culture*, vol. V: *C*, ed. by Thomas N. Hall (forthcoming), who provides a thorough summation of recent scholarship. On CCCC 9, see Montague Rhodes James, *A Descriptive Catalogue of the Manuscripts in the Library of Corpus Christi College, Cambridge*, 2 vols (Cambridge, 1912), I, 21–30; Mildred Budny, *Insular, Anglo-Saxon, and Early Anglo-Norman Manuscript Art at Corpus Christi College, Cambridge: An Illustrated Catalogue*, 2 vols (Kalamazoo, 1997), I, 609–22; Gameson, *Manuscripts*, no. 54; Gneuss, *Handlist*, no. 36. On Cotton Nero E. I, see Gameson, *Manuscripts*, no. 397; Gneuss, *Handlist*, nos 344–45.

[66] More precisely, an origin in the diocese of Noyon-Tournai within the archdiocese of Reims has been suggested by Jackson and Lapidge, 'Contents of the Cotton-Corpus Legendary', pp. 133–34; and by Michael Lapidge, 'Roman Martyrs and their Miracles in Anglo-Saxon England', in *Miracles and the Miraculous in Medieval Germanic and Latin Literature*, ed. by K. E. Olsen, A. Harbus, and T. Hofstra (Leuven, 2004), pp. 95–120 (p. 113).

[67] Augustine, *Sermo* 370.2–4 (*PL* 39.1657–79). Two other copies of this sermon, which was included by Paul the Deacon as a reading for the feast of the Purification (PD I.65), appear in

Ambrose's commentary on Luke (fols 142^v–143^r),[68] and an anonymous and unpublished sermon (inc. 'Conueniendum est in unum') at folios 143^r–144^r which is also known from a slightly later copy in Cambridge, Pembroke College, MS 25, folios 27^r–28^v, a version of the Homiliary of Saint-Père de Chartres produced at Bury St Edmunds at the end of the eleventh or very beginning of the twelfth century.[69] The four sermons in Cotton Nero E. I Part 2 are two sermons by Augustine for the nativity of John the Baptist (fols 29^v–30^r and 30^{r-v}),[70] a *Sermo de natiuitate sanctae Mariae* (*BHL* 5341) excerpted from the apocryphal *Gospel of pseudo-Matthew* (fols 116^v–18^r),[71] and the ninth-century All Saints sermon beginning 'Legimus in ecclesiasticis historiis' (fol. 151^{r-v}).[72] Of the forty-three hagiographic texts in CCCC 9, only one, Alcuin's sermon on the nativity of St Vedast (*BHL* 8509) at pp. 145–47, styles itself a *homilia* or *sermo* rather than a *vita* or *passio* or an account of miracles.[73] None of these sermons is very surprising to find in an

---

Durham, Cathedral Library, MS B. II. 2 (s. xi^{ex}, Durham), fols 49^v–50^r; and Worcester, Cathedral Library, MS F. 92 (s. xi/xii or xii^{in}, Worcester), fols 162^r–163^r.

[68] Ambrose, *In Lucam* II.58–62, ed. by M. Adriaen, CCSL, 14 (Turnhout, 1957), pp. 56–57, here rubricated 'sermo beati Ambrosii episcopi'.

[69] See James E. Cross, *Cambridge Pembroke College MS. 25: A Carolingian Sermonary Used by Anglo-Saxon Preachers*, King's College London Medieval Studies, 1 (London, 1987), p. 25, who identifies copies in other manuscripts of the Homiliary of Saint-Père de Chartres.

[70] Augustine, *Sermo* 293(a).2–5 and *Sermo* 292(c), ed. by Germain Morin, *Miscellanea Agostiniana*, vol. I: *Sancti Augustini sermones post Maurinos reperti* (Rome, 1930), pp. 223–26 and 351–52 respectively.

[71] *The Apocryphal Gospels of Mary in Anglo-Saxon England*, ed. by Mary Clayton, CSASE, 26 (Cambridge, 1998), pp. 323–27.

[72] This sermon is not listed by Jackson and Lapidge in their inventory of 'The Contents of the Cotton-Corpus Legendary', possibly because it is difficult to tell whether this text formed part of the original collection or is a slightly later addition. In their analysis of the collection, Jackson and Lapidge (p. 132) accept the original limits of the legendary in Cotton Nero E. I Part 2 as extending through fol. 155^v (in agreement with Gneuss, *Handlist*, no. 344), but in their itemization of the contents of that volume (pp. 137–41) they list texts only through fol. 151^r, leaving fols 151^r–155^v unaccounted for. The three items occupying those folios are a copy of 'Legimus in ecclesiasticis historiis' (fol. 151^{r-v}), a set of *Miracula s. Leonis papae* (fols 151^v–153^v), and twelve Office lections and a Mass for the nativity of St Nicholas of Myra (fols 153^v–155^v). These three items are judged 'local Worcester supplements' to the collection, probably not much later than the main part, by E. Gordon Whatley in his entries on 'Leo IX, miracula' and 'Nicolaus, lectiones' in 'Acta Sanctorum', pp. 292–95 and 361–63 (quotation at p. 294). Gneuss, *Handlist*, no. 344, dates fols 1–155 inclusive to s. xi$^{3/4}$.

[73] Alcuin, *Adhortatio ad imitandas uirtutes s. Vedasti* (*AASS* Februarii, I, 800; *PL* 101.678–81). See Jullien and Perelman, *Clavis Scriptorum Latinorum Medii Aevi*, II, 8–9. A French translation

eleventh-century English legendary. The feasts and saints which they celebrate (Purification, nativity of John the Baptist, Nativity of the Virgin, All Saints, and Vedast) are all standard fixtures of the late Anglo-Saxon calendar, and it is particularly telling that all five of these feasts and saints are ones for which we find new and supplementary sermons added to English Paul the Deacon manuscripts at very nearly the same time, so that the homiliaries can be shown to follow a pattern of development that is closely parallelled in the 'Cotton-Corpus Legendary'.

In the final quarter of the eleventh century another large legendary was compiled at Salisbury, evidently relying on the same now-lost exemplar as the saints' lives in Cotton Nero E. I and CCCC 9, and the result is the two-volume collection now classed as Salisbury, Cathedral Library, MSS 221 and 222, which are appropriately referred to together as the Salisbury recension of the 'Cotton-Corpus Legendary'.[74] Salisbury 221 contains sixty-seven saints' *vitae* or *passiones* from January to June, complemented by an additional set of readings for fifty-six saints from June to early October in Salisbury 222 (the remainder of October through December evidently having been lost). The only text within this entire two-volume collection that is explicitly labelled a sermon or homily rather than a saint's *vita* or *passio* is the copy of Alcuin's *Sermo in natale s. Vedasti* (*BHL* 8509) in Salisbury 222, folios 242ʳ–243ᵛ, which parallels the copy in CCCC 9, and which is here rubricated 'Homelia in die natalis sancti Vedasti pontifici'.

In the first quarter of the twelfth century, the Salisbury canons took their hagiographic research a step further by compiling an additional collection of saints' *vitae* and *passiones* as supplements to the already extensive collection in Salisbury 221 and 222, and the result this time was the two relatively small legendaries now classed as Dublin, Trinity College, MS 174 and Salisbury, Cathedral Library, MS 223. Trinity 174 is a composite manuscript made up of six booklets containing twenty-seven saints' *passiones* and *vitae*, a double Mass for martyrs, and fourteen

---

is given by Christiane Veyrard-Cosme, *L'œuvre hagiographique en prose d'Alcuin: Vitae Willibrordi, Vedasti, Richarii: Édition, traduction, études narratologiques*, Per Verba: Testi mediolatini con traduzione, 21 (Florence, 2003), pp. xxxviii–xl.

[74] On Salisbury 221 and 222, see Schenkl, *Bibliotheca*, nos 908–09; Thomas Duffus Hardy, *Descriptive Catalogue of Materials Relating to the History of Great Britain and Ireland, to the End of the Reign of Henry VII*, 3 vols, Rolls Series 26 (London, 1862–71; repr. New York, 1963), I.1, 71, 301, 317, 396; Madan, Craster, and Denholm-Young, *Summary Catalogue*, II.2, 1212–13 (nos 8688–89); Ker and Piper, *Medieval Manuscripts in British Libraries*, IV, 257–62; Webber, *Scribes and Scholars*, pp. 154–57, 169, and 170; Gameson, *Manuscripts*, nos 896–97; Gneuss, *Handlist*, nos 754.5–6.

sermons or texts rubricated as sermons.[75] The fourteen sermons in Trinity 174 include texts for Saints Barnabas, Julian of Le Mans, Luke, Nicholas, Servatius of Tongres, Stephen, Vincent of Saragossa, and the crucifix of Beirut, plus a sermon by Laurence of Novara on almsgiving at folios 99^r–103^v and an unidentified and incomplete sermon on the Apostles' Creed at folios 121^r–123^r.[76] The sermons on Servatius, on the miracles wrought by the crucifix of Beirut, and on almsgiving by Laurence of Novara are the earliest such texts in an English manuscript. The other half of this legendary, Salisbury 223, contains thirty-three hagiographic texts for the feasts of various saints from Boniface (5 June) to Fides (6 October), with readings for several continental saints who are virtually unknown in English legendaries prior to this, namely Archadius, Concordius, Dioscorus, Gertrude of Nievaux, Iohannes Penariensis, Sabinianus, and Ursinus.[77] Salisbury 223 also contains an unpublished tract on the Conception of the Virgin Mary at folios 19^v–20^r,[78] and one genuine sermon, a copy of pseudo-Augustine, *Sermo* 196 at folios 25^v–27^r, attributed to Pope St Leo the Great ('Sermo sancti Leonis pape in natale sancti Iohannis Baptistae').[79] This last sermon was included in the eighth-century Homiliary of Alan of Farfa (II.37) as a reading for the nativity of John the Baptist, and that continues to be its designated function here.[80]

---

[75] On Trinity 174, see Schenkl, *Bibliotheca*, no. 3312; Mario Esposito, 'On Two Hagiographical Manuscripts in the Library of Trinity College, Dublin', *Journal of Theological Studies*, 14 (1913), 72–77 (pp. 74–77); Paul Grosjean, 'Catalogus codicum hagiographicorum latinorum Bibliothecarum Dublinensium', *Analecta Bollandiana*, 46 (1928), 81–148 (pp. 88–91); M. L. Colker, *Trinity College Library Dublin: Descriptive Catalogue of the Mediaeval and Renaissance Latin Manuscripts*, 2 vols (Dublin, 1991), I, 320–30; Webber, *Scribes and Scholars*, pp. 143, 158; Gameson, *Manuscripts*, no. 202; Gneuss, *Handlist*, no. 215.

[76] Full identifications of all these texts (except for the unidentified sermon on the Apostles' Creed) are given by Colker, *Trinity College Library Dublin: Descriptive Catalogue*, I, 320–30.

[77] On Salisbury 223, see Schenkl, *Bibliotheca*, nos 908–09; Hardy, *Descriptive Catalogue*, I.1, 71, 107, 239; Madan, Craster, and Denholm-Young, *Summary Catalogue*, II.2, 1211–12 (no. 8687); Ker and Piper, *Medieval Manuscripts in British Libraries*, IV, 262–64; Webber, *Scribes and Scholars*, pp. 169–70; Gameson, *Manuscripts*, no. 898.

[78] I have an edition in progress.

[79] Pseudo-Augustine, *Sermo* 196, *In natale s. Ioannis Baptistae* (*PL* 39.2111–13), also printed as pseudo-Maximus of Turin, *Sermo* 65 (*PL* 57.661–64); *CPPM* I, no. 981.

[80] Hosp, 'Il sermonario di Alano di Farfa (*Continuazione*)', pp. 232–33; Grégoire, *Homéliaires liturgiques médiévaux*, p. 173. Another copy of pseudo-Augustine, *Sermo* 196 in an English manuscript from about a generation earlier appears in Durham A. III. 29, fols 189^r–191^v.

In addition to these full-blown legendaries, there are quite a few smaller and more eclectic manuscripts from the period containing texts on just one or two saints. Among these is Cambridge, Corpus Christi College, MS 312, a *libellus* of materials pertaining to St Augustine of Canterbury written at St Augustine's Abbey towards the middle of the twelfth century, preserving a set of materials that had been assembled probably in the 1090s by the monastic hagiographer Goscelin.[81] Like a number of other eleventh- and twelfth-century manuscripts, CCCC 312 was designed to provide a complete set of texts for the Office celebration of a particular saint's feast.[82] It includes Goscelin's *Historia maior* and *Historia minor* of St Augustine (*BHL* 777 and 778) as well as Goscelin's account of Augustine's miracles (*BHL* 779), a series of lections for the feast of St Augustine and for ferial days and the octave, a neumed antiphon for St Augustine, prayers for the vigil of the feast of St Augustine, and an unpublished sermon by Goscelin for the feast of St Augustine, which is 26 May. This sermon is a tour-de-force of ecclesiastical rhetoric that boldly promotes Augustine as the patron saint and spiritual father of the English, a latter-day Moses who led the English to salvation and who is destined to represent the English before God on Judgement Day (just as Patrick is said in Irish tradition to be the destined spokesperson for the Irish at Judgement Day[83]).

[81] On CCCC 312, see James, *Descriptive Catalogue of the Manuscripts in the Library of Corpus Christi College Cambridge*, II, 112–14; Gneuss, *Handlist*, no. 89; K. D. Hartzell, *Catalogue of Manuscripts Written or Owned in England up to 1200 Containing Music* (Woodbridge, 2006), p. 51 (no. 36).

[82] For discussion of several such hagiographic *libelli*, see Francis Wormald, 'Some Illustrated Manuscripts of the Lives of the Saints', *Bulletin of the John Rylands Library*, 35 (1952–53), 248–66; Dolbeau, 'Typologie et formation des collections hagiographiques', pp. 160–61; Philippart, *Les légendiers latins*, pp. 99–101; David N. Dumville, *Liturgy and the Ecclesiastical History of Late Anglo-Saxon England*, Studies in Anglo-Saxon History, 5 (Woodbridge, 1992), pp. 108–10; *Three Eleventh-Century Anglo-Latin Saints' Lives*, ed. and trans. by Love, pp. xiii–xiv, xxxii–xxxiii; Éric Palazzo, 'Le rôle des *libelli* dans la pratique liturgique du haut Moyen Age: histoire et typologie', *Revue Mabillon*, n.s., 1 (1990), 9–36 (pp. 9, 18, 20, 22 n. 64, and 23); Pierre-Marie Gy, 'The Different Forms of Liturgical "Libelli"', in *Fountain of Life: In Memory of Niels K. Rasmussen, O.P.*, ed. by Gerard Austin (Washington, D.C., 1991), pp. 23–34 (pp. 27 and 29–30); and Ute Kleine, 'Stumme Seiten: Beobachtungen und Thesen zu Herstellung und Gebrauch von hagiographischen Büchern im Hochmittelalter', *Frühmittelalterliche Studien*, 38 (2004), 371–91. *Libelli* devoted to saints' miracles are discussed by Réginald Grégoire, *Manuale di agiologia: Introduzione alla letteratura agiografica*, 2nd edn, Bibliotheca Montisfani, 12 (Fabriano, 1996), pp. 150–53.

[83] Some notes on the Patrician tradition are gathered by Thomas N. Hall, 'Medieval Traditions about the Site of Judgment', in *Four Last Things: Death, Judgment, Heaven, and Hell in the*

This is a very rare example of a sermon composed in England before the twelfth century for the liturgical commemoration of an English saint. The only other extant copy appears in London, British Library, Cotton MS Vespasian B. XX (s. xii[in]), folios 86[r]–93[v], which is also from St Augustine's Abbey.[84] Since Goscelin's sermon was written expressly for the celebration of St Augustine's feast at St Augustine's Abbey, and since the only two known copies are in manuscripts produced there, it is entirely possible that this sermon was never known outside of Canterbury during the Middle Ages.

A *libellus* of materials pertaining to St Benedict of Nursia, the father of Benedictine monasticism, is preserved in Cambridge, St John's College, MS 164, written at St Augustine's Abbey in the tenth century.[85] Its contents include Adrevald of Fleury's *Translatio s. Benedicti* (*BHL* 1117), Adrevald's treatise on the *Miracula s. Benedicti* (*BHL* 1123), two neumed hymns, and an incomplete copy of the sermon on St Benedict by Odo of Cluny at folios 89[r]–98[v].[86] Odo's sermon on St Benedict was originally written for Cluniac observance of the octave of the feast of St Benedict (18 July) and was read annually at Cluny and Fleury by the close of the eleventh century.[87] The copy in St John's 164 is the earliest surviving copy of this sermon in an English manuscript.[88]

Middle Ages: 1993 Proceedings of the Illinois Medieval Association, ed. by Allen J. Frantzen, Essays in Medieval Studies, 10 (Chicago, 1994), pp. 79–97 (pp. 88–90 and n. 47).

[84] The copy of the sermon in Cotton Vespasian B. XX occupies a separate quire written in a mid-twelfth-century hand (see Gameson, *Manuscripts*, no. 414). An edition of Goscelin's sermon is forthcoming by Shannon Ambrose.

[85] On St John's 164, see Schenkl, *Bibliotheca*, no. 2640; M. R. James, *A Descriptive Catalogue of the Manuscripts in the Library of St John's College Cambridge* (Cambridge, 1913), pp. 197–99; Gneuss, *Handlist*, no. 153; Hartzell, *Catalogue*, pp. 117–18 (no. 56).

[86] Odo of Cluny, *Sermo 3, De s. Benedicto abbate* (*PL* 133.721–28), ending incomplete, and with text missing between folios 96 and 97 owing to the loss of a leaf.

[87] Ernst Sackur, *Die Cluniacenser in ihrer kirchlichen und allgemeingeschichtlichen Wirksamkeit bis zur Mitte des elften Jahrhunderts*, 2 vols (Halle, 1892–94; repr. Darmstadt, 1965), II, 335; Jean Longère, 'La prédication sur saint Benoît du Xe au XIIIe siècle', in *Sous la règle de saint Benoît: structures monastiques et sociétés en France du Moyen Age à l'époque moderne. Abbaye bénédictine Sainte-Marie de Paris, 23–25 Octobre 1980* (Geneva, 1982), pp. 433–60 (pp. 433–36); Pellegrin, 'Notes sur quelques recueils de vies de saints', p. 253; Walter Berschin, *Biographie und Epochenstil im lateinischen Mittelalter*, 4 vols in 5, Quellen und Untersuchungen zur lateinischen Philologie des Mittelalters, 8–10 and 12.1–2 (Stuttgart, 1986–2001), IV.1, 31–32.

[88] Later copies of Odo's sermon on St Benedict appear in New York, Pierpont Morgan Library, MS 926 (s. xi[3/4]), fols 76[v]–77[v]; Durham A. III. 29, fols 222[v]–227[r]; and Worcester F. 94, fols 45[v]–49[v].

Cambridge, Trinity Hall, MS 21 is yet another hagiographic *libellus*, this time containing texts chosen primarily but not exclusively for the celebration of the feast of St Martin, the sixth-century Bishop of Tours.[89] The manuscript includes Sulpicius Severus's *Vita s. Martini Turonensis* (*BHL* 5610–16), Gregory of Tours's *De transitu s. Martini* (*BHL* 5619–21), Gregory's *Vita s. Britii* (*BHL* 1452), John of Naples's *Vita s. Nicolai* (*BHL* 6104–05), and two extracts from Gregory of Tours's *De miraculis s. Martini* (*BHL* 5622–23) at folios 67ᵛ–69ʳ, both rubricated as sermons and both attributed, rather implausibly, to Ambrose ('Sermo sancti Ambrosii de transitu sancti Martini' and 'Item alius quando corpus eius translatum est'). Remember that Ælfric tells the monks of Eynsham that if no sermons designated for a particular saint's feast are available, then one should adapt something suitable for the occasion. This is exactly what has happened in the case of these two excerpts from Gregory's treatise on Martin's miracles, which circulated in numerous *libelli* devoted to Martin, which are sometimes referred to as *Martinelli* or 'little collections of texts pertaining to St Martin'. Other examples of *Martinelli* from Anglo-Saxon England which include these same excerpts from Gregory of Tours's *De miraculis s. Martini* adapted as sermons are Hereford, Cathedral Library, MS O. VI. 11 (s. xiˣ) and Vatican City, Biblioteca Apostolica Vaticana, MS Reg. lat. 489, folios 61–124 (s. xi¹).[90]

Hereford, Cathedral Library, MS P. II. 5, Part 2 (fols 146–54) is a single booklet of hagiographic texts copied in England early in the twelfth century.[91] It

---

[89] On Trinity Hall 21, see Schenkl, *Bibliotheca*, no. 2821; M. R. James, *A Descriptive Catalogue of the Manuscripts in the Library of Trinity Hall* (Cambridge, 1907), pp. 37–39; Gameson, *Manuscripts*, no. 184; Gneuss, *Handlist*, no. 201.

[90] See the discussion by Whatley, 'Acta Sanctorum', pp. 330–32. These *Martinelli* are not always stand-alone *libelli*: the Martin set (consisting of Sulpicius's *Vita s. Martini* chs 2–6, Gregory of Tours's *Historia Francorum* I.48 and *De virtutibus s. Martini* I.4 (*BHL* 5621), and Sulpicius's *Epist*. 3 *ad Bassulam* (*BHL* 5613)) in Avranches, Bibliothèque municipale, MS 29 (s. x/xi, southern England; later provenance Mont Saint-Michel), fols 99ʳ–105ʳ, is preceded by ninety-eight folios of pseudo-Bede sermons and followed by an extract from Augustine's *De diversis quaestionibus LXXIII*. For details, see the *Catalogue général des manuscrits des Bibliothèques publiques de France. Départements IV: Arras, Avranches, Boulogne* (Paris, 1872), pp. 443–44; and Gneuss, *Handlist*, no. 782. Two further *Martinelli* are noted by Gneuss, *Handlist*, nos 296 (London, British Library, Additional MS 40074) and 378.5 (London, British Library, Cotton MS Tiberius D. IV, fols 1–105).

[91] On Hereford P. II. 5, Part 2, see Schenkl, *Bibliotheca*, no. 4201; Arthur Thomas Bannister, *A Descriptive Catalogue of the Manuscripts in the Hereford Cathedral Library* (Hereford, 1927), pp. 119–20; R. A. B. Mynors and R. M. Thomson, *Catalogue of the Manuscripts of Hereford Cathedral Library* (Cambridge, 1993), p. 76; Gameson, *Manuscripts*, no. 316.

contains just two items, a *Passio s. Margaritae* (*BHL* 5306) at folios 146ʳ–149ʳ, followed at folios 149ʳ–153ᵛ by a sermon on St Mary Magdalene usually attributed to Odo of Cluny (*BHL* 5439–41).[92] The sermon on Mary Magdalene attributed to Odo, here rubricated as a 'uita sancte Marie Magdalene', was frequently employed for readings in the Night Office on the feast of Mary Magdalene (22 July), especially in northern France, by the late eleventh century.[93] Its authorship by Odo has recently been called into question by Dominique Iogna-Prat, who finds no evidence that it was ever known at Cluny and who thinks it was written instead sometime between 860 and 1040, perhaps at Vézelay, where it was first divided for reading in the monastic Night Office and where a strong cult to Mary Magdalene was established in the eleventh century.[94] The only other copy of this sermon on Mary Magdalene in an English manuscript through the early twelfth century is in Worcester F. 94, folios 49ᵛ–51ʳ.

London, British Library, Additional MS 19835 is a manuscript written in Normandy or England around the turn of the twelfth century.[95] It contains Heiric of Auxerre's *Collectanea* (consisting of extracts from Orosius, Suetonius, and Valerius Maximus), miscellaneous theological treatises including excerpts from Jerome and Augustine on the Psalms, a treatise on the Greek alphabet, some letters by Fulbert of Chartres, and portions of three sermons by Fulbert on the Nativity and Purification of the Virgin at folios 24ʳ–25ᵛ. These three sermons are Fulbert's *Sermones* 5, 4, and 3 according to the numbering assigned to them in *PL* 141.319–25.[96] The small corpus of Marian sermons authored by Fulbert of Chartres (952–1028) played a prominent role in the advancement of the Marian cult in England in the

---

[92] Odo of Cluny, *Sermo 2, In veneratione s. Mariae Magdalenae* (*PL* 133.713–21).

[93] Victor Saxer, *Le culte de Marie Madeleine en occident des origines à la fin du moyen âge*, Cahiers d'archéologie et d'histoire, 3 (Auxerre, 1959), pp. 71, 174, 180, 313–18.

[94] Dominique Iogna-Prat, 'La Madeleine du *Sermo in veneratione sanctae Mariae Magdalenae* attribué à Odon de Cluny', *Mélanges de l'École Française de Rome: Moyen Âge*, 104 (1992), 37–70. Direct influence of the Vézelay cult on the English veneration of Mary Magdalene is emphasized by Veronica Ortenberg, 'Le culte de sainte Marie Madeleine dans l'Angleterre anglo-saxonne', *Mélanges de l'École Française de Rome: Moyen Âge*, 104 (1992), 13–35 (pp. 34–35), and Ortenberg, *The English Church and the Continent*, p. 254.

[95] On BL Add. 19835, see *Catalogue of the Additions to the Manuscripts in the British Museum* [. . .]: *Additional MSS. 19,720–24,026* (London, 1965), p. 9; Gameson, *Manuscripts*, no. 348; Gneuss, *Handlist*, no. 281.3.

[96] Sermons 5 and 4 are also edited by J. M. Canal, 'Texto crítico de algunos sermones marianos de San Fulberto de Chartres o a él atribuibles', *Recherches de théologie ancienne et médiévale*, 30 (1963), 55–87 and 329–33 (pp. 331–33 and 56–61 respectively).

late eleventh and early twelfth centuries, to judge from the number of copies surviving in manuscripts produced during this period.[97] His fourth sermon, for the Nativity of Mary (inc. 'Approbatae consuetudinis est'), commands an especially interesting place in the history of Marian literature because of its frank endorsement of the apocryphal nativity legend in the *Libellus de nativitate s. Mariae* (a revision of the *Gospel of pseudo-Matthew*)[98] and also because of the story it tells of the Archdeacon Theophilus, an early Faust figure who in a rash moment deeded his soul to the devil, then changed his mind and prayed for help from the Virgin Mary, who interceded on his behalf and liberated Theophilus from his diabolical contract. The story of Theophilus's charter with the devil and of Mary's intercession was better known in Anglo-Saxon England (and is probably better known today) through the seventh-century Greek legend known as the *Penitence of Theophilus*, a text translated into Latin in the ninth century and included in that form in both recensions of the 'Cotton-Corpus Legendary' plus two other Anglo-Saxon manuscripts.[99] But the version of this story in Fulbert's *Sermo* 4 also reached a wide

---

[97] On Fulbert's Marian sermons, see J. M. Canal, 'Los sermones marianos de San Fulberto de Chartres († 1028)', *Recherches de théologie ancienne et médiévale*, 29 (1962), 33–51, which should be read in conjunction with the (perhaps overly) stern critique by Henri Barré, 'Pro Fulberto', *Recherches de théologie ancienne et médiévale*, 31 (1964), 324–36, who points out several errors and gaps in Canal's reconstruction of the transmission of Fulbert's works, both in Canal's 'Los sermones marianos' and in his 'Texto crítico' (cited in the previous note). Canal later responded to Barré's criticisms by publishing some revisions and additions in 'Los sermones marianos de San Fulberto de Chartres: Conclusión', *Recherches de théologie ancienne et médiévale*, 33 (1966), 139–46. The collective findings of Canal and Barré concerning the authenticity and transmission of Marian sermons attributed to Fulbert are summarized by R. Laurentin, 'L'œuvre mariale de Fulbert de Chartres', *Revue des sciences philosophiques et théologiques*, 50 (1966), 544–45. Important accounts of Fulbert's Mariology are provided by Henri Barré, *Prières anciennes de l'Occident à la Mère du Sauveur: Des origines à saint Anselme* (Paris, 1963), pp. 150–55; Paul Viard, 'Fulbert de Chartres', in *Dictionnaire de spiritualité*, V, cols 1605–11 (cols 1607–10); Jacques Pintard, 'Saint Fulbert à l'origine du culte chartrain de la Nativité de Notre-Dame', in *De cultu mariano*, ed. by Lécuyer and others, III, 551–69; Fassler, 'Mary's Nativity, Fulbert of Chartres, and the *Stirps Jesse*'; and Luigi Gambero, *Mary in the Middle Ages: The Blessed Virgin Mary in the Thought of Medieval Latin Theologians*, trans. by Thomas Buffer (San Francisco, 2005), pp. 81–87.

[98] Fulbert's use of and remarks on the *Libellus de nativitate s. Mariae* are most fully examined by Rita Beyers in her edition of the *Libellus* in *Libri de nativitate Mariae*, Corpus Christianorum, Series Apocryphorum, 10 (Turnhout, 1997), pp. 140–46.

[99] See Mary C. Clayton, 'Theophilus, historia', in *Sources of Anglo-Saxon Literary Culture*, vol. I, ed. by Biggs and others, pp. 453–55, and on knowledge of the Theophilus legend in Anglo-Saxon England, Clayton, *Cult of the Virgin Mary*, pp. 71–72, 109, 114–18, and 240–41, who

audience since this sermon soon became a standard reading for the feast of Mary's Nativity in French and Italian homiliaries and was in fact quite arguably the most influential sermon for the Nativity of Mary written in the eleventh century.[100] Copies of this sermon appear in BL Add. 19835 as well as six other English manuscripts of the late eleventh or early twelfth century, including three of the augmented versions of Paul the Deacon's Homiliary mentioned earlier.[101] Three other sermons by Fulbert, his *Sermones* 1, 7, and 8, appear together in Durham, Cathedral Library, MS B. II. 11 (s. xi^ex, Durham), folios 133^r–134^v.[102]

The first thirty-five folios of London, British Library, Harley MS 3020 is a dossier of texts on the lives of early Wearmouth-Jarrow saints copied probably at Glastonbury in the late tenth or early eleventh century.[103] It includes the earliest extant copy of Bede's *Historia abbatum* (*BHL* 8968) and the anonymous *Vita ss. Ceolfridi, Eosterwini, Sigfridi et Hwætberhti* (*BHL* 1726), preceded at folios 1^r–6^r by Bede's *Homilia* I.13 for the feast of Benedict Biscop (*BHL* 1101), the seventh-century founder of the twin monasteries at Wearmouth and Jarrow and a figure for whom Bede had an especially strong personal devotion. This homily is a meditation on Christ's invitation to his disciples in Matthew 19 to renounce their

judges the *Penitentia Theophili* to be 'one of the most important texts inspiring devotion to Mary in late Anglo-Saxon England' (p. 118).

[100] Forty-three manuscripts containing this sermon are listed by Canal, 'Los sermones marianos', pp. 36–37 and 330. Another nine are identified by Barré, 'Pro Fulberto', pp. 325–27, who suggests the number could be significantly enlarged. Canal later identified ten more manuscripts in his 'Conclusión', pp. 141–42. A detailed reading of this sermon in light of the Marian liturgy developed at Chartres in the eleventh century (primarily by Fulbert himself) is provided by Fassler, 'Mary's Nativity, Fulbert of Chartres, and the *Stirps Jesse*', pp. 402–16.

[101] CUL Kk. 4. 13 (s. xi/xii, Norwich), fols 158^r–159^v; Cambridge, Corpus Christi College, MS 332 (s. xii^1 or xii^1/4, Rochester; see Gameson, *Manuscripts*, no. 81); Pembroke 24 (s. xi^2, N. France; provenance Bury St Edmunds by s. xi/xii), fols 140^r–145^v; Cambridge, Trinity College, MS B. 14. 30 (s. xi^ex, Exeter; Leicester), fols 48^r–56^v; Oxford, Bodleian Library, MS Digby 39 (s. xii^in, Abingdon), fols 40^r–44^r; Worcester F. 94, fols 77^v–78^v (incomplete) and 219^r–220^v. A later copy appears in Hereford, Cathedral Library, MS P. VIII. 7 (s. xii^2, Hereford), fols 108^v–110^v, in yet another modified Paul the Deacon Homiliary. Of these, only Pembroke 24 and Worcester F. 94 are cited in the lists of manuscripts by Canal and Barré.

[102] On Durham B. II. 11, see Rud, *Codicum manuscriptorum catalogus*, pp. 106–09; Schenkl, *Bibliotheca*, no. 4395; Mynors, *Durham Cathedral Manuscripts*, p. 38. Viard, 'Fulbert', col. 1606, doubts the authenticity of *Sermo* 7.

[103] On Harley 3020, see *Catalogue of the Harleian Manuscripts*, II, 725–26; James P. Carley, 'More Pre-Conquest Manuscripts from Glastonbury Abbey', *ASE*, 23 (1994), 265–81; Whatley, 'Acta Sanctorum', p. 108; Gneuss, *Handlist*, no. 433; Hartzell, *Catalogue*, p. 304 (no. 162).

families and earthly possessions and come follow him, a choice Bede finds exemplified in Benedict Biscop, who gave up secular pursuits and dedicated himself to a life of monastic discipline and learning and who accordingly received the hundredfold reward Christ promised to his followers, especially those who uphold the virtue of virginity. The great historical irony of the transmission history of Bede's gospel homilies is that as a collection they remained virtually unknown in England prior to the twelfth century, while perfectly good copies were made at St Gallen, Cluny, and other continental centres during the Anglo-Saxon period based on Insular exemplars that have since vanished.[104] The primary reason why any of Bede's gospel homilies were known in Anglo-Saxon England is not because copies of the entire collection were readily available but because thirty-seven of the fifty homilies were incorporated into Paul the Deacon's Homiliary and were thus presumably read during the monastic Night Office at some English centres.[105] *Homilia* I.13 on Benedict Biscop is not among these (no doubt because Paul the Deacon, writing for Frankish monks and ecclesiasts, had little use for a homily celebrating what his audience would have regarded as an obscure Northumbrian saint), and the copy of this homily in Harley 3020 happens to be the only complete copy in an Anglo-Saxon manuscript. The only other pre-Conquest witness to Bede's homily on Benedict Biscop is an incomplete copy in the closely contemporary manuscript Lincoln, Cathedral Library, MS 182 (s. x/xi, Abingdon),[106] where the homily (at fols 39^r–40^v) ends at a point in the text corresponding to line 99 in Hurst's edition (CCSL, 122, pp. 88–91). Lincoln 182 is the only pre-Conquest English manuscript containing all of Bede's gospel homilies, but as this particular homily shows, it is not the best witness to the collection, and one has to turn to some of the continental manuscripts to find copies closer to Bede's original. After Harley 3020 and Lincoln 182, the next copy of Bede's homily on Benedict Biscop in an English

[104] See the brief *conspectus codicum* compiled by D. Hurst in Bede, *Opera homiletica. Opera rhythmica*, ed. by Hurst and J. Fraipont, CCSL, 122 (Turnhout, 1955), pp. xvii–xxi.

[105] According to the reconstruction of the original contents of Paul the Deacon's Homiliary by Grégoire, *Homéliaires liturgiques médiévaux*, pp. 423–78, the homilies included are Bede, *Hom.* I.3–4, 7–12, 14–16, 18–21, and 24; II.2–9, 11–14, 16–20, and 22–25. The readings in Paul the Deacon's Homiliary taken from works by Bede are surveyed by Smetana, 'Paul the Deacon's Patristic Anthology', pp. 79–80. See also Joyce Hill, 'Carolingian Perspectives on the Authority of Bede', in *Innovation and Tradition in the Writings of the Venerable Bede*, ed. by Scott DeGregorio, Medieval European Studies, 7 (Morgantown, 2006), pp. 227–49 (pp. 231–33)

[106] On Lincoln 182, see Schenkl, *Bibliotheca*, no. 4027; R. M. Thomson, *Catalogue of the Manuscripts of Lincoln Cathedral Chapter Library* (Cambridge, 1989), pp. 146–47; Gneuss, *Handlist*, no. 274.

manuscript appears in the first volume of the great three-volume Worcester homiliary, Worcester F. 92, folios 154ᵛ–155ᵛ, which is likewise an incomplete copy, in this case ending at a point corresponding to Hurst's line 93, thus stopping short of naming Benedict Biscop, who is first introduced in line 98. The copy in Worcester F. 92, in other words, seems to have been edited to excise all hagiographic content and render a purely exegetical homily on Matthew 19. 27–29.

London, British Library, Harley MS 3908 is a collection of materials devoted entirely to St Mildrith of Thanet.[107] Like CCCC 312, Harley 3908 is a hagiographic *libellus* produced at St Augustine's Abbey under the direction of Goscelin (if not actually written by Goscelin himself, which is a distinct possibility). The contents are Goscelin's *Vita Deo dilectae virginis Mildrethae* (*BHL* 5960), a set of Office lections and a Mass for Mildreth's feast, a set of antiphons and responses entitled *Historia de s. Mildrethae* accompanied by musical notation, the *Translatio s. Mildrithae* (*BHL* 5961), and a homily. This homily (at fols 40ʳ–41ᵛ) is an abbreviated copy of Gregory the Great's twelfth gospel homily (CCSL, 141, pp. 80–83, lines 1–66) and is the only text in the manuscript not by Goscelin and not composed originally in honour of St Mildreth. It immediately follows a set of eight Office lections composed by Goscelin, and the homily itself is divided for lections 9–12. Remember that Ælfric's instructions for selecting readings for a saint's feast in the Night Office include the provision that if no sermon on the saint is available to be read for the third set of readings, which typically comprise lections 9 through 12, then one should take that set of readings from a gospel homily. Harley 3908 offers a perfect illustration of that practice.

London, British Library, Royal MS 8. B. XIV is a dossier of materials pertaining to the seventh-century Breton hermit St Judoc, consisting of an incomplete copy of Isembard of Fleury's *Vita, inventio, et miracula s. Iudoci* (*BHL* 4505–10), now lacking the first five chapters, plus Mass-sets for the Invention and Translation of St Judoc, two hymns, a prayer, a metrical *Vita s. Iudoci*, and three sermons.[108] The

---

[107] On Harley 3908, see *Catalogue of the Harleian Manuscripts*, III, 95; D. W. Rollason, 'Goscelin of Canterbury's Account of the Translation and Miracles of St. Mildrith (*BHL* 5961/4): An Edition with Notes', *Mediaeval Studies*, 48 (1986), 139–210 (pp. 149–50); Richard Sharpe, 'Words and Music by Goscelin of Canterbury', *Early Music*, 19 (1991), 94–97; Gameson, *Manuscripts*, no. 452; Gneuss, *Handlist*, no. 439.5; Hartzell, *Catalogue*, pp. 305–06 (no. 164).

[108] On Royal 8. B. XIV, see G. F. Warner and J. P. Gilson, *Catalogue of Western Manuscripts in the Old Royal and King's Collections*, 4 vols (London, 1921), I, 224–25; Whatley, 'Acta Sanctorum', pp. 275–76; Gneuss, *Handlist*, no. 474.5; Michael Lapidge, 'A Metrical *Vita S. Iudoci* from Tenth-Century Winchester', *Journal of Medieval Latin*, 10 (2000), 255–306 (pp. 264–65); Hartzell, *Catalogue*, p. 322 (no. 180).

first of these sermons (at fols 120ʳ–121ᵛ) is a sermon by Isembard (*BHL* 4509) that comes at the very end of his life of St Judoc and that regularly occurs as part of that text.[109] The second sermon (at fols 129ᵛ–131ᵛ) is a copy of Alcuin's sermon for the nativity of St Vedast (*BHL* 8509), which has here been revised as a sermon in honour of Judoc through the substitution of Judoc's name for Vedast's. And the third sermon (at fols 131ᵛ–133ᵛ) is Lupus of Ferrières's *Sermo in festivitate s. Iudoci confessoris* (*BHL* 4510d).[110] The part of the manuscript containing Isembard's *Vita, inventio, et miracula s. Iudoci*, as well as the Mass-sets, the hymns, and the prayer, was written on the Continent in the early eleventh century, very likely at Saint-Josse-sur-Mer in Brittany, the home base of Judoc's cult. But the rest of the manuscript, containing the metrical life of Judoc and the final two sermons, is written in Anglo-Caroline script of the later eleventh century, an indication that the manuscript was completed in England in the late eleventh century, when these last texts were added to the earlier continental core. Michael Lapidge has argued that the poem on St Judoc was composed in the late tenth century at Winchester, where one of Judoc's relics was taken in the early tenth century and where an active Judoc cult developed during the course of the tenth century.[111] The sermons by Alcuin and Lupus of Ferrières are thus Winchester supplements to this Judoc *libellus*, which provides our best evidence for the continued vitality of a Judoc cult in England through the eleventh century.

The middle part of London, British Library, Royal MS 13. A. X, comprising folios 63–103, is an originally distinct group of five quires constituting a *libellus* devoted to the sixth-century Welsh-born Breton saint Machutus or Malo, written in the late tenth century.[112] It contains Bili's *Vita s. Machuti* (*BHL* 5116a), a hymn

---

[109] Isembard's sermon is unpublished. Twelve manuscripts containing Isembard's *Vita, inventio, et miracula s. Iudoci* (and so presumably the *sermo* as well) are identified by Baudouin de Gaiffier, 'Isembard de Fleury-sur-Loire, auteur de la *Vita S. Iudoci* (*BHL* 4505–10)', *Jahrbuch der Gesellschaft für niedersächsische Kirchengeschichte*, 77 (1979), 9–12 (p. 10).

[110] Edited by Wilhelm Levison, 'Eine Predigt des Lupus von Ferrières', in *Kultur- und Universalgeschichte: Walter Goetz zu seinem 60. Geburtstage dargebracht von Fachgenossen, Freunden und Schülern* (Leipzig, 1927), pp. 3–14, repr. in Levison, *Aus Rheinischer und Fränkischer Frühzeit: Ausgewählte Aufsätze* (Düsseldorf, 1948), pp. 557–66, relying on Royal 8. B. XIV, which apparently preserves the only surviving copy.

[111] Michael Lapidge, 'Tenth-Century Anglo-Latin Verse Hagiography', *Mittellateinisches Jahrbuch*, 24–25 (1989–90), 249–60 (pp. 255–56); Lapidge, 'Metrical *Vita S. Iudoci*'.

[112] On Royal 13. A. X, see Warner and Gilson, *Catalogue of Western Manuscripts*, II, 79–80; Gneuss, *Handlist*, no. 482. Dumville, *Liturgy and the Ecclesiastical History*, p. 110, claims the manuscript was 'probably written at Winchester', which would make sense given the Winchester focus of the Anglo-Saxon cult of St Machutus, summarized by Whatley, 'Acta Sanctorum', pp. 307–10.

to St Machutus, and a sermon for the feast of St Machutus at folios 98ʳ–103ᵛ. The sermon, known only from this manuscript, is an expanded version of Alcuin's sermon for St Vedast (*BHL* 8509) which has been modified for the 15 November feast of St Machutus.[113]

New York, Pierpont Morgan Library, MS 926 is a composite manuscript written in several stages at St Albans over the course of the late eleventh and early twelfth centuries.[114] Its contents consist of several hagiographic and liturgical texts for use in Office celebrations of various saints' feasts, including Anastasius's translation of Leontius's *Vita s. Iohannis Eleemosinarii* (*BHL* 4388), three hymns to St Alban, a hymn to St Dunstan, Ethelhard's *Vita s. Dunstani* (*BHL* 2343), a *Vita s. Alexii* (*BHL* 286), a set of versicles, antiphons, and responses for the feast of St Birinus, and Odo of Cluny's sermon on St Benedict at folios 76ᵛ–77ᵛ (another copy of which appears in St John's 164, mentioned above).

Another composite manuscript that has been confected from several originally separate booklets written in the late eleventh and early twelfth centuries, this time at Abingdon, is Oxford, Bodleian Library, MS Digby 39.[115] This is a cluster of primarily hagiographic texts including the *Passio s. Theclae* (*BHL* 8020n), *Miracula s. Eadmundi* (*BHL* 2395), *Translatio beati Iacobi apostoli* (*BHL* 4067), *Vita s. Birini* (*BHL* 1361), Osbern of Canterbury's *Vita et translatio s. Elphegi* (*BHL* 2518–19), and three sermons for saints. The sermons are Fulbert of Chartres's *Sermo* 4 for the Nativity of Mary at folios 40ʳ–44ʳ (the Theophilus sermon mentioned earlier under BL Add. 19835) and two sermons for the feast of St Birinus: the first (at fols 50ʳ–52ʳ) excerpted from Bede's *Historia ecclesiastica* III.7, and the second (at fols

---

[113] The sermon, rubricated 'Homelia in natale sancti Machutis Christi confessoris atque pontificis', is edited by Robert Brown and David Yerkes, 'A Sermon on the Birthday of St. Machutus', *Analecta Bollandiana*, 99 (1981), 160–64. The interpolated passages not deriving from Alcuin are identified by François Dolbeau, 'Les sources d'un sermon en l'honneur de saint Malo', *Analecta Bollandiana*, 101 (1983), 417–19, who detects borrowings from two other sermons: Caesarius of Arles, *Sermo* 223, and pseudo-Augustine, *Sermo* 209.

[114] On Pierpont Morgan 926, see K. D. Hartzell, 'A St. Albans Miscellany in New York', *Mittellateinisches Jahrbuch*, 10 (1975), 20–61; R. M. Thomson, *Manuscripts from St Albans Abbey 1066–1235*, 2 vols (Woodbridge, 1982), I, 115–16; Gameson, *Manuscripts*, nos 608–12; Gneuss, *Handlist*, no. 865; Hartzell, *Catalogue*, pp. 351–54 (no. 207).

[115] On Digby 39, see W. D. Macray, *Catalogi codicum manuscriptorum bibliothecae Bodleiana pars nona* (Oxford, 1883), cols 35–36; Hardy, *Descriptive Catalogue*, I.1, 238, and I.2, 534–35; Madan, Craster, and Denholm-Young, *Summary Catalogue*, II.1 (no. 1640); David Townsend, 'An Eleventh-Century Life of Birinus of Wessex', *Analecta Bollandiana*, 107 (1989), 129–59 (p. 132); *Three Eleventh-Century Anglo-Latin Saints' Lives*, ed. by Love, pp. xlix–lxxxviii; Gameson, *Manuscripts*, nos 708–11; Gneuss, *Handlist*, no. 609.

52^r–56^r) a variation on Alcuin's sermon for St Vedast (*BHL* 8509). These two sermons for Birinus are the same two sermons for Birinus found in Durham A. III. 29, folios 332^v–335^r. The second of these, a thinly disguised revision of Alcuin's sermon for St Vedast with Birinus's name inserted in place of Vedast's, is one we have already seen several times before and which we are now in a position to recognize as one of the best represented Latin sermons for a saint in English manuscripts through the early twelfth century, with two unrevised copies as originally intended for Vedast in CCCC 9 and Salisbury 222 (the Worcester and Salisbury recensions of the 'Cotton-Corpus Legendary') and with adaptations for other saints in Durham A. III. 29 (for Birinus), Royal 8. B. XIV (for Judoc), Royal 13. A. X (for Machutus), and Digby 39 (for Birinus).[116] These multiple revisions of Alcuin's sermon for the purpose of venerating other saints who lacked their own Office literature echo a phenomenon that is even more prevalent in continental hagiography since this very same sermon by Alcuin, originally conceived as a tribute to Vedast, is elsewhere refashioned as a sermon in honour of Saints Arnulf, Bertin, Corbinianus, Emmeram, Frodobert, Rupert of Worms, and Sabinus.[117] In both English and continental hagiographic traditions, in other words, Alcuin's sermon for St Vedast functioned as what is sometimes referred to as a model sermon, a generic template that can be used as the basis for a variety of novel compositions honouring any number of saints (and a type of sermon especially favoured by lazy preachers).[118]

Conclusions

Nearly all of the manuscripts mentioned here post-date Ælfric, and most are so far removed from his time and place that I doubt they offer much help in identifying

---

[116] The copy of this sermon in Digby 39, as revised for Birinus, is edited by Love, *Three Eleventh-Century Anglo-Latin Saints' Lives*, pp. 119–22.

[117] See François Dolbeau, 'Le légendier de l'abbaye cistercienne de Clairmarais', *Analecta Bollandiana*, 91 (1973), 273–86 (p. 276); and Dolbeau, 'À propos d'un sermon sur s. Possesseur, évêque de Verdun', *Analecta Bollandiana*, 98 (1980), 386. Similarly, a ninth-century sermon for the feast of St Marsus of Auxerre that has been recrafted as a sermon for St Felix (and divided for eight lections) is discussed by Van Egmond, 'Audience of Early Medieval Hagiographical Texts', pp. 64–65.

[118] For discussion of a model sermon collection by the fifteenth-century Franciscan preacher Johannes von Werden, see John W. Dahmus, '*Dormi secure*: The Lazy Preacher's Model of Holiness for his Flock', in *Models of Holiness in Medieval Sermons*, ed. by Kienzle and others, pp. 301–16.

the saints' feasts which Ælfric would have observed at Eynsham in the first or second decade of the eleventh century. On this point for the time being the most valuable resource will have to remain Lapidge's essay on Ælfric's *sanctorale*.[119] On the main question raised at the beginning of this essay, however, concerning the texts Ælfric has in mind when he refers to sermons appropriate for reading in the Night Office on a saint's feast, this inventory offers some guidance on the kinds of texts that were available for this purpose in England up through the early Norman period. We know that Ælfric had access to a version of Paul the Deacon's Homiliary,[120] as well as a large legendary that in some respects resembled the 'Cotton-Corpus Legendary',[121] and both of these collections would have furnished him with sermons for saints' feasts. I would not discount the possibility, however, that the Eynsham monks may also have had access to one or more small individual *libelli* for saints such as those noted above for Augustine of Canterbury, Benedict, Judoc, Machutus, Martin, Mildreth, and the early Wearmouth-Jarrow saints. So many of these manuscripts survive from the eleventh century (and at least one from the mid-tenth century, the *libellus* for St Benedict in Cambridge, St John's College, MS 164) that they must have been current during Ælfric's lifetime, and these would have been easier to produce and to consult than a large homiliary or legendary.

Possibly the most illuminating feature of these manuscripts as they relate to the practice Ælfric describes is the presence of *lectio* numbers in the margins of both homiliaries and hagiographic manuscripts signalling the division of sermons for reading in the Night Office precisely according to the method outlined in Ælfric's *Letter*. The three examples touched on earlier from Harley 652 (lections for the feasts of Saints Mildreth, Hadrian, Laurence, Iustus, Honorius, and Theodore), Harley 3908 (lections for the feast of St Mildreth), and Lincoln 158 (lections for the nativity of John the Baptist) are representative of a common practice and could easily be multiplied. Ælfric is sometimes depicted as a sort of temperamental renegade who did not always see eye to eye with his contemporaries and forebears on questions of liturgy and ecclesiastical politics, but on this particular point, concerning the use of sermons for saints in the monastic Night Office, he was evidently right in step with the dominant European custom.

---

[119] Michael Lapidge, 'Ælfric's *Sanctorale*', in *Holy Men and Holy Women*, ed. by Szarmach, pp. 115–29.

[120] As was first demonstrated by Smetana, 'Aelfric and the Early Medieval Homiliary'.

[121] See Whatley, 'Cotton-Corpus Legendary'.

HOMILETIC CONTEXTS FOR ÆLFRIC'S HAGIOGRAPHY: THE LEGEND OF SAINTS CECILIA AND VALERIAN

Robert K. Upchurch

It might seem odd to find a chapter on Ælfric's *Legend of Cecilia* in a volume concerned with Old English sermons. Ælfric himself, however, routinely combined hagiographical material in the *Sermones catholici* (*Catholic Homilies*) and homiletic material in the *Lives of Saints*. Indeed, he spent much energy transforming saints' legends into preaching texts before deciding to let the distinct genres stand alone in the same collection.[1] Because the story of Cecilia and Valerian belongs among his later works and is an exemplary narrative intended for devotional reading, not a sermon to be preached from the pulpit, it requires some effort for a modern reader to discern how Ælfric intends to edify the faith of the English through an account of these Roman virgin spouses and martyrs. By reading the *Legend of Cecilia* (*LS* II.34) in light of sermons in the *Lives* and *Sermones catholici* we can best see the appeal the story had for him and the lessons he expected the audience to draw from it.[2]

This chapter opens by looking at those sermons of Ælfric that help us to interpret the hagiography of chaste marriage as it is represented in the *Legend of Cecilia*. Having mapped out a homiletic context for understanding the saints as

---

[1] Regarding the mix of saints' lives and sermons in the *Catholic Homilies* and Ælfric's changing approach to writing hagiography, see Malcolm Godden, 'Experiments in Genre: The Saints' Lives in Ælfric's *Catholic Homilies*', in *Holy Men and Holy Women: Old English Prose Saints' Lives and their Contexts*, ed. by Paul E. Szarmach (Albany, 1996), pp. 261–87. On the mix of genres in the *Lives of Saints*, see Joyce Hill, 'The Dissemination of Ælfric's *Lives of Saints*', in ibid., pp. 235–59 (pp. 236–42).

[2] *Ælfric's Lives of Saints*, ed. by Walter W. Skeat, 2 vols in 4 parts, EETS: OS, 76, 82, 94, 114 (London, 1881–1900; repr. as 2 vols, London, 1966).

personifications of different types of chastity (ranging from marital celibacy to spiritual purity), I examine ways in which the Old English version of the story of Cecilia and Valerian provides a hagiographical context for Ælfric's homiletics. In this section I focus on his personification of the saints as symbols of the ever-virginal but ever-bearing Church and call attention to editorial decisions he makes in order to illustrate in the hagiography points of doctrine and belief he expounds in the homilies. One of the most striking features of Ælfric's homiletics of chastity is the extent to which laymen and clerics are jointly involved in producing 'spiritual children' for the Church, and I conclude with the suggestion that he includes Cecilia and Valerian in the *Lives* to garner support of reformed monastic priests at the expense of unreformed, married ones. In reading the *Legend of Cecilia* against the homilies, I hope to demonstrate the usefulness of the sermons in opening up broader perspectives from which to analyse and understand his adaptations of individual saints' legends and even his aims for the collection of *Lives* as a whole.[3]

Homiletic Contexts for Ælfrician Hagiography

Among the five homilies, twenty-six legends, two Old Testament narrative pieces, and three tracts that made up the *Lives* as Ælfric appears to have issued it, his sermon *De memoria sanctorum* (*Memory of the Saints, LS* I.16) most clearly expresses his hope that his audience would regard Cecilia and Valerian as personifications of chastity, an essential virtue for Christians intent on meriting everlasting life with God.[4] He probably intended the sermon to introduce the *Lives*, and when read as

---

[3] My methods and concerns are indebted to the work (among others) of Mary Clayton, Malcolm Godden, Peter Jackson, Clare Lees, Hugh Magennis, and Gordon Whatley. Nor am I the first to use Ælfric's homilies to shed light on the *Legend of Cecilia*, as Bernadette Moloney and Liesl R. Smith do in their dissertations, respectively, 'A Critical Edition of Ælfric's Virgin-Martyr Stories from *The Lives of Saints*' (unpublished doctoral dissertation, University of Exeter, 1980), pp. 163–80, and 'Virginity and the Married-Virgin Saints in Ælfric's *Lives of Saints*: The Translation of an Ideal' (unpublished doctoral dissertation, University of Toronto, 2000), pp. 81–124 and 178–91. Because published examples using this approach are uncommon, however, I want to emphasize here the interconnectedness of ideas in the *Lives of Saints* and the *Sermones catholici*, and to focus attention on the latter's usefulness for delimiting reasons which motivate Ælfric's selections and treatments of legends in the *Lives*. All translations are my own.

[4] Unfortunately, Skeat concluded that, even though Ælfric wrote and included as an appendix to the *Lives* three tracts (*Interrogationes Sigeuulfi in Genesin, De falsis diis*, and *De duodecim abusiuis*), they 'do not form a necessary part of the Homilies on the Saints' Lives' and omits them from his edition (*Lives of Saints*, II, p. ix and n. 1). However, the tracts must be read in conjunction with

an introductory piece to the collection, it suggests that he wants Christians to understand the stories of saints struggling against their pagan antagonists as depictions of their own battles to fend off vice and cultivate virtue in their ongoing spiritual warfare against the devil.[5] The sermon does not begin by addressing spiritual warfare. Instead, Ælfric reviews chronologically different types of saints (Old Testament and New Testament figures, post-apostolic martyrs, and confessors), whom he pairs with their exemplary characteristics. Abraham, for example, is lauded for great faith and obedience, Christ for humility, and the martyrs for unswerving devotion. This survey of ancient holy men and women positions the entire collection against a backdrop of Christian history in which God has been at work in the lives of his saints and sets the stage for the discussion in the second half of the homily of the spiritual battles facing Anglo-Saxon believers.[6]

Ælfric's discussion of the spiritual warfare waged by all Christians on the front lines of the interior makes evident his hope that those reading or hearing the *Lives* read aloud would see their own psychomachia being played out in the hagiography in the rest of the collection.[7] Like the saints of old, English Christians can win

---

the legend and homilies printed by Skeat in order to gain the fullest sense of the didactic scope of the collection. All are cited fully in notes below. On the contents of the collection as it was originally issued, see Hill, 'Dissemination', p. 237.

[5] James R. Hurt's article, 'A Note on Ælfric's *Lives of Saints*, No. XVI', *ES*, 51 (1970), 231–34, makes these points in detail. Peter Clemoes first observed that Ælfric may have intended *De memoria sanctorum* as an introduction to the *Lives* ('The Chronology of Ælfric's Works', in *The Anglo-Saxons: Studies in Some Aspects of their History and Culture, Presented to Bruce Dickins*, ed. by P. A. M. Clemoes (London, 1959), pp. 212–47 (p. 222)): 'It places the passions of martyrs in an historical perspective and relates them to the reader's struggle against sin. It has been removed from first place in [London, British Library, Cotton MS Julius E. VII], though it is still not assigned to any specific occasion; but in [Cambridge, University Library, MS] Ii. I. 33 it retains the rub[r]ic appropriate to an initial position: *Incipit sermo de memoria sanctorum*.' The sermon, however, survives in the most complete manuscript of the *Lives* (London, British Library, Cotton MS Julius E. VII) as its fifteenth item. For a complete list of contents that compares the scribal numbering to the ordering of the texts in Skeat's edition where *De memoria sanctorum* is item 16, see Hill, 'Dissemination', p. 241.

[6] Hurt, 'Note on Ælfric's *Lives of Saints*', p. 231.

[7] Ælfric discusses the spiritual warfare that engages mind and body in at least three other places in the *Lives*: the *De oratione Moysi* (*LS* I.13, lines 41–43, p. 286), *De auguriis* (*LS* I.17, lines 1–46, pp. 364 and 366) and *Passio Machabeorum* (*LS* II.25, lines 688–704, p. 112). A good example from the *Sermones catholici* is his homily for the Nativity of St John the Baptist (*Ælfric's Catholic Homilies: The First Series, Text*, ed. by Peter Clemoes, EETS: SS, 17 (Oxford, 1997), lines 161–84, pp. 384–85). Raymon S. Farrar observes generally that, '[t]he saint, whether historical or not, is a quasi-allegorical figure, manifesting some aspect of the Christian life — and the

everlasting glory if they subdue devilish vice with godly virtue.[8] So that Christians may identify and stave off Satan's temptations, he enumerates at length the eight capital sins, 'þe us onwinnað swiðe' (*LS* I.16, line 267, p. 354; 'which attack us exceedingly') and the eight chief virtues, 'ða magan oferswiðan þas foresædan deoflu' (lines 312–13, p. 358; 'which are able to overcome the aforesaid devils'). Because the catalogues of vices and virtues follow the paring of saints with their exemplary traits, the lists encourage Christians to make connections between their internal spiritual warfare and the external events recounted not only in the first half of the sermon but in narratives from scripture and sacred texts elsewhere in the *Lives*. Each *miht* ('virtue') Christians are exhorted to embody in *De memoria sanctorum* represents a point of contact with saints who exhibit *gemetegung* ('moderation'), *clænnyss* ('chastity', 'purity'), *cystignyss* ('generosity'), *geðyld* or *þolmodnys* ('patience'), *gastlice blys* ('spiritual joy'), *anrædnyss godes weorces* ('the constancy of a good work'), *soðe lufu to gode* ('true love towards God'), and *eadmodnyss* ('humility').[9] Read thus, the stories of the saints become 'emblematic narratives' in which 'inner experience, either psychological or spiritual, is reflected by external events of the narrative', and Ælfric implies that being equipped for and winning spiritual warfare entails an ability to draw inspiration from the legends in the *Lives*.[10]

totality of hagiography may well provide a psychomachia of the ideal mental states (and their active consequences) of the practicing Christian — and hence reflecting, in miniature, Christ Himself': 'Structure and Function in Representative Old English Saints' Lives', *Neophilologus*, 57 (1973), 83–93 (p. 87).

[8] *LS* I.16, lines 219–24, p. 352.

[9] The section enumerating the eight chief virtues runs from lines 312 to 363 in *LS* I.16, pp. 358–62. For the purposes of this chapter, I have focussed only on the virtues personified by the saints, but as Hurt ('Note on Ælfric's *Lives of Saints*', p. 234) points out, Ælfric is also warning his audience against the vices personified by the saints' adversaries. Almachius, Cecilia's antagonist, personifies pride, for example, and she roundly criticizes and even taunts him for his presumption (*LS* II.34, lines 313–19 and 324–31, p. 374). Other passages in the *Lives* that call attention to the sin of pride are *LS* I.1, lines 107–09 (p. 16), *LS* I.16, lines 306–11 (p. 358), and a passage from *De duodecim abusiuis huius seculi* (ed. by Richard Morris in *Old English Homilies and Homiletic Treatises [. . .] of the Twelfth and Thirteenth Centuries, First Series*, EETS: OS, 29 and 34 (London, 1867–68; repr. as one volume, 1998), pp. 107–19 (pp. 113, line 30 – 115, line 11)). Examples from the *Sermones catholici* are *CH* I.9, lines 157–63 (p. 254), *CH* I.10, lines 177–81 (p. 264), which follows a passage listing many of virtues in *De memoria sanctorum*, and *CH* II.40, lines 279–82 (*Ælfric's Catholic Homilies: The Second Series, Text*, ed. by Malcolm Godden, EETS: SS, 5 (London, 1979) p. 344), where pride is listed with other capital sins.

[10] Thomas D. Hill, 'Imago Dei: Genre, Symbolism, and Anglo-Saxon Hagiography', in *Holy Men and Holy Women: Old English Prose Saints' Lives and their Contexts*, ed. by Paul E. Szarmach (Albany, 1996), pp. 35–50 (p. 45).

If the list above helps to delimit the didactic ambit of the legends in the *Lives*, then *clænnyss*, the second item, is the virtue that the virgin spouses Cecilia and Valerian most clearly personify. Ælfric's definition of *castitas* in *De memoria sanctorum* hints at how a lay audience might regard the chaste marriage featured in the legend as a reflection, albeit an imperfect one, of their own Christian wedlock. He defines chastity this way in the sermon:

> Seo oðer miht is *castitas*, þæt is clænnyss on ænglisch, þæt is þæt se læweda hine healde butan forligre on rihtum synscipe mid gesceadwisnysse and se gehadoda godes ðeowa healde his clænnysse: þonne bið oferswyðed swa eac seo galnyss. (*LS* I.16, lines 321–25, p. 358)

> [The second virtue *castitas*, 'chastity' in English, is that the layman keep himself free from adultery in proper marriage with rationality and that the servant of God in holy orders preserve his chastity: then sexual desire will be overcome just so.]

Chastity for the layman consists of fidelity to one's spouse and of rational propriety regarding sexual intercourse. The phrase *mid gesceadwisnysse* ('with rationality'), which qualifies 'proper marriage', alludes to the observance of rules governing when a couple was and was not permitted to have sex, and through such self-control the virtue of *clænnyss* overcomes the vice of *ungemetegod galnyss* (*LS* I.16, line 276, p. 356; 'immoderate sexual desire').

Seen in the light of sermons in the *Sermones catholici* that review such regulations in detail, the brief allusion in *De memoria sanctorum* to the need for control over one's sexual appetites attests to Ælfric's confidence that the phrase 'with rationality' will bring to the minds of his audience any number of ways they should moderate their sexual activity.[11] The following definition of chastity explains clearly that to conduct a marriage with reason — here *alyfedlice* ('in the permitted manner') — is to limit sex to those times when procreative intercourse is permissible: '[þ]æt is þæs læwedan mannes clænnys. þæt he his æwe healde. and alyfedlice for folces eacan bearn gestreone' (*CH* II.6, lines 137–38, p. 57; '[t]he chastity of a layman is that he keep his marriage law and beget children in the permitted manner for the increase of people'). Because sex is intended only for procreation, Ælfric prohibits it when a woman is menstruating, pregnant, or post-menopausal.[12] Not

---

[11] In this section, I summarize many points I treat in greater detail in my 'For Pastoral Care and Political Gain: Ælfric of Eynsham's Preaching on Marital Celibacy', *Traditio*, 59 (2004), 39–78 (esp. pp. 39–60).

[12] See *CH* II.6, lines 115–26 (p. 56) and *SH* II.19, lines 111–16, in *Homilies of Ælfric: A Supplementary Collection*, ed. by John Pope, EETS: OS, 259–60 (London, 1967–68), p. 628. Post-menopausal abstinence is a regulation unique to Ælfric; the others are common to penitential literature.

only was intercourse regulated according to natural cycles, but it was also forbidden during whole seasons of the Church year, Lent for example, in addition to many important feast days and festivals.[13] 'Ne gesceop se ælmihtiga god. men for galnysse' (*CH* II.19, line 172, p.185; 'The almighty God did not create men for the sake of sexual desire'), Ælfric admonishes in another sermon and unflatteringly compares rational humans who cannot control their cravings to irrational but *clænan* ('pure', line 177, p. 185) animals that have intercourse only at set times.[14] Since obedience to the *regol* ('rule') governing marital chastity guarantees husbands and wives will be 'fulfremed on læwedum hade' (*SH* II.19, line 115, p. 628; 'perfected in the layman's state'), their *clænnyss* for him symbolizes the sincerity and integrity of their faith.

Because celibacy figures so prominently in Ælfric's idealization of Christian marriage, there can be little wonder why he chooses for the *Lives* four legends about virgin spouses, three of which feature husbands and wives as saints.[15] Certainly Cecilia, whose desire 'on clænnysse criste [. . .] þeowian' (*LS* II.34, line 19, p. 356; 'to serve [. . .] Christ in chastity') is honoured by God, and Valerian, to whom God grants any wish because he 'lufa[ð] clænnysse' (line 85, p. 360; 'loves chastity'), are fitting personifications of the virtue that God, according to Ælfric, loves 'especially' above all others.[16] Chastity, however, represents more than abstinence from sexual intercourse for him: the saints' extraordinary physical

---

[13] Ælfric specifically advises laymen to abstain 'on halgum timan, and on ðam Leneten-fæstene, and on ælcum ymbren-fæstene' ('at holy times, and at Lent, and at each Ember fast': *The Homilies of the Anglo-Saxon Church: The First Part, Containing the Sermones catholici or Homilies of Ælfric*, ed. and trans. by Benjamin Thorpe, 2 vols (London, 1844–46), II, 608). Ember fasts were observed on the Wednesday, Friday, and Saturday of the weeks following the third Sunday of Advent, Pentecost Sunday, the Exaltation of the Cross (14 September), and the first Sunday in Lent.

[14] See also Ælfric's comments at *CH* I.1, lines 150–54 (p. 184) and *CH* I.6, lines 79–97 (pp. 226–27).

[15] In addition to Cecilia and Valerian, Ælfric includes Julian and Basilissa (*LS* I.4) and Chrysanthus and Daria (*LS* II.35). The fourth virgin spouse is Æthelthryth, who practices chaste marriage in spite of her second husband's strenuous objections. For an analysis that explains how Ælfric reshapes her legend to emphasize mutually pursued marital celibacy, see Peter Jackson, 'Ælfric and the Purpose of Christian Marriage: A Reconsideration of the *Life of Æthelthryth*, lines 120–30', *ASE*, 29 (2000), 235–60. I have recently edited and translated Ælfric's lives of Julian and Basilissa, Cecilia and Valerian, and Chrysanthus and Daria, as well as their closest Latin source texts in *Ælfric's Lives of the Virgin Spouses* (Exeter, 2007).

[16] From a list of eight virtues, Ælfric singles out chastity as the one prized *huru* ('especially') by God in *CH* II.1, lines 277–85, at line 284 (p. 10).

commitment also symbolizes their spiritual purity — a faith undefiled by unbelief or inconstancy. In this way Cecilia and Valerian hold an especial appeal for him as emblems of the earthly Church, a fellowship of believers made up of men and women, married and unmarried, religious and lay, who collectively embody the virginity and fruitfulness of Christ's bride.

In Ælfric's homiletic treatments of divine spiritual marriage, he emphasizes that married folk too are brides of Christ and thus should exhibit virginity by means of their steadfast belief and fecundity by giving birth to spiritual children.[17] Like the Church who refuses to commit spiritual adultery by fornicating with other gods, believers worship Christ alone and are not allured by superstition or sorcery. These virgins, in short, remain *anræd* ('constant') in their belief.[18] Such Christians outwardly manifest this fundamental inward steadfastness in two aspects embodied by the Church, her *gastlic þeaw* ('spiritual behaviour') and *gastlic bearteam* ('spiritual procreation of children').[19] For couples, 'spiritual behaviour' means living *rihtlice* (Assmann III, line 135, p. 29; 'properly') and would include obedience to the rules and regulations mentioned above that affected their physical *clænnyss*. Spiritual fruitfulness, on the other hand, refers to the Church's inexhaustible capacity for giving birth to new members who are baptized into her faith and belief.

---

[17] His treatment of the allegory is indebted to Old Testament accounts of Israel's unfaithfulness toward God and to patristic interpretation: concerning the biblical sources, see, for example, Exodus 31. 6 and 34. 15–16, Deuteronomy 31. 16, Judges 2. 17, and Hosea 2. 2–5; for the patristic allegory Ælfric relies on Bede who most likely relied on Augustine. Malcolm Godden points to Bede's *In Lucae evangelium expositio* (ed. by D. Hurst, CCSL, 120 (Turhout, 1960) II.2271–74): *Ælfric's Catholic Homilies: Introduction, Commentary, and Glossary*, ed. by Malcolm Godden, EETS: SS, 18 (Oxford, 2000), p. 277; for a representative passage of Augustine, see his *De sancta virginitate*, ed. and trans. by Patrick Walsh (Oxford, 2001), pp. 66–147, at pp. 70–73 (para. 6). In this and the next paragraph, I summarize from a lengthy discussion in Upchurch, 'For Pastoral Care and Political Gain', pp. 60–71.

[18] This is a connection that Ælfric emphasizes throughout the *Lives* by characterizing virgin saints such as Agnes, Agatha, Cecilia, and Chrysanthus and Daria as being *anræd* ('constant, resolute'). See, respectively, *LS* I.7 (Agnes), lines 88 (p. 174), 122 (p. 176), and 274 (p. 186); *LS* I.8 (Agatha), line 65 (p. 198); *LS* II.34 (Cecilia), lines 156 (p. 364) and 325 (p. 374); and *LS* II.35 (Chrysanthus and Daria), line 122 (p. 384). I am grateful to Gordon Whatley for drawing my attention to Ælfric's preference for translating *constans* with *anræd* and to these examples. Ælfric employs the language of other passages concerning the spiritual chastity of the church in his definition of *fortitudo*, which he glosses in Old English as *strængð oððe anrednys* (*LS* I.1, lines 164–67, at line 165 (p. 20); 'strength or steadfastness').

[19] *Angelsächsische Homilien und Heiligenleben*, ed. by Bruno Assmann, BaP, 3 (Kassel, 1889; repr. Darmstadt, 1964), Homily 3, line 129, p. 29.

For devout lay believers this means teaching spiritual truths they have been able to grasp and exhorting others to good deeds by leading exemplary lives.

It is extraordinary that Ælfric credits the laity with any ability to teach, and this willingness explains why he reconfigures the saints' conversionary activity and teaching as spiritual childbearing, as will be discussed below. By teaching he does not mean scriptural exegesis, which remains the privilege of the clergy. Teaching for laymen rather consists of positively impacting others with their upright lives and even sharing spiritual truths and doctrines they have learned. In the following passage, he identifies the motivation (a yearning for eternal life), method (teaching by example), and manner (living temperately and cultivating virtues) of laymen who 'teach properly':

> [S]ume læwde men sind swa geworhte. þæt hí mid onbryrdnysse þæs upplican eðles syllað gode bysne oðrum geleaffullum. and symle tæcað riht þæs ðe hi magon tocnawan be ðam yttrum andgitum. þeah ðe hí ne cunnon ða incundan deopnysse godes lare asmeagan; And ðonne hí on heora flæsclicum lustum gemetegode beoð. and on woruldlicum gewilnungum ne beoð to grædige. and eac wið oðrum unðeawum þurh godes ege hí sylfe healdað. þonne styrað hí eac oðrum mannum ðurh heora lifes rihtwisnysse. and gestrynað gode sume oðerne mannan oððe má. (*CH* II.38, lines 55–66, p. 320)

> [Certain laymen are so made that they, with devotion to the heavenly homeland, give a good example to other believers and always teach properly that which they are able to recognize with the outer senses, although they are not able to interpret the inner depth of God's doctrine. And when they are moderate in their physical desires, and are not too greedy in worldly desires, and also guard themselves against other vices by means of the fear of God, then they also restrain other men by means of the righteousness of their life and acquire for God some other person or more.]

The final clause is particularly striking for the fact that Ælfric elsewhere uses the verb *gestrynan* ('to acquire' or 'to beget') to describe the work of priests actively engaged in spiritual procreation.[20] Not incidentally, this passage occurs in the context of an explication of the Parable of the Talents (Matthew 25. 14–30), at the end of which the lord who is angry with the servant who buried his money gives it to the faithful servant who has doubled his. In Ælfric's interpretation, the lazy servant/bad cleric loses his original *pund* ('pound') of *incund angit* ('inner understanding', *CH* II.38, line 147, p. 323) when the lord gives it to the faithful servant/devout layman, who in addition to his sensory comprehension of the truths of

---

[20] See, for example, *CH* II.6, lines 140–42 and 150–53 (p. 57) and *SH* II.18, lines 154–57 and 166–68 (p. 597).

God's world possesses deeper insight to His doctrines.[21] I will return in the final section to discuss Ælfric's blurring of the lines between devout laymen and good clerics, but for the present, the passage is most significant for the way in which it models the laity's involvement in spiritual procreation.[22]

Ælfric does not specify when laymen may instruct other people or what Christian tenets are suitable for them to teach, but his comments regarding baptism in a sermon for Epiphany suggest both a context for and the content of such teaching, and invoke a moment when priest and laymen are jointly engaged in the Church's work of bringing forth new believers. Adult baptism would have been rare in late Anglo-Saxon England, so most common were christenings where children 'fullodon ðurh geleafan þæs fæder. and ðære meder. and se godfæder wæs þæs cildes forspreca. and borh wið god þæt hit heolde þone cristendom be godes tæcunge' (*CH* II.3, lines 252–55, p. 26; 'were baptized on account of the faith of the father and mother, and the godfather was the child's advocate and pledge to God that he will preserve his Christianity according to God's teaching').[23] One context for lay teaching, then, is the home or foster home wherein parents and godparents would instruct children, adolescents, and young adults in the rudiments of Christian doctrine and practice while living out an upright life amidst various relatives, friends, or servants, depending on one's social status. The doctrinal content of those discussions becomes clearer when Ælfric reviews the baptismal scrutiny, in which a godfather renounces the devil and affirms the verity of the Trinity and a belief in the resurrection of the body. These last two doctrines are also mentioned in the creed, which along with the Lord's Prayer, all Christians were to know, and these texts too contain basic tenets laymen could master and share. Having covered the layman's obligation to teach, Ælfric closes the sermon with a reminder that should

---

[21] Ælfric's interpretation of the parable differs markedly from his source, a homily on the same text by Pope Gregory (Godden, *Introduction, Commentary, and Glossary*, pp. 647–48).

[22] In *CH* II.5, lines 115–16 (p. 45), Ælfric, following Pope Gregory, identifies labourers in God's vineyard as those who, among other virtues, 'cariað mid wacelum mode hú hí oðra manna sawla gode gestrynan. and mid him to ðam écan life gelædan' ('with a vigilant mind care about how they may acquire other men's souls for God and may lead them with them to everlasting life').

[23] In this passage Ælfric is explaining the origin of a practice he has learned about from *ealdum gesetnyssum* (line 247, p. 26; 'old compositions'), and so he continues, 'nu stent ðeos gesetnys on godes gelaðunge. þæt man ða unsprecendan cild fullige. and hi beoð gehealdene þurh oðra manna geleafan' (lines 257–59, p. 26; 'now this ordinance remains in God's church so that one may baptize children who are unable to speak and so that they will be preserved by means of the faith of other men').

laymen wish to merit everlasting life, then '[i]s nu for ði micel neod gehwám þæt hé leornige æt his làreowe hú hé his cristendom healdan sceole. mid þam soðan geleafan' (*CH* II.3, lines 287–88, p. 27; 'it is now therefore very necessary for everyone to learn from his teacher how he ought to preserve his Christianity with true faith'). In view of this transfer of belief from priest to layman, which involves both in similar activities, and Ælfric's promotion of the clerical virtue of celibacy among the laity, he clearly was willing and he believed his audience was prepared to see Cecilia and Valerian as reflections of a Church whose members dutifully carry out their work as virgin brides of Christ and mothers to other believers.[24]

Hagiographic Contexts for Ælfrician Homiletics

When Ælfric decides to include an Old English version of the *Passio Sanctae Ceciliae* in the *Lives of Saints*, he inherits a Latin legend whose core narrative lends itself to an allegorical interpretation of its virginal yet fruitful spouses as figures of the Church.[25] As Sherry Reames explains, the author of the *passio* models Cecilia and

---

[24] The point is bolstered elsewhere in the *Lives*; see, for instance, Agnes's description of herself as Christ's bride, which concludes with this rhetorically heightened passage: "'Þam anum ic healde minne truwan æfre, þam ic me befæste mid ealre estfulnysse. Þonne ic hine lufige, ic beo eallunga clæne; þonne Ic hine hreppe, ic beo unwemme; ðonne Ic hine underfó, ic beo mæden forð and þær bærn ne ateoriað on ðam brydlace. Þær is eacnung buton sare and singallic wæstmbærnyss'" (*LS* I.7, lines 56–62, p. 172; "'To Him alone I always keep my faith, to Him I entrust myself with all devotion. When I love Him, I am entirely pure; when I touch Him, I am undefiled; when I receive Him, I am still a virgin, and the marriage does not lack children. There is conception without sorrow and continual fruitfulness'"). This legend too features a series of conversions that, when read symbolically, focus attention on the growth of the Church: see, for example, Agnes's role in the conversion of Constantia, Constantine's daughter, and of Gallicanus, her suitor. Alison Gulley also draws attention to the prominent role of conversion in Ælfric's *Legend of Cecilia*, though in service of a different argument: "'Seo fæmne þa lærde swa lange þone cniht oðþæt he ge-lyfde on þone lifigendan god'": The Christian Wife as Converter and Ælfric's Anglo-Saxon Audience', *Parergon*, 19 (2002), 39–51.

[25] Patrick Zettel has demonstrated that Hereford, Cathedral Library, MS P. VII. 6 is the closest among those manuscripts that he associates with the so-called Cotton-Corpus Legendary, a hypothetical, ninth-century collection of saints' lives preserved now in eleventh- and twelfth-century English manuscripts: 'Ælfric's Hagiographic Sources and the Latin Legendary Preserved in B. L. MS Cotton Nero E I + CCCC MS 9 and Other Manuscripts' (unpublished doctoral dissertation, Oxford University, 1979), pp. 257–58. My study of over one hundred manuscripts of the *passio* confirms Zettel's identification of the Hereford manuscript as a reliable guide to the sort of text from which Ælfric worked, though, as he observed, it is not an exact match (p. 314). The

Valerian's chaste marriage on that in an earlier work in order to present an 'ideal of perfection' that would evoke the figure of the Church:[26]

> Betrothal to Christ, renouncing all rival loves, bearing fruit in the conversion of others, and remaining faithful even in the face of death — this is what Christian perfection means in the *Passio*, and it is necessarily exemplified not only in Cecilia herself but also in the whole chain of saints who proceed from her. Cecilia wins over Valerian, her bridegroom; together they convert his brother Tiburce; Tiburce and Valerian go on to convert Maximus [their torturer], who in turn converts others — and so on and on, the *Passio* suggests, until the end of time.[27]

Since Ælfric utilizes the allegory of spiritual marriage in his sermons to personify Christians as virgins who preserve their chastity by means of steadfast belief and celibate bodies, and who figuratively bear offspring by teaching the faith, he undoubtedly recognized the legend's potential to model the Church's 'spiritual behaviour' and 'spiritual procreation of children' in all its complexity. The majority of Ælfric's editorial changes concentrate more attention on spiritual procreation than behaviour, and they signal that his homiletic interest in metaphorical motherhood extends to the hagiography.[28] Accordingly, the following discussion focuses

---

differences in the Hereford text of Cecilia and that of Cambridge, Corpus Christi College, MS 9, pp. 323–36 raise the possibility that Hereford P. 7. vi is not a 'later and expanded version of the Cotton-Corpus collection' as Zettel (following Levison) supposed but preserves textual traditions that bypassed Worcester where the earliest surviving copies of Cotton-Corpus were made (p. 39). On the relationships among the various 'recensions' of the legendary, see E. Gordon Whatley's entry for 'Cotton-Corpus Legendary' in *Sources of Anglo-Saxon Literary Culture*, vol. V: C, ed. by Thomas N. Hall (Kalamazoo, forthcoming). An edition and translation of the Hereford P. 7. vi text, as well as variants from CCCC9, are found in *Ælfric's Lives of the Virgin Spouses*, pp. 172–217.

[26] The author borrows the episode in which Maxima persuades Martinianus to adopt marital chastity from Victor of Vita's late fifth-century *History of the Vandal Persecution* (Hippolyte Delehaye, *Étude sur le légendier romain: Les saints de novembre et de décembre*, Subsidia Hagiographica, 23 (Brussels, 1936), pp. 78–79). The episode is found in *Victoris episcopi vitensis Historia persecutionis Africanae provinciae*, ed. by Michael Petschenig, Corpus Scriptorum Ecclesiasticorum Latinorum, 7 (Vienna, 1881), pp. 13–17; and, for a translation, see *Victor of Vita: History of the Vandal Persecution*, trans. by John Moorhead (Liverpool, 1992), p. 15 (Book I, §31–32).

[27] Sherry L. Reames, 'The Cecilia Legend as Chaucer Inherited It and Retold It: The Disappearance of an Augustinan Ideal', *Speculum*, 55 (1980), 38–57 (p. 42).

[28] In addition to the fact that generally Cecilia and Valerian's physical virginity, steadfast faith, and refusals to sacrifice to idols represent 'spiritual behaviour', there are particular moments Ælfric seems deliberately to evoke a personification of the Church. His report that Valerian *gebeah to gode* (*LS* II.34, line 53, p. 358; 'turned to God'), confesses 'Unus deus, unus fides, unum baptisma' (line 62, p. 358; 'one God, one faith, one baptism'), and agrees to undertake chaste marriage

on those changes that strengthen parallels between the conversionary activity of the saints and the fruitfulness of the Church. I begin by establishing that Ælfric understood the saints' teaching and exhortation as spiritual procreation. Then, taking as a cue the passage on teaching quoted above from the sermon for Epiphany, I focus on the motivation, method, and manner of the teacher-saints who model for the laity the process of producing spiritual progeny.

Ælfric's revision of the angel's response to Valerian's request that his brother Tiburtius be saved attests that he equates teaching and spiritual procreation, which in turn associates the saints' conversion of others with the fruitfulness of the Church. In the *passio* the angel uses a monetary metaphor to tell Valerian that Tiburtius will be saved: "'sicut te per famulam suam Ceciliam lucratus est Dominus ita per te quoque tuum lucrabitur fratrem, et cum eodem ad martyrii palmam attinges'" (Hereford P. 7. vi, fol. 74vb; "'just as the Lord redeemed you through His servant Cecilia, so in the same way he will He redeem your brother thorough you, and you will attain the palm of martyrdom together with him'"). Ælfric, however, prefers a metaphor of procreation to connect the notions of rebirth and belief, and he links being born again to teaching. Specifically, he substitutes for *lucror* ('to gain') the verbs *gestrynan* ('to beget') and *gelyfan* ('to believe') and adds a reference to Cecilia's instruction to create this new reply: "'þin broðor tiburtius bið *gestryned* þurh þe to þam ecan life swa swa þu *gelyfdest* on god þurh cecilian lare and git sceolan begen (þu and þin broðor) beon gemartyrode samod'" (*LS* II.34, lines 95–98, pp. 360 and 362; "'your brother Tiburtius will be born into everlasting life through you, just as you believed in God through Cecilia's instruction; and you both, you and your brother, will be martyred together'").[29]

---

recalls a description in the *Sermones catholici* of a Church, composed of husbands and wives, who maintains her 'þæs geleafan mægðhad' ('virginity of belief') and 'þe wurðað ænne soðne god. and nele forligerlice to leasum hæðengylde bugan' ('who honours one true God and does not wish adulterously to turn to false idolatry'; *CH* II.39, lines 79–81, p. 329).

[29] The construction of the phrase *bið gestryned* [. . .] *to þam ecan life* suggests that Ælfric intends it to mean 'will be born into everlasting life' rather than 'will be acquired for the everlasting life', although he is well aware of the link between spiritual procreation and spiritual profit. A parallel construction supporting this reading is that from his sermon for Christ's Nativity in the Second Series, where he writes that 'Ure ealda fæder adam us gestrynde to deaðe. and crist us gestrynð gastlice to ðan ecan life. gif we forbugað deofles lare. and beoð urum drihtne gehyrsume on his bebodum' (*CH* II.1, lines 117–20, p. 6; 'Our old father Adam begot us into death, and Christ begets us spiritually to the everlasting life if we shun the devil's teaching and are obedient to our Lord in his commandments'). Other examples are *CH* I.35, lines 40–46 (p. 477) and *CH* II.39, lines 87–90 (p. 330).

This rewriting has three effects. First, it projects the metaphor of generation back into the narrative and recasts Cecilia's conversion of Valerian on their wedding night as spiritual childbearing.[30] Second, it patterns the subsequent conversions in the legend as spiritual procreation. And third, it highlights the transfer of belief from one person to another by means of personal interaction as Cecilia and Valerian beget Tiburtius, Tiburtius and Valerian beget Maximus, and Maximus begets the pagans who hear his report of seeing the brothers' souls ascend to heaven; the cycle returns to Cecilia, who converts another four hundred pagans before she is locked in her bath. That she also continues to instruct her *mædena* (line 359, p. 376; 'virgins') after her bungled beheading and entrusts them to the Pope's care just before she dies suggests that there will be no end to Cecilia's offspring, no interruption to the growth of the Church.

Motivation

If the saints' teaching and converting symbolize spiritual procreation for Ælfric, then he exhibits a concomitant interest in sharpening the legend's focus on their motivations for doing so. As in the sermon for Epiphany, where laymen instruct others because of their own 'devotion to the heavenly homeland', the reality of an afterlife in which God metes out eternal reward or punishment animates the faith of the teacher-saints in the *Legend of Cecilia* and motivates them to share it. This broad vision of the Church at work in the world helps to explain why Ælfric suppresses the Latin text's lengthy debates over whether or not everlasting life is real and why he introduces verbal alterations that focus attention on the hope that sustains a Christian's commitment to spiritual purity, practice, and proselytizing.[31]

Ælfric introduces much earlier than the *passio* the idea that the *þa ecan life* ('the everlasting life') is the animating force of Christianity, and he makes more plain the eternal stakes of the protagonists' evangelical impulses. 'Another life' does not become a central topic for discussion in the Latin legend until Cecilia catechizes

---

[30] This association explains the significance of Ælfric's decision to report that Cecilia 'lærde swa lange þone cniht oð þæt he gelyfde on þone lifigendan god' (lines 49–50, p. 358; 'instructed the young man for a long time until he believed in the living God'). Valerian eventually goes to Pope Urban who 'his geleafan him tæht' (line 70, p. 360; 'taught him his faith'), but in the *passio*, only Urban is said to teach Valerian; see note 38 below.

[31] See for example the nearly 850-word debate between Tiburtius and Valerian, and Almachius at Hereford P. 7. vi, fols 77va–78ra, which Ælfric omits. It would also be uncharacteristic for him to preserve exchanges of this length.

Tiburtius, but Ælfric identifies Cecilia's love of eternity as the source of her fervent devotion to God in his second sentence. There he explains that Cecilia meditates on the scriptures and the teachings of God because '[þ]eos halige fæmne hæfde on hire breoste swa micele *lufe to þam ecan life*' (*LS* II.34, lines 5–6, p. 356, my emphasis; 'this holy virgin had in her breast so great *a love for the everlasting life*'). This love of heaven that fuels her asceticism also sparks her efforts to convert her new husband, who, after he becomes a Christian, requests only that his brother be permitted to have eternal life too. So it is that Ælfric's angel promises Valerian that Tiburtius will be born again *to þam ecan life* ('to the everlasting life') rather than simply 'redeemed' as in the *passio*.[32] Tiburtius apparently internalizes Cecilia's lesson that rewards and punishments will be meted out not in '"illa [. . .] uita que isti uite succedit"' (Hereford P. 7. vi, fol. 75va; '"that [. . .] life which follows this life"') but '"on þam ecan life þe æfter þysum cymð"' (*LS* II.34, line 151, p. 364' '"in the everlasting life which comes after this one"'), for he later tells Maximus that he and his brother die joyfully because they are going '"to beteran life [. . .] to þam ecan life"' (lines 231 and 233, p. 368; '"to a better life [. . .] to the everlasting life"'). By repeating 'the everlasting life', Ælfric brings into sharp focus the way in which the promise of eternity enables Christians to maintain a proper perspective on temporal existence and reminds the audience why the legend's teacher-saints continue spreading the faith even under duress.

Method

We noted earlier that laymen are to teach the spiritual truths they apprehend either by example or by explanation, and Cecilia provides Ælfric an exemplary teacher who instructs others by her way of life and by her elucidation of Christian doctrine. The *passio* is notable for the number of instances in which the saints instruct others, and Ruth Waterhouse observed thirty years ago that he uses more direct speech in the *Legend of Cecilia* than in any of the other lives in the collection.[33] If such speeches normally allow the saint to assume the role of preacher, then the voice of a saint/preacher also becomes that of a lay teacher, and the

---

[32] Quoted above on p. 276.

[33] Ruth Waterhouse, 'Ælfric's Use of Discourse in Some Saints' Lives', *ASE*, 5 (1976), 83–103 (p. 86). Bernadette Moloney, however, shows that Waterhouse's conclusions regarding Ælfric's assignment of direct and indirect speech to good and bad characters, respectively, in the *Legend of Cecilia* must be qualified: 'Another Look at Ælfric's Use of Discourse in Some Saints' Lives', *ES*, 63 (1982), 13–19 (p. 16).

majority of speeches Ælfric preserves in his adaptation reinforce points of doctrine or practice he makes elsewhere.[34]

This tendency is especially true of Cecilia's responses to the four questions Tiburtius poses during the 'catechetical conversation' that leads to his conversion, but for the sake of brevity I focus only on her answer to the second question as it demonstrates best how a saint's speech can work as a set piece modelling succinct encapsulations of basic Christian principles.[35] Having been prompted by Cecila's comment that people who believe that earthly life is the only life should be afraid to die, Tiburtius asks her whether there is another life, who can confirm it, why the one God of Christianity has three names, and who has been to the other life and returned to earth to guarantee that it exists. Each of Cecilia's answers parallels or echoes passages in other of Ælfric's sermons.[36] In her summary statement regarding

---

[34] On the saint's function as preacher in Ælfric's early saints' lives, see Godden, 'Experiments in Genre', p. 266.

[35] The phrase 'catechetical conversation' is Pauline Thompson's from an unpublished paper, 'The Saint as Catechist in Ælfric's Life of St Cecilia' (International Society of Anglo-Saxonists, Helsinki, 2001), in which she examines Ælfric's treatment of these four questions, especially the second. Her interest in these questions lies primarily in how the answers reflect his views of 'human responsibility and divine grace in the conversion process', whereas I simply want to draw attention to their function in the hagiography of reinforcing points Ælfric makes in the homilies. I am grateful to Professor Thomson for providing me with a copy of her paper, which forms part of a book-length study of Ælfric's virgin martyrs that she is preparing.

[36] Compare Cecilia's answer to the first question (LS II.34, lines 141–53, p. 364) with lines 33–71 of De falsis diis (SH II.21, pp. 678–80), which Ælfric appends to the Lives, and CH I.32, lines 195–229, pp. 457–58. Parallels for her response to Tiburtius's third question (LS II.34, lines 163–70, pp. 364 and 366) are found in several sermons: concerning the unity of the Trinity, see LS I.1, lines 14–19 (pp. 10 and 12) and 31–41 (p. 12), SH II.21, lines 20–24 (p. 677), the passage from Interrogationes Sigeuulfi in Genesin cited in the following note, and CH I.8, lines 206–10 (p. 248); regarding her comparison of the Trinity to man's 'andgit and wylla and gewittig gemynd' (LS II.34, line 169, p. 366; 'understanding and will and conscious memory'), see LS I.1, lines 112–22 (pp. 16 and 18), lines 192–95 in 'A Critical Edition of Ælfric's Translation of Alcuin's Interrogationes Sigwulfi Presbiteri and of the Related Texts De Creatore et Creatura and De Sex Etatibus Huius Seculi', ed. by William P. Stoneman (unpublished doctoral dissertation, University of Toronto, 1982), p. 131, and CH I.20, lines 190–212 (pp. 341–42), all of which are cited in Godden, Introduction, Commentary, and Glossary, p. 164; and for other instances in which Ælfric uses frofer gast (LS II.34, line 166, p. 366; 'Comforting Spirit') to refer to the Holy Spirit, see CH I.20, lines 84–85 (p. 338) and CH I.22, lines 175–78 (pp. 360–61). A representative sermon that treats in more detail the points which Cecilia mentions in her summary of Christ's life in answer to Tiburtius's fourth question (LS II.34, lines 177–82, p. 366) is CH I.1, lines 236–93 (pp. 187–89).

the Trinity that constitutes her response to the question about who can confirm the existence of the everlasting life, it is not impossible to hear Ælfric's idealized lay teacher instructing a child, godchild, relative, or friend:

> Ealle gesceafta scyppend ænne sunu gestrynde and forðteah þurh hine sylfne þone frofer gast; þurh þone sunu he gesceop ealle gesceafta þe syndon and hi ealle gelyffæste þurh þone lifigendan gast. (*LS* II.34, lines 175–60, p. 365)

> [The Creator of all creatures begot a Son and brought forth by His own means the Comforting Spirit; through the Son He created all creatures that exist and endowed them all with life through the living Spirit.]

The doctrine of the Trinity was one of Ælfric's 'key concerns', so it is not surprising that two other texts in the *Lives* contain similar formulations and that *De memoria sanctorum*, the opening sermon itself, begins and end with an evocation of the triune God.[37] Not every speech, of course, works so patently to cement in the audience's minds such fundamental tenets of the faith, but most reinforce principles expounded elsewhere in the *Lives* and the *Sermones catholici* and model a concision and lucidity that would assist any Christian in explaining his or her faith.

Manner

If Ælfric's attention to why and what the saints teach can be understood as attempts to associate their actions with the procreative activity of the Church, then he also appears interested in highlighting the spirit in which her members become mothers to other believers. Like the devout laymen in the sermon for Epiphany who live temperately in order to admonish others to good deeds, the saints exhort others with mild, alluring speech. It seems that for Ælfric a desire to attract others to the everlasting life is necessary for successful spiritual generation, and his decision to set the scene of Cecilia's initial encounter with Valerian in the bed rather than the bed chamber best illustrates this concern. In the *passio*, after the newly-weds enter the nuptial chamber on their wedding night, Cecilia addresses Valerian

---

[37] Respectively, Godden, *Introduction, Commentary, and Glossary*, p. 164; *De falsis diis* (*SH* II.21, lines 1–24, p. 677) and *Interrogationes Sigeuulfi in Genesin* ('Ælfric's Translation of Alcuin's *Interrogationes Sigwulfi Presbiteri*', ed. by Stoneman, lines 554–65, pp. 236–37); and *LS* I.16, lines 1–4 (p. 336) and 382–84 (p. 362). It is also worth remarking that *De falsis diis* opens with Ælfric's reminder that Scripture taught the worship of one God and a quotation of Ephesians 4. 5–6, whose one deity, faith, and baptism Valerian confirms when visiting Pope Urban (see note 30 above).

as '"dulcissime atque amantissime juvenis"' (Hereford P. 7. vi, fol. 74ʳᵃ; '"sweetest and most beloved young man"') and then springs on him her announcement that she is guarded by an angel who will kill him should he try to defile her. Remarkably, Ælfric recasts the encounter as a pillow talk, and now in bed with her new husband, Cecilia 'makes love' to Valerian with her beauty, wisdom, and language and 'thus allured him to God':

> Hi wurdon þa gebrohte on bedde ætgædere, and Cecilia sona þæt snotere mæden gespræc hire brydguman and þus to Gode tihte: 'Eala, þu min leofa man, ic þe mid lufe secge, Ic habbe Godes encgel þe gehylt me on [lufe] and gif þu wylt me gewemman he went sona to ðe and mid gramum þe slihð þæt þu sona ne leofast. Gif þu þonne me lufast and butan laðe gehylst on clænum mægðhade Crist þonne lufað þe and his gife geswutelað þe sylfum swa swa me.' (LS II.34, lines 28–37. pp. 356 and 358)

> [They were then brought into bed together, and immediately Cecilia, the wise virgin, spoke to her bridegroom and thus allured him to God: 'Oh, my beloved husband, I say to you with love, I have an angel of God who guards me in love, and if you wish to defile me, he will turn to you at once and in anger strike you so that instantly you will not live. Therefore, if you will love me and will guard me without harm in pure virginity, then Christ will love you and will reveal his grace to you just as to me.']

Using spiritual fervour instead of sexual ardour, Cecilia expresses her true affection for her bridegroom verbally rather than physically, when she, not Pope Urban (as in the *passio*), 'þa lærde swa lange þone cniht oð þæt he gelyfde on þone lifigendan god' (lines 49–50, p. 358; 'instructed the youth for a long time until he believed in the living God').[38] As was the case in Ælfric's initial description of Cecilia as a woman who possessed a great 'love of the everlasting life', this initial use of *tihtan* to connote allurement colours subsequent occurrences of the verb that he adds to the narrative and infuses other encounters with a similar desire.

It is appropriate, I think, to characterize as loving the manner in which Christians talk to others about their faith in the *Legend of Cecilia*. Ælfric has the brothers approach Maximus with *tihtinge* (LS II.34, line 234, p. 368; 'encouragement'); he substitutes *heo tihte* (line 300, p. 372; 'she allured') for the inexpressive *dicit* (Hereford P. 7. vi, fol. 79ʳᵃ; 'she said') to characterize Cecilia's interaction with the crowd who gathers to bewail her death; and he writes simply that she *tihte* (line 358, p. 376; 'encouraged') the faithful just before her death. The timbre of these voices is less that of the prophet Jonah than the apostle John, who, in Ælfric's words, *tihte* the people of Asia from their pagan temples *mid geswæsum wordum*

---

[38] In the *passio* Urban is depicted as 'edocens eum omnem fidei regulam' (Hereford P. 7. vi, fol. 74ᵛᵃ; 'instructing him in the whole rule of the faith').

(*CH* I.4, line 204, p. 213; 'with pleasing words'). The love that marks these martyrs' discourse is rooted in a desire for the everlasting life against which any physical
passion or craving for worldly delights pales in comparison. The resulting image is
that of a chaste couple and their spiritual children who represent a Church sound
in its doctrine and speaking not as noisy gongs or clanging cymbals but, as Tiburtius attributes to Cecilia, with the tongues of angels.[39]

Conclusion

Having demonstrated that Ælfric rewrites the *Legend of Cecilia* to model for laymen their role in the procreative activity of the Church, I conclude with thoughts
about why he develops in the sermons ideas of chastity, purity, and spiritual marriage that blur the lines between priests and laymen, and why he includes in the
Lives of Saints a model of sanctity that promotes these same ideals. Put simply,
when read in the context of writings that promote celibacy and spiritual purity
among the laity and that take clergymen to task for their lack of these virtues, the
Legend of Cecilia may work subtly to erode the laity's support for married or otherwise unreformed priests and to redirect it to a reformed, monastic priesthood.[40]
The longstanding practice of clerical marriage in the English church distressed
Ælfric, and he registered his objections to it throughout his career. Displaying none
of Cecilia's mildness towards his wayward Christian brothers, he castigates them
as lawbreakers and heretics in pastoral letters, calls them perverts in a sermon to be
delivered from the pulpit, and infers that they are retrogrades in a legend to be read
in private.[41] He astonishingly suggests they divorce their wives, though he admits
he cannot force them to do so.[42] On the other hand, he considered reformed
monastic priests like himself to be set apart by their absolute celibacy, chosen by the
virgin Christ to administer Communion in purity, and thus able to deliver superior

---

[39] *LS* II.34, lines 173–74 (p. 366).

[40] Malcolm Godden suggested this possibility to me. I have put forth this idea as it relates to
Ælfric's homilies on marital celibacy in 'For Pastoral Care and Political Gain'.

[41] For lawbreakers, see *Die Hirtenbriefe Ælfrics in altenglischer und lateinischer Fassung*, ed.
by Bernard Fehr, BaP, 9 (Hamburg, 1914), I, §14 (p. 4) and II, §87 (p. 46); for heretics, see
Assmann II, line 199 (p. 22); for perverts, see *CH* II.6, line 156 (p. 57); and for retrogrades, see
LS I.10, lines 202–33 (pp. 232 and 234).

[42] Fehr 2, §111 (*Die Hirtenbriefe Ælfrics*, p. 48); see also Fehr 2, §88–91 (ibid., p. 46) and Fehr
I, §17 (ibid., p. 5) for his demand that priests put away their wives.

pastoral care.[43] Certainly they are never distracted by biological children and are free to attend to the well-being of their spiritual offspring.[44]

It is the laity, these children, whose material and ideological support Ælfric hopes to gain, and this struggle explains his keenness to alienate the laity from married clergymen and ally them to monastic priests. He accomplishes the former in a sermon when he censures married priests as perverts and questions their spiritual fitness by pointing out they live in violation of scriptural precedent and canon law.[45] Less aggressively, sermons like those surveyed in the section on 'Homiletic Contexts for Ælfrician Hagiography', which promote among the laity chastity — whether marital celibacy or spiritual purity — as the virtue loved 'especially' by God, also point up the undistinguished nature of a priesthood who cannot best the *clænnyss* of the devout layman.[46] When Ælfric applies such homiletics to the hagiography, as we saw in the section on 'Hagiographic Contexts for Ælfrician Homiletics', he endorses in the *Legend of Cecilia* a model of sanctity that attributes to lay folk an asceticism, orthodoxy, and learnedness that only reinforces the ordinariness of the unreformed, uneducated, non-monastic clergyman. Skilfully, however, he is careful to unite the laity to the monastic priesthood by calling attention to their shared values in sermons as well as saints' lives like the *Legend of Cecilia*. The very *clænnyss* that permits laymen to discount a married priest allows them to join the reformed clergy in a monk-like pursuit of holiness. Charged thus with preserving the chastity appropriate to them and with teaching and bearing spiritual children, the laity is allied to monastic priests and saints like Cecilia and Valerian as virgin brides of Christ and mothers to other believers.

When we recall that Cecilia and Valerian personify a virtue applied to laymen and priests in *De memoria sanctorum*, then it becomes clear how Ælfric could understand the saints' *clænnyss* as symbolic of the *anrædnyss* ('constancy') his countrymen needed to muster in the ongoing spiritual warfare against the devil, plagued as England was (to his mind) with clergy lacking honour and lay folk wanting piety. In *De oratione Moysi* (*The Prayer of Moses*, *LS* I.13) Ælfric again urges the audience into spiritual battle, this time with the promise of safety for their souls and nation if lay and cleric would 'god wurðian mid soðre anrædnysse' (line 178, p. 296'

---

[43] See *LS* I.10, lines 222–31 (p. 234).

[44] For Ælfric's rebukes to priests for being biological fathers, see Fehr 3, §41 (*Die Hirtenbriefe Ælfrics*, p. 62) and Fehr III, §81 (ibid., p.176).

[45] *CH* II.6, lines 144–66 (p. 57).

[46] See note 17 above.

'honour God with true constancy'). Likewise, he reiterates his hope that stories such as the *Legend of Cecilia* will strengthen Christians in the midst of their struggles to remain steadfast in the faith. Just as Aaron and Hur came to Moses' aid while he prayed for Joshua's victory over the Amalekites (Exodus 17. 10–13), so too will God come to succour English Christians who pray for assistance amid the warfare of their souls. Lest they wonder how to recognize God's help when it comes, Ælfric reminds them that 'þonne we bec rædað oððe rædan gehyrað, þonne sprecð god to us þurh þa gastlican rædincge' (*LS* I.13, lines 62–63, pp. 286 and 288; 'when we read or hear books read, then God speaks to us through the spiritual reading').[47] Undoubtedly he imagined God speaking to Anglo-Saxon Christians through his homilies and hagiography, and undoubtedly he heard Him in the *Legend of Cecilia* urging layman and priest alike to the chastity and constancy that would guarantee them victory here and in the hereafter.[48]

---

[47] This reminder echoes the Latin Preface of the *Lives* where Ælfric says he writes 'studentes aliis prodesse edificando ad fidem lectione huius narrationis, quibuscumque placuerit huic operi operam dare, siue legendo, seu audiendo, quia estimo non esse ingratum fidelibus' ('desiring, by edifying in the faith through the reading of this narrative, to profit any others whom it pleases to give their attention to this work either by reading or listening, for I do not reckon it to be disagreeable to the faithful'): *Ælfric's Prefaces*, ed. and trans. by Jonathan Wilcox, Durham Medieval Texts, 9 (Durham, 1994), pp. 119 and 131; *LS* I.Preface, lines 2–5 (p. 2).

[48] I would like to thank Jenny Adams, Karen Upchurch, and the editor for their comments and criticisms.

ÆLFRIC'S OR NOT? THE MAKING OF A *TEMPORALE* COLLECTION IN LATE ANGLO-SAXON ENGLAND

Loredana Teresi

C ambridge, Corpus Christi College, MS 302 and London, British Library, Cotton MS Faustina A. XI are two closely related copies of an Anglo-Saxon *temporale*, that is, a collection of homilies for the Proper of the Season[1] strictly following the liturgical year. Ker dates CCCC 302 to some time between the end of the eleventh and the beginning of the twelfth century.[2] It contains Ælfric's *Hexameron* followed by another thirty-three items in Old English.[3] Some folios are missing in the codex, so that the original number of items that the

---

[1] The Proper of the Season includes feasts other than saints' days (Proper of the Saints). The term *temporale* refers to movable feasts, i.e. those feasts which follow the lunar calendar, as suitably and concisely elucidated by Lapidge in his essay on Ælfric's *sanctorale*: 'The liturgical year consists of two great, overlapping cycles of feasts: the *temporale* and the *sanctorale*. The *temporale* consists of those Sundays (and associated days) linked to Easter; and because Easter originated as a feast (Passover or *pasch*) in the Hebrew lunar calendar, it falls on a different Sunday — and hence different calendar day — each year. The *sanctorale*, on the other hand, consists of those feasts that are celebrated each year on the same day of the Roman or solar calendar'. Michael Lapidge, 'Ælfric's Sanctorale', in *Holy Men and Holy Women: Old English Prose Saints' Lives and their Contexts*, ed. by Paul E. Szarmach (Albany, 1996), pp. 115–29 (p. 115). For further details, see Gregory Dix, *The Shape of the Liturgy*, 2nd edn (London, 1945), pp. 333–85. CCCC 302 is not, strictly speaking, a *temporale* collection, since it also includes items belonging to the Proper of the Saints.

[2] See N. R. Ker, *Catalogue of Manuscripts Containing Anglo-Saxon* (Oxford, 1957), pp. 95–99 (no. 56) and Helmut Gneuss, *Handlist of Anglo-Saxon Manuscripts: A List of Manuscripts and Manuscript Fragments Written or Owned in England up to 1100*, MRTS, 241 (Tempe, 2001), p. 36 (no. 86).

[3] Ker's itemization differs from the numbering of homilies in the various editions. See Table 1 below.

manuscript contained cannot be ascertained.[4] Cotton Faustina A. IX was written
in the first half of the twelfth century,[5] and contains thirty-eight items — all in Old
English, as in CCCC 302 — but some folios have been lost, so that it is difficult
to determine the original number of items.[6] The origin and provenance of the two
manuscripts are still unknown, but they have been associated by various scholars
with the south-east.[7] Both manuscripts show a combination of Ælfrician and
anonymous homilies. In its present state, CCCC 302 covers the first half of the
liturgical year, from the First Sunday in Advent to Rogationtide.[8] As can be seen
from Table 1,[9] where the items are listed in the first column, twenty-seven texts are

[4] Ker, *Catalogue*, p. 98, gives the following collation: '1–11[8], 12[8] wants 2 after p. 188, 13–14[8]. 3 and 6 in quire 14 are half-sheets. Leaves missing at end'.

[5] See Ker, *Catalogue*, pp. 190–93 (no. 153).

[6] Collation: '1 one (f. 2), 2–7[8], 8[8] wants 1 before f. 51, 9–12[8], 13[4], 14[8], 15[8] wants 2 after f. 102, 16–21[8], 22[8] wants 4 after f. 159, 23–25[8], 26[12] wants 10–12, probably blank, after f. 196. Blank parchment leaves have been inserted in place of the leaves missing from quires 8 and 22. A quire is missing after f. 50' (Ker, *Catalogue*, p. 193). On the two manuscripts, see also Loredana Teresi, 'A Computer-Assisted Analysis of Spellings in Two Vernacular Manuscripts of the Transition Period: Cambridge, Corpus Christi College 302 and London, British Library, Cotton Faustina A. ix' (unpublished doctoral thesis, University of Manchester, 1998).

[7] See, for example, *Homilies of Ælfric: A Supplementary Collection*, ed. by John C. Pope, 2 vols, EETS: OS, 259–60 (London, 1967–68), I, 50–52; and D. G. Scragg, 'The Corpus of Vernacular Homilies and Prose Saints' Lives before Ælfric', *ASE*, 8 (1979), 223–77 (p. 247).

[8] Rogationtide, also called 'letania maiore', refers to the three days (Monday, Tuesday, and Wednesday) of fasting and penitence preceding Ascension. The term 'letania maiore' in Roman liturgy referred to St Mark's feast (25 April), while in Gallican liturgy it corresponded to the three days of penitential processions before Ascension established by Bishop Mamertus in Vienna (*c.* 470). Ælfric and the various Anglo-Saxon homiliaries that have survived follow the Gallican use. For further details, see *Eleven Old English Rogationtide Homilies*, ed. by Joyce Bazire and James E. Cross (Toronto, 1982), pp. xv–xxv; *Anglo-Saxon Litanies of the Saints*, ed. by Michael Lapidge, Henry Bradshaw Society Publications, 106 (London, 1991), pp. 8–11; Lapidge, 'Ælfric's *Sanctorale*', p. 127, n. 10; and Stephen J. Harris's study of 'The Liturgical Context of Ælfric's Homilies for Rogation' in this volume.

[9] The first two columns give the itemization as in Ker's *Catalogue*, followed by a translation of the rubric accompanying the various items, when present. Defective texts, with missing parts due to accidental loss of folios/pages or quires, are shown by the use of '[…]' at the beginning or at the end of the rubric, as applicable. The third column shows the Cameron number: see Angus Cameron, 'A List of Old English Texts', in *A Plan for the Dictionary of Old English*, ed. by Roberta Frank and Angus Cameron (Toronto, 1973), pp. 25–306. Column four quotes the printed editions of the various homilies: *Angelsächsische Homilien und Heiligenleben*, ed. by Bruno Assmann, BaP, 3 (Kassel, 1889); *Eleven Old English Rogationtide Homilies*, ed. by Bazire and

by Ælfric, one is by Wulfstan, and six are anonymous. Cotton MS Faustina A. IX's collection stretches from the second Sunday after Epiphany[10] to Pentecost, and includes thirty-three items by Ælfric and five anonymous ones. The comparison shows how similar the two collections are.

Table 1

CCCC 302	Cotton Faustina A. IX	Cameron no.	Edition[1]
Rubric missing [*Hexameron*]		B 1.5.13	Crawford
1st Sunday in Advent		B 1.1.41	*CH* I.39
2nd Sunday in Advent		B 1.1.42	*CH* I.40
3rd Sunday in Advent		B 1.3.18	*LS* I.17
4th Sunday in Advent		B 2.2.4	Bethurum VIIIb
Christmas		B 1.1.3	*CH* I.2
St Stephen		B 1.1.4	*CH* I.3
St John		B 1.1.5	*CH* I.4
	[. . .] *Rubric missing* [2nd Sunday after Epiphany?]	B 1.2.5	*CH* II.4

Cross; *The Homilies of Wulfstan*, ed. by Dorothy Bethurum (Oxford, 1957); Tolliver Cleveland Callison III, 'An Edition of Previously Unpublished Anglo-Saxon Homilies in MSS. CCCC 302 and Cotton Faustina A. ix' (unpublished doctoral dissertation, University of Wisconsin, 1973); *Ælfric's Catholic Homilies: The First Series, Text*, ed. by Peter Clemoes, EETS: SS, 17 (Oxford, 1997); *Exameron Anglice, or the Old English Hexameron*, ed. by S. J. Crawford, BaP, 10 (Hamburg, 1921); *Ælfric's Catholic Homilies: The Second Series, Text*, ed. by Malcolm Godden, EETS: SS, 5 (London, 1979); *The Blickling Homilies of the Tenth Century*, ed. by Richard Morris, EETS: OS, 58, 63, 73 (London, 1874–80; repr. as one volume, 1967); *Wulfstan: Sammlung der ihm zugeschriebenen Homilien nebst Untersuchungen über ihre Echtheit*, vol. I: *Text und Varianten*, ed. by A. S. Napier (Berlin, 1883; repr. with a supplement by K. Ostheeren, Dublin, 1967); *Homilies of Ælfric*, ed. by Pope; *The Vercelli Homilies and Related Texts*, ed. by D. G. Scragg, EETS: OS, 300 (Oxford, 1992); *Ælfric's Lives of Saints*, ed. by Walter W. Skeat, EETS: OS, 76, 82, 94, 114 (London, 1881–1900; repr. as 2 vols, 1966); Loredana Teresi, '*Be Heofonwarum 7 be Helwarum*: A Complete Edition', in *Early Medieval English Texts and Interpretations: Studies Presented to Donald G. Scragg*, ed. by Elaine Treharne and Susan Rosser, MRTS, 252 (Tempe, 2003), pp. 211–44; and *Vier altenglische Predigten aus der heterodoxen Tradition, mit Kommentar, Übersetzung und Glossar sowie drei weiteren Texten im Anhang*, ed. by H. L. C. Tristram (Inaugural-diss. Freiburg-im-Breisgau; privately printed, 1970).

[10] The first item begins imperfectly and the rubric has been lost, but the second item in the manuscript is a homily for the third Sunday after Epiphany, and therefore it seems reasonable to assume that the preceding item was meant for the second Sunday after Epiphany, as it is in other collections, such as Cambridge, Corpus Christi College, MS 198 and Cambridge, Corpus Christi College, MS 162.

CCCC 302	Cotton Faustina A. IX	Cameron no.	Edition[1]
	3rd Sunday after Epiphany	B 1.1.9	*CH* I.8
2nd Sunday after Epiphany	**4th Sunday after Epiphany**	**B 1.8.5**	**Assmann II**
3rd Sunday after Epiphany	**5th Sunday after Epiphany**	**B 3.2.5**	**Teresi / Callison 2**
4th Sunday after Epiphany	**6th Sunday after Epiphany**	**B 3.2.6**	**Assmann XIV**
5th Sunday after Epiphany	**7th Sunday after Epiphany**	**B 3.2.7**	**Callison 1**
Septuagesima	Septuagesima	B 1.2.6a	*CH* II.5a
De alleluia	*De alleluia*	B 1.2.6b	*CH* II.5b
Sexagesima	Sexagesima	B 1.2.7	*CH* II.6
Quinquagesima	Quinquagesima [...][2]	B 1.1.11	*CH* I.10
Ash Wednesday		B 1.3.13	*LS* I.12
1st Sunday in Lent	[...] *Rubric missing* [1st Sunday in Lent?]	B 1.1.12	*CH* I.11
Monday after 1st Sunday in Lent	Monday after 1st Sunday in Lent	B 1.2.8	*CH* II.7
2nd Sunday in Lent	2nd Sunday in Lent	B 1.2.9	*CH* II.8
3rd Sunday in Lent	3rd Sunday in Lent	B 1.4.4	*SH* I.4
4th Sunday in Lent	4th Sunday in Lent	B 1.1.13	*CH* I.12
	4th Sunday in Lent	B 1.2.13	*CH* II.12a
	4th Sunday in Lent	B 1.2.14	*CH* II.12b
	4th Sunday in Lent	B 1.3.14	*LS* I.13
5th Sunday in Lent	5th Sunday in Lent	B 1.2.15	*CH* II.13
Friday before Palm Sunday	Friday before Palm Sunday	B 1.5.4	Assmann V
Palm Sunday	Palm Sunday	B 1.1.15	*CH* I.14
Monday in Passion week	Monday in Passion week	B 1.2.16	*CH* II.14
	Monday in Passion week	B 3.2.21	Callison 3
Maundy Thursday	Maundy Thursday	B 3.2.22	Assmann XIII
	Easter	B 1.1.17	*CH* I.15
Easter [...][3]	Easter	B 1.2.18	*CH* II.15
	Easter	B 1.2.19	*CH* II.16a
	Wednesday in Easter week	B 1.2.20	*CH* II.16b
	1st Sunday after Easter	B 1.1.18	*CH* I.16
[...] *Rubric missing* [2nd Sunday after Easter?]	2nd Sunday after Easter [...][4]	B 1.1.19	*CH* I.17
	[...] *Rubric missing* [3rd Sunday after Easter?]	B 1.6.3 + B 1.4.20	Napier VIII + *SH* II.19

CCCC 302	Cotton Faustina A. IX	Cameron no.	Edition[1]
	4th Sunday after Easter	B 1.4.7	*SH* I.7
	[6th Sunday after Easter?][5]	B 1.4.8	*SH* I.8
In letania maiore		B 1.1.20	*CH* I.18
Monday in Rogationtide		B 3.2.35	Bazire-Cross 5
Monday in Rogationtide		B 1.1.21	*CH* I.19
Tuesday in Rogationtide		B 3.2.40	Scragg 10
Tuesday in Rogationtide [. . .]	*De fide catholica*	B 1.1.22	*CH* I.20
	Ascension	B 1.1.23	*CH* I.21
	Sunday after Ascension	B 1.4.9	*SH* I.9
	Pentecost	B 1.1.24	*CH* I.22
	Pentecost	B 1.4.10	*SH* I.10

[1] When a homily in a given edition is composed of different parts, the various parts will be distinguished by the use of alphabetical letters (e.g. *CH* II.23a vs 23b).

[2] Since a folio and a quire seem to be missing, the manuscript very likely contained *LS* I.12 as well. See Ker, *Catalogue*, p. 190, and *First Series*, ed. by Clemoes, p. 79.

[3] Only one folio is missing, the second of a quire of eight; no homilies have therefore been lost.

[4] Only one folio is missing.

[5] The rubric in the manuscript reads '*Dominica V post octaua*', that is the 6th Sunday after Easter, perhaps a corruption for '*Dominica V post pascha*'.

The two manuscripts have twenty-one items in common which are arranged in the same order and mostly follow the same distribution within the liturgical year.[11] The exceptions are Assmann II, Teresi, Assmann XIV, and Callison 1 (listed in bold in Table 1), which are assigned to the second through fifth Sundays after Epiphany in CCCC 302 and to the fourth through seventh Sundays after Epiphany in

[11] Item 9 in CCCC 302 and item 3 in Cotton Faustina A. IX (B 1.8.5, Assmann II) are adapted from Ælfric's *Letter to Sygefyrð*. According to Clemoes, it is 'an unofficial *ad hoc* homily formed by simply cutting out the introductory portion of the letter': P. A. M. Clemoes, 'The Chronology of Ælfric's Works', in *The Anglo-Saxons: Studies in Some Aspects of their History and Culture Presented to Bruce Dickins*, ed. by Peter Clemoes (London, 1959), pp. 212–47; repr. with the same title, as a monograph, *OEN* Subsidia, 5 (Binghamton, 1980), p. 19, n. 1. See also Jonathan Wilcox, 'The Transmission of Ælfric's *Letter to Sigefyrth* and the Mutilation of MS Cotton Vespasian D. xiv', in *Early Medieval English Texts*, ed. by Treharne and Rosser, pp. 285–300 (p. 290): 'the tract is pared down, lacking both the preface and the audience addresses, reduced to a piece of general edification on chastity good for any occasion and used in these manuscripts for two different Sundays following Epiphany'. Note also that Teresi, Assmann XIV, and Callison 1 are only found in CCCC 302 and Cotton Faustina A. IX. On anonymous items, see Scragg, 'Corpus of Vernacular Homilies', pp. 245–47.

Cotton Faustina A. IX.[12] The similarity in content is also parallelled by textual closeness, showing that the two manuscripts evidently derive from a common ancestor, probably at some remove from both. As Clemoes puts it: 'N's and O's texts of their *CH* I items share many readings — alterations and corruptions — which are not authentic and are peculiar to them as a pair and which prove that these two manuscripts represent a common line of transmission'.[13]

Ker and Clemoes had also noted the similarity between this pair of codices and a third manuscript: Cambridge, University Library, MS Ii. 4. 6, probably written at the New Minster in Winchester around the middle of the eleventh century.[14] It contains a comparable set of *temporale* from the second Sunday after Epiphany

---

[12] The discrepancy between the two sets of dates may reflect the flexibility of the period between Epiphany and Septuagesima, in which the number of Sundays can range from one to six (on Cotton Faustina A. IX having an entry for an impossible seventh Sunday see below, p. 306. The complex framework of the Easter season developed gradually in time. The Council of Nicea (325) established that Easter would fall on the first Sunday after the full moon following the Spring equinox (21 March), i.e. in a period between 22 March and 25 April (*termini pascales*). Up to the fifth century, Lent ended on Holy Thursday, when the Paschal *Triduum* (Good Friday, Holy Saturday, and Easter Sunday) began, each day on the preceding evening. Fasting began on the first Sunday in Lent and ended on Holy Thursday, thus lasting for forty days (Sundays were also counted, although they were outside the fasting time). Eventually, however, the fasting season started to be counted backwards from Easter Sunday rather than Holy Thursday, and the Sundays were excluded from the computation. Consequently four more days were added at the beginning of the period, from Ash Wednesday, to make up the forty days of fasting. The Easter season was then extended to fifty days, by starting on the preceding Sunday (Sunday in Quinquagesima) and including all the Sundays again in the calculation, up to Easter. The number of days was then brought up to sixty by including the week before the Sunday in Quinquagesima and the three days after Easter (Wednesday in Easter week representing the end of Sexagesima). Finally, from the seventh century onwards, Septuagesima was formed by adding a week before Sexagesima and all the remaining days in Easter week. Up to six Sundays are therefore possible, between Epiphany and Septuagesima, when Easter is late, and only one Sunday when Easter is early. For further information on the liturgical year, see Cyrille Vogel, *Medieval Liturgy: An Introduction to the Sources*, rev. and trans. by William Storey and Niels Rasmussen (Washington, D.C., 1986), pp. 304–14. Note that, in medieval counting, as with the Roman system, the point of departure had to be included in the sum; so, for example, the octave of Pentecost is a Sunday, because eight days are reckoned between the two Sundays, since both Sundays are included in the sum.

[13] *First Series*, ed. by Clemoes, p. 69. Clemoes's 'N' is Cotton Faustina A. IX and 'O' is CCCC 302. Clemoes quotes as evidence a few readings from *CH* I.10 (lines 8, 11, 27, 31, and 62) where the two manuscripts agree against all other witnesses.

[14] Ker, *Catalogue*, pp. 31–35 (no. 21); see also Clemoes, 'Chronology', pp. 17–18. On the manuscript's Winchester origin, see T. A. M. Bishop, *English Caroline Minuscule* (Oxford, 1975), p. xv, n. 2.

(beginning imperfectly) to the first Sunday after Pentecost,[15] but incorporates only homilies by or based on Ælfric.[16] Table 2 shows a comparison of the homilies in the three collections.[17]

Table 2

CUL Ii. 4. 6	Cotton Faustina A. IX	CCCC 302
		[*Hexameron*] (Crawford)
		1st Sunday in Advent (*CH* I.39)
		2nd Sunday in Advent (*CH* I.40)
		3rd Sunday in Advent (*LS* I.17)
		4th Sunday in Advent (Bethurum VIIIb)
		Christmas (*CH* I.2)
		St Stephen (*CH* I.3)
		St John (*CH* I.4)
[...] [2nd Sunday after Epiphany?] (*CH* II.4)	[...] [2nd Sunday after Epiphany?] (*CH* II.4)	
[3rd Sunday after Epiphany?] (*CH* I.8)	3rd Sunday after Epiphany (*CH* I.8)	
[4th Sunday after Epiphany?] (*CH* II.23b)		
	4th Sunday after Epiphany (Assmann II)	2nd Sunday after Epiphany (Assmann II)
	5th Sunday after Epiphany (Teresi)	3rd Sunday after Epiphany (Teresi)
	6th Sunday after Epiphany (Assmann XIV)	4th Sunday after Epiphany (Assmann XIV)

[15] The homily for the first Sunday after Pentecost is followed by two Rogationtide homilies by Ælfric (*CH* I.18 and 19, the latter ending imperfectly), starting on a new page.

[16] The collection includes two composite homilies for Rogationtide (Bazire and Cross 6 and 7) containing anonymous as well as Ælfrician material: see M. R. Godden, 'Old English Composite Homilies from Winchester', *ASE*, 4 (1975), 57–65.

[17] The liturgical assignments given in the table are those found in the manuscripts and not in the editions. When rubrics are missing, probable reconstructions are supplied in square brackets, while question marks indicate uncertainty.

CUL Ii. 4. 6	Cotton Faustina A. IX	CCCC 302
	7th Sunday after Epiphany (Callison 1)	5th Sunday after Epiphany (Callison 1)
Septuagesima (*CH* II.5)	Septuagesima (*CH* II.5)	Septuagesima (*CH* II.5)
Sexagesima (*CH* II.6)	Sexagesima (*CH* II.6)	Sexagesima (*CH* II.6)
Quinquagesima (*CH* I.10)	Quinquagesima [...] (*CH* I.10)	Quinquagesima (*CH* I.10)
Ash Wednesday (*LS* I.12)		Ash Wednesday (*LS* I.12)
1st Sunday in Lent (*CH* I.11)	[...] [1st Sunday in Lent?] (*CH* I.11)	1st Sunday in Lent (*CH* I.11)
1st Sunday in Lent (*CH* II.7)	Monday after 1st Sunday in Lent (*CH* II.7)	Monday after 1st Sunday in Lent (*CH* II.7)
2nd Sunday in Lent (*CH* II.8)	2nd Sunday in Lent (*CH* II.8)	2nd Sunday in Lent (*CH* II.8)
3rd Sunday in Lent (*SH* I.4)	3rd Sunday in Lent (*SH* I.4)	3rd Sunday in Lent (*SH* I.4)
4th Sunday in Lent (*CH* I.12)	4th Sunday in Lent (*CH* I.12)	4th Sunday in Lent (*CH* I.12)
4th Sunday in Lent (*CH* II.12a)	4th Sunday in Lent (*CH* II.12a)	
4th Sunday in Lent (*CH* II.12b)	4th Sunday in Lent (*CH* II.12b)	
4th Sunday in Lent (*LS* I.13)	4th Sunday in Lent (*LS* I.13)	
5th Sunday in Lent (*CH* II.13)	5th Sunday in Lent (*CH* II.13)	5th Sunday in Lent (*CH* II.13)
	Friday before Palm Sunday (Assmann V)	Friday before Palm Sunday (Assmann V)
Palm Sunday (*CH* II.14) Note on *Swigdagas* Palm Sunday (*CH* I.14)	Palm Sunday (*CH* I.14) Monday in Passion week (*CH* II.14)	Palm Sunday (*CH* I.14) Monday in Passion week (*CH* II.14)
	Monday in Passion week (Callison 3)	
	Maundy Thursday (Assmann XIII)	Maundy Thursday (Assmann XIII)
Easter (*CH* I.15)	Easter (*CH* I.15)	
Easter (*CH* II.15)	Easter (*CH* II.15)	Easter (*CH* II.15) [...]
? (*CH* II.16a)	Easter (*CH* II.16a)	
? (*CH* II.16b)	Wednesday in Easter week (*CH* II.16b)	
? (*CH* I.16)	1st Sunday after Easter (*CH* I.16)	
3rd Sunday after Easter (*CH* I.17)[1]	2nd Sunday after Easter [...] (*CH* I.17)	[...] [2nd Sunday after Easter?] (*CH* I.17)

CUL Ii. 4. 6	Cotton Faustina A. IX	CCCC 302
	[. . .] [3rd Sunday after Easter?] (composite homily[2])	
5th Sunday after Easter (*SH* I.7)	4th Sunday after Easter (*SH* I.7)	
6th Sunday after Easter (*SH* I.8)	6th Sunday after Easter (*SH* I.8)[3]	
Monday in Rogationtide (Bazire-Cross 6)		
Tuesday in Rogationtide (Bazire-Cross 7)		
Wednesday in Rogationtide (*CH* I.18)		*In letania maiore* (*CH* I.18)
		Monday in Rogationtide (Bazire-Cross 5)
		Monday in Rogationtide (*CH* I.19)
		Tuesday in Rogationtide (Scragg 10)
	? (*CH* I.20)	Tuesday in Rogationtide [. . .] (*CH* I.20)
Wednesday in Rogationtide (*CH* II.22)		
Ascension (*CH* I.21)	Ascension (*CH* I.21)	
Sunday after Ascension (*SH* I.9)	Sunday after Ascension (*SH* I.9)	
Pentecost (*CH* I.22)	Pentecost (*CH* I.22)	
Pentecost (*SH* I.10)	Pentecost (*SH* I.10)	
1st Sunday after Pentecost (*SH* I.12)		
Monday and Tuesday in Rogationtide (*CH* I.18)		
? (*CH* I.19)		

[1] The rubrics in *CH* I.17 and *SH* I.7 and 8 in this manuscript assign the homilies to the '*Dominica II post octaua paschae*', '*Dominica IIII post octaua paschae*', and '*Dominica V post octaua paschae*', respectively, but maybe '*post octaua paschae*' is a corruption for '*post pascha*'.

[2] A composite homily formed by joining together excerpts from Napier VIII (*De septiformi spiritu*) and *SH* II.19 (*De doctrina apostolica*); see below, p. 301 and note 40.

[3] The rubric reads '*Dominica V post octaua*'; see above, note 5 to Table 1.

On the basis of this similarity, in his essay on the chronology of Ælfric's works, Clemoes had argued that the three manuscripts witnessed a common phase of reorganization and expansion of Ælfric's liturgical homilies for the Proper of the Season, which Ælfric himself had arranged in a *temporale* collection — what Clemoes called TH I — around 1002–05.[18] He claimed that the three manuscripts were based on 'a series by Ælfric for the Proper of the Season from Christmas to the Sunday after Pentecost', which originally probably included homilies for feasts not represented in the three compilations, such as Circumcision and Epiphany, as, in his opinion, Ælfric would not have left them out.[19] His hypothesis was later reinforced by his analysis of the transmission of the First Series of the *Catholic Homilies*, which showed that the three manuscripts were the main witnesses of what he considered the δ phase of Ælfric's reworking and reissuing of the homilies.[20] In particular, CUL Ii. 4. 6 on the one hand and CCCC 302 and Cotton Faustina A. IX on the other represented two distinct stages within this phase that we may call δ^1 and δ^2. The first stage (δ^1, represented by CUL Ii. 4. 6) would be characterized by an expanded version of *CH* I.17, which is not found in the manuscripts belonging to the α–γ phases, but appears in the δ–ζ manuscripts.[21] The second stage (δ^2, represented by the ancestor of Cotton Faustina A. IX and CCCC 302) would include two authentic expansions in *CH* I.8 and 16 which are not found in CUL Ii. 4. 6 (δ^1) but which reappear in the manuscripts of the subsequent phases (ϵ–ζ).[22] This distinction holds also for a series of readings that

[18] Clemoes, 'Chronology', pp. 17 and 34.

[19] Clemoes, 'Chronology', p. 18. In his opinion, Ælfric would have later extended the series throughout the year in TH II, a series 'more strictly confined to pericope homilies', now partly surviving in London, British Library, Cotton MS Vitellius C. V ('H'); Cambridge, Trinity College, MS B. 15. 34 ('U'); and Oxford, Bodleian Library, MS Bodley 343 ('B'). The whole series would contain seventy-two homilies, divided into two volumes, and Trinity B. 15. 34 would be a witness of the second volume, ending imperfectly (pp. 20–22). A pericope is the portion of Gospel to be read during Mass, and a pericope homily expounds the gospel reading for the day.

[20] Clemoes distinguishes between six main phases in Ælfric's reworking of the series, designated by Greek letters from α to ζ, 'the first three being marked by revision and the second three mainly by supplementation and reorganization': α ('A'), β ('Da', 'Ea', and F), γ ('K'), δ ('M', 'N', and 'O'), ϵ ('Q'), and ζ ('Bc', 'Hc', and 'U') (*First Series*, pp. 64–97).

[21] The long passage by Ælfric expanding the homily is printed by Clemoes in Appendix B, as text 3 (*First Series*, pp. 535–42).

[22] These expansions are printed as texts 1 and 2 in Clemoes' Appendix (*First Series*, pp. 533–35); they are witnessed only by Cotton Faustina A. IX, as CCCC 302 does not contain these homilies.

are not found in the manuscripts of the first three phases (α–γ) or in CUL Ii. 4. 6 (δ^1),[23] but which occur in Cotton Faustina A. IX and/or CCCC 302,[24] as well as in manuscripts of phases ε and ζ. Given the overall similarity of the collections in the three manuscripts, and given their differentiation into two subsequent stages of the δ phase, Clemoes concluded that they 'represent two stages in the development of a set within Ælfric's scriptorium' and that Ælfric himself was responsible for the collection.[25]

Clemoes's latter assertion, which had already been spelled out in his work on the chronology of Ælfric's work, was questioned by Pope in his edition of the Supplementary Series. The evidence yielded by the homilies Pope edited (and *SH* I.9 in particular) convinced him that CUL Ii. 4. 6, Cotton Faustina A. IX, and CCCC 302 had a faulty ancestor in common. He rejected the idea of Ælfric having issued two similar collections at different times (one with the expansion of *CH* I.16 and the other without it), since the three manuscripts contained errors that Pope felt would not have been tolerated by Ælfric long enough to be copied twice, in two subsequent collections. He therefore claimed that the faulty ancestor in common between CUL Ii. 4. 6, Cotton Faustina A. IX, and CCCC 302 had to be placed already at some remove from Ælfric. He considered the expanded version of *CH* I.16 in Cotton Faustina A. IX as the probable work of an interpolator and cast strong doubts on Ælfric's responsibility for the compilation of the *temporale* as a whole.[26] Of course, when Pope published his edition, Clemoes's work on the transmission of the First Series of the *Catholic Homilies* was not yet accessible, and therefore he could not verify his hypothesis against those data, as Clemoes himself remarks in his discussion of Pope's objections.[27]

One alternative explanation, however, is suggested by Clemoes himself: 'The alternative is to suppose that two people outside the author's scriptorium independently of one another used much the same items at much the same time to organize much the same series.'[28] Clemoes dismisses this idea as implausible, given the striking similarity between the collections. However, if one conflates all the *temporale*

---

[23] For example, *tobræc* changed to *oferswiðde* in *CH* I.15 (line 151), or *þæt is* and *anum* added in *CH* I.18 (lines 155 and 183, respectively).

[24] Depending on which manuscript contains that particular homily.

[25] *First Series*, ed. by Clemoes, p. 72.

[26] *Homilies*, ed. by Pope, I, 46–47 and 334–35.

[27] *First Series*, ed. by Clemoes, p. 71.

[28] *First Series*, ed. by Clemoes, p. 72.

items for the relevant period from Ælfric's *Catholic Homilies* and *Lives of Saints* (column 4 in Table 3 below), one obtains exactly the same type of collection, with exactly the same items in exactly the same order — with the exclusion of the homilies for Rogationtide, which will be discussed later — as is found in CUL Ii. 4. 6, Cotton Faustina A. IX, and CCCC 302 (columns 1–3).

Table 3

CUL Ii. 4. 6	CF A. IX	CCCC 302	*CH* and *LS*	*SH*	Customary Occasion
		Crawford			
		CH I.39	*CH* I.39		1st Sunday in Advent
		CH I.40	*CH* I.40		2nd Sunday in Advent
		LS I.17			
		Bethurum VIIIb			
		CH I.2			
		CH I.3			
		CH I.4			
CH II.4	*CH* II.4		*CH* II.4		2nd Sunday after Epiphany
CH I.8	*CH* I.8		*CH* I.8		3rd Sunday after Epiphany
CH II.23b					
	Assmann II	Assmann II			
	Teresi	Teresi			
	Assmann XIV	Assmann XIV			
	Callison 1	Callison 1			
CH II.5	*CH* II.5	*CH* II.5	*CH* II.5		Septuagesima
CH II.6	*CH* II.6	*CH* II.6	*CH* II.6		Sexagesima
CH I.10	*CH* I.10	*CH* I.10	*CH* I.10		Quinquagesima
LS I.12		*LS* I.12	*LS* I.12		Ash Wednesday
CH I.11	*CH* I.11	*CH* I.11	*CH* I.11		1st Sunday in Lent
CH II.7	*CH* II.7	*CH* II.7	*CH* II.7		1st Sunday in Lent[1]
CH II.8	*CH* II.8	*CH* II.8	*CH* II.8		2nd Sunday in Lent
SH I.4	*SH* I.4	*SH* I.4		*SH* I.4	3rd Sunday in Lent
CH I.12	*CH* I.12	*CH* I.12	*CH* I.12		4th Sunday in Lent
CH II.12	*CH* II.12		*CH* II.12		4th Sunday in Lent
LS I.13	*LS* I.13		*LS* I.13		4th Sunday in Lent
CH II.13	*CH* II.13	*CH* II.13	*CH* II.13		5th Sunday in Lent

CUL Ii. 4. 6	CF A. IX	CCCC 302	*CH* and *LS*	*SH*	Customary Occasion
	Assmann V	Assmann V			
CH II.14	*CH* I.14	*CH* I.14	*CH* I.14		Palm Sunday[2]
Note on	*CH* II.14	*CH* II.14	*CH* II.14		Palm Sunday[3]
Swigdagas			Note on		Note on *Swigdagas*
CH I.14			*Swigdagas*		
	Callison 3				
	Assmann XIII	Assmann XIII			
CH I.15	*CH* I.15		*CH* I.15		Easter
CH II.15	*CH* II.15	*CH* II.15	*CH* II.15		Easter
CH II.16a	*CH* II.16a		*CH* II.16a		Easter
CH II.16b	*CH* II.16b		*CH* II.16b		Easter[4]
CH I.16	*CH* I.16		*CH* I.16		1st Sunday after Easter
CH I.17	*CH* I.17	*CH* I.17	*CH* I.17		2nd Sunday after Easter[5]
	composite homily				
SH I.7	*SH* I.7			*SH* I.7	4th Sunday after Easter
SH I.8	*SH* I.8			*SH* I.8	5th Sunday after Easter
CH I.21	*CH* I.21		*CH* I.21		Ascension
SH I.9	*SH* I.9			*SH* I.9	1st Sunday after Ascension
CH I.22	*CH* I.22		*CH* I.22		Pentecost
SH I.10	*SH* I.10			*SH* I.10	Pentecost
SH I.12				*SH* I.12	1st Sunday after Pentecost

[1] The rubrics in Cotton Faustina A. IX and CCCC 302 assign this homily to the following Monday.

[2] CUL Ii. 4. 6 shows a transposition in the order of *CH* I.14 and *CH* II.14.

[3] Again, Cotton Faustina A. IX and CCCC 302 assign this homily to the following Monday.

[4] The rubric in Cotton Faustina A. IX assigns this item to Wednesday in Easter week.

[5] As already noted, *CH* I.17 and *SH* I.7 and 8 in CUL Ii. 4. 6 end the rubric with *post octaua paschae* rather than *post pascha*, so they are assigned to the third, fifth, and sixth Sundays after Easter rather than second, fourth, and fifth. Probably a mistake, but *CH* I.16 has no rubric, so it is difficult to tell. Also *SH* I.8 in Cotton Faustina A. IX unexpectedly displays the rubric *dominica V post octaua*.

Save for the inclusion of certain Supplementary Homilies (column 5), there are no items in common between CUL Ii. 4. 6 and either Cotton Faustina A. IX or

CCCC 302 (or both) that are not part of this conflated set. These supplementary items have most probably been included in order to fill some problematical gaps in the collection: the third Sunday in Lent, the fourth and fifth Sundays after Easter, the first Sunday after Ascension, and (only in CUL Ii. 4. 6) the first Sunday after Pentecost. These feasts are all obvious gaps that anyone trying to build up a *temporale* for this extension would have tried to fill with available material.[29] If Ælfric's Supplementary Homilies for these feasts were commonly available, it would not be surprising if two people independently had chosen to insert them in the collection, in the appropriate places.

In the light of this conflated set, the 'striking' similarity between CUL Ii. 4. 6 and the other two manuscripts becomes far less 'striking' or enlightening.[30] Anyone who had access to Ælfric's material (the two series of *Catholic Homilies*, his *Lives of Saints*, and the few supplementary items needed to fill the gaps) would have been able to make a similar collection. Of course, it could have been Ælfric himself, or someone in his scriptorium, as Clemoes argues. It is well known, however, that Ælfric sent everything he wrote to Canterbury — not only his new works but also his reworkings and updated versions — and that this material was then copied out again, sometimes altered, and then sent on to other destinations all over the country.[31] It is possible that someone who had access to Ælfric's series (and also his isolated homilies, perhaps, since we are not sure how the supplementary items edited by Pope circulated) decided at some point to put the various *temporale* items together, in the order in which they had been issued by Ælfric (i.e. First Series, Second Series, *Lives of Saints*, and then supplementary items), and that this process took place twice independently, in two different places (or in the same place, maybe Canterbury, at different times), but yielding out a similar result.[32] The fact

---

[29] On feast days and Masses in Anglo-Saxon England, see Ursula Lenker, *Die westsächsische Evangelienversion und die Perikopenordnungen im angelsächsischen England*, Texte und Untersuchungen zur englischen Philologie, 20 (Munich, 1997).

[30] The similarity would have been striking if the three manuscripts had had, for example, Assmann V in common (as the only Friday in Lent) or Callison 3, since that would have been harder to explain without resorting to a common source.

[31] See *First Series*, ed. by Clemoes, pp. 162–63, and *Second Series*, ed. by Godden, p. lxv.

[32] There is evidence that these types of collection were being made, outside Ælfric's scriptorium, in late Anglo-Saxon England. Oxford, Bodleian Library, MSS Bodley 340 + 342, for example, is a witness to the fact that, somewhere in the south-east (very likely Canterbury), both *temporale* and *sanctorale* items from Ælfric's two series of *Catholic Homilies* were put together (probably with the author's permission) in a homiliary following the liturgical year, at the end of

that the collections in Cotton Faustina A. IX and CCCC 302 show an updated version of the First Series of *Catholic Homilies* might then be explained by the fact that the compiler of the collection in their common ancestor had access to a more recent version of these homilies (δ^2), rather than having to postulate that Ælfric himself had 'updated' the collection in his own scriptorium. Clemoes's attribution of the collection to Ælfric was based on the fact that it was unlikely that someone had modified an existing *temporale* by replacing all the First Series items with updated versions that had meanwhile become available, whilst it would have been normal in Ælfric's scriptorium to prepare a new *temporale* with additions and revisions in some of the homilies. If the two collections (the one in CUL Ii. 4. 6 and that in the ancestor of CCCC 302 and Cotton Faustina A. IX) were prepared independently, however, Clemoes's arguments lose strength.

Godden's study of the development and circulation of the Second Series of *Catholic Homilies* does not seem to refute the hypothesis of an independent origin for the two collections. He agrees with Clemoes's theory of the Ælfrician authorship of two subsequent stages of the *temporale*, but his opinion is founded on the same assumption that 'the overall similarity of content and arrangement' between CUL Ii. 4. 6 and Cotton Faustina A. IX — which has proved to be more illusory than real — can only be explained with the two collections going 'back independently to a source within Ælfric's scriptorium'.[33] Moreover, some of his assertions on the two collections seem to cast doubts on Clemoes's reconstruction, rather than confirm it, since he admits that 'The precise relationship of M and N [CUL

the tenth century, and later supplemented by anonymous pieces either to fill gaps or to replace some Ælfrician items (presumably without Ælfric's consent). A similar collection, but only with *temporale* homilies, is found in Cambridge, Corpus Christi College, MS 162, which, in D. G. Scragg's words, 'provides evidence of a move, probably in Canterbury, towards the provision of a *temporale* sequence beginning at Septuagesima (such as is witnessed in at least one later manuscript) at the very end of the tenth century or at the latest in the early years of the eleventh': 'Cambridge, Corpus Christi College 162', in *Anglo-Saxon Manuscripts and their Heritage*, ed. by Phillip Pulsiano and Elaine M. Treharne (Aldershot, 1998), pp. 71–83 (p. 80). See also Scragg, 'Corpus of Vernacular Homilies', pp. 237–40, and Kenneth Sisam, 'MSS. Bodley 340 and 342: Ælfric's *Catholic Homilies*', *RES*, 7 (1931), 7–22; 8 (1932), 51–68; and 9 (1933), 1–12; repr. in his *Studies in the History of Old English Literature* (Oxford, 1953; repr. 1998), pp. 148–98. The cluster of homilies for Sundays after Pentecost in the Taunton fragment might also represent an independent attempt to combine homilies in a *temporale*: see Mechthild Gretsch, 'The Taunton Fragment: A New Text from Anglo-Saxon England', *ASE*, 33 (2004), 145–93, and Aidan Conti's study of 'The Circulation of the Old English Homily in the Twelfth Century' in this volume.

[33] *Second Series*, ed. by Godden, p. xlix.

Ii. 4. 6 and Cotton Faustina A. IX] is a difficult issue'.[34] Godden observes, for example, that although CUL Ii. 4. 6 shows several additional passages by Ælfric in its First Series homilies, no additions are found in its Second Series items,[35] a fact which is difficult to explain if the collection was compiled by Ælfric himself, but very easy to account for if it was the work of somebody putting the various items together as they had them.

Another fact that casts doubts on Ælfric's authorship of CUL Ii. 4. 6 is its use of *CH* II.23b, a piece originally employed by Ælfric as an appendix to his homily for the third Sunday after Pentecost (*CH* II.23a) and later incorporated in a homily for the thirteenth Sunday after Pentecost (*SH* II.17).[36] The piece expounds Matthew 8. 23–27, which is normally the pericope for the fourth or fifth Sundays after Epiphany.[37] Though lacking a rubric in the manuscript, the homily appears to correspond to the fourth Sunday, since it follows an item composed for the third Sunday after Epiphany (*CH* I.8). Ælfric's comment at the beginning of *CH* II.23b, however, shows that he intended the homily to be read on neither of these two Masses: 'Mine gebroðru we wyllað eow gereccan sume cristes wundra. to getrymmincge eoweres geleafan; We sind gecnæwe þæt we hit forgymeleasedon on ðam dæge þe mann þæt godspel rædde. ac hit mæg eow nu fremian. swa micclum swa hit ða mihte' (*CH* II.23, lines 127–30, p. 217; 'My brothers, we will explain to you some of the miracles of Christ, for the strengthening of your belief. We are aware that we neglected it on the day when the Gospel was read, but it can now benefit you as much as it could then'). It is probable, therefore, as Pope claims, that somebody else assigned this piece to the fourth Sunday after Epiphany, on the basis of the gospel reading on which it was centred:

> Clearly [this homily] was not designed as a complete sermon, but its position in M is understandable when we observe that the first of the two gospel-texts it sets forth (*Matthew* viii. 23–27 and *Mark* v. 1–20) is normally the pericope for the fourth Sunday after Epiphany. Probably the scribe himself or his supervisor made the assignment in an effort to supply a gap in the series without admitting non-Ælfrician material.[38]

---

[34] *Second Series*, ed. by Godden, p. xlviii. This statement appears in the section in which Godden describes the various manuscripts that contain the Second Series homilies, and does not mention CCCC 302 ('O') because he has not discussed it yet.

[35] *Second Series*, ed. by Godden, p. lxxxvi.

[36] See *Homilies*, ed. by Pope, II, 563–64, and Malcolm Godden, *Ælfric's Catholic Homilies: Introduction, Commentary, and Glossary*, EETS: SS, 18 (Oxford, 2000), p. 550.

[37] See Lenker, *Die westsächsische Evangelienversion*, pp. 303 and 326.

[38] *Homilies*, ed. by Pope, I, 41. Godden also suggests that *CH* II.23 might freely have been used at this point in CUL Ii. 4. 6 since it could not be included in its proper place in the *temporale* (the

If the transposition had been Ælfric's own choice, and if he had been responsible for both collections, the homily would have been very likely retained for the fourth Sunday after Epiphany in the ancestor of Cotton Faustina A. IX and CCCC 302; its compiler, however, seems to have made quite a different choice — Cotton Faustina A. IX inserts Assmann II, while CCCC 302 has Assmann XIV — thus showing that the gap was probably still there when the collection was assembled.

Another element, according to Godden, that proves Ælfric's authorship of CUL Ii. 4. 6 and the ancestor of Cotton Faustina A. IX and CCCC 302 is 'the comprehensive and well-organized nature of the collection[s], with all the relevant items for Sundays from the *Catholic Homilies* and the *Lives of Saints* included and six later homilies by Ælfric covering the gaps'.[39] Table 3, however, shows that not all the gaps were filled: even imagining a most basic liturgical cycle comprising only Sundays and Ascension, one striking absence is a homily for the third Sunday after Easter. No text is supplied for the occasion in CUL Ii. 4. 6 and CCCC 302, while Cotton Faustina A. IX covers the festival with a composite homily drawn from Ælfric's *De septiformi spiritu* (Napier VIII) and *De doctrina apostolica* (*SH* II.19) — a combination described by Godden as 'possibly by Ælfric'.[40] A few items for Sundays after Epiphany are also missing, although this particular absence raises the issue (to be addressed later) of where the original collection began.[41] If the two collections were made independently by someone other than Ælfric, the gaps could be easily explained in terms of lacunae in the material available to the compiler; an

---

third Sunday after Pentecost), as the collection originally extended only through the first Sunday after Pentecost (*Second Series*, pp. lxxxvi–lxxxvii). Masses, however, and consequently homilies, could not be stopped at Pentecost. The remaining Masses would have had to be celebrated anyway, whether they were in the collection or not. It is far more probable, therefore, that *CH* II.23 was moved to the Fourth Sunday after Epiphany, on the basis of the pericope, by somebody other than Ælfric, as the latter had assigned it by choice to a different date.

[39] *Second Series*, ed. by Godden, p. lxiv.

[40] *Second Series*, ed. by Godden, p. xlviii; see also Clemoes, 'Chronology', p. 5. See, however, the convincing arguments against Ælfric's responsibility for the combination by Pope (*Homilies*, II, 614–15). As Pope remarks, the presence of the compilation in Cotton Faustina A. IX would seem to indicate that Ælfric's homily for this Sunday (Assmann VI) had not been written yet (*Homilies*, ed. by Pope, I, 45).

[41] Clemoes himself remarks that very likely Ælfric had not yet written homilies for Sundays after Epiphany beyond the fourth Sunday, because the three existing manuscripts of this alleged Ælfrician *temporale* (CUL Ii. 4. 6, CCCC 302, and Cotton Faustina A. IX) cover these feasts with items from other sources ('Chronology', pp. 18–19).

equally simple explanation, moreover, would account for the way in which the gaps were filled in the ancestor of CCCC 302 and Cotton Faustina A. IX, mainly by using compilations and/or anonymous material.[42]

Furthermore, the very nature of Ælfric's previous work — that is, the issuing of the First and Second Series of the *Catholic Homilies* and the *Lives of Saints* — seems to speak against the idea of Ælfric's authorship of the two *temporale* collections. The Second Series does not 'complement' the First: nearly half of it is made up of items for feasts that had already been covered in the First Series; Ælfric himself states in the Latin preface to the First Series, moreover, that the two series can be put together or read in alternating years in order not to bore the audience, thus showing that he was not thinking in terms of a complete *temporale*.[43] The probable lack at this stage of a homily for the third Sunday after Easter (mentioned above) also draws into question the idea of a plan to create a complete *temporale* collection, since this occasion was one of the 'great fifty days' leading from Easter to Pentecost — one of the fundamental clusters of the liturgical year[44] — and would have been essential in a series from Septuagesima to Pentecost.[45]

---

[42] The presence in CUL Ii. 4. 6 and Cotton Faustina A. IX of items from the Supplementary Series homilies may seem at first to argue for Ælfric's authorship of the two collections. However, the distribution of *SH* I.4 on the one hand and *SH* I.7, 8, 9, and 10 on the other makes other explanations possible. *SH* I.4 is found in all three manuscripts (CUL Ii. 4. 6, Cotton Faustina A. IX, and CCCC 302) and seems to have enjoyed a wider circulation as well (Cambridge, Corpus Christi College, MS 303; Cambridge, Corpus Christi College, MS 198; London, British Library, Cotton MS Vitellius C. V; Oxford, Bodleian Library, MS Hatton 114; and London, British Library, Cotton MS Vespasian D. XIV). Pope remarks that there are no shared errors between the three manuscripts in this homily. The remaining four, on the other hand (*SH* I.7, 8, 9, and 10), seem to have been restricted to very few manuscripts: as a group they are only found in CUL Ii. 4. 6, Cotton Faustina A. IX and Cambridge, Trinity College, MS B. 15. 34; *SH* I.8 also appears in Oxford, Bodleian Library, MS Bodley 343 and London, British Library, Cotton MS Cleopatra B. XIII; *SH* I.9 is also found in Oxford, Bodleian Library, MS Junius 121. These homilies do not appear in CCCC 302, not even where they would have been expected (i.e. for the fourth and fifth Sundays after Easter), whilst in CUL Ii. 4. 6 and Cotton Faustina A. IX they show some shared errors that would point to a common source. It is possible, therefore, that the original compilation from which Cotton Faustina A. IX and CCCC 302 derived their material only had *SH* I.4, and that Cotton Faustina A. IX acquired the other homilies later, from a source close to the ancestor of CUL Ii. 4. 6.

[43] *CH* I, *Praefatio*, lines 27–30, pp. 173–74.

[44] The term 'Pentecost' originally designated the whole fifty-day period, and only later came to indicate the final day (Vogel, *Medieval Liturgy*, p. 311).

[45] This series is the nucleus that Clemoes, Godden, and Pope all agree must have been in the original collection, though Clemoes believed that the collection was much broader; see below.

Another aspect of Ælfric's work that challenges Ælfric's authorship of the collections is his consistent mixing of *temporale* and *sanctorale* items in the *Catholic Homilies* and *Lives of Saints*. The practice seems to indicate that the two types of items were not 'separated' in his mind, even though he always states in the rubric the liturgical destination of each piece.

It is possible, as Clemoes and Godden assert, that it was Ælfric who put the items together; it is equally possible in my opinion, however, that it was someone else, someone who felt the need to combine the items he had available in the sequence of the liturgical year, perhaps on the basis of a *temporale* capitulary or lectionary.[46] If so, the compiler would have been someone, as Pope puts it, 'close enough to the author to include everything that was available in its then latest form'.[47]

As already mentioned, according to Clemoes, the original range of the Ælfrician collection extended from Christmas to the octave of Pentecost. He considered the current beginning of CCCC 302 as only partially reflecting the beginning of the original collection, partly because Ælfric usually began the liturgical year with Christmas and not with Advent,[48] and partly because the homilies for the first and

---

[46] As in CCCC 162; see note 32 above. Capitularies are lists of the gospel pericopes to be read during Mass for the various feasts of the year, arranged in liturgical order. They only mark the beginning and the end of passages, and are generally appended to gospel books. Lectionaries give the whole pericopes, arranged according to the liturgical year. For liturgical books in Anglo-Saxon England in general, see Helmut Gneuss, 'Liturgical Books in Anglo-Saxon England and their Old English Terminology', in *Learning and Literature in Anglo-Saxon England: Studies Presented to Peter Clemoes on the Occasion of his Sixty-fifth Birthday*, ed. by Michael Lapidge and Helmut Gneuss (Cambridge, 1985), pp. 91–141, and *The Liturgical Books of Anglo-Saxon England*, ed. by Richard W. Pfaff, *OEN*, Subsidia, 23 (Kalamazoo, 1995). See also Lenker, *Die westsächsische Evangelienversion* and 'The West Saxon Gospels and the Gospel-Lectionary in Anglo-Saxon England: Manuscript Evidence and Liturgical Practice', *ASE*, 28 (1999), 141–78.

[47] *Homilies*, ed. by Pope, I, 48. It may also well be that Ælfric had really planned to compose a *temporale* at some point, but did not write enough homilies during his lifetime to complete it, or maybe he did so later, in what Clemoes called TH 2. Clemoes himself, however, observed that some of the gaps (either in terms of homilies in general or in 'pericope' homilies in particular) still remain in the extant Ælfrician canon (e.g. no homilies for the third and fourth Sundays in Advent; for the first Sunday after Epiphany and for any Sundays beyond the third; for the fourteenth, fifteenth, eighteenth, nineteenth, and twentieth Sundays after Pentecost, and any Sundays beyond the twenty-third; and no pericope homily for the first Sunday in Advent), although he was confident that the whole set existed in Ælfric's time, as noted above. See Clemoes, 'Chronology', pp. 22–23.

[48] Vogel points out that 'the liturgical year never did come to have an absolutely fixed beginning'. The starting date was 1 March in early Roman liturgical use, but it was pushed back

second Sundays in Advent (*CH* I.39 and 40) appeared to belong to a different phase (β) of Ælfric's reworking of that series. Moreover, he thought that the original collection probably contained various other items (e.g. *CH* II.2 for St Stephen, *CH* I.5 for Holy Innocents, *CH* I.6 for Circumcision, *CH* I.7 and *CH* II.3 for Epiphany, and all the homilies for Fridays in Lent: *SH* I.2, 3, 5, and 6) totalling around forty pieces which he laid down neatly in a table in his introduction to the edition of the First Series homilies.[49] Clemoes explained this supposed range of the collection (from Christmas to Pentecost) with the key role that the first Sunday after Pentecost had acquired in the Middle Ages as 'the climax of the liturgical celebrations which since Christmas had commemorated the chief events in Christ's life and the descent of the Holy Spirit'.[50] Pope, however, was more inclined to believe that the original collection, whoever its author might be, should be restricted only to homilies for Sundays from Septuagesima (*CH* II.5) to the octave of Pentecost (*SH* I.10), with the inclusion of Ascension as the only week day. His assumption was mainly based on the fact that this range — Sundays from Septuagesima to the octave of Pentecost — was the cluster that resulted from putting together all the items that the two branches (CUL Ii. 4. 6 on the one hand, and Cotton Faustina A. IX or CCCC 302 — or both — on the other) had in common, since he believed that the three manuscripts had a common ancestor at some point.[51] This resulting

---

to 25 December in the Old Gelasian Sacramentary, with Christmas shifting from the *sanctorale* to the *temporale*, as the opening day of the liturgical year, and further pushed back to the first Sunday in Advent, around the eighth or ninth century (*Medieval Liturgy*, pp. 311–12). Ælfric discusses the problem of the beginning of the year in *CH* I.6, lines 129–61, where he also mentions that some service-books begin with Advent: 'Sume ure þeningbec onginnað on aduentum domini' (lines 137–38, pp. 228–29). On the Old Gelasian Sacramentary (Vatican City, Biblioteca Apostolica Vaticana, Reg. 316) and related issues, see C. E. Hohler, 'Some Service-Books of the Later Saxon Church', in *Tenth-Century Studies: Essays in Commemoration of the Millennium of the Council of Winchester and Regularis Concordia*, ed. by David Parsons (London, 1975), pp. 60–83 and 217–27, and Yitzhak Hen, 'The Liturgy of St Willibrord', *ASE*, 26 (1997), 41–62.

[49] Clemoes, 'Chronology', pp. 18–19, and *First Series*, ed. by Clemoes, pp. 78–83.

[50] Clemoes, 'Chronology', p. 19.

[51] *Homilies*, ed. by Pope, I, 42–45. The homily for Ash Wednesday (*LS* I.12) and those for Monday and Wednesday in Easter week (*CH* II.16a and 16b) were apparently all read on the preceding Sundays; see Godden, *Introduction, Commentary, and Glossary*, pp. 500–01. Pope leaves out the dubious common items at the beginning of CUL Ii. 4. 6 and Cotton Faustina A. IX because of the way in which the former manuscript seemed to have been put together, with a central cluster of homilies to which other items had been added at the beginning and at the end. As noted by Ker, the collection in CUL Ii. 4. 6 was the work of two scribes, one copying items 4–18 (from Septuagesima to Palm Sunday) and the other copying items 1–3 (for Sundays after

cluster had the advantage of being liturgically homogeneous, in that all its festivals would depend on Easter:

> It is true that Ælfric himself began the year with Christmas in both series of the Catholic Homilies and the Lives of Saints; but he or anyone else would have found it convenient, in planning a Temporale for a portion of the year only, to limit it to festivals of which the date is governed by Easter. The Sundays in Advent and after Epiphany depend on Christmas; all the rest, except the Saints' days, on Easter.[52]

His conclusion was also corroborated, in his view, by the disagreement of the Rogationtide homilies in the three manuscripts.[53] If the original *temporale* in CUL Ii. 4. 6 and in the ancestor of Cotton Faustina A. IX and CCCC 302 was restricted to Sundays, as he believed, Rogationtide pieces would have been excluded (since they were intended for reading on the Monday, Tuesday, and Wednesday before Ascension), and their divergence in the three manuscripts would be easily explained as being the result of later independent additions. Clemoes, however, challenged this inference, claiming that it might equally be that Ælfric's items for Rogationtide were included in the set and the differences among the manuscripts arose during transmission.[54] An original cluster extending from Septuagesima to Pentecost, as postulated by Pope, would still not oppose the hypothesis that the two collections were made independently, since the compilers might have taken the homilies they needed — for the range they had planned — from the various

---

Epiphany) and 19–37 (from Easter onwards). Item 3 finishes on the ninth line, and the rest of the page is blank. Moreover, the following two leaves (the last two leaves of the quire) have been excised. This arrangement led Ker and Pope to believe that items 4–18 were copied first, and then the second scribe finished copying the original section (up to the octave of Pentecost), and later added a few homilies, which were not in the original collection, on a new quire at the beginning of the manuscript, as well as the two Rogation pieces at the end. The way the manuscript was put together would prove, according to Pope, that the first three items (i.e. the homilies for the second, third, and fourth Sundays after Epiphany), just like the last two (the two Rogationtide homilies), were not part of the original collection, which only included Sundays from Septuagesima to the octave of Pentecost. Clemoes, however, argued that the possibility of the two scribes dividing the workload in half, and copying the two parts at the same time, could not be ruled out. In that case, the blank page after item three could be explained by that scribe finishing the part assigned to him and then helping the other scribe finish the other section. See Ker, *Catalogue*, p. 35; *Homilies*, ed. by Pope, I, 40–41; and *First Series*, ed. by Clemoes, pp. 72–74.

[52] *Homilies*, ed. by Pope, I, 47. CCCC 162 also seems to contain an independent cluster beginning at Septuagesima. See Scragg, 'Cambridge, Corpus Christi College 162', pp. 75–76.

[53] See the items between *SH* I.8 and *CH* I.21 in Table 2.

[54] *Homilies*, ed. by Pope, I, 44–45; *First Series*, ed. by Clemoes, p. 75.

series by Ælfric, as explained above, to the same effect. It would be perhaps more difficult to believe that they had exactly the same range in mind, but it is not implausible, since they might have had the same liturgical needs; it is not even necessary, in fact, since the two sets are different, and might have been different straight from the beginning.

With what materials the original collection in the common ancestor of Cotton Faustina A. IX and CCCC 302 began is still a matter for debate: the former is defective at the beginning and the latter seems unreliable, as it does not constitute an exhaustive cluster for the Christmas cycle, nor even a basic one, since fundamental feasts like Epiphany are not represented.[55] Even the reconstruction of the section devoted to Sundays after Epiphany is problematic, because the two manuscripts disagree.[56] CCCC 302 has four homilies (Assmann II, Teresi, Assmann XIV, and Callison 1) assigned to the second through fifth Sundays, whilst Cotton Faustina A. IX has now six homilies (*CH* II.4 and *CH* I.8, followed by the same homilies found in CCCC 302), assigned to the second (though the rubric is missing) through seventh Sundays. If their ancestor was using anonymous homilies and other material available to fill the gaps left by Ælfric, it would be reasonable to expect them to have *CH* II.4 and *CH* I.8 for the second and third Sundays, and four additional items to cover the remaining Sundays (first, fourth, fifth, and sixth, as only six are required). It is not possible to determine whether Cotton Faustina A. IX had a homily for the first Sunday after Epiphany, because that part of the manuscript was lost; what is left of the collection, however, certainly shows this expected pattern, so perhaps Cotton Faustina A. IX is closer to its ancestor in this respect than is CCCC 302. The presence of a homily for an alleged seventh Sunday might seem puzzling at first, but a number of capitularies and lectionaries exist that include pericopes for up to ten Sundays after Epiphany.[57] More interestingly, as Lenker shows, some of these capitularies and lectionaries provide for exactly seven Sundays after Epiphany, as with Cotton Faustina A. IX,[58] and some for five

---

[55] Its apparently incongruous mixing of *temporale* and *sanctorale* items was, in fact, a standard practice for the Christmas season, as can be seen, for example, from capitularies that distinguished between the two cycles. See Lenker, *Die westsächsische Evangelienversion*, p. 69.

[56] Whatever evidence might be drawn from a comparison of CUL Ii. 4. 6 and Cotton Faustina A. IX is inconclusive, in my opinion, since, as I have shown, the two collections might be totally independent.

[57] See Lenker, *Die westsächsische Evangelienversion*, pp. 167–68, 301–06, and 506.

[58] Cambridge, Trinity College, MS B. 10. 4 (s. xi^{1/4}, Canterbury, Christ Church? or Peterborough?); London, British Library, Royal MS 1. D. IX (s. xi^{in}, Canterbury, Christ Church or

Sundays, as with CCCC 302.[59] The capitulary in London, British Library, Cotton MS Tiberius A. II is particularly noteworthy in this regard because it separates *temporale* and *sanctorale* items in two distinct groups. The manuscript was written on the Continent (possibly at Lobbes) and given to King Æthelstan by Otto I in the first half of the tenth century. Æthelstan eventually donated it to Christ Church, Canterbury, and it was still there in the eleventh and twelfth centuries.[60] It might have therefore influenced other books that were produced in Canterbury, both in terms of capitularies/lectionaries and homiliaries.

The exact number of items for Sundays after Epiphany that were in CCCC 302 and Cotton Faustina A. IX's common ancestor cannot be determined with certainty. It is possible that CCCC 302 removed some items, or that Cotton Faustina A. IX added some. The absence in CCCC 302 of the Ælfrician homilies for these feasts is, however, puzzling. If they were removed, why remove Ælfrician items rather than anonymous homilies, since the compilation shows that the latter were only meant to fill gaps? And if the scribe decided to remove some items from the section, why remove the first two rather than the last two? Or, if the two Ælfrician items were never there, why was it so? Even if these questions cannot be answered, either way it seems that the compilers in some cases considered anonymous items 'equal' to or even 'better' than Ælfrician homilies[61] — unless we assume that Ælfric's items were accidentally lost at some point in CCCC 302's transmission and were no longer available, and that the number of homilies for Sundays after

Peterborough?, prov. s. xi (prob. by 1018) Canterbury, Christ Church), London, British Library, Loan MS 11 (*c.* 1020, Canterbury, Christ Church or Peterborough?, prov. Windsor, St George's Chapel); London, British Library, Harley MS 76 (s. xi[1], prob. Canterbury, Christ Church, prov. s. xi[ex] Bury St Edmunds); Cambridge, St John's College, MS 73 (s. xi/xii, Bury St Edmunds); Hanover, Kestner-Museum, MS WM XXIa. 36 (*c.* 1020, Canterbury, Christ Church, prov. Germany by s. xi, prov. Lüneburg, Abbey of St Michael), all deriving from a common ancestor (Lenker, 'The West Saxon Gospels and the Gospel-Lectionary', p. 166, n. 114). Dates, origin, and provenance are taken from Gneuss, *Handlist*, nos 172, 447, 501, 413, 149, and 831.

[59] London, British Library, Cotton MS Tiberius A. II (s. ix/x or x[in], Lobbes, prov. England (royal court) before 939, prov. Canterbury, Christ Church s. x[1]); Florence, Biblioteca Medicea Laurenziana, Plut. xvii. 20 (s. xi[2/4], Canterbury, Christ Church?, prov. Continent s. xi); and Warsaw, Biblioteka Narodowa, i. 3311 (s. x/xi) (Gneuss, *Handlist*, nos 362, 827, and 942).

[60] See Simon Keynes, 'King Athelstan's Books', in *Learning and Literature in Anglo-Saxon England*, ed. by Lapidge and Gneuss, pp. 143–201 (pp. 147–53).

[61] For a similar example, see Bodley 340 + 342, where an anonymous homily for Christmas (Scragg 5) has replaced Ælfric's Christmas items from his two series of *Catholic Homilies*. See Scragg, 'Corpus of Vernacular Homilies', p. 238.

Epiphany was consequently reduced and their order rearranged to its present state. The supplementation of Ælfrician Rogationtide pieces with anonymous items in the manuscript, however (Bazire and Cross 5 and Scragg 10; see Table 1), would seem to confirm that both may have been viewed with equal favour.

Whoever made the collection in the ancestor of CCCC 302 and Cotton Faustina A. IX, and whatever its original nature, what can be reconstructed from a comparison of the two manuscripts shows that although the collection was certainly built around Ælfric's work, it diverges from Ælfric's dictates and views in various respects. First of all, it does not comply with Ælfric's directive that no homilies should be delivered on *swigdagas* ('silent days'), that is, Maundy Thursday, Good Friday, and Holy Saturday in Passion week,[62] since both manuscripts contain an anonymous homily for Thursday (Assmann XIII). This feature is not highly surprising, since, as Hill observes, 'Ælfric's position appears not to have been symptomatic of a widespread practice within the secular church, nor did he establish a trend even amongst those who knew and respected his work';[63] even Wulfstan, for instance, composed a homily for Maundy Thursday (Bethurum XV). Hill and Wilcox mention, even more poignantly, the marginal note in Cambridge, Corpus Christi College, MS 178, p. 229, in which a certain Coleman has insolently commented on Ælfric's proscription: 'Ac þis ne þynceð no us well gesæd' ('But this does not seem to us well said'), a line akin to that appearing in Oxford, Bodleian Library, MS Hatton 114, fol. 86ʳ: 'Ðis nis no well gesæd' ('This is not well said').[64] Secondly, the two manuscripts mix Ælfric's homilies with anonymous material and with apocryphal matter, which he considered unacceptable and would not have wanted to be found side by side with his works. Furthermore, some of his homilies show corruptions and additions,[65] which he explicitly forbids in the well-known final passage in his Old English preface to the First Series of *Catholic Homilies*.[66]

---

[62] 'Ne mot nan man secgan spell. on þam ðrim swigdagum', *CH* II.14, line 357 ('No one may deliver a homily on the three silent days').

[63] Joyce Hill, 'Ælfric's "Silent Days"', in *Sources and Relations: Studies in Honour of J. E. Cross*, ed. by Marie Collins, Jocelyn Price, and Andrew Hamer, special issue, *Leeds Studies in English*, n.s., 16 (1985), 118–131 (p. 123).

[64] Hill, 'Ælfric's "Silent Days"', p. 121; Jonathan Wilcox, 'Transmission of Literature and Learning: Anglo-Saxon Scribal Culture', in *A Companion to Anglo-Saxon Literature*, ed. by Phillip Pulsiano and Elaine Treharne (Oxford, 2001), pp. 50–69 (p. 65); and N. R. Ker, 'Old English Notes Signed "Coleman"', *Medium Ævum*, 18 (1949), 29–31.

[65] See *First Series*, ed. by Clemoes, p. 69.

[66] *CH* I, *Praefatio*, lines 128–34 (p. 177).

CCCC 302 shows further features that deviate from Ælfric's views. For example, it repeats material. Two homilies in the collection — items 12 (Callison 1)[67] and 33 (Scragg 10) — are extremely close, the former being just a 'cropped' version of the latter, reproducing, with very little change, the part of Scragg 10 which is concerned with the transience of life and of earthly riches, from the reference to St James onwards.[68] This repetition of material goes against Ælfric's inclinations, as can be seen from his note to *CH* I.12 in London, British Library, Royal MS 7. C. XII, fol. 64ʳ. Here, a passage of twenty-six lines in *CH* I.12 is marked for deletion with the author's explanation that the passage had been expanded in a homily in the Second Series and that it should therefore be removed from this homily, in order not to bore the listener.[69] In addition to such repetition, CCCC 302 leaves out his homilies for the second and third Sundays after Epiphany, replacing them with others from different sources. Finally, it begins its liturgical cycle with Advent, in a way that goes against Ælfric's views, as they can be inferred both from his practice (with the two series of *Catholic Homilies* beginning at Christmas) and from his discussion of the issue in *CH* I.6, mentioned above.

Ælfric's influence is still remarkable, as can be inferred from the fact that even at such late date, the bulk of the collection is mainly Ælfrician; this influence, however, appears to coexist with other attitudes, convictions, and practices. As Wilcox notes, 'Ælfric's sense of his work as an authorized and fixed text was not compatible with the practice of early medieval vernacular textual transmission'.[70] Furthermore, the dissemination of his *Catholic Homilies*, as Godden observes, 'from the very first took a form which showed little respect for Ælfric's wishes, breaking up his two series and mixing their contents with other homilies not by him and not approved of by him'.[71] The extant collections in CCCC 302 and Cotton Faustina A. IX, although mainly centred on Ælfric's work, are among the witnesses of this

---

[67] This homily also appears in Cotton Faustina A. IX, as item 6.

[68] This homily survives in nine different versions. For further details, see *Vercelli Homilies*, ed. by Scragg, pp. 191–95, and Jonathan Wilcox, 'Variant Texts of an Old English Homily: Vercelli X and Stylistic Readers', in *The Preservation and Transmission of Anglo-Saxon Culture*, ed. by Paul E. Szarmach and Joel T. Rosenthal, Studies in Medieval Culture, 40 (Kalamazoo, 1997), pp. 335–51. At least one of the scribes in the transmission was aware of this repetition, since some readings in the second text seem influenced by the first.

[69] See Sisam, 'MSS. Bodley 340 and 342', pp. 173–74.

[70] Wilcox, 'Transmission of Literature and Learning', p. 63.

[71] *Second Series*, ed. by Godden, p. lxii.

state of affairs, in various respects, and call for further study to unveil the secrets that their compilations still hold.

Summing up, although the *temporale* collection in CUL Ii. 4. 6 and that from which CCCC 302 and Cotton Faustina A. IX derive are very similar, they are not necessarily related. It is possible that Ælfric was responsible for both collections (or for one of them), but it is far more likely that the two collections were made independently by other churchmen. The manuscripts that contain the collections are a long way from Ælfric, and might well be the work of others, possibly based in Canterbury, where there seems to have been a tradition of arranging homilies in liturgical cycles.[72] The evidence we have is far from conclusive, and current theories on the development, chronology, and dissemination of the *CH* manuscripts need to be reconsidered and re-examined. Further study is needed — especially in the relationship between all the collections we have, the liturgical practices of the various late Anglo-Saxon religious centres, and the liturgical books that have survived — in order to throw light on the genesis and development of the homiletic collections of the late Anglo-Saxon period.[73]

---

[72] It is possible, however, that it was a widespread practice and that evidence from other centres has not survived. See note 32 above.

[73] I wish to thank Patrizia Lendinara, Don Scragg, Jon Wilcox, and Gabriella Mazzon for their valuable help and support during the preparation of this essay, and Aaron Kleist for his immeasurable patience as editor.

WULFSTAN AS READER, WRITER, AND REWRITER

Andy Orchard

By the time he died, on 28 May 1023, Archbishop Wulfstan II of York had been a powerful political figure for decades, a national spokesman and commentator who had managed to survive and even thrive as a member of the *witan* ('counsellors') during the turbulent transition between the reigns of the Anglo-Saxon Æthelred II (who ruled 978–1013 and again 1014–16) and his Danish conqueror Cnut (who ruled 1016–35), for both of whom Wulfstan wrote laws.[1] It is apt testament to the troubled times in which he lived that among the many alliterative doublets with which he peppers his prose, the phrase *bryne and blodgite* ('burning and bloodletting'), which is found no fewer than nine times in extant Old English, should appear only in works that for one reason or another have been associated with Wulfstan.[2]

We know little of Wulfstan's life: he is a mystery until he begins to attest charters as Bishop of London (996–1002/03) with the distinctive cognomen *Lupus* ('Wolf') and becomes successively Bishop of Worcester and (at first in controversial plurality) Archbishop of York.[3] The always interesting but often unreliable

---

[1] Wulfstan is generally agreed to have had a hand in the formulation of the lawcodes V–X Æthelred, I–II Cnut, and the 1018 edict of Cnut (see A. G. Kennedy, 'Cnut's Law Code of 1018', *ASE*, 11, (1983), 72–81); other codes associated with his name include *Edward and Guthrum, Grið, Að, Gepyncðo, Hadbot, Mircena laga, Norðleoda laga, Episcopus, Rectitudines, Gerefa*, and *Norðymbra preosta lagu*.

[2] The phrase appears, with variants, at Bethurum V.103, XX(BH).51, XX(C).64, and XX(EI).56; Napier XXVII.129/2, XXXV.170/1, XXXVI.172/18, XLVII.243/2, and L.268/21. For the attribution of these latter texts to Wulfstan, see below, p. 318 and the reference given in note 26 on p. 319.

[3] For succinct accounts of Wulfstan's life and career, see *The Homilies of Wulfstan*, ed. by Dorothy Bethurum (Oxford, 1957), pp. 54–68; Dorothy Bethurum, 'Wulfstan', in *Continuations*

Liber Eliensis ('Book of Ely') speaks of a brother, Brihthelm, who succeeded him as bishop, as well as other family members,[4] and it is therefore fitting that today Wulfstan's remains lie buried in Ely Cathedral alongside those of another loyal but rather less lucky servant of Æthelred, Ealdorman Byrhtnoth of Essex, who fought and died in 991 at the watershed Battle of Maldon, commemorated in the splendid Old English poem of the same name.[5] Both men can be said to symbolize the range of choices available to Anglo-Saxons (or at least to prominent and politically active ones) in the wave of the successive Viking raids and incursions that culminated in the reign of Cnut, namely acceptance (and accommodation) or resistance (and annihilation).

Byrhtnoth, an old warhorse ready for one last charge, chose option (b): a doomed resistance that if it was memorable and magnificent was still rash and reckless. According to two versions of the *Anglo-Saxon Chronicle*, it was the defeat at Maldon that led directly to Æthelred's disastrous policy of paying off the raiders, a piece of evil counsel (*unræd*) that Wulfstan (a later counsellor of the same badly counselled king) was still deploring decades later, in three of the five manuscripts

---

and Beginnings, ed. E. G. Stanley (London, 1966), pp. 210–46; and *Sermo Lupi ad Anglos*, ed. by Dorothy Whitelock (London, 1939; 3rd edn London, 1963), pp. 7–17. Particularly valuable in this respect are a series of studies by Dorothy Whitelock, including 'Wulfstan and the So-called Laws of Edward and Guthrum', *English Historical Review*, 56 (1941), 1–21; 'Archbishop Wulfstan, Homilist and Statesman', *Transactions of the Royal Historical Society*, 4th series, 24 (1942), 25–45; 'Wulfstan and the Laws of Cnut', *English Historical Review*, 63 (1948), 433–52; 'Wulfstan's Authorship of Cnut's Laws', *English Historical Review*, 70 (1955), 72–85; and 'Wulfstan at York', in *Franciplegius: Medieval and Linguistic Studies in Honor of Francis Peabody Magoun*, ed. by Jess B. Bessinger, Jr, and Robert P. Creed (New York, 1965), pp. 214–31. An invaluable collection of important essays is *Wulfstan, Archbishop of York: Proceedings of the Second Alcuin Conference*, ed. by Matthew Townend, Studies in the Early Middle Ages, 10 (Turnhout, 2004). For a useful account of the early charters witnessed by Wulfstan, as well as for some provocative suggestions concerning his attitudes towards the infamous St Brice's Day Massacre of Danes in England on 13 November 1002, see Jonathan Wilcox, 'The St. Brice's Day Massacre and Archbishop Wulfstan', in *Peace and Negotiation: Strategies for Coexistence in the Middle Ages and the Renaissance*, ed. by Diane Wolfthal, Arizona Studies in the Middle Ages and the Renaissance, 4 (Turnhout, 2000), pp. 79–91.

[4] See further Janet Fairweather, *Liber Eliensis: A History of the Isle of Ely from the Seventh Century to the Twelfth* (Woodbridge, 2005); and *Homilies*, ed. by Bethurum, pp. 55–56.

[5] See in general *The Battle of Maldon AD 991*, ed. by Donald G. Scragg (Oxford, 1991); Scragg's own edition and translation of the poem appears on pp. 15–36. See too John Crook, '"Vir optimus Wlstanus": The Post-Conquest Commemoration of Archbishop Wulfstan of York at Ely Cathedral', in *Wulfstan, Archbishop of York*, ed. by Townend, pp. 501–24.

and in two of the three versions of the mighty *SERMO LUPI AD ANGLOS QUANDO DANI MAXIME PERSECUTI SUNT EOS* ('SERMON OF "WOLF" TO THE ENGLISH WHEN THE DANES WERE AFFLICTING THEM MOST GREATLY'),[6] on which his modern reputation has largely come to rest.[7] One notes the anglicized word-order in this rubric, where Latin would prefer 'eos persecuti sunt', as well as the fact that the precise date of the *Sermo Lupi ad Anglos* is still in dispute: the traditional 1014 date favoured by almost all modern commentators is based on that found in just one manuscript, London, British Library, Cotton MS Nero A. I (Bethurum XX(EI), version I), which contains annotations in Wulfstan's own hand,[8] and continues the rubric given above with the words *QUOD FUIT ANNO MILLESIMO .XIIII. AB INCARNATIONE DOMINI NOSTRI IESU CRISTI* ('WHICH OCCURRED IN THE YEAR 1014 FROM THE INCARNATION OF OUR LORD JESUS CHRIST').[9] It is, however, worth pointing out that this date is clearly written over an erasure in the Cotton manuscript, and it has been argued that the date given in the C-version of the *Sermo Lupi* (based on Cambridge, Corpus Christi College, MS 201), namely 1009, more accurately reflects the time when the English were most greatly

---

[6] Cf. Bethurum XX(C).123 and XX(EI).125–6: 'We him gildað singallice, 7 hi us hynað dæghwamlice' ('we pay them continually, and they humiliate us daily').

[7] The standard edition, containing in many cases the definitive discussion, remains that of Whitelock, *Sermo Lupi*. See too, for example, Stephanie Dien, '*Sermo Lupi ad Anglos*: The Order and Date of the Three Versions', *NM*, 76 (1975), 561–70; Stephanie Hollis (*née* Dien), 'The Thematic Structure of the *Sermo Lupi*', *ASE*, 6 (1977), 175–95; Raachel Jurovics, '*Sermo Lupi* and the Moral Purpose of Rhetoric', in *The Old English Homily and its Backgrounds*, ed. by Paul E. Szarmach and Bernard F. Huppé (Albany, 1978), pp. 203–20; Michael Cummings, 'Paired Opposites in Wulfstan's *Sermo Lupi ad Anglos*', *Revue de l'Université d'Ottawa*, 50 (1980), 233–43; J. E. Cross, 'Literary Impetus for Wulfstan's *Sermo Lupi*', *Leeds Studies in English*, n.s., 20 (1989), 271–91; and Alice Cowan, '*Byrstas* and *bysmeras*: The Wounds of Sin in the *Sermo Lupi ad Anglos*', in *Wulfstan, Archbishop of York*, ed. by Townend, pp. 397–411. See too Melissa Bernstein, 'The Electronic Sermo Lupi ad Anglos' <http://english3.fsu.edu/~wulfstan/>.

[8] See note 20 below.

[9] For an attempt to identify the date of first performance still more closely to 16 February 1014, see Jonathan Wilcox, 'Wulfstan's *Sermo Lupi ad Anglos* as Political Performance: 16 February 1014 and Beyond', in *Wulfstan, Archbishop of York*, ed. by Townend, pp. 375–96, as well as his earlier 'The Wolf on Shepherds: Wulfstan, Bishops, and the Context of the *Sermo Lupi ad Anglos*', in *Old English Prose: Basic Readings*, ed. by Paul E. Szarmach, Basic Readings in Anglo-Saxon England, 5 (New York, 2000), pp. 395–418.

afflicted.[10] The problems of assessing the multiple manuscripts and versions of uncertain date that characterize Wulfstan's most famous work are both magnified and multiplied when attempting to ascertain the chronology and authorship of other works attributed to Wulfstan's hand, and are emblematic of the complex difficulties of attempting to capture a character who clearly dominated his age.

At all events, and evidently punning on the second element of Æthelred's name, the A-version of the *Anglo-Saxon Chronicle* for 991, after giving a brief account of the circumstances surrounding the Battle of Maldon and the death of Byrhtnoth, describes the ruinous plan to pay off the Vikings as follows (emphasis added): 'þæne *ræd* ger*æd*de ærest Syric arcebisceop' ('The first to counsel that counsel was Archbishop Sigeric').[11] By contrast, Wulfstan (to whom two poems in various versions of the *Anglo-Saxon Chronicle* have been uncertainly attributed)[12] has only a single usage of the word *unræd* ('evil counsel') in all his preaching works, fittingly enough in a brief passage which he puts in the mouth of the prophet Jeremiah, but which can perhaps be read as Wulfstan's way of aligning himself with Jeremiah, and saying 'I told you so' (Bethurum XI.206–09):[13]

---

[10] See now Simon Keynes, 'An Abbot, an Archbishop, and the Viking Raids of 1006–7 and 1009–12', *Anglo-Saxon England*, 36 (forthcoming).

[11] *The Anglo-Saxon Chronicle: A Collaborative Edition*, vol. V: *MS. C*, ed. by Katherine O'Brien O'Keeffe (Cambridge, 2001), p. 86.

[12] The poems in question are s.a. 959 (DE versions) and 975 (D version) respectively; see further, Karl Jost, 'Wulfstan und Die Angelsächsische Chronik', *Anglia*, 47 (1923), 105–23. It is also worth pointing out that in two of the three versions of his *Sermo Lupi* Wulfstan makes use of the compound *wæpengewrixl* ('weapon-exchange'; Bethurum XX(C).100 and XX(EI).103) that otherwise only appears in the *Chronicle*-poem on *The Battle of Brunanburh* (s.a. 937; line 51). See further Richard Dance, 'Sound, Fury, and Signifiers; or Wulfstan's Language', in *Wulfstan, Archbishop of York*, ed. by Townend, pp. 29–61 (p. 60).

[13] Here and throughout I give references to *Homilies*, ed. by Bethurum, but have recast the text according to punctuation and lineation of the manuscripts, the better to give a sense of the formal structures of Wulfstan's prose. Here I follow Cambridge, Corpus Christi College, MS 201, p. 64, lines 35–39 (cf. Oxford, Bodleian Library, MS Hatton 113, fol. 26ᵛ, lines 1–7). All translations are my own, except those from the Vulgate, which follow the Douai-Rheims version. For further discussion of the principles involved, see Andy Orchard, 'On Editing Wulfstan', in *Early Medieval English Texts and Interpretations: Studies Presented to Donald G. Scragg*, ed. by Elaine Treharne and Susan Rosser, MRTS, 252 (Tempe, 2003), pp. 311–40; and 'Re-Editing Wulfstan'. Criticisms of Bethurum's editorial approach and often inaccurate reporting of manuscripts can be found in Christine Franzen, *The Tremulous Hand of Worcester: A Study of Old English in the Thirteenth Century* (Oxford, 1991), pp. 32–33; Ian McDougall, 'Some Remarks on Dorothy Bethurum's Treatment of Glosses in MS. Bodleian Hatton 113', *ANQ*, 8 (1995), 3–4; and

1   Hwæt onfundon eowre yldran ·
2   þurh ænig ðyngc on me ·
3   þæs þe heom þuhte ·
4   þæt ful riht nære ·

5   nu hi swa swiðe awændan hi fram me ·
6   7 ferdan on unriht ·
7   7 unræde filigdon ·
8   7 unriht lufedon ·
9   7 unnytte wurdon ·
10 nu lange him sylfum ·

[Did your elders find out about anything from me that seemed to them not wholly correct? Now they have so greatly turned from me, and passed into injustice, and followed evil counsel, and loved injustice, and become themselves useless now for a long time.]

Strong stuff, and doubtless what many may have thought about the disastrous end of Æthelred's reign. In fact, this passage represents a considerable expansion of the words of Jeremiah 2. 5 ('Haec dicit Dominus quid inuenerunt patres uestri in me iniquitatis'; 'Thus saith the Lord: What iniquity have your fathers found in me?'), with the omission of the direct attribution of these words to God, and the piquant proviso that the Old English term *yldran* means not simply 'elders' or 'ancestors' (compare Latin *patres*, 'fathers'), but also 'superiors': taken in his own voice, Wulfstan's words could be construed as a mark of frustration with the ruling elite that he had joined.

Wulfstan's additions to Jeremiah (essentially, lines **5–10** above) are clearly and characteristically signalled both in style and structure: an envelope-pattern of phrases beginning with *nu* ('now', **5** and **10**) marks off a series of four clauses containing four finite verbs (*ferdan* [. . .] *filigdon* [. . .] *lufedon* [. . .] *wurdon*) and four negative compounds (*unriht* [. . .] *unræde* [. . .] *unriht* [. . .] *unnytte*) that gradually bring the problem home to the guilty 'themselves' (*him sylfum*, **10**). Such negative compounds in *un-* are indeed a characteristic feature of Wulfstan's writing,[14] and Wulfstan adopts here the words of a fiery Old Testament preacher,

Jonathan Wilcox, 'Napier's "Wulfstan" Homilies XL and XLII: Two Anonymous Works from Winchester?', *JEGP*, 90 (1991), 1–19 (p. 8, n. 31).

[14] See Mabel Falberg Dobyns, 'Wulfstan's Vocabulary: A Glossary of the Homilies with Commentary' (unpublished doctoral dissertation, University of Illinois at Urbana-Champaign, 1973), p. 6, speaking of noun-compounds: 'One group of more than 30 different nouns have the prefix *un-*, with one form, *unriht*, being mentioned 42 times. In this group not only did *un-* indicate antithesis — *unhæl* ("sickness, infirmity, disease"), *unclænnes* ("impurity"), *ungod* ("evil"), and intensification — *unwrenc* ("wicked trick, evil design"), *unweod* ("ill weed"), *ungyld* ("excessive tax"),

but adapts them to make them his own. Such dramatic recasting of biblical prose, let alone that of other authors (including himself), can be said to be the hallmark of Wulfstan's distinctive prose style, one that caused Wulfstan's works to be both widely heard and broadly read not only in his own time but also into the twelfth century. If after Wulfstan's death it is the writings of his contemporary and chief vernacular source Ælfric that came to eclipse those of his ecclesiastical superior, no one can doubt the immediate and electrifying (and at times terrifying and stulti-fying) impact of what Wulfstan wrote and spoke on his contemporary audience.

Modern readers, or more particularly modern editors, distinguish between (for example) sermons, homilies, political speeches, poems, pastoral letters, charters, laws, and works of socio-political analysis, but it is far from clear that Wulfstan (who apparently wrote all of the above, as well as a body of Latin writings that are increasingly being identified)[15] did so, at least in literary terms.[16] It is demonstrable that the same characteristic phrasing appears throughout, though even here there are pitfalls: as a powerful and evidently widely respected figure, Wulfstan's works were often imitated by contemporary and later writers, in ways often difficult to distinguish from his own revisions.[17] Even after his death, for a hundred years or

but also pejorative force — *uncræft* ("decit, evil practice, guile"), *unlagu* ("injustice, evil law, viola-tion of law"), *unlar* ("evil teaching, false doctrine"), *unweder* ("bad weather, bad season").'

[15] Thomas N. Hall, 'Wulfstan's Latin Sermons', in *Wulfstan, Archbishop of York*, ed. by Townend, pp. 93–139.

[16] The number, range, and quality of editions containing works related wholly or partly to Wulfstan is great; the basic editions include *Wulfstan: Sammlung der ihm zugeschriebenen Homilien nebst Untersuchungen über ihre Echtheit*, vol. I: *Text und Varianten*, ed. by Arthur S. Napier (Berlin, 1883; repr. with a bibliographical appendix by Klaus Ostheeren, Dublin, 1967); *Die Gesetze der Angelsachsen*, ed. by Felix Liebermann, 3 vols (Halle, 1903–16; repr. Aalen, 1960); *Homilies* ed. by Bethurum; 'A Late Old English Handbook for the Use of a Confessor', ed. by Roger Fowler, *Anglia*, 83 (1965), 1–34; *Wulfstan's Canons of Edgar*, ed. by Roger Fowler, EETS: OS, 266 (Oxford, 1972); *Die 'Institutes of Polity, Civil and Ecclesiastical'*, ed. by Karl Jost, Swiss Studies in English, 47 (Bern, 1959); *The Benedictine Office*, ed. by James Ure (Edinburgh, 1957). In addition, the interested reader has to consult numerous articles arguing for the authenticity or otherwise of specific texts, including in particular the following: Whitelock, 'Wulfstan and the So-called Laws of Edward and Guthrum'; Whitelock, 'Archbishop Wulfstan, Homilist and Statesman'; Dorothy Bethurum, 'Archbishop Wulfstan's Commonplace Book', *PMLA*, 57 (1942), 916–29; Whitelock, 'Wulfstan and the Laws of Cnut'; Angus McIntosh, 'Wulfstan's Prose', *Publications of the British Academy*, 35 (1949), 109–42; Karl Jost, *Wulfstanstudien*, Swiss Studies in English, 23 (Bern, 1950); Whitelock, 'Wulfstan's Authorship of Cnut's Laws'; *Homilies*, ed. by Bethurum; and Whitelock, 'Wulfstan at York'.

[17] See, for example, Wilcox, 'Napier's "Wulfstan" Homilies XL and XLII'; Jonathan Wilcox, 'The Dissemination of Wulfstan's Homilies: The Wulfstan Tradition in Eleventh-Century

so, Wulfstan continued to be copied verbatim and imitated and 'improved', with varying success.[18] He also left his mark in other ways, in manuscripts now identified as having been compiled at his behest, and comprising what is often misleadingly called his 'Commonplace Book' ('Handbook' would be a better term),[19] and in contemporary manuscripts associated with Worcester and York where his own handwriting has been identified writing, rewriting, correcting, and 'improving' a wide range of existing texts, including his own.[20]

Vernacular Preaching', in *England in the Eleventh Century*, ed. by Carola Hicks, Harlaxton Medieval Studies, 2 (Stamford, 1992), pp. 199–217; Donald Scragg, *Dating and Style in Old English Composite Homilies*, H. M. Chadwick Memorial Lectures, 9 (Cambridge, 1998); and Jonathan Wilcox, 'Wulfstan and the Twelfth Century', in *Rewriting Old English in the Twelfth Century*, ed. by Mary Swan and Elaine M. Treharne, CSASE, 30 (Cambridge, 2000), pp. 83–97.

[18] See, for example, J. E. Cross, 'Wulfstan's *De Anticristo* in a Twelfth-Century Worcester Manuscript', *ASE*, 20 (1991), 203–20; Stephen Morrison, 'A Reminiscence of Wulfstan in the Twelfth Century', *NM*, 96 (1995), 229–34; and Wilcox, 'Wulfstan and the Twelfth Century'.

[19] Bethurum, 'Archbishop Wulfstan's Commonplace Book'; Hans Sauer, 'Zur Überlieferung und Anlage von Erzbischof Wulfstans "Handbuch"', *Deutsches Archiv für Erforschung des Mittelalters*, 36 (1980), 341–84; translated into English as 'The Transmission and Structure of Archbishop Wulfstan's "Commonplace Book"', in *Old English Prose: Basic Readings*, ed. by Paul E. Szarmach, Basic Readings in Anglo-Saxon England, 5 (New York, 2000), pp. 339–93. See too Joyce Hill, 'Archbishop Wulfstan: Reformer?', in *Wulfstan, Archbishop of York*, ed. by Townend, pp. 309–24 (pp. 320–24); and J. E. Cross, 'Atto of Vercelli, *De pressuris ecclesiasticis*, Archbishop Wulfstan, and Wulfstan's "Commonplace Book"', *Traditio*, 48 (1993), 237–46.

[20] Neil Ker, 'The Handwriting of Archbishop Wulfstan', in *England Before the Conquest: Studies in Primary Sources Presented to Dorothy Whitelock*, ed. by Peter Clemoes and Kathleen Hughes (Cambridge, 1971), pp. 315–31; the manuscripts in question are Cambridge, Corpus Christi College, MS 190, pt 1 (s. xi¹), pp. iii–xii and 1–294; Copenhagen, Kongelige Bibliotek, Gl. Kgl. Sam. MS 1595 4⁰ (s. xi¹), fols 48ʳ, 65ᵛ–66ᵛ, and 81ʳ; London, British Library, Additional MS 38651 (s. xiⁱⁿ), fols 57–58; London, British Library, Cotton MS Claudius A. III (s. x/xi¹), fols 31–86 and 106–50; London, British Library, Cotton MS Nero A. I (Worcester or York, s. xiⁱⁿ), fols 70–177; London, British Library, Cotton MS Tiberius A. XIII (Worcester, s. xi¹–xiᵉˣ), fols 1–118; London, British Library, Cotton MS Vespasian A. XIV (Worcester or York, s. xi¹), fols 114–79; London, British Library, Harley MS 55 (s. xi¹), fols 1–4; Oxford, Bodleian Library, MS Hatton 20 (S.C. 4113) (890–97); Oxford, Bodleian Library, MS Hatton 402 (S.C. 4117) (Brittany, s. ix²; France, s. x); Rouen, Bibliothèque municipale, MS 1382 (U109), fols 173ʳ–198ᵛ; and York, Minster Library, MS Add. 1 (s. xi¹–s. xi²). Facsimiles of a number of annotations in Wulfstan's hand are found in *A Wulfstan Manuscript Containing Institutes, Laws and Homilies (British Museum Cotton Nero A.I)*, ed. by H. R. Loyn, EEMF, 17 (Copenhagen, 1971), both on the folios mentioned and as an Appendix. See too *Wulfstan Texts and Other Homiletic Materials*, ed. by Jonathan Wilcox, ASMMF, 8 (Tempe, 2000), and *Worcester Manuscripts*, ed. by Christine Franzen, ASMMF, 6 (Tempe, 1998).

The first serious attempt to attribute a distinct canon of surviving works to Wulfstan is now more than three centuries old, when in 1705 the great Humfrey Wanley identified the Latin nom de plume *Lupus* ('wolf') found in Cambridge, Corpus Christi College, MS 201 with that of Wulfstan, and attributed as many as fifty-three sermons to his hand.[21] Despite undoubted advances in understanding of Wulfstan as an author since then, resulting in an initial reluctance to accept all of Wanley's attributions as genuine,[22] it is chastening to note that successive trends and developments in scholarship have seen a slow drift back to Wanley's position, with a comparatively small number of additions; the case of Wulfstan offers a stark warning to modern scholarship of the dangers of ignoring past work. Modern Wulfstan-scholarship rests on the monumental edition of Arthur S. Napier, the first volume of which isolates no fewer than sixty-two separate texts which the editor believed might plausibly have some connection with Wulfstan;[23] alas, the second volume, in which he was to have determined precisely which of the texts he considered authentic, was never published, and it was left to Karl Jost (in an analytical monograph) and to Dorothy Bethurum and Dorothy Whitelock (in successive editions) to spell out criteria for inclusion in what was swiftly recognized was only a part of Wulfstan's burgeoning canon.[24]

Bethurum's edition is particularly unfortunate in this respect, since she prints only those works previously edited by Napier which she considered 'homiletic' (a term which perhaps wisely she does not closely define), even though she accepts that Wulfstan was the author of Napier XXIII, XXIV, XXV, XXXV, XXXVI, XXXIX, L, LI, LII, LIII, LIX, LX, and LXI, as well as the opening of Napier XLVII (242.23–243.21); the result is that these texts have languished in limbo

---

[21] George Hickes, *Linguarum ueterum septentrionalium thesaurus grammatico-criticus et archaeologicus*, 3 vols: I.1: *Institutiones Grammaticae Anglo-Saxonicae et Moeso-Gothicae*; I.2: *Institutiones Grammaticae Franco-Theotiscae*; II.1: *Grammaticae Islandicae Rudimenta*; II.2: *De antiquae Litteraturae Septentrionalis Utilitate; siue de Linguarum ueterum Septentrionalium usu Dissertatio, Epistolaris ad Bartholomæum Showere*; III: *Antiquae Literaturae Septentrionalis Liber Alter: seu Humphredi Wanleii Librorum ueterum Septentrionalium* [. . .] *Catalogus* (Oxford, 1703–05), III, 140–43.

[22] In his ground-breaking dissertation, *Über die Werke des altenglischen Erzbischofs Wulfstan* (Weimar, 1882), Arthur S. Napier pronounced as genuine only what are now known as Bethurum VI, VII, XIII, XX, and XXI, on the basis of manuscript rubrics containing Wulfstan's pen name *Lupus*.

[23] *Wulfstan: Sammlung*, ed. by Napier.

[24] Jost, *Wulfstanstudien*; *Homilies*, ed. by Bethurum; and *Sermo Lupi*, ed. by Whitelock.

somewhat in discussions of Wulfstan's work. Bethurum likewise dismissed out of hand (again, without really explaining why) a further set of texts (Napier XXIX, XXXI, XLIII, XLIV, XLV, XLVI, LVII, and LXII) which she regarded as containing genuine Wulfstan-material, but not having come from Wulfstan himself.[25] Meanwhile, Jonathan Wilcox goes further than Bethurum in attributing still further texts to Wulfstan's hand.[26] Other attempts to summarize the present still far from settled position have been offered in two recent doctoral theses.[27]

The first difficulty in establishing a canon of Wulfstan's preaching texts lies in the leaking boundaries of the genres in which Wulfstan worked. While some modern scholarship has tended to attempt a distinction between general addresses of exhortation that are not connected to specific dates or events in the Church calendar (usually designated 'sermons'), and those addresses which have a particular place in the ecclesiastical cycle (generally termed 'homilies'), which are often individually based on a designated biblical passage (the so-called *pericope*), such a nice distinction is relatively recent, and is unsupported not only by the medieval evidence, but even by earlier editions still in frequent use.[28] Similarly, Wulfstan frequently employed the same words, themes, and stylistic tics in his law-codes as in his preaching and seems to have drawn little distinction between the two genres;[29] as Patrick Wormald succinctly puts it: 'The simple truth is that [Wulfstan's] earlier laws are heavily homiletic, and his later homilies are very like laws.'[30] Jonathan Wilcox explains further:

> Wulfstan's homiletic works are rarely expositions of a pericope; generally they expound straightforward catechetical instruction or centre on eschatological themes, especially in relation to a perception of current moral and political decline. His other writings share

[25] *Homilies*, ed. by Bethurum, pp. 36–41.

[26] Wilcox, 'Dissemination of Wulfstan's Homilies', pp. 200–01.

[27] Don William Chapman, 'Stylistic Use of Nominal Compounds in Wulfstan's Sermons' (unpublished doctoral dissertation, University of Toronto, 1996), pp. 201–08; and Sara María Pons-Sanz, 'The Norsified Vocabulary in the Works of Archbishop Wulfstan II of York' (unpublished doctoral dissertation, University of Cambridge, 2004), pp. 5–20.

[28] So, for example, while most recent scholars would accept that Wulfstan is better known for sermons and Ælfric for homilies, they are also used to citing *Homilies*, ed. by Bethurum, for Wulfstan, and refer to the *Sermones catholici* of Ælfric.

[29] Mark K. Lawson, 'Archbishop Wulfstan and the Homiletic Element in the Laws of Æthelred II and Cnut', in *The Reign of Cnut, King of England, Denmark, and Norway*, ed. by Alexander Rumble (Leicester, 1994), pp. 141–64.

[30] Patrick Wormald, 'Archbishop Wulfstan: Eleventh-Century State-Builder', in *Wulfstan, Archbishop of York*, ed. by Townend, pp. 9–27 (p. 17).

similar preoccupations. Instruction is pursued in the pastoral letters, while the degenera-
tion of society is addressed in the law-codes and, in a more general way, by the *Institutes
of Polity*. There is a substantial overlap between Wulfstan's sermons and his legal writings.
He uses both to teach "God's law [. . .] preach right and forbid wrong". Such overlap is
particularly obvious in pieces like Napier LIX–LXI, where homiletic injunctions are
created from a collection of legal statements. Nevertheless, Wulfstan's legal writings have
a different status from his homiletic writings: the law-codes reflect the outcome of legisla-
tive meetings of the king and his counselors.[31]

Other works in still other genres, many of them sharing the same core style and
themes that are usually characterized as distinctively 'Wulfstanian', have been
identified, notably the *Canons of Edgar*, edited by Roger Fowler, some parts of the
so-called *Benedictine Office*, edited by James Ure, and, as Wilcox notes, the various
texts collected together by Karl Jost under the umbrella title of *Institutes of Polity*.[32]
Yet all of these texts share material in common with Wulfstan's acknowledged
preaching texts.

No doubt in large part because of the pitfalls of making secure attributions to
Wulfstan, much of the scholarship devoted to him has focussed on discussions of
Wulfstan's distinctive style (which is to say arguments that his style *is* distinctive
at all).[33] The essence of that style seems to lie in its heavy reliance on emphasis
through repetition at every level of discourse. At the sub-verbal level, sounds are
matched in purple passages of alliteration and assonance, while words, formulas,
themes, and entire compositions are repeated, notably in the various versions of the
celebrated *Sermo Lupi*.[34] It has also become commonplace in discussions of
Wulfstan's style to compare and contrast it with that of his celebrated and prolific
contemporary Ælfric, who also provided Wulfstan with a significant number of his
vernacular sources. The comparison is an unfair one on many levels. In the

---

[31] Wilcox, 'Dissemination of Wulfstan's Homilies', p. 201.

[32] For the relevant editions and attributions, see note 16 above.

[33] Still extremely valuable is McIntosh, 'Wulfstan's Prose'. A useful and more recent overview
is provided by Dance, 'Sound, Fury, and Signifiers'. See also, for example, Chapman, 'Stylistic Use
of Nominal Compounds'; Andy Orchard, 'Crying Wolf: Oral Style and the *Sermones Lupi*', *ASE*,
21 (1992), 239–64; Pons-Sanz, 'Norsified Vocabulary'; and Scragg, *Dating and Style*.

[34] So, for example, Frank Stanton, *Anglo-Saxon England*, 3rd edn (Oxford, 1971), p. 460,
notes that Wulfstan's celebrated *Sermo Lupi* (Bethurum XX) 'makes its effect by sheer monotony
of commination', while Hollis, 'Thematic Structure', p. 175, points out of the same work that
'even its admirers have regarded it as little more than a stringing together of the nation's sins and
tribulations which impresses by its horrific accumulation of detail'. The best analysis of Wulfstan's
style remains McIntosh, 'Wulfstan's Prose'; see further Orchard, 'Crying Wolf'.

combined reckoning of Ælfric's various series of *Catholic Homilies*, Malcolm Godden has calculated that 'there are about 5056 separate headwords in the text [. . .]. There are also 430 proper names';[35] Wulfstan's corpus of such writings is admittedly considerably smaller, but the disparity is still striking: in the fullest available glossary to the Wulfstan material edited by Bethurum I count some 2043 headwords, and only sixty-nine proper names.[36] Even here, direct comparison is misleading, since the basis for categorization is different in each case (and somewhat inconsistent in both): the proper names included by Mabel Dobyns in Wulfstan's total include *Antecrist* ('Antichrist', 29 times), *Crist* ('Christ', 40 times), *Drihten* ('Lord', 74 times), and *God* ('God', 499 times), as well as several national designations, including *Engle, Englisc* ('[the] English', 25 times) and *Denisc* ('Danish', 3 times); Godden uses a different base-line. In general, however, any adjustments would only emphasize the disparity further: Wulfstan has his own rather limited idiolect, and in general seems to stick closely to it. Likewise, in Bethurum's edition of Wulfstan's sermons, only once is a single patristic source named: *Gregorius* (Gregory the Great, at Bethurum Xc.48), while Ælfric fairly peppers his writings with dozens of the names of the more than one hundred authorities he cites and echoes.[37] Such a broad difference is in part a measure of the very different audiences both men addressed but, given the way in which Wulfstan habitually recast Ælfric's carefully crafted and equally distinctive prose, may well also be a mark of a distinct difference in temperament that would have made them uncomfortable collaborators.

Wulfstan's strong sense of rhythm has often been commented on, even if some previous attempts to classify his works as poetry seem a little misguided.[38] It has likewise frequently been noted that Wulfstan has a fondness for intensifying adverbs such as *oft* ('often'), *swyðe* ('greatly'), *georne* ('readily'), *gelome* ('frequently'),

---

[35] Malcolm Godden, *Ælfric's Catholic Homilies: Introduction, Commentary, and Glossary*, EETS: SS, 18 (Oxford, 2000), p. 671.

[36] Dobyns, 'Wulfstan's Vocabulary'; see too Loring Holmes Dodd, *A Glossary of Wulfstan's Homilies*, Yale Studies in English, 35 (New York, 1908; repr. Hildesheim, 1968), based on Napier's edition. The figures here are based on the work of Dobyns.

[37] Michael Lapidge, *The Anglo-Saxon Library* (Oxford, 2006), pp. 250–66, identifies no fewer than 107 authors or anonymous texts and genres used by Ælfric, not including biblical and liturgical sources; cf. Godden, *Introduction, Commentary, and Glossary*, pp. xxxviii–lxii. A further invaluable resource is the *Fontes Anglo-Saxonici* database, <http://fontes.english.ox.ac.uk/>, where the present disparity in the successful sourcing of Ælfric and Wulfstan is glaringly apparent.

[38] See especially E. Einenkel, 'Der *Sermo ad Anglos*: ein Gedicht', *Anglia*, 7 (1884), 200–03.

and *wide* ('widely'), sometimes in comparative or superlative forms (*geornor, gelomor, oftor, oftost, swyðor, swyðost, widdast* are all attested), and that he often readily combined them widely into greatly repeated adverbial phrases (such as [*ealles*] *to swyðe* ('[all] too greatly'), *swyðe georne* ('very readily'); [*ealles*] *to wide* ('[all] too widely'), *wide 7 side* ('far and wide'); *oft 7 gelome* ('often and frequently'); [*ealles*] *to gelome* ('[all] too frequently')). Wulfstan is also particularly associated with the opening address *Leofan men(n)* ('Dear people'), although the phrase is clearly not his alone; it contrasts with such formulations as 'Menn þa leofestan' ('Dearest people') found widely elsewhere in earlier collections of homilies, most notably in the Vercelli Book, where it occurs no fewer than eighty-nine times, appearing in all but five of the twenty-three homilies in the manuscript,[39] and forming the opening address in fifteen of them.[40] Of the twenty-seven Old English sermons by Wulfstan edited by Bethurum (counting her three versions of the *Sermo Lupi* as separate texts), all but four contain the phrase *Leofan men(n)*,[41] which is found in total some sixty times, and in some sermons the phrase recurs often: Bethurum VII has six examples (VII.3, 19, 26, 78, 88, and 104), and Bethurum Xc no fewer than nine (X.3, 20, 39, 71, 76, 118, 121, 141, and 196). But while the frequency of this characteristic phrase in Wulfstan's works has often been remarked upon, it is striking that he seems to have employed it frequently not simply to open his addresses, but also to close them: in seven of the sermons edited by Bethurum the final occurrence of the phrase is combined with an exhortation of the form *utan* ('let us [. . .]') that is again typical of (but not unique to) Wulfstan's preaching style.[42] The distinctly brief sermon Bethurum XXI notably begins with the phrase 'Leofan men, utan understandan' ('Dear people, let us understand [...]', XXI.4), a first-person formulation that seems a variant on the second-person 'Leofan men(n), understandað' ('Dear people, understand') found widely elsewhere.[43] Likewise, Bethurum XIX (which immediately follows one of the two versions of Bethurum XXI in CCCC 201) begins 'Leofan men, utan spyrian' ('Dear people, let us inquire'), perhaps suggesting that if a wider selection of Wulfstan's

---

[39] The exceptions are Vercelli Homilies III, V, VI, VII, and XXIII. Homily III opens with the parallel phrase 'Broðor þa leofestan' ('Dearest brothers'), which clearly derives from the equivalent Latin homiletic opening *Fratres carissimi*.

[40] Vercelli Homilies II, IV, VIII, IX, XI, XII, XIII, XIV, XV, XVI, XVII, XVIII, XIX, XX, and XXI.

[41] The exceptions are Bethurum VIIIb, Xa, XII, and XVIb.

[42] See Bethurum II.68, III.74, VI.214, VIIa.17, Xc.196, XIII.53, and XV.69.

[43] See Bethurum Ib.3, VII.3, VIIIc.100, and XIII.3; Napier XXV.122/12 and XXVII.128/2.

preaching had survived, we would recognize still more combinations of stock and reworked themes.

Bethurum attempted to characterize Wulfstan's preaching as being focussed on four areas: 'Eschatological Homilies' (Bethurum I–V), 'The Christian Faith' (Bethurum VI–XII), 'Archiepiscopal Functions' (Bethurum XIII–XVIII), and 'Evil Days' (Bethurum XIX–XXI). But just as there is considerable leakage between the various genres of text that Wulfstan appears to have composed, so too there is notable overlap between the sermons in each of Bethurum's categories: obviously, 'Eschatological Homilies' and those on 'Evil Days' are as interrelated as 'The Christian Faith' and 'Archiepiscopal Functions'. It seems fairer to focus on the very public role that Wulfstan seems to accord himself, and on his repeated preoccupation with the proper responsibilities of different levels of a society in crisis.

Indeed, one of the most striking aspects of all of Wulfstan's extant work is the high seriousness with which he seems to have taken his episcopal role; many of Wulfstan's writings address the function of the bishop, both implicitly and explicitly.[44] Given the general lawlessness of the times in which he lived, it is perhaps unsurprising that so much of Wulfstan's focus is on the failure of bishops to instil a greater sense of respect, discipline, and authority in the beleaguered nation; characteristic (and often repeated in various forms) is the following blast (Bethurum XVII.36–43; Oxford, Bodleian Library, MS Hatton 113, fol. 94ʳ, lines 3–13):

1   Bisceopas syndan bydelas 7 godes lage lareowas ·
2   7 hy sculan georne oft 7 gelome clypian to criste
3   7 for eall cristen folc þingian georne ·
4   7 hi scylan georne godes riht bodian
5   7 æghwylc unriht georne forbeodan ꞉

6   7 se ðe oferhogie þæt he heom hlyste ·
7   hæbbe him gemæne þæt wið god sylfne ·
8   7 gyf bisceopas forgymað þæt hi synna ne styrað
9   ne unriht forbeodað ne godes riht ne cyðað ·
10   ac clumiað mid ceaflum þær hi scoldan clypian · et reliqua ·[45]

---

[44] Bethurum (*Homilies*, pp. 225–50) organizes seven sermons under the general heading 'Archiepiscopal Functions', but as we shall see, many others of his works focus on the same broad theme.

[45] In the version of this passage found in London, British Library, Cotton MS Cleopatra B. XIII, the final phrase *et reliqua* is replaced by 'wa him þære swigean' ('woe to them in their silence'), a reading that is reflected in some of the parallel passages below. Intriguingly, yet a further version appears earlier in Hatton 113, fol. 83ʳ, lines 2–9, following a general rubric *BE GODES BYDELUM* ('CONCERNING GOD'S PREACHERS'): 'Godcundlice bydelas 7 godes lage

[Bishops are preachers, and teachers of God's law, and they ought eagerly oft and again to cry out to Christ, and intercede eagerly for all Christian folk, and they ought eagerly to preach God's justice and eagerly forbid every injustice; and he who scorns to listen to them, let him settle that with God himself; and if bishops neglect to rebuke sins and to forbid injustice and to proclaim God's justice, but mumble with their jaws when they should cry out, and so on.]

The layout here reflects a more relaxed attitude to punctuation in this particular manuscript than that found in the passage cited earlier, though here too manuscript punctuation plays a key role in revealing the rhetorical and syntactical structure. The passage divides easily into two, with the first half (**1–5**) consisting of an opening 'line' characterized by medial rhyme (*bydelas* [...] *lareowas*) followed by four others which fail to exhibit the feature, followed by a second half (**6–10**) in which this pattern is reversed (cf. *oferhogie* [...] *hlyste*; *gemæne* [...] *sylfne*; *forgymað* [...] *styrað*; *forbeodað* [...] *cyðað*). Quite apart from the insistent alliteration (every single 'line' has either inter- or intralinear alliteration, or both), repeated diction (note especially the fourfold repetition of *georne* in **2–5**, highlighted by the patterned syntax of '7 hy sculan georne [...] 7 hi scylan georne' in **2** and **4**), and other kinds of sound- and wordplay (such as the progression 'bydelas [...] bodian [...] forbeodan [...] forbeodað', or the chiasmus 'riht [...] unriht [...] unriht [...] riht', both of which straddle the natural divide), the passage concludes with a self-alliterating phrase ('ac clumiað mid ceaflum þær hi scoldan clypian', **10**) that obviously appealed to Wulfstan, so frequently does he recycle it. Indeed, given the fact that the verb *clumian* only appears in extant Old English in passages written by Wulfstan himself, one might almost describe the phrase as his trademark.

Certainly, a clearly related passage towards the end of the longest version of the *Sermo Lupi* comparing the plight of the Anglo-Saxons with that of the indigenous Britons they forcibly replaced returns to the same theme (Bethurum XX(EI).176; Cotton Nero A. I (MS I), fol. 114ᵛ, lines 8–23):

1 An þeodwita wæs on brytta tidum · gildas hatte ·
2 Se awrat be heora misdædum ·
3 hu hy mid heora synnum swa oferlice swyþe god gegræmedan ·
4 þæt he let æt nyhstan engla here heora eard gewinnan ·
5 7 brytta dugeþe fordon[46] mid ealle ;

lareowas sculon · swyðe georne oft 7 gelome · godes riht cyðan 7 unriht forbeodan · 7 se ðe oferhogie þæt he heom hlyste · hæbbe him gemæne þæt wið god sylfne · 7 gyf bisceopas forgymað · þæt hi synna ne styrað ne unriht forbeodað · ac clummiað [*pace* Bethurum, who reads *clumiað*] mid ceaflum þær hy sceoldan clypian · wa heom þære swigean ·'

[46] The MS reads *fordom*.

6 7 þæt wæs geworden (þæs)[47] þe he sæde ·

7 þurh ricra reaflac · 7 þurh gitsunge wohgestreona ;

8 Ðurh leode unlaga · 7 þurh wohdomas ;

9 Ðurh biscopa[48] asolcennesse · 7 þurh lyðre yrhðe godes bydela ꞉

10 þe soþes geswugedan · ealles to gelome ·

11 7 clumedan mid ceaflum · þær hy scoldan clypian ;

12 Ðurh fulne eac · folces gælsan · 7 þurh oferfylla 7 mænigfealde synna ·

13 heora eard hy forworhtan · 7 selfe hy forwurdan ;

[There was a national spokesman in the time of the Britons called Gildas. He wrote about their misdeeds, how they through their sins so very greatly angered God that in the end he allowed an army of the English to conquer their country and utterly destroy the flower of the British; and that came about, as he said, through the plundering of the powerful and through greed for ill-gotten gains; through wrongful laws of the people and through crooked judgements, through the laziness of bishops and through the vile cowardice of the preachers of God, who all too frequently were silent about the truth, and mumbled with their jaws, where they ought to cry out. And also through the lust of the people and through the excessive appetites and manifold sins they lost their land and perished themselves.]

This self-contained passage breaks up a sequence of five successive examples of sentences beginning with the phrase (*w*)*uton* + infinitive, Wulfstan's usual mode of concluding his sermons, and signals the piece as an add-in theme in this longest of the three versions of the *Sermo Lupi* (or a theme subsequently deleted).[49] A later hand (not that of Wulfstan) has signalled the ultimate source here and has written '[*Gil*]*dae Libellus*' ('the little book of Gildas') in the margin at folio 114ᵛ, lines 10–11, a reference to the *De excidio Britanniae* by the sixth-century monk Gildas that, like so many of his sources, Wulfstan seems to have known second-hand. In fact, Wulfstan's ultimate source is a letter from Alcuin to Archbishop Æthelhard, decrying the lack of moral courage shone in the face of Viking depredations in his own day:

Legitur in libro Gildi, Britonum sapientissmi, quod idem ipsi Britones propter rapinas et auaritiam principum, propter iniquitatem et inustitiam iudicum, propter desidiam et

---

[47] *þæs* added above line.

[48] *-pa* corrected from *-pas* (dittography).

[49] The whole sequence runs as follows: 'uton don swa us neod is [XX(EI).174] [...] [Gildas passage] [...] uton don swa us þearf is [XX(EI).186] [...] uton don swa us þearf is [XX(EI).190] [...] uton God lufian 7 Godes lagum fylgean [XX(EI).192–93] [...] uton word 7 weorc rihtlice fadian [XX(EI).195]'.

pigritiam predicationis episcoporum, propter luxuriam et malos mores populi patriam perdiderunt.[50]

[One reads in the book of Gildas, wisest of the Britons, that in fact the Britons themselves, through the pillaging and greed of the leaders, through the injustice of the judges, through the laziness and slackness of the bishops, through the lasciviousness and wicked morals of the people, lost their homeland.]

The same passage occurs in no fewer than four manuscripts associated with Wulfstan's so-called Handbook, and is certainly the ultimate source.[51] It is important to highlight the fact that the rhetorical strategies employed here in Latin in fact match closely Wulfstan's own in Old English: copious alliteration (*Legitur in libro*; *pigritiam predicationis*; *malos mores*; *populi patriam perdiderunt*), repeated words (notably *propter*), and repeated syntactical structures (*propter* + accusative + genitive). Wulfstan maintains the basic fourfold division of blame between leaders, judges, bishops, and the people (in that order), but noticeably increases dramatically the repetitive verbal element (the Latin *propter* features four times, the Old English equivalent *þurh* no fewer than eight, with two renderings each per *propter*, as it were). In Wulfstan's scheme, as revealed by the manuscript punctuation, the leaders (**7**), the judges (**8**), and the people (**12**) get a line each, while the role of the bishops is significantly expanded, threefold (**9–11**). The litany of despair and destruction that concludes each of the two parts of this passage (*fordon* (**5**) [...] *forworhtan* (**13**) [...] *forwurdan* (**13**)) seems particularly artful, and again transcends the source. The close links between the rhetoric and aural embellishments employed by Alcuin in Latin and Wulfstan in Old English are particularly striking and suggest Wulfstan's sensitivity to the sounds and structure of the texts he is appropriating. Apparently, those who criticize Wulfstan's prose style for its demonstrable repetitiveness would do well to read what he read.

In the Cotton manuscript, the text of the *Sermo Lupi* begins at the head of folio 110ʳ, preceded (at the top of 109ʳ) by a further text that has the rubric *BE ÐEODWITAN* ('CONCERNING NATIONAL SPOKESMEN'), a precursor

---

[50] Text from *Two Alcuin Letter-Books*, ed. by Colin Chase (Toronto, 1975), p. 74, lines 109–13; see too Gareth Mann, 'The Development of Wulfstan's Alcuin Manuscript', in *Wulfstan, Archbishop of York*, ed. by Townend, pp. 235–78 (pp. 245–46).

[51] London, British Library, Cotton MS Vespasian A. XIV, fol. 146ʳ; Cambridge, Corpus Christi College, MS 190, p. 173 (which seems textually even closer than what is cited above); Cambridge, Corpus Christi College, MS 265, p. 7; Oxford, Bodleian Library, MS Barlow 37, p. 34. In the Vespasian manuscript (from which the text above is taken) the passage is underlined, perhaps by Wulfstan himself.

to Wulfstan's use of the same term to describe Gildas himself ('An þeodwita wæs on brytta tidu*m* · gildas hatte ·', **1**). The opening lines of this brief text repeat the same familiar theme (WPol 2.1: 41; Cotton Nero A. I, fol. 109ʳ, lines 2–14):

1   Cyningan 7 biscpan ꞉ eorlan 7 heretogan ꞉
2   gerefan 7 deman ꞉ larwitan 7 lahwitan gedafenað mid rihte ·
3   for gode 7 for worolde · þæt hy ánræde weorðan · ꞉ godes riht lufian ;·

4   7 biscpas syndan bydelas · 7 godes lage lareowas ·
5   7 hy scylan bodian · 7 unriht forbeodan ꞉
6   7 se þe oferhogige · þæt he heom hlyste ꞉
7   hæbbe him gemæne · þæt wið god sylfne ;
8   7 gif biscpas forgymað · þæt hy synna ne styrað ꞉
9   ne unriht forbeodað · ne godes riht ne cyðað ꞉
10   ac clumiað mid ceaflum · þær hi scoldan clypian ꞉ wa heom þære swigean ;

[For kings and bishops, earls and chiefs, reeves and judges, scholars of lore and scholars of law, it is properly fitting before God and the world that they become resolute, and love God's justice; and bishops are preachers, and teachers of God's law, and they ought to preach and forbid injustice; and he who scorns to listen to them, let him settle that with God himself; and if bishops neglect to rebuke sins and to forbid injustice and to proclaim God's justice, but mumble with their jaws when they should cry out, woe to them for their silence.]

This passage, while clearly related to the two others cited previously, shows still further artistry with regard to clausal arrangement: most of the lines given here split easily into two (compare the arrangement signalled by the punctuation in previous passages cited), linked by medial and end-rhyme on a limited number of endings (viz. *-e* and *-an*); almost the whole of Bethurum XXI, which directly follows the *Sermo Lupi* in the Cotton manuscript (fols 115ᵛ–116ʳ) is built on the same conceit, which seems to be a particular feature of Wulfstan's later style.[52]

    A few folios earlier on in the same Cotton manuscript Wulfstan essentially repeats the same mantra, with some minor variations, at the beginning of a text which its editor entitles 'Ermahnung an die Bischöfe' ('Exhortation to the Bishops';[53] Cotton Nero A. I, fol. 100ᵛ, lines 1–8):

1   Biscpas scoldan symle · godes riht bodian · 7 unriht forbeodan ·
2   7 witodlice sona swa biscpas rihtes adumbiað ·
3   7 sona swa hy eargiaþ[54] 7 hy rihtes forscamiað ·

---

[52] See further Orchard, 'On Editing Wulfstan', especially the Appendixes.

[53] WPol 4, *'Institutes of Polity'*, ed. by Jost, p. 262. For a detailed discussion of this passage, see Wilcox, 'The Wolf on Shepherds', pp. 403–04.

[54] Corrected from *eargeaþ*.

4   7 clumiað mid ceaflum þonne hy scoldan clypian ·
5   sona heora wyrðmynt bið waniende swiðe ;

[Bishops should continually preach God's justice and forbid injustice, and certainly, as soon as bishops grow dumb, and as soon as they shun and are ashamed of justice, and mumble with their jaws when they ought to cry out, their glory is greatly diminished.]

The first sixteen words of this passage (**1–2**, up to *adumbiað*) are apparently written in Wulfstan's own hand; the final six words of the text as a whole (fol. 102ʳ, lines 3–4) are in the same hand, a curious circumstance that lends a particular immediacy to the text as a whole, as if it had Wulfstan's special endorsement. The *biscpas* spelling, found twice in these opening words, likewise seems only to survive in texts that, like this one, are closely related to Wulfstan, and may reflect his habitual orthography.[55] It is at all events clear from these evidently closely related but quite distinctive passages the extent to which Wulfstan not only adapted his sources, but also his own earlier words.

So, for example, among the more curious examples of Wulfstan's reading and writing are some rather unimpressive verses in honour of the Archbishop copied in his own hand in London, British Library, Cotton MS Vespasian A. XIV, fol. 148ᵛ:

1   Qui legis hunc titulum Domino da[56] uota tonanti ·
2   Archipontifice pro Wulfstano uenerando ;

3   Floret in hoc opere pia mentio praesulis archi ·
4   Wulfstani cui det Dominus pia regna polorum ·
5   'Et sibi commissos tueatur ab hoste maligno ;'[57]

6   Pontificis bonitas manet hoc memoranda ierarchi ·
7   Wulfstani supero qui sit conscriptus in albo ;

8   Est laus Wulfstano mea pulchritudo benigno ·
9   Pontifici cui sit Dominus sine fine serenus ;

10   Comere me comiter iussit ita praesulis archi
11   Wulfstani pietas, data sit cui arce corona ·

---

[55] The *biscpas*-spelling is found further on in the same text, at W Pol 4, *Institutes of Polity*, ed. by Jost, p. 267, as well as in the law-code VI Æthelred 2.2 in the manuscript Cotton Claudius A. III, annotated by Wulfstan (cf. Ker, 'Handwriting', p. 321). The same form, as well as two variant forms (*biscpæs* and *biscpan*) are found in the law-code *Grið*, also associated with Wulfstan (at 11, 19.1, and 24), in the same Cotton Nero A. I manuscript as the previous few quotations.

[56] A marginal hand, apparently Wulfstan's own, has toned down the abrupt impact of the imperative *da* ('give'), by apparently inserting the words [*Si*] *uolueris* ('If you are willing').

[57] This line has been squeezed into the margin.

12 Praesule Wulfstano hoc opus est consente paratum ·
13 Pollice quod docto impressit subtilis aliptes ·[58]

[You who read this subscription, give votive offerings to the Lord God on behalf of the venerable Archbishop Wulfstan. In this work flourishes honourable mention of Archbishop Wulfstan, to whom may the Lord grant the holy Kingdom of Heaven. [And let him guard those entrusted to him from the evil enemy.] The goodness of Archbishop Wulfstan remains to be commemorated in this [work]; and may he be inscribed in the album of heaven. My beauty is praise to kindly Bishop Wulfstan, to whom may the Lord be eternally gentle. The piety of Archbishop Wulfstan ordered me to be composed courteously thus, to whom may a crown be granted in the citadel [of heaven]. This work has been prepared with the consent of Bishop Wulfstan, which the clever anointer impressed with a learned thumb.]

These are certainly odd verses to have been inscribed in Wulfstan's own hand, offering as they do shameless prayers for his salvation. Line 5 seems obviously interpolated, not least by the way it has been crammed into the margin as an afterthought in the manuscript itself; even had the layout of line 5 been more regular, it would likely have been detected as a later addition, breaking as it does a clear sequence of six couplets combining mention of Wulfstan by name and rank with wishes for his commemoration.[59] The final line varies the theme a little, suggesting that the work in question has had the support of Wulfstan, and giving (as it were) his thumbs-up. It is tempting to suggest that Wulfstan himself added line 5 to temper the prayers for his own salvation by sparing a thought for his flock. In the context of the Anglo-Danish atmosphere that pervades the final decades of Wulfstan's life, it is intriguing to note that these verses seem close to the kind of pure praise poetry for a nobleman that is so familiar from Old Norse poetry, and so notably absent from the Anglo-Saxon written record.[60]

The explicit naming of Wulfstan six times in what I take to be the original twelve lines of the poem and the relentless repetition (again reminiscent of Wulfstan's vernacular works) of his (archi)episcopal rank (*Archipontifice* [. . .] *praesulis archi* [. . .] *Pontificis* [. . .] *ierarchi* [. . .] *Pontifici* [. . .] *praesulis archi* [. . .]

---

[58] For a facsimile, see *Wulfstan Manuscript*, ed. by Loyn, Appendix. See too Ker, 'Handwriting', p. 326.

[59] Ker, 'Handwriting', p. 326, notes that the margin has been trimmed, but that Wulfstan 'wrote *item* against each new couplet, but only traces of the word remain'.

[60] For an overview of contemporary practice, see, for example, Roberta Frank, 'Cnut in the Verse of his Skalds', in *Reign of Cnut*, ed. by Rumble, pp. 106–24; and Matthew Townend, 'Contextualizing the *Knútsdrápur*: Skaldic Praise-Poetry at the Court of Cnut', *ASE*, 30 (2001), 145–79.

Praesule) can be matched by other kinds of patterned repetition elsewhere in the core poem (*da* [. . .] *det* [. . .] *data sit*; *in hoc opera* [. . .] *hoc* [. . .] *hoc opus*; *pia mentio* [. . .] *pia regna* [. . .] *pietas*), and such features, such as word- and sound-play (*Domino da uota tonanti*; *Comere me comiter*), together with the poem's clear penchant for polysyllabic words even at the end of hexameter lines (words of four or more syllables include *Archipontifice* [. . .] *uenerando* [. . .] *Pontificis* [. . .] *memoranda ierarchi* [. . .] *pulchritudo* [. . .] *Pontifici*), must have made the poem extremely impressive even to the most illiterate (which is to say un-Latinate) audience. Indeed, the level of Latinity of the poet himself is open to doubt: several lines have abnormal scansion or questionable forms.[61] Particularly intriguing in this respect is the use of the active infinitive *comere* (literally 'to adorn') in line 10, following the verb *iussit* ('ordered'), where the passive form *comeri* ('to be adorned') would seem preferable grammatically, albeit that the scansion would preclude its use here, since in Old English it is by contrast the active form that would be required: the celebrated inscription on the so-called Alfred Jewel (*Aelfred mec heht gevvyrcan*, 'Ælfred ordered me to be made') offers a useful parallel. No one supposes that King Alfred himself created the jewel that bears his name, so it is perhaps surprising that a number of scholars have suggested that Wulfstan was both the author and the scribe of these verses.[62] Confected as they are from a series of more-or-less formulaic phrases,[63] these verses are not of the highest quality, but that is hardly a reason

---

[61] Notable here is the scansion of *pŭlchrĭtūdŏ* (line 8), which is hard to parallel elsewhere; the whole phrase *cŏm ĭtĕr iŭssĭt ĭtă* (line 10, presumably scanned thus) is likewise distinctly curious. The form *consente* (line 12, presumably for *consentiente*) seems unique.

[62] See further Mann, 'Development of Wulfstan's Alcuin Manuscript', p. 235; Patrick Wormald, 'Archbishop Wulfstan and the Holiness of Society', in his *Legal Culture in the Early Medieval West: Law as Text, Image and Experience* (London, 1999), pp. 225–51 (p. 228); and *The Copenhagen Wulfstan Collection: Copenhagen Kongelige Bibliotek Gl. kgl. sam 1595*, ed. by James E. Cross and Jennifer Morrish Tunberg, EEMF, 25 (Copenhagen, 1993), pp. 45–47. On the background to this important manuscript, containing several Latin texts now attributed to Wulfstan, see Johan Gerritsen, 'The Copenhagen Wulfstan Manuscript: A Codicological Study', *ES*, 79 (1998), 501–11.

[63] So, for example, to take line 1 as an example: the phrase *Qui legis hunc titulum* is found in a number of epigraphical verses, as well as in some verses by the Carolingian poet Theodulf of Orléans (*Carmina* 40.17); the phrase *uota tonanti* also appears three times in the verses of Theodulf's contemporary and rival, the Anglo-Saxon Alcuin (*Carmina* 88.4.11, 89.8.3, and 90.25.3). Likewise, line 5 seems almost entirely created from existing fragments of earlier verses: the phrase *sibi commissos* can be found in poems by Bede (*Hymn* 2.303) and Milo of Saint-Amand (*De sobrietate* 2.895); *ab hoste maligno* twice in poems by Alcuin (*Carmina* 69.193 and 124.10); and *tueatur ab hoste* by Hibernicus Exul (*Carmina* 21.1). Other phrases also found widely in the

to suppose that Wulfstan composed them himself. Nonetheless, as the apparent copyist of these poor if flattering verses, Wulfstan demonstrates a healthy concern for his own status, reputation, and ultimate salvation.

A thankfully shorter but no less pitiful poem that fawns on Wulfstan in a similar way is found in the lower margin of a cartulary relating to the endowment of the church of Worcester (London, British Library, Cotton MS Tiberius A. XIII, fol. 101ᵛ):

> 1 Sit pariter Lupo pax uita longa salusque
> 2 Iungere gaudemus lapidem disiungere necne
> 3 Laetatur pius his iunctis nostri memor et sit.[64]

[May there be for the wolf ['Wulf'] peace, long life, and salvation alike. We rejoice to join the stone ['stan'] and not to separate from [it]. When these things are joined together, the pious one is happy, and may he remember us.]

This rather laboured poem of doubtful scansion and morphology (one longs to emend *Laetatur* to *Laetetur*, to preserve the necessary subjunctive sense 'May [the pious one] be happy') turns in a somewhat clunky fashion on the conceit that the Latin words *Lupo* [...] *lapidem* ('wolf [...] stone'), emphasized through assonance and alliteration, equate in Old English to the constituent elements (*Wulf* [...] *stan*) of the bishop's own name. Presumably these verses derive from some toady

---

verses of Anglo-Latin or Carolingian poets include *regna polorum* (line **4**; cf. e.g. Aldhelm, *Carmina ecclesiastica* 3.31 and *Carmen de uirginitate* 2160; Boniface, *Carmina* 1.51; Alcuin, *Carmina* 1.974 and 91.3.2; Hrabanus Maurus, *Carmina* 89.17; Walahfrid Strabo, *Carmina* 23.1.161 and *Vita S. Galli* 1.1418; *pia regna poli* is found in Theodulf of Orléans, *Carmina* 71.38). More intriguing is the poet's use of the rare form *aliptes* (line **13**, literally 'wrestling-master'), which is found twice in the *Satires* of Juvenal (3.76 and 6.422; the latter line concludes with the cadence *impressit aliptes*), as well as the phrase *pollice* [...] *docto* (line **13**), which is found elsewhere apparently only in Prudentius (*Psychomachia* 1.364). In late Anglo-Saxon England, knowledge of the verses of both Juvenal and Prudentius (as well as Aldhelm, Bede, and a range of Carolingian authors) has only been demonstrated thus far for Wulfstan's contemporary and namesake, Wulfstan Cantor of Winchester, whose versified life of St Swithun is the longest Anglo-Latin poem extant. In this context, it is perhaps worth noting that ending a hexameter with any quadrisyllabic form is relatively unusual; ending one with the term *ierarchi* seems to be a feature all but unique to these verses on Wulfstan, and to Wulfstan of Winchester, who employs the same form in the same position no fewer than four times (Swith. praef.211; 1.161, 449; 2.1027). On the poetic style of Wulfstan of Winchester's poem, see Michael Lapidge, *The Cult of St Swithun*, Winchester Studies, 4.2 (Oxford, 2003), pp. 341–64.

[64] Compare Stephen Baxter, 'Archbishop Wulfstan and the Administration of God's Property', in *Wulfstan, Archbishop of York*, ed. by Townend, pp. 161–205 (p. 161).

in Wulfstan's service; certainly it seems striking, given Wulfstan's own penchant for reading and recycling Alcuin's works (as seen above), that the hexameter cadence *uita salusque* that may lie behind line **1** here should appear three times in Alcuin's verse.[65] Once again one notes repetitive elements even in this short text (*Iungere* [...] *disiungere* [...] *iunctis*), a feature to which the poem's addressee has shown himself especially sensitive.

Yet despite our growing knowledge of Wulfstan's sources and reading, the precise roots of Wulfstan's style remain hard to determine, although many aspects of it can be paralleled in pre-existing collections of sermons, notably the Vercelli Book.[66] More intriguing is a clear parallel in form and phrasing between what might be called one of Wulfstan's signature themes and a passage from a poem in the Exeter Book, describing the fate of the sinful at Doomsday (*Christ C* 1609–12):

> Ðær sceolan þeofas   ond þeodsceaþan,
> lease ond forlegene,   lifes ne wenan,
> ond mansworan   morþorlean seon,
> heard ond heorogrim.[67]

[There must [go] thieves and mighty ravagers, the false and the adulterers, not hope for life, and perjurors see retribution for crime, hard and fiercely grim.]

The source of this passage has been traced to a combination of a number of biblical passages from the Pauline Epistles.[68] One such is I Corinthians 6. 9–10:

---

[65] Alcuin, *Carmina* 1.640, 31.7, and 104.3.4. The triad *pax uita salusque* appears in variant forms in Alcuin, *Carmina* 40.13 and 76.3.3, as well as in verses by Theodulf of Orléans (*Carmina* 41.4.2) and Sedulius Scottus (*Carmina* 1.3.4). Given the metrical solecisms in the other verses on Wulfstan already cited, it is striking that in the opening line of this poem there seem to be unusual scansions of *Lŭpo* and *vītā*. It is tempting to suggest that the two poems were the work of a single indifferent poet.

[66] Scragg, *Dating and Style*.

[67] Text from *The Anglo-Saxon Poetic Records*, ed. by G. P. Krapp and E. V. K. Dobbie, 6 vols (New York, 1931–42), III, 48; the manuscript reads *moþorlean* at 1611b, but the emendation is universally accepted. On the date of the manuscript, cf. Bernard J. Muir, *The Exeter Anthology of Old English Poetry: An Edition of Exeter Dean and Chapter MS 3501*, rev. 2nd edn (Exeter, 2000), I, 1: 'The combined codicological and literary evidence indicates that the anthology was designed and copied out *circa* 965–75, making it perhaps the oldest surviving book of vernacular poetry from Anglo-Saxon England.' While there remains some dispute about the last assertion here, there is no doubt that the Exeter Book is earlier than any of Wulfstan's surviving works.

[68] See further Frederick M. Biggs, *The Sources of 'Christ III': A Revision of Cook's Notes*, OEN Subsidia, 12 (Binghamton, 1986), p. 38.

An nescitis quia iniqui regnum Dei non possidebunt nolite errare neque fornicarii neque idolis seruientes neque adulteri neque molles neque masculorum concubitores neque fures neque auari neque ebriosi neque maledici neque rapaces regnum Dei possidebunt.

[Know you not that the unjust shall not possess the kingdom of God? Do not err: Neither fornicators nor idolaters nor adulterers: nor the effeminate nor liars with mankind nor thieves nor covetous nor drunkards nor railers nor extortioners shall possess the kingdom of God.]

A further relevant passage is I Timothy 1. 9–10:

Sciens hoc quia iusto lex non est posita sed iniustis et non subditis impiis et peccatoribus sceleratis et contaminatis patricidis et matricidis homicidis fornicariis masculorum concubitoribus plagiariis mendacibus periuris et si quid aliud sanae doctrinae aduersatur.

[Knowing this: that the law is not made for the just man but for the unjust and disobedient, for the ungodly and for sinners, for the wicked and defiled, for murderers of fathers and murderers of mothers, for manslayers, for fornicators, for them who defile themselves with mankind, for menstealers, for liars, for perjured persons, and whatever other thing is contrary to sound doctrine.]

Whatever the ultimate source, this passage from *Christ C* is lavishly embellished aurally, with lines of cross-alliteration (1609 and 1611) alternating with lines of double alliteration (1610 and 1612). The use of alliterating doublets in these lines is also striking: no fewer than three are clearly signalled (*þeofas ond þeodscaþan*; *lease ond forlegene*; *heard ond heorogrim*), and even though such alliterating doublets are found commonly throughout *Christ C*, the collocation here is surely deliberate.[69] The parallels with Wulfstan's acknowledged works seem clear; one might cite, for example, the following (Bethurum VII.128–34; CCCC 419, pp. 176, line 16 – 177, line 12; parallels with *Christ C* are highlighted in bold italics):

1 *Ðyder scylan* manslagan · *7 þider scylan* manswican ;
2 *Ðider scylan* æwbrecan · 7 þa fulan *forlegenan* ·

---

[69] Alliterating doublets are found in the a-lines of *Christ C* in the following lines: 877 (*beorht ond bliþe*), 883 (*trume ond torhte*), 884 (*singað ond swinsiaþ*), 896 (*beorhtra ond blacra*), 909 (*eadgum ond earmum*), 913 (*lufsum ond liþe*), 917 (*wordum ond weorcum*), 933 (*trume ond torhte*), 951 (*weccað ond woniað*), 954 (*swar ond swiðlic*), 980 (*stið ond stæðfæst*), 997 (*cirm ond cearu*), 998 (*gehreow ond hlud*), 1004 (*innan ond utan*), 1018 (*hwit ond heofonbeorht*), 1070 (*ece ond edgeong*), 1071 (*neode ond nyde*), 1127 (*dysge ond gedwealde*), 1196 (*to hleo ond to hroþer*), 1207 (*wunde ond wite*), 1236 (*wordum ond weorcum*), 1239 (*blæde ond byrhte*), 1256 (*blædes ond blissa*), 1407 (*earg ond unrot*), 1408 (*dugeþum ond dreamum*), 1411 (*sar ond swar*), 1443 (*hosp ond heardcwide*), 1523 (*hat ond heorogrim*), 1528 (*yrre ond egesful*), 1564 (*won ond wliteleas*), 1583 (*þeawa ond geþonca*), 1610 (*lease ond forlegene*), 1612 (*heard ond heorogrim*), and 1648 (*hafað ond healdeð*).

3 *þider scylan mansworan* · 7 *morð*wyrhtan ·
4 *þider scylan* gitseras · ryperas · 7 reaferas · 7 þas woruldstruderas ·
5 *þider scylan þeofas · 7 þeodsceaðan* ·
6 *Ðider scylan* wiccan · 7 wigeleras · 7 hrædest to secganne ·
7 ealle þa manfullan þe ær yfel wohrton ·
8 7 noldan geswican ne wið god þingian ;[70]

[Thither must [go] adulterors and those foul fornicators, thither must [go] perjurors, thither must [go] misers, robbers, and plunderers and mighty despoilers, thither must [go] thieves and mighty ravagers, thither must [go] sorcerers and soothsayers, and to say it quickest, all those evil people who did wickedness before, and did not want to cease nor intercede with God.]

It seems unlikely (though not impossible) that Wulfstan had direct knowledge of *Christ C*; both texts, however, may well be drawing on a pre-existing sermon tradition that employed the same trope. Particularly interesting in this respect is the way Wulfstan seems characteristically happy to repeat the phrase *þider scylan* seven times in this passage, where the poet of *Christ C* has the equivalent *Ðær sceolan* just once; one is reminded of the way in which Wulfstan doubled the syntactical repetitions already explicit in Alcuin, his source, in the passage on Gildas quoted above.

Wulfstan relied on a variety of texts in producing his speeches and sermons, but rarely signals them or indeed seems to rely on them too slavishly. By contrast,

---

[70] Cf. Bethurum XIII.92–97: '*Ðyder sculan* manslagan, *7 ðider sculan mansworan*; *þyder sculan* æwbrecan 7 ða fulan *forlegenan*; *ðider sculan* wiccan 7 bearn*myrð*ran; *ðider sculan þeofas 7 ðeodscaðan*, ryperas 7 reaferas, 7, hrædest to secganne, ealle þa manfullan þe God gremiað, butan hy geswican 7 ðe deoppor gebetan' ('Thither must [go] manslayers, and thither must [go] perjurors; thither must [go] adulterors and those foul fornicators; thither must go sorcerers and child-murderers, thither must [go] thieves and mighty ravagers, robbers and plunderers, and to say it quickest, all those evil people who anger God, unless they cease and the more deeply make amends'). Other parallels include Napier XLII.204/1–4: '*Ðider scylan þeofas and þeodsceaðan*; *þider scylan* wiccan and wigleras, and raðest is to sæcgenne, ealle þa manfullan, þe ær yfel worhton and noldon geswican ne wið god þingian'; Napier L.266/24 – 267/1: 'He sceal mandæde men þreagean þearle mid woroldlicre steore, and he sceal *morð*wyrhtan, hlafordswican and *manswaran*, mannslagan and mægslagan, cyrichatan and sacerdbanan, hadbrecan and æwbrecan, *þeofas and þeodsceaþan*, ryperas and reaferas, *leoger*as and liceteras, wedlogan and wærlogan hatian and hynan and eallum godes feondum styrnlice wiðstandan'; Napier LX.309/27 – 310/6: 'Her syndan on earde godcundnessæ wiðersacan and godes lage oferhogan, manslagan and mægslagan, cyrichatan and sacerdbanan, hadbrecan and æwbrecan, myltestran and bearn*myrð*ran, *þeofas and þeodscaðan*, ryperas and reaferas, *leoger*as and liceteras and leodhatan hetele ealles to manege, þe ðurh mansylene bariað þas þeode, and wedlogan and wærlogan and lytle getrywða to wide mid mannum.'

Ælfric is relatively scrupulous about signalling his debts,[71] and while he will often eloquently translate his Latin source into elegant Old English, he does not usually stray far from its sense. Wulfstan apparently has few such scruples, and (as we have seen) happily recasts, embellishes, and generally appropriates the material he uses, so that it smacks of his own all too imitable style. As often, the differences in outlook and methodology between Ælfric and Wulfstan are instructive: the sheer number of sources identified as having been used by Ælfric dwarfs the comparatively few sources so far found for Wulfstan, a distinction only partly due to their respective attitudes towards fidelity to their source.

A final example of Wulfstan's use and adaptation of earlier works brings together a number of the aspects of his reading, writing, and rewriting that have been discussed above. While scholars have long supposed, based partly on surviving correspondence (notably the so-called pastoral letters),[72] that Wulfstan used Ælfric as a kind of research assistant, drafting preliminary versions that Wulfstan then recast in his own style, it now seems more likely that Wulfstan, like so many contemporary and later authors, made use of pre-existing manuscript collections of Ælfric's works when composing derivative works of his own.[73] In identifying no fewer than 'eighteen texts by Ælfric used in Wulfstan's writings altogether: the five pastoral letters, a Latin tract (*Decalogus Moysi*), and twelve homilies and tracts in Old English', Malcolm Godden suggests in particular that Wulfstan may have made use of selections of Ælfrician material resembling those found in existing manuscripts such as Cambridge, Corpus Christi College, MS 178 (likely written at Worcester in the first half of the eleventh century) or Oxford, Bodleian Library, MS Hatton 115 (written in the second half of the eleventh century and at least

---

[71] Cf. Godden, *Introduction, Commentary, and Glossary*, p. xxxix: 'Citations in individual texts are frequent: often he names a particular authority at the head of a text, perhaps as a routine assertion of the authority behind his argument, sometimes giving the impression that the whole homily is in the voice of one of the fathers.'

[72] The letters are conveniently collected in *Die Hirtenbriefe Ælfrics in altenglischer und lateinischer Fassung*, ed. by Bernard Fehr, BaP, 9 (Hamburg, 1914; repr. with a supplementary introduction by Peter Clemoes, Darmstadt, 1966), pp. 222–27.

[73] Malcolm Godden, 'The Relations of Wulfstan and Ælfric: A Reassessment', in *Wulfstan, Archbishop of York*, ed. by Townend, pp. 353–74. Godden is reacting to suggestions, such as that made by J. E. Cross and Andrew Hamer, eds, *Wulfstan's Canon Law Collection*, Anglo-Saxon Texts, 1 (Cambridge, 1999), pp. 22–23 and 29, who describe Ælfric as essentially a part of Wulfstan's team of helpers.

subsequently kept at Worcester).[74] A further manuscript, Cambridge, Corpus Christi College, MS 188, containing an augmented version of Ælfric's First Series of *Catholic Homilies*, dating from the first half of the eleventh century, and at one time perhaps kept at Hereford, contains a unique version of *CH* I.17 that is of particular relevance here, adding as it does a passage on Doomsday that is not found elsewhere, part of which reads as follows (my layout):

1 Nu is eac sé tima þe se ylca apostol paulus
2 fores?de gefyrn timotheae þam bisceope ·
3 þæt on ðam endenextan dagum beoð frecenfulle tída
4 and menn lufiað to swiðe þas swicolan woruld ·
5 and hí beoð grædige góldes and seolfres ;
6 On modignysse áhafene and huxlice tælende;
7 Heora fæderum and moddrum hi beoð ungehyrsume;
8 Unðancwyrðe on ðeawum · and forscyldgode on d?dum ·
9 butan ælcere trywðe · and bútan soðre sibbe;
10 Mid leahtrum afyllede · and unlíðe him betwynan;
11 Ungehéaldsume · and butan wélwillendnysse;
12 Melderas and toðundene · and heora lustas lufigende
13 swiðor þonne hi lufion ðone lyfiendan god;
14 Hi habbað arfæstnysse híw and wiðsácað þære mihte ;
15 Nu is ðeos woruld gemencged mid swylcum mannum to swiðe ·
16 and hi þa bilewitan men mid heora menigfealdum leahtrum
17 to yfelnysse tihtað and to árleasum dædum ·
18 for ðan ðe sé awyrgeda gást wunað on swylcum mannum ·
19 and hí synd deofles lima swá swá heora dæda swuteliað ;[75]

[Now is also the time that the same apostle Paul predicted formerly to Timothy the bishop that in the last days there will be terrible times, and people will love too greatly this treacherous world; and they will be greedy for gold and silver, puffed-up with pride and speaking arrogantly; they will be disobedient to their fathers and mothers, thoughtless in their customs and damned in their deeds without any loyalty and without true reconciliation; filled with sins and unkind to each other; disloyal and without benevolence, the betrayers and the puffed-up, and loving their lusts more than they love the living God: they have the appearance of righteousness and they scorn its reality. Now this world is mingled with such people too much, and they entice the innocent people to wickedness with their manifold sins, and they are the devil's limbs, just as their deeds reveal.]

[74] Godden, 'Relations of Wulfstan and Ælfric', p. 363–69; on CCCC 178, see now Mary Clayton, 'Ælfric's *De auguries* and Corpus Christi College Cambridge 178', in *Latin Learning and English Lore: Studies in Anglo-Saxon Literature for Michael Lapidge*, ed. by Katherine O'Brien O'Keeffe and Andy Orchard, 2 vols (Toronto, 2005), II, 376–94.

[75] *Ælfric's Catholic Homilies: The First Series, Text*, ed. by Peter Clemoes, EETS: SS, 17 (Oxford, 1997), p. 540, lines 157–71.

Ælfric's clearly signalled source here (if indeed he is the author, as seems generally supposed) is another passage from one of the Pauline Epistles, specifically II Timothy 3. 1–5, which is itself notable for its rhetorical phrasing:

> Hoc autem scito
> quod in nouissimis diebus instabunt tempora periculosa
> et erunt homines se ipsos amantes
> cupidi elati superbi blasphemi parentibus inoboedientes
> ingrati scelesti sine affectione sine pace
> criminatores incontinentes inmites sine benignitate
> proditores proterui tumidi uoluptatium amatores
> magis quam Dei habentes speciem
> quidem pietatis uirtutem autem eius abnegantes et hos deuita.

> [Know also this, that in the last days shall come dangerous times. Men shall be lovers of themselves, covetous, haughty, proud, blasphemers, disobedient to parents, ungrateful, wicked, without affection, without peace, slanderers, incontinent, unmerciful, without kindness, traitors, stubborn, puffed up, and lovers of pleasure more than of God: having an appearance indeed of godliness but denying the power thereof. Now these avoid.]

But, in contrast to Wulfstan's free treatment of Alcuin's Latin seen above, a comparison of the Latin and the Old English demonstrates how closely Ælfric has rendered his source in phrasing and diction, even to the extent that the Old English adjectives beginning with *un-* map on precisely to Latin adjectives beginning with *in-*.[76] Like Wulfstan, but with more fidelity to the text he is adapting, Ælfric allows the rhetorical structure of his source to dictate his own basic strategy, while making the piece his own.

Now although this unique passage in CCCC 188 does not feature on Godden's list of Wulfstan's Ælfrician sources, a clear echo is found in Bethurum V.8–26 (CCCC 201, pp. 68, line 34 – 69, line 10, with parallel phrases highlighted in bold italics):

1 Vres drihtenes apostolas axodan hwilum hine silfne ·
2 ymbe ðisse worlde geendunge ·

3 Ða sæde he heom hwilce earfoðnessa ·
4 7 hwilce gedrecednessa ·
5 sculon on worlde ·
6 ær ðam ende geweorðan ·
7 swilce næfre ær ne gewurdan ·
8 ne næfre eft ne gewurðað ·
9 7 þæt godspel cweð ·

---

[76] So *ungehyrsume* 7; = *inoboedientes*; *Undancwyrðe* 8 = *ingrates*; *unliðe* 10 = *inmites*; *Ungeheáldsume* 11 = *incontinentes*.

10 Wa ðam wifum þe þonne timað ·
11 7 on þam earmlican timan ·
12 heora cild fedað ·

13 La nyde hit sceal
14 eac on worlde ·
15 for folces synnum ·
16 yfelian swiðe ·

17 Forðam *nu is se tima*
18 *þe paulus se apostol*
19 *gefirn foresæde* ·

20 He *sæde* hwilum
21 þam biscope timothee ·
22 *þæt on ðam endenyhstan dagum* · þisse worlde
23 *beoð fræcenlice tida* for manna synnum ·
24 *7 men* þonne *lufiað* he cwæð ·
25 ealles *to swiðe þas swicolan world* ·
26 *7 beoð* ofer*grædige* worldgestreona
27 7 to manega wurðað to wlance ·
28 7 ealles to rance ·
29 7 to gilpgeorne ·
30 7 sume wurðað egeslice godcundnessa hyrwende ·
31 7 boclare leande ·
32 7 lufigende unriht ·
33 7 sume wurðað swicole ·
34 7 swæslice ficole ·
35 7 butan getrywðum *forscildgode* on synnum ·
36 7 gecnawe se ðe cunne ·

37 *nu is se tima* ·
38 þæt *þeos world is gemæncged* ·
39 *mid mænigfealdan* mane ·
40 7 mid felafealdan facne ·
41 7 þæs hit is þe wyrse wide on worlde
42 ealswa þæt godspel cwæð ·[77]

[Our Lord's apostles once asked him about the end of this world. Then he told them that such hardships and sufferings should occur in the world before the end as had never occurred, nor ever would again. And the Gospel said: Woe to the women who are pregnant then, and bring up their children in that miserable time. Behold, it needs must also become very terrible in the world as a result of people's sins, for now is the time that the Apostle Paul spoke of; once he said to Bishop Timothy that in the last days of this world

---

[77] I have silently expanded suspensions, and restored some letters deleted by a later reader.

there would be dreadful times as a result of men's sins, and, as he says, men will love this deceptive world all too much, and be too greedy for worldly wealth, and too many will become too arrogant, and altogether too proud and boastful, and some will become terrible scoffers at piety and revilers of book-learning, and lovers of wrong, and some will become treacherous and beguilingly fickle, and steeped in sins without any truth. And let them recognize it who can, now is the time that this world is mingled with manifold wickedness and multifarious crime, and for that reason it is the worse widely in the world, just as the Gospel says.]

The division into constituent clauses (again revealed and emphasized through manuscript punctuation) reveals something of Wulfstan's clear sense of rhetorical structure. Manuscript pointing highlights the rhyming doublets 'hwilce earfoð-nessa 7 hwilce gedrecednessa' (**3–4**), 'to wlance 7 ealles to rance' (**27–28**), and 'swicole 7 swæslice ficole' (**33–34**) as well as the present-past-future sequence in 'geweorðan […] gewurdan […] gewurðað' (**6–8**); the impressive stream of eleven clauses in a sequence all commencing with '7' are likewise thrown into relief, leading up to a final segment (**37–42**) that opens with a phrase ('nu is se tima', **37**) that echoes one from earlier in the passage (**17**), and closes with another ('ealswa þæt godspel cwæð', **42**) that has a similar parallel earlier in the piece (**9**). This segment is likewise notable for its continued assonance, alliteration, and sound-play ('gem*æn*cged **m**id **m***æn*igfealdan **m***an*e'; '*felafeal*dan **f**acne'; '**w**yrse **w**ide on **w**orlde'), features that are found elsewhere in the passage.[78] Wulfstan has clearly elaborated greatly on Ælfric's prose, evidently augmenting it with stock themes and phrases of his own. Of the forty-two clauses identified here, no fewer than twenty-four have clear echoes elsewhere in preaching material associated with Wulfstan, as follows:

2   cf. Bethurum II.12 (*þisse worulde geendung*).

5–6   cf. Bethurum II.19–20 (*scoldan geweorðan ær ðam ende wide on worulde*).

7–8   cf. Bethurum III.59–60 and Napier XLII.192/8 (*swylce æfre ær næs ne eft ne geweorþeð*).

9   cf. Bethurum V.26 and Xc.115 (*ealswa þæt godspel cwæð*).

12   cf. Bethurum VI.165 (*cild fedeð*).

---

[78] So, for example, this passage (**10**) contains the only example of the verb *tyman* in the sermons edited by Bethurum, presumably to chime with the noun *tima* that immediately follows (**11**), and which appears three times in the passage (at **11**, **17**, and **37**), and nine times in the sermon as a whole (Bethurum V.13, 15, 24, 41, 46, 62 (twice), 98, and 102).

13   cf. Bethurum V.40 (*sceal hit nyde*), XX(BH).5 (*hit sceal nyde*), XX(C).9 (*hit sceal nyde*), and XX(EI).9 (*hit sceal nyde*).
15   cf. Bethurum XX(EI).9 (*for folces synnan*).
16   cf. Bethurum V.41, XX(BH).5, XX(C).9, and XX(EI).10 (*yfelian swiðe*).
17   cf. Bethurum V.24 (*nu is se tima*).
23   cf. Bethurum III.43 (*for manna synnum*).
25   cf. Bethurum VI.115; VIIa.13; Xc.90, 93, and 197; XI.116 and 160; XIII.60; XIV.27; XV.62; XVII.69 and 77; XX(BH).34 and 106; XX(C).41 and 148; and XX(EI).40 and 150; Napier XXXVII.179/27; XL.189/9; XLIII.209/24; XLVII.243/13; L.273/14; and LIX.309/6 (*ealles to swyðe*).
28–29 cf. Bethurum VIIIc.171 (*ne beon ge to rance ne to gylpgeorne*).
32   cf. Bethurum VI.115 and XI.209 (*unriht lufode*).
33–34 cf. Bethurum Ib.16–17 (*swæslice swicole*), VIIIc.157 (*ne to swicole ne to ficole*), and IX.126 (*manswican þe on ða wisan swæslice swiciað*).
36   cf. Bethurum V.32; XV.49; XX(BH).45 and 84; XX(C).58 and 96; and XX(EI).50 and 99; Napier XXVII.129/9; XLVII.243/16; and L.268/29 (*gecnawe se ðe cunne*).
37   cf. Bethurum V.15 (*nu is se tima*).
39–40 cf. Napier XLII.194/20 (*facne and manfullum cræfte*).
41   cf. Bethurum Ib.18; II.20; and III.5 and 54; and Napier L.270/20 (*wide on worulde*).
42   cf. Bethurum V.12 and Xc.115 (*ealswa þæt godspel cwæð*).

Even in adapting Ælfric, Wulfstan takes pains to make the piece his own. While Wulfstan's customary recycling of his own characteristic phrases is obviously in evidence here, other aspects of the vocabulary of this passage are in fact rather rare within his corpus (notably *ofergrædige*, **26**) and support the notion that Wulfstan is relying heavily on Ælfric here. The opening of this passage clearly renders Matthew 24. 15 ('Interrogatus Iesus a discipulis de consummatione seculi'), and the wording here is so strikingly close to Ælfric's translation in *SH* II.18, lines 229–31 ('Sermo de die iudicii') that its editor was moved to exclaim that 'When we find Wulfstan using the same introduction to his sermon entitled *Secundum Marcum* (Bethurum V), we may be sure he took it from Ælfric':[79]

[79] *Homilies of Ælfric: A Supplementary Collection*, ed. by John C. Pope, EETS: OS, 259–60 (London, 1967–68), p. 610.

Ða halgan *apostolas* þe mid him þam Hælende ferdon,
þa þe he her on worulde wunode mid mannum,
ahsodan hyne endemys be *þissere worulde geendunge*;

[The holy apostles who travelled with the Saviour, those who dwelt here in the world
with men, they asked him together about the ending of this world.]

Pope gives a further two examples where this same homily of Ælfric seems to have
been used elsewhere in Bethurum V. The passage is again steeped in aural effects,
including alliteration, rhyme, and insistent (if not absolutely regular) use of the
two-stress rhythmical phrases that are Wulfstan's hallmark. As we have seen
throughout, when Wulfstan adopts, he adapts, even when drawing on prose stylists
as accomplished as Alcuin and Ælfric, and even when the work that he remakes is
his own.

Alas, Wulfstan's success in recasting what he wrote has been masked and obscured by later Wulfstan-imitators who in some cases produced work that is hard
to distinguish from Wulfstan's own. And thus his literary legacy has languished,
from a potent combination of uncertainty and insouciance, though his name lives
on. To most modern readers, Ælfric seems humble; Wulfstan not. Ælfric was a
monk, a Mass-priest, and an abbot; Wulfstan an archbishop, a law-maker, and a
confidant of kings. The two most justly famous and celebrated of late Anglo-Saxon
prose stylists are perhaps bound to be locked in an invidious comparison that leaves
neither side truly revealed. But just as Wulfstan was not Byrhtnoth, and chose not
to oppose what he could not destroy, so too he is not Ælfric, whose writings have
in modern scholarship wholly eclipsed his own. We need to understand Wulfstan
on his own terms, and not simply as a less learned, less polished, less measured
author than Ælfric: it is an over-simplification to say that while Ælfric wrote for
the cloister, Wulfstan wrote for the court. It is truer to say that while Ælfric
teaches and explains, Wulfstan preaches and proclaims. For all that, Wulfstan's is
a unique voice from a troubled time, and even now he deserves to be heard.[80]

[80] I am grateful to Samantha Zacher and Simon Keynes for reading through this paper and
for making a number of valuable suggestions.

Appropriation

OLD WINE IN A NEW BOTTLE: RECYCLED INSTRUCTIONAL MATERIALS IN *SEASONS FOR FASTING*

Mary P. Richards

Late Old English poetry is an untidy body of materials that some readers might consider uninviting as well. The poems range from occasional, for example the metrical entries in the *Anglo-Saxon Chronicle*, to devotional, such as portions of the Benedictine Office. Several are hortatory, eschatological, or gnomic. Many are translations, however loose, from Latin sources, primarily prose. As such, these poems generally treat the material of Anglo-Saxon prose, even so far as employing a 'prosaic' vocabulary.[1] Although they draw upon older poetic formulas and diction, they tend to be less strict in their adherence to the metrical principles of classical Old English verse, in part because of changes in the language, in part owing to lesser skilled poets.[2] And they often rely upon 'fillers', formulaic phrases that contribute little to meaning but serve the requirements of stress and

---

[1] On the literary and stylistic affiliations of *Seasons for Fasting*, see Mary P. Richards, 'Prosaic Poetry: Late Old English Poetic Composition', in *Old English and New: Studies in Language and Linguistics in Honor of Frederic G. Cassidy* (New York, 1992), pp. 85–92. On prosaic style generally, see E. G. Stanley, 'Studies in the Prosaic Vocabulary of Old English Verse', *NM*, 72 (1971), 385–418, and Roberta Frank, 'Poetic Words in Old English Prose', in *From Anglo-Saxon to Early Middle English: Studies Presented to E. G. Stanley*, ed. by Malcolm Godden, D. Gray, and T. Hoad (Oxford, 1994), pp. 87–107.

[2] See, for example, the recent studies by Charles D. Wright, 'More Old English Poetry in Vercelli Homily XXI', in *Early Medieval English Texts and Interpretations: Studies Presented to Donald G. Scragg*, ed. by Elaine Treharne and Susan Rosser, MRTS, 252 (Tempe, 2003), pp. 245–62, and Thomas A. Bredehoft, 'Ælfric and Late Old English Verse', *ASE*, 33 (2004), 77–107 (pp. 82–97).

alliteration. Nevertheless, there is much of interest in these late poems. They seem to represent a shift in taste coincidental with the extraordinary prose works of Ælfric and Wulfstan composed during the late tenth and early eleventh centuries. In fact, the learning and range of these prose writings are largely echoed in the surviving poetry from the period with the exception of such texts as the *Chronicle* poems and *The Battle of Maldon*.

This description of late poetical material will provide a context for the subject of the present essay, the Old English poem known as *Seasons for Fasting (SF)*.[3] As it survives, in a sixteenth-century transcript made by Laurence Nowell in London, British Library, Additional MS 43703, *SF* runs some 229½ lines divided into twenty-nine stanzas.[4] It was incomplete at the time Nowell copied it from the now-burnt London, British Library, Cotton MS Otho B. XI, as we know from Humphrey Wanley's earlier description.[5] The poem merits our attention because it embodies many of the themes, compositional methods, and sources found throughout late Anglo-Saxon writing. Furthermore, it is the earliest surviving piece of sustained stanzaic poetry in English. Whereas the poet has clear links to certain

---

[3] The standard edition is by Elliott Van Kirk Dobbie in *The Anglo-Saxon Minor Poems*, Anglo-Saxon Poetic Records, 6 (New York, 1942), pp. 98–104. Both Hoyt St. Clair Greeson, Jr, in 'Two Old English Observance Poems: "Seasons for Fasting" and "The Menologium" – An Edition' (unpublished doctoral thesis, University of Toronto, 1970), and Chadwick B. Hilton in 'An Edition and Study of the Old English "Seasons for Fasting"' (unpublished doctoral thesis, University of Tennessee , 1983), add valuable observations about the text and its background. In the years since its discovery, *SF* has had a number of commentators, most notably L. Whitbread, 'Notes on the Seasons for Fasting', *NQ*, 191 (1946), 249–52; F. Holthausen, 'Ein altenglisches Gedicht über die Fastenzeiten', *Anglia*, 71 (1952–53), 191–201; Roy F. Leslie, 'Textual Notes on *The Seasons for Fasting*', *JEGP*, 52 (1953), 555–58; and Kenneth Sisam, 'Seasons of Fasting', in his *Studies in the History of Old English Literature* (Oxford, 1953; repr. 1998), pp. 45–60.

[4] Carl T. Berkhout provides an up-to-date assessment and bibliography regarding Nowell in his contribution, 'Laurence Nowell (1530 – *ca* 1570)', in *Medieval Scholarship: Biographical Studies on the Formation of a Discipline*, vol. II: *Literature and Philology*, ed. by Helen Damico with Donald Fennema and Karmen Lenz (New York, 1998), pp. 3–17, with discussion of *SF* on p. 10.

[5] Roland Torkar offers a thorough reconstruction of Cotton Otho B. XI in *Eine altenglische Übersetzung von Alcuins 'Die Virtutibus et Vitiis,' Kap. 20 (Liebermanns Judex)* (Munich, 1981), esp. pp. 39–43. Before the manuscript burned, Wanley indicated that it was '*truncatum etiam in fine*' and transcribed lines 1–7a in his *Librorum Veterum Septentrionalium Catalogus*, vol. II of George Hickes, *Linguarum veterum septentrionalium thesaurus grammatico-criticus et archaeologicus*, 3 vols (Oxford, 1703–05), p. 219. A full stanza, lines 87–94, was printed earlier by Abraham Wheloc in his *Historiae Ecclesiasticae Gentis Anglorum Libri V* (Cambridge, 1643–44), p. 96.

contemporary poems, particularly the metrical *Creed* and, to a lesser extent, *Judgment Day II*, a rendition of Bede's poetical *De die iudicii*, his working methods resemble those of composite homilists, who drew on materials from Ælfric, Wulfstan, and others to address the occasion or topic at hand. The goal of this essay is to elucidate the sources and assembly of the extraordinary poem *Seasons for Fasting* and to demonstrate its uniqueness in the Old English tradition of recycled homiletic materials.

Paul Szarmach has argued that these anonymous homilists often began with a core text and expanded it by means of accretions often drawn from the works of Ælfric and Wulfstan.[6] Donald Scragg and others have demonstrated how the Insular practice of reusing homiletic materials originated with the Benedictine Revival and established a method of stylistic expansion that influenced Wulfstan, in particular, and continued long after the Archbishop's death.[7] Poets from the late tenth/early eleventh centuries also participated in this process, borrowing imagery, formulas, and occasionally even entire passages from earlier Old English poetry, even as they relied upon Latin sources.[8] In aim and subject matter, however, the *SF* poet more nearly resembles contemporary prose writers, the composite homilists, in his choice of topical and hortatory materials at the nexus of law and homily, as Patrick Wormald so cogently described Wulfstan's later writings.[9]

A brief overview of *SF* will illustrate its homiletic affinities. The controlling theme is the proper observance of fasts by the laity and priesthood. In three introductory stanzas, the poet opens with the example of Moses to communicate the

---

[6] See his 'The Vercelli Homilies: Style and Structure', in *The Old English Homily and its Backgrounds*, ed. by Paul E. Szarmach and Bernard F. Huppé (Albany, 1978), pp. 241–67, esp. pp. 244–52.

[7] Scragg, *Dating and Style in Old English Composite Homilies*, H. M. Chadwick Memorial Lectures, 9 (Cambridge, 1999).

[8] The poet of the Old English poetic *Menologium*, for example, quotes three lines from the Old English metrical Psalter. For a discussion of the implications of this phenomenon, see M. J. Toswell, 'The Metrical Psalter and *The Menologium*: Some Observations', *NM*, 94 (1993), 249–57. Further insight into the intertextuality of Old English poetry will be forthcoming from Andy Orchard's Anglo-Saxon Formulary Project, currently underway at the University of Toronto. See Orchard's description in 'Looking for an Echo: The Oral Tradition in Anglo-Saxon Literature', *Oral Tradition*, 18 (2003), 225–27.

[9] Wormald pursues this idea in depth in 'Archbishop Wulfstan and the Holiness of Society', in *Anglo-Saxon History: Basic Readings*, ed. by David Pelteret (New York, 1999), pp. 191–224, repr. in Wormald's *Legal Culture in the Early Medieval West: Law as Text, Image and Experience* (London, 1999), pp. 225–51.

importance of following spiritual leaders who convey and abide by God's law, including the injunction to fast. He concludes the introductory portion of the poem with a brief mention of Christ's sacrifice and resurrection and moves to the first major topic, the four seasonal observances known in England as Ember fasts.[10] Within the ten following stanzas, the poet describes these fasts and argues for their traditional English dates as prescribed by Gregory the Great. At the same time, he admonishes his audience not to accept the rival continental practices that have recently appeared in some areas.[11] This topical material today is probably the most interesting part of the poem, as indicated by the modern title assigned to it. But in fact, the Ember controversy constitutes only one-third of the extant stanzas. An equal number, stanzas 14 through 23, address the meaning and proper observance of the Lenten fast, a frequent topic for homilists. Here the poet cites the traditional examples of Moses, Elias, and Christ, and concludes with a call to beware the devil, who stands ready to accost every sinner just as he did Christ in the desert. The final group of stanzas, 24 through 29, deals with unobservant priests who mislead their flocks. Shifting strategy, the poet launches a tirade against lax priests who set a poor example by eating delicacies and drinking wine at taverns during periods when fasts should be observed. His portrait of such priests as 'gleemen' offering toasts rather than spiritual guidance links back to his concern that the laity are not receiving sound advice about Ember observances.

The most recent commentator on the poem, Hugh Magennis, places it in the context of teachings about fasting, gluttony, and drunkenness in Anglo-Saxon England. He calls the poem 'a statement of ecclesiastical authority which draws securely upon the embracing tradition of Christian regulatory teaching, in which eating and drinking have a moral and spiritual rather than a social significance'.[12] He links *SF* to ecclesiastical prose writings, with special emphasis on its connections to Alcuin's *De uirtutibus et uitiis* and to a range of Old English homilies

---

[10] Each of the four dates, along with English tradition, is discussed thoroughly in G. G. Willis, *Essays in Early Roman Liturgy* (London, 1964), pp. 64–75.

[11] Greeson, 'Two Old English Observance Poems', pp. 28–33, shows how murky the issue of Ember dates would have been in tenth-century England.

[12] Magennis, *Anglo-Saxon Appetites: Food and Drink and their Consumption in Old English and Related Literature* (Dublin, 1999), p. 92. In a shorter analysis, Patrick Wormald calls *SF* a poem about legal obligation: 'BL, Cotton MS. Otho B. xi: A Supplementary Note', in *The Defence of Wessex: The Burghal Hidage and Anglo-Saxon Fortifications*, ed. by David Hill and Alexander R. Rumble (Manchester, 1996), pp. 59–68 (p. 63). Greeson, 'Two Old English Observance Poems', p. 1, describes *SF* as an 'observance' poem in that it urges the proper observance of penitential times.

(many with identifiable Latin sources).[13] Not surprisingly, most of the homilies relate to the Lenten season. Although Magennis's analysis is enlightening, the totality of the poem is more complex, and indeed more interesting, than these prose sources would imply. For example, *SF* bears a number of connections to materials collected in the companion set of homilies and ecclesiastical institutes preserved in Oxford, Bodleian Library, MSS Hatton 113–14 and Junius 121, attributed most recently by Helmut Gneuss to Worcester in the third quarter of the eleventh century.[14] Similarly, the poem has affinities with certain items preserved in versions of the collection known as Wulfstan's Commonplace Book, associated with Worcester and York. As mentioned previously, *SF* also shares a poetic tradition with other late Old English poetry, including a close relationship to the versified *Creed*, part of the Benedictine Office in Junius 121.[15] Overall, the three major subjects of the poem — the dates for Ember fasts, the Lenten fast, and the gluttonous behaviour of certain priests — seem to have led the poet to three distinct sets of sources, the aspect of his compositional method to be discussed in this essay. I hope to show that he pursued his themes sequentially, as homilists often did, and that in so doing, he reflected and even surpassed Wulfstan's wide-ranging interest in prescriptive materials. Going beyond the authors of composite homilies who cut, pasted, and expanded selections from earlier works, our poet drew from a greater variety of sources, such as computistical materials, and perhaps his own personal observations to produce a unique result.

As mentioned above, the subject of the first major section of *SF* is the four seasonal fasts, known in Anglo-Saxon England as *ymbrendagas* (Ember days) or *ymbrenfæstena* (Ember fasts), celebrated on a Wednesday, Friday, and Saturday in late February or March, June, September and December.[16] In particular, the poet

---

[13] Magennis, *Anglo-Saxon Appetites*, pp. 93–100. An especially useful study of Alcuin's work as it was transformed into Old English homiletic prose is Paul E. Szarmach, 'Vercelli Homily XX', *Mediaeval Studies*, 35 (1973), 1–26.

[14] Gneuss *Handlist of Anglo-Saxon Manuscripts: A List of Manuscripts and Manuscript Fragments Written or Owned in England up to 1100*, MRTS, 241 (Tempe, 2001), pp. 120–21.

[15] Richards, 'Prosaic Poetry', pp. 85–87.

[16] Although the *SF* poet never uses the word *ymbre*, it is exclusively English. The *OED* speculates that it could be a corruption of Old English *ymbrene*, meaning 'period or revolution of time', more specifically 'season, or time of year'. Ælfric uses both *ymbre* and *ymbrene* with their different senses in his writings; citations can be found in *A Microfiche Concordance to Old English*, ed. by Antonette diPaolo Healey and Richard L. Venezky (Toronto, 1980). Alternatively, *ymbrene* could be a corruption of the Latin *quattuor tempora*, possibly related to Gmc. *quatember*.

addresses the controversy centred upon the dates of the spring and summer fasts. According to English tradition, the spring fast was to be observed in the first week of Lent and the summer fast in the week following Pentecost Sunday.[17] Continental practice, by contrast, assigned the spring fast to the first week of March and the summer fast to the second week of June. Both traditions observe the third and fourth Ember fasts in the week preceding the autumnal equinox and the week prior to the Nativity. All four dates are covered in our poem on lines 48–50, 58–62, 67–70, and 72–73, respectively.

The English dates, first ascribed to Gregory by Ecgberht of York, persisted without question until the aftermath of the Benedictine Revival, when calendars reflecting the continental usage began to appear at centres such as Worcester and Winchester.[18] Reaction to this incursion can be witnessed in the evolving legislation drafted by Archbishop Wulfstan known as the royal codes Æþelred V and VI, composed about 1008–09. Here the statement that festivals and fasts should be observed 'swa swa þa heoldon þa ða betst heoldon' (V. 15, 'just as they are observed according to the best practice') is expanded with '7 ymbren fæstena, swa swa Sanctus Gregorius Angelcynne sylf hit gedihte' (VI. 23, 'and Ember fasts, just as St Gregory himself prescribed it for the English').[19] These legal statements may well have influenced the poet of *SF*, especially as he seems to be writing to a mixed audience including the laity.[20] Nevertheless, the topic of Ember fasts is an unusual focus for a work in Old English. Although these occasions are often mentioned in sermons on fasting, they normally do not receive extended treatment. For that we must look to computistical materials, and these indeed seem to be a significant inspiration for the first portion of the poem.

As materials for determining the Anglo-Saxon calendar, particularly in regard to calculating the dates for moveable feasts, computus tables and charts often included information about the seasonal fasts. Compiled about 978 in Winchester, the highly influential computus appearing in London, British Library, Cotton MS

---

[17] The Ember days rulings are discussed by G. G. Willis in *Further Essays in Early Roman Liturgy*, Alcuin Club Collections, 50 (London, 1968), pp. 227–29. See also Heinrich Henel, *Studien zum altenglischen Computus* (Leipzig, 1934), pp. 60–64, and Sisam, 'Seasons of Fasting', p. 49 and n. 1.

[18] Sisam, 'Seasons of Fasting', p. 49 and n. 2.

[19] *Die Gesetze der Angelsachsen*, ed. by F. Liebermann, vol. I: *Text und Übersetzung* (Halle, 1903; repr. Scientia Aalen, 1960), p. 260, §15, and p. 252, §22.3–§23.

[20] See Magennis, *Anglo-Saxon Appetites*, pp. 88–89, and Chadwick B. Hilton, 'The Old English *Seasons for Fasting*: Its Place in Vernacular Complaint Tradition', *Neophilologus*, 70 (1986), 155–59.

Tiberius B. V (fols 2^r–19^r) and in the contemporary Leofric Missal (Oxford, Bodleian Library, MS Bodley 579, fols 38^r–58^r) presents the English dates; a statement in the Leofric Missal introduces them as follows: 'Haec sunt ieiunia quae Sanctus Gregorius Genti Anglorum predicare precepit' ('These are the fasts which St Gregory prescribed publicly for the people of England').[21] This computus was known, for example, to Byhrtferth of Ramsey, who composed a handbook to it, the *Enchiridion*, in Latin and Old English about 1011. Here Byrhtferth not only set forth the English dates, but he also included statements in Old English directing priests to know the correct dates for Ember fasts and exhorting them to fast accordingly:

> Þæt sceolon preostas witan mid fullum gerade þæt feower ymbrenfæstenu beoð on twelf monðum. (II. 1. 388–89)

> [Priests must know with perfect understanding that there are four Ember fasts in the twelve months.]

> And ic þe bebeode þæt þu þa twelf ymbrendagas gehealde, and ealle þa ymbrendagas glædlice gehealde þe ealde uðwitan gesetton eallum folce to ecere blisse. (Postscript, lines 38–40)[22]

> [And I exhort you to hold the twelve Ember-days and all the Ember-days that old scholars established as an eternal joy for all people.]

Our poem preserves a possible link to the *Enchiridion* through its use of two technical terms in stanza 6. Here Gregory's directions for fasting to the English people are introduced:

> And we þa mearce sceolan
> heoldan higefæste   *** mid Anglum,
> swa hie gebrefde us   beorn on Rome,
> Gregorius,   gumena papa. (*SF*, lines 43b–46)

> [And we ought to observe resolutely those occasions … with the English, just as the man in Rome, Gregory, the people's pope, wrote them down briefly for us.]

---

[21] Quoted from F. E. Warren's edition (Oxford, 1883), p. 53, by Greeson, 'Two Old English Observance Poems', pp. 73–74, n. 11. In the introduction to their edition of *Byrthferth's Enchiridion*, EETS: SS, 15 (Oxford, 1995), Peter S. Baker and Michael Lapidge describe the version of the computus in these two manuscripts as the standard 'which influenced virtually all later computi produced in England', p. xlv.

[22] *Byrthferth's Enchiridion*, ed. by Baker and Lapidge, pp. 81 and 245. In 'Doctrine and Diagrams: Maintaining the Order of the World in *Byhrtferth's Enchiridion*', in *The Christian Tradition in Anglo-Saxon England: Approaches to Current Scholarship and Teaching*, ed. by Paul Cavill (Cambridge: Brewer, 2004), pp. 121–37, Philippa Semper discusses the pedagogical aspects of the manual, esp. p. 127. Semper addresses Byrhtferth's presentation of the Ember fasts in diagrams and text on pp. 32–33.

Mearce appears twice in Byhrtferth's work as it is used in *SF*, referring to a term, that is 'a lunar date from which a feast is calculated'.[23] Interestingly, the corresponding passage in the *Enchiridion* explicates the meaning of Latin mnemonic verses for determining the term of Easter. By using *mearce* as he does, our poet is therefore able to convey the precise distinction between the English and continental dates for the Ember fasts. Another rare usage is *SF gebrefde*, literally 'written down briefly', said of directions for determining leap year and for the proper conduct of the Passover feast in Byhrtferth's work.[24] In so characterizing Gregory's prescription to the English nation, our poet emphasizes the connection between the lunar calendar and the spiritual imperative. At the very least we can conclude that the *SF* poet was familiar with the Old English terminology of observance as reflected in Byhrtferth's handbook, and probably was influenced as well by the Latin computus of his time. In fact, the traditional association of these materials with Latin mnemonic poems on the dates of Easter and Lent could have offered inspiration to versify, if one were needed.[25] A copy of the computus prefaced by such poems and including a statement prescribing the English dates for Ember fasts actually appears in eleventh-century matter added to the beginning of the homiletic collection in Hatton 113, which, it may be recalled, has affinities with *SF*.[26] This collocation of texts, apparently contemporary with the remainder of the manuscript, offers further evidence for the conscious association of computistical and prescriptive materials that is evidenced in our poem.

After introducing the issue of Gregory's dates for the English observances, the poet devotes the next four stanzas of the first section to each of the Ember fasts in turn. In so doing, the poet conveys his awareness that the first two fasts of the year require special attention by describing their dates and celebrations in more specific language than the others. Compare, for example, the description of the second fast:

> On þære wucan   þe æfter cumeð
> þam sunnandæge   þe geond sidne wang
> Pentecostenes dæg   preostas nemnað. (*SF*, lines 58–60)

[in the week which comes after the Sunday which throughout the wide land priests call the day of Pentecost.]

---

[23] *Byrhtferth's Enchiridion*, ed. by Baker and Lapidge, p. 452.

[24] *Byrhtferth's Enchiridion*, ed. by Baker and Lapidge, p. 437.

[25] See *Byrhtferth's Enchiridion*, ed. by Baker and Lapidge, commentary on the Easter cycle, pp. 320–21.

[26] N. R. Ker, *Catalogue of Manuscripts Containing Anglo-Saxon* (Oxford, 1957), p. 398, item 81; see also above, p. 349.

with the third:

> On þære wucan   þe ærur byð
> emnihtes dæge   ælda beornum. (*SF*, lines 67–68)

[in the week which is before the day of Equinox for the children of men.]

Moreover, the poet's treatment of Gregory's admonition as well as the dates of the four fasts seems to draw upon a Latin text on the Ember fasts, found in five manuscripts of the so-called Commonplace Book associated with Archbishop Wulfstan.[27] The full piece, entitled *De ieiunio quattuor temporum*, has been described and edited by James Cross.[28] The opening to this piece, expanded by a statement of Gregory's prescription for the English, comprises the shorter version that appears in two of the five manuscripts.[29] Since none of the additional material in the longer version is adopted by our poet, it appears that he drew upon this shorter text to support his argument. Its influence on *SF* becomes clear when poetic references to the first fast are compared to the corresponding Latin descriptions:

> We þæt forme sceolan   fæsten heowan
> on þære ærestan   wucan lengtenes
> on þam monþe   þe man Martius
> geond Romwara   rice nemneð. (*SF*, lines 47–50)

[We must observe that first fast in the first week of Lent in the month which is called March throughout the kingdom of Rome.]

Sed sanctus Gregorius hêc ieiunia genti Anglorum sic predicare precepit: Ieiunium primum in prima ebdomada quadrigesime. (Cross, p. 75)

---

[27] For an overview of this collection in its various manifestations, see Hans Sauer, 'The Transmission and Structure of Archbishop Wulfstan's "Commonplace Book"', in *Old English Prose: Basic Readings*, ed. by Paul E. Szarmach, Basic Readings in Anglo-Saxon England, 5 (New York, 2000), pp. 339–93. Thomas N. Hall now identifies this Latin text as a sermon by Wulfstan on the basis of its inclusion in a collection of his Latin works in Copenhagen, Kongelige Bibliotek, Gl. Kgl. Sam. MS 1595 (1st quarter, 11th century, Worcester (and York?)), at fols 23v–25r. See Hall, 'Wulfstan's Latin Sermons', in *Wulfstan, Archbishop of York: The Proceedings of the Second Alcuin Conference*, ed. by Matthew Townend, Studies in the Early Middles Ages, 10 (Turnhout, 2004), pp. 93–139 (p. 97).

[28] Cross expands upon Sauer's work, first published in 1980, in 'A Newly-Identified Manuscript of Wulfstan's "Commonplace Book", Rouen, Bibliothèque Municipale, MS 1382 (U.109), fols 173r–198v', *Journal of Medieval Latin*, 2 (1992), 63–83. Latin quotations are from this article.

[29] The manuscripts in question are Cambridge, Corpus Christi College, MS 190, pp. 225–27, and London, British Library, Cotton MS Nero A. I, fols 173r–174r. Cross, 'Newly-Identified Manuscript', p. 66, asserts that the expanded sermon in the other three collections was made 'under the direction, at least, of Archbishop Wulfstan'.

[But St Gregory prescribed these fasts to the people of England thus: the first fast in the first week of Lent.]

Quae tempora ieiuniorum ita praecepit Romana auctoritas obseruare, ut in primo mense, quem Martium uocant. (Cross, p. 73)

[The Roman authority undertook to observe times of fasting, as in the first month which they call March.]

And for the fourth fast:

> We þæt feorþe sceolen   fæsten gelæstan
> on þære wucan   þe bið ærur full
> dryhtnes gebyrde. (*SF*, lines 71–73a)

[We must observe that fourth fast in the week which is complete before the birth of the Lord.]

Ieiunium quartum in integra ebdomada ante natale Domini. (Cross, p. 75)

[The fourth fast in the full week before the birth of the Lord.]

We can even trace the influence of the short Ember text into stanza 11 following the descriptions of the fasting dates, where the poet sets forth the days of the week for the seasonal observances:

> On þissum fæstenum   is se feorþa dæg
> and sixta samod   seofoþa getinge
> to gelæstanne. (*SF*, lines 79–81a)

[During these fasts is the fourth day, and the sixth together with the seventh, to be performed.]

iiii et vi feria et sabbato ieiunandum sit. (Cross, p. 73)

[The fourth and sixth days and Saturdays should be observed as fast days.]

The stanza concludes with instructions to observe the fast until nones phrased similarly to those in Wulfstan's Lenten sermon in Old English:

> Emb þa nigoþan tyd,   nan is on eorþan,
> butan hine unhæl   an geþreatige,
> þe mot, æt oþþe wæt   ærur þicgan. (*SF*, lines 83–85)

[Concerning the none hour, there is no one on earth, unless sickness afflicts him, who may taste food or drink beforehand.]

Þæt æfre ænig cristen man ænig dæge ær nontide naðor ne abyrige ne ætes ne wætes butan hit for unhæle sy.[30]

---

[30] *The Homilies of Wulfstan*, ed. by Dorothy Bethurum (Oxford, 1957), XIV, lines 16–18, p. 233. Similar admonitions appear in a variety of homiletic texts for Lent and Rogation Days, as

[That no Christian man should ever partake of either food or drink before noontime unless it be for sickness.]

This sermon appears uniquely in Hatton 113, part of the core collection preserving many of the sources of *SF*.

In sum, for his treatment of the particulars of the Ember fasts, our poet is indebted to a Latin text presumably associated with Wulfstan. For his information about the computus, the poet seems to have been influenced by an Old English handbook, Byrhtferth's *Enchiridion*, from which he has adopted two key terms used in determining moveable feasts. Finally, the poet has made his first use of Lenten material, this authored by Wulfstan, before moving to the second portion of the poem to treat the Lenten fast in detail. Prior to doing so, he reminds his audience not to believe 'southerners' from the Continent who advocate other Ember dates which they claim to have been issued by Moses (!) and instead to look further south, to Gregory in Rome, for guidance on this matter.[31]

In the second part of *SF*, the types of sources and working methods used by our poet change as he moves to a topic, the Lenten fast, treated widely in traditional homiletic materials, including the writings of Ælfric and Wulfstan.[32] Although we can identify a few specific sources here, the poet employs an array of conventional themes, images, and biblical references probably stored in his memory. Our first example conveys the complexity of the situation. It appears that the poet may have known and used the version of Ælfric's Second Series homily for the First Sunday in Lent, very possibly in the composite version known as Napier LV that appears in Hatton 114, the collection that seems to underlie so much of his work.[33] In *SF*,

---

indicated by Roberta Frank in 'Old English *æræt* – "too much" or "too soon"?', in *Words, Texts and Manuscripts: Studies in Anglo-Saxon Culture Presented to Helmut Gneuss on the Occasion of his Sixty-fifth Birthday*, ed. by Michael Korhammer, Karl Reichl, and Hans Sauer (Cambridge, 1992), pp. 293–303.

[31] For background to the hostility towards Breton pilgrims and other religious exiles during the reign of King Athelstan (924 x 929), and the resistance to ensuing Benedictine reforms that had continental (Frankish) roots, see Caroline Brett, 'A Breton Pilgrim in England in the Reign of King Athelstan', in *France and the British Isles in the Middle Ages and Renaissance: Essays by Members of Girton College, Cambridge, in Memory of Ruth Morgan*, ed. by Gillian Jondorf and D. N. Dumville (Woodbridge, 1991), pp. 43–69, esp. pp. 44–48.

[32] In addition to Ælfric's First and Second Series homilies for the First Sunday in Lent, treated hereafter, see for example, Blickling Homily III for the same occasion in *The Blickling Homilies*, ed. by Richard Morris, EETS: OS, 58, 63, 73 (London, 1874–80; repr. as one volume, 1967), pp. 27–39.

[33] *Ælfric's Catholic Homilies: The Second Series, Text*, ed. by Malcolm Godden, EETS: SS, 5 (Oxford, 1979), no. 7, lines 11–13. The composite homily, containing lines 1–37 and 89–179

as the poet recounts the history of the Lenten fast, we find wording close to the revised version in Ælfric's Second Series homily:

> [Moyses] þæt fæsten heold   feowertig daga
> and nyhta samod,   swa he nahtes anbat
> ær he þa deoran æ   dryhtnes anfenge. (*SF*, lines 108–10)

[Moses held that fast forty days and nights together, so he tasted nothing before he received the precious law of the Lord.]

> Se heretoga Moyses fæste feowertig daga and feowertig nihta tosamne to ði þæt he moste godes æ underfon. (*CH* II.7, lines 11–13)

[The army leader Moses fasted forty days and forty nights together so that he might receive God's law.]

The corresponding passage from Ælfric's First Series homily for the same occasion, also found in Hatton 114, reads as follows:

> Moyses se heretoga fæste eac feowertig daga. 7 feowertig nihta. to ðy þæt he moste underfon godes æ. (*CH* I.11, lines 182–83).

[Moses the army leader fasted likewise forty days and forty nights in order that he might receive God's law.][34]

An obvious difference between the two versions of the homily is the word *tosamne* added to the revision and reflected in *SF samod*. Moreover, the revised version omits an important aspect of the First Series text, namely Ælfric's statement that the forty-day fast 'was made possible only by divine power, for Moses and Elijah as much as for Christ'.[35]

> Ac [Moyses] ne fæste na þurh his agene mihte, ac þurh godes; eac se witega helias. fæste eallswa lange; eac þurh godes mihte. (*CH* I.11, lines 184–85)

[But Moses did not fast through his own power, but through God's; likewise the prophet Elijah fasted just as long, also through God's power.]

---

from Ælfric, is printed in *Wulfstan: Sammlung der ihm zugeschreibenen Homilien nebst Untersuchungen über ihre Echtheit*, vol. I: *Text und Varianten*, ed. by A. S. Napier (Berlin, 1883; repr. with a bibliographical supplement by Klaus Ostheeren, Dublin, 1967), pp. 282–89. The passage in question is at p. 285, lines 16–18, with Ostheeren's notes on p. 360. Its wording is identical to that quoted above. See also Karl Jost, *Wulfstanstudien*, Swiss Studies in English, 23 (Bern, 1950), pp. 261–62.

[34] Translation quoted from *Ælfric's Catholic Homilies: The First Series, Text*, ed. by Peter Clemoes, EETS: SS, 17 (1997), no. 11, lines 82–84.

[35] Discussed by Malcolm Godden in *Ælfric's Catholic Homilies: Introduction, Commentary, and Glossary*, EETS: SS, 18 (Oxford, 2000), p. 93.

Only the point about Elijah is retained in the Second Series homily and in Napier LV; the statement about Moses is omitted in both texts. The former idea seems to underlie the poet's depiction of Elijah's fast:

> Eft Helias,   eorl se mæra,
> him on westene   wiste geþigede,
> þær him symbelbread   somod mid wætere
> dryhtnes engla sum   dihte togeanes,
> and se gestrangud wearð   styþum gyfle
> to gefæstenne   feowertig daga
> and nihta samod. (SF, lines 120–26a)

> Se mære þegen   mihta ne hæfde
> to astigenne   stæppon on ypplen
> ær him þæt symbel wearþ   seald fram engle. (SF, lines 129–31)

[Again, Elijah himself, the famous man, consumed food in the desert, where for him one of the angels of the Lord set out feast bread along with water, and he came to be strengthened with sustaining food in order to fast forty days and nights together. [. . .] The glorious thane had not the power to ascend the steps to the summit before the feast was given to him by the angel.]

Thus, while SF 120–26 renders the narrative in I Kings 19. 4–8, the commentary offered in lines 129–31 implies Ælfric's interpretation of the episode. The poet does not offer any such statement about either Moses or Christ. The omission is another possible connection with the revised version of Ælfric's Lenten homily.

In stanza 18, as Hans Schabram has shown, the poet adopts an idea, ultimately from Malachi 2. 7, expressed in the Old English and Latin versions of an anonymous sermon for Ash Wednesday found in Cambridge, Corpus Christi College, MS 190:[36]

> Sint for englas geteald   eorþbugendum
> þa þe dryhtnes word   dædum lærað. (SF, lines 136–37)

Schabram translates the vexed passage from the poem as follows: 'Angels are considered as earth dwellers who teach the word of God by deeds', an allusion to priests who serve both as God's angels and messengers on earth.[37] The corresponding passage from the Old English homily in CCCC 190 reads:

---

[36] Schabram, 'Zur Interpretation der 18. Strophe des altenglischen Gedichts The Seasons for Fasting', Anglia, 110 (1992), 296–306, quotations at p. 305.

[37] Schabram, 'Zur Interpretation der 18 Strophe', p. 306. An interesting counterpoint to the idea of priests as God's messengers/angels appears in Blickling Homily IV for the Third Sunday in Lent, where priests who do not rightly serve the laity are likened to fallen angels who contended against God and were cast into hell. See Blickling Homilies, ed. by Morris, p. 49.

Forðan se sacred is gecyged godes engel, þæt is godes boda.[38]

[Therefore the priest is called God's angel, that is, God's messenger.]

This source provides yet another link to Wulfstan's Commonplace Book as a working context for our poet. His subsequent exhortation to fast from sinful deeds reflects the liturgy for the Lenten season, as Hoyt Greeson has shown, but, more importantly for this study of sources, it appears in the material drawn from Ælfric's *CH* II.7 in Napier LV.[39]

The remaining influences upon the poet's treatment of the Lenten fast may well reside in his memory rather than direct borrowing.[40] For instance, his mention of Christ's willingness to be baptized and to fast forty days even though sinless, as an example to others, reflects the orthodox view.[41] Greeson points out the correspondence in phrasing regarding this matter between *SF* 157b *nanuht gyltig* and the phrase *nanre synne forgifenysse* in Ælfric's Second Series homily on the Epiphany (II.3, line 198).[42] It is worth noting that this homily appears only in three surviving manuscript collections, but two of these have connections to the Worcester area.[43] Further, the poet's description of the devil's works, in which the devil attempts to place his arrows in the bodies of his victims, and the remedy against this assault, namely seeking the shield of the Lord and his holy angels, echoes the ideas and some of the vocabulary in Cynewulf's *Christ II*, lines 763b–80a.[44] Wulfstan offers a similar depiction of the devil's weapons in sermons addressed to priests and to the laity on the efficacy of baptism, found in Bethurum VIIIb, lines 34–35, and VIIIc,

---

[38] Schabram, 'Zur Interpretation der 18 Strophe', p. 305.

[39] Greeson, 'Two Old English Observance Poems', p. 237. *CH* II.7, lines 35–37, is quoted in Napier LV.12–13.

[40] Mary Swan offers a provocative analysis of the function of memory in late Old English homiletic composition in 'Memorialized Readings: Manuscript Evidence for Old English Homily Composition', in *Anglo-Saxon Manuscripts and their Heritage*, ed. by Phillip Pulsiano and Elaine M. Treharne (Aldershot, 1998), pp. 205–17. The work of the *SF* poet reflects many of her observations about the role of memory in the transmission of this material.

[41] See, for example, Matthew 3. 15 and Augustine, *In Iohannis euangelium tractatus CXXIV*, ed. by R. Willems, CCSL, 36 (Turnhout, 1954), V.5.

[42] Greeson, 'Two Old English Observance Poems', p. 239.

[43] On this relationship, see *Old English Homilies from MS Bodley 343*, ed. by Susan Irvine, EETS: OS, 302 (Oxford, 1993), pp. li–lii. The manuscript firmly attributed to Worcester is Cambridge, Corpus Christi College, MS 178.

[44] Printed in *The Exeter Book*, ed. by George Philip Krapp and Elliott Van Kirk Dobbie, Anglo-Saxon Poetic Records, 3 (New York, 1936), pp. 3–49, at p. 24.

lines 65–66, one copy of the latter appearing in Hatton 113, folios 16–21. In these sermons, the chrism anointed on the chest and shoulders serves as God's shield 'þæt deofol ne mæg ænig his ættenra wæpna him on afæstnian' (Bethurum VIIIc, lines 65–66, 'so that the devil may not fasten any of his poison weapons upon him'). If Wulfstan is our poet's immediate (possibly remembered) source, the image here makes a neat link with the previous reference to Christ's baptism.[45] The poet concludes this section with a reminder that the forty-day Lenten fast must be observed until nones without partaking of meat or fish (*SF*, lines 181–83). Similar directives appear in almost every Anglo-Saxon discussion of Lenten observances, from Theodulf's *Capitula* through Wulfstan's works. In sum, our poet has drawn from conventional materials, themes, and images in his treatment of the Lenten fast. Although we can identify some specific influences, the most noteworthy of those being the passages from Ælfric quoted in Napier LV, he obviously drew upon a broad knowledge of the literature related to his topic and freshened his references primarily by directly addressing his audience, telling them, for instance, that they, like Elijah, need the Lord's help to ascend to glory (*SF*, lines 148–51).

In the last section of *SF*, the poet makes several shifts in perspective and tone. He begins by setting forth certain expectations of priests: that they sing daily Mass; that they exhort their listeners to fast properly and to make amends for their sins with alms; and that they lead exemplary lives as an inspiration to their congregants. Precedents for these directives appear in the writings of both Ælfric (Old English letter for Wulfsige) and Wulfstan (especially his *Canons of Edgar* and the derivative *Northumbrian Priests' Law*).[46] In particular, *Canons* 48, 49, and 59 speak directly to these topics by advising priests to be versed in the feasts and fasts of the Church and to speak with one voice about these to the laity, lest they be misled, and to be neither *ealuscopas* ('ale-house singers') nor gleemen, but rather bear themselves wisely and worthily.[47] These statements are echoed by items 11 and 41 in *Northumbrian Priests' Law*.[48] But next, our poet turns from offering directions for priests to address *folces mann* in the second person, as an individual who may be

---

[45] See also Greeson, 'Two Old English Observance Poems', p. 240.

[46] Ælfric's letter for Wulfsige II, Bishop of Sherborne, has been edited and translated by Dorothy Whitelock in *Councils and Synods with Other Documents relating to the English Church*, vol. I.1, A.D. 871–1066 (Oxford, 1981), pp. 191–226, esp. §§ 61–66, 74–78. For *Wulfstan's Canons of Edgar* see the edition by Roger Fowler, EETS: OS, 266 (Oxford, 1972). For the *Northumbrian Priests' Law*, see *Die Gesetze*, ed. by Liebermann, I, 380–85, esp. §§ 11, 41, 57.

[47] *Wulfstan's Canons of Edgar*, ed. by Fowler, pp. 12–15.

[48] *Die Gesetze*, ed. by Liebermann, I, 381–82.

confronted with badly behaving clergy. In lines derived ultimately from Ezekiel 34. 18–19, as Schabram has shown, the poet instructs his audience not to follow sinning priests and drink the dirty water of iniquity, but instead to drink the clear water of the teaching of glory, in other words, divine truth.[49] In this the poet may have been inspired by a passage from the English translation of Gregory's *Cura Pastoralis*:[50]

> Nu þa, folces mann   fyrna ne gyme,
> þe gehalgod mann   her gefremme,
> ac þu lare scealt   lustum fremman
> ryhthicgennde   þe he to ræde tæchð,
> drince he him þæt drofe,   [duge hlutter þe]
> wæter of wege,   þæt is wuldres lare. (*SF*, lines 202–07)[51]

[Now then, man of the people, heed not sins the ordained man commits here, but you ought, thinking rightly, to perform gladly the doctrine which he teaches with good counsel; though he drink the dirty water, you ought to drink that [pure water] from the way, that is, the teaching of glory.]

> Sua ða lareowas hi drincað suiðe hluter wæter, ðonne hi ðone
> godcundan wisdom leorniað, 7 eac ðonne hie hiene lærað; ac hie
> hit gedrefað mid hira agnum unðeawum, ðonne ðæt folc bisenað
> on hira unðeawum, nals on hira lare.[52]

[Thus the teachers drink very pure water when they learn the divine wisdom, but also when they teach it; but they defile it with their own vices when they set an example to the people by their vices, not by instruction.]

Given that Gregory's chapter, in which this sentence appears, is devoted to criticism of teachers who do not live up to their teaching, our poet may well have had these ideas in mind even as he struggled to incorporate them into poetry.[53]

At this point in the poem, the poet gives way to personal observations about bad priestly behaviour and expresses his outrage at what he has witnessed. As Magennis shows, the poet's attack follows Alcuin's three-part definition of gluttony,

---

[49] Schabram, '*The Seasons for Fasting* 206f. Mit einem Beitrag zur ae. Metrik', in *Britannica: Festschrift für Hermann M. Flasdieck*, ed. by Wolfgand Iser and Hans Schabram (Heidelberg, 1960), pp. 221–40.

[50] Schabram, '*Seasons for Fasting* 206f.', pp. 225–27.

[51] Line 206b retains the MS reading over Dobbie's emendation.

[52] *King Alfred's West-Saxon Version of Gregory's Pastoral Care*, ed. by Henry Sweet, EETS: OS, 45 and 50 (Oxford, repr. 2001), p. 31, lines 3–6.

[53] *King Alfred's West-Saxon Version of Gregory's Pastoral Care*, ed. by Sweet, pp. 29–32.

originally in *De uirtutibus et uitiis*, but also widely known in Anglo-Saxon England and used, for example, by Ælfric in another Second Series Lenten homily.[54] First, the bad priests eat and drink too soon:

> Sona hie on mergan mæssan syngað
> and forþegide, þurste gebæded,
> æfter tæppere teoþ geond stræta. (*SF*, lines 213–15)

[Promptly in the morning they sing Mass and, having consumed [it], urged by thirst they roam through the streets in pursuit of the tapster.]

Secondly, they consume delicacies:

> Ostran to æte and æþele wyn
> emb morgentyd. (*SF*, lines 219–20a)

[oysters for food and fine wine during the morning time.]

And thirdly, they eat and drink too much:

> Hi þonne sittende sadian aginnað,
> [win seniað,] syllað gelome,
> cweðað goddlife gumena gehwilcum
> þæt wines dreng welhwa mote,
> siþþan he mæssan hafað, meþig þicgan,
> etan ostran eac and oþerne
> fisc of flode. (*SF*, lines 224–30a)[55]

[Sitting then, they begin to sate [themselves], bless the wine, pour repeatedly, say 'good life' to each of men, say that anyone weary after he has Mass may partake of a drink of wine, eat oysters as well and other fish from the sea.]

This performance of gluttony leads the poet to compare the erring priests to dogs and wolves, who also are unable to restrain themselves before food.

> Þæs þe me þingeð
> þæt hund and wulf healdað þa ilcan
> wisan on worulde and ne wigliað
> hwænne hie to mose fon, mæða bedæled. (*SF*, lines 220b–23)

---

[54] Magennis, *Anglo-Saxon Appetites*, pp. 93–94. See also *CH* II.12, lines 493–99, and N. R. Ker, 'Three Old English Texts in a Salisbury Pontifical, Cotton Tiberius C. i', in *The Anglo-Saxons: Studies in Some Aspects of their History and Culture Presented to Bruce Dickins*, ed. by Peter Clemoes (London, 1959), pp. 262–79, at p. 276. Frank, 'Old English *æræt*', p. 300, cites these passages from *SF* as further evidence of the Anglo-Saxon prohibition against early eating.

[55] Line 225a emended per Sisam, Leslie, and others.

[It seems to me that the hound and wolf act the same way in the world and do not hesitate when they seize food, lacking all continence.]

In his pastoral letters, as noted above, Ælfric wrote frequently about proper behaviour for priests and condemned excess in food and drink. However, he expressly forbids gluttonous priests to participate in Mass in his second Old English letter to Wulfstan, quoted from Junius 121 by Fehr:

Seðe aniges þinges onbyrigð, ætes oððe wætes, ostran oððe ofæt, wines oððe wæteres, ne ræde he pistol ne godspell to mæssan.[56]

[He who tastes anything of food or drink, oyster or fruit, should not read the epistle or gospel at Mass.]

This injunction gives special force to the poet's complaint in the closing lines of *SF* and reinforces Magennis's suggestion that *SF* 225a *win seniað* may involve Eucharistic parody.[57] Wulfstan's *Canons of Edgar*, also copied into Junius 121, draw upon Ælfric's letters for some of their formulations and likewise speak to the kind of behaviour condemned by our poet.[58] In short, even the poet's indignation at the sinful examples presented by gluttonous priests is rooted in contemporary writings found, as it happens, in manuscript collections of materials related to all three of his major topics.

It becomes clear, then, that by the eleventh century, instructional materials could be packaged quite differently from their original contexts and used in the service of current debates. *Seasons for Fasting* stands apart from Old English composite homilies on fasting, not the least because it is a poem. The first section has a distinctively nationalistic flavour that appears, for example, in topical poetry from the *Anglo-Saxon Chronicle*. The middle portion presents the poet's doctrinal points, while the conclusion attacks specific abuses in priestly behaviour. There is little overlap among the types of materials that influenced each part of the poem, though admittedly we can see evidence of Wulfstan's writings in all three. The poet moves from more technical sources treating the dates of Ember fasts, to an array of Lenten sermons, and finally to regulatory texts about the proper conduct and duties of priests.

---

[56] *Die Hirtenbriefe Ælfrics in altenglischer und lateinischer Fassung*, ed. by Bernhard Fehr, BaP, 9, repr. with a supplement to the introduction by Peter Clemoes (Darmstadt, 1966), pp. 146–221 (p. 180, lines 31–35).

[57] See Hilton, 'Old English *Seasons for Fasting*', pp. 155–59, and Magennis, *Anglo-Saxon Appetites*, p. 92.

[58] See note 47 above.

SF is so unusual in respect to its sources and influences that it is difficult to contextualize even within the ragtag field of late Old English poetry. It has been compared most often to the verse *Menologium*, a metrical calendar of sorts that draws from an array of liturgical texts such as missals and sacramentaries.[59] *Menologium* seems to have been composed as a means to help the unlettered (at least in Latin) determine the feasts of the liturgical calendar, for it describes these in reference to each other, rather than to lunar calculations, beginning and ending with the Feast of the Nativity of Christ.[60] Its cyclical structure, together with short but lyrical evocations of the seasons, suggests an Irish influence on the poet.[61] The poet even quotes three lines from the Old English metrical Psalms in celebration of Easter.[62] However, with their topical references and treatments of the liturgical calendar, the features common to *SF* and *Menologium* seem more to reflect general concerns of the era than a similar purpose.

Probably owing to their interest in the calendar, both poems were copied into manuscripts with the *Anglo-Saxon Chronicle*. But whereas *Menologium* appears in formal prefatory material in London, British Library, Cotton MS Tiberius B. I, *SF* occurred originally in a group of miscellaneous texts copied at the end of the now-burnt London, British Library, Cotton MS Otho B. XI, at some remove from the *Chronicle* text in that codex.[63] Both poems also express a nationalistic, even contemporary, viewpoint, with *Menologium* celebrating the feasts of Saints Gregory and Augustine and probably alluding to the injunction from the law code

---

[59] The text has been edited by Dobbie in *Anglo-Saxon Minor Poems*, pp. 49–55, and by Greeson, 'Two Old English Observance Poems', pp. 196–212. Kemp Malone published a translation, 'The Old English Calendar Poem', in *Studies in Language, Literature, and Culture of the Middle Ages and Later*, ed. by E. Bagby Atwood and Archibald A. Hill (Austin, 1969), pp. 193–99.

[60] Greeson, 'Two Old English Observance Poems', pp. 111–20. Pauline Head, 'Perpetual History in the Old English *Menologium*', in *The Medieval Chronicle: Proceedings of the 1st International Conference on the Medieval Chronicle, Driebergern/Utrecht, 13–16 July 1996*, ed. by Erik Kooper, Costerus New Series, 120 (Amsterdam, 1999), pp. 155–62.

[61] Greeson, 'Two Old English Observance Poems', pp. 169–72, and Elaine Tuttle Hansen, *The Solomon Complex*, McMaster Old English Studies and Texts, 5 (Toronto, 1988), pp. 117–20. See also John Hennig, 'The Irish Counterparts of the Anglo-Saxon *Menologium*', *Mediaeval Studies*, 14 (1952), 98–106.

[62] See above, note 8.

[63] The manuscript context for *Menologium* is discussed by Katherine O'Brien O'Keeffe in *The Anglo-Saxon Chronicle: A Collaborative Edition*, vol. V: *MS. C* (Cambridge, 2001), pp. xxv–xcii. For Cotton Otho B. XI, see Torkar, *Eine altenglische Übersetzung*, pp. 39–43.

V Æthelred in the closing lines.[64] In *SF*, however, these types of references are limited to the first section of the poem, whereas they appear at intervals throughout *Menologium*. Moreover, the latter has been well characterized as a catalogue poem, one with an ordered list of items (in this case, liturgical feasts) amplified by brief commentary.[65] It makes no argument, nor does it contain homiletic exposition, both prominent features of *SF*. So whereas that portion of *SF* influenced by Byrhtferth's Handbook on the computus, dealing with matters related to the calendar, resembles aspects of the *Menologium*, the rest of *SF* does not. While *Menologium* aims to inform its audience, the *SF* poet hopes to inform and to motivate his listeners.

Considering its compositional process, the only candidate for a core text in *SF* would be the short Latin history of Ember fasts, associated with Wulfstan's so-called Commonplace Book, described above. Whereas Old English composite homilies normally incorporated Old English texts, perhaps our poet turned to a Latin source because he could not locate one in English other than computistical material. Certainly he relied upon Old English sources for the remainder of the poem as he moved from traditional Lenten themes to admonitions about proper fasting. In fact, the very variety of his materials links *SF* to specific manuscript collections associated with Worcester, and it is reasonable to speculate upon his possible connection to Wulfstan's circle there. But the urgency of his topic, the poetic form, or both somehow freed the poet to expand the conventions of composite homilists and to create a new type of work from traditional methods and materials. This innovation, as we have seen, involved the integration of topical materials with computistical and hortatory elements, resulting in a new stanzaic mode of composition.[66]

---

[64] *Die Gesetze*, ed. by Liebermann, I, 240, §15.

[65] Nicholas Howe, *The Old English Catalogue Poems*, Anglistica, 23 (Copenhagen, 1985), pp. 74–86.

[66] I thank Professor Eric Stanley for his helpful suggestions in the course of completing this essay.

THE CIRCULATION OF THE OLD ENGLISH HOMILY IN THE TWELFTH CENTURY: NEW EVIDENCE FROM OXFORD, BODLEIAN LIBRARY, MS BODLEY 343

Aidan Conti

Presently, study into the role and use of English as one of three languages of literate discourse in England after 1066 finds itself in the throes of a fundamental reassessment.[1] Traditionally, the century and a half following the Norman Conquest, and the twelfth century in particular, which witnessed a dramatic decrease in the production of newly written material in English, has been regarded as the nadir of English literary history.[2] Indeed, the period's reputation as a renaissance rests largely, if not solely, on the production of Latin material by such figures as Anselm, Walter Map, William of Malmesbury, and John of Salisbury.[3] Yet, even as the number of original vernacular literary works once thought

---

[1] The period is now the focus of a project funded by the Arts and Humanities Research Council (AHRC) of Great Britain, 'The Production and Use of English Manuscripts 1060 to 1220', directed by Mary Swan and Elaine Treharne, details of which can be found at <http://www.le.ac.uk/ee/em1060to1220/index.htm>.

[2] On the views of English literary history leading to this type of assumption and its development, see A. G. Rigg, *A History of Anglo-Latin Literature* (Cambridge, 1992), esp. pp. 1–6.

[3] The idea of a twelfth-century renaissance was popularized by Charles Haskins, *The Renaissance of the Twelfth Century* (Cambridge, MA, 1927). On the justification of the term, as well as England's relation to the period, see R. W. Southern, 'The Place of England in the Twelfth-Century Renaissance', *History*, 45 (1960), 200–16. For further discussion of the term 'renaissance' and England's place in the period, see Christopher Brooke, *The Twelfth-Century Renaissance* (London, 1969), and more recently Rodney M. Thomson, 'England and the Twelfth-Century Renaissance', *Past and Present*, 101 (1983), 3–21, repr. in *England and the Twelfth-Century Renaissance* (Aldershot, 1998).

to have been written in the twelfth century, such as *The Owl and the Nightingale*,[4] decreases upon the closer scrutiny of modern scholarship, present-day studies have more accurately depicted the varied role that English material played in a wide range of literary production in the twelfth century.[5] Indeed, a full understanding of the marked and continued interest in the Old English homily in the twelfth century stands within a broader tradition of interaction between the Anglo-Norman present and the Anglo-Saxon past.[6]

The continued copying and employment of Old English material, which took place in a wide range of texts,[7] has perhaps been most widely discussed in relation to the outburst of historical writing in the early part of the twelfth century that underscores the interdependence of English, Latin, and French.[8] The persistence of English as a contemporary historical medium is demonstrated in the continued updating of the *Peterborough Chronicle*.[9] Additionally, the *Anglo-Saxon Chronicle* underpins much of Geffrey Gaimar's versified Anglo-Norman *Histoire des Engleis*.[10] The *Anglo-Saxon Chronicle* had an even broader and, contemporarily speaking, more profound influence on historical writing in Latin of such writers as Henry of Huntingdon, William of Malmesbury, and John of Worcester.[11] Anglo-Norman

---

[4] This poem, once dated to *c.* 1189–1216, has been recently reassigned to the second half of the thirteenth century; see Neil Cartlidge, 'The Date of *The Owl and the Nightingale*', *Medium Ævum*, 65 (1996), 230–47. For the argument for an earlier date, see Eric Stanley, *The Owl and the Nightingale* (London, 1960, repr. Manchester, 1972), p. 19.

[5] See, for example, Elaine Treharne, 'English in the Post-Conquest Period', in *A Companion to Anglo-Saxon Literature*, ed. by Phillip Pulsiano and Elaine Treharne (Oxford, 2001), pp. 403–14.

[6] On the literature, language, and multilingualism of the period, see Ian Short, 'Language and Literature', in *A Companion to the Anglo-Norman World*, ed. by Christopher Harper-Bill and Elisabeth van Houts (Woodbridge, 2003), pp. 191–213.

[7] For a list of the range of material written and copied in English in the twelfth century, see Elaine Treharne and Mary Swan, 'Introduction', in *Rewriting Old English in the Twelfth Century*, ed. by Mary Swan and Elaine M. Treharne, CSASE, 30 (Cambridge, 2000), pp. 1–10 (pp. 1–2).

[8] For a useful introduction to the subject, see Elisabeth van Houts, 'Historical Writing', in *Companion to the Anglo-Norman World*, ed. by Harper-Bill and van Houts, pp. 103–21.

[9] See *The Anglo-Saxon Chronicle*, vol. VII: *MS E*, ed. by Susan Irvine (Cambridge, 2004); see also the still useful introduction in Cecily Clark, *The Peterborough Chronicle: 1070–1154*, 2nd edn (Oxford, 1970).

[10] See Alexander Bell, *L'estoire des Engleis*, Anglo-Norman Texts, 14–16 (Oxford, 1960), esp. pp. lii–lxxvii.

[11] For Henry, see Diana Greenway, *Henry Archdeacon of Huntingdon: Historia Anglorum*, Oxford Medieval Texts (Oxford, 1998), pp. lxxxv–cvii, esp. pp. xci–xcviii. For William, see the

efforts to grapple with the Anglo-Saxon past not only reused Old English material but reinvented it; Henry of Huntingdon relied on the *Anglo-Saxon Chronicle* in his history, but also attempted to mirror the metre of Old English verse in his Latin rendering of the *Chronicle* poem *The Battle of Brunanburh*.[12]

Thus, the period witnessed a sustained and profound interest in English works even if the impetus to produce new works in English decreased to a trickle. Nowhere is the interest more pronounced than in the continued copying, compilation, and reworking of Old English homiletic material in the twelfth century. Of the twenty-seven surviving manuscripts containing predominately Old English material that were written about 1100 or later, nine are homiletic and hagiographic collections, making these texts the most common to have been copied after the Conquest.[13] Clearly, in the twelfth century there was still an interest in exegesis of

---

commentary of R. A. B. Mynors with R. M. Thomson and M. Winterbottom, *William of Malmesbury: Gesta regum Anglorum; The History of the English Kings*, Oxford Medieval Texts, 2 vols (Oxford, 1998), vol. II. For John, see Patrick McGurk and Reginald Darlington, *The Chronicle of John of Worcester*, vols II and III, Oxford Medieval Texts (Oxford, 1995–98), III, pp. xix–xl (esp. pp. xx–xxvi).

[12] See A. G. Rigg, 'Henry of Huntingdon's Metrical Experiments', *Journal of Medieval Latin*, 1 (1991), 60–72.

[13] This number includes one manuscript dated s. xiii[in] and one dated to about 1200 by N. R. Ker, *A Catalogue of Manuscripts Containing Anglo-Saxon* (Oxford, 1957; repr. with suppl. 1990), pp. xviii–xix, as well as one manuscript omitted in Ker's catalogue but mentioned in a footnote (p. xix, n. 2). Another manuscript (London, British Library, Cotton MS Otho A. XIII), reported to have been written around the time of Henry II, was described by Wanley but lost in the fire of Ashburnham House. As Ker noted, no clear line between Old and Middle English can be drawn, and so he excluded from his count some manuscripts containing English, but whose links to the Anglo-Saxon past he found 'tenuous' such as the Lambeth homilies (London, Lambeth Palace Library, MS Lambeth 487) and Vespasian homilies (London, British Library, Cotton MS Vespasian A. XXII) both of which contain material derived from Old English sources, as well as two other manuscripts written in the twelfth century, the Ormulum (Oxford, Bodleian Library, MS Junius 1) and the Trinity homilies (Cambridge, Trinity College, MS B. 14. 52). Increasingly, there has been a tendency to include implicitly the Lambeth, Vespasian, and, perhaps to a lesser extent, Trinity homilies as part of Old English in the twelfth century; see Treharne and Swan, 'Introduction', pp. 1–2. Although only parts of the collections derive from Anglo-Saxon material, the reuse of Ælfric's work in the Lambeth and Vespasian homilies is fundamental to issues raised here. On the Lambeth homilies, see Mary Swan, 'Ælfric's *Catholic Homilies* in the Twelfth Century', in *Rewriting Old English*, ed. by Swan and Treharne, pp. 62–82 (pp. 71–76); Celia Sisam, 'The Scribal Tradition of the *Lambeth Homilies*', *RES*, n.s. 2 (1951), 105–13. On the Vespasian homilies, see Mary Richards, 'MS Cotton Vespasian A. XXII: The Vespasian Homilies', *Manuscripta*, 22 (1978), 97–103.

homiletic material in English as well as the sermon and exhortatory material of pre-Conquest origin.

The example provided by the work of Ralph d'Escures, an Anglo-Norman abbot who became Bishop of Rochester (1108–14) and then Anselm's little-known successor as Archbishop of Canterbury (1114–22), demonstrates the way in which new and old material was commingled in twelfth-century manuscripts for contemporary uses.[14] The only known work attributed to Ralph is a short Latin homily on the active and contemplative life designated for the Feast of the Assumption of the Blessed Virgin Mary (15 August).[15] Ralph's own prefatory remarks indicate that he originally delivered the piece, which represents his attempt to reconcile the gospel lection for the day with the celebrated feast, in Norman French on more than one occasion and then translated his work into Latin at the request of his superiors.[16] Presumably, after Ralph left for England in 1102 the homily was translated into an Old (or early Middle) English version, which survives in a single manuscript witness, London, British Library, Cotton MS Vespasian D. XIV, folios 4–169, dated to the middle part of the twelfth century.[17] The manuscript itself may have originated in Rochester, or Christ Church, Canterbury,[18] the very places at which Ralph's career in England was centred, which may suggest that the Archbishop himself or someone close to the Archbishop played a role in the translation of the homily. The Latin version of Ralph's homily also enjoyed a fairly widespread circulation; in manuscripts dated to the first half of the

[14] The only full treatment of the life of Ralph d'Escures is Mary Amanda Clark, 'Ralph d'Escures: Anglo-Norman Abbot and Archbishop' (unpublished doctoral dissertation, University of California at Santa Barbara, 1975).

[15] See Richard Sharpe, *A Handlist of the Latin Writers of Great Britain and Ireland before 1500*, Publications of the Journal of Medieval Latin, 1 (Turnhout, 1997; reissued with additions and corrections 2001), p. 447, no. 1242.

[16] 'Quid ad gloriosam Virginem Dei Genitricem lectio ista pertineat, ut in eius festiuitate legatur, plerique solent quaerere: unde quid ego sentirem, in conuentu fratrum prout potui uulgariter jam plusquam semel exposui. Et quia quod dixi auditoribus placuit, dicta letteris mandare ab eisdem et maxime a dominis abbatibus Willelmo Fiscanensi, Arnulpho Troarnensi, jussus, imo coactus sum': *PL* 158.644C–D.

[17] The homily is found on fols 151ᵛ–157ᵛ; see Ker, *Catalogue*, no. 209, pp. 271–77. On the compilation of Cotton Vespasian D. XIV, see Rima Handley, 'British Museum MS. Cotton Vespasian D. xiv', *NQ*, n.s., 21 (1974), 243–50.

[18] See Elaine M. Treharne, 'The Dates and Origins of Three Twelfth-Century Old English Manuscripts', in *Anglo-Saxon Manuscripts and their Heritage*, ed. by Phillip Pulsiano and Elaine M. Treharne (Aldershot, 1998), pp. 227–53 (p. 236).

twelfth century the homily was integrated into circulating versions of Paul the Deacon's homiliary, and shortly after Ralph's death the homily circulated under a false attribution to Anselm.[19] The translation into English of Ralph's work indicates that Anglo-Norman and Latin versions of the homily were not sufficient for the needs of contemporary clergy or laity. That this recently composed work circulated with pre-Conquest Anglo-Saxon material suggests that older vernacular material was instrumental in meeting the continued need for homiletic material in English.[20]

Yet, the examination of individual manuscripts suggests no single, overarching motivation behind the continued compilation of Old English material; in many cases, the particular purpose behind the compilation of a manuscript remains difficult to ascertain.[21] Recently, an increasing amount of work has attempted to examine post-Conquest homiletic manuscripts in terms of their monastic production,[22] aided by the examinations of manuscript production at Worcester, Rochester, and Christ Church, Canterbury.[23] Newer post-Conquest secular foundations, on the other hand, seemed not to have valued Anglo-Saxon vernacular compositions.[24] That monastic cathedrals should maintain an interest in Old

---

[19] See André Wilmart, 'Les Homilies attribuées à St. Anselme', in *Archives d'histoire doctrinale et littéraires du moyen âge*, vol. II (Paris, 1927), pp. 1–29 (pp. 18–19).

[20] A fuller treatment of the English translation of Ralph d'Escures has recently appeared: see Elaine Treharne, 'English Prose Texts and their Audience in the Mid-Twelfth Century', in *Writers of the Reign of Henry II: Twelve Essays*, ed. by Ruth Kennedy and Simon Meecham-Jones (New York, 2006), pp. 169–86. I am grateful to Elaine Treharne for sharing a prepublication copy of this work with me.

[21] On this subject supported by a range of examples from several manuscripts, see Susan Irvine, 'The Compilation and Use of Manuscripts Containing Old English in the Twelfth Century', in *Rewriting Old English*, ed. by Swan and Treharne, pp. 41–61.

[22] See for example, Treharne, 'Dates and Origins', p. 231.

[23] For Worcester, see E. A. McIntyre, 'Early Twelfth-Century Worcester Cathedral Priory, with Special Reference to Some of the Manuscripts Written There' (unpublished doctoral thesis, University of Oxford, 1978). For Rochester, see Mary P. Richards, *Texts and their Traditions in the Medieval Library of Rochester Cathedral Priory*, Transactions of the American Philosophical Society, 78.3 (Philadelphia, 1988). For Christ Church, Canterbury, see Teresa Webber, 'Script and Manuscript Production at Christ Church, Canterbury after the Norman Conquest', in *Canterbury and the Norman Conquest: Churches, Saints and Scholars, 1066–1109*, ed. by R. Eales and R. Sharpe (London, 1995), pp. 144–56.

[24] See Teresa Webber, *Scribes and Scholars at Salisbury Cathedral Library c. 1075–c. 1125* (Oxford, 1992).

English material is perhaps understandable; the monastic cathedral has been described as a particularly Anglo-Saxon establishment, and in these centres one might expect a more determined interest in Anglo-Saxon works.[25]

In addition to examining sets of manuscripts within the context of a particular religious institution, recent scholarship has examined post-Conquest manuscripts to determine the textual transmission of pre-Conquest works, to chart the evolution from Old to Middle English, and — perhaps one of the most interesting trends in Anglo-Saxon studies and one that mirrors present attitudes in medieval textual studies — to analyse these manuscripts and the texts therein in their own right, not simply as derivative material. In considering the evolving methods used in examining and studying post-Conquest Old English material in general and homilies in particular, the case of Oxford, Bodleian Library, MS Bodley 343 is demonstrative.

The manuscript, which has been dated on palaeographical grounds to the second half of the twelfth century, is important for several reasons.[26] Not only does the manuscript preserve the only extant versions of some pre-Conquest vernacular material, such as the second part of Ælfric's exposition for St Vincent's day,[27] it also contains significant reworkings of earlier material, such as Ælfric's *Life of St Martin*.[28] Furthermore, Bodley 343 is the sole twelfth-century manuscript to reproduce vernacular homilies of Wulfstan.[29] The manuscript also contains several later

---

[25] See Janet Burton, *Monastic and Religious Orders in Britain: 1000–1300* (Cambridge, 1994), pp. 14–15; and also David Knowles, *The Monastic Order in England*, 2nd edn (Cambridge, 1963), p. 129.

[26] For the generally accepted date of the manuscript, see Ker, *Catalogue*, no. 310, pp. 368–75. It should be noted, however, that the dating in F. Madan, H. H. E. Craster, and N. Denholm-Young, *A Summary Catalogue of Western Manuscripts in the Bodleian Library at Oxford*, vol. II.1 (Oxford, 1922), no. 2406, suggests the more specific third quarter of the twelfth century for the bulk of the manuscript, and the second half or the third quarter of the twelfth century for the Latin items that are the focus of the following discussion. A. S. Napier writing before Ker and the *Summary Catalogue* suggested 'about the third quarter of the twelfth century' in *History of the Holy Rood-Tree*, EETS: OS, 103 (London, 1894), p. ix.

[27] See Susan Irvine, 'Bones of Contention: The Context of Ælfric's Homily on St Vincent', *ASE*, 19 (1990), 117–32.

[28] See Susan Rosser, 'Old English Prose Saints' Lives in the Twelfth Century: The *Life of Martin* in Bodley 343', in *Rewriting Old English*, ed. by Swan and Treharne, pp. 132–42.

[29] See Jonathan Wilcox, 'Wulfstan and the Twelfth Century', in *Rewriting Old English*, ed. by Swan and Treharne, pp. 83–97.

additions of which *The Grave* has perhaps drawn the most attention.[30] This juxta-position of conservatism and progressiveness appears also in the lexicon employed in the manuscript which contains, for example, the last attestation of *þeowman* ('slave'),[31] in many ways a typical Old English compound, and, on the other hand, the first example of *degan* ('to die').[32] Indeed, among the small group of post-Conquest copies of Old English material, Bodley 343 is distinctive in both its contents and size.[33]

Although Bodley 343 has received a fair share of modern attention, the most notable manifestation of which is Susan Irvine's edition of seven homilies unique to the manuscript, no definitive evidence has nailed down a provenance or origin of the manuscript; Worcester and environs remains, however, the consensus candidate.[34] The earliest record of the manuscript comes from the first donation in 1602–03 by Sir Robert Cotton to Sir Thomas Bodley, who had resolved to re-create the public library at Oxford. The renowned palaeographer and cataloguer Humfrey Wanley conjectured that Bodley 343 represented the *Sermones Anglici*

---

[30] Edited by R. Buchholz, 'Die Fragmente der Reden der Seele and den Leichnam in zwei Handschriften zu Worcester and Oxford', *Erlanger Beiträge zur englischen Philologie*, 6 (1890), 11; see also A. Schröer, '"The Grave"', *Anglia*, 5 (1882), 289–90.

[31] See D. A. E. Pelteret, *Slavery in Anglo-Saxon England from the Reign of Alfred until the Twelfth Century* (Woodbridge, 1995), p. 314.

[32] See Antonette diPaolo Healey and others, *The Dictionary of Old English Fascicle F and Fascicles A–E (with revisions)*, CD-ROM (Toronto, 2003), *s.v.* dēgan. The attestation is defended against the counter-claims of the Canterbury Psalter by David McDougall and Ian McDougall, 'Some Notes on Notes on Glosses in the *Dictionary of Old English*', in *Anglo-Saxon Glossography*, ed. by R. Derolez (Brussels, 1992), pp. 115–38 (p. 124). See also Richard Dance, 'Is the Verb *Die* Derived from Old Norse? A Review of the Evidence', *ES*, 81 (2000), 368–83.

[33] It has been suggested that Bodley 343 is the widest and tallest of post-Conquest religious manuscripts containing English because it contains both Latin and Old English items; see Elaine Treharne, 'The Production and Script of Manuscripts Containing English Religious Texts in the First Half of the Twelfth Century', in *Rewriting Old English*, ed. by Swan and Treharne, pp. 11–40 (pp. 14–15), who compares the size of five other post-Conquest manuscripts with Bodley 343. It should be noted that Treharne reports folio measurements, which by her own admission may not represent the original size due to the possibility of trimming after original composition, rather than the measurements of the written space on the folio. Indeed, parts of the red titles to the Old English items on fols 65ʳ and 66ʳ have been excised due to trimming which suggests that at least part of the manuscript was larger at the time of composition.

[34] See *Old English Homilies from MS Bodley 343*, ed. by Susan Irvine, EETS: OS, 302 (Oxford, 1993), p. lii.

donated by Cotton,[35] as one of the eleven volumes listed in the library's 'Register of Benefactors' under the year 1603,[36] an identification that has been accepted by the *Summary Catalogue*.[37] The range of texts in the manuscript and the varying lines of transmission represented by the texts have suggested that the codex was compiled in or around Worcester.[38] However, differing analyses of the language of parts of the manuscript have produced other suggestions. Although Irvine's linguistic analysis of the seven items of her edition supports Worcester,[39] the south has also been proposed,[40] and another, less commonly accepted, analysis based on comparison with charter evidence has asserted that the language of the manuscript represents the dialect of the Worcester-Hereford border.[41]

Yet, despite all this attention lavished on the vernacular items perserved in the manuscript, scant attention has been paid to the series of Latin homilies that occupy folios xi[r]–xxxix[v], the overwhelming portion of the first scribe's stint in the manuscript. Until recently, scholars described only in passing the sixty-seven distinct items in this series of homilies, each of which is distinguished by a large

---

[35] 'Hunc cod. unum eorum esse puto, quem D. Thomæ Bodleio, ad instruendam Bibliothecam ab eo constructam dono dedit. D. Robertus Cottonus. Brucæus', in H. Wanley, *Antiquæ literaturæ septentrionalis liber alter seu* [...] *librorum vett. septentrionalium* [...] *catalogus historico-criticus*, vol. II of George Hickes, *Linguarum veterum septentrionalium thesaurus grammitco-criticus et archaeologicus*, 3 vols (Oxford, 1703–05), p. 25. The two volumes have been reprinted as no. 248 in the series English Linguistics 1500–1800 (A Collection of Facsimile Reprints), ed. by R. C. Alston (Menston, 1970).

[36] R. W. Hunt, *A Summary Catalogue of Western Manuscripts in the Bodleian Library at Oxford*, vol. I: *Historical Introduction and Conspectus of Shelf-Marks* (Oxford, 1953), pp. 76–122; the Cotton benefaction is listed at pp. 86–87.

[37] Hunt, *Summary Catalogue*, I, 86, no. 300 in order of acquisition. See also, Colin G. C. Tite, '"Lost or Stolen or Strayed": A Survey of Manuscripts Formerly in the Cotton Library', in *Sir Robert Cotton as Collector: Essays on an Early Stuart Courtier and his Legacy*, ed. by C. J. Wright (London, 1997), pp. 262–306 (p. 263).

[38] See *Old English Homilies*, ed. by Irvine, pp. li–lii, and more recently 'Compilation and Use of Manuscripts', pp. 59–60.

[39] *Old English Homilies*, ed. by Irvine, pp. lv–lxxvii.

[40] See *Homilies of Ælfric: A Supplementary Collection*, ed. by John C. Pope, EETS: OS, 259–60 (London, 1967–68), I, 18.

[41] See Peter Kitson, 'When Did Middle English Begin? Later Than You Think!', in *Studies in Middle English Linguistics*, ed. by J. Fisiak, Trends in Linguistics, Studies and Monographs, 103 (Berlin, 1997), pp. 221–69, and also 'Old English Dialects and the Stages of the Transition to Middle English', *Folia Linguistica Historica*, 11 (1992 [for 1990]), 27–87.

decorated initial, usually followed by a smaller, often red or green, initial beginning the pericope; indeed, several descriptions miscounted or misnumbered the items.[42] The discrepancy in the varying tallies may be explained by the presence of one non-homiletic piece consisting of seven manuscript lines summarizing the life of James, the son of Alpheus, author of the epistle bearing his name.[43] Another possible source for the discrepancy may be the several sets of paired homilies intended for the same occasion: one on the epistle, the other for the gospel reading for the day.[44] The fullest published assessment to date of these homilies appeared as part of Susan Irvine's study of the Old English homilies in Bodley 343 in which initial lines of each of these Latin items were published as part of the description, examination, and contextualization of the manuscript.[45] Irvine suggests further that the Latin expositions

> rely heavily on the Church Fathers and [...] may be a fairly recent rewriting of inherited patristic teaching [...] they may have been intended for liturgical use, for preaching or reading aloud rather than for private reading [and] included in an otherwise Old English manuscript because they were thought suitable for a readership or audience whose first language was English and whose knowledge of Latin was limited.[46]

Indeed, these homilies, which present commonplace teaching, even if not directly reliant on the church fathers, bear an important relation to preaching and the vernacular in the twelfth century, which will be further explored in the following discussion. This Latin section of the manuscript, Irvine concludes, argues against an exclusively antiquarian motive behind the compilation of the manuscript.

Based on Irvine's work, it is now possible to establish that the Latin homilies of Bodley 343 constitute a version of the recently entitled Carolingian Homiliary of Angers, a collection that has been most thoroughly examined by Raymond Étaix,

---

[42] *Ælfric's Catholic Homilies: The Second Series, Text*, ed. by Malcolm Godden, EETS: SS, 5 (London, 1979), p. xxxvii, equivocates: 'About sixty-seven short Latin homilies.' Ker, *Catalogue*, no. 310, item 5, counts 'sixty-five short homilies on the Gospels', which is repeated by Pope in *Homilies*, I, 14. *Ælfric's Catholic Homilies: The First Series, Text*, ed. by Peter Clemoes, EETS: SS, 17 (Oxford, 1997), p. 3, numbers sixty-five items and dubs them 'expositions'.

[43] Item number *xviii*; see further, pp. 392–94 below. For the sake of convenience, when discussing the collection of Latin items as a whole, the term 'homilies' will be used.

[44] These are items *ii* and *iii*, *xi* and *xii*, *xix* and *xx*, *xxii* and *xxiii*, *lxvii* and *l*. A further discussion of the sequence and itemization of the homilies follows.

[45] See Irvine, *Old English Homilies*, pp. xxiv–xxviii.

[46] Irvine, *Old English Homilies*, pp. xxviii–xxix.

who describes eleven full as well as five partial manuscript witnesses.[47] A previous description of the homiliary dubbed the collection the 'homiliarium gothicum', based on the witness of a Toledo manuscript once believed to have been written in the ninth or tenth century, but now dated to the late twelfth century.[48] The tentative title proposed by Étaix reflects not the place of origin of the homiliary, which remains unestablished, but the most complete, as well as the earliest, manuscript known to Étaix, namely Angers, Bibliothèque municipale, MS 236.[49] The identification of this homiliary in Bodley 343 is not only significant — it both elucidates a considerable part of the contents of the manuscript and demonstrates a more diffuse circulation of the text than previously known — but it is also timely because the most recently discovered, or perhaps rediscovered, Old English text, namely the so-called Taunton fragments, represents a fragmentary bilingual version of the Homiliary of Angers.[50]

[47] Raymond Étaix, 'L'homéliaire carolingien d'Angers', *Revue Bénédictine*, 104 (1994), 148–90. I am profoundly grateful to the late Abbé Étaix for his generous correspondence which made this identification and much of this work possible. For a more detailed account of this identification, see the appendix that follows. To distinguish items as they appear in the Homiliary of Angers, I have retained the Arabic numbers used in Étaix's reconstruction and designate the item as part of the homiliary by the prefixed abbreviation HA (e.g. HA 1). When discussing items as they appear in Bodley 343, I have retained Irvine's system of lower-cased Roman numerals, and where appropriate labelled the item with the designation of *Sermo* (e.g. *Sermo lviii*), concerning which see note 54 below.

[48] See J. F. Rivera Recio, 'El "homiliarum gothicum" de la biblioteca capitular de Toledo, homiliario romano del siglo IX/X', *Hispania Sacra*, 4 (1951), 147–67. Rivera Recio later accepted a much later dating of the manuscript to the late twelfth century; see A. M. Mundó, 'Datación de códices visigóthicos toledanos', *Hispania Sacra*, 18 (1965), 1–25 (p. 18). This homiliary is not a version of the Homiliary of Toledo as cited by Henri Barré, *Les homéliaires carolingiens de l'école d'Auxerre: authenticité, inventaire, tableaux comparitifs, initia*, Studi e Testi, 225 (Vatican City, 1962), p. 3, where Rivera Recio's 'homiliarium gothicum' is cited next to G. Morin, 'Homiliae Toletanae', in *Liber Comicus sive Lectionarius Missae quo Toletana Ecclesia ante annos mille et ducentos utebatur*, Anecdota Maredsolana, 1 (Maredsous, 1893), pp. 406–25. A more recent examination of the Homiliary of Toledo is that of Reginald Grégoire, 'L'homéliaire de Tolede', in *Les homéliaires du moyen âge: inventaire et analyse des manuscrits*, Rerum Ecclesiasticarum Documenta, Series Maior, Fontes 6 (Rome, 1966), pp. 161–85, with nineteen of the unedited homilies printed as appendix 2, pp. 197–230.

[49] Étaix, 'L'homéliaire carolingien d'Angers', pp. 149 and 174.

[50] The Taunton fragments (Taunton, Somerset, Somerset County Record Office, DD/SAS C/1193/ 77), tentatively dated on palaeographical grounds to the mid-eleventh century, were published after this contribution had been submitted; see Mechthild Gretsch, 'The Taunton Fragment: A New Text from Anglo-Saxon England', *ASE*, 33 (2004 [2005]), 145–93 (Recent

The circulation of this homiliary in eleventh- and twelfth-century England in both Latin and English necessitates a brief appraisal of the work, its use and content. Although Étaix gave a thorough account of the manuscript witnesses identified at the time of his writing, few of the homilies themselves have been published,[51] and little has been done to characterize the homiliary, its style, sources, and audience. The designation 'homiliary' has support in some of the manuscript witnesses in which each item is rubricated as a 'homelia' or 'omelia'; furthermore, as a homiliary, the collection provides expositions of pericopes for Sundays following the order of the liturgical year and provides four items for the common of saints. However, the material in the collection frequently exhibits catechetical and admonitory characteristics more frequently characterized by sermons,[52] a situation which highlights some of the difficulties in making this modern distinction.[53] Consequently, readers expecting the systematic exposition of scripture characteristic of the 'named' Carolingian homiliaries of Haymo and Heiric and the works that make up the collection of Paul the Deacon will be surprised by the inconsistency in the Homiliary of Angers's treatment of scriptural material.[54]

---

issues of *Anglo-Saxon England* have in fact appeared in the year after their publication date, in this case, instalments were generally received by libraries in Summer 2005). Shortly after publication of the Taunton fragments, Helmut Gneuss reported that Bodley 343 contained two of the Taunton homilies ('The Homiliary of the Taunton Fragments', *NQ*, n.s., 52 (2005), 440–42). Efforts have been made to incorporate the Taunton discovery into this paper, which, however, could not be completely rewritten. These circumstances, however, should serve to highlight the importance of twelfth-century manuscripts for the study of Anglo-Saxon England, and underscore research activity and opportunities in the period.

[51] In addition to the nine homilies published by Étaix, 'L'homéliaire carolingien d'Angers', pp. 177–89, two of the homilies were published by Rivera Recio, 'El "homiliarium gothicum"', pp. 162–63.

[52] On this distinction, see Thomas N. Hall, 'The Early Medieval Sermon', in *The Sermon*, ed. by Beverly Mayne Kienzle, Typologie des sources du moyen âge occidental, 81–83 (Turnhout, 2000), pp. 203–69 (p. 205): 'a *sermon* is fundamentally a catechetical or admonitory discourse built upon a theme or topic not necessarily grounded in Scripture, whereas a *homily* is a systematic exposition of a pericope (a liturgically designated passage of Scripture, usually from a Gospel or Epistle) that proceeds according to a pattern of *lectio continua*, commenting on a given passage verse by verse or phrase by phrase.' See also Barré, *Les homéliaires carolingiens*, pp. 13–14.

[53] For the idea that homilies include sermons, see Mary Clayton, 'Homiliaries and Preaching in Anglo-Saxon England', *Peritia*, 4 (1985), 207–42 (p. 208).

[54] Following the terminology of Étaix, I call the works homilies. However, in reference to specific items of the homiliary as it appears in Bodley 343, I have adopted the title *Sermo* followed by the item number as printed by Irvine, e.g. *Sermo xxii*; this designation, which has no

The homilies exhibit a simple Latin style and a correspondingly simple structure. In several cases, the homily paraphrases or quotes the biblical lection for the day with regular exegetical interjections preceded by *id est*. The pattern is clearly demonstrated in the homily for Christmas day (HA 1) which elucidates the first fourteen verses of John:

> *Et Verbum caro factum est et habitauit in nobis,* id est habitauit in mundo triginta et tribus annis et modo habitauit in nobis per fidem rectam et operibus bonis. Tunc fuit Ioannes Babtista *missus a Deo ut periberet testimonium de lumine,* hoc est de Christo qui est lux uera. Non erat Iohannes lux, nisi tunc prophetabat de lumine, hoc est de Christo qui *inluminat omnem hominem uenientem in hunc mundum.* Unde ipse ait: *Quamdiu in mundo sum, lux sum mundi. Et sui eum non receperunt,* id est pessimi Iudei quos creauit, quibus dedit legem, non crediderunt, non receperunt eum in cordibus suis. *Quotquot autem receperunt eum dedit eis potestatem fieri filios Dei,* id est sanctos apostolos qui eum crediderunt dedit eis gratiam Spiritus sancti uirtutem facere in hunc mundum.[55]

> [*And the Word was made flesh, and dwelt among us,* this means he lived in the world for thirty-three years and now he has lived among us through correct faith and in good works. Then John the Baptist was *sent from God to give testimony of the light,* that is of Christ who is the true light. John was not the light, but he prophesied then about the light, that is about Christ who *enlighteneth every man that cometh into this world.* Whence He said, *As long as I am in the world, I am the light of the world. And his own received him not,* which means the wicked Jews whom he created, to whom he gave the law, they did not believe, they did not receive him in their hearts. *But as many as received him, he gave them power to be made the sons of God,* which means the holy apostles who believed in him, he gave to them the grace of the Holy Spirit to make virtue in this world.]

The exposition avoids large, more complex theological questions that the passage might elicit in favour of a basic historical elucidation that clarifies the most basic meaning of the scriptural passage and the roles that the various figures play in Christian history.

In other cases, the homilist, following the basic form of the early medieval sermon rather loosely,[56] makes a noted effort to distinguish his literal exposition of the biblical reading for the day from the spiritual interpretation (*de interpretatione*

---

manuscript support, has the advantage of distinguishing the homilies as they appear in Bodley 343 from their numbering in the Homiliary of Angers.

[55] Quoted from Étaix, 'L'homéliaire carolingien d'Angers', pp. 177–78, lines 10–21. All translations are my own unless noted otherwise.

[56] For a useful sketch of the elements of the medieval sermon, see Thomas L. Amos, 'Early Medieval Sermons and their Audience', in *De l'homélie au sermon: histoire de la prédication médiévale*, Actes du Colloque international de Louvain-la-Neuve, ed. by Jaqueline Hamesse and Xavier Hermand (Louvain-la-Neuve, 1993), pp. 1–14 (pp. 6–7).

spiritale) of the reading. In HA 10 (*Sermo vi*), an item devised around the pericope for the fourth Sunday in Lent (John 6. 5–14), the homilist begins by informing the audience that it is appropriate first to hear about and understand the story and the miracles of the Lord which he reveals openly before his disciples and people.[57] An account of the feeding of the crowd from five loaves and two fish follows, sometimes paraphrasing, sometimes quoting the Bible. The homilist then states that he has related what happened and that it is time to relate the spiritual interpretation.[58] The populace is equated with the human race; the fish, the two testaments; the grass, sin or vice trampled down; the twelve baskets, the twelve bodies of the twelve apostles which are filled with the spiritual understanding of the Lord. The basic method presents the passage as an allegory in which the literal items can be replaced with their spiritual sense. The implication resulting from the explanation is that the audience should see itself as the populace that Jesus fed, and like that populace should be filled and satiated with the teaching of the Lord. Once the miracle has been explained, the homilist states 'Ecce, nos, fratres, repleti sumus et saciati de doctrina Domini',[59] equating his present audience with that of Jesus. This is in a sense a tropological understanding of the passage; from it the audience learns to confess and do penance for sins. These actions in turn will pave the way for practitioners to merit eternal life.

Clearly, there is a high degree of commonplace teaching involved in this kind of approach to gospel readings. To make the point, one need only look at the similarity between the Homiliary of Angers and other, unrelated works. For example, HA 7 (*Sermo lxiv*) for the fourth Sunday after Epiphany relates the pericope (Matthew 8. 23), then recounts Jesus's ability to make the wind and sea obey during the storm at sea. Following the narration, individual elements are identified with their spiritual meanings: the ship is the Church; the wind represents the world. The

---

[57] 'Oportet nos, fratres karissimi, primum audire et intelligere de ystoria et de miraculis Domini quę ostendit coram discipulis suis et coram populo': fol. xii^vb, 15–17 (*Sermo vi*, p. 238, lines 2–3). In order to provide the greatest accesibility possible to references of unpublished texts in Bodley 343, I cite folio, column, and line numbers and provide in parentheses references to the text in Aidan Conti, 'Preaching Scripture and Apocrypha: A Previously Unidentified Homiliary in an Old English Manuscript, Oxford, Bodleian Library, Bodley 343' (unpublished doctoral thesis, University of Toronto, 2004) in the form of item number, page number, and continuous line numbers.

[58] 'Iam diximus de factis; dicamus de spiritali interpretatione': fol. xiv^ra, 6–7 (*Sermo vi*, p. 239, line 18).

[59] Fol. xiv^ra, 18–19 (*Sermo vi*, p. 239, line 25).

same expositional technique is seen in an item corresponding to the same day in a series of Middle English metrical homilies.[60] The homilist introduces his exposition by recounting the story found in the Gospel (1–22). The ship is then identified as the Church:

> Al hali kirc, als thinc me,
> Mai bi this schippe takened be,
> That Crist rad in and his felawes,
> Imang dintes of gret quawes. (lines 23–26)[61]

> [All holy church, it seems to me,
> may be signified by this ship
> in which Christ and his companions rode
> amongst the blows of great waves.]

By extended analogy, the church floats above the sea of this world ('hali kirc [. . .] Fletes abouen this werldes se', lines 28–29), a metaphor that is explicitly explained later: 'Bot for our godspel spekes of se, | Quarbi this werld mai bisend be' (lines 93–94).[62] If this type of spiritual exegesis seems mundane, one modern critic notes that

> Such *topoi* are doubly interesting, first because their diffusion makes them, as it were, part of the mentality of their time; and second because a good preacher could impart a personal touch to them that could make them effective even from a purely literary view.[63]

Despite the relatively commonplace nature of the exegesis in the Homiliary of Angers, the homilist, unlike the more famous named homilists of the Carolingian era who relied heavily on the accepted, orthodox exegesis of the church fathers, writes 'original' work.[64] The specific language he uses frequently belongs to no early source material. In some cases, however, there are links to sources, tenuous parallels in themes and language, especially to Gregory the Great and pseudo-Jerome.[65] A

---

[60] J. Small, *English Metrical Homilies from Manuscripts of the Fourteenth Century* (Edinburgh, 1867). The homily for the third Sunday after the Octave of Epiphany is on pp. 134–44.

[61] Small, *English Metrical Homilies*, p. 135.

[62] Small, *English Metrical Homilies*, p. 138.

[63] David L. D'Avray, 'Sermons after 1200', in *Medieval Latin: An Introduction and Bibliographical Guide*, ed. by F. A. C. Mantello and A. G. Rigg (Washington, D.C., 1996), pp. 662–69 (p. 665).

[64] See Étaix, 'L'homéliaire carolingien d'Angers', pp. 175–76.

[65] For a brief list of parallels (without full quotations of the parallels themselves), see Étaix, 'L'homéliaire carolingien d'Angers', p. 176.

fitting example is provided for in the homily for the first Sunday in Lent (HA 11; *Sermones ii* and *iii*) which elaborates on the three temptations of Jesus. The Angers homilist states that the devil wanted to tempt Jesus in the same three ways in which he tempted Adam, the first man, namely by gluttony, avarice, and pride ('Voluit eum diabolus temptare in ipsis tribus modis quomodo Adam temptauit primum hominem, id est gula et avaricia et superbia').[66] These words essentially paraphrase and truncate an idea whose ultimate source is Gregory's *Homiliae in Euangelia* XVI:

> Antiquus hostis contra primum hominem parentem nostrum in tribus se temptationibus erexit, quia hunc uidelicet gula, uana gloria et auaritia temptauit [...] Sed quibus modis primum hominem strauit, eisdem modis secundo homini temptato succubuit [...]. Sed eisdem modis a secundo homine uincitur, quibus primum hominem se uicisse gloriatur.[67]

> [The ancient enemy set himself against the first man, our forebear, in three temptations. He tempted him by gluttony, by vainglory, and by avarice [...]. But by those same means, by which he overcame the first man, he surrendered when the second man was tempted [...]. But by those same means, by which he boasted that he had overcome the first man, he was overcome by the second man.]

After the juxtaposition of temptations, the Angers homilist introduces the question concerning which spirit led Jesus into the desert where he fasted: 'Quidam fratres dubitare solent a quo spiritu ductus est Iesus an a suo an ab alieno.'[68] Again, we see a clear rephrasing of Gregory's formulation: 'Dubitari a quibusdam solet a quo spiritu sit Iesus ductus in desertum.'[69] The homilist shows a slightly more creative refashioning method in converting Gregory's matter of fact 'hoc audire aures expauescunt' ('the ears are terrified to hear this')[70] in relation to the supposed tempation of Jesus into an exhortation: 'Quod auribus audiuimus, expauescamus!' ('Let us greatly fear what our ears have heard!').[71] One of the more interesting topoi borrowed from Gregory is the idea that the devil is the head of all the wicked and the wicked, namely Pilate and the Jews, are his limbs:

---

[66] Fol. xi[va], 5–9 (*Sermo ii*, p. 229, lines 3–4).

[67] Quoted from Gregory the Great, *Homiliae in Evangelia*, ed. by Raymond Étaix, CCSL, 141 (Turnhout, 1999), pp. 109–15 (pp. 111–12), lines 31–53.

[68] 'Certain brothers are accustomed to doubt by which spirit Jesus was led, whether by his own or another's': fol. xi[va], 10–12 (*Sermo ii*, p. 229, lines 4–5).

[69] 'Certain persons are accustomed to question by what spirit Jesus was led into the desert' (*Homiliae in Evangelia* XVI, lines 1–2, ed. by Étaix, p. 110).

[70] *Homiliae in Evangelia* XVI, line 9 in ed. by Étaix, p. 110.

[71] Fol. xi[vb], 21–22 (*Sermo ii*, p. 231, line 29).

Certe iniquorum omnium diabolus caput est, et huius capitis membra sunt omnes iniqui. An non diaboli membrum Pilatus? An non diaboli membra Iudaei persequentes et milites crucifigentes fuerunt? Quid ergo mirum si se ab illo permisit in montem duci, qui se pertulit etiam a membris illius crucifigi?[72]

[Indeed, the devil is the head of all the wicked, and the limbs of this head are all the wicked. Was not Pilate a limb of the devil? And were not the Jews who persecuted him, and the soldiers who crucified him, limbs of the devil? Why then should we wonder if he allowed himself to be crucified by his members?]

The Angers homilist turns Gregory's questions into statements of fact:

Non est mirandum si se permisit capiti iniquorum temptare quando postea permisit se membris illius flagellare et crucifigare. Caput iniquorum diabolus est. Membra eius fuit Pilatus et mali Iudei et milites.[73]

[One should not wonder if he allowed himself to be tempted when after he allowed himself to be flagellated and crucified by his members. The head of the wicked is the devil. His limbs were Pilate and the Jews and the soldiers.]

Interesting, in addition to the reuse of the topos, is the use of active infinitive forms (*temptare, flagellare, crucifigare*) where the syntax, bolstered by reference to Gregory, requires passive infinitives.[74] Although this feature is not consistent throughout the entirety of the homiliary, such linguistic peculiarities may, pending the judicial assesment of all the material, assist in determining the vernacular background of the homiliary's author.

Similar to the way in which the homilist incorporates material from Gregory, material from pseudo-Jerome is recycled. For example, in the same homily for the first Sunday in Lent, the homilist depicts the devil's final attempt to tempt Jesus. According to the gospel account: 'et ostendit ei omnia regna mundi et gloriam eorum et dixit illi, "haec tibi omnia dabo si cadens adoraueris me"'.[75] The

---

[72] *Homiliae in Evangelia* XVI, lines 10–14, ed. by Étaix, p. 110.

[73] Fol. xi[vb], 26–32 (*Sermo ii*, p. 231, lines 31–34).

[74] The appearance of these forms in Bodley 343 is not a scribal idiosyncracy. Three other manuscripts have been affected by the anomalous spellings to different degrees. Angers 236, fol. 21[r], lines 2–3 has 'temptare [...] flagellare [...] crucifigere'. In Grenoble, Bibliothèque municipale, MS 278, fol. 5[r], lines 1–3, the first two infinitives have been corrected, but the scribe's mechanical technique has created an anomalous third infinitive form: 'temptari [...] flagellari [...] crucifigeri'. Uppsala, Universitetsbibliotek, MS C 148, fol. 57[r], lines 6–8, has the active forms of the infinitives as well 'temptare [...] flagellare [...] crucifigere' but has reconstrued other parts of the sentence to make these active forms work within a new syntax.

[75] Matthew 4. 8–9: 'and shewed him all the kingdoms of the world and the glory of them, and said to him: "All these I will give to thee, if falling down thou wilt adore me"'.

Homiliary of Angers, however, conflates elements from the third-person narrative into the speech of the devil, and presents a devil who adds the extra incentive of gold and silver. The devil states, 'Si cadens adoraueris me, omnia regna mundi, aurum et argentum dabo tibi'.[76] The addition of the gold and silver seems to come from an elaboration in pseudo-Jerome's *In euangelium secundum Mattheum*: 'et ostendit ei omnia regna mundi, id est aurum, argentum'.[77] Indeed, Étaix reports several parallels in the homiliary with pseudo-Jerome, probably an Irishman working on the Continent in the second half of the eighth century.[78]

On two occasions the homilist refers explicitly to patristic authority. The first in the homily for the third Sunday after Pentecost (HA 28, *Sermo xxvii*) offers a reference to Gregory's classification of the nine orders of angels.[79] On the other occasion, the homilist refers to Augustine, but does so in such a way that the mention of the father may have been employed only to bolster the homilist's credentials, so to speak. In HA 5 (*Sermo lxii*) for the second Sunday after Epiphany, based on John 2. 1–11, the homilist presents the transformation of the water in the water pots into wine as a cause of celebration for Jesus's disciples who find reason to praise and esteem ('laudare et magnificare') the act. In the explanation of the spiritual sense of the homilist's version of the narrative, the audience is informed that although some say that Moses was the first to receive testamental law, and some say that John the Baptist drank the passion before Christ, Augustine says that the holy apostle Paul, who tasted divine mysteries, began to praise and esteem that the great divine mysteries had been observed in the advent of the Lord.[80]

In the loose adaptation of sources and in the sources themselves, the Angers homilist distinguishes himself from the more studied source material used in the more familiar Carolingian homiletic collections, such as the homiliaries of Smaragdus and Hrabanus Maurus, which frequently refer to the same patristic sources for

---

[76] 'If falling down you will adore me, I will give to you all the kingdoms of the world, gold and silver': fol. xi^vb, 11–13 (*Sermo ii*, p. 230, lines 23–34).

[77] 'He showed him all the kingdoms of the world, that is gold and silver' (*PL* 30.542B).

[78] See Étaix, 'L'homéliaire carolingien d'Angers', p. 176.

[79] See Gregory, *Homiliae in Euangelia* XXXIV, ed. by Étaix, pp. 299–319 (pp. 305–06, sect. 7, lines 148–77).

[80] 'aliqui dicunt quod Moyses fuit qui primus accipit legem; aliqui dicunt quod Iohannes baptista fuit qui ante bibit passionem quam Christus; sed Augustinus dicit quod beatus Paulus apostolus qui congustasset diuina misteria, cepit laudare et magnificare quod magna diuina misteria fuerunt obseruata in aduentu Domini': fol. xxxvii^ra, 24–31 (*Sermo lxii*, pp. 337–38, lines 28–31).

exegesis of the Gospels.[81] Consequently, whereas those homiliaries imbued with patristic authority generated material suitable for monastic use, the Homiliary of Angers shows no such affinity.[82] With respect to the use and audience of the homiliary,[83] Étaix has ruled out its use in the Night Office,[84] where lessons were taken from a homily attributed to one of the church fathers or a pope.[85] Another possible use for Carolingian homiliaries may have been devotional reading,[86] but the sparse, schematic treatment of scriptural material in the Homiliary of Angers makes it an unlikely candidate for such reflection.

Although the boundaries between the genres and uses of homiliaries appear to have been quite fluid,[87] it appears that the Homiliary of Angers addressed another function of homiliaries, namely that of providing models to preachers for their addresses to lay audiences, a proposition further supported by the fragmentary vernacular translation in the Taunton fragments.[88] The need for preaching to the laity was well acknowledged in the Carolingian period as is borne out by the many synods and councils that addressed the issue,[89] and the role of the supposedly uninvolved monastic communities in pastoral care in England may be greater than

---

[81] On the standard use of certain patristic sources for specified gospel expositions, see Étaix, 'L'homéliaire carolingien d'Angers', pp. 175–76: see also Barré, *Les homéliaires carolingiens*, p. 140.

[82] See D'Avray, 'Sermons after 1200', p. 665.

[83] On the uses of homliaries, see Barré, *Les homéliaire carolingiens*, pp. 4–30.

[84] Étaix, 'L'homéliaire carolingien d'Angers', p. 177: 'In ne s'agit certainement pas d'un homéliaire qui a servi pour les lecteurs de l'office de nuit: le format réduit des manuscrits ne convenait pas pour la lecture publique et aucune trace de divisions en leçons n'a été relevée.'

[85] See John Harper, *The Forms and Orders of Western Liturgy from the Tenth Century to the Eighteenth Century* (Oxford, 1991), p. 87.

[86] See Barré, *Les homéliaire carolingiens*, p. 140.

[87] On the distinctions and their interrelatedness, see Clayton, 'Homiliaries and Preaching', pp. 216–17.

[88] See Étaix, 'L'homéliaire carolingien d'Angers', p. 177, where he suggests that the homilies are blueprints for sermons for preachers.

[89] See Thomas Leslie Amos, 'The Origin and Nature of the Carolingian Sermon' (unpublished doctoral dissertation, Michigan State University, 1983), especially pp. 30–31, 117, 143, and 163. On the provisions of the Anglo-Saxon Council of Clofeshoh in particular, see Catherine Cubitt, 'Pastoral Care and Conciliar Canons: The Provisions of the 747 Council of *Clofesho*', in *Pastoral Care before the Parish*, ed. by John Blair and Richard Sharpe (Leicester, 1992), pp. 193–211.

previously imagined.[90] Perhaps the best noted example of such a homiliary is the Saint-Père de Chartres (or Pembroke)–type homiliary,[91] for which we have manifestations of its use in vernacular Old English and Old Norse material.[92] Indeed, in at least one manuscript witness, Grenoble 278, several items from the Saint-Père homiliary circulated together with the Homiliary of Angers.[93] Before the publication of the Taunton fragments, no vernacular manifestation of the Homiliary of Angers was known, although given the commonplace nature of its contents parallels to vernacular material were readily detectable, if not demonstrably traceable to use of the homiliary itself.[94]

Furthermore, the contents of the Angers homiliary itself give some indications of its intended audience. The homilist appears to have in mind married participants, obviating a monastic audience.[95] In the homily for the feast day for St Andrew (30 November) (HA 54, *Sermo lii*), the homilist urges his audience to imitate the life of the apostles, stating 'Si habes uxores, tibi sint quasi non habentes'.[96] Morever, the following statement addresses the audience's worldly possessions: 'Si

[90] See Alan Thacker, 'Monks, Preaching and Pastoral Care in Early Anglo-Saxon England', in *Pastoral Care before the Parish*, ed. by Blair and Sharpe, pp. 137–70, and also John Blair, *The Church in Anglo-Saxon Society* (Oxford, 2005).

[91] See Barré, *Les homéliaires carolingiens*, p. 24.

[92] For Old English, see James Cross, *Cambridge Pembroke College MS. 25: A Carolingian Sermonary used by Anglo-Saxon Preachers*, King's College London Medieval Studies, 1 (London, 1987). For Old Norse, see Thomas N. Hall, 'Old Norse-Icelandic Sermons', in *The Sermon*, ed. by Kienzle, pp. 661–709 (pp. 672–73).

[93] See Étaix, 'L'homéliaire carolingien d'Angers', pp. 160–64; on the Saint-Père items in the manuscript, see Cross, *Cambridge, Pembroke College MS. 25*, p. 1.

[94] See, for example, Michael Cummings, 'Napier Homily 55 and Belfour Homily 10 on the Temptations in the Desert', *NM*, 80 (1979), 315–24 (p. 319, n. 21), which notes parallels between *Sermo ii* and an Old English homily for Lent found later in the manuscript, now edited as Irvine V, in *Old English Homilies*, ed. by Irvine, pp. 116–45.

[95] The use of the address *fratres* or *fratres karissimi* in the homiliary does not exclude a lay audience as it was a common designation used for all Christians in the *ad populum* sermons of both Caesarius of Arles and Hrabanus Maurus. Also in the vernacular, Ælfric uses *broþor* and *gebroþra* for all fellow Christians; see Gretsch, 'Taunton Fragment', p. 192.

[96] 'If you have wives, let them be to you as if you did not have them': fol. xxxii[ra], 31–32 (*Sermo lii*, p. 315, lines 28–29). The use of the plural wives with the singular subject is somewhat odd in its grammar, but makes sense within the rhetoric of the passage especially considering the following 'possessiones'.

habes possessiones mundi, sint tibi quasi dimittendas.'[97] Presumably a monastic audience, which would have renounced worldly possessions at least in name and would have no wives to renounce, would not have needed this injunction.

The idea that the Homiliary of Angers provided blueprints for sermons, which would enable a preacher to use the exegetical topoi therein in a vernacular sermon tailored and expanded to suit individual needs, fits in well with the hortatory and pastoral elements of the homiliary, as well as with the witnesses themselves in which scribes (or later compilers and preachers) did not hesitate to modify the text of these utilitarian works according to their needs.[98] Indeed, there are indications within the homiliary itself that these pieces were to be delivered by a *sacerdos*: 'Et nos sacerdotes debemus preuidere et timere ut semper sine intermissione ammone-amus uos ut legem ac mandata Domini custodiatis.'[99] Normally, the reader might assume that the subject, 'nos', encompasses both the speaker and the audience, a subject that builds on the communal identity of speaker and listener, as is often the case in sermons. Yet, the distinction between the main subject, 'nos', and the addressed audience, 'uos', demonstrates a breakdown in this communal identity, a clear demarcation separating the priest from, one assumes, his lay audience.

Yet, in some cases the laity seems not to be the only audience addressed. For example, *Sermo xxxiv* (HA 21)[100] on the expulsion of the buyers and sellers in the temple, is seen as a condemnation of the priests of the day because they cultivated this activity on account of their desire for gold and silver.[101] The condemnation is not confined to the past as the homilist draws his conclusions: 'Sic ad sensum, fratres: mali episcopi et mali sacerdotes qui dona spiritus sancti accipiunt et pro munere illa uendunt foras de templo Christi eicientur.'[102] Elsewhere the homilist

---

[97] 'If you have worldly possessions, let them be as if they should be cast away by you': fol. xxxii[ra], 32–33 (*Sermo lii*, p. 315, line 29).

[98] See Étaix, 'L'homéliaire carolingien d'Angers', p. 149: 'Il s'agit en effet d'ouvrages utilitaires: les scribes n'hésitaient pas á modifier le texte selon les besoins.'

[99] 'And we, priests, must foresee and fear so that we may continuously without intermission incite you to observe the law and mandates of the Lord': fol. xxxix[ra], 14–17 (*Sermo lxv*, p. 342, lines 35–37).

[100] The homily appears to have been designated for *pascha annotina* in the Angers manuscript, but for the First Sunday after Pentecost in others. See further below, p. 389.

[101] 'mali sacerdotes nutriebant omnia illa propter concupiscentiam auri et argenti': fol. xxvi[ra], 13–15 (*Sermo xxxiv*, p. 288, lines 23–24).

[102] 'So to the meaning, brothers: wicked bishops and wicked priests who receive the gifts of the Holy Spirit and sell them for favours are cast out from the temple of Christ': fol. xxvi[ra], 19–22 (*Sermo xxxiv*, p. 288, lines 26–27).

notes, 'multi <sunt> episcopi et sacerdotes […] qui magis intrant sacerdotale offi-
cium pro lucro terreno quam pro desiderio celesti'.[103] At first, it may seem contrary
to a preacher's own interests to highlight the shortcomings of his colleagues and
superiors. Emphasizing the sins of those in whom the laity was compelled to put
its faith for eternal life could seriously undermine the moral authority of the clergy.
As a result, it is possible to read such statements as assurances to the present lay
audience, guarantees that although these kinds of priests do exist, the local clergy
was not prone to the same faults of those subjects of the sermons themselves.

Additionally, the real 'audience' of any homiliary is manifold. As a document
the homiliary could serve not only as an outline of suitable preaching material for
priests, but also as a text addressed to the ordained, reinforcing the importance of
their standing within the greater community. As a result, every preacher who
picked up a copy of the Homiliary of Angers and used it in public discourse acted
as both a reader and author. Presently, there is little evidence that the homilies of
the Homiliary of Angers were delivered in their present form. We see little of the
rhetorical patterning often used to elevate the speech of the presenter. Furthermore, the quality of the Latin is often ungrammatical to such an extent that it
seems to have caused significant problems for copyists. Consequently, one imagines
that the homilies represent outlines, quick glosses on important points in the daily
biblical lection for a preacher who would deliver his sermon in the vernacular,
rather than the specific sermon itself.[104]

Evidence that the homiliary provided notes, rather than the fixed text, is
provided when one considers parts of the vernacular rendering afforded by the
Taunton fragments. In the beginning of the homily for the Fifth Sunday after
Pentecost (HA Fourth), the homilist contrasts divine clemency with human desire
for vengeful punishment. We sin daily against the Lord, the audience is informed,

---

[103] 'Many are the priests and bishops who enter into the priesthood for earthly profit rather
than on account of a heavenly desire': fol. xxix^va, 31–33 (Sermo xliv, p. 304, lines 35–37).

[104] Indeed, the vernacular in the Taunton fragments can be viewed in the same way. As an
alternating line-by-line translation, the Old English need not represent a sermon itself but
vernacular notes for material to be included therein or presented to the laity. That a homiliary
would provide 'reference' material for use in preaching, rather than a sermon to be delivered
verbatim, is not new; see Milton McC. Gatch, 'The Office in Late Anglo-Saxon Monasticism',
in Learning and Literature in Anglo-Saxon England: Studies Presented to Peter Clemoes on the
Occasion of his Sixty-fifth Birthday, ed. by Michael Lapidge and Helmet Gneuss (Cambridge,
1985), pp. 341–62, esp. pp. 359 and 357, where with respect to Ælfric's Second Series of Catholic
Homilies, Gatch states, 'the preacher or reader is given materials and helpful notes to use more or
less as he will in devising alternatives to the sermons of the First Series'.

but he does not kill us, nor reject, nor condemn, but always waits so that we amend ourselves for the better.[105] The Latin text of the Taunton fragments presents the juxtaposition using an anomalous mix of tenses and moods: 'Nos fratres cotidie peccauimus contra Dominum in multis modis [...]. Ille nos occidat, non spernit, non condempnat [...]. Set semper nos exspectet ut nos emendemus in melius.'[106] Although inconsistencies in tense and mood are present in almost every Latin manuscript of the homily, the English translator does not repeat these errors but produces relatively cogent English:

> Leofe breoðre deghwamlice we syngiað ongean ure drihten on felæ wisan [...] Hæ ne ofsleþ us, ne he us ne tostryegdeð, ne us ne niðrað [...] Æac efre he us onbydeð þ we gebetæð þa yfela cystas ðe we don habbað.
>
> [Dear brethren, daily we sin against our Lord in many ways [...]. He does not kill us; nor does He destroy us; nor does He condemn us [...]. Also, He is always waiting for us to repair the wicked deeds that we perpetuated.][107]

Although the English translation here demonstrates lexical peculiarities,[108] the syntax and form demonstrate that it is not the work of a word-by-word glossator. The translation works phrase by phrase, sentence by sentence in an attempt to transform the Latin into a workable vernacular interpretation, lending support to the hypothesis that the homiliary was used to instruct either the laity or unlearned clergy, or possibly both these groups.

Issues regarding the use and audience of the homiliary are perhaps compounded by questions about the date of its original composition. Although Étaix envisaged the work of a tenth-century pastor, there is little firm evidence to further the conjecture.[109] The earliest identified manuscripts of the homiliary date to the eleventh century, and more likely to the second half of that century rather than the first.[110]

---

[105] 'Nos, fratres, cothidie peccamus contra Dominum in multis modis. Ille nos non occidit, non spernit, non condemnat sed semper nos expectat ut nos emendemus in melius': from Berlin, Staatsbibliothek, MS Lat. oct. 359, fol. 105ʳ. This manuscript provides the most 'grammatical' rendering of the passage in question.

[106] P. 5, lines 4–10 (p. 1 according to the correct reordering in Grestch, 'Taunton Fragment', p. 151).

[107] P. 5, lines 5–14 (p. 1 according to the correct reordering in Gretsch; translation from Gretsch, 'Taunton Fragment', p. 151).

[108] See Gretsch, 'Taunton Fragment', esp. pp. 178 and 181.

[109] Étaix, 'L'homéliaire carolingien d'Angers', p. 177.

[110] See Étaix, 'L'homéliaire carolingien d'Angers', p. 158, n. 6. As noted above, the earliest manuscript known to Étaix was Angers 236. The Taunton fragments now have some claim to the

Furthermore, the order of the pericopes of the homiliary, which conform to the standard Romano-Frankish system that gradually became the standard throughout Western Europe after the mid- to late eighth century, provides no evidence with which to date and localize the evangelary (or evangeliary) on which the homiliary's pericopes are based.[111] Nevertheless, the homiliary does demonstrate some conservative elements, the most notable of which is the preservation of biblical readings associated with the Vetus Latina. For example, HA 45 (*Sermo xliii*) is based on the story of the barren fig tree and the cure of the infirm woman (Luke 13. 6–13). In describing the infirm woman the most common Vulgate reading appears as 'inclinata'; however, the Homiliary of Angers presents the woman as 'incuruata' a reading associated with two Vetus Latina manuscripts, the codex Brixianus (Brescia, Biblioteca Civica Queriniana) and the codex Palatinus (Vienna, Österreichische Nationalbibliothek, cod. lat. 1185).[112] Additionally, in HA 11 (*Sermo ii*) when Jesus states his final rebuke to the tempting Satan, he orders 'Vade retro Sathanas' in at least two manuscripts, Bodley 343 and Uppsala, Universitetsbibliotek, MS C 148.[113] Jerome explicitly rejected the addition of 'retro' into Jesus's command.[114]

---

earliest manuscript of the homiliary given their tentative dating to around the middle of the eleventh century (Gretsch, 'Taunton Fragment', p. 149). However, like Angers 236, the Taunton fragments may date to the second half of the century; see Gretsch, 'Taunton Fragment', p. 193, n. 121.

[111] The literature on this subject is quite extensive. The development of the system was investigated by T. Klauser, *Das römische Capitulare evangeliorum: Texte und Untersuchungen zu seiner ältesten Geschichte*, vol. I: *Typen*, Liturgiegeschichtliche Quellen und Forschungen, 28 (Munster, 1935), and W. H. Frere, *Studies in Early Roman Liturgy*, vol. II: *The Roman Lectionary*, Alcuin Club Collections, 30 (London, 1934) and Frere, *Studies in Early Roman Liturgy*, vol. III: *The Roman Epistle-Lectionary*, Alcuin Club Collections, 31 (London, 1935); and thereafter further revised by A. Chavasse, 'Les plus anciens types du lectionaire et de l'antiphonaire romains de la messe', *Revue Bénédictine*, 62 (1952), 3–94. Useful and more basic introductions can be found in Aimé Georges Martimort, *Les lectures liturgiques et leurs livres*, Typologie des sources du Moyen Âge occidental, 64 (Turnhout, 1992), and Cyrille Vogel, *Medieval Liturgy: An Introduction to the Sources*, rev. and trans. by William Storey and Niels Rasmussen (Washington, D.C., 1986). A fuller discussion of the liturgical year in the Homiliary of Angers and the differences in Bodley 343 can be found in Conti, 'Preaching Scripture and Apocrypha', pp. 64–72.

[112] See J. Wordsworth and H. I. White, *Nouum Testamentum Domini Nostri Iesu Christi Latine Secundum Editionem Sancti Heironymi*, Pars Prior: Quattor Evangelia (Oxford, 1889–99), pp. 405–6 and p. xxxi.

[113] See Bodley 343, fol. xi^{vb}, line 15, and Uppsala, Universitetsbibliotek, MS C 148, fol. 56^{v}, line 10.

[114] See Jerome, *Commentariorum in Matheum libri IV*, ed. by David Hurst and M. Adriaen, CCSL, 77 (Turnhout, 1969), bk. I, lines 378–85: '*Tunc dixit ei Iesus: vade satanas; scriptum est:*

Nevertheless, the reading dominated early gospel books with both Celtic and Vetus Latina associations.[115] Moreover, the 'retro' reading was vehemently defended by Ælfric, based on a seemingly errant claim that Jerome used the reading in a letter.[116] These readings cannot pinpoint the date of composition of the homiliary, but do suggest that the collection at least relied on older, and by the eleventh century antiquated, versions of the Gospels.

Although Bodley 343 contains one of the more complete versions of the Homiliary of Angers, the manuscript does present some peculiarities and unique features in its presentation of the homiliary. While a full discussion of the differences and peculiarities of each manuscript witness to the homiliary has yet to be conducted, the most remarkable idiosyncrasies of the Bodley version will be dis-

Dominum Deum tuum adorabis et illi soli servies [. . .] Petro enim dicitur: *Vade retro me satana*, id est sequere me qui contrarius es uoluntati meae; hic uero audit: *Vade satanas*, et non ei dicitur retro, ut subaudiatur: uade in ignem aeternum qui praeparatus est tibi et angelis tuis' ('Then Jesus said to him: *Begone Satan; for it is written, The Lord thy God shalt thou adore, and him only shalt thou serve* [. . .] for it is said to Peter: *Go behind me, Satan*, that is follow me, you who are contrary to my will; but he (Satan) hears, "Vade satanas", and "retro" is not said to him so that "Go to the eternal fire which is prepared for you and your angels" is understood').

[115] These are Dublin, Trinity College Library, MS 52, 'Book of Armagh'; London, British Library, Egerton MS 609; Paris, Bibliothèque nationale de France, fonds latin 9389, 'Echternach Gospels'; Lichfield, Cathedral Library, 'Lichfield Gospels'; Dublin, Trinity College Library, MS 58, 'Book of Kells'; Oxford, Bodleian Library, MS Auct. D. 2. 19, 'Macregol' or 'Rushworth Gospels'; Cambridge, Corpus Christi College, MS 286, 'Gospels of St Augustine of Canterbury' where the reading 'retro' is written over an erasure and is of an indistinguishable date; and London, British Library, Harley MS 1775, in which 'retro' is the initial reading of the first hand. See further Wordsworth and White, *Nouum Testamentum*, pp. 51, xi–xiv, 707–08, and 713–16. The 'retro' reading is also reported in Paris, Bibliothèque nationale de France, fonds latin 11553, 'Codex Sangermanensis'.

[116] See Malcom Godden, *Ælfric's Catholic Homilies: Introduction, Commentary and Glossary*, EETS: SS, 18 (Oxford, 2000), p. 90. The full text of Ælfric's defense is found in *First Series*, ed. by Clemoes, p. 270, app. crit. to line 110 in EKM: 'Quidam dicunt non dixisse saluatorem satane uade retro sed tantum uade sed tamen in rectioribus et uestustioribus exemplaribus habetur uade retro satanas. Sicut interpretatio ipsius nominis declarat. Nam diabolus deorsum ruens interpretatur. Apostolo igitur petro dicitur a christo uade retro me id est sequere me. Diabolo non dicitur uade retro me sed uade retro sicut iam diximus. Et sic scripsit beatus hieronimus in una epistola' ('Certain people say that the Saviour did not say, "Satane, uade retro", but only "Vade", but in the more correct and older exemplars "Vade retro, Satanas" is upheld, just as an explanation of Satan's name demonstrates, for "devil" is interpreted as "Deorsum ruens" (falling down). Therefore, to the apostle Peter "Vade retro me", that is "Follow me", is said by Christ. "Vade retro me" is not said to the devil, but "Vade retro" just as we have said, and so did St Jerome write in an epistle').

cussed here. First, one notes that the Bodley version of the homiliary conforms more precisely to the 'standard' system of pericopes for the Sundays following Pentecost than does the 'original' state of the collection, best represented by the Angers manuscript.[117] The Angers manuscript, as well as several others, places the homily based on John 3. 1 (HA 21) in a position before the homily for Litanies (or Rogationtide); as a result, in these manuscripts, HA 21 acts as an exposition for *pascha annotina*, the celebration of the previous year's Easter. In Bodley 343, and other manuscripts, this reading is placed in the position for the First Sunday after Pentecost, thereby shifting all the Sundays after Pentecost in this second state of the homiliary to one Sunday after those in the original state.[118] Consequently, the original state of the collection provides for twenty-five Sundays after Pentecost whereas the 'normalized' version presents twenty-six.

Another example of the way in which Bodley 343 deviates from Étaix's reconstructed Homiliary of Angers is that, like many manuscript witnesses of the homiliary, Bodley 343 integrates homilies from the common of saints into the *temporale* cycle. In the case of HA 57, the common for a confessor, Bodley 343 has located the homily between items for the Second and Third Sundays in Advent and it may therefore have been intended for St Nicolaus's Day, 6 December.[119] The other item for the common of saints, HA 59, the common for a virgin (*Sermo xli*), has been placed in between items for the Seventeenth and Eighteenth Sundays after Pentecost (which are the Sixteenth and Seventeenth Sundays after Pentecost in the reconstructed series), a date for which the existing evidence from Anglo-Saxon England and the later uses of Hereford, Sarum, and York provide no clue for what virgin feast day the homily was intended.[120]

---

[117] See Étaix, 'L'homéliaire carolingien d'Angers', p. 175.

[118] And thereby conforming more to Chavasse's B family of Type 3; see Chavasse, 'Les plus anciens types du lectionnaire'; see also A. Wilmart, 'Le *Comes* de Murbach', *Revue Bénédictine*, 30 (1913), 25–69.

[119] See Ursula Lenker, *Die westsächsische Evangelienversion und die Perikopenordnungen im angelsächsischen England*, Texte und Untersuchungen zur englischen Philologie, 20 (Munich, 1997), p. 373, ‡ 153.

[120] For Anglo-Saxon evangelaries, see Lenker, *Die westsächsische Evangelienversion*. On the later uses of Hereford, Sarum, and York respectively, see W. Henderson, *Missale ad Usum Percelebris Ecclesiae Herfordensis* (Farnborough, 1874; repr. 1967); J. Wickham Legg, *The Sarum Missal: Edited from Three Early Manuscripts* (Oxford, 1916; repr. 1969); W. Henderson, *Missale ad Usum Insignis Exxlesiae Eboracensis*, 2 vols, Publications of the Surtees Society, 59 and 60 (Durham, 1874).

Perhaps the most striking feature of the Bodley version of the Homiliary of Angers is the way in which the Bodley version begins and ends. In other witnesses to the homiliary, expositions on the Gospel and epistle for a particular day are regularly rubricated as one item;[121] however, there is at least one exception.[122] In Bodley 343, expositions of the epistle and gospel readings are separated so that one item in the Homiliary of Angers, such as HA 11 for Quadragesima, may appear as two separately rubricated items in Bodley 343, namely *Sermones ii* and *iii*. The most remarkable manifestation of this difference occurs in the separation of the gospel and epistle expositions for HA 10 (Quinquagesima) where the homily has been divided in such a way that the second part, the exposition of I Corinthians 13. 4, begins the entire collection in Bodley 343, while the first part of the exposition, that based on Luke 13. 6, ends the collection.[123] All other manuscript witnesses of the homiliary begin at an early point in the year (generally Christmas, though some manuscripts lack items at the beginning) and then continue sequentially through the liturgical year.[124] One plausible explanation for the awkward ordering in Bodley 343 lies in the relatively common use of booklets as textual repositories in the Anglo-Saxon and post-Conquest period.[125] Indeed, the use of booklets appears to account for the complexity of Bodley 343's compilation and 'its reliance on so many lines of transmission' with respect to its vernacular items.[126] In this instance, it appears that the first scribe of Bodley 343, or one of his predecessors, copied the Homiliary of Angers from a booklet consisting of two or more gatherings which at one point were separated and then put back together and possibly reassembled in the wrong order. A later scribe, perhaps the first scribe of

---

[121] Two examples are HA 10 and 11; see Étaix, 'L'homéliaire carolingien d'Angers', p. 150.

[122] Namely, HA 35 and 36, individual items based on I Corinthians 6. 10 and Luke 16. 1 for the Ninth (or Tenth) Sunday after Pentecost.

[123] Gneuss, 'The Homiliary', p. 441, discusses the unusual arrangement of the sequence in Bodley 343.

[124] The one exception to this may be Uppsala, Universitetsbibliotek, MS C 60 which presents 25, 21, 26–29, 36–49, 54, 50, 53, 58, 57, 2, 22. However, the number of missing items makes certainty difficult.

[125] See Pamela R. Robinson, 'Self-Contained Units in Composite Manuscripts of the Anglo-Saxon Period', in *Anglo-Saxon Manuscripts: Basic Readings*, ed. Mary P. Richards, Basic Readings in Anglo-Saxon England, 2 (New York, 1994), pp. 25–35; reprinted from *ASE*, 7 (1978), 231–38.

[126] See *Old English Homilies*, ed. by Irvine, p. liii.

Bodley 343, then copied the work 'as is' without attempting to reconcile the anomalous sequence of items.

Before returning to the question of the place of the homiliary in the manuscript it is perhaps worth looking at those items in Bodley 343 that have not been identified as part of the Homiliary of Angers. While some of these homilies remained unidentified elsewhere (namely *vii, xi, xii, xix*), others offer points of comparison with known works. The most exciting of these items, *Sermo x*, is a previously unrecognized Latin translation of pseudo-Eusebius Alexandrinus's *De Christi passione*.[127] Formerly, the Latin translation of *De Christi passione* was known only from its appearance in the composite *Sermo de confusione diaboli*, which conflates two originally independent expositions.[128] To this anonymous author are attributed twenty-two 'short yet influential texts',[129] several of which were translated into Old Russian, Old Slavonic, Georgian, Armenian, Arabic, and Syriac.[130] Identification of the author has aroused considerable interest and debate in which the leading candidate was initially Eusebius of Emesa,[131] then Eusebius of Alexandria,[132] before the present nomenclature was adopted.[133] To confuse the matter

---

[127] See M. Geerard, *Clavis patrum graecorum*, vol. III (Turnhout, 1979), p. 74, no. 5526. The homily is edited in B. de Montfaucon, *Joannis Chrysostomi Opera Omnia*, 2nd edn, vol. XI (Paris, 1838), cols 867–71, under the title *In sancta et magna Parasceve, et in sanctum passionem Domini*. The text is also found in *Patrologia Graeca*, ed. by Jacques-Paul Migne, 161 vols (Paris, 1857–86), 62, 721–24. A new edition based on a more thorough survey of the materials promised by E. von Dobschütz never appeared, nor did the edition of the late Guy Lafontaine, cited as in preparation by Geerard, *Clavis patrum graecorum*.

[128] Edited with an introduction by E. K. Rand, 'Sermo de confusione diaboli', *Modern Philology*, 2 (1904), 261–78; for two later witnesses, see Z. Izydorczyk, 'Two Newly Identified Manuscripts of the *Sermo de confusione diaboli*', *Scriptorium*, 43 (1989), 253–55. The text is also edited with a fuller apparatus by O. Hey, 'Eine Predigt über Christi Höllenferht', *Archiv für lateinische Lexicographie und Grammatik*, 14 (1906), 253–68.

[129] Izydorczyk, 'Two Newly Identified Manuscripts', p. 253.

[130] See Geerard, *Clavis patrum graecorum*, pp. 61–75, nos 5510–32 for further details.

[131] See L.-F.-A. Maury, 'Histoire d'un évangile apocryphe: l'Évangile de Nicodeme', in *Croyance et Légendes de l'Antiquité* (Paris, 1863), pp. 289–332 (p. 323).

[132] See Rand, 'Sermo de confusione diaboli', pp. 262–64.

[133] There is no concrete evidence for the date of this work. The general hypothesis asserts the fifth or the sixth century; see Rand, 'Sermo de confusione diaboli', pp. 262–63; E. von Dobschütz, 'Nicodemus, Gospel of', in *A Dictionary of the Bible*, ed. by J. Hastings, vol. III (New York, 1919), pp. 544–47 (p. 545); D. Sheerin, 'St John the Baptist in the Lower World', *Vigiliae Christianae*, 30 (1976), 1–22 (p. 17).

further only slightly, in the Middle Ages *De Christi passione* appears to have circulated amongst the works of St John Chrysostom.[134] At its core, the homily depicts a version of Christ's descent into Hell that differs in important ways from the more popular *Gospel of Nicodemus*.[135] Because these differences centre around the same basic story, some scholars have argued that the pseudo-Eusebius Alexandrinus material represents the source for the *Gospel of Nicodemus* descent,[136] others that pseudo-Eusebius used an early version of the *Descensus ad inferos* in his homilies;[137] yet more recently a compromise position, asserting a common foundation, has been posited.[138]

Another item unique to the Bodley 343 recension of the Homiliary of Angers consists of seven manuscript lines that briefly describe the genealogy and life of James the Lesser:

> Iste Iacobus filius Alphei fuit quia et frater Domini nominatur. Tres enim sorores fuerunt, Maria mater Domini et Maria Iacobi et Ioseph mater, <et Maria mater> filiorum Zebedei. Tante et enim sanctitatis iste Iacobus fuisse (xx^ra) narratur ut propter eius necem dicat Ioseph subuersam esse Ierusalem. Hic autem post passionem Domini anno tricesimo suum feliciter consummauit martirium.[139]

> [This James was the son of Alpheus and is therefore called brother of the Lord. For there were three sisters, Mary the mother of the Lord, and Mary the mother of James and Joseph, and Mary the mother of the sons of Zebedee. And this James is said to have been of such sanctity that Josephus says that Jerusalem was destroyed on account of his death. Moreover, he auspiciously suffered martyrdom in the thirtieth year after the Lord's passion.]

This brief notice, perhaps a marginal note from an exemplar here copied into the main body of text, represents a studied representation of this 'frater Domini'. The relationship of the so-called brothers of Jesus as expressed in the Bodley notice has

---

[134] Indeed, it seems that for this reason it was first edited along with other *spuria* in the *opera* of John Chrysostom by Henry Savile in *S. Ioannis Chrysostomi Opera Graece: octo voluminibus* (Eton, 1613).

[135] On these differences, see J. A. MacCulloch, *The Harrowing of Hell: A Comparative Study of an Early Christian Doctrine* (Edinburgh, 1930), pp. 174–91.

[136] See Maury, 'Histoire', p. 323.

[137] See for example, Constantin von Tischendorf, *Evangelia apocrypha*, 2nd edn (Leipzig, 1876; repr. Hildesheim, 1966), p. lxviii; Lipsius, *Die Pilatus-Akten kritische untersucht* (Kiel, 1871), p. 7; and Dobschütz, 'Nicodemus', p. 545.

[138] See for example, MacCulloch, *Harrowing of Hell*, p. 185.

[139] See fols xix^vb, 34 – xx^ra, 3 (*Sermo xviii*, pp. 262–63).

its origins in Jerome,[140] but finds its nearest related and fullest expression in Haymo's *Epitome historiae sacrae*:

> Sciunt etiam qui diligenter explorauerunt, quia frater Domini sit dictus, tamquam cognatus sit. Hic enim mos Hebraeorum, cognatos uel propinquos fratres dicere uel appellare. Frater igitur Domini sic dictus est, quia de Maria sorore matris Domini, et patre Alpheo genitus est; unde Iacobus Alphei appellatur. Sed, quoniam nunc se ingessit occasio, de duobus Iacobis omnem quaestionem rescindamus, et altius generis eorum repetamus originem. Maria mater Domini, et Maria mater Iacobi, fratris Domini, et Maria <mater Iacobi>[141] fratris Ioannis euangelistae, sorores fuerunt, de diuersis patribus genitae, sed de eadem matre, scilicet Anna.[142]

> [Those who have carefully investigated this matter also know that he is called 'brother of the Lord' as if he is his kinsman. For this is the custom of the Hebrews, to call or refer to one's cousins or close relatives as 'brothers'. Thus the 'brother' of the Lord is so called because he was born of the sister of Mary, the mother of the Lord, and his father was Alpheus; this is why he is called James, son of Alpheus. But since the opportunity has now presented itself, we open up the whole question concerning the two Jameses and repeat the origin of their noble lineage. Mary, the mother of the Lord, and Mary, the mother of James, the Lord's brother, and Mary the mother of James, the brother of John the Evangelist, were sisters, born from different fathers but from the same mother, namely Anne.]

In addition, the final two sentences of the Bodley genealogy are equally erudite. The reference to Josephus's recording of James's sanctity and the ensuing destruction of Jerusalem is borrowed from Jerome's *De uiris inlustribus*.[143] The final details regarding James's death are borrowed from Bede's *Commentarius in epistolas septem catholicas*.[144] On the one hand, this display of erudition suggests that not all users

---

[140] 'Restat conclusio, ut Maria ista quae Jacobi minoris scribitur mater, fuerit uxor Alphaei, et soror Mariae matris Domini, quam Mariam Cleophae Joannes euangelista cognominat, siue a patre, siue gentilitate familiae aut quacunque alia causa ei nomen imponens': *Aduersus Heluidium de Mariae uirginitate perpetua*, §13 (*PL* 23.206A).

[141] Emendation suggested by B. de Gaiffier, 'Le *Trinubium Annae*: Haymon d'Halberstadt ou Haymon d'Auxerre?', *Analecta Bollandiana*, 90 (1972), 289–98 (p. 289).

[142] §2.3 in *PL* 118.823D–24B.

[143] 'Tradit idem Iosephus tantae eum sanctitatis fuisse et celebritatis in populo, ut propter eius necem creditum sit subuersam Hierosolymam' ('Josephus records that he (James) was of so great sanctity and renown among the people, that it was believed that Jerusalem was destroyed on account of his death'): chap 2, p. 8, lines 6–8, in E. C. Richardson, *Hieronymi Liber de uiris inlustribus. Gennadii Liber de uiris inlustribus*, Texte und Untersuchungen zur Geschichte der altchristlichen Literatur, 14 (Leipzig, 1896).

[144] 'Constat enim quia beatus Iacobus tricesimo post passionem domini anno suum consummauit martyrium' ('For it is clear that blessed James suffered martyrdom in the thirtieth year after

of the Homiliary of Angers shared the lack of patristic knowledge displayed within the homilies themselves and consequently were not as unlettered as those to whom the contents of the homiliary were addressed. On the other, the learned lines demonstrate that at some point it was deemed necessary to specify the precise James who authored the epistle lest contemporary or future users of the homiliary be in doubt.

The other two identifiable items in Bodley 343 reveal a different textual tale. *Sermones lv* and *lvi* are adaptations, or blunderings, of Gregory's *Homiliae in Euangelia* VI and VII. It is unclear whether the state of the texts in Bodley 343 is the result of scribal transmission which transversed several different hands or if there are deliberate attempts to rewrite the patristic texts. One example demonstrates the phenomenon. In *Homilia* VII, Gregory states 'quisquis auaritiae aestibus anhelat' ('whoever pants in the heat of avarice'). The Bodley 343 version of the homily restates this as 'quisquis auaritie uestibus se uelat' ('whoever hides himself in the clothes of avarice'). The former scenario, which posits error, seems the more plausible because at this point the Bodley text of the homiliary shows serious flaws. In the homily that precedes the adaptations of Gregory (*Sermo liv*, HA 57), a large section elaborating on the way in which one should use the five senses to attain eternal life is missing; hearing is the only sense that is discussed in the Bodley version. Furthermore, the unidentified homily that follows the Gregorian adaptations has several points of intransigent text that figure to be the result of copying errors on the part of the Bodley scribe or perhaps his predecessors.

The recent publication of the Taunton fragments affirms an English antecedent to Bodley 343 in an Anglo-Saxon or Anglo-Norman manuscript[145] and bolsters the argument that the homiliary was used for explicating basic exegesis to the laity in

---

the Lord's passion'): Prol, lines 23–24, in Bede, *Opera Exegetica*, ed. by M. L. W. Laistner and D. Hurst, CCSL, 121 (Turnhout, 1983).

[145] There is no other predecessor in England based on examination of catalogue descriptions for manuscripts cited as either 'Homiliaries, Latin' or 'Homilies and sermons in Latin, anonymous or not identified' in Helmut Gneuss, *Handlist of Anglo-Saxon Manuscripts: A List of Manuscripts and Manuscript Fragments Written or Owned in England up to 1100*, MRTS, 241 (Tempe, 2001) and Helmut Gneuss, 'Addenda and Corrigenda to the *Handlist of Anglo-Saxon Manuscripts*', *ASE*, 32 (2003 [2004]), 293–305, as well as those listed under 'Homiliae' and 'Homiliary (Latin)' in Richard Gameson, *The Manuscripts of Early Norman England (c. 1066–1130)* (Oxford, 1999). In the case of Gneuss no. 268.6 (Gameson no. 324) Hertford, Hertfordshire Record Office (now Hertfordshire Archives and Local Studies (HALS) at Hertford County Hall), Gorhambury, X.D.4.B and X.D.4.C for which I could find no outside description, I examined the detached manuscript leaves themselves.

the vernacular, making it an important text in the study of Old English homiletics. However, as we have noted earlier, the story of Bodley 343 does not only look backwards, but forwards. My investigation into the Homiliary of Angers has revealed a later (albeit partial) English witness to the homiliary in Cambridge, St John's College, MS C. 12 (s. xiii).[146] The manuscript contains the following:

> fols 140^v–141^r: HA 5; Second Sunday after Epiphany; cf. *Sermo lxii*;
> fol. 141^r: HA 6; Third Sunday after Epiphany; cf. *Sermo lxiii*;
> fol. 141^{r-v}: HA 7; Fourth Sunday after Epiphany; cf. *Sermo lxiv*;
> fol. 141^v: HA 8; Septuagesima; cf. *Sermo lxv*;
> fols 141^v–142^r: HA 9; Sexagesima; cf. *Sermo lxvi*;
> fol. 142^r: the gospel-based exposition, or first part of HA 10; Quinquagesima; cf. *Sermo lxvii*;
> fol. 142^{r-v}: HA 14; Fourth Sunday in Lent; cf. *Sermo vi*;
> fol. 142^v: an incomplete version of *De Christi passione*; cf. *Sermo x*.[147]

Several indicators, such as the separation of the gospel exposition of HA 10 (an exclusive feature of the John's and Bodley manuscripts) and the common inclusion of *De Christi passione*, reveal a close relationship between the two witnesses. Perhaps most suggestive, however, are similarities relating to the codicological aspects of the homiliary in each of these manuscripts. In St John's College, C. 12, the Homiliary of Angers occupies part of the sixteenth quire (fols 139–44), which appears not to have been part of the manuscript's original compilation, or at least not part of the largest section (now non-contiguous) of the manuscript; quire 16 lacks the small divot, approximately one centimetre wide, found in the top of the folios in half of the other quires, namely 1, 2, 8, 9, 10, 12, 14, and 15. If the Homiliary of Angers was indeed copied out in its entirety originally, the text would have occupied approximately twenty folios, a good size for a small but thorough

---

[146] Montague Rhodes James, *A Descriptive Catalogue of the Manuscripts in the Library of St John's College, Cambridge* (Cambridge, 1913), no. 62, pp. 82–86 (p. 85); also available online at <http://www.joh.cam.ac.uk/library/special_collections/manuscripts/medieval_manuscripts/medman/C_12.htm>. The English origin of the manuscript is suggested by a bidding prayer wherein the speaker is the Archbishop of Canterbury. I am extremely grateful to Jonathan Grove who was able to provide an initial examination of the manuscript to confirm its contents.

[147] Foliation presented here represents the present-day order and sequence of folios based on my own examination of the manuscript. The folio numbers hand-written in the manuscript do not match the present position of folios in the present binding.

collection of sermon notes.[148] If the homiliary circulated as a portable, unbound book it would have been more likely to be disassembled and misbound with other materials. As it stands, the number and changes of hands, as well as codicological complications, renders suggestions regarding the collection's origin and provenance speculative at best. However, tentative links to Canterbury for other parts of the manuscript hint at an origin that would dovetail nicely with the suggestion that much of Bodley 343's vernacular material originates from the south-east.[149] Whether future work can confirm or refute any origin or provenance, the appearance of a related version of the Homiliary of Angers in this thirteenth-century English manuscript suggests that when the first scribe of Bodley 343 produced his copy, the act was not motivated by antiquarian interests; however old the homiliary itself may be, it was actively copied in England as early as the eleventh century, again in the twelfth, and at least once again in the thirteenth. Given the use and the nature of the text discussed here, this rate of preservation is more significant than the raw number of manuscripts might suggest.

The curious situation regarding the relationship of HA to the whole of St John's College, C. 12 is parallelled to a large extent in the example of Bodley 343. The prevailing description espoused by Susan Irvine and Malcolm Godden contends that Bodley 343 is written in seven sections, each formed by a group of quires ending with a blank space before a new quire begins;[150] this characterization has been relied upon for other work involving the manuscript.[151] The implications of this description are somewhat misleading, however, for, as Clemoes noted in his assessment, not every section ends with blank space.[152] The third section, (c), as defined by Irvine and Godden, ends with a half-line that had been squeezed below the margin of folio 20^v, the last folio of the ninth quire. Indeed, the second scribe of the manuscript is compelled to fit text below the margin with some regularity, although never as much as on folio 20^v.[153] Furthermore, a space of five lines at the

---

[148] The written space of fol. 142^v is approximately 18.5 cm x 13.5 cm. The written space and size of folios in other quires differs, sometimes significantly.

[149] See *Homilies*, ed. by Pope, I, 18.

[150] See *Old English homilies*, ed. by Irvine, p. xx, and compare *Second Series*, ed. by Godden, p. xxxvii, which does not assert that blank space ends each section, but that a quire division coincides with each section.

[151] See, for example, Wilcox, 'Wulfstan in the Twelfth Century', p. 83.

[152] See *First Series*, ed. by Clemoes, pp. 1–5.

[153] Compare, for example, fols 23^v, 27^r, 29^r, 36^r, 36^v, 39^r, 148^r, 163^r, 164^v, 165^v.

bottom of folio 11ᵛ prompted Clemoes, contrary to Irvine and Godden, to end the third section, (c), at this point, the only section break not to coincide with a quire division.[154] Additionally, fourteen lines of blank space, not accounted for in any sectional division, are found on folio 166ᵛ after a Latin dialogue on the creed and before the English text resumes below on the first of the folio's two columns.

Although the idea that sections coincide with quire groupings does not always attain, palaeographers agree that the manuscript is the work of two scribes; the first responsible for folios viʳ–xxxixᵛ (quires 1–6) the second for folios 1ʳ–170ʳ (quires 7–29). As a result, it is not clear that the Homiliary of Angers, and the remainder of the first scribe's work, was originally bound with that of the second scribe; indeed, the different, presumably early modern, folio-numbering systems may bear this out. However, a lack of uniformity in the quality of the folios that persists throughout the manuscript suggests that the Homiliary of Angers was not necessarily a separable unit bound into the manuscript at a later date.[155] Perhaps given the large dimensions of Bodley 343 and the complex textual history of its vernacular items, the manuscript was compiled as a formal copy of preaching and instructional material that had been circulating in booklets previously. Whether the manuscript was originally intended to be a joint production of the two scribes or not, we have evidence that the twelfth-century scribe responsible for copying the Homiliary of Angers also copied Old English material, namely folios viʳ–xʳ, the first section, of Bodley 343. Consequently, it appears that this Latin homiliary, with its focus on the basic, catechetical elements of Christian faith and its emphasis on promoting actions to ensure the salvation of Christian souls, was a suitable companion to Old English material and to those engaged in the continued use of Anglo-Saxon homilies; although the homiliary appears in Latin in Bodley 343, the translation in the Taunton fragments attests to its use in English-speaking circles.

To retrieve the motivations for the compilation of Bodley 343 itself is difficult. As has been noted, the manuscript bears few of the marks that distinguish manuscripts used for preaching.[156] As it stands, the manuscript could well have served as a compendious resource of preaching material, which also included quasi-historical material, such as the *History of the Holy-Rood Tree*, as well as guidelines on the interpretation of the Old Testament in the form of Ælfric's letter to Sigeweard (who is unnamed in the Bodley version) and on episcopal duties in the form

---

[154] See *First Series*, ed. by Clemoes, pp. 2–3.

[155] See Conti, 'Preaching Scripture and Apocrypha', pp. 54–55.

[156] See Irvine, 'Compilation and Use of Manuscripts', p. 59.

of Ælfric's letters to Wulfstan, all of which would have made the codex a rather encyclopaedic volume covering a range of concerns for an individual involved in ecclesiastical duties and pastoral care. The Homiliary of Angers, a text designed for basic biblical exposition, adds a new dimension to the story of the manuscript, as well as to the types of material used for the teaching of the Bible in post-Conquest England. Bodley 343 and the Taunton translation demonstrate the homiliary's intimate relationship to the vernacular and bolster the notion that content, not language, should guide the discussion of sources for popular preaching.[157] Copies from the eleventh through the thirteenth centuries indicate the work's persistence and suggest the persistence of oral, biblical exposition in English. Indeed, the textual evidence in Bodley 343 attests to a probable vibrant traffic in Anglo-Saxon material in the century following the Norman Conquest, a traffic that likely took place in the form of portable booklets of various sizes; such a hypothesis best accounts for the varied textual traditions that underpin the compilation of Bodley 343 and are reinforced by the anomalous sequence of the Homiliary of Angers found therein.[158] If, on the one hand, the Conquest inspired a monastic antiquarian reaction which maintained English ways despite the Norman conquerors,[159] on the other hand, it has long been suggested that English preaching continued in the post-Conquest parish.[160] Additionally, the evidence afforded by the adaptation of Old English material for a contemporary audience seen elsewhere in the Lambeth and Vespasian homilies further supports the continued circulation of post-Conquest material in English and demonstrates more than antiquarian motivations and reactions.[161] While the number of extant manuscripts do not fully show the range of the circulation of the Old English homily in the twelfth century, the range of

[157] See Thomas L. Amos, 'Preaching and the Sermon in the Carolingian World', in *De Ore Domini: Preacher and the Word in the Middle Ages*, ed. by Thomas L. Amos, Eugene Green, and Beverly Mayne Kienzle (Kalamazoo, 1989), pp. 41–60.

[158] For a forceful restatement of the importance of booklets at some stage in the transmission of texts found in Bodley 343, see Irvine, 'Compilation and Use of Manuscripts', p. 57.

[159] For this sentiment, see Michael Clanchy, *From Memory to Written Record: England 1066–1307*, 2nd edn (Oxford, 1993), p. 212. For a view that imparts less reactionism to these monastic scholars and perhaps a more genuine fervour for understanding the historical past and rehabilitating it to fit their historical present, see Southern, 'Place of England', p. 208.

[160] See, for example, John Moorman, *Church Life in England in the Thirteenth Century* (Cambridge, 1955), esp. p. 78.

[161] See Swan, 'Ælfric's *Catholic Homilies*', pp. 74–75, and Richards, 'MS Cotton Vespasian A. XXII', pp. 98 and 103.

textual traditions found in many post-Conquest manuscripts bears out the widespread nature of this phenomenon even as modern scholarship pieces together the various roles that the Old English homily played in the pivotal twelfth century. During the course of the century and thereafter, the patristic-based homily, the staple of Carolingian biblical exposition, gave way to the thematic, scholastic sermon, marking a profound shift in the Church's view of the role of preaching and coinciding with the widespread trends in learning and its institutionalization sweeping through post–Gregorian reform Europe. Yet a shift is not a clean break; amidst these changes, traditional homiletic material from the past continued to be recast and transformed to serve a contemporary purpose.[162]

[162] In addition to those who have been thanked in the course of this paper, I am also extremely grateful to Andy Orchard, Antonette diPaolo Healey, Ian McDougall, and Christopher A. Jones for comments on various aspects of this work.

Appendix

The Latin Homilies of Bodley 343 (fols xiʳ–xxxixᵛ)[163]

Folio reference	Item no.	Pericope	Feast day	Outside Identification
xiʳ	*i*	I Corinthians 13. 4	Quinquagesima	HA 10.2
xiᵛ–xiiʳ	*ii*	Matthew 4. 1	Quadragesima	HA 11.1
xiiʳ	*iii*	II Corinthians 6. 1	Quadragesima	HA 11.2
xiiʳ–xiiiʳ	*iv*	Matthew 17. 10	2nd Sunday in Lent	HA 12
xiiiʳ⁻ᵛ	*v*	Luke 11. 14	3rd Sunday in Lent	HA 13
xiiiᵛ– xivʳ	*vi*	John 6. 5	4th Sunday in Lent	HA 14
xivʳ⁻ᵛ	***vii***	Matthew 15. 21	?In Lent	
xivᵛ–xvᵛ	*viii*	John 8. 46	5th Sunday in Lent	HA 15
xvᵛ–xviʳ	<u>*ix*</u>	Matthew 21. 1	Palm Sunday	HA 55 (1st Sunday in Advent)
xviʳ–xviiʳ	***x***			*De Christi passione*
xviiʳ⁻ᵛ	***xi***	I Corinthians 5. 7	Easter Sunday	
xviiᵛ–xviiiʳ	***xii***	Mark 16. 1	Easter Sunday	
xviiiʳ–xixʳ	*xiii*	John 20. 24	1st Sunday after Easter	HA 16
xixʳ	*xiv*	John 10. 11	2nd Sunday after Easter	HA 17
xixʳ	*xv*	John 16. 16	3rd Sunday after Easter	HA 18
xixʳ⁻ᵛ	*xvi*	John 16. 5	4th Sunday after Easter	HA 19
xixᵛ	*xvii*	John 16. 23	5th Sunday after Easter	HA 20
xixᵛ–xxʳ	***xviii***			The genealogy of James
xxʳ	***xix***	James 5. 16	Rogationtide	
xxʳ⁻ᵛ	*xx*	Luke 11. 5	Rogationtide (Litanies)	HA 22
xxᵛ–xxiʳ	*xxi*	Mark 16. 14	Ascension	HA 23
xxiʳ	*xxii*	John 15. 26	6th Sunday after Easter	HA 24
xxiʳ⁻ᵛ	*xxiii*	John 14. 23	Pentecost	HA 25

[163] For the Latin homilies of Bodley 343, the following table retains the Latin-numeral system printed by Irvine in *Old English Homilies*. Items that do not form part of the identified Homiliary of Angers are presented in bold-faced font. Homilies that appear in the Bodley 343 version in a sequence that deviates from that of the Homiliary of Angers are underlined. Abbreviations and short titles found for items outside Bodley 343 are those used in the preceding piece.

Folio reference	Item no.	Pericope	Feast day	Outside Identification
xxi^v	*xxiv*	John 3. 1	1st Sunday after Pentecost	HA 21 (Pascha annotina)
xxi^v–xxii^v	*xxv*	John 16. 9	2nd Sunday after Pentecost	HA 26 (1st)
xxii^v–xxiii^r	*xxvi*	John 14. 6	3rd Sunday after Pentecost	HA 27 (2nd)
xxiii^{r–v}	*xxvii*	Luke 15. 1	4th Sunday after Pentecost	HA 28 (3rd)
xxiii^v	*xxviii*	Matthew 5. 20	7th Sunday after Pentecost	HA 31 (6th)
xxiii^v–xxiv^r	*xxix*	Matthew 16. 13	Peter and Paul, 29 June	HA 32
xxiv^{r–v}	*xxx*	Mark 8. 1	8th Sunday after Pentecost	HA 33 (7th)
xxiv^v	*xxxi*	Matthew 7. 15	9th Sunday after Pentecost	HA 34 (8th)
xxiv^v–xxv^r	*xxxii*	I Corinthians 6. 10	10th Sunday after Pentecost	HA 35 (9th)
xxv^{r–v}	*xxxiii*	Luke 16. 1	10th Sunday after Pentecost	HA 36 (9th)
xxv^v–xxvi^r	*xxxiv*	Luke 19. 41	11th Sunday after Pentecost	HA 37 (10th)
xxvi^{r–v}	*xxxv*	Luke 18. 10	12th Sunday after Pentecost	HA 38 (11th)
xxvi^v	*xxxvi*	Mark 7. 31	13th Sunday after Pentecost	HA 39 (12th)
xxvi^v–xxvii^v	*xxxvii*	Luke 10. 23	14th Sunday after Pentecost	HA 40 (13th)
xxvii^v	*xxxviii*	Luke 17. 11	15th Sunday after Pentecost	HA 41 (14th)
xxvii^v–xxviii^r	*xxxix*	Matthew 6. 24	16th Sunday after Pentecost	HA 42 (15th)
xxviii^r	*xl*	Luke 7. 11	17th Sunday after Pentecost	HA 43 (16th)
xxviii^{r–v}	*xli*	Matthew 13. 44	Unknown	HA 59 (Common for a Virgin)
xxviii^v	*xlii*	Luke 14. 1	18th Sunday after Pentecost	HA 44 (17th)
xxviii^v–xxix^r	*xliii*	Luke 13. 6	19th Saturday after Pentecost	HA 45 (18th)
xxix^{r–v}	*xliv*	Matthew 22. 23	19th Sunday after Pentecost	HA 46 (18th)
xxix^v–xxx^r	*xlv*	Matthew 9. 1	20th Sunday after Pentecost	HA 47 (19th)

Folio reference	Item no.	Pericope	Feast day	Outside Identification
xxx^r	*xlvi*	Matthew 22. 2	21st Sunday after Pentecost	HA 48 (20th)
xxx^r	*xlvii*	John 4. 46	22nd Sunday after Pentecost	HA 49 (21st)
xxx^r–v	*xlviii*	Matthew 18. 23	23rd Sunday after Pentecost	HA 50 (22nd)
xxx^v–xxxi^r	*xlix*	Matthew 22. 15	24th Sunday after Pentecost	HA 51 (23rd)
xxxi^r–v	*l*	Matthew 9. 18	25th Sunday after Pentecost	HA 52 (24th)
xxxi^v	*li*	Matthew 13. 24	26th Sunday after Pentecost	HA 53 (25th)
xxxi^v–xxxii^r	*lii*	Matthew 4. 18	St Andrew, 30 November	HA 54
xxxii^r–v	*liii*	Luke 21. 25	2nd Sunday in Advent	HA 56
xxxii^v	*liv*	Matthew 25. 14	St Nicolaus, 6 December	HA 57 (Common for a Confessor)
xxxii^v–xxxiii^v	**lv**	Matthew 11. 2	3rd Sunday in Advent	Gregory, *Homiliae in Euangelia* VI
xxxiii^v–xxxiv^r	**lvi**	John 1. 19	4th Sunday in Advent	Gregory, *Homiliae in Euangelia* VII
xxxiv^r–xxxv^r	**lvii**	Matthew 10. 16	Unknown	
xxxv^r	*lviii*	John 1. 1	Christmas	HA 1
xxxv^r–xxxvi^r	*lix*	Luke 2. 21	Octave of Christmas, 1 January	HA 2
xxxvi^r–v	*lx*	Matthew 2. 1	Epiphany, 6 January	HA 3
xxxvi^v–xxxvii^r	*lxi*	Luke 2. 42	1st Sunday after Epiphany	HA 4
xxxvii^r–v	*lxii*	John 2. 1	2nd Sunday after Epiphany	HA 5
xxxvii^v–xxxviii^r	*lxiii*	Matthew 8. 1	3rd Sunday after Epiphany	HA 6
xxxviii^r–v	*lxiv*	Matthew 8. 23	4th Sunday after Epiphany	HA 7
xxxviii^v–xxxix^r	*lxv*	Matthew 20. 1	Septuagesima	HA 8
xxxix^r–v	*lxvi*	Luke 8. 4	Sexagesima	HA 9
xxxix^v	*lxvii*	Matthew 20. 18	Quinquagesima	HA 10.1

Preaching Past the Conquest: Lambeth Palace 487 and Cotton Vespasian A. XXII

Mary Swan

Introduction: Materials

Old English preaching, and the production of preaching texts, did not stop at 1066. Along with other pre-Conquest Old English compositions, many homilies were recopied, and reused, from the late eleventh to the early thirteenth century.[1] Current research on these post-Conquest Old English homiletic texts indicates that they were very likely to be copied for practical use in preaching in church or monastic settings, as well as perhaps for private devotional reading. Homiletic Old English manuscripts written in the later eleventh and twelfth centuries include some of the most important witnesses to the works of Ælfric, and show pre-Conquest preaching texts being modified structurally and linguistically for new audiences.

Manuscripts dating from between the later eleventh and early thirteenth centuries which contain Old English homilies are the following:

Cambridge, Corpus Christi College, MS 421 (s. xi[1], s. xi 3rd quarter; earlier sections probably Canterbury, later sections probably Exeter)[2]

---

[1] For an overview of post-Conquest Old English production, see *Rewriting Old English in the Twelfth Century*, ed. by Mary Swan and Elaine M. Treharne, CSASE, 30 (Cambridge, 2000). A comprehensive new survey of the field is being undertaken by the Arts and Humanities Research Council–funded project 'The Production and Use of English Manuscripts 1060 to 1220' <http://www.le.ac.uk/ee/em1060to1220>, which will run from 2005 to 2010, and will produce a full catalogue of all surviving manuscripts containing Old English produced in this period.

[2] Manuscript datings and origins are taken from Neil R. Ker, *Catalogue of Manuscripts Containing Anglo-Saxon* (Oxford, 1957; repr. with supplement 1990); *Ælfric's Catholic Homilies:*

London, Lambeth Palace Library, MS 489 (s. xi 3rd quarter, very probably Exeter)

Oxford, Bodleian Library, MSS Hatton 113, 114 (s. xi 3rd quarter, very probably Worcester)

Oxford, Bodleian Library, MS Junius 121 (s. xi 3rd quarter, very probably Worcester)

London, British Library, Cotton MS Cleopatra B. XIII (s. xi 3rd quarter, very probably Exeter)

Cambridge, Corpus Christi College, MS 302 (s. xii^{in}, origin unknown; possibly Essex)

London, British Library, Cotton MS Faustina A. IX (s. xii end of first quarter, origin unknown) [3]

Oxford, Bodleian Library, MS Hatton 116 (s. xii; about a decade later than Cotton Faustina A. IX, possibly Worcester) [4]

Cambridge, Corpus Christi College, MS 367, fols 3–6, 11–29 (s. xii, origin not known, but possible south-eastern; perhaps Rochester; in Worcester by some point in the twelfth century)

London, British Library, Cotton MS Vespasian D. XIV (s. xii$^{med.}$ for first scribe and s. xii^2 for second and third scribes, probably Rochester) [5]

Cambridge, Corpus Christi College, MS 303 (s. xii^2, probably Rochester)

Oxford, Bodleian Library, MS Bodley 343 (s. xii$^{med.}$, West Midlands, possibly Hereford) [6]

Cambridge, University Library, MS Ii. 1. 33 (s. xii^2, origin not known but possibly Rochester or Christ Church, Canterbury)

The First Series, Text, ed. by Peter Clemoes, EETS: SS, 17 (Oxford, 1997); *Ælfric's Catholic Homilies: The Second Series, Text,* ed. by Malcolm Godden, EETS: SS, 5 (London, 1979); and Elaine Treharne, 'The Production and Script of Manuscripts Containing English Religious Texts in the First Half of the Twelfth Century', in *Rewriting Old English,* ed. by Swan and Treharne, pp. 11–40.

[3] Treharne, 'Production and Script', p. 21.

[4] Treharne, 'Production and Script', p. 21.

[5] Treharne, 'Production and Script', p. 34.

[6] For the localization of the dialect of this manuscript in the vicinity of Hereford, as opposed to the usual suggestion of Worcester as its place of origin, see Peter Kitson, 'Old English Dialects and the Stages of the Transition to Middle English', *Folia Linguistica Historica,* 11 (1992 [for 1990]), 27–87.

London, British Library, Cotton MS Vespasian A. XXII (*c.* 1200, very probably
    Rochester)
London, Lambeth Palace Library, MS 487 (*c.* 1200, West Midlands)[7]
This essay will consider two of the manuscripts from the later chronological
extreme of the above list — Lambeth 487 and Cotton Vespasian A. XXII —
chosen to enable an examination of Old English preaching texts at their farthest
remove from the pre-Conquest period. Its focus will be on the physical characteristics of the two manuscripts and what these can reveal about how, and why, they
were made and about the use of Old English homilies at the turn of the thirteenth
century.

London, Lambeth Palace Library, MS 487

Lambeth 487 is a collection of homiletic and devotional texts. It is a small manuscript. Jonathan Wilcox gives the dimensions of the leaves as 176–78 x 134 mm,
and notes that the original width of the parchment, before the addition of mending
strips was *c.* 127 mm, and that the written area is *c.* 144–60 x 81 mm.[8] The manuscript is not especially luxurious or striking; it has no illustrations, although space
has been left for some initial letters at the opening of items to be filled in,
presumably more elaborately than the rest of the script. This has not been done,
and the only use of colour other than black is the red ink used for some titles and
quotations.

    The manuscript contains nineteen items, the first eighteen of which were all
written by a single scribe in around the year 1200,[9] and the nineteenth by a second
scribe in the mid-thirteenth century. Items 1 to 18, then, were written out as a set,
and possibly as a single project. They consist of devotional texts of a variety of
kinds: some framed with the rhetorical markers of homilies, and others not. The
Church festivals to which the items refer include Palm Sunday, three Sundays in

---

    [7] Ker, *Catalogue*, p.222, also records the evidence for the existence of London, British Library,
Cotton MS Otho A. XIII, now destroyed by fire, and known from Wanley's transcripts of incipits
and explicits. This manuscript might have contained Old English homilies and have been written
after the Conquest.

    [8] *Wulfstan Texts and Other Homiletic Materials*, ed. by Jonathan Wilcox, ASMMF, 8
(Tempe, 2000), pp. 72–78 (p. 73).

    [9] Ker does not include Lambeth 487 or Cotton Vespasian A. XII in his *Catalogue* on the
grounds of what he describes as their 'tenuous' connection with Old English manuscripts (p.xix).
He also notes that both manuscripts 'may have been written before 1200' (p. xix).

Lent, and the Nativity, and three of the texts include gospel commentaries. All but two of these items are in prose. The exceptions are item 6, *Pater Noster*, a rhyming commentary on the Lord's Prayer, which contains many direct audience addresses by its narrative voice which are like those used in preaching, and item 18, *Poema Morale* (sometimes known as *Conduct of Life*).

Some of the items in Lambeth 487, including the *Pater Noster*, a piece on the creed which follows it in the manuscript, and the *Poema Morale*, show an interest in themes and a spiritual sensibility much closer to post-Conquest than to Anglo-Saxon England, and five of the items in the manuscript which have no apparent connections to Old English texts (items 7, 13, 15, 16, and 17) also survive in more or less similar form in the contemporary (or very slightly earlier) manuscript Cambridge, Trinity College, MS B. 14. 52, which appears to have no direct links with Old English traditions.[10]

Five of the homiletic texts in Lambeth 487 have been identified as reusing the work of named Old English homilists. Item 2 includes an adapted passage from Wulfstan's *Be Godcundre Warnunge*;[11] an Ælfrician source has recently been found for part of the closing section of item 3;[12] items 9 and 11 reuse material from Ælfric's *Catholic Homilies*; and item 10 is an adapted rewriting of a pre-Conquest source homily which itself combined excerpts from five different Ælfrician texts. In her article on the scribal tradition of the Lambeth homilies, moreover, Celia Sisam includes item 1 in a list of texts in the manuscript which 'certainly go back

---

[10] The manuscript is edited by Richard Morris, *Old English Homilies and Homiletic Treatises [. . .] of the Twelfth and Thirteenth Centuries*, First Series, EETS: OS, 29 and 34 (London, 1867–68; repr. as one volume, 1988), pp. 1–190. In the Notes and Emendations to the volume, Morris comments on some of the comparisons between items in Lambeth 487 and earlier Old English texts, but he does not provide thorough collations. Some of the manuscript's contents are edited by Sarah M. O'Brien, 'An Edition of Seven Homilies from Lambeth Palace Library MS 487' (unpublished doctoral thesis, University of Oxford, 1985). The prose items in the manu-script are described by Veronica O'Mara in O. S. Pickering and V. M. O'Mara, *The Index of Middle English Prose, Handlist XIII: Manuscripts in Lambeth Palace Library* (Cambridge, 1999), pp. 40–43, and the whole manuscript is described in Wilcox, *Wulfstan Texts*, pp. 72–78. For further discussion of Trinity B. 14. 52, see below.

[11] Item 2 is analysed by Jonathan Wilcox, 'Wulfstan and the Twelfth Century', in *Rewriting Old English*, ed. by Swan and Treharne, pp. 83–97.

[12] By Elaine Treharne, in a recent conference paper, 'Unoriginal Sin: Textually Transmitted Deviancy in Old English Prose'. This source identification will be published by Treharne in *Living Through Conquest* (Oxford, forthcoming).

to Old English', and although no Old English source has so far been identified for this item, its tone and thematic focus make Sisam's suggestion very plausible.[13]

In earlier articles on aspects of Lambeth 487,[14] I proposed that items 9, 10, and 11 show similar modifications to their Ælfrician sources; in particular the omission of references to specifically monastic topics, and patterns of expansion of phrases for reiterative stress and addition of single words and word couplets for added emphasis. Some degree of this sort of stylistic reworking can be seen in many adaptations of Ælfrician preaching texts from the late tenth century onwards,[15] but it is notable that the modification of the Old English sources in these items matches the verbal and stylistic characteristics of the preacherly/narrative voice of Lambeth 487 items 1–18 as a whole: the voice generated is one which is closer to relatively formal spoken than formal written style, and which does not echo Ælfric's carefully balanced phrases and avoidance of rhetorical excess. Moreover, since the modifications to the Ælfrician sources of items 9, 10, and 11 are not attested in any other surviving versions of the Ælfrician texts in question, it is reasonable to propose that this distinctive reshaping is the work of the Lambeth 487 scribe and not inherited by him or her from an exemplar.

Another striking feature which unifies almost all of the items in Lambeth 487 is the insertion of short quotations in Latin which either provide authoritative-sounding statements for translation into English or serve as the subject for exegesis in English. The addition of Latin snippets to reused Old English homiletic texts is a very rare phenomenon: the only other example identified to date is London, British Library, Cotton MS Tiberius A. III, item 16, compiled in the mid-eleventh

---

[13] Celia Sisam, 'The Scribal Tradition of the *Lambeth Homilies*', *RES*, n.s., 2 (1951), 105–13 (p. 110, n. 4).

[14] See Swan, 'Old English Made New: One Catholic Homily and its Reuses', *Leeds Studies in English*, n.s., 28 (1997), 1–18; 'Ælfric's *Catholic Homilies* in the Twelfth Century', in *Rewriting Old English*, ed. by Swan and Treharne, pp. 62–82; 'Imagining a Readership for Post-Conquest Old English Manuscripts', in *Imagining the Book*, ed. by John Thompson and Stephen Kelly (Turnhout, 2005), pp. 145–57; and 'Mobile Libraries: Old English Manuscript Production in Worcester and the West Midlands, 1090–1215', to be published in *Essays in Manuscript Geography: Vernacular Manuscripts of the English West Midlands from the Conquest to the Sixteenth Century*, ed. by Wendy Scase, Texts and Cultures of Northern Europe, 10 (Turnhout, forthcoming 2007).

[15] An overview of the reuse of the *CH* is given in Swan, 'Ælfric as Source: The Dissemination of Ælfric's *Catholic Homilies* from the Late Tenth to Twelfth Centuries' (unpublished doctoral thesis, University of Leeds, 1993).

century.[16] In Lambeth 487, then, this feature turns the manuscript into something unlike almost all composite anonymous reshapings of Old English homiletic texts, and into something more like early Middle English homilies, in which the threading through of Latin quotations and English translations of them is much more common.

I have discussed elsewhere the effect of the Latin quotations in Lambeth 487 on the style and content of the items in which they are included — namely, to add authority and to prompt English exegesis.[17] The Latin quotations are also of interest for what they reveal about the production of the manuscript. They are in the main scribal hand, but are in red ink — a rare and visually conspicuous form of marking in such an unadorned manuscript — and can be demonstrated to have been written after the main text was completed, since some of them are squashed into their spaces, and in one case, space has been left but not filled. This space appears about a third of the way into item 10, 'De octo uiciis et de doudecim abusiuis huius seculi', which does not open with a homiletic formula of address but is homiletic in style in important ways: it is full of exhortation and instruction conveyed in a preacherly voice, and it ends with the traditional formula 'Quod ipse prestare dignetur qui uiuit et regnat deus per omnia secula seculorum. Amen'[18] ('May God, who lives and reigns for ever and ever, himself deign to grant this. Amen').[19] The section of item 10 in question is set out with space for a Latin quotation which is not present in the surviving versions of the composite piece which it copies. Morris gives the text from Lambeth 487 as follows:

> Þenne we sculan witan þet ure wununge nis nauht her; as is on heuene; gif we hopiað to gode swa þe apostel seide bi him and bi oðran rihtwise. [Nostra autem conuersatio in celis est.] þet is ure wununge is on heuene. þider we sculen hihgen of þissere erfeðnesse.[20]

> [Then we must know that our dwelling-place is not here; but it is in heaven; if we trust in God as the apostle said about him and about other righteous people [Nostra autem conversation in celis est.] that is our dwelling-place is in heaven. We must hurry there from this tribulation.]

[16] See Clare A. Lees, 'Liturgical Traditions for Palm Sunday and their Dissemination in Old English Prose' (unpublished doctoral thesis, University of Liverpool, 1985), pp. 93–110, and Swan, 'Ælfric as Source', pp. 168–74.

[17] Swan, 'Lambeth Palace 487 and Reading for the Ear', to be published in *Recovering Reading*, ed. by John Thompson and Stephen Kelly.

[18] *Old English Homilies*, ed. by Morris, p. 119, lines 18–20.

[19] I am grateful to William Flynn for assistance with this translation.

[20] *Old English Homilies*, ed. by Morris, p. 105, lines 30–35.

Here, Morris has supplied in square brackets the Latin biblical quotation which would be intended to serve as a prompt for the Old English translation 'þet is ure wununge is on heuene'. Not only does Lambeth 487 not include the Latin quotation, however, but the space it leaves for it is too small to fit the quotation in full, though it may be sufficient were the quotation heavily abbreviated.

Another picture is offered by one of the two surviving versions of Lambeth 487's composite source: Cambridge, Corpus Christi College, MS 178 (s. xi¹, at Worcester in the eleventh century, and possibly written there). In an appendix to his edition of Lambeth 487, Morris gives the corresponding section of CCCC 178 thus:

> Þonne sceole we witan þæt ure wunung nis na her. ac is on heofenum gif we hopiað to gode; þyder we sceolan efstan of þissere earfoðnysse.[21]

> [Then we must know that our dwelling-place is not here. But it is in heaven if we trust in God; we must hasten there from this tribulation.]

It is clear from this comparison that the Lambeth compiler has altered his or her source to add the planned Latin quotation and to turn the Old English biblical snippet quoted without attribution in the source text, as represented by CCCC 178, into something explicitly signalled as a translation of the Latin which was to precede it. Presumably the trigger for the planned Latin phrase is the compiler's recollection of the Latin source of 'ure wununge nis nauht her; ac is on heuene', but extensive adaptations are made to the passage to insert the quotation and its translation. Rather than simply supplying the Latin, followed by 'þet is', as happens elsewhere in item 10, the Lambeth 487 compiler has inserted a reference to Paul, space for the Latin quotation, and its English translation. The effect of all this is rather clumsy: as well as loosening Ælfric's rhythm, the words 'ure wununge [...] is on heuene' feature twice very close together.

The plans visible in Lambeth 487, and described above, for a rather heavy-handed explicitness in the rendering of its source make item 10 similar in rhetoric, register, and voice to the other items in the manuscript with identified Old English sources, and strengthen the case for a single adapter for each of them. The range of links to Old English traditions in the form of the reuse of Ælfric and Wulfstan texts in Lambeth 487 shows that its adapter — or the adapter of an earlier version of the same set of items, if we allow for the possibility of Lambeth 487 copying these items unaltered from an already-adapted immediate source — must have had access to at least a limited selection of Old English material and have chosen to use

---

[21] *Old English Homilies*, ed. by Morris, p. 298, lines 12–14.

this as part of his or her source library.[22] In her important study of Lambeth 487, Sisam addresses the question of the process of adaptation in the manuscript. She argues that such adaptation would need to be made in the form of revisions on the page, prepared in advance of the use of the manuscript for preaching: '[i]t would not be easy for a preacher, as he delivered his sermon, to adapt impromptu archaic or unfamiliar forms, syntax, or vocabulary. These he might alter in his copy, and the alterations would be incorporated by the next scribe who made a fair copy such as MS. Lambeth 487.'[23] Sisam discusses the difficulty of making corrections to a vellum copy of a text and surmises that because of this difficulty some archaic forms would be left by the updating corrector of a manuscript and others altered. Sisam's suggestion, however, does not easily account for the density of alterations to word order and vocabulary in some parts of the manuscript: in particular in item 10, as described above, and also item 11.[24] Many of these alterations are not at all vital to an attempt to render tenth-century homilies intelligible to a late twelfth- or early thirteenth-century audience, and thus are unlikely to have been made with the deliberation required of manuscript-to-manuscript copying or erasure and correction. This flexibility of adaptation, and in particular the alteration of word and phrase order within sentences and the expansion of single words into memorable couplets, is more likely to be an indicator of the use of memorialized reproduction in at least one stage of the textual transmission process.[25]

In her consideration of the process behind the introduction of dialect changes, Sisam does consider the possibility that a scribe might 'memorize phrases or sentences' from the source manuscript and 'write them down in the forms he was accustomed to'.[26] Using this hypothesis, we might imagine an updating scribe in the late twelfth or early thirteenth century reading a phrase from a pre-Conquest

---

[22] Even if we allow for the possibility of an intermediate, exact source for these items in Lambeth 487, this source is very likely to be post-Conquest, given the layer of lexical updating to the Old English ultimate sources.

[23] Sisam, 'Scribal Tradition', p. 112.

[24] Examples of this degree of alteration in item 11, whose source is Ælfric's First Series homily for Palm Sunday, include the substitution of 'etelice forgulte' ('grievously sinned') for the source's 'forwyrhte' ('forfeited'), and 'tuhte and spuhte' ('incited and beguiled') for 'tihte' ('incited'). See *Old English Homilies*, ed. by Morris, p. 123, lines 5–6, and *CH* I.14, line 169, p. 296.

[25] See Mary Swan, 'Memorialized Readings: Manuscript Evidence for Old English Homily Compilation', in *Anglo-Saxon Manuscripts and their Heritage*, ed. by Phillip Pulsiano and Elaine M. Treharne (Aldershot, 1998), pp. 205–17, for an analysis of possible indicators of reproduction of Old English prose from memory.

[26] Sisam, 'Scribal Tradition', p. 112.

Old English source manuscript, internalizing it, and then writing out the updated version as it was formulated in his or her head.[27] The possibility of a scribe working in this way has important implications for the study of recopying in general, and also of translation from Latin into Old English, since if we accept that it is a likely working practice, we cannot assume that minor changes within sentences are always the result of error, or of a copyist not working directly with a written exemplar. It is comparable with the techniques by which today's language students are trained to produce fluent written translations into English from another language: not to work word-by-word with the eye and risk producing stilted Modern English, but rather to translate phrase-by-phrase with the brain, to produce accurate but fluent copy and thus a smoother and more context-sensitive rewriting.

In apparent contrast to this fluency of translation and adaptation, the construction of Lambeth 487 is inconsistent. As well as the patchy filling-in of red Latin words and phrases, there are major inconsistencies of lineation and many striking errors and corrections made by the scribe. The whole manuscript is ruled up for writing, including the folios containing the later text at the end (fols 65^v–67^r). The appearance of the lineation on these last folios is the same as that elsewhere in the manuscript, which implies that the whole volume was ruled up before writing began. If this is the case, some aspects of the lineation seem very strange: in many openings a different number of lines is ruled on each page, and numbers of lines per page are not consistent across gatherings either. Only ruling the folios after their collation into the volume could produce this result. In some cases the lineation of the left-hand page of an opening continues further down into the bottom margin than that on the right-hand page. This discrepancy cannot be explained by an item or a section of an item ending at the end of the left-hand page and therefore being squashed in by the scribe; neither do such points coincide with the ends of gatherings. Sometimes where the number of lines ruled on each page of an opening differs the writing space is equal, but the lines are closer together on one page. A scenario which would account for all of these aspects of ruling is that the scribe had assembled the source manuscripts for all of items 1–17 and for some reason ruled the manuscript into which they were to be written page-by-page as each page was about to be written, but that the sequence of manuscript preparation

---

[27] For discussions of this sort of practice, see M. Benskin and M. Laing, 'Translations and Mischsprachen in Middle English Manuscripts', in *So meny people longages and tonges: Philological Essays in Scots and Mediaeval English Presented to Angus McIntosh*, ed. by M. Benskin and M. L. Samuels (Edinburgh, 1981), pp. 55–106 (p. 66), and Roy Michael Liuzza, 'Scribal Habits: The Evidence of the Old English Gospels', in *Rewriting Old English*, ed. by Swan and Treharne, pp. 143–65.

changed for the final stage — the folios which are ruled but not written on — because the scribe planned to copy out an additional text which was due to be made available but was not to hand at the point of ruling, and so he or she ruled up extra folios for this purpose.

Other oddities of compilation include the abrupt ending of item 7. This text ends imperfectly one quarter of the way along the fourth line of folio 27ᵛ. It is followed by one blank line and then the opening of item 8. If the imperfect ending to item 7 occurred at the end of a quire, it could be explained by the assumption that the following quire had been lost from the manuscript, but this is not the case. The most likely explanation for this feature of the manuscript is that the Lambeth scribe's exemplar for item 7 was missing the end of the text, but if so it is surprising that the Lambeth scribe was content to leave it unfinished, rather than supplying the end of the narrative from another manuscript or from memory.[28] One further feature which is not easy to explain is the occurrence in item 10 of a run-on phrase written against the final line in the right-hand margin of a folio half-way through the item. This folio is not at the end of a quire, so there is no obvious reason for the scribe to have written the run-on phrase at its foot.

In addition to the oddities of compilation described above, Lambeth 487's scribe made many copying errors, which have been commented on by Morris and Sisam amongst others.[29] In many places across the whole manuscript the scribe has written words or whole phrases wrongly. These errors of copying fall into two categories: firstly, dyslexia-like inversions and confusion of letters and sometimes words (for example 'þewas' for 'weges' in item 10, 'focl' for 'folc' and 'eclicnew' for 'elc icnew' in item 9, and 'swnan' for 'snow' in item 4[30]); and, secondly, apparent misreadings of minims and letter forms (for example 'denað' for 'deriað' in item 10 and 'denan' for 'derian' in item 11, 'imede' for 'iernede' and 'butas' for 'buton' in item 9; 'þe' for 'we' in items 9 and 10; 'ȝis' for 'ȝif' in item 10; 'hu' for 'nu' in item 10; 'siriat' for 'smat' three times in item 14; and 'hm' for 'hin' in item 18[31]).

---

[28] Cambridge, Trinity College, MS B. 14. 52 contains the full text of this item. See Morris, *Old English Homilies*, pp. 15–23.

[29] See the marginal notes to the edition in *Old English Homilies*, and also pp. 306–30; and Sisam, 'Scribal Tradition', pp. 110–13.

[30] *Old English Homilies*, ed. by Morris, p. 119, line 4; p. 87, line 15; p. 89, line 31; and p. 43, line 3, respectively.

[31] *Old English Homilies*, ed. by Morris, p. 101, line 2; p. 121, line 29; p. 93, line 33; p. 95, line 32; p. 97, line 11 and p. 105, line 28; p. 103, line 35; p. 107, line 16; p. 141, lines 5, 10, and 15; and p. 167, line 115, respectively.

These apparent misreadings of letter forms would imply miscopying from a written exemplar, but some of the confusions of words in Lambeth 487 seem more like mishearings: 'seoffimede mede' in item 9, which Morris suggests should read 'seolfne imedemede', and 'touþe' for 'to þe' in item 6.[32] A cluster of errors at the end of item 14 also implies that this section of the text was not fully understood by the scribe.[33]

On some occasions the scribe has corrected his or her own errors. Some of these corrections show confusion over the presence or absence of initial 'h' and also possible mishearing: 'halie' crossed out and replaced by 'alle' in item 7; 'ali' marked for replacement with 'halie' in item 9; and 'ic him' with the 'him' marked for replacement with 'em', in item 10.[34] Although the majority of the serious garblings occur in the Old English–related items, the lower-level errors are spread fairly evenly across the whole manuscript.

These plentiful and strange mistakes, and the inconsistencies in the manuscript makeup, demonstrate that Lambeth 487 is not the high-quality formal production of a prestigious scriptorium, or of a highly trained scribe. It could be argued that at this period the context of production of vernacular homiletic material, especially with such strong links to Anglo-Saxon traditions, is unlikely to be high status and well equipped. If Lambeth 487 was produced as part of the primary activity of a scriptorium in any major monastic house, the level of error it contains would surely at least have been corrected, and in all probability not tolerated in the first place. The majority of other post-Conquest Old English homiletic manuscripts are written in a script which is not formal in character,[35] and in her study of five post-Conquest Old English religious manuscripts, most of which are thought to have been made in important monastic scriptoria such as Rochester and Worcester,[36] Treharne describes these as 'non-elaborate in format [. . .] utilitarian volumes',[37]

---

[32] *Old English Homilies*, ed. by Morris, p. 97, line 35; and p. 61, line 3, respectively.

[33] *Old English Homilies*, ed. by Morris, p. 145.

[34] *Old English Homilies*, ed. by Morris, p. 73, line 21; p. 91, line 36; and p. 119, line 8, respectively.

[35] Treharne (private communication, 14 November 2005) identifies Cambridge, Corpus Christi College, MS 367, Parts I and II; Oxford, Bodleian Library, MS Hatton 115, fols 148–55; and Cambridge, Corpus Christi College, MS 303 as showing 'non-formal, non-high grade script'.

[36] Cambridge, Corpus Christi College, MS 302; London, British Library, Cotton MS Faustina A. IX; Oxford, Bodleian Library, MS Hatton 116; Cambridge, Corpus Christi College, MS 303; and London, British Library, Cotton MS Vespasian D. XIV. The information on places and dates noted here draws on Treharne, 'Production and Script'.

[37] Treharne, 'Production and Script', p. 39.

but the lack of deluxe features and the functional but not highly formal script style of these manuscripts should not detract from the relative accuracy of their copying of source texts. If Lambeth 487 was produced outside a major scriptorium, and in a less professional manner and context than these other examples, this might explain its inaccuracies; furthermore, if its scribe was also to be its preacher or its reader, then such slips might be more tolerable and could be rectified in performance were the homiletic items to be preached. The likelihood that a faulty text is a serious impediment to the performance of a homily is diminished, moreover, if we consider the possibility that a written preaching text is not bound to be read out word-by-word by a preacher as if it were a complete script, but rather provides a more or less precise cue, clause by clause or sentence by sentence, for what a preacher will say in any given preaching event.

London, British Library, Cotton MS Vespasian A. XXII

The second late Old English homiletic manuscript to be discussed has a construction which is dramatically more uneven than that of Lambeth 487, in that its Old English homiletic texts are short and probably incomplete, and in terms of quantity they form a small part of the codex. The majority of the contents of Cotton Vespasian A. XXII are Latin texts written down in the twelfth and thirteenth centuries, almost certainly at Rochester.

The Latin texts form what are now described as Parts 1, 2, and 4 of the manuscript; one quire of the manuscript, however, Part 3, contains four short texts in Old English. The latter appear in a single scribal hand which is usually dated to around the year 1200, but which Elaine Treharne would date a little earlier; to the last decade or so of the twelfth century.[38] Part 3 of the manuscript is neatly written, and its layout shows apparent unachieved plans to add coloured initials and titles, which suggests that this section of the manuscript was intended to be seen and valued. The format of Part 3 has one exceptionally striking feature: the relevant folios are ruled for, and the Old English items written in, two columns, unlike almost all of the rest of the manuscript. This two-column format for Old English homiletic prose is almost unique.[39] In terms of contents, two of the four Old

---

[38] I am grateful to Elaine Treharne for estimating this date.

[39] One other late Old English homiletic manuscript — Bodley 343, probably from the West Midlands — also has some two-column text, which is mostly for some of its Latin items, but includes some Old English text added to the end of a Latin leaf (for the pages containing two-

English texts in Cotton Vespasian A. XXII are versions of pieces from the First Series of Ælfric's *Catholic Homilies*, whilst the other two, which are short passages of the sort often excerpted from Old English homiletic prose, are not securely sourcable to any other pre- or post-Conquest English or Latin texts.

The Old English contents of Cotton Vespasian A. XXII have been discussed in print by Mary Richards and Jonathan Wilcox.[40] Robert McColl Millar and Alex Nicholls have published a detailed comparison of the first Old English item, a version of Ælfric's 'De initio creaturae', with other versions of that homily. The manuscript's Latin contents have been described by Richards, Wilcox, and others as part of the manuscript context of the Old English pieces, but to date the detail of the second, third, and fourth Old English pieces, and the rationale behind the composition of the whole manuscript, have not been scrutinized. What follows will move from some observations on the Old English items in the manuscript to the detail of its compilation and what that implies about when, and why, it was assembled.

The four Old English items that form Part 3 of Cotton Vespasian A. XXII also comprise the eighth quire of the manuscript and are just about at the centre of the codex. Old English item 1 is the version of Ælfric's 'De initio creaturae'. Item 2 is a version of the parable of the king who rewards his friends and punishes his enemies. The connections between this version and that given by Anselm in his 'De similitudine inter Deum et quemlibet regem suos Iudicantem' have been noticed,[41] but as Richards observes, this does not mean that item 2 has to be a direct translation from Anselm. If it is, this is the only translation of Anselm into Old English of which I am aware, though we do have evidence, in the form of a list of the contents of the library of Rochester Priory, for the presence of at least two Anselm manuscripts — sets of his letters and writings on the Psalms — at Rochester by

---

column Latin text, see *Old English Homilies from MS Bodley 343*, ed. by Susan Irvine, EETS: OS, 302 (Oxford, 1993), p. xx).

[40] Richards, 'Texts and their Traditions in the Medieval Library of Rochester Cathedral Priory', *Transactions of the American Philosophical Society*, 78 (1988); 'Innovations in Ælfrician Homiletic Manuscripts at Rochester', *Annuale Medievale*, 19 (1979), 13–26; and 'MS Cotton Vespasian A. XXII: The Vespasian Homilies', *Manuscripta*, 22 (1978), 97–103. Wilcox, *Wulfstan Texts*, pp. 46–52.

[41] The first published description of this similarity was John Wells, *A Manual of the Writings in Middle English* (New Haven, 1916), p. 285. Richards notes this in 'MS Cotton Vespasian A. XXII', p. 99.

1202.[42] Item 3 is a brief piece based on Ephesians 6. 11, a description of the weapons needed by a Christian warrior, which has no identified source. Item 4 is an even shorter piece which corresponds to the gospel text of Ælfric's First Series homily for the Fourth Sunday after Pentecost (*CH* I.24).

No other manuscript contains these same four pieces, so no possible exemplar for the whole of the Old English quire has been identified, Both of the Ælfric-derived pieces, however, have connections with the versions of those texts in other Rochester-related manuscripts of the *Catholic Homilies*, and in particular with the two-volume set Oxford, Bodleian Library, MSS Bodley 340 and 342, which was written in the early eleventh century, was almost certainly at Rochester by the early thirteenth century, and shows signs of use in the eleventh and twelfth centuries. Peter Clemoes notes in his edition of the First Series of the *Catholic Homilies* that, in his view, Vespasian Old English item 1 was copied from Bodley 342, and item 4 from Bodley 340.[43] The nature of the connections between these versions of the two *Catholic Homilies*, and the very limited length of item 4, make it impossible to be sure about a direct source–product relationship between the two manuscripts, but Vespasian items 1 and 4 indeed have some distinctively Rochester-like traits, as does item 2. Although item 2 has no complete identified source, Robert McColl Millar and Alex Nicholls make the very interesting connection of one passage from item 2 with the 'regular' version of Ælfric's 'De initio creaturae',[44] but not with item 1's version, which abbreviates the relevant passage. My analysis of this passage in item 2 leads me to agree with McColl Millar and Nicholls that item 2 does draw on the 'regular' text of 'De initio creaturae' and not that in item 1. The connections between the Ælfrician homily and the corresponding passage in item 2 are loose, and of a type best explained by the writer of item 2 using the 'regular' Ælfric homily from memory of a 'Rochester-type' copy, rather than from a written

[42] London, British Library, Cotton MS Nero A. VII, described in Helmut Gneuss, *Handlist of Anglo-Saxon Manuscripts: A List of Manuscripts and Manuscript Fragments Written or Owned in England up to 1100*, MRTS, 241 (Tempe, 2001), p. 65. See also W. B. Rye, 'Catalogue of the Library of the Priory of St. Andrew, Rochester, A.D. 1202', *Archaeologia Cantiana: Transactions of the Kent Archaeological Society*, 3 (1860), 47–64 (p. 56, item 84; and p. 58, item 139).

[43] *First Series*, ed. by Clemoes, p. 136.

[44] Robert McColl Millar and Alex Nicholls, 'Ælfric's *De initio creaturae*', in *The Preservation and Transmission of Anglo-Saxon Culture*, ed. by Paul E. Szarmach and Joel T. Rosenthal (Kalamazoo, 1997), pp. 431–61 (pp. 447–48, n. 8), which gives Morris, p. 233, lines 9–16 (the passage in Vespasian item 2) as compared with *CH* I.1, lines 8–11, p. 178, and *Old English Homilies*, ed. by Morris, p. 219, lines 1–3 (Vespasian item 1).

exemplar. Such a scenario of reuse of pre-Conquest preaching materials from memory implies that, at the time Cotton Vespasian A. XXII is being made, Old English preaching texts are either still being studied and memorized for future use, or are still being preached aloud — or both.

Some elements of one of the Vespasian Old English items also echo Lambeth 487. Item 16 of Lambeth 487 is entitled 'Estote Fortes in Bello'. This item shares two Latin quotations from the Ephesians chapter with Vespasian item 3, and its Old English list of weapons shares four items with the equivalent list in Vespasian item 3. These overlaps are shared by item 30 in Trinity B. 14. 52, which is close, but not identical, to Lambeth item 16,[45] and which also contains the two Latin quotations and four list items in question. This resemblance between an item in the Vespasian Homilies, which are not usually judged to have post-Conquest sources, and Trinity B. 14. 32, which is usually considered to have no pre-Conquest Old English sources, suggests that the relationship between these two homiletic connections, and their respective range of sources, needs to be reconsidered. The resemblances noted above are not sufficiently strong or extensive to posit a direct relationship between Vespasian and either Lambeth or Trinity, but they might perhaps suggest a lost shared indirect Old English and Latin source-text for both Vespasian item 3 and Lambeth item 16 / Trinity item 30 circulating quite widely in the late twelfth century.

One further, slight, connection exists between Cotton Vespasian A. XXII and Lambeth 487, in the form of the alteration in both manuscripts of an Ælfrician reference to the Jews to 'hethen' ('the heathen').[46] This correspondence is perhaps indicative either of wider late twelfth-century Old English usage for which we have no other evidence or, once again, of indirect sources shared by, or some other form of acquaintance between, Lambeth 487 and Cotton Vespasian A. XXII. Such an acquaintance would require particular textual transmission connections between the West Midlands and Rochester at this date, and this possibility is further discussed below.

One feature which unifies all four of the Cotton Vespasian A. XXII Old English pieces is their incompleteness. Item 1 occupies four and three-quarter pages

---

[45] The two texts are compared by O'Brien, 'Edition of Seven Homilies', pp. 255–68. The significant differences between them imply that, although the two texts are certainly closely related (O'Brien suggests that they might both derive from an English translation of a text originally written in Latin), the one manuscript was not the direct exemplar for the other.

[46] Vespasian item 4, *Old English Homilies*, ed. by Morris, p. 245, line 1, as compared with Ælfric's First Series homily for the Fourth Sunday after Pentecost (*CH* I.24, line 5, p. 371).

of the manuscript. It differs substantially from the 'regular' Ælfric version of 'De initio creaturae' in that it has a unique, added opening section and also misses out the last few lines of the 'regular' version, instead giving a simple clause wrapping up the partial Ælfric sentence at which it stops reproducing the Ælfric text. It is clear that the scribe's intention was to write more of this item, since the end of the last folio on which it is written was left blank, and this blank space would be just about the right size to take the remainder of the 'regular' version of 'De initio creaturae'. Item 2 occupies just under three and a half pages in the manuscript and, like item 1, is incomplete as it stands: it ends abruptly, and just over half of its final page was left blank by the Old English scribe, as if more text was to be added. Similarly, item 3, which occupies only about three-fifths of a manuscript page, is clearly unfinished as it stands. It ends abruptly, with a Latin quotation which is not translated into Old English, and the rest of the page was left blank by the Old English scribe, as was the following page. Item 4 occupies just a quarter of a page, and the following two folios of the Old English quire were left blank by the Old English scribe.

The incompleteness of the Old English items in Cotton Vespasian A. XXII is striking, and suggests that their scribe had only intermittent access to source manuscripts. Relatively little concerted work has been done on the availability of pre-Conquest Old English texts in the centres which we believe to be producing copies and adaptations of them at this date, but it is clear that the range of Old English texts available to a late twelfth-century compiler, and the ease or difficulty of gaining sustained access to them, will have had a fundamental effect on the extent and nature of their reuse. An alternative explanation for the incomplete state of the Old English items in Cotton Vespasian A. XXII might be that the scribe intended to modify each piece so that it was not the same as its exemplar, left space to add his or her own endings, but never got around to doing so. As has been noted, we can show that at least one manuscript of Ælfric's *Catholic Homilies* was very likely in Rochester Priory library in the early thirteenth century, but that does not tell us precisely how accessible it or any other potential Old English source-manuscripts were to a scribe at this date. The Rochester textual connections of the Vespasian Old English items match the strong indications that its Latin texts in parts 1, 2, and 4 were written in and for Rochester.

The place of the Old English quire — Part 3 — in the manuscript is difficult to assess, not least because we have no certain knowledge of exactly when any of the four parts was bound in with the others. Wilcox summarizes his deductions from internal evidence about the sequence of assemblage of the whole codex: a thir-teenth-century table of contents 'refers [...] to the contents of Part 1 and Part 4', and a much later hand — possibly in about 1360 — adds to the table of contents a reference to Part 2.[47] Wilcox implies that Part 3 must have been added at some time after about 1360, and before the addition of an early modern table of contents which includes all four parts of the manuscript.

My examination of the format of the Old English items relative to other parts of the manuscript leads me to think that the Old English quire might have been part of the manuscript by a date right at the beginning of, or possibly earlier than, Wilcox's implied range, as will now be argued. Wilcox has noted that the Old English quire in Cotton Vespasian A. XXII — Part 3 — is surrounded by a bifolium which forms folios 51 and 59* of the manuscript.[48] The first folio of this bifolium also serves the function of finishing off the last item of Part 2, an account of the disputes between Henry and Thomas à Beckett. Wilcox notes that the Latin script on this folio, folio 51, is larger than that in the preceding pages; I judge it to be in a different, but contemporary, hand. The final leaf of the bifolium is blank, like the leaf before it from the end of the Old English quire. Apart from the Old English quire, the only other pages of the whole manuscript to be ruled for two columns are a single opening, which is also a bifolium, much later in the manuscript: folios 126ᵛ and 127ʳ. This opening comes just after the end of an item in Part 4, and it and the couple of folios which follow it and complete the manuscript are written on in a hand of around 1360,[49] and they contain material in Latin relating to Rochester. At least one, and possibly two, hands of about the same date as that on 126ᵛ and 127ʳ (and maybe including that same hand) have also annotated some of the formerly blank Old English folios in the manuscript, also with Rochester notes. Some of these later Latin notes on the Old English folios observe the two-column ruling, and others do not.

This overview of the layout and collation of Cotton Vespasian A. XXII allows us to identify precisely which elements of the manuscript construction pose problems, or apparent inconsistencies, and thus to draw out their implications. Three aspects of the inconsistencies can be identified: first, the lineation of the Old English quire is often irregular from page to page; second, it is also often irregular across bifolia, which might imply that the quire was ruled after it was assembled; third, the lineation is also irregular across individual openings, so on the face of it, ruling once assembled is not very likely, unless the person doing the ruling went

---

[47] Wilcox, *Wulfstan Texts*, p. 48.

[48] There are two page 59s in the modern foliation: one is identified as simply 59 and the second as 59*.

[49] I am grateful to Elaine Treharne for estimating this date, and for very helpful conversations about Lambeth 487 and Cotton Vespasian A. XXII.

page by page. Ruling the quire in this way is unnecessarily complicated, but it is the only scenario which accounts for all of the irregularities. This hypothesis may be challenged, however, by folios 126^v and 127^r, which appear to have roughly equal ruling; this is hard to discern with confidence, partly because the ruling lines are now faint, and partly because the Latin notes are not as neatly set out as the Old English texts, so they sometimes mislead the eye when looking for ruling lines.

The drawing of the two columns and their lines, in terms of implement used and character of the lines drawn, is very similar across all of the Old English quire and folios 126^v and 127^r, and so it is reasonable to assume that that these folios were all prepared by the same person at the same time, and for the same purpose, and that 126 and 127 were not designed to sit so far apart from what is now the Old English quire, separated from it by many folia ruled for a single column. The bifolium 126 and 127 could, of course, have begun its assembled life as the outer bifolium of what is now the Vespasian Old English quire before getting removed from the rest of that quire. In that case, the double-column format would extend across the whole quire of ten, except for its first and last page.

For what purpose all of these two-column folia might have been prepared is another vexing question. As mentioned above, two-column layout is almost never used for Old English homiletic prose, so preparing folia in this way must surely normally mean that they are intended to take Latin text. If that was the case, then the Old English Vespasian texts were perhaps written on a spare quire which had been found to be superfluous to its intended, Latin purpose.

One deduction which can be made from these features is that the Old English quire and the final quire of Part 4 must have been available in a single place, presumably at the same time, and that they were perhaps bound up at the same time too; either into a single manuscript — Cotton Vespasian A. XXII — or into two separate booklets. Then, later, in around 1360, both the Old English quire and the 126/127 bifolium were written on by the Latin note-writer or -writers; it is highly likely that by this time they were already part of the same codex. We know that the 51/59* bifolium was added to Part 2 at the same time as, or very soon after, the text of Part 2 was written; that is, in around 1214. This sequence leaves, then, two possibilities for the incorporation of the Old English quire into Cotton Vespasian A. XXII: either it was put into its current position in 1214, along with the 51/59* bifolium; or it was originally put into the final quire of the manuscript, along with and between folios 126^v and 127^r and was later moved forward into the centre of the manuscript.

It is possible that the Old English texts were written out very close in time to the Latin in Part 2. Our understanding of Old English script style and fashion, and how it relates to Latin and Anglo-Norman scripts, in the eleventh and twelfth centuries, is still very incomplete,[50] but if most Old English copying this late is carried out as a supplementary, possibly marginal, scriptorium activity, then it might be the case that English script styles were changing more slowly, and were less driven by dictates of fashion, than were Latin and French styles. If this were so, then a scribe who wrote both Latin and Old English might use a hand for the former which looks to us to be later than the hand used for the latter, when in fact the scribe's Latin hand is simply more up-to-date than his or her English one.

Another way to argue the possibility for discrepant scribal hands across Old English and Latin is to imagine that scribes copying Old English this late are more likely to be old than young, since in that case they might have been taught by scribes who had direct acquaintance with pre-Conquest Old English. McColl Millar and Nicholls suggest that 'some aspects of script, lexis and language' of Vespasian Old English item 1 might indicate that 'the copyist was an old man with experience of Old English towards the end of its currency'.[51] Whether this hypothesis can be sustained on the evidence so far assembled is not clear, and until it is, it is wiser to be cautious about a scenario which might shore up the stereotype of late post-Conquest Old English as the antiquarian hobby of a few superannuated and culturally isolated scribes.

The major question remaining, then, is why the Old English quire was included in Cotton Vespasian A. XXII. The easiest answer to offer is, of course, that it simply got bound up in the manuscript, initially at the end of the manuscript, because it included blank spaces and pages which could be used by the fourteenth-century Latin annotator. A much more speculative answer, by contrast, might take note of the large number of items in the rest of the manuscript which relate not just to Rochester, but more precisely to pre-Conquest Rochester, including a list of the Archbishops of Canterbury and Bishops of Rochester from the birth of Christ onwards, a list of the kings of Kent, and two lists of donations to the priory which separate pre-Conquest gifts from post-Conquest ones, and thus demonstrate an acute awareness of the Conquest as a significant dividing line for Rochester. If Cotton Vespasian A. XXII as we have it was assembled by the mid- to late fourteenth century, its range of contents might be united by a concern with Rochester matters and Rochester Englishness, and the four Old English texts might provide

---

[50] The data gathered and analysed by the 'English Manuscripts 1060 to 1220' project will allow this question to be addressed in detail.

[51] McColl Millar and Nicholls, 'Ælfric's *De initio creaturae*', p. 446.

an anchor to pre-Conquest language and Englishness a very long way into post-Conquest England.

Conclusions: Functions

The confident and creative recasting of a pre-Conquest Old English devotional text seen in Lambeth 487 makes it clear that the necessary conditions for such vernacular homiletic production were all in place in at least one part of the country in the late twelfth or early thirteenth century. Those conditions include intellectual resources such as training in reading and writing Old English, physical resources such as materials and space for writing, access to Old English source-manuscripts, impetus for production, and plans for the use of the resulting new Old English texts. Lambeth 487 is certainly evidence of Old English homilies being remade into texts usable for reading, and quite possibly for preaching too, in this late period.

The question of the reading or preaching of the Old English homiletic texts in Cotton Vespasian A. XXII has been pondered by Mary Richards, who suggests that these texts are for the teaching of the 'unlettered clergy' by parish priests around Rochester, and notes 'clear evidence that two of the Vespasian homilies were intended for oral delivery in the first-person asides interpolated into the texts'.[52] The examples Richards refers to here are in Old English item 1 ('me scel sigge, an oðre stowe',[53] 'I will say in another place') and item 2 ('Ac we sede ʒehw',[54] 'But we said to you'). McColl Millar and Nicholl also comment on the first of these interpolations, noting that nothing in the Old English Vespasian pieces could constitute the later reference this remark signals.[55] Nor is there in the Old English Vespasian pieces any passage which would be the earlier reference implied by the second interpolation. The first of these interpolations is not in any other version of the Ælfrician source-homily, and the second is in an item which has no known source. They both offer relatively strong indications that the Old English quire in Cotton Vespasian A. XXII as it stands is not complete, and they both also imply that item 1 as written was intended primarily for a reading audience who could be expected to have encountered the earlier reference, and to come to the later one, as they read

---

[52] Richards, 'MS Cotton Vespasian A. XXII', pp. 98, 103, and 99 (quote).

[53] *Old English Homilies*, ed. by Morris, p. 219, line 14.

[54] *Old English Homilies*, ed. by Morris, p. 237, line 32.

[55] McColl Millar and Nicholls, 'Ælfric's *De initio creaturae*', p. 432.

through the now-missing Old English texts which must have included them. Such a scenario would mean that the Old English pieces in Cotton Vespasian A. XXII were not primarily intended to be preached as they stood, but of course it does not rule out the possibility that they were written down in Cotton Vespasian A. XXII as a collection of useful materials which the writer thought he or she might later quarry to make English preaching texts. Against this, one might of course argue the possibility that this remark is meant to be remembered by a regular preaching audience who could be expected to be present at a sequence of preaching events — which would imply that the quire was meant for use in preaching to a monastic, not a parish, audience. In short, the evidence offers a multiplicity of possible interpretations: the pieces were intended for direct oral delivery, as raw material for subsequent sermon production, for use in a secular setting, or for ministry to a monastic audience — or for some combination of the above.

The possibility of connections between Rochester and the West Midlands in the post-Conquest period, particularly with regard to the considerable Old English copying activity going on in both areas, merits further attention. Other codicological evidence, including reassembling of manuscripts by joining of existing and newly written sections from different areas of England to form new codices, the splitting and rebinding of volumes, and the correction and glossing of earlier texts, suggests that from the late eleventh to early thirteenth century in particular parts of England, pre-Conquest homiletic manuscripts were being exported and imported and remade.[56] Such a network of exchange and adaptation of pre-Conquest Old English homilies stretching to almost two hundred years after their composition shows clearly that Old English homilies occupied a significant place in the reading and preaching of Anglo-Norman England.

---

[56] See Swan, 'Mobile Libraries'.

ANGLO-SAXON HOMILIES
IN THEIR SCANDINAVIAN CONTEXT

Christopher Abram

The influence of Anglo-Saxon homiletics transcends both the temporal and spatial boundaries of Anglo-Saxon England. Other essays in this volume (and elsewhere) have discussed the continuing production and use of Old English homilies in post-Conquest England; less widely studied has been the transmission, dissemination, and influence of Anglo-Saxon homilies abroad. In medieval Norway and Iceland, the influence of Anglo-Saxon homiletics was of importance in the creation of a corpus of vernacular preaching and devotional material suitable to the needs of a fledgling church. This influence manifested itself in three main ways: (1) the physical transit of homiletic manuscripts from England to Scandinavia; (2) the use of sources of an English provenance, either in Latin or the vernacular, in translated Old Norse-Icelandic homilies; and (3) the adoption of motifs, rhetorical techniques, and prose stylistics drawn directly from the Old English tradition in original Old Norse compositions.

In comparison with the Anglo-Saxon corpus, the number of surviving Old Norse-Icelandic homilies is small.[1] Some thirty-three manuscripts (many mere fragments) exist, containing approximately 150 texts of homilies (or parts of homilies) in Old Norse, mostly originating in Iceland.[2] These manuscripts range

---

[1] In this article, I use 'Old Norse-Icelandic' to refer to the literary corpus as a whole, and 'Norwegian' or 'Icelandic' where the geographical provenance of a text or manuscript is germane to the discussion.

[2] Thomas N. Hall, 'Old Norse-Icelandic Sermons', in *The Sermon*, ed. by Beverly Mayne Kienzle, Typologie des sources du moyen âge occidental, 81–83 (Turnhout, 2000), pp. 661–709, lists and describes the extant manuscripts of Old Norse homilies (pp. 691–704).

in date from the middle of the twelfth to the middle of the sixteenth century.[3] Two main manuscript compilations of Old Norse-Icelandic homilies survive: the 'Icelandic Homily Book' (Stockholm, Kunglinga Biblioteket, Cod. Holm. Perg. 15 quarto (s. xiii[in], Iceland, provenance unknown): henceforth cited as IHB) and the 'Norwegian Homily Book' (Copenhagen, Arnamagnæanske Institut, 619 quarto (s. xiii[in], Norway, provenance probably Bergen): henceforth cited as NHB). These collections attest both to the early phases of Christian literary production in their respective countries and to a common Norwego-Icelandic textual tradition: the two codices contain closely related texts of eleven homilies that indicate the existence of a common exemplar.[4] Both manuscripts date from the beginning of the thirteenth century, although they are believed to contain versions of texts composed up to a century earlier.

Remarkably few homilies in Latin have survived from medieval Scandinavia, although this imbalance in favour of the vernacular probably reflects the agendas of post-medieval manuscript collectors rather than the reality of medieval manuscript production. In the modern era, too, Old Norse-Icelandic homilies have mainly endured critical neglect incommensurate with their crucial importance as witnesses to the earliest phases of literacy and Christian instruction in Scandinavia. Whereas homilies in both Old English and Latin are recognized as central to the study of Anglo-Saxon literary and religious culture, specialists in Old Norse-Icelandic — spoilt for choice, perhaps, so far as vernacular prose literature is concerned — have tended to marginalize utilitarian Christian texts. As such, a good deal of potentially useful work remains to be done on Old Norse-Icelandic homilies: a number of texts remain unedited; the influence of homiletic writings on other genres has yet to be traced; and, while the sources of many Old Norse-Icelandic homilies have already been identified, the circumstances by which these sources came to be disseminated in Scandinavia often remain obscure.

---

[3] The oldest Icelandic manuscript in existence is Copenhagen, Arnamagnæanske Institut, 237a folio (s. xii[med], Iceland, provenance unknown), two leaves previously used as binding strips that contain fragmentary vernacular versions of a church dedication homily and Gregory's *Homilia in Euangelia* XXXIV.

[4] For a description of these manuscripts, see Hall, 'Old Norse-Icelandic Sermons', pp. 692–97. Citations are taken from the following editions: IHB from *The Icelandic Homily Book. Perg. 15 40 in the Royal Library, Stockholm*, ed. by Andrea de Leeuw wan Weenan, Íslensk handrit: Icelandic Manuscripts, Series in Quarto, 3 (Reykjavik, 1993), and NHB from *Gamal Norsk Homiliebok. Cod. AM 619 4°*, ed. by Gustav Indrebø (Oslo, 1931). The texts common to both collections are identified and discussed by Indrebø in his edition of NHB, pp. 42–57.

England was undoubtedly one of the most important conduits through which Christianity and its appurtenances reached Scandinavia; English missionaries were involved in the conversion effort from the beginning, and English influence is apparent in many aspects of early Scandinavian ecclesiastical culture, most particularly in Norway.[5] The transmission of the texts most needful for a fledgling church to possess, homilies not least among them, was an important part of this process.

Anglo-Saxon Homiletic Manuscripts Exported to Scandinavia

Numerous fragments of liturgical manuscripts of established English provenance survive in libraries in Norway and Sweden. Medieval book-lists suggest that English liturgical materials also made their way to Iceland.[6] The only extant Anglo-Saxon homiletic manuscripts to have survived in a Scandinavian milieu, however, are found in Denmark. A collection of fragments of Ælfric's First Series of *Catholic Homilies* has been found in Copenhagen, discovered as binding strips for a post-medieval codex (Copenhagen, Rigsarkivet, Aftagne Pergamentfragmenter 63–64, 669–71, and 674–98 (s. xi[in], England, provenance unknown)).[7] No satisfactory provenance for these fragments has been established, and there is as yet no evidence as to when they (or the manuscript from which they were extracted) reached

---

[5] See Absalom Taranger, *Den Angelsaksiske Kirkes Inflydelse paa den Norske* (Kristiania, 1890); Lesley Abrams, 'The Anglo-Saxons and the Christianization of Scandinavia', *ASE*, 24 (1995), 213–49, and 'Eleventh-Century Missions and the Early Stages of Ecclesiastical Organisation in Scandinavia', *Anglo-Norman Studies*, 17 (1994), 21–40; F. Berkeli, 'The Earliest Missionary Activities from England to Norway', *Nottingham Medieval Studies*, 15 (1971), 27–37; and Stefan Hallberg, 'Tysk eller Engelsk Mission? Om de tidiga Kristna låneorden', *Maal og Minne* (1986), 42–49.

[6] Hall, 'Old Norse-Icelandic Sermons', pp. 673–74, n. 20, and Tryggvi J. Oleson, 'Book Collections of Mediaeval Icelandic Churches', *Speculum*, 32 (1957), 502–10.

[7] Helmut Gneuss, *Handlist of Anglo-Saxon Manuscripts: A List of Manuscripts and Manuscript Fragments Written or Owned in England up to 1100*, MRTS, 241 (Tempe, 2001), no. 816.6. Fragments from the same manuscript are also found in the library of The Arnamagnaean Institute, Copenhagen (no shelf-mark: Gneuss, *Handlist*, no. 811.5) and in The Hague (Koninklijke Bibliotheek, MS 133. D. 21: Gneuss, *Handlist*, no. 830). The Copenhagen fragments have been edited by Else Fausbøll, *Fifty-Six Ælfric Fragments: The Newly-Found Copenhagen Fragments of Ælfric's 'Catholic Homilies' with Facsimiles*, Publications of the Department of English, University of Copenhagen, 14 (Copenhagen, 1986). See also Fausbøll, 'More Ælfric Fragments', *ES*, 76 (1995), 302–06, and *Ælfric's Catholic Homilies: The First Series, Text*, ed. by Peter Clemoes, EETS: SS, 17 (Oxford, 1997), pp. 58–59.

Scandinavia: there is no reason to assume that transmission occurred before the dismemberment of the manuscript, presumably at the hands of a Renaissance antiquarian.[8]

Our sole extant witness to the export of manuscripts of Anglo-Saxon homilies to Scandinavia in the Middle Ages, therefore, is the 'Copenhagen Wulfstan Collection' (Copenhagen, Kongelige Bibliotek, Gl. Kgl. Sam. MS 1595 (s. xi[in], Worcester, provenance possibly Roskilde)), a version of Archbishop Wulfstan's Handbook, annotated in the author's own hand, produced at Worcester between 1002 and 1023.[9] It contains texts of seventeen Latin *sermones* believed to be the work of Wulfstan, alongside eight by Abbo of Saint-Germain-des-Prés. The Copenhagen Wulfstan Collection has been in Denmark, so far as we can tell, for almost its entire history; indeed, Johann Gerritsen has argued that the compilation of the manuscript was expedited in order that it be presented to Gerbrand, the Englishman who was to be consecrated as bishop of the Danish see at Roskilde, in (or soon before) 1022. Gerbrand would have taken the book with him to Roskilde as part of his episcopal library.[10]

The Copenhagen Wulfstan Collection did not influence the course of Old Norse-Icelandic homiletics. Danish texts are not usually admitted to the Old Norse-Icelandic corpus, since Denmark diverged linguistically and culturally from Norway and Iceland at an early stage; it is unlikely that Old Norse-Icelandic homilies were ever composed in a Danish milieu. If Gerritsen's conjecture about the manuscript's origins and its journey to Roskilde is correct, however, the Copenhagen Wulfstan Collection provides us with the earliest indication that there was a Scandinavian context for Anglo-Saxon homilies as early as the first quarter of the eleventh century. Homiletic texts, in Latin but bearing a distinctively Anglo-Saxon stamp (in the case of the Wulfstan texts), were among the written materials perceived as being useful to a bishop taking over a recently established Danish see. With the production of this manuscript expressly for export, the Anglo-Saxon ecclesiastical establishment is seen, at its highest level, to concern itself with the textual needs of a Scandinavian church: as well it might during the reign of the

---

[8] Fausbøll, *Fifty-Six Ælfric Fragments*, pp. 108 and 113–14.

[9] Gneuss, *Handlist*, no. 814. The manuscript has been reproduced in facsimile: *The Copenhagen Wulfstan Collection: Copenhagen Kongelige Bibliotek Gl. kgl. sam 1595*, ed. by James E. Cross and Jennifer Morrish Tunberg, EEMF, 25 (Copenhagen, 1993).

[10] Johann Gerritsen, 'The Copenhagen Wulfstan Manuscript: A Codicological Study', *ES*, 79 (1998), 501–11 (pp. 509–11).

Danish King of England, Cnut. That the manuscript was produced at Worcester is unsurprising, considering Wulfstan's connection with that centre.

Latin Texts of an Anglo-Saxon Provenance as Sources of Old Norse-Icelandic Homilies

The extant corpus of Old Norse-Icelandic homilies comprises a mixture of original and translated texts. Norwegian and Icelandic homilists clearly possessed a range of standard Latin sources: a book-list of 1318 from Vellir in Svarfaðadalur, for example, reveals that the church there — the benefice of the schoolmaster at Hólar, the leading centre of ecclesiastical education in medieval Iceland — owned, alongside three books of homilies in Icelandic, a copy of *Homiliae Gregorii* and of *Homiliae Augustini*.[11] Gregory appears to have been a particular favourite of Scandinavian authors: a complete translation of the *Homiliae xl in Euangelia* into Icelandic was made in the early twelfth century, and although the original manuscript is lost, there are numerous texts in existence (both Icelandic and Norwegian) that derive from it.[12] Owing to the low rate of survival for Latin manuscripts from medieval Norway and Iceland, it is difficult to assess in what form, and by what means, the works of the standard homiletic authors were disseminated in these countries. It seems likely, for example, that a version of Paul the Deacon's homiliary was in circulation in Norway in the twelfth century, but no Scandinavian manuscript of that popular and widely disseminated work has itself survived.[13] The corpus as it stands provides us with ample evidence of what Thomas Hall calls the 'fertile reception history' of Old Norse-Icelandic homilies, as they were copied, recopied, and transmitted between Norway and Iceland.[14] It is much more difficult to discern the circumstances in which they were originally composed or to identify

[11] Oleson, 'Book Collections', p. 509. On the library and school at Hólar, see Guðbrandur Jónsson, *Dómkirkjan á Hólum í Hjaltadal: lýsing íslenzkra miðaldakirkna*, Safn til sögu Íslands og íslenzkra bókmennta, 5 (Reykjavik, 1919–29).

[12] Hall, 'Old Norse-Icelandic Sermons', pp. 674–76; see also Kirsten Wolf, 'Gregory's Influence on Old Norse-Icelandic Religious Literature', in *Rome and the North: The Early Reception of Gregory the Great in Germanic Europe*, ed. by Rolf H. Bremmer, Jr, Kees Dekker, and David F. Johnson, Medievalia Groningana, 4 (Paris, 2001), pp. 255–74.

[13] Ian J. Kirby, 'Christian Prose, 2: West Norse', in *Medieval Scandinavia: An Encyclopedia*, ed. by Phillip Pulsiano (New York, 1993), p. 79.

[14] Hall, 'Old Norse-Icelandic Sermons', p. 674.

how, when, or where their sources became available to Norwegian and Icelandic authors. In the few instances where it has proved possible to observe more precisely the route of transmission of these sources, however, it has become apparent that Old Norse-Icelandic homilists not infrequently used English books as their main exemplars.

One such book may be Cambridge, Pembroke College, MS 25 (s. xi[ex], England, provenance Bury St Edmunds), a manuscript which contains a copy of the Homiliary of Saint-Père de Chartres.[15] Written in the second half of the eleventh century, probably at Bury St Edmunds, this manuscript, though relatively late, stands at the end of a textual tradition that stretches back for at least a century, and probably rather more: the terminus ad quem for the compilation of the first Anglo-Saxon version of this homiliary must be placed before the compilation of the Vercelli Book, since texts from the Pembroke-type homiliary were among the sources used in the composition of the Vercelli Homilies. Four texts from the Vercelli Book (Homilies III, XIX, XX, and XXI) and five other Old English homilies (Tristram III, Assmann XI and XII, and Belfour V and VI) have all been shown to be based, at least partially, upon Latin sources drawn from the Pembroke-type homiliary.[16]

The influence of this collection upon vernacular homiletics was not restricted to Anglo-Saxon England. A homily rubricated *In capite ieiunii* for Ash Wednesday in IHB was identified by Joan Turville-Petre as a compilation of extracts from a selection of Latin texts including the pseudo-Augustinian *Sermo* 254, Theodulf of Orléans's *Capitula*, the *Collectio canonum Hibernensis*, Alcuin's *De uirtutibus et uitiis*, and Isidore's *De ecclesiasticis officiis*; she noted that Vercelli III is a near-identical rendering of the same passages into Old English and posited the existence of a common Latin source available to both the Anglo-Saxon and Icelandic translators.[17] Subsequently, Helen Spencer discovered that this Latin homily was still extant (Turville-Petre had assumed it to be lost), and that its earliest copy was to be found in Pembroke 25, where it bears the rubric *Omelia in Dominica ii in Quadragesima*.[18] It is not possible to say for certain that the Icelandic homily was

---

[15] Gneuss, *Handlist*, no. 131.

[16] James E. Cross, *Cambridge Pembroke College MS. 25: A Carolingian Sermonary Used by Anglo-Saxon Preachers*, King's College London Medieval Studies, 1 (London, 1987).

[17] Joan Turville-Petre, 'Translations of a Lost Penitential Homily', *Traditio*, 19 (1963), 51–78. The text in IHB is found at fols 29[v], line 8 – 31[r], line 11.

[18] Helen Spencer, 'Vernacular and Latin Versions of a Sermon for Lent: "A Lost Penitential Homily" Found', *Mediaeval Studies*, 44 (1982), 271–305; Cross, *Cambridge Pembroke College MS. 25*, p. 27.

translated directly from the Pembroke 25 text, merely that Pembroke 25 represents the extant version of the Saint-Père homiliary closest to that used by the Scandinavian translator. That said, the available witnesses to the Saint-Père homiliary have strong English connections.[19] It seems reasonable therefore to assume that, as Hall puts it, 'The Old Icelandic Homily Book was composed with the aid of an English homiliary designed as a resource for vernacular preaching, and both the substance and the liturgical setting of the Icelandic Rogationtide sermon can be traced to tenth-century English practice'.[20]

The type of source found useful by the authors of the Vercelli Homilies in the tenth century was still being transmitted in vernacular versions in the second half of the twelfth century, when Oxford, Bodleian Library, MS Bodley 343 (s. xii[1], English West Midlands, provenance probably Worcester) — a 'conservative and backward-looking' (to use Spencer's phrase) compilation of pre-Conquest homilies — was put together: this codex contains Belfour V and VI, which are both derived from the same Pembroke-type homily as Vercelli III and the IHB homily for Ash Wednesday.[21] The textual tradition of the Pembroke-type *Omelia in Dominica ii in Quadragesima* was still alive and active in England in the period when the Icelandic translation came to be made.

A second text found in Pembroke 25 has identifiable, though less well-defined, connections with Old Norse-Icelandic homiletics. A homily for All Saints, found in variant versions in NHB and IHB (and also partially in a third manuscript, a single leaf from Iceland that survives as Copenhagen, Arnamagnæanske Institut, 655 XIII quarto (s. xiii[ex], Iceland, provenance unknown)), has as its main source the pseudo-Bedan sermon 'Legimus in ecclesiasticis historiis', now attributed to Ambrosius Autpertus.[22] This text is usually found in augmented versions of the

---

[19] Spencer, 'Vernacular and Latin Versions', pp. 278–79. The sole remaining continental copy of the Saint-Père homiliary, whence the compilation takes its name, is Chartres, Bibliothèque municipale, MS 25 (s. x/xi, France). Dating from the tenth or eleventh century, Chartres 25 is the oldest surviving witness to the homiliary's textual tradition. It was badly damaged by fire in 1944, and its relationship to the Pembroke-type homiliary has never been established.

[20] Hall, 'Old Norse-Icelandic Sermons', p. 673.

[21] Spencer, 'Latin and Vernacular Versions', p. 271. For a detailed description of Bodley 343, see *Old English Homilies from MS Bodley 343*, ed. by Susan Irvine, EETS: OS, 302 (Oxford, 1993), pp. xviii–xlviii.

[22] IHB, fols 18[v]1–22[r]6; NHB, pp. 143–47. For the Latin source, see James E. Cross, '"Legimus in ecclesiasticis historiis" – A Sermon for All Saints and its Use in Old English Prose', *Traditio*, 33 (1977), 103–55.

homiliary of Paul the Deacon, a work that, as previously mentioned, was probably known in medieval Norway and Iceland. It was popular in Anglo-Saxon England: Gneuss lists sixteen separate extant manuscripts of the homiliary as having been written or owned in England before 1100.[23] Even so, if the passages extracted from 'Legimus in ecclesiasticis historiis' by the translator of the Old Norse-Icelandic homily were simply taken from Paul the Deacon, there would be no reason in particular to assume that it was an English version of the homiliary to which he turned. In addition, however, there is a version of this text in Pembroke 25, and it seems likely that the Old Norse-Icelandic homily may have been translated from a version related to this manuscript rather than from a copy of Paul's homiliary.

The Old Norse-Icelandic homily for All Saints is far from being a simple translation of 'Legimus in ecclesiasticis historiis': passages of this sermon, often rather abridged, are incorporated into the first section of a more or less original composition that may also draw upon Honorius Augustodunensis's *Sermo de omnibus sanctis* (although the correspondences with the latter text are generally thematic rather than textually precise).[24] In two instances there are readings in the Old Norse-Icelandic text that appear to agree with the Pembroke 25 version of the homily in opposition to the readings of the main Paul the Deacon tradition. There are no important differences between the Norwegian and Icelandic renderings of these citations of the Latin, although the Icelandic text as a whole contains a significant amount of material (for which no source has been identified) that NHB lacks.

'Legimus in ecclesiasticis historiis' begins with a quotation from Bede's *Historia ecclesiastica* that reads, in the version preserved in the homiliary of Paul the Deacon,

> Legimus in ecclesiasticis historiis quod Sanctus Bonifatius, qui quartus a beato Gregorio Romane urbis episcopatum tenebat, suis precibus a Foca cesare impetraret donar[i] ecclesie Christi templum Romae ab antiquis Panteon ante uocabatur quia hoc quasi simulacrum omnium uideretur esse deorum. In quo, eliminata omni spurcitia, fecit ecclesiam sanctae dei genetricis atque omnium martyrum Christi ut, exclusa multitudine demonum, multitudo ibi sanctorum in memoria habetur.[25]

> [We read in ecclesiastical histories that St Boniface, who was the fourth Bishop of Rome from the blessed Gregory, by his request succeeded in gaining from the Emperor Foca for Christ's church a Roman temple, which from antiquity had been called 'Pantheon'

---

[23] Gneuss, *Handlist*, p. 175. See also now Joyce Hill's 'Ælfric's Manuscript of Paul the Deacon's Homiliary: A Preliminary Analysis', in this volume.

[24] See Oddmund Hjelde, *Norsk preken i det 12. århunde. Studier i Gammel Norsk Homiliebok* (Oslo, 1990), pp. 367–75.

[25] Cross, '"Legimus in ecclesiasticis historiis"', lines 1–5.

because it was regarded as a representation of all the gods. Having removed such rubbish, he founded in it a church dedicated to the holy mother of God and all martyrs of Christ, so that, a multitude of demons having been cast out, a multitude of saints might be remembered there.]

In NHB, the translation of this passage runs thus:

> Sva er sagt á bócum at hæilagr Bonefatius pafe er hinn fiorðe var fra Gregorio let kirkiu vigia í Ruma-borg guði til dyrðar ok ollum hælgum mǫnnum hans. er aðr hafðe veret allra diofla blot-staðr. því at þat syndisc maclect at þar heldesc mining allra hæilagra. er áðr var braut reken saurgan allra diofla.[26]

> [Thus it says in books that holy Boniface, who was the fourth pope from Gregory, had a church in Rome dedicated to the glory of God and all his saints, which formerly had been a sacrifice-place of all devils, because it seemed fitting that the remembrance of the saints should be kept there, when first the defilement of all devils was driven away.]

The Old Norse-Icelandic translation has been somewhat abbreviated. *Ecclesiasticis historiis* has been replaced with the less specific *bocum*; the Roman emperor is not named; nor is the Pantheon. In the Latin the explanation of the temple as *simulacrum omnium deorum* ('a representation of all the gods') requires the reader to understand the meaning of 'Pantheon'; perhaps the author of the Old Norse-Icelandic version did not possess this knowledge, or else thought that his audience would not. His interpretation that this temple *hafðe veret allra diofla blot-staðr* is not a direct translation of the Latin text. I would argue that *blot-staðr* (literally 'place of sacrifice', the word *blót* being a standard part of the Norse terminology for heathen worship) must represent *templum*: if *allra diofla blot-staðr* is meant to represent *simulacrum omnium deorum*, then it must be counted as a misunderstanding of the exemplar, and it leaves *templum* untranslated. It is possible that *allra diofla* could stand for *omnium deorum*, making the commonplace equation between the old gods and devils, but *blot-staðr* and *simulacrum* belong to entirely different semantic fields.[27] There is, however, an alternative explanation for the Old Norse-Icelandic text's reading, if we prefer not to impugn the translator's Latinity. In the version of 'Legimus in ecclesiasticis historiis' preserved in Pembroke 25, there is an extra word not found elsewhere in the textual tradition of Paul the Deacon: *idolorum* ('of idols') has been inserted between *templum* and *Romae*. *Blot-staðr diofla* is a highly satisfactory rendering of *templum idolorum* into

---

[26] NHB, p. 143, lines 26–31. The IHB version differs from NHB only in replacing *kirkiu* ('church') with *hús* ('house').

[27] As pointed out by Hjelde, *Norsk preken*, p. 368.

Old Norse. This reading in the Scandinavian homily thus places it in a textual tradition with very strong English connections.

The second apparent point of contact between the Pembroke 25 version of this homily and the Old Norse-Icelandic translations occurs in a stylized list of the torments endured by Christian martyrs.

His subiectum est triumphale martyrum nomen qui per diuersa tormentorum genera Christi passionem non lassescentibus precordium mentibus imitabantur: alii ferro perempti, alii flammis exusti, alii flagris uerberati, alii uectibus perforati, alii cruciati patibulo, alii pelagi periculo, alii uiui decoriati, alii uinculis mancipati, alii linguis priuati, alii lapidibus obruti, alii frigore adflicti, alii fame cruciati, alii uero truncatis manibus siue ceteris caesi[s] membris spectaculum contumeliê in populis nudi propter nomen domini portantes.[28]

[The triumphant name of martyr has been given to those who, with unwearied mind, in body imitated the passion of Christ through various modes of torment: some slain by the sword, others burned in flames, others flogged with whips, others pierced by arrows, others fixed to a cross, others by the peril of the sea, others flayed alive, others hung in chains, others deprived of their tongues, others afflicted by cold, others tortured by hunger, others, with hands or other members cut off, [shown] naked as a spectacle for the contempt of the populace, for bearing the name of the Lord.]

The Old Norse-Icelandic translation of this passage has a different introduction, and its version of the list shows a characteristic tendency to abbreviate:

Þessa hotið æignasc oc pinslar-vattar guðs þæir er fyr-lito þessa heims lif ok boðorð hæiðinna konunga. Sumir vǫru sverði hognir. en sumir í eldi brendir. sumir í vatne cafðer. en sumir stongum barðir. sumir hængdir. en sumir í hvéle brotner. sumir sveltir. en af sumum qvicum skin flegit.[29]

[This festival is also concerned with those martyrs who forsook the life of this world and the bidding of heathen kings. Some were cut down by the sword, and some burned in fire; some submerged in water, and some beaten with staves; some hanged, and some broken on a wheel; some starved, and the skin was flayed alive from some.]

---

[28] Cross, "'Legimus in ecclesiasticis historiis'", lines 124–30.

[29] NHB, p. 145, lines 10–13. The introductory phrase *þæir er fyr-lito þessa heims lif ok boðorð hæiðinna konunga* picks up an idea that the Latin has after the list of torments: 'Hi sunt triumphatores et amici dei qui, contemnentes sceleratorum iussa principum modo coronantur et accipiunt palmas laborum, quia fundati sunt supra firmam petram, id est, Christum' (lines 130–32; 'They are conquerors and friends of God, who, scorning the commands of sinful rulers soon are crowned and receive the palms of their labours, seeing that they are founded upon the firm rock, which is Christ').

In this instance, the translation is linked to Pembroke 25 by the reading *sumir í vatne cafðer* ('some [were] submerged in water'), when the Paul the Deacon text lacks a verb in the phrase *alii pelagi periculo* ('some by danger at sea'). Pembroke 25, once again in opposition to the rest of the tradition, provides a verb for this clause and reads *pelagi periculo demersi* ('some [were] submerged in danger at sea').[30] Even if the translation is not exact, the Old Norse-Icelandic homily once again preserves a reading found also in Pembroke 25 that is absent from any extant text of Paul's homiliary. It is not the only text to do so: as Cross notes, a version containing a phrase including the verb *demersi* seems to underlie the reading found in Ælfric's homily *Natale omnium Sanctorum* from the First Series of *Catholic Homilies*: *sume on widdre sæ besencte* ('some [were] submerged in the wide sea').[31] Ælfric's homily is closely based upon 'Legimus in ecclesiasticis historiis', and Cross believes that a text related to that of Pembroke 25 (although not Pembroke 25 itself, which post-dates Ælfric) may have been the version that he used.[32]

In both of the foregoing examples, one point becomes particularly apparent: the Old Norse-Icelandic homilies are based, wholly or partially, upon Latin texts that circulated widely in Anglo-Saxon England, that continued to be used in English centres after the Conquest, and that were also used by the authors of Old English homilies.[33] Another example of this trend is perhaps found in a homily for Advent in IHB, which combines two homilies by Caesarius of Arles in a manner very similar to the Old English Assmann XI.[34] It is not possible as yet to determine precisely how and in what form these Latin sources of an English provenance reached Scandinavia, but Pembroke 25 should probably serve as a starting point for further study in this direction: its homily for *Dominica ii in Quadragesima* provides the best and earliest text of the source upon which the Icelandic sermon for Ash

---

[30] One other manuscript examined by Cross includes a verb in its version of the list of martyrs' torments: the 'Newberry Library Homiliary' (Chicago, Newberry Library, MS 1, s. x^{cx}, France, prov. unknown), reads *periculo pelagi iactati* ('placed in danger at sea').

[31] *CH* I.36, line 76 (p. 488).

[32] Cross, '"Legimus in ecclesiasticis historiis"', p. 129.

[33] 'Legimus in ecclesiasticis historiis' was also a source for another of Ælfric's homilies, *In Dominica Palmarum* (*CH* I.14), again from the First Series of *Catholic Homilies*, and for the *Passio S. Mauricii et sociorum eius* from Ælfric's *Lives of Saints* (*LS* II.28), Blickling XIV, and the *Old English Martyrology*. See Cross, '"Legimus in ecclesiasticis historiis"', pp. 129–34.

[34] See Hans Bekker-Nielsen, 'En nørron adventspraediken', *Maal og Minne* (1959), 48–52; Joan Turville-Petre, 'Sources of the Vernacular Homily in England, Norway and Iceland', *Arkiv för nordisk filologi*, 75 (1960), 168–82 (pp. 179–80, n. 1).

Wednesday was based, and the homily for All Saints found in NHB and IHB has significant variant readings in common with the Pembroke text of 'Legimus in ecclesiasticis historiis'.

Ælfric in Old Norse-Icelandic Translation

The source identifications outlined above were first suggested to scholars by the correspondences between certain Old Norse-Icelandic homilies and their Old English counterparts, which were sufficiently close as to suggest a common Latin source. In a few cases, however, it can be demonstrated that Old Norse-Icelandic texts are derived directly from the Anglo-Saxon *vernacular* tradition. Most conspicuously, texts based upon two homilies by Ælfric are preserved in the important Icelandic miscellany *Hauksbók* (Copenhagen, Arnamagnænske Institut, 544 quarto, (*c.* 1290–1334, Iceland)).[35] The first piece, entitled *Um þat hvaðan otru hofst* in *Hauksbók*, is based upon Ælfric's *De falsis diis* (*SH* II.21); the second, untitled but beginning 'Hinn helgi byskup [. . .]', is an imprecation against witchcraft that is partly based upon his Old English homily *De auguriis* (*LS* I.17), a text that was usually transmitted alongside the *Lives of Saints*.[36] There was initially some doubt about the proximate source of the Old Norse-Icelandic homily *Um þat hvaðan otru hofst*: its relationship to Ælfric's *De falsis diis* was indubitable, but it was suggested that the similarities between the two texts were best explained by positing the existence of a common Latin exemplar.[37] Work by John Pope and Arnold Taylor subsequently established, however, that the Icelandic homily is a translation out of Old English, although the translator apparently used a copy of Ælfric's text slightly different to those found in extant manuscripts.[38] While *Um þat hvaðan otru hofst* paraphrases *De falsis diis* at points, at other times the parallels are so close that the Icelandic author must have had a text of the Anglo-Saxon

---

[35] *Hauksbók udgiven efter de Arnamagnænske håndskrifter no. 371, 544 og 675, 40 samt forskellige papirshåndskrifter af det kongelige nordiske Oldskrift-selskab*, ed. by Eiríkur Jónsson and Finnur Jónsson (Copenhagen, 1892–96), pp. 156–64 and 167–69.

[36] *LS* I.17 (*Ælfric's Lives of Saints*, ed. by Walter Skeat, EETS: OS, 76, 82, 94, 114 (London, 1881–85; repr. in 2 vols, 1966), I, 364–83). See I. Reichborn-Kjennerud, 'Et kapitel av *Hauksbók*', *Maal og Minne* (1934), 144–48.

[37] Turville-Petre, 'Sources of the Vernacular Homily', p. 175, n. 2.

[38] *Homilies of Ælfric: A Supplementary Collection*, ed. by John C. Pope, EETS: OS, 259–60 (London, 1967–68), II, 676–712; Arnold Taylor, '*Hauksbók* and Ælfric's *De Falsis Diis*', *Leeds Studies in English*, 3 (1969), 101–09.

exemplar in front of him. The *Hauksbók* homilies are better termed adaptations of Ælfric's sermons than translations, perhaps, but nevertheless they provide us with clear evidence of the transmission of Old English homilies into Scandinavia and their use by authors of Old Norse-Icelandic texts. As with the Copenhagen Wulfstan Collection, moreover, certain evidence (albeit circumstantial) links the *Hauksbók* homilies to Worcester. The text of *De falsis diis* closest to the Icelandic translation is found in Cambridge, Corpus Christi College, MS 178 (s. xi^in, Worcester).[39] This codex is also one of only five to contain a text of Ælfric's *De auguriis* alongside *De falsis diis*, leading Taylor to conjecture that the two Old English homilies were transmitted together, and in a manuscript similar to CCCC 178.[40]

Composite Old Norse-Icelandic Homilies Based upon Old English Texts

Ælfric's influence on the Old Norse-Icelandic corpus was not restricted to the two texts that were translated in their entirety. In NHB, there is an admonitory sermon dealing with basic Christian behaviour (and particularly behaviour in church) entitled *Sermo ad populum*, which is apparently a reworking of material drawn mainly from two Old English texts: the *Prayer of Moses* from Ælfric's *Lives of Saints* (*LS* I.13), and the pseudo-Wulfstanian Napier XXIX. Joan Turville-Petre examined the Norwegian *Sermo ad populum* in the light of the Old English material and concluded, once more, that 'the Latin sources used by Ælfric's predecessors, and by Ælfric himself for some of his later works were available in some form to Icelandic and Norwegian scholars writing about a century later'.[41] The ideas found in the *Sermo ad populum* she traced back to a complex of authorities including Caesarius of Arles, Alcuin, and the Hiberno-Latin tract *De duodecim abusiuis saeculi*. These authors doubtless are the ultimate sources for various sections of the Norwegian homily, but, as I have recently argued elsewhere, there is good reason to suppose that the *Sermo ad populum* was composed by a homilist familiar with their ideas as filtered through Old English texts.[42]

NHB's *Sermo ad populum* appears to be a 'cut and paste' homily; the author does not restrict himself to any one source, but rather excerpts passages relating to

---

[39] Gneuss, *Handlist*, no. 54.

[40] Taylor, '*Hauksbók* and Ælfric's *De Falsis Diis*', p. 108.

[41] Turville-Petre, 'Sources of the Vernacular Homily', p. 182.

[42] Christopher Abram, 'Anglo-Saxon Influence in the Old Norwegian Homily Book', *Mediaeval Scandinavia*, 14 (2004), 1–35 (pp. 9–22). See also Hjelde, *Norsk preken*, pp. 113–29.

his theme from a number of texts. It is possible that in some instances his composition is based upon recall rather than a direct consultation of the source text; what
is certain, in my view, however, is that in composing this sermon he turned to Old
English homilies rather than to their Latin sources, both as general inspiration and
as specific models for particular sections of his address. His indebtedness to the
vernacular tradition is signalled by a combination of thematic correspondences,
verbal echoes, and style. The use of repetitive word-pairs, especially alliteration, is
a feature characteristic of Wulfstanian (and pseudo-Wulfstanian) prose, and is
found also in those passages of NHB's *Sermo ad populum* that run parallel to the
pseudo-Wulfstanian composition, Napier XXIX.[43] Compare, for example, the
following passages from the introductions of the two texts:

> Goðer brøðer ok systr lyðið til hvat hinar hælgu bøc segia ok bioða os at ver lifim retlega
> lif vno. ok með mykilli þolenmøðe. ok þionum sua drotne varum. ok gefum goða gaoum
> at þvi er ver hetum guði þa er ver tocum við cristni [. . .] Nu vilium ver yðr þes biðia ok
> bioða af guðs hende at þer haldeð væl cristindom yðan. ok vereð lyðnir til guðs boðorðe.
> fyrir þvi at mæira þorf eigum vér til þes en ver kunnim ætla.[44]

> [Good brothers and sisters, listen to what the holy books say and bid us, that we should
> live our life correctly, and with great patience. And thus let us serve our Lord, and let us
> give good heed to him whom we call God since we accepted Christianity [. . .] Now we
> wish to bid and entreat you, on God's behalf, that you hold your Christianity well, and
> be obedient to God's commandments, because we have more need of this than we can
> estimate.]

> Men ða leofestan, gehyrað, hwæt us halige bec beodað, þæt we for godes lufan and for his
> ege ure lif rihtlice libban and mid eaðmedum urum drihtne hyron and urne cristendom
> and ure fulluht wel healdon [. . .] We halsiað eow and beodað, þæt ge god lufian and him
> eallunga gehyrsume beon, forðam us ys neod, þæt we eow rihtlice tæcon, and eow ys
> oferþearf, þæt ge hit rihtlice healdon.[45]

> [Beloved men, listen to what the holy books bid us, that we live our life correctly for love
> and fear of God and obey our Lord with humility, and hold to our Christianity and our
> baptism well [. . .] We beseech you and bid that you love God and are entirely obedient

---

[43] Inna Koskenniemi, *Repetitive Word Pairs in Old and Early Middle English Prose: Expressions of the Type 'Whole and Sound' and 'Answered and Said'*, Annales Universitatis Turkensis,
Series B, 107 (Turku, 1968), pp. 47–51. On Wulfstan's use of the word-pair, see also Andy Orchard, 'Crying Wolf: Oral Style and the *Sermones Lupi*', *ASE*, 21 (1992), 239–64 (pp. 248–49).

[44] NHB, p. 35, lines 18–21, and p. 36, lines 2–4.

[45] *Wulfstan: Sammlung der ihm zugeschriebenen Homilien nebst Untersuchungen über ihre
Echtheit*, vol. I, *Text und Varianten*, ed. by Arthur Napier (Berlin, 1883), p. 134, lines 11–14, and
p. 135, lines 5–8.

to him, because it is needful for us that we teach you correctly, and <u>for you it is most needful</u>, that you keep it correctly.]

The correspondences between these two passages are not exact, and it seems unlikely that the Norwegian homily has been translated off the page from a manuscript containing Napier XXIX. But phrases like those underlined in the passages above all represent phraseology of a type that is extremely characteristic of certain rhetorical formulas used frequently by some Anglo-Saxon homilists, Wulfstan and his imitators foremost among them.

Thematically, NHB and Napier XXIX remain close to each other as they generalize about the types of sin that their audiences should avoid and the particular dangers of pride, although NHB contains a list of capital sins that more closely resembles a version, presumably derivative of Caesarius of Arles, that Ælfric includes in his Second Series homily *In dedicatione ecclesiae* (*CH* II.40).[46] When, however, Napier XXIX moves on to its main theme — the importance of confession, a topic in which the Norwegian homilist is not interested — NHB immediately departs from it, turning instead to a section from Ælfric's *Prayer of Moses* as it expounds upon the importance of prayer and correct behaviour in church. Although the NHB text displays yet again a tendency to abbreviate, it has enough significant details in common with the *Prayer of Moses* to suggest direct influence, as is demonstrated by its section on prayer:

> Ok æicci þyccir fiandanom iam-illt sem þat er hann hœyrir menn biðia sér miscunnar til guðs. fyrir þui at sva mælte guð sialfr. Ðat er þer biðid til min. þa mæle þer við mik sialfan. En þa er þer heyrið lesnar bœcr minar. þa heyri þer orð min sialfs. <u>Hværr maðr á at biðia fyrir ser sem hann cann ok hann hefir numet. fyrir þvi at vár droten can allar tungur.</u> ok hvarge sem maðr er stadr þa er ret at hann biði ser goz.[47]

> [And nothing seems so ill to the devil as that when he hears men pray to God for mercy. For, as God himself has said: 'It is when you pray to me, then you speak with me myself. And when you hear my books read, then you hear my own words.' <u>Every man has to pray for himself as he is able and as he has learnt, because our Lord knows all languages.</u> And wherever one is located it is appropriate that one should pray to God.]

---

[46] NHB, p. 35, lines 24–32; *CH* II.40, lines 279–82 (*Ælfric's Catholic Homilies: The Second Series, Text*, ed. by Malcolm Godden, EETS: SS, 5 (London, 1979), p. 344). See Abram, 'Anglo-Saxon Influence', pp. 12–13. The sources of *In dedicatione ecclesiae* have been identified as part of the *Fontes Anglo-Saxonici* Project: M. Godden, 'The Sources of Ælfric, *Catholic Homilies* II.40 (Cameron B.1.2.49)', in *Fontes Anglo-Saxonici: A Register of Written Sources Used by Anglo-Saxon Authors [CD-ROM Version 1.1]*, ed. by Fontes Anglo-Saxonici Project (Oxford, 2002).

[47] NHB, p. 36, lines 8–14:

Nis nan þincg swa lað þam geleafleasum deofle swa þæt hine man gebidde bealdlice to Gode [...] þonne we us gebiddað mid bylewitum mode, þonne sprece we soðlice to Gode sylfum swa, and þonne we bec rædað oððe rædan gehyrað, þonne sprecð God to us þurh þa gastlican rædincge. Se man mot hine gebiddan swa swa he mæg and cann, forðan þe se ælmihtiga God cann ælc gereord tocnawan, and on ælcere stowe man mot mærsian his drihten, and hine gebiddan beo þærþær he beo.[48]

[There is no thing so hateful to the faithless devil as that a man should pray earnestly to God [...] when we pray with a mild heart, truly we speak to God himself, and when we read the books, or hear them read, then God speaks to us through the spiritual reading. The man must pray to him just as he is able and knows, because almighty God can understand all languages, and in every place must a man praise his Lord, and pray to him wherever he may be.]

The phrase about praying as best as one is able, because God knows all languages (underlined in the above passages) is particularly suggestive of direct influence rather than of a shared source, since these two phrases express in such similar terms an idea — that God knows all languages — that has not been identified as existing anywhere else in homiletic literature.[49] Shared details like this one, when taken together with the general thematic congruencies and stylistic commonalities, relate the Norwegian *Sermo ad populum*, conclusively in my view, to the Anglo-Saxon tradition of vernacular homiletics. Again, this Norse author may also have gained exposure to Old English preaching texts and techniques at Worcester. Napier XXIX exists in but one copy: Oxford, Bodleian Library, MS Hatton 113 (s. xi[med], Worcester), an Anglo-Saxon manuscript whose Worcester provenance is undoubted. The other main analogue to the *Sermo ad populum*, Ælfric's *Prayer of Moses*, is preserved in the same manuscript.

Stylistic and Rhetorical Influence of Anglo-Saxon Homiletics upon Original Old Norse-Icelandic Compositions

As well as being used as proximate sources for Old Norse-Icelandic homilies, the English tradition of vernacular preaching could also transmit motifs that could be adopted and adapted by Scandinavian authors for use in their original compositions. At the level of motif study, it is often difficult to separate the Old English versions from their ultimate Latin sources, unless the presentation of the motif

---

[48] *LS* I.13, lines 50–51 and 60–67 (pp. 286 and 288).

[49] Mattias Tveitane, 'Vár drotten kann allar tungur', *Maal og Minne* (1964), 106–12; Abram, 'Anglo-Saxon Influence', pp. 15–16.

takes on a distinctive form in its vernacular contexts. An example of this process can be seen in a Norwegian homily for Christmas Day: this text, which is a rather unusual mélange of apocryphal motifs, is parallelled, particularly in its stereotyped descriptions of heaven and hell, by a number of anonymous Old English homilies. It is certainly not a direct translation of any one Anglo-Saxon text, but the motifs with which the Norwegian author embellishes his descriptions of the joys of heaven and the pains of hell are drawn from a distinctively Insular tradition: rhetorical techniques such as 'negative specification', 'numerical *gradatio*', word-pairs, and inversion are combined with variants on the well-known 'seven joys' topos in similar ways by the author of the NHB text and in several Old English descriptions of heaven and hell.[50] An example of the degree of similarity between the two traditions may be given by comparing the description of heaven found in NHB with that of Napier XXIX.

> Þar er æigi hungr ne þorste. ne ælli. ne myrcr. ne óp ne ræimr ne væinan. ne gratr. ne sorg. ne sarlæicr. Þar er lios fyri utan myrcr. ok líf fyrir utan dauða. œska fyrir utan ælli. Hæilsa fyrir utan sótt.[51]

> [There is neither hunger nor thirst, nor old age, nor darkness; neither weeping nor wailing, nor crying; neither sorrow nor pain. There is light without darkness, and life without death; youth without ageing, health without illness.]

> Ðær is ece leoht buton þystrum; nis þær adles granung, ac þær is geogoð buton ylde; þær is ece lif butan ateorunge and ece gefea butan ælcum ende. ne bið þær unrotnes æfter gefean, ac þær ðurhwunað aa seo ece bliss; ne bið þær hungor ne þurst ne ænig gewinn, ac þær byð seo ece rest, and haligra symbelnys þær þurhwunað a butan ende.[52]

> [There is eternal light without darkness; there is no groaning of disease, but there is youth without old age; there is eternal life without weariness and eternal joy without any end. There is no sorrow after the joy, but eternal bliss always remains there; there is neither hunger nor thirst nor any strife, but there is the eternal rest, and holy festivity goes on for ever without end.]

The correspondences between these two passages are not sufficiently close to speak of Napier XXIX as a source for the Norwegian homily; rather, when taken together with the other stylistic, rhetorical, and thematic similarities between

---

[50] Abram, 'Anglo-Saxon Influence', pp. 22–28; Hildegard L. C. Tristram, 'Stock Descriptions of Heaven and Hell in Old English Prose and Poetry', *NM*, 79 (1978), 102–13, and Thomas D. Hill, 'The Seven Joys of Heaven in "Christ III" and Old English Homiletic Texts', *NQ*, 214 (1969), 165–66.

[51] NHB, p. 32, lines 11–14.

[52] *Wulfstan: Sammlung*, ed. by Napier, p. 142, line 26 – p. 143, line 1.

NHB's Christmas homily and Old English texts, they suggest that the author was familiar with certain trends in Old English homiletics and was composing his text in imitation of them. Further confirmation of the Norwegian author's compositional debt to anonymous Old English homilies is provided by his use of the famous 'men with the tongues of iron' motif, in which the pains of hell are implied by their inexpressibility in human speech. This topos was extremely widespread, owing to its origin in Virgil and inclusion in the popular apocryphon the *Visio Pauli*; it was not, however, static and developed in distinctive ways in different textual traditions.[53] In NHB the topos is expressed thus:

> Oc þo at hværr maðr hæfði hundrað hofða. ok í hværiu hofði være .c. tunga or iarne. ok þær allar mælte fra uphafe hæi þessa. alt til veraldar enda. þa mætte þær æigi sægia allt þat hit illa er í helviti er.[54]

> [And though each man had a hundred heads and in each head there were a hundred tongues of iron, and they all spoke from the beginning of this world up until the end of the world, they would not be able to say all the evil that is in hell.]

As I have shown in a previous article, this reformulation of the motif is almost unique in its combination of details: that there are a hundred heads, each containing a hundred iron tongues, and that they all speak from the beginning to the end of the world. There is, however, an Old English sermon that in its presentation of the 'men with the tongues of iron' motif agrees with NHB in every respect: *Be Heofonwarum and be Helwarum*, a text found in two post-Conquest manuscripts, London, British Library, Cotton MS Faustina A. IX (s. xii[in], south-east England, provenance unknown) and Cambridge, Corpus Christi College, MS 302 (s. xi/xii, south-east England, provenance unknown).[55]

---

[53] Ernst Robert Curtius, *European Literature and the Latin Middle Ages*, trans. by W. R. Trask (London, 1979), pp. 159–62, and Pierre Courcelle, 'Histoire du cliché virgilien des cent bouches', *Révue des études Latines*, 33 (1955), 231–40.

[54] NHB, p. 34, lines 2–6.

[55] Abram, 'Anglo-Saxon Influence', pp. 28–33. The provenance of CCCC 302 and Cotton Faustina A. IX has not satisfactorily been established, although both manuscripts originated in south-east England, and possibly at St Paul's, London. See Elaine M. Treharne, 'The Production and Script of Manuscripts Containing English Religious Texts in the First Half of the Twelfth Century', in *Rewriting Old English in the Twelfth Century*, ed. by Mary Swan and Elaine M. Treharne, CSASE, 30 (Cambridge, 2000), pp. 11–40 (p. 20).

Þeah ænig man hæfde .c. heafda and þæra heafda æghwilc hæfde .c. tungan and hi wæron ealle isene and ealle spræcon fram frymðe þyssere worulde oð ende ne mihton hi asecgan þæt yfel þe on helle is.[56]

[Though any man had a hundred heads and each of those heads had a hundred tongues, and they were all iron; and though they all spoke from the beginning of this world until the end, they would not be able to say the evil that is in hell.]

The Norwegian homily and the Old English *Be Heofonwarum and be Helwarum* together make up a unique subcategory of this widespread and influential motif. Even though this type of material might well have beeen transmitted mnemonically rather than mechanically by copying, it seems quite unlikely that the two versions of this motif would develop collaterally identical variations upon the Latin tradition. When combined with the other similarities between the Norwegian Christmas homily and Old English texts, we are left with the impression that the Norse author may not have had any single identifiable source text, but that his composition was profoundly influenced by English vernacular preaching.

Possible Routes of Dissemination

Having established that a small group of Old Norse-Icelandic homilies were based upon, or influenced by, Anglo-Saxon exemplars, either in Latin or Old English, it remains to ask the following questions: when, where, and how did Scandinavian homilists gain access to their sources, or become exposed to Anglo-Saxon homiletics more generally? I believe that it is possible to identify two English centres as being most likely to have provided material used by Norwegian or Icelandic authors, on the basis of two principle criteria: first, that they possessed manuscripts containing homilies that we know to have been translated into Old Norse; second, that at the time that the Old Norse-Icelandic homilies were being composed (over the course of the twelfth century), texts of the type identified above as having been used by Old Norse-Icelandic authors remained in use and in production.

On the basis of the evidence assembled in this article, two obvious possibilities for monastic foundations involved with the dissemination of Anglo-Saxon material into Scandinavia offer themselves. Bury St Edmunds, the home of the Pembroke 25 homiliary, is certainly one, although it must be remembered that other copies

---

[56] '*Be Heofonwarum 7 be Helwarum*: A Complete Edition', ed. by Loredana Teresi, in *Early Medieval English Texts and Interpretations: Studies Presented to Donald G. Scragg*, ed. by Elaine Treharne and Susan Rosser, MRTS, 252 (Tempe, 2003), pp. 211–44 (p. 229).

of this collection must also have existed and that its influence is apparent in Old English homilies written at other centres. But Bury had close ties with the Norwegian Church throughout the twelfth and thirteenth centuries: the Archbishop of Nidaros, Eystein, the most prominent Scandinavian churchman of his day, lived in the abbot's house at Bury for several months during his stay in England between 1180 and 1183.[57] It is tempting to associate this attested intercourse between Bury and the Church in Norway with the transmission of manuscripts across the North Sea.

Second, there is Worcester. There is no clear evidence to suggest that twelfth-century Worcester was regularly visited by Scandinavian clergy, yet Worcester may well have had a crucial role in shaping the course of Old Norse-Icelandic homiletics. The extant manuscripts indicate that the Old English homilies used by Scandinavian authors would have been available to them at Worcester; more importantly, perhaps, Worcester represents the most conspicuous example of the persistence of Old English preaching and the continuing production of homiletic manuscripts containing texts from the Anglo-Saxon vernacular tradition, into the twelfth century (and even beyond). Worcester began the transmission of Anglo-Saxon homilies into Scandinavia with the production of the Copenhagen Wulfstan Collection for export to Denmark; the possibility that this centre continued to play an important role in the transmission of Anglo-Saxon literary culture into Norway and Iceland in the post-Conquest period is one that will, I feel sure, repay much more detailed investigation.

[57] See Henry Goddard Leach, *Angevin Britain and Scandinavia*, Harvard Studies in Comparative Literature, 6 (Cambridge, MA, 1921), pp. 90–96, and Abram, 'Anglo-Saxon Influence', pp. 6–7.

Anglo-Saxon Homiliaries
in Tudor and Stuart England

Aaron J Kleist

If the history of the Anglo-Saxon homiliary in the centuries surrounding the Conquest is complex, scarcely less so is the tale of its dispersal following the monastic dissolution of 1535–40. In the face of negligent custodians and anti-clerical despoilers, manuscripts were exported wholesale, bought up by private collectors, or used in scouring candlesticks or yet more ignoble purposes. Recent studies have highlighted the zealous work of figures such as Matthew Parker to preserve and consolidate these texts, as well as the labours of those like John Joscelyn who inaugurated the modern study of Old English. In fact, however, the forty-two collections of sermons designated as homiliaries by N. R. Ker's *Catalogue of Manuscripts Containing Anglo-Saxon* — collections found in a total of some thirty-five manuscripts — passed through a remarkable panoply of hands during this period. In the two centuries of Tudor and Stuart reign, over three dozen figures may arguably or demonstrably be associated with these texts. Their range is considerable: politicians and courtiers, diplomats and administrators, scholars and schoolmasters, nobles and knights, theologians, alchemists, archbishops, jurists, heralds, historians, librarians, and antiquaries — whether native to English soil or visitors from the Continent, all held volumes of Old English homilies in their hands.

Imposing categories on such diversity of material and persons is by nature problematic. A number of challenges are posed by Ker's designation of certain texts as 'homiliaries'; some of these are dealt with in the Appendix to this volume. Further concerns involve the extent to which such homiliaries may be shown to have been used. Only rarely, such as with annotations in Parker's hand, does evidence allow us to establish whether individuals actually read the homilies in their possession. A signature on a frontispiece may indicate little other than the fact of ownership; what aspects of the manuscript were of interest or what motivations may have prompted its acquisition may ultimately remain obscure. While not a few prominent early Anglo-Saxonists do not appear among the lists below, moreover — Robert Recorde (*c.* 1510–58), William L'Isle (*c.* 1569–1637), and William Somner (bap. 1598, d. 1669), to name a few — it is certainly conceivable that they might have consulted these manuscripts without leaving visible marks. The boundaries of the era in question, finally, are less than straightforward. The figures below are grouped by reference to the Tudor and Stuart periods, attempting to distinguish between the first wave of interest in Anglo-Saxon manuscripts and its ongoing development in the seventeenth century; all too often, however, there is overlap between the Elizabethan and Jacobean ages. Even referring to the Tudors and Stuarts, of course, belies the discontinuity of their history — particularly in the latter case, where execution, restoration, and revolution separate James I from Anne, last of the Stuart line.

However impossible such concerns, however, they need not unduly encumber the present undertaking. The following simply seeks to provide a starting point and reference for future scholarship in the area. Entries are cross-referenced throughout to homiliaries in the Appendix. A maximum of five honours per person are listed as representative. Ongoing degrees such as knighthood or appointments where the final date is uncertain are indicated by the use of 'from', as in 'Keeper of the Records in the Tower of London from 1563'; otherwise, boundaries of terms served are indicated where known. In certain cases, individuals tangentially related to the homiliaries are described, such as Thomas Hearne [S10B]; other entries seek to clarify difficult genealogical relationships, as with Christopher Hatton [T6B], whose immediate family includes at least three others of the same name. Where figures' dates overlap the Elizabethan and Jacobean periods, cross-references indicate in which category they are treated. Finally, selective bibliographies are provided with each entry to aid those going on to more detailed studies.

The Tudors: 1509–1603

Alphabetical Order		Chronological Order		
[T1]	Beale, Robert (1541–1601)	(1470/71–1530)	[T18]	Wolsey, Thomas
[T2]	Bodley, Sir Thomas (1545–1613)	(1504–75)	[T10]	Parker, Matthew
[T3]	Bowyer, William (d. 1569/70)	(1505/06–58)	[T16]	Talbot, Robert
[T4]	Cope, Sir Walter (1553?–1614)	(1520–76)	[T12]	Pilkington, James
[T5]	Cradock[e], Edward (fl. 1552–94)	(1526/27–85)	[T14]	Russell, Sir Francis
[T6]	Ferrar, R. (d. 1572)	(1527–99)	[T13]	Pilkington, Leonard
[T6B]	[Hatton, Sir Christopher (*c.* 1540–91)]	(1529–1603)	[T7]	Joscelyn, John
[T7]	Joscelyn, John (1529–1603)	(1530 – *c.* 1570)	[T9]	Nowell, Laurence
[T8]	Lambarde, William (1536–1601)	(1530/31?–1604)	[T17]	Whitgift, John
[T9]	Nowell, Laurence (1530 – *c.* 1570)	(1536–1601)	[T8]	Lambarde, William

Alphabetical Order		Chronological Order		
[T10]	Parker, Matthew (1504–75)	[(c. 1540–91)]	[T6B]	[Hatton, Sir Christopher]
[T11]	Parker, Sir John (1548–1618/19)	(1541–1601)	[T1]	Beale, Robert
[T12]	Pilkington, James (1520–76)	(1545–1613)	[T2]	Bodley, Sir Thomas
[T13]	Pilkington, Leonard (1527–99)	(1548–1618/19)	[T11]	Parker, Sir John
[T14]	Russell, Sir Francis (1526/27–85)	(fl. 1552–94)	[T5]	Cradock[e], Edward
[T15]	Scory, John (d. 1585)	(1553?–1614)	[T4]	Cope, Sir Walter
[T16]	Talbot, Robert (1505/06–58)	(d. 1569/70)	[T3]	Bowyer, William
[T17]	Whitgift, John (1530/31?–1604)	(d. 1572)	[T6]	Ferrar, R.
[T18]	Wolsey, Thomas (1470/71–1530)	(d. 1585)	[T15]	Scory, John

The Stuarts: 1603–1714

Alphabetical Order		Chronological Order		
[S1]	Bagford, John (1650/51–1716)	(1551–1623)	[S4]	Camden, William
[S2]	Barlow, Thomas (1608/09–91)	(c. 1560–1621)	[S3]	Bowyer, Robert
[S3]	Bowyer, Robert (c. 1560–1621)	(1563/64–1641)	[S16]	Spelman, Sir Henry
[S4]	Camden, William (1551–1623)	(1571–1631)	[S5]	Cotton, Sir Robert Bruce
[S5]	Cotton, Sir Robert Bruce (1571–1631)	(1577–1635)	[S8]	Elsynge, Henry
[S6]	Cotton, Sir Thomas (1594–1662)	(1584–1652)	[S20]	Young, Patrick
[S6B]	[Cotton, Sir John (1621–1702)]	(1584–1654)	[S15]	Selden, John
[S7]	Dugdale, Sir William (1605–86)	(1591–1677)	[S11]	Junius, Francis
[S8]	Elsynge, Henry (1577–1635)	(1592–1661)	[S12]	Le Neve, Sir William
[S8B]	[Harley, Robert (1661–1724)]	(c. 1593–1653)	[S18]	Whelock, Abraham
[S9]	Hatton, Christopher (1605–70)	(1594–1662)	[S6]	Cotton, Sir Thomas
[S10]	Hatton, Christopher (1632–1706)	(1598–1673)	[S17]	Theyer, John
[S10B]	[Hearne, Thomas (1678–1735)]	(1605–70)	[S9]	Hatton, Christopher
[S11]	Junius [Du Jon], Francis (1591–1677)	(1605–86)	[S7]	Dugdale, Sir William
[S12]	Le Neve, Sir William (1592–1661)	(1608/09–91)	[S2]	Barlow, Thomas
[S13]	Marshall, Thomas (1621–85)	(1618–89)	[S19]	Voss, Isaac
[S14]	Pepys, Samuel (1633–1703)	(1621–85)	[S13]	Marshall, Thomas
[S15]	Selden, John (1584–1654)	(1621–1702)]	[S6B]	[Cotton, Sir John]
[S16]	Spelman, Sir Henry (1563/64–1641)	(1632–1706)	[S10]	Hatton, Christopher
[S17]	Theyer, John (1598–1673)	(1633–1703)	[S14]	Pepys, Samuel
[S18]	Whelock, Abraham (c. 1593–1653)	(1650/51–1716)	[S1]	Bagford, John
[S18B]	[Willis, Browne (1682–1760)]	(1661–1724)	[S8B]	[Harley, Robert]
[S19]	Voss [Vossius], Isaac (1618–89)	(1678–1735)	[S10B]	[Hearne, Thomas]
[S20]	Young [Junius], Patrick (1584–1652)	(1682–1760)	[S18B]	[Willis, Browne]

The Tudors: 1509–1603

[T1] Beale, Robert (1541–1601), diplomat, administrator, and antiquarian; Secretary to Sir Francis Walsingham (Principal Secretary and Privy Counsellor to Queen Elizabeth), Clerk of the Queen's Privy Council from 1572, and Secretary of the Queen's Council of the North. Educated in civil law, logic, and rhetoric, Beale's scholarly reputation led to diplomatic missions on the Continent from the 1560s to the 1580s as well as service under Walsingham and ultimately Queen Elizabeth. Controversially, in parliament and in his writings he defended puritan positions, bringing him into sharp dispute with John Whitgift, Archbishop of Canterbury [T17 below]. A member of the Society of Antiquaries, Beale amassed a considerable library, nearly all of which passed into the Yelverton collection, now at the British Library. One manuscript perhaps owned by Beale is London, British Library, Royal MS 7. C. XII [App 1.1.9], the unique witness to the earliest known stage of Ælfric's First Series of *Catholic Homilies*, with notes in Ælfric's own hand; what appears to be Beale's name, now erased but partially legible, appears on fol. 4ʳ of the manuscript, following the name of cardinal Thomas Wolsey [T18 below] inscribed two folios before.[1]

[T2] Bodley, Sir Thomas (1545–1613), scholar, diplomat, and founder of the Bodleian Library at Oxford; Fellow of Merton College, Oxford, 1564–86; Oxford's first lecturer in Greek from 1565; Member of Parliament from 1584; and Knight from 1604. The son of a Protestant reformer, Bodley lived with his family in exile on the Continent during the reign of Mary before coming to Oxford as a student in 1559. There he developed an unusual competence in Greek and Hebrew, befriended Sir Henry Savile, who would assist him with the organization of the Bodleian, and came under the patronage of Robert Dudley, Earl of Leicester, and Sir Francis Walsingham, principal secretary to Queen Elizabeth (cf. Robert Beale [T1 above]). From 1585 to 1597 he was engaged in diplomatic missions on the Continent, most notably as Elizabeth's ambassador to the Dutch United

---

[1] For more on Robert Beale, see *Elizabethan Government and Society: Essays Presented to Sir John Neale*, ed. by S. T. Bindoff, J. Hurstfield, and C. H. Williams (London, 1961); Patrick Collinson, *The Elizabethan Puritan Movement* (Berkeley, 1967); Conyers Read, *Mr Secretary Walsingham and the Policy of Queen Elizabeth*, 3 vols (Oxford, 1925); Swen Voekel, "'Upon the Suddaine View': State, Civil Society and Surveillance in Early Modern England', *Early Modern Literary Studies*, 4 (1998), 1–27; and the *Oxford Dictionary of National Biography*, ed. by H. C. G. Matthew and Brian Harrison (Oxford, 2004) [hereafter *ODNB*], IV, 519–22. I am indebted to Caitlin Cogan and Rob Price for their help in verifying bibliographical details cited in this study.

Provinces. Suffering from ill health and disillusioned by the frustrations of public service, Bodley devoted his last fifteen years to founding the centre that would bear his name: the Bodleian Library at Oxford, designed to replace the collection donated by Humphrey, Duke of Gloucester (1390–1447) that was dispersed in the sixteenth century. Contributors to the project included William Camden and Sir Robert Cotton [S4 and S5 below]; Anglo-Saxon homiliaries contributed by Bodley to the library included Oxford, Bodleian Library, MSS Bodley 340 + Bodley 342 [App 1.1.10] and Oxford, Bodleian Library, MS Bodley 343 [App 1.1.11 and 2.6].[2]

[Bowyer, Robert (*c.* 1560–1621): see S3 below]

[T3] Bowyer, William (d. 1569/70),[3] antiquary; Bailiff of the Borough of Westminster by 1560; Member of Parliament for Westminster in 1563; and Keeper of the Records in the Tower of London from 1563 (the official patent for which office being issued in 1567). As Keeper, Bowyer was responsible for the single largest collection of government documents and was one of the first to attempt systematically to produce digests of its contents. A collector of manuscripts, he acquired not only the C version of the *Anglo-Saxon Chronicle* (London, British Library, Cotton MS Tiberius B. IV, fols 3–86 and 88–90) and a copy of Alfred's *Cura Pastoralis* (London, British Library, Cotton MSS Otho B. II + Otho B. X, fols 61, 63, and 64), but also an Anglo-Saxon homiliary: Oxford, Bodleian Library, MSS Bodley 340 + Bodley 342 [App 1.1.10]. On Bowyer's death, the homiliary may have passed to his son, Robert Bowyer [S3 below], from whom it was acquired by Sir Walter Cope [T4 below] before 1602.[4]

[Camden, William (1551–1623): see S4 below]

[T4] Cope, Sir Walter (1553?–1614), administrator; Knight from 1603; Member of Parliament, 1604 and 1614; Chamberlain of the Exchequer from 1609; Public

---

[2] For more on Sir Thomas Bodley, see for example Ian Philip, *The Bodleian Library in the Seventeenth and Eighteenth Centuries,* (Oxford, 1983); David J. B. Trim, 'Sir Thomas Bodley and the International Protestant Cause', *Bodleian Library Record,* 16 (1999), 314–40; David Vaisey, 'The Legacy of Sir Thomas Bodley', *Bodleian Library Record,* 17 (2002), 419–30; and *ODNB,* VI, 411–15.

[3] N. R. Ker states that 'The date of Bowier's death is not known, but it was probably in or before 1576, when his post of Keeper of the Records in the Tower was given to Michael and Thomas Henneage [brothers, 1540–1600 and *c.* 1532–95, respectively]': *Catalogue of Manuscripts Containing Anglo-Saxon* (Oxford, 1957), p. liv.

[4] For more on William Bowyer, see for example Ker, *Catalogue,* p. liv; May McKisack, *Medieval History in the Tudor Age* (Oxford, 1971); and *ODNB,* VI, 997.

Registrar-General of Commerce from 1611 or 1612; and Master of the Court of Wards from 1612. Secretary from the mid-1570s to Sir William Cecil, Elizabeth's Secretary of State, and factotum and friend to Sir Robert Cecil, William's son, Cope rose through the family's patronage to become an influential figure in national administration. Trusted in affairs of finance and diplomacy, he came to be on close terms with James I and the royal family. To Cope belonged Oxford, Bodleian Library, MSS Bodley 340 + Bodley 342 [App 1.1.10], a manuscript he likely obtained prior to 1602 from Robert Bowyer [S3 below], who may in turn have inherited it from his father William [T3 above] on the latter's death in 1569 or 1570.[5]

[Cotton, Sir Robert Bruce, first baronet (1571–1631): see S5 below]

[Cotton, Sir Thomas, second baronet (1594–1662): see S6 below]

[T5] Cradocke [or Cradock], Edward (fl. 1552–94), theologian and alchemist; Lady Margaret Professor of Divinity at Oxford, 1565–94; and Rector, St Mary Aldermary, London, 1570–94. Coming to the Professorship without degrees in theology, Cradocke not only completed a bachelor's and a doctorate in the subject in the next two years, but held the post — elected biennially by doctors and senior students of theology — for an unprecedented three decades. A Catholic under Mary I, Cradocke returned to the Anglican Church with the accession of Elizabeth in 1558, and served in 1562 on a synod convened by Archbishop Matthew Parker [T10 below] to revise the Thirty-Nine Articles of Anglican doctrine. Parker further distinguished Cradocke in 1570 by helping appoint him to a London benefice, the rectorship of St Mary Aldermary, and to be a preacher at Canterbury Cathedral the same year. In 1571 or 1572, he published *The Shippe of Assured Safetie*, a treatise on divine providence written at Oxford during a time of plague. Throughout his career, moreover, he pursued the philosopher's stone, viewing alchemy as a spiritually salutary calling. Found at Tavistock Abbey in 1566, Cambridge, Corpus Christi College, MS 201, Part I [App 3.2] appears to have spent some time in Cradocke's library: John Joscelyn [T7 below], transcribing pp. 101–03 of CCCC 201 into his notebook, notes that the section comes *ex Oxoniensi libro D[octoris] Cradoke* (London, British Library, Cotton MS Vitellius D. VII, fol. 145[r]; 'from an Oxford book belonging to Doctor Cradock'). From Cradock the manuscript

---

[5] See further Alan Haynes, *Robert Cecil, First Earl of Salisbury: Servant of Two Sovereigns* (London, 1989); Theodore K. Rabb, *Jacobean Gentleman: Sir Edwin Sandys, 1561–1629* (Princeton, 1998); Andrew G. Watson, 'The Manuscript Collection of Sir Walter Cope (d. 1614)', *Bodleian Library Record*, 12 (1987), 262–97; and *ODNB*, XIII, 316–17.

passed into the hands of Parker, perhaps out of gratitude for Parker's assistance in his appointments to London and Canterbury.[6]

[Elsynge, Henry (bap. 1577, d. 1635): see S8 below]

[T6] Ferrar, R. (d. 1572), Member of Parliament for Tavistock in west Devon. A servant of the Bedford family, Ferrar was responsible for the discovery in 1566 of London, British Library, Cotton MS Vitellius C. V [App 1.1.7] and (probably) Cambridge, University Library, MS Ii. 4. 6 [App 1.2.1] in the monastic library of Tavistock Abbey. Ferrar delivered the manuscripts to Francis Russell, second Earl of Bedford [T14 below], who in 1567 presented CUL Ii. 4. 6 to Matthew Parker [T10 below]; Cotton Vitellius C. V was still in Bedford's possession in 1584, but passed thereafter into the possession of Sir Robert Cotton [S5 below], perhaps following Bedford's death in 1585.[7]

[T6B] [Hatton, Sir Christopher (c. 1540–91), politician and courtier; Justice of the Peace for Northamptonshire from 1569; Member of Parliament from 1571; Knight, 1577; Knight of the Garter, 1588; and Lord Chancellor from 1587. From the time he first attracted Elizabeth's attention in 1564, Hatton rose swiftly in the Queen's favour, receiving appointments and estates and increasing royal confidence and affection. Deft in the art of courtly love, Hatton at once charmed the Queen with his lifelong devotion and offered her a personal friendship, becoming for many years her daily companion. From the late 1570s he regularly served as spokesman for Elizabeth in parliament, promoting royal policy in the Commons; as a member of the privy council from 1578, England's relations with the Continent and negotiations regarding a possible royal marriage were among his concerns. Hatton's religious convictions were somewhat unclear: rumoured to have Catholic sympathies, publicly he took a strong anti-papal stance while also opposing the puritans — positions shared by a figure he vigorously supported, John Whitgift, Archbishop of Canterbury from 1583 [T17 below]. On Hatton's death, his library and estates passed to his nephew, Sir William Newport, who then took Hatton's name. When William died without sons in 1597, the inheritance passed to another relative named Sir Christopher Hatton (d. 1619), whose son

---

[6] For additional material on Cradocke, see Edward Cradocke, 'A Treatise Touching the Philosopher's Stone', in *Alchemical Poetry 1575–1700, from Previously Unpublished Manuscripts*, ed. by Robert M. Schuler, English Renaissance Hermeticism, 5 (New York, 1995), pp. 3–48; and *ODNB*, XIII, 923.

[7] On Ferrar, see Ker, *Catalogue*, p. 35.

(Christopher, first Baron Hatton [S9 below]) and grandson (Christopher, first Viscount Hatton [S10 below]) would collect and ultimately bequeath Anglo-Saxon homiliaries to the Bodleian Library.[8]]

[T7] Joscelyn, John (1529–1603), scholar and cleric; Fellow of Queens College, Cambridge, *c.* 1549–57; Latin Secretary to Archbishop Matthew Parker from 1559; Prebend of Hereford, 1560–77; Rector of Hollingborne, Kent, from 1577. The third son of Hertfordshire gentry, Joscelyn began his career at Cambridge in 1545. He took his undergraduate degree in 1549 and was admitted as Fellow of Queens College, after which he lectured in Latin and Greek before taking his MA in 1552. Though he initially subscribed to Catholicism under Mary I, he displayed Protestant convictions after resigning his fellowship in 1557. His scholarly reputation, however, endured, calling him to the attention of Archbishop Matthew Parker [T10 below], who enlisted him as his Latin secretary in 1559. Their collaboration thereafter was a watershed for medieval and particularly for Anglo-Saxon studies. To facilitate Parker's search for precedent in the early English Church for Anglican doctrine, Joscelyn assiduously collected Old English material, borrowing or copying manuscripts in situ. A careful student both of texts and language, he annotated and compiled notes on Anglo-Saxon material, leading to both publications such as Parker's edition of Ælfrician works in *A Testimonie of Antiquitie* (*c.* 1566) and linguistic tools such as his (unfinished) Old English–Latin dictionary, compiled with Parker's son John [T11 below].

Ten manuscripts containing Anglo-Saxon homiliaries are known to have passed through Joscelyn's hands. Four are from the college that would inherit Parker's collection. Cambridge, Corpus Christi College, MS 178 [App 1.1.2] Joscelyn used for his glossary in London, Lambeth Palace Library, MS 692. Cambridge, Corpus Christi College, MS 201 [App 3.2] he annotated and partly transcribed in his notebook, London, British Library, Cotton MS Vitellius D. VII, noting that its current owner was Edward Cradocke [T5 above]. Cambridge, Corpus Christi College, MS 198 [App 1.1.4], on which Parker drew along with London, British Library, Cotton MS Faustina A. IX [App 1.2.6] for *A Testimonie of Antiquitie*, Joscelyn appears to have consulted at Worcester before it passed into Parker's keeping around the last quarter of the sixteenth century. At some point, Joscelyn

---

[8] On Hatton, see for example Eric S. Brooks, *Sir Christopher Hatton: Queen Elizabeth's Favourite* (London, 1947); D. Allen Carroll, 'Christopher Hatton's Ciphers', *Manuscripta*, 40 (1996), 54–57; Collinson, *Elizabethan Puritan Movement*; Alice Gilmore Vines, *Neither Fire Nor Steel: Sir Christopher Hatton* (Chicago, 1978); and *ODNB*, XXV, 817–23.

foliated the manuscript, added folio numbers to the original contents-list, made numerous interlinear glosses, recorded variant readings from other manuscripts, and underlined words which he then included in his Old English word-lists (Lambeth 692, fols 24ʳ–25ᵛ) and in his Old English dictionary (London, British Library, Cotton MSS Titus A. XV–XVI). He cross-referenced homilies in CCCC 198, furthermore, to those in other homiliaries, such as Oxford, Bodleian Library, MSS Hatton 113 + 114 [App 1.1.12] and Cambridge, Corpus Christi College, MS 421 [App 4.1]. CCCC 421 thus comprises the fourth homiliary known to have been consulted by Joscelyn, though it is likely that he also knew Cambridge, Corpus Christi College, MSS 419 + 421 [App 3.3 and 4.1], as its Parkerian tables of contents likewise cross-references homilies in CCCC 198.

At least three homiliaries from Sir Robert Cotton's collection [S5 below] also were known to Joscelyn. Cotton Faustina A. IX [App 1.2.6], first of all, contains annotations by Joscelyn in various parts of the manuscript. On the one hand, next to Ælfric's *Letter to Sigefyrth*, Joscelyn entered the preface to the letter reproduced from London, British Library, Cotton MS Vespasian D. XIV [App 2.4]; from the latter manuscript, Joscelyn also copied the letter into London, British Library, Cotton MS Vespasian D. VII, noting variants found in Faustina's version. Based on Joscelyn's work, Parker printed the preface to the *Letter to Sigefyrth* in *A Testimonie of Antiquitie*. On the other hand, next to an Ælfrician homily for Easter which Parker would showcase in the *Testimonie*, Joscelyn entered variant readings for the homily and cross-references to leaf-numbers in the *Testimonie*. In Cotton Vespasian D. VII, finally, Joscelyn noted that Faustina belonged to William Bowyer [T3 above]. Second, there is London, British Library, Cotton MS Otho B. X + Oxford, Bodleian Library, MS Rawlinson Q. e. 20 [App 2.3]. A number of leaves originally formed part of separate manuscripts but were owned and perhaps inserted into Cotton Otho B. X by Joscelyn: fols 29–30; fol. 51 (originally belonging to London, British Library, Cotton MS Otho C. I, vol. I); and fol. 165. Joscelyn's ownership of the volume is evidenced by his notes to that effect in Cambridge, Corpus Christi College, MS 9 + London, British Library, Cotton MS Nero E. I. The volume was one of many that passed into the hands of Sir Robert Cotton [S5 below], either during Joscelyn's lifetime or after his death; Cotton references Joscelyn's prior ownership of the manuscript in London, British Library, Harley MS 6018, when recording the loan of the volume to William Camden [S4 below]. Third, there is Cotton Vespasian D. XIV [App 2.4], from which Joscelyn copied the *Letter to Sigefyrth* into Cotton Vespasian D. VII and the letter's preface into Cotton Faustina A. IX. Laurence Nowell's ownership [T9 below] of Cotton Vespasian D. VII Joscelyn notes in Cotton Vespasian D. VII.

Last we come to the homiliaries at Oxford. Oxford, Bodleian Library, MSS Bodley 340 + Bodley 342 [App 1.1.10] was owned by William Bowyer [T3 above] and possibly thereafter by his son Robert [S3 below]; the family's association with the manuscript is corroborated by Joscelyn, who cross-references a text in CCCC 198 to 'sermo 13 in libro M. bower' (fol. 266ʳ), *liber* likely referring to Bodley 342 and *bower* meaning either William or Robert.⁹ Hatton 113 + 114 [App 1.1.12] Joscelyn consulted at Worcester alongside CCCC 198, perhaps in or after the 1560s. Joscelyn wrote marginal notes in the volumes and drew on Hatton 113 for his glossaries in Lambeth 692. Finally, there is Oxford, Bodleian Library, MS Hatton 115 + Kansas, Kenneth Spencer Research Library, MS Pryce C2:2 [App 3.5], which Joscelyn also consulted in the course of his pursuit of Anglo-Saxon precedent for Parker.¹⁰

[Junius [Du Jon], Francis [Franciscus] (1591–1677): see S11B below]

[T8] Lambarde, William (1536–1601), lawyer, public servant, and historian; possibly Member of Parliament, 1563 and 1566; County Commissioner of the Peace for Kent from 1579; Associate Bencher from 1579 and then Bencher of Lincoln's Inn from 1597; and Keeper of Records in the Tower of London from 1601. Educated possibly at Jesus College, Cambridge from 1549 and at Lincoln's Inn from 1556, Lambarde may have represented Aldborough, Yorkshire in the parliamentary sessions of 1563 and 1566–67; in the latter capacity, he may be identified with the 'William Lambert' who successfully argued for the House of Commons's right, in the face of Elizabethan opposition, to debate the issue of royal succession, thus defending the House's right to free speech. At Lincoln's Inn, encouraged by fellow antiquarians Lawrence Nowell and Matthew Parker [T9 and T10 below], Lambarde engaged in research into Anglo-Saxon and Norman laws, publishing his findings in *Archaionomia, siue de priscis Anglorum legibus* (London, 1568); the

---

⁹ Ker, *Catalogue*, p. 367.

¹⁰ Further studies on Joscelyn include Janet Bately, 'John Joscelyn and the Laws of the Anglo-Saxon Kings', in *Words, Texts, and Manuscripts: Studies in Anglo-Saxon Culture Presented to Helmut Gneuss on the Occasion of his Sixty-fifth Birthday*, ed. by M. Korhammer, Karl Reichl, and Hans Sauer (Cambridge, 1992), pp. 435–66; Judith Sanders Gale, 'John Joscelyn's Notebook: A Study of the Contents and Sources of B.L., Cotton MS. Vitellius D. vii' (unpublished master's thesis, University of Nottingham, 1978); Timothy Graham, 'The Old English Prefatory Texts in the Corpus Canterbury Pontifical', *Anglia*, 113 (1995), 1–15; Angelika Lutz, 'Das Studium der Angelsächsischen Chronik im 16. Jahrhundert: Nowell und Joscelyn', *Anglia*, 100 (1982), 301–56; James L. Rosier, 'The Sources of John Joscelyn's Old English-Latin Dictionary', *Anglia*, 78 (1960), 28–39; and *ODNB*, XXX, 714–15. See also Ker, *Catalogue*, p. lii.

book was only the second volume to print Old English, following Parker's *A Testimonie of Antiquitie* (London, *c.* 1566), and in 1644 was re-edited by another student of Anglo-Saxon, Abraham Whelock [S18 below]. Following his appointment as Commissioner of Sewers for Kent in 1568, Lambarde embarked on the first county history, a history of Kent drawing on such early sources as William I's Domesday Book; Lambarde published his work in 1576, but ceased research into the history of other counties on learning of a similar undertaking by William Camden [S4 below; see also Sir William Dugdale, S7 below]. As part of the county commission of the peace for Kent from 1579, he kept a record of observations regarding government, the 'Ephemeris'; this work he followed with an influential legal study, the posthumously published *Archeion* (London, 1635), setting forth a governmental model whose basic principles might be traced to Anglo-Saxon jurisprudence. Lambarde provides evidence to the Parkerian ownership of Cambridge, Corpus Christi College, MS 201 [App 3.2] when, copying pp. 97–101 into the commonplace book of his friend Nowell in 1571, he notes that his source was *liber* [...] *Mathaei Cantuariensis Archiepiscopi* (University of California at Los Angeles, University Research Library, Department of Special Collections, MS 170/159, fol. 210^r; 'a book [...] of Matthew Archbishop of Canterbury'). As Lambarde appears not to have been aware of CCCC 201 when he published his *Archaionomia*, between 1568 and 1571 Parker thus likely assumed ownership of the manuscript.[11]

---

[11] Additional studies of Lambarde's life and works include James D. Alsop and Wesley M. Stevens, 'William Lambarde and the Elizabethan Polity', *Studies in Medieval and Renaissance History*, 8 (1986), 231–65; Carl T. Berkhout, 'William Lambarde's Old English Ex Libris', *NQ*, 31 (1984), 297–98; Ronald E. Buckalew, 'Nowell, Lambarde, and Leland: The Significance of Laurence Nowell's Transcript of Ælfric's Grammar and Glossary', in *Anglo-Saxon Scholarship: The First Three Centuries*, ed. by Carl T. Berkhout and Milton McC. Gatch (Boston, 1982), pp. 19–50; Wilbur Dunkel, *William Lambarde, Elizabethan Jurist 1536–1601* (New Brunswick, 1965); Raymond J. S. Grant, *Laurence Nowell, William Lambarde and the Laws of the Anglo-Saxons*, Costerus, 108 (Amsterdam, 1996); A. Kent Hieatt, 'King Arthur in William Lambarde's *Archaionomia* (1568)', *ANQ*, 5 (1992), 78–82; *William Lambarde and Local Government*, ed. by Conyers Read (Ithaca, 1962); Wilfrid Prest, 'William Lambarde, Elizabethan Law Reform, and Early Stuart Politics', *Journal of British Studies*, 34 (1995), 464–80; Makoto Sasaki, 'A Note on the Tudor Studies of Anglo-Saxon Laws to William Lambarde', *Law Review of Komazawa University*, 24 (1982), 53–88; Kenneth Sisam, 'The Authenticity of Certain Texts in Lambarde's Archaionomia 1568', in *Studies in the History of Old English Literature* (Oxford, 1953; repr., 1998), pp. 232–58; E. G. Stanley, 'Old English = "Anglo-Saxon": William Lambarde's Use in 1576', *NQ*, 42 (1995), 437; Richard J. Terrill, 'William Lambarde: Elizabethan Humanist and Legal Historian', *Journal of Legal History*, 6 (1985), 157–78; Retha Warnicke, *William Lambarde, Elizabethan Antiquary 1536–1601* (Chichester, 1973); Patrick Wormald, 'The Lambarde

[Le Neve, Sir William (bap. 1592, d. 1661): see S12 below]

[T9] Nowell, Laurence (1530 – *c.* 1570), antiquarian; Member of Parliament for Knaresborough, Yorkshire, 1559. Not to be confused with Laurence Nowell, dean of Lichfield (*c.* 1516–76), who shared Nowell's paternal grandparents. A student of Anglo-Saxon from about 1561, Nowell transcribed and translated a number of Old English works, such as Ælfric's *Grammar* and the *Old English Bede*. Evincing a keen interest in Anglo-Saxon law-codes, he produced the first critical edition and translation of the laws of Alfred (London, British Library, Henry Davis MS 59 (M 30)), a work used by his close friend, William Lambarde [T8 above] in his 1568 *Archaionomia*. In Anglo-Saxon poetry he was scarcely less invested, acquiring the *Beowulf* manuscript in 1563 (London, British Library, Cotton MS Vitellius A. XV) and ultimately familiarizing himself with as much as half of the extant poetic corpus. A pioneer of early Anglo-Saxon studies, perhaps his greatest contribution to the field was his compilation of the first Old English dictionary, the *Vocabularium Saxonicum*, which circulated in manuscript until published finally in 1952. A wide-ranging traveller, Nowell left England in 1567 for the Continent, studying over the next two years in the Universities of Paris, Vienna, and Freiburg im Breisgau. After hearing nothing from him in the two years that followed, however, his brothers successfully petitioned to have him declared dead; Lambarde, Nowell's executor, oversaw the transfer of the latter's estate with the exception of Nowell's library, which he retained. One Anglo-Saxon homiliary owned and glossed by Nowell was that in London, British Library, Cotton MS Vespasian D. XIV [App 2.4]; from the manuscript he produced an Old English word-list in London, Lambeth Palace Library, MS 692, perhaps underlining less common words in Cotton Vespasian D. XIV in the process. John Joscelyn [T7 above] noted Nowell's ownership of Cotton Vespasian D. XIV when copying Ælfric's *Letter to Sigefyrth* from now-lost leaves therein to London, British Library, Cotton MS Vespasian D. VII.[12]

Problem: Eighty Years On', in *Alfred the Wise: Studies in Honour of Janet Bately*, ed. by Jane Roberts and Janet L. Nelson with Malcolm Godden (Cambridge, 1997), pp. 237–75; and *ODNB*, XXXII, 287–90.

 [12] Nowell is the subject of numerous studies, including Carl T. Berkhout, 'Laurence Nowell (1530–ca. 1570)', in *Literature and Philology*, ed. by H. Damico, D. Fennema, and K. Lenz, special issue, *Medieval Scholarship: Biographical Studies on the Formation of a Discipline*, 2 (1998), 3–17; Berkhout, 'The Pedigree of Laurence Nowell the Antiquary', *English Language Notes*, 23 (1985), 15–26; Pamela M. Black, 'Laurence Nowell's "Disappearance" in Germany and its Bearing on the Whereabouts of his *Collectanea*, 1568–1572', *English Historical Review*, 92

[T10] Parker, Matthew (1504–75), clergyman, administrator, and antiquarian; Fellow (from 1527) and then Master (1544–53) of Corpus Christi College, Cambridge; Dean of the College of Stoke by Clare, 1535–48; Vice-Chancellor of Cambridge, 1545–*c*. 1553; and Archbishop of Canterbury, 1559–75. Prior to the ascent of Mary I in 1553, Parker was a man whose career flourished on multiple fronts. A member of Corpus Christi College, Cambridge from *c*. 1520, he took thereafter a series of degrees: his BA in 1525, MA in 1527 or 1528, BTh in 1535, and DTh in 1538. Simultaneously, he advanced within the administrative structure, becoming master of Corpus and then vice-chancellor of the university. Perhaps influenced at Cambridge by the evangelical reformer Thomas Bilney (*c*. 1495–1531), moreover, Parker came to the attention of Queen Anne Boleyn, who shared Bilney's views of the central role of grace and faith, the primacy of scripture over ecclesiastical authority, and the importance of preaching for conveying Christian doctrine. Having been ordained priest in 1527, Parker became royal chaplain first to Anne in 1535 and then to Henry VIII in 1537. Anne made Parker Dean of Stoke by Clare and before her execution commended to his spiritual care her daughter, Elizabeth. Henry's recommendation, in turn, led to Parker's appointment as prebend of Ely in 1541 and master of Corpus in 1544; the benefices of rector at Ashen, Essex (1543–46), Burlingham St Andrew, Norfolk (1544–50), and Landbeach, Cambridgeshire (from 1545) shortly followed. Henry's son Edward VI (1547–53) continued the preferential trend, presenting Parker in 1552 to the deanery of Lincoln and the prebendary of Corringham in Lincoln Cathedral. In 1547, however, two years before the legalization of clerical marriage, he married Margaret Harleston, with whom he had been living since 1544. Strong opposition to such marriage by Catholic Mary led to him being stripped of his offices between 1553 and 1554. While he did not join other married priests in continental exile, he did live in hiding, perhaps near Cambridge, and once was severely injured when a forced flight by night led to his falling from his horse. His circumstances would again change dramatically, however, with the accession of

(1977), 345–53; Black, 'Some New Light on the Career of Laurence Nowell the Antiquary', *Antiquaries Journal*, 62 (1982), 116–23; Buckalew, 'Nowell, Lambarde, and Leland'; Grant, *Laurence Nowell, William Lambarde*; Grant, 'Laurence Nowell's Transcript of BM Cotton Otho B. xi', *ASE*, 3 (1974), 111–24; Thomas G. Hahn, 'The Identity of the Antiquary Laurence Nowell', *English Language Notes*, 20 (1983), 10–18; Lutz, 'Das Studium der Angelsächsischen Chronik im 16. Jahrhundert'; *Laurence Nowell's 'Vocabularium Saxonicum'*, ed. by Albert H. Marckwardt, *University of Michigan Studies in Language and Literature*, 25 (1952); Retha M. Warnicke, 'The Laurence Nowell Manuscripts in the British Library', *British Library Journal*, 5 (1979), 201–02; and *ODNB*, XLI, 237–39.

Elizabeth. Recommended to the Queen not only by her mother but by Parker's demonstration of considerable administrative gifts at Stoke by Clare and Cambridge, between 1558 and 1559 Parker found himself appointed Archbishop of Canterbury. In this role, he faced the formidable challenge of stabilizing the English Church in the aftermath of Marian turmoil and charting its theological course amidst challenges from recusant Catholics and Protestants calling for further reform. In 1563, under his direction, the Church established the Thirty-Nine Articles, which set forth the defining tenets of Anglican doctrine. He engaged the heated debate over ecclesiastical vestments, oversaw and contributed greatly to the development of the so-called Bishops' Bible, and defended Episcopal versus Presbyterian church governance. In seeking to justify the theological positions of the new English Church, moreover, he pursued historical precedent, showing that in departing from Rome the Church was actually remaining true to traditional English belief. As a result, he turned to antiquarian studies and to the ecclesiastical writings of the Anglo-Saxons in particular, looking for Reformed theology in early English teaching, for evidence of corruption in the Roman Church, and for examples of vernacular translations of scripture. To this end, he began acquiring books. Prompted in part by a request from Elizabeth in 1760 to collect English materials to assist a group of German Protestant historians, he began in earnest to compile lists of desired texts and to set about obtaining or borrowing volumes to be copied. While in many cases (though by no means all) such volumes were returned to their owners, Parker also was not hesitant about making 'improvements' to the books that came into his hands, trimming, reordering, augmenting, dividing, and rebinding manuscripts in a fashion less than consonant with modern archival practice. Assisted by his son John Parker [T11 below], scholars such as William Lambarde [T8 above], and above all by his Latin secretary John Joscelyn [T7 above], moreover, Parker studied and annotated numerous works thus acquired, publishing or sponsoring the publication of editions deemed supportive of his views. Of the many examples that might be offered in this regard, two are of particular interest to Anglo-Saxonists. *A Testimonie of Antiquitie*, on the one hand, was the first book printed with Anglo-Saxon characters; published by John Day for Parker around 1566, in it Parker reproduced a number of texts by Ælfric of Eynsham to support the Protestant view of transubstantiation. The next work containing Old English to be published thereafter was the second edition of the *Defence of Priestes Mariages*, Parker's expansion of an anonymous work (also possibly by Parker) that incorporates four quoted passages in the same Anglo-Saxon type.

Parker's research into Ælfrician material and the subject of priestly marriage, among others, led him to make active use of Anglo-Saxon homiliaries. They were fifteen in number, ten being labelled by Parker as follows:

Primus liber homiliarum: Cambridge, Corpus Christi College, MS 162 [App 1.2.2]. The manuscript was one of only four that came to Parker from unknown sources — Cambridge, Corpus Christi College, MS 188 [App 1.1.3], Cambridge, Corpus Christi College, MS 302 [App 1.2.3], and Cambridge, Trinity College, MS B. 15. 34 [App 1.2.5] being the others — though CCCC 162 and 188 may have been among the 'iii saxon bokes. found in the church of heref.' sent to Parker by John Scory [T15 below].[13] CCCC 162 shows numerous signs of the Archbishop's handiwork. Parker was responsible for having a contents list added, a leaf from a printed missal inserted as a frontispiece, and twenty-two pages (now constituting CCCC 162, Part II, pp. 139–60) taken from Cambridge, Corpus Christi College, MS 178 to augment the volume [App 3.1]. He also had the assembled manuscript rebound, with sixteenth-century endleaves and a sixteenth-century vellum leaf separating the two Parts. Pagination, notes, and marks appear in the 'well-known and conspicuous red pencil used perhaps by Parker himself and certainly by his son John'.[14] One such annotation, next to the homily for Easter Sunday (§38.32), notes that the Ælfrician material therein is 'in libello impresso' ('printed in the booklet') — that is, in Parker's *A Testimonie of Antiquitie*; CCCC 162 was thus likely one of the 'diuerse bookes of sermons' Parker consulted before publishing Ælfric's *CH* II.15 (*A Testimonie*, fol. 61ᵛ).

Secundus liber homiliarum: Cambridge, Corpus Christi College, MS 178 [App 1.1.2 and 3.1]. CCCC 178 was owned by Parker and shows ample evidence of his use. He was responsible for the pagination of rectos in red pencil; the inclusion of a table of contents; the rubrication of the opening homily in the collection; the transfer of eleven leaves originally between pp. 30 and 33 to CCCC 162, pp. 139–60 [App 3.1]; and the insertion of a supply leaf at pp. 31–32, on which he had copied the opening of *CH* I.24 from CCCC 162, p. 160. Parker's binders, who commonly employed blank portions of parchment documents as endleaves, used pieces from an early sixteenth-century account-roll (concerning the estate of John de Vere, thirteenth Earl of Oxford (1442–1513)) for pp. v–vi; other fragments of the account-roll appear as pp. 459–60 of CCCC 178, pp. xxv–xxviii of Cambridge,

---

[13] Montague Rhodes James, *A Descriptive Catalogue of the Manuscripts in the Library of Corpus Christi College, Cambridge*, 2 vols (Cambridge, 1912), I, 445; see also Mildred Budny, *Insular, Anglo-Saxon, and Early Anglo-Norman Manuscript Art at Corpus Christi College, Cambridge: An Illustrated Catalogue*, 2 vols (Kalamazoo, 1997), I, 572–73, who concludes that CCCC 188 is perhaps a more likely candidate than CCCC 162. On the unknown origin of these items in Parker's collection, see Ker, *Catalogue*, p. liii.

[14] Ker, *Catalogue*, p. liii.

Corpus Christi College, MS 191 (recording payments in 1511 and 1512), and pp. i–vi and 435–38 of Trinity B. 15. 34 [App 1.2.5].[15] Underlining and other marks in the conspicuous red pencil used by Parker and his son John are found on pp. 50–54 and 163. (The second half of the manuscript (Ker no. 41B), which Joscelyn used for his glossary in London, Lambeth Palace, MS 692, fol. 16, also includes a note in red pencil on p. 291: 'In hoc libro facilius discitur Lingua Saxonica' ('In this book the Saxon language is the more easily learned').) As the heading to the contents page and the Parkerian '2' across the fore-edge of the leaves show, the manuscript was Parker's *Secundus liber* [*homiliarium*].

Tertius liber homiliarum: Cambridge, Corpus Christi College, MS 188 [App 1.1.3]. Like CCCC 162 above, this manuscript was one of four that came to Parker from unknown sources, though it may have been sent from Hereford by John Scory. CCCC 188 shows numerous signs of the Archbishop's handiwork. Parker was responsible for having a contents list added; endleaves inserted and the volume bound; portions of damaged leaves reconstructed with vellum strips or patches (e.g. on pp. 3–4 and 7–12); parts of certain texts furnished on supply leaves, such as the beginning of the *Hexameron* on pp. 1–2 and the end of *CH* I.29 and beginning of *CH* I.30 on pp. 317–22 (Ker no. 43.31–32); and portions of other texts erased, such as the opening of the last, imperfect article on p. 460 (*SH* II.18 (no. 43.46)) and the end of *CH* I.15 on p. 165 (no. 43.16) — in the latter case, probably because the preceding leaves were loose and displaced in Parker's time, so that the ending appeared to be acephalous. Parker himself attempted to indicate the proper order of the leaves, misbound in or prior to the thirteenth century, with catchwords and page references (pp. 82, 83, and 440 (erroneously for 444)); he also identified one of the homilies whose beginning he had supplied (*CH* I.30 (no. 43.32)), and (probably) paginated the rectos of the manuscript in red pencil.

Quartus liber homiliarum: Cambridge, Corpus Christi College, MS 198 [App 1.1.4 and 1.3.1]. Features which Parker added (or caused to be added) to this manuscript include a composite endleaf (fol. i*, made of a reused fragment of a fifteenth-century list of kitchen expenses sandwiched between two sixteenth-century unwatermarked paper leaves[16]); a title for the book at the top of the frontispiece ('Sermones saxonici lx^a', fol. ii*^r); potentially the frontispiece itself; a list of contents (fol. ii*^v); an ascription of the book to Ælfric ('Ælfricus abbas transtulit', fol. 1^r); a short set of catchwords to guide the reordering of leaves when

---

[15] See Ker, *Catalogue*, p. xlii, and Budny, *Illustrated Catalogue*, I, 549.

[16] Budny, *Illustrated Catalogue*, I, 557 and 559.

rebinding (fols 374ᵛ, 375ᵛ, and 376ᵛ); foliations throughout in red crayon (some-what imperfectly, as at fols 223 and 245); a new binding; and a 'tidied' ending, the opening of an incomplete homily on the last page (*De uirginitate*, fol. 394ᵛ) having been erased. Responsibility for the frontispiece is debated: Ker observes that Parker liked frontispieces and had a habit of inserting them even when they bore little relation to the manuscript's contents; Budny, however, suggests that 'they most probably form an integral part of this book', with the image perhaps added along with homiletic interpolations (fols 321–27 and 367–77) in the second half of the eleventh century.[17] Parker drew on CCCC 198 along with London, British Library, Cotton MS Faustina A. IX [App 1.2.6] for his publication in *A Testimonie of Antiquitie* (London, *c.* 1566) of a key Ælfrician homily for Easter (*CH* II.15).

Quintus liber homiliarum: Cambridge, Corpus Christi College, MS 302 [App 1.2.3]. Like CCCC 162, CCCC 188, and Trinity B. 15. 34, CCCC 302 came to Parker from unknown sources. He was responsible for having the table of contents made, paper and parchment flyleaves and supply leaves inserted, and the volume rebound; pagination, notes, and marks appear in the red pencil used by Parker and his son John.

Sextus liber homiliarum: Cambridge, Corpus Christi College, MS 421 [App 4.1]. The collection includes a Parkerian table of contents, pagination in red pencil on the rectos of pp. 3–353, and sixteenth-century parchment flyleaves on pp. v–viii.

Septimus liber homiliarum: Cambridge, Corpus Christi College, MS 419 + Cambridge, Corpus Christi College, MS 421, pp. 1 and 2 [App 3.3]. CCCC 419, which follows CCCC 421 in Parker's collection, is annotated by the Archbishop and paginated on rectos in red pencil. Parker transplanted CCCC 419's frontis-piece to CCCC 421, pp. 1–2, flipping the page to move the image to the recto, and inserted a thirteenth-century Psalter leaf as the frontispiece of CCCC 419, pp. ix–x. To him is likely due the insertion of sixteenth-century parchment leaves in CCCC 419, pp. v–viii and 367–70, along with the Parkerian tables of contents in CCCC 419, fol. 'ii'ᵛ and CCCC 421, fol. 'ii'ʳ, with their cross-references to homilies in CCCC 198 [App 1.1.4].

Octauus liber homiliarum: Cambridge, University Library, MS Ii. 1. 33 [App 2.1]. CUL Ii. 1. 33 includes a Parkerian table of contents, the Parkerian title 'hom. 51', and a sixteenth-century parchment flyleaf typical of Parker's binders.[18] The

---

[17] Ker, *Catalogue*, pp. 76 and xli, and Budny, *Illustrated Catalogue*, I, 558.

[18] See Ker, *Catalogue*, p. xlii.

manuscript was ostensibly included in Parker's literary bequest to Corpus Christi College on his death in 1575, but in fact given by him to Cambridge University Library in 1574.

Nonus liber homiliarum: Cambridge, Corpus Christi College, MS 303 [App 1.2.4 and 1.3.2 below]. CCCC 303 also shows characteristic signs of Parker's ownership: a table of contents in the Archbishop's hand,[19] parchment flyleaves from his binders, and the 'tidying' of the opening of the manuscript to remove the acephalous first entry (Ker no. 57.1). This last involved cutting away all but a narrow strip of a preceding leaf (to which the last of the flyleaves then was attached) and erasing and pasting over the last lines of the homily on what is now page 1.

Decimus liber homiliarum: Cambridge, Trinity College, MS B. 15. 34 [App 1.2.5]. Like CCCC 162, CCCC 188, and CCCC 302, Trinity B. 15. 34 came to Parker from unknown sources. To him are likely due the pagination of rectos in red pencil and the conclusion to the last entry being appended on a sixteenth-century supply leaf; he was also responsible for having a table of contents incorporated and having the volume rebound. Only five Old English manuscripts survive in bindings of the sixteenth century, of which this is one. Among the flyleaves inserted by the binders are early sixteenth-century account-rolls relating to one William Colne. On Parker's death, Trinity B. 15. 34 passed to his son John Parker (1548–1619), whose signature is found on the opening pastedown; the volume appears as number 44 in the list of John's manuscripts in London, Lambeth Palace Library, MS 737.

In addition to the above, five other homiliaries passed through Parker's hands. Cambridge, Corpus Christi College, MS 367 [App 1.1.5] was owned by Parker, who had it bound together with a copy of Ælfric's *De temporibus anni* (CCCC 367, pt. II, fols 1, 2, and 7–10 (Ker no. 62)), the *Vision of Leofric* (fols 48ᵛ–50ᵛ (Ker no. 64)), and other fragments prior to his death in 1575.

Cambridge, University Library, MS Ii. 4. 6 [App 1.2.1] was discovered in 1566, perhaps along with London, British Library, Cotton MS Vitellius C. V [App 1.1.7], in the monastic library of Tavistock Abbey by R. Ferrar [T6 above], a servant of Sir Francis Russell, Earl of Bedford [T15 below]; the following year, Bedford presented it to Parker, who placed his distinctive stamp on the manuscript. He had a table of contents added, an extract from his *A Testimonie of Antiquitie* inserted after the Ælfrician homily which it quotes (*CH* II.15 (no. 21.20)), and the volume bound, his binders characteristically including metal bosses, a title-

---

[19] Identified informally by Dr Tim Bolton on 19 January 2005.

label for the cover, and binding and supply leaves.[20] He also 'tidied' the initial and final entries in the volume: the first, acephalous homily he attempted to excise by pasting fol. 7 to fol. 6, pasting fol. 9 to fol. 8, and erasing what text remained visible on fol. 9[v]; the missing conclusion to the last homily he had copied onto supply leaves inserted for the purpose. The manuscript was one of those left by Parker to Cambridge University Library in 1574.

London, British Library, Cotton MS Faustina A. IX [App 1.2.6] and London, British Library, Cotton MS Vespasian D. XIV [App 2.4] both contain key annotations by Joscelyn [see T7 above] on which Parker drew when printing the preface to the *Letter to Sigefyrth* and an Ælfrician homily for Easter (*CH* II.15) in *A Testimonie of Antiquitie*. To Parker's circle is also due the addition in Cotton Faustina A. IX of a supply leaf (fol. 1) with its Parkerian title on the recto: 'Sermones anglicæ siue Saxonicæ 36' — '36' referring to the number of Anglo-Saxon homilies ostensibly found therein.[21]

Finally, it was Parker who joined Part I of Cambridge, Corpus Christi College, MS 201 [App 3.2] to Part II, pp. 179–272, a Latin and Old English copy of the *Capitula* of Theodulf of Orléans; Part II had formerly been bound with CCCC 191, which in turn had been joined to Cambridge, Corpus Christi College, MS 196 up until the thirteenth century. Found at Tavistock Abbey in 1566, Part I appears to have rested for a time in the collection of Edward Cradocke [T5 above]; from Cradocke the manuscript passed into the hands of Parker, perhaps out of gratitude for Parker's role in appointing Cradocke in 1570 to the Church of St Mary Aldermary in London and to Canterbury Cathedral as a preacher that same year. William Lambarde [T8 above], in any event, copying pp. 97–101 into the commonplace book of his friend Laurence Nowell [T9 above] in 1571, noted that his source was *liber* [...] *Mathaei Cantuariensis Archiepiscopi* (University of California at Los Angeles, University Research Library, Department of Special Collections 170/159, fol. 210[r]; 'a book [...] of Matthew Archbishop of Canterbury'). As Lambarde appears not to have been aware of CCCC 201 in 1568, when he

---

[20] Some of these leaves, concerning a will of which Richard Tottenham (Abbot of Quarr, 1508–21) was an executor, appear also in Cambridge, Corpus Christi College, SP. 438; see Ker, *Catalogue*, pp. xli, 34, and 35.

[21] Certain multi-part homilies are counted as single units in modern editions (*CH* II.5 (Ker no. 153.7–8), 12 (no. 153.16–17), and 16 (no. 153.27–28)), which may account for the discrepancy between Parker's count (36) and that of Ker (38). (Treating the three multi-part homilies as single units results in my own count (35), three less than Ker's.)

published his *Archaionomia*, between 1568 and 1571 Parker thus likely assumed ownership of the manuscript.

On CCCC 201 Parker left his typical marks. In addition to joining Part I to Part II, he paginated the manuscript in red pencil, added both paper and parchment sixteenth-century flyleaves, 'tidied' its first page by erasing thirty-eight lines of an acephalous text, filled the space with a contents-list perhaps written by his son John, and had the volume rebound. Fragments of one of the flyleaves, a sixteenth-century court-case record, also appear in two other manuscripts rebound by Parker: Cambridge, University Library, MS Kk. 3. 18, and Cambridge, Trinity College, MS R. 5. 34 (725). Budny posits that the record may conceivably have served as a wrapper for CUL Kk. 3. 18 when Parker acquired that manuscript from Robert Talbot.[22] Both Joscelyn and Parker annotated CCCC 201, with Parker quoting from p. 82 (Wulfstan's *Sermo Lupi ad Anglos* (Ker no. 49B.40)) in his *De antiquitate Britannicæ ecclesiæ* (London, 1572), p. 63. As CCCC 201 is either absent from or appears as a late addition in the copies of Parker's bequest to Corpus Christi, it appears not to have come immediately to the college on his death in 1575 (Ker, *Catalogue*, p. 90). Rather, for a time it may have formed part of the collection of John Parker [T11 below].[23]

---

[22] Budny, *Illustrated Catalogue*, I, 480.

[23] Recent studies of Parker include Nancy C. Bjorklund, 'Matthew Parker and the Reform of the English Church During the Reigns of Henry VIII and Edward VI' (unpublished doctoral dissertation, University of California, Irvine, 1987; abstract in *Dissertation Abstracts International-A*, 48 (1987), 1522); Robert Bowers, 'The Chapel Royal, the First Edwardian Prayer Book, and Elizabeth's Settlement of Religion, 1559', *Historical Journal*, 43 (2000), 317–44; Eric J. Carlson, 'Clerical Marriage and the English Reformation', *Journal of British Studies*, 31 (1992), 1–31; Patrick Collinson, 'Episcopacy and Quasi-Episcopacy in the Elizabethan Church', in *Miscellanea historiae ecclesiasticae*, ed. by Bernard Vogler (Brussels, 1987), VIII, 229–38; Bruce Dickins, 'The Making of the Parker Library', *TCBS*, 6 (1972), 19–34; Timothy Graham, 'Matthew Parker and his Manuscripts: A Study of an Elizabethan Library and its Use', in *A History of Libraries in Britain and Ireland*, vol. I, ed. by Elisabeth Leedham-Green and Teresa Webber (Cambridge, 2005), pp. 322–41; Graham, 'Matthew Parker and the Conservation of Manuscripts: The Case of CUL MS Ii. 2. 4', *TCBS*, 10 (1995), 630–41; Graham, 'A Parkerian Transcript of the List of Bishop Leofric's Procurements for Exeter Cathedral: Matthew Parker, the Exeter Book, and Cambridge University Library MS Ii.2.11', *TCBS*, 10 (1994), 421–55 + plates; *The Recovery of the Past in Early Elizabethan England: Documents by John Bale and John Joscelyn from the Circle of Matthew Parker*, ed. by Timothy Graham and Andrew G. Watson (Cambridge, 1998); Graham, 'The Beginnings of Old English Studies: Evidence from the Manuscripts of Matthew Parker', in *Back to the Manuscripts: Papers from the Symposium 'The Integrated Approach to Manuscript Studies: A New Horizon' Held at the Eighth General Meeting of the Japan Society for Medieval English Studies, Tokyo, December 1992*, ed. by Shuji Sato (Toyko, 1997), pp. 29–50; Suzanne C. Hagedorn,

[T11] Parker, Sir John (1548–1618/19), antiquarian; Knight from 1603.[24] The elder of two surviving sons of Matthew Parker [T10 above], John and his brother Matthew (1551–74) spent five of their early years living in hiding with their father in Norfolk, after married clergy fell into disfavour with the ascent of Mary in 1553. On Elizabeth's succession in 1558 and his father's subsequent appointment as Archbishop of Canterbury, John lived not in the ecclesiastical palaces but in one of two houses purchased by the Archbishop in Lambeth and in Bekesbourne, Kent — the displacement itself testifying to the continuing controversy under Elizabeth surrounding clerical matrimony. On his brother's death, John inherited the two properties along with St Mary's Hostel, Cambridge, purchased for their mother before her death in 1570; the libraries of these three houses are inventoried in London, Lambeth Palace Library, MS 737, a book owned and signed by John. Two homiliaries appear as part of this inventory. In Cambridge, Trinity College, MS B. 15. 34 [App 1.2.5], John's signature is found on the opening pastedown; the volume appears as number 44 in Lambeth 737. Cambridge, Corpus Christi College, MS 201 [App 3.2] is either absent from or appears as a late addition in the copies of Parker's bequest to Corpus Christi; consequently, it appears not to have come immediately to the college on his death in 1575, but may for a time have

'Matthew Parker and Asser's *Ælfredi regis res gestæ*', *Princeton University Library Chronicle*, 51 (1989), 74–90; Christopher Haigh, *English Reformations: Religion, Politics, and Society Under the Tudors* (Oxford, 1993); C. P. Hall, 'The Guild of Corpus Christi and the Foundation of Corpus Christi College: An Investigation of the Documents', in *Medieval Cambridge: Essays on the Pre-Reformation University*, ed. by P. Zutshi (Rochester, 1993), pp. 65–91; Catherine Hall, 'Matthew Parker as Annotator: The Case of Winchester Cathedral MS XXB', *TCBS*, 10 (1995), 642–45; Hall, 'Matthew Parker in Cambridge: An Exhibition in the Parker Library, October 1993 – February 1994', *OEN*, 27 (1993), A1–A8; Theodore H. Leinbaugh 'Ælfric's Sermo de Sacrificio in Die Pascae: Anglican Polemic in the Sixteenth and Seventeenth Centuries', in *Anglo-Saxon Scholarship*, ed. by Berkhout and Gatch, pp. 51–68; Peter J. Lucas, 'A testimonye of verye ancient tyme? Some Manuscript Models for the Parkerian Anglo-Saxon Type-designs', in *Of the Making of Books: Medieval Manuscripts, their Scribes and Readers: Essays Presented to M. B. Parkes*, ed. by P. R. Robinson and Rivkah Zim (Aldershot, 1997), pp. 147–88; Diarmaid MacCulloch, *The Later Reformation in England, 1547–1603* (New York, 1990); R. I. Page, *Matthew Parker and his Books, Sandars Lectures in Bibliography Delivered on 14, 16, and 18 May 1990 at the University of Cambridge* (Kalamazoo, 1993); Richard Rex, *Henry VIII and the English Reformation* (Basingstoke, 2006); Vivienne Sanders, 'The Household of Archbishop Parker and the Influencing of Public Opinion', *Journal of Ecclesiastical History*, 34 (1983), 534–47; and *ODNB*, XLII, 707–28.

[24] Alastair Bellany and Andrew McRae state that John sat in the parliaments of 1589, 1593, 1601, and 1604 (*Early Stuart Libels: An Edition of Poetry from Manuscript Sources* <http://www.earlystuartlibels.net/htdocs/pdf/esl.pdf> [accessed 1 July 2007], p. 189, n. 83), but I have been unable to corroborate this information.

formed part of John Parker's collection, being possibly the 'Miscellan[ea] quedam saxonicè' appearing as number 102 in the Lambeth 737 list.[25]

[T12] Pilkington, James (1520–76), preacher and bishop; Fellow of St John's College, Cambridge, from *c.* 1539; Regius Professor of Divinity, Cambridge from 1559; Master of St John's, 1559–61; and Bishop of Durham from 1561. With much of James's career was intertwined that of his younger brother, Leonard [T13 below]. Both fled to the Continent after Mary I came to power in 1553; under Elizabeth, both returned to their undergraduate college of St John's, where James and Leonard were successively appointed Master. Both took decisive stands in the hotly contested subject of priestly marriage by taking wives — James once, in or before 1564, the relationship perhaps initially being kept secret; Leonard twice, first while on the Continent and then as a widower in 1597, two years before his death. In 1564, three years after James's appointment as bishop, he brought his brother to Durham with him, previously having lamented the challenges of the diocese and feelings of isolation. While James was far more antagonistic to Catholicism than his brother, both were committed to Protestant education, James founding in 1556 a grammar school in Rivington, Lancashire of which Leonard became overseer on James's death in 1576. One of the brothers — either James in 1574 or Leonard in 1599[26] — gave to the University of Cambridge a key volume of Ælfrician homilies, Cambridge, University Library, MS Gg. 3. 28 [App 1.1.1].[27]

[T13] Pilkington, Leonard (1527–99), clergyman and academic; Fellow of St John's College, Cambridge, 1546–*c.* 1553 and from 1559; Master of St John's, 1561–64; Regius Professor of Divinity, Cambridge, 1561–62; and Prebendary of Durham, 1567–99. Much of Leonard's career was centred around his college of St John's: graduating with a BA in 1544, he was appointed fellow there in 1546,

---

[25] See further Carl T. Berkhout, 'The Parkerian Legacy of a Scheide Manuscript: William of Malmesbury's Gesta Regum Anglorum', *Princeton University Library Chronicle*, 55 (1994), 277–86; and Sheila Strongman, 'John Parker's Manuscripts: An Edition of the Lists in Lambeth Palace MS 737', *TCBS*, 7 (1977), 1–27.

[26] See Ker, *Catalogue*, p. 21, and *Ælfric's Catholic Homilies: The First Series, Text*, ed. by Peter Clemoes, EETS: SS, 17 (Oxford, 1997), p. 25, and Ker, p. liv, for these assertions, respectively.

[27] On James Pilkington, see Felicity Heal, *Of Prelates and Princes: A Study of the Economic and Social Position of the Tudor Episcopate* (Cambridge, 1980); David Marcombe, 'A Rude and Heady People: The Local Community and the Rebellion of the Northern Earls', in *The Last Principality: Politics, Religion and Society in the Bishopric of Durham, 1494–1660*, ed. by D. Marcombe (Nottingham, 1987), pp. 117–51; Brett Usher, 'Durham and Winchester Episcopal Estates', *Journal of Ecclesiastical History*, 49 (1998), 393–406; and *ODNB*, XLIV, 318–21.

mathematical examiner in 1548, lecturer in mathematics in 1550, senior fellow in 1551, lecturer in Hebrew in 1561, and ultimately Master of the college in 1561, succeeding his older brother James [T12 above]. A hiatus in his advancement came with the accession of Mary I in 1553, when he was ejected from his fellowship and fled with James to the Continent; to this post Leonard was restored under Elizabeth after the death of his wife Katherine, whom he had married while in exile. In 1564, three years after James's consecration as Bishop of Durham and Leonard's installation as Master, James had Leonard appointed to the rectory of Whitburn, Durham, and then installed as a canon of Durham Cathedral in 1567. On his death, Leonard bequeathed to the University of Cambridge seventeen books and possibly one Anglo-Saxon homiliary: Cambridge, University Library, MS Gg. 3. 28 [App 1.1.1], though the volume may have been given to Cambridge by James in 1574.[28] Leonard's signature appears on fol. 1 of the homiliary.[29]

[T14] Russell, Sir Francis (1526/27–85), second Earl of Bedford from 1555; Lord Warden of the Stannaries, 1559–80; Knight of the Garter, 1564; Member, Queen's Council of the North from 1561; and Lieutenant-General in the North from 1565. Sir Francis was the son of John Russell, privy councillor and lord privy seal to Henry VIII. Associated with Elizabeth from the time of Wyatt's rebellion (1544), he became a close friend of William Cecil, later her chief counsellor, who deployed him on diplomatic missions in Scotland and the Continent. Personally, he was a staunch supporter of evangelical Protestantism, though he appears not to have played a major role in advocating for Protestant reform in parliament. His library reveals a considerable interest in the works of continental reformers, and included in addition two Anglo-Saxon homiliaries: London, British Library, Cotton MS Vitellius C. V [App 1.1.7] and Cambridge, University Library, MS Ii. 4. 6 [App 1.2.1], discovered in the monastic library of Tavistock Abbey in 1566 by one of his servants, one R. Ferrar [T6 above]. In 1567, Bedford presented CUL Ii. 4. 6 to Matthew Parker [T10 above]; Cotton Vitellius C. V remained in Bedford's possession at least until 1584, but passed thereafter into the possession of Sir Robert Cotton [S5 below], perhaps following Bedford's death in 1585.[30]

---

[28] See Ker, *Catalogue*, p. liv versus Ker, p. 21 and *First Series*, ed. by Clemoes, p. 25.

[29] For Leonard Pilkington, see H. C. Porter, *Reform and Reaction in Tudor Cambridge* (Cambridge, 1958); and *ODNB*, XLII, 323–24.

[30] Portraits of Russell appear in Cristina H. Garrett, *The Marian Exiles: A Study in the Origins of Elizabethan Puritanism* (Cambridge, 1938; repr. 1966); *History of Parliament, Commons, 1509–58*, ed. by S. T. Bindoff (London, 1982), III, 230–31; and *ODNB*, XLVIII, 238–41.

[T15] Scory, John (d. 1585), clergyman; Dominican friar, *c.* 1530–38; Bishop of Rochester, 1551–52; Bishop of Chichester, 1552–53; and Bishop of Hereford, 1559–1685. Volatile and contentious, Scory was an influential figure in the early Anglican Church. A gifted preacher, he came to the notice of Archbishop Thomas Cranmer after the dissolution in 1538 of the Dominican house in which Scory had been a friar. Initially commissioned by Cranmer to evangelize his Canterbury diocese, Scory would prove a trial both to his conservative parishioners and to his patron, being the subject of protest and then imprisonment for his inflammatory sermons. It was likely Scory's initiative that led in September 1553 to the mass distribution of an unpublished treatise by Cranmer condemning the Mass; Cranmer was immediately arrested, and Scory went into exile the following June. Settling in Emden, Germany, Scory turned the town into a centre of Protestant printing, publishing not only works by English reformers, such as Cranmer's influential *Defensio de uerae doctrinae de sacramentis* (Emden, 1557), but personal translations of church fathers such as Augustine, seeking like Matthew Parker [T10 above] to demonstrate the consonance of Anglican doctrine with that of the early Church. As the senior ranking bishop in exile, Scory was assured a prominent post following Elizabeth's accession, and indeed found himself appointed to the bishopric of Hereford, where he spent his last days wrestling with a staunchly conservative parish marked by Catholic sympathies. It was from Hereford that Scory sent 'iii saxon bokes' to Matthew Parker, two of which may have been Cambridge, Corpus Christi College, MS 188 [App 1.1.3] and MS 162, Part I [App 1.2.2].[31]

[Selden, John (1584–1654): see S15 below]

[Spelman, Sir Henry (1563/64–1641): see S16 below]

[T16] Talbot, Robert (1505/06–58), antiquarian; Prebendary and Canon, Norwich Cathedral, 1547–58. Educated at New College, Oxford, where he received his BA in 1525 and MA in 1529, Talbot went on to serve as schoolmaster in Essex and to hold ecclesiastical benefices in various counties before being associated with

---

[31] See James, *Corpus Christi*, I, 445, and Budny, *Illustrated Catalogue*, I, 572–73, who concludes that CCCC 188 is perhaps a more likely candidate than CCCC 162. Scory's life is treated in Edward J. Baskerville, *A Chronological Bibliography of Propaganda and Polemic Published in English Between 1553 and 1558: From the Death of Edward VI to the Death of Mary I* (Philadelphia, 1979); Collinson, *Elizabethan Puritan Movement*; Heal, *Of Prelates and Princes*; Diarmaid MacCulloch, *Thomas Cranmer: A Life* (New Haven, 1996); Andrew Pettegree, 'The English Church at Emden', in *Marian Protestantism: Six Studies*, ed. by Andrew Pettegree (Brookfield, 1996), pp. 10–38; and *ODNB*, XLIX, 322–24.

Norwich Cathedral in 1547. The first person known to collect and read Anglo-Saxon manuscripts after the Dissolution, Talbot influenced a number of other leading figures in the field. He exchanged Old English materials with John Leland (*c.* 1503–52) and Robert Recorde (*c.* 1512–58); his library was consulted by John Bale (1495–1563); and his leading work, *Annotationes Itinerarii Antonini*, a topographical examination of the Antonine Itinerary or register of roads in Roman Britain, was extracted by William Camden [S4 below] and published by Thomas Hearne [S10B below] in the early eighteenth century. Talbot's interests included linguistic as well as topographical matters, his Old English–Latin word-list being the first of its kind in early modern England. On his death, his library was scattered, but certain volumes, such as Talbot's autograph of the *Annotationes* (Cambridge, Corpus Christi College, MS 379) and transcripts of Anglo-Saxon charters (Cambridge, Corpus Christi College, MS 111), passed into the hands of Matthew Parker [T10 above]. Two homiliaries have tangential connections to Talbot: annotations in his hand appear in London, British Library, Cotton MS Vespasian D. XIV [App 2.4], and fragments of one of the flyleaves in Cambridge, Corpus Christi College, MS 201, Part I [App 3.2] appear in Cambridge, University Library, MS Kk. 3. 18, for which they may conceivably have served as a wrapper when Parker acquired CUL Kk. 3. 18 from Talbot.[32]

[Theyer, John (bap. 1598, d. 1673): see S17 below]

[Whelock [or Wheelocke], Abraham (*c.* 1593–1653): see S18 below]

---

[32] On Talbot, see *Recovery of the Past*, ed. by Graham and Watson; Timothy Graham, 'Robert Talbot's "Old Saxonice Bede": Cambridge University Library, MS Kk. 3. 18 and the "Alphabeticum Norwagiaum" of British Library, Cotton MSS, Domitian A. IX', in *Books and Collectors, 1200–1700: Essays Presented to Andrew Watson*, ed. by J. P. Carley and C. G. C. Tite (London, 1997), pp. 295–316; Graham, 'The Earliest Old English Word-List from Tudor England', *Medieval English Studies Newsletter*, 35 (1996), 4–7; Graham, 'Early Modern Users of Claudius B. IV: Robert Talbot and William L'Isle', in *The Old English Hexateuch: Aspects and Approaches*, ed. by Rebecca Barnhouse and Benjamin C. Withers (Kalamazoo, 2000), pp. 271–316; N. R. Ker, 'Medieval Manuscripts from Norwich Cathedral Library', *TCBS*, 1 (1949–53), 1–28 (repr. in *Books, Collectors and Libraries: Studies in the Medieval Heritage*, ed. by A. G. Watson (London, 1985), pp. 243–72); R. I. Page, 'A Sixteenth-Century Runic Manuscript', in *Studies in Honour of René Derolez*, ed. by A. M. Simon-Vandenbergen (Gent, 1987), pp. 384–90 (repr. in Page, *Runes, and Runic Inscriptions* (Rochester, 1995), pp. 289–94); C. E. Wright, 'Robert Talbot and Domitian A. IX', *Medium Ævum*, 6 (1937), 170–71; and *ODNB*, LIII, 722–23. See also Budny, *Illustrated Catalogue*, I, 480, and Ker, *Catalogue*, p. 1.

[T17] Whitgift, John (1530/31?–1604), administrator and archbishop; Lady Margaret Professor of Divinity, Cambridge, 1563–69; Master of Trinity College, Cambridge, from 1570; Bishop of Worcester from 1577; Member of the Privy Council from 1586; and Archbishop of Canterbury, 1583–1604. Throughout his career, Whitgift was a strong denouncer of the papacy, an advocate of Calvinist doctrine, and a defender of episcopal versus presbyterian church government. The last issue, which sharply divided the university, set him in opposition to Thomas Cartwright, a subsequent Lady Margaret professor, against whom Whitgift wrote with the support of Archbishop Matthew Parker [T10 above]. His stance against the puritans also brought him into conflict with Robert Beale [T1 above], while his greatest ally in this regard was Sir Christopher Hatton [T6B above]. One of the manuscripts bequeathed by Whitgift to Trinity College was Cambridge, Trinity College, MS B. 15. 34 [App 1.2.5], a volume previously belonging to Parker.[33]

[T18] Wolsey, Thomas (1470/71–1530), royal minister; Royal Chaplain from 1507; Dean of Lincoln Cathedral and Royal Almoner to Henry VIII from 1509; Dean of York from 1513; Bishop of Lincoln and then Archbishop of York from 1514; Cardinal from 1515; and Lord Chancellor from 1516. Rising swiftly under Henry VIII, Wolsey soon became the controlling figure in state matters. The endeavours to which he brought his considerable gifts and energy were manifold, furthering royal aims regarding diplomatic relations on the Continent, war with France, control of the nobility, the legal system, and perhaps most of all the Great Matter of 1527, facilitating Henry's divorce of Catherine of Aragon and marriage to Anne Boleyn. Hesitant in the face of the diplomatic ramifications of such a divorce, and increasingly blamed for royal failure to obtain it, Wolsey incurred the displeasure both of Henry and of Anne, a longstanding rival for Henry's political favour. By 1528 Wolsey had been forced to resign as lord chancellor; by 1530 his downfall was complete after being charged with high treason. During his ascendancy, however, Wolsey consciously cultivated an opulence in keeping with his status as royal representative, spending considerable sums on art, architecture, music, and centres of learning, particularly at Oxford. One manuscript likely

---

[33] For more on Whitgift, see L. H. Carlson, 'Archbishop Whitgift: His Supporters and Opponents', *Anglican and Episcopal History*, 57 (1987), 285–301; E. Gilliam and W. J. Tighe, 'To "Run With the Time": Whitgift and the Lambeth Articles, and the Politics of Religious Controversy in Late 16th Century England', *Sixteenth Century Journal*, 23 (1992), 325–40; Peter Lake, *Moderate Puritans and the Elizabethan Church* (Cambridge, 1982); Lake, *Anglicans and Puritans? Presbyterianism and English Conformist thought from Whitgift to Hooker* (Cambridge, 1988); and *ODNB*, LVIII, 717–28.

owned by Wolsey is London, British Library, Royal MS 7. C. XII [App 1.1.9], the unique witness to the earliest known stage of Ælfric's First Series of *Catholic Homilies*, with notes in Ælfric's own hand; Wolsey's name appears on fol. 2[r] of the manuscript, two folios before that of Robert Beale [T1 above].[34]

[Young [Junius], Patrick (1584–1652): see S20 below]

The Stuarts: 1603–1714

[S1] Bagford, John (1650/51–1716), bookseller and antiquarian. Originally a shoemaker, and with little academic education, from 1686 Bagford collected and traded books around Holborn, supplying such major collectors as Samuel Pepys [S14 below] and Edward and Robert Harley [S8B below]; for the last, Bagford assembled from gathered materials a set of texts for which he is chiefly remembered: the Bagford Ballads. During these years, he became friends with a number of manuscript scholars, including Humfrey Wanley (1672–1726), with whom he attempted to refound the Society of Antiquaries in 1707, and Thomas Hearne [S10B below], whom he met at Oxford and who became a lifelong collaborator. Bagford provided Hearne with material for his private collections and printed work, Hearne published a 1715 study by Bagford on historical artefacts in London, and both contributed to a 1721 edition of Chaucer. One fragment found by Bagford, used as a pastedown by a binder and collected by Bagford as an Anglo-Saxon specimen, was London, British Library, Harley MS 5915, fol. 13 [App 1.1.8]. After Bagford's death, it was purchased along with the rest of his manuscripts by Edward Harley.[35]

[S2] Barlow, Thomas (1608/09–91), Keeper of the Bodleian Library from 1652 to 1660; Lady Margaret Professor of Divinity from 1660; Provost of Queen's Col-

---

[34] Further studies of Wolsey include J. D. Alsop, 'The Structure of early Tudor Finance, 1509–1558', in *Revolution Reassessed: Revisions in the History of Tudor Government and Administration*, ed. by C. Coleman and D. R. Starkey (Oxford, 1986), pp. 135–62; *Cardinal Wolsey: Church, State and Art*, ed. by S. J. Gunn and P. G. Lindley (Cambridge, 1991); Peter J. Gwyn, *The King's Cardinal: The Rise and Fall of Thomas Wolsey* (London, 1990); Mervyn E. James, *Society, Politics and Culture: Studies in Early Modern England* (Cambridge, 1986); Helen Miller, *Henry VIII and the English Nobility* (Oxford, 1986); and *ODNB*, LX, 17–38.

[35] On Bagford, see Milton McC. Gatch, 'John Bagford, Bookseller and Antiquary', *British Library Journal*, 12 (1986), 150–71; Gatch, 'John Bagford as a Collector and Disseminator of Manuscript Fragments', *The Library*, 6th series, 7 (1985), 95–114; and *ODNB*, III, 228–29.

lege, Oxford from 1657; Archdeacon of Oxford from 1664; and Bishop of Lincoln from 1675. Barlow was a firm believer in monarchical authority and in Calvinist doctrine, a staunch opponent of Catholicism, and a notable teacher of philosophy at Oxford. He was also the subject of some controversy, being seen by many as threading his way through the shifting politics of the English Civil War and Restoration by shifting sides — or at least emphasizing on different occasions various aspects of his beliefs. In 1659, during his tenure at the Bodleian, the library acquired the considerable collection of John Selden [S15 below], consisting of some eight thousand printed works and manuscripts. It was likely sequent to this period, however, that he entered a note in Oxford, Bodleian Library, MS Hatton 116 [App 1.3.8; see also App 3.6] identifying a Latin collect on p. 398 as corresponding to 25 November, St Katherine's Day, as the manuscript was not bequeathed to the Bodleian by Sir Christopher Hatton [T6B above] until 1675.[36]

[S3] Bowyer, Robert (*c.* 1560–1621), parliamentary official; Keeper of the Records in the Tower of London, 1604–12; Member of Parliament, 1605–10; and Clerk of the Parliaments, 1610–21. Not to be confused with his grandfather (d. 1552) or his father's brother (d. 1567/68), both of the same name. A student of law in the 1580s, Bowyer came to the notice of Thomas Sackville, later Lord Treasurer and Earl of Dorset, whom he served as secretary. Under Sackville's patronage, Bowyer secured various political posts, in 1594 possibly being chosen to serve as deputy to John Parker [T11 above] in a chancery post — albeit one into which Parker ultimately was not sworn. In 1604 he was appointed Keeper of the Tower records along with Henry Elsynge [S8 below], his relative by marriage to Bowyer's niece, Blanche Highgate. From his father William [T3 above], himself formerly a Keeper of Tower records, Robert inherited a number of volumes from his father's personal collection. Some of these came to augment the library of Sir Robert Cotton [S5 below]; indeed, Ker describes Robert as 'perhaps the most important collector of Old English manuscripts, apart from John Joscelyn [T7 above], from whom

---

[36] Additional information on Barlow may be found in Mark Goldie, 'Danby, the Bishops, and the Whigs', in *The Politics of Religion in Restoration England*, ed. by T. Harris, P. Seaward, and M. Goldie (Oxford, 1990), pp. 75–106; Ian M. Green, *The Re-establishment of the Church of England, 1660–1663* (Oxford, 1978); James R. Jacob, *Henry Stubbe, Radical Protestantism and the Early Enlightenment* (Cambridge, 1983); J. W. Packer, *The Transformation of Anglicanism, 1643–1660, with Special Reference to Henry Hammond* (Manchester, 1969); Paul Seaward, *The Cavalier Parliament and the Reconstruction of the Old Regime, 1661–1667* (Cambridge, 1989); John Spurr, *The Restoration Church of England, 1646–1689* (New Haven, 1991); and *ODNB*, III, 927–32.

Cotton may have acquired manuscripts directly' (*Catalogue*, p. lvi). Oxford, Bodleian Library, MSS Bodley 340 + Bodley 342 [App 1.1.10], however, took another path: inherited likely from his father on William's death in 1569 or 1570, from Robert it passed into the hands of Sir Walter Cope [T4 above], who bequeathed it to the Bodleian Library in 1602.[37]

[S4] Camden, William (1551–1623), antiquary and herald; Second Master of Westminster School, 1575–93; Master of Westminster, 1593–97; Prebend of Ilfracombe, Salisbury Cathedral, 1589–1623; and Clarenceux King of Arms, 1597–1623. Ultimately responsible in 1620 for endowing the Camden professorship of history at Oxford University, Camden was an academic marked initially by a difficult relationship with the institution: a religious conservative in a centre of puritan support, he was twice denied a fellowship between 1566 and 1569, unsuccessful in petitioning for his BA in 1570 and for an MA in 1588, awarded the former degree at last in 1574, having left Oxford without one, and offered the latter degree in recognition of his achievements in 1613 — a distinction he would then reject. In 1575 he took up a post at Westminster School, one of the most prestigious in the nation; William Cecil, Lord Burghley presided over it from 1576 and was instrumental in encouraging Camden's research. Working with the support of such antiquarians as William Lambarde [T8 above; see also Sir William Dugdale, S7 below], Camden's study of primary historical sources — including topographical, philological, numismatic, and other non-literary evidence, in which he was a pioneer — resulted in 1586 in the publication of the *Britannia*, a collection of documentation from pre-Roman Britain. An instant success, the *Britannia* was enlarged and reprinted five times in Camden's lifetime and continued to be published over the eighteenth and early nineteenth centuries. In this work, as in papers presented in the Society of Antiquaries later to be published by Thomas Hearne [S10B below], Camden modelled a careful, methodological approach that would influence and garner interest in the field of material and cultural history. In 1595, he published what would become for over a century the standard Greek grammar in Britain. In 1597, he was appointed Clarenceux King of Arms, one of the three chief offices in the College of Arms, which met in the same house as the Society of Antiquarians and arbitrated heraldic matters related to genealogies, titles, and degrees in the kingdom. In 1603 and 1605, he published two additional historical studies: *Anglica, Normannica, Hibernica, Cambrica, a veteribus scripta,*

---

[37] On Bowyer, see Robert Bowyer, *The Parliamentary Diary of Robert Bowyer, 1606–7*, ed. by David Harris Wilson (Minneapolis, 1931); and *ODNB*, VI, 995.

an edition of early English chronicles, and *Remaines of a Greater Worke Concerning Britain*, material accessory to the *Britannia* which included an anthology of medieval poetry and a study of the English language; the *Remaines* he largely derived from the library of his former student and longstanding friend, Sir Robert Cotton [S5 below]. It was with Cotton's help that Camden produced his final major work, the *Annales rerum Anglicarum, et Hibernicarum, regnante Elizabetha*, the first biography of Elizabeth, which he completed in 1617; it was also to Cotton that Camden bequeathed the bulk of his library. One Cotton manuscript borrowed by Camden was London, British Library, Cotton MS Otho B. X + Oxford, Bodleian Library, MS Rawlinson Q. e. 20 [App 2.3]; Cotton records the loan in London, British Library, Harley MS 6018.[38]

[Cope, Sir Walter (1553?–1614): see T4 above]

[S5] Cotton, Sir Robert Bruce, first baronet (1571–1631), politician and antiquary; Justice of the Peace for Huntingdonshire, 1601, and for Westminster, *c.* 1628; Member of Parliament for Newton, Isle of Wight, 1601, for Huntingdonshire, 1604, 1606, and 1610, for Old Sarum, 1624, and for Thetford, 1625; Knight from 1603; and Baronet from 1611. Not to be confused with Sir Robert Cotton MP (1644–1717), son of Sir Thomas Cotton [S6 below], or Robert Cotton, fifth baronet (1669–1749), son of Sir John Cotton, third baronet [S6B below]. Though a student at Jesus College, Cambridge from 1581 to 1585 or 1586, and at the Middle Temple from 1589, perhaps more formative for Cotton were his early years at Westminster School with William Camden [S4 above], alongside whom he would

---

[38] Resources on Camden include George C. Boon, 'Camden and the Britannia', *Archaeologia Cambrensis*, 136 (1988), 1–19 + plates; William Camden, *The History of the Most Renowned and Victorious Princess Elizabeth Late Queen of England*, ed. by W. T. MacCaffrey (Chicago, 1970); Richard L. DeMolen, 'The Library of William Camden', *Proceedings of the American Philosophical Society*, 128 (1984), 326–409; Wyman H. Herendeen, 'Wanton Discourse and the Engines of Time: William Camden – Historian among Poets-Historical', in *Renaissance Rereadings: Intertext and Context*, ed. by M. C. Horowitz, A. J. Cruz, and W. A. Furman (Urbana, 1988), pp. 142–56; Herendeen, 'William Camden: Historian, Herald, and Antiquary', *Studies in Philology*, 85 (1988), 192–210; Herendeen, '"Like a Circle Bounded in Itself": Jonson, Camden, and the Strategies of Praise', *Journal of Medieval and Renaissance Studies*, 11 (1981), 137–67; Bernard Nurse, 'The 1610 Edition of Camden's *Britannia*', *Antiquaries Journal*, 73 (1993), 158–60; Stuart Piggott, 'William Camden and the *Britannia*', *Proceedings of the British Academy*, 37 (1951), 199–217; Elisabeth M. C. van Houts, 'Camden, Cotton and the Chronicles of the Norman Conquest of England in 1066', *British Library Journal*, 18 (1992), 148–62; Daniel R. Woolf, *The Idea of History in Early Stuart England: Erudition, Ideology and the 'Light of Truth' from the Accession of James I to the Civil War* (Toronto, 1990); and *ODNB*, IX, 603–14.

pursue historical and etymological research in the Society of Antiquaries from the late 1580s. After an outbreak of plague in London forced a hiatus in meetings from 1594 to 1598, Cotton petitioned Elizabeth and subsequently James I to found a permanent academic centre for antiquarian study and to create a national library for the purpose by merging his library with the royal one. As debates in parliament came increasingly to hinge on historical precedent for matters of contemporary politics, however, both the Society of Antiquaries and Cotton's library came to be seen as dangerous. Cotton's petition was unsuccessful, the Society ceased meeting in 1607, and the days of open access to Cotton's library were numbered. Though an influential advisor to the monarch and privy council throughout the reigns of James and Charles I, Cotton fell into disfavour after 1627 when in print he urged the monarch to be advised by his whole council rather than by a particular peer — in this case, Charles's favourite, Sir George Villiers, Duke of Buckingham. Charles impounded Cotton's library in 1629 and briefly imprisoned Cotton himself, allowing him only sporadic access to his library before his death despite pardoning him in 1630. Among the numerous scholars indebted to the library for their research were Sir Henry Spelman and John Selden [S16 and S15 below], the latter of whom likely helped Sir Thomas Cotton preserve the collection during the Civil War; like Camden, both Spelman and Selden consulted manuscripts containing Anglo-Saxon homiliaries. Seven such manuscripts were to be found in Cotton's collection: London, British Library, Cotton MS Faustina A. IX [App 1.2.6], which Cotton acquired from Henry Elsynge [S8 below] in October 1597; Cotton MS Julius E. VII [App 1.3.5], which may have been bound with Cotton MS Tiberius B. II and separated by Cotton prior to being catalogued in 1621; Cotton MS Otho B. X + Oxford, Bodleian Library, MS Rawlinson Q. e. 20 [App 2.3], which Cotton obtained from John Joscelyn [T7 above], whose prior ownership Cotton references in London, British Library, Harley MS 6018, when recording the loan of the volume to Camden; Cotton MS Vespasian D. XIV [App 2.4], formerly owned by Laurence Nowell [T9 above]; Cotton MS Vitellius C. V [App 1.1.7], which Cotton likely obtained from Sir Francis Russell [T14 above] and which he signed on the recto of the opening folio, which had been reversed; Cotton MS Vitellius D. XVII [App 2.5], which also appears in his catalogue of 1621; and Oxford, Bodleian Library, MS Bodley 343 [App 1.1.11 and 2.6], which he gave to Oxford's Bodleian Library perhaps in 1601 or 1603.[39]

---

[39] A number of essays treat Robert Cotton, including James P. Carley and Colin G. C. Tite, 'Sir Robert Cotton as Collector of Manuscripts and the Question of Dismemberment: British Library MSS Royal 13 D. I and Cotton Otho D. VIII', *The Library*, 6th series, 14 (1992), 94–99;

[S6] Cotton, Sir Thomas, second baronet (1594–1662), landowner; Member of Parliament in 1624, 1625, 1628, and 1640. Not to be confused with his paternal grandfather (b. in or before 1544, d. 1592) or paternal uncle (b. 1572) of the same name. Perhaps chiefly invested in the management of his estates, Thomas nonetheless shared his father's antiquarian interests. He successfully petitioned for the return of the manuscripts library which had been impounded under Charles I, expanded it, and preserved it thereafter through the English Civil War and Interregnum — a task made the more challenging by Thomas's perceived royalist sympathies and the potentially subversive nature of the collection, which had been confiscated to prevent its use in arguments over political precedent. Thomas's name appears on fols 2^r and 3^r respectively of London, British Library, Cotton MS Faustina A. IX [App 1.2.6] and Cotton MS Julius E. VII [App 1.3.5]. Cotton Faustina A. IX he loaned in 1641 to Sir William Le Neve [S12 below] along with Cotton MS Vitellius C. V [App 1.1.7], and in the same year loaned Cotton MS Vitellius D. XVII [App 2.5] to John Selden [S15 below].[40]

[S6B] [Cotton, Sir John, third baronet (1621–1702), landowner and politician; Member of Parliament for Huntingdonshire, 1661 and 1665. Not to be confused with his son, John Cotton (d. 1681), his grandson, Sir John Cotton, fourth baronet (c. 1680–1731), or his cousin, Sir John Cotton, sixth baronet (d. 1752). A royalist sympathizer, he nonetheless played no part in the Civil War and in 1688 accepted the deposition of Charles II's brother, the Catholic James II, in favour of Charles's nephew William III. It was under William in 1700 or 1701 that he sold to the nation the family library of books and some 958 manuscripts.[41]]

David Howarth, 'Sir Robert Cotton and the Commemoration of Famous Men', *British Library Journal*, 18 (1992), 1–28; Roger B. Manning, 'Antiquarianism and the Seigneurial Reaction: Sir Robert and Sir Thomas Cotton and their Tenants', *Historical Research*, 63 (1990), 277–88; Graham Parry, *The Trophies of Time: English Antiquaries of the Seventeenth Century* (Oxford, 1995); Kevin Sharpe, *Sir Robert Cotton 1586–1631: History and Politics in Early Modern England* (Oxford, 1979); Elizabeth Cover Teviotdale, 'Some Classified Catalogues of the Cottonian Library', *British Library Journal*, 18 (1992), 74–87; Colin G. C. Tite, 'The Early Catalogues of the Cotton Library', *British Library Journal*, 6 (1980), 144–57; Tite, '"Lost or Stolen or Strayed": A Survey of Manuscripts Formerly in the Cotton Library', *British Library Journal*, 18 (1992), 107–47; Tite, *Sir Robert Cotton and his Library* (London, 1993); Tite, *The Manuscript Library of Sir Robert Cotton*, Panizzi Lectures, 1993 (London, 1994); van Houts, 'Camden, Cotton and the Chronicles', pp. 148–62; *Sir Robert Cotton as Collector: Essays on an Early Stuart Courtier and his Legacy,* ed. by C. J. Wright (London, 1997); and *ODNB*, XIII, 674–79.

[40] See *ODNB*, XIII, 628.

[41] See *ODNB*, XIII, 628.

[S7] Dugdale, Sir William (1605–86), antiquarian and herald; Blanch Lyon Pursuivant, 1638–39; Rouge Croix Pursuivant from 1639; Norroy King of Arms, *c.* 1660–77; Garter King of Arms from 1677; Knight from 1677. Born in Warwickshire, Dugdale's earliest antiquarian interests involved a history of the county and gentry therein. The project brought him into contact in 1638 with the octogenarian Sir Henry Spelman [S16 below], who became his patron. Spelman recommended Dugdale to Thomas Howard, Earl of Arundel, for the position of herald, and recommended to Dugdale the project that would make his reputation: a historical study of English monasticism. Working with Roger Dodsworth (bap. 1585, d. 1654), and assisted in his study of Old English by William Somner (bap. 1598, d. 1669), Dugdale published the *Monasticon Anglicanum* in three volumes (1655, 1661, and 1673); in distinct contrast to Elizabethan and Jacobean scholarship, which had viewed monasticism with suspicion or disdain, the work established monastic history as a legitimate field for investigation. In 1656, the year after the initial appearance of the *Monasticon*, Dugdale at last published *The Antiquities of Warwickshire*, by now the product of some twenty-five years' work; a careful and thorough study, it follows in the tradition of the county histories by William Lambarde and William Camden [T8 and S4 above]. Other antiquarian research was made possible by Sir Christopher Hatton, first Baron Hatton [S9 below], whom Dugdale met in 1638 and who arranged access to repositories of records such as the Tower of London. Sir Thomas Cotton [S6 above] opened his father's library to Dugdale as well. Two projects of particular interest for Anglo-Saxon studies Dugdale finished in 1664: *Concilia* and *Archaeologus*, the first volumes of which Spelman published in 1639 and 1628 respectively, but which remained unfinished at Spelman's death in 1641. The *Concilia* examined the councils of the Anglo-Saxon Church; the *Archaeologus* defined legal terms found in Anglo-Saxon and Norman documents. On his death, Dugdale's papers passed into Oxford's Ashmolean Museum, established by Dugdale's son-in-law, Elias Ashmole. Beforehand, however, one homiletic collection passed through Dugdale's hands: Oxford, Bodleian Library, MSS Hatton 113 + 114 [App 1.1.12; see also 1.3.7 and 3.4], to which in 1644 he added tables of contents on paper leaves at the end of each volume (Hatton 113, fols 145–46, and Hatton 114, fols 248–49), noting in the process that they were owned by Christopher, first Baron Hatton (Oxford, Bodleian Library, MS Dugdale 29 (6519), fol. 'iv'ᵛ).[42]

---

[42] Dugdale appears as the subject of H. A. Cronne, 'The Study and Use of Charters by English Scholars in the Seventeenth Century: Sir Henry Spelman and Sir William Dugdale', in *English Historical Scholarship in the Sixteenth and Seventeenth Centuries*, ed. by Levi Fox (London, 1956),

[S8] Elsynge, Henry (bap. 1577, d. 1635), parliamentary official and scholar; Keeper of the Records in the Tower of London, 1604–12; and Clerk of the Parliaments, 1621–35. Not to be confused with his father (d. 1582) and son (bap. 1606, d. 1656) of the same name. History primarily remembers Elsynge as a historian of Parliament, a codifier of parliamentary procedure, and a preserver of parliamentary records. His career was intertwined with Robert Bowyer [S3 above], to whom he was related, confusingly, by two indirect means. On the one hand, Elsynge was married to Bowyer's niece, that is, Bowyer's sister's daughter Blanche (Elsynge) Highgate. On the other hand, Elsynge's mother had married Bowyer's elder half-brother, Henry Knyvett: Knyvett was the son of Agnes Harcourt by her first husband, John Knyvett, while Bowyer was Agnes's son by her second husband, William Bowyer [T3 above]; it was Henry Knyvett whom Elsynge's mother, Frances Browne, married two years after the death of Elsynge's father in 1582. Elsynge, therefore, was Robert Bowyer's 'nephew' twice over — both by Elsynge's own marriage and by that of Elsynge's mother; Bowyer's will, however, suggests that the childless Bowyer viewed Elsynge almost like a son. The two were appointed jointly as Keepers of Tower records in 1604, Elsynge assisted Bowyer on the latter's appointment as Clerk of the Parliaments in 1610, and he succeeded Bowyer to the post in 1621. It was from Bowyer's father William, however, that Elsynge acquired London, British Library, Cotton MS Faustina A. IX [App 1.2.6], as attested by John Joscelyn [T7 above] in London, British Library, Cotton MS Vespasian D. VII. From Elsynge, the manuscript passed into the collection of Sir Robert Cotton [S5 above] in 1597.[43]

[S8B] [Harley, Robert, first Earl of Oxford and Mortimer (1661–1724), politician; Member of Parliament for Tregony, 1689, and for New Radnor, 1690–*c.* 1711; Speaker of the House of Commons, 1701–05; Secretary of State for the Northern Department, 1704–08; Chancellor of the Exchequer, 1710–11; and Lord High

---

pp. 73–91; Linda L. Giese, 'An Anonymous Seventeenth-Century Bodleian Manuscript Dictionary: Its Authorship and Significance to Old English Studies', *Bodleian Library Record*, 14 (1992), 145–57; Ann Hughes, *Politics, Society and Civil War in Warwickshire, 1620–1660* (Cambridge, 1987); Stanley G. Mendyk, *Speculum Britanniae: Regional Study, Antiquarianism, and Science in Britain to 1700* (Toronto, 1989); Parry, *Trophies of Time*; David Yerkes, 'Dugdale's *Dictionary* and Somner's *Dictionarium*', *English Language Notes*, 14 (1976), 110–12; and *ODNB*, XVII, 153–57.

[43] On Elsynge, see Henry Elsynge, *The Manner of Holding Parliaments in England* (repr. South Hackensack, 1971); Elizabeth R. Foster, *The Painful Labour of Mr. Elsyng* (Philadelphia, 1972); and *ODNB*, XVIII, 339–40.

Treasurer, 1711–14. The son of a staunch Presbyterian and supporter of parliament during the Civil War, Harley's fortunes rose when in the revolution of 1688 he fought with his father for William, prince of Orange. The following year saw his election to parliament, where mastery of internal procedure and external media — the hiring of writers such as Daniel Defoe and Jonathan Swift to draft pamphlets against his opponents — brought him prominence and power. In 1700–01, he worked with William III on the conditions for the house of Hanover to succeed Anne Stuart, William's heir. Thereafter, with William's and Anne's support, he served repeated terms as Speaker of the House of Commons, became one of Anne's closest advisers, became Northern Secretary of State, and was instrumental in bringing about England's union with Scotland. Though a leader of the Whigs, however, he became disillusioned with the party and was forced to resign his offices in 1708 after alienating his former political allies Lord Godolphin and the Duke of Marlborough. Harley's misfortunes were not to last: by 1710, his influence with Anne had again become such that he displaced Godolphin, was elevated to the peerage, and was appointed Chancellor of the Exchequer and then Lord High Treasurer until Anne's death in 1714. This would be the pinnacle of his career: despite his work on the Hanoverian succession, Harley was stripped of all offices with the ascent of George I, who condemned Harley's support of the 1713 treaty of Utrecht that had ended the War of the Spanish Succession and betrayed (in the King's view) English allies such as Hanover. After his death, however, Harley's influence on scholarship would be immense as a result of his vast library, catalogued by his librarian, Humphrey Wanley (1672–1726). In 1753, the manuscripts collected by Harley and his son Edward (1689–1741) were sold to parliament by Edward's wife and daughter, the Countess of Oxford and the Duchess of Portland. When the British Museum was founded that same year, these volumes became part of the Manuscripts Foundation Collections. One fragment in the collection was London, British Library, Harley MS 5915, fol. 13 (part of the same manuscript as Cambridge, Magdalene College, MS Pepys 2981, no. 16 [App 1.1.8]); it formerly had been owned by John Bagford [S1 above], who had collected it along with other binding scraps as a historical specimen.[44]

---

[44] Further information on Harley may be found in Edward S. Roscoe, *Robert Harley, Earl of Oxford, Prime Minister 1710–1714* (London, 1902); C. E. Wright, *Fontes Harleiani: A Study of the Sources of the Harleian Collection of Manuscripts Preserved in the Department of Manuscripts in the British Museum* (London, 1972); and *ODNB*, XXV, 317–26.

[S9] Hatton, Christopher, first Baron Hatton (bap. 1605, d. 1670), politician and landholder; Member of Parliament, 1625, 1626, and 1640; Knight of the Bath, 1626; Privy Councillor, 1642/43–48 and from 1662; Baron of Kirkby from 1643; and Governor of Guernsey from 1662. The male heir of Sir Christopher Hatton [T6B above], Elizabeth's lord chancellor, Hatton was a prominent landholder of Northamptonshire and active in local politics, serving as MP for Peterborough and Higham Ferrers as well as Clitheroe in Lancashire. A Royalist, Hatton spent much of the Interregnum in France, returning to England to attempt to preserve and then reclaim his estates. A charter member of the Royal Society following the Restoration, Hatton was a patron of Sir William Dugdale [S7 above] and a collector of manuscripts and books. Among his works acquired by 1644 were three Anglo-Saxon homiliaries: Oxford, Bodleian Library, MSS Hatton 113 + 114 [App 1.1.12, 1.3.7, and 3.4], Hatton 115 [App 3.5], and Hatton 116 [App 1.3.8 and 3.6]; these on his death passed to his son Christopher, first Viscount Hatton [S10 below].[45]

[S10] Hatton, Christopher, first Viscount Hatton (bap. 1632, d. 1706), politician and military officer; Gentleman of the Privy Chamber from 1662; Member of Parliament, 1663; Captain from 1667 and then Captain of Grenadiers from 1687 in the Earl of Manchester's Foot; second Baron Hatton from 1670; Viscount Hatton of Gretton from 1683. A Royalist like his father, Christopher, first Baron Hatton [S9 above], Hatton went into exile with him to Paris during the Interregnum and then prospered through a series of advancements after the Restoration. On his father's death in 1670, Hatton succeeded him as Baron Hatton and as Governor of Guernsey, on which island his wife and mother were killed when gunpowder exploded after a lightning strike. A supporter of Charles II, he attempted to be noncommittal during the Glorious Revolution of 1688 which deposed Charles's brother, the Catholic James II, in favour of Charles's nephew William III; by 1696, however, he had affirmed William's right to the throne. Of the manuscripts bequeathed by Hatton to the Bodleian Library in 1675, four were Anglo-Saxon homiliaries: Oxford, Bodleian Library, MSS Hatton 113 + 114 [App 1.1.12, 1.3.7, and 3.4], Hatton 115 [App 3.5], and Hatton 116 [App 1.3.8 and 3.6]. Shortly thereafter, the Library lent these volumes to Thomas Marshall [S13 below], who lent them to Francis Junius [S11 below], who left them again to the Bodleian on his death in 1678 as part of his bequest of manuscripts.[46]

---

[45] See *ODNB*, XXV, 823–24.

[46] See Philip, *Bodleian Library in the Seventeenth and Eighteenth Centuries*; H. D. Turner, 'Charles Hatton: A Younger Son', *Northamptonshire Past and Present*, 3 (1965), 255–61; and *ODNB*, XXV, 824–25.

[S10B] [Hearne, Thomas (bap. 1678, d. 1735), antiquary and publisher; Library Assistant, Bodleian Library, Oxford, 1701–12; and Second Librarian, Bodleian Library, 1712–16. Working under John Hudson (1662–1719) as an Oxford librarian, Hearne helped to update the Bodleian catalogues, published various volumes, and assisted antiquarians with their research. Among the editions he published during this period were a series of Latin classics; a collection of correspondence between library founder Sir Thomas Bodley [T2 above] with his first librarian, Thomas James (*Reliquiae Bodleianae* (London, 1703)); and a life of King Alfred that had been compiled by Sir John Spelman (1594–1643), son of Sir Henry Spelman [S16 below]. Among the scholars he assisted was John Bagford [S1 above], working on such projects as an edition of Chaucer that would ultimately be published by William and Timothy Thomas in 1721. Perhaps the strongest influence on Hearne's academic interests and beliefs, however, was the antiquary Thomas Smith (1638–1710), who reinforced Hearne's non-juror principles — his conviction, that is, against taking oaths — and left him his manuscripts. Hearne's stance on oaths would hinder his professional progress, leading him to decline such posts as the librarianship of the Bodleian. Increased opposition from university authorities on this and other issues finally led to Hearne's forcible termination as librarian when in 1716 Hudson had the library locks changed. Thereafter, he made his living as a publisher of private works, including an edition of selected papers of the Elizabethan Society of Antiquaries, William Camden's *Annales rerum Anglicarum* [S4 above], and a copy of *The Battle of Maldon*, printed from a transcript made for him by David Casley (deputy keeper and then keeper of the Royal and Cotton libraries, 1718–54) of the original Cottonian manuscript, lost in the 1731 Ashburnham House fire. One other manuscript damaged and disordered in the fire was London, British Library, Cotton MS Otho B. X + Oxford, Bodleian Library, MS Rawlinson Q. e. 20 [App 2.3]; directly following the conflagration, one leaf found its way into the hands of a 'commoner' of Christ Church, Oxford, the son of the antiquarian Browne Willis [S18B below]. On 15 November, three weeks after the fire, Willis in turn gave it to Hearne; the leaf is now Rawlinson Q. e. 20.[47]]

---

[47] Studies of Hearne include T. A. Birrell, 'Anthony Wood, John Bagford and Thomas Hearne as Bibliographers', in *Pioneers in Bibliography*, ed. by R. Myers and M. Harris (Winchester, 1988), pp. 25–39; C. S. Briggs, 'Thomas Hearne, Richard Richardson, and the Osmondthick Hoard', *Antiquaries Journal*, 58 (1978), 247–59; Robert Easting, 'The Middle English "Hearne fragment" of *St Patrick's Purgatory*', *NQ*, 35 (1988), 436–37; J. C. Findon, 'The Nonjurors and the Church of England, 1689–1716' (unpublished doctoral dissertation, University of Oxford,

[S11] Junius [Du Jon], Francis [Franciscus] (1591–1677), antiquarian and philologist; Pastor at Hillegersberg, The Netherlands, 1617–19. Not to be confused with his father, a French nobleman of the same name (1545–1602). Born in Heidelberg, Germany, and raised in the Netherlands, Junius studied at Leiden University from 1608 and at Middelburg from 1614 to 1615, receiving the philological and theological training that would shape his career. After serving as minister in the Dutch Church, he left for England in 1621, where he served as tutor and then librarian to the family of Thomas Howard, Earl of Arundel. With the encouragement of the Earl, a keen collector of art, Junius drew on classical quotations to compile an encyclopaedia of artists and artefacts (published posthumously in 1694) and *De pictura ueterum* (London, 1637), which set forth a history of theories of art as well as artistic instruction. In 1642 he returned to the Netherlands, where he remained for thirty-three years; it was here that his research into the origins of Dutch brought him unrivalled expertise in older Germanic languages. In this pursuit he was aided by the library of his nephew Isaac Voss [S19 below], with whom he lived from 1655, and by repeated visits to parts of Scandinavia and to England, interacting with such scholars as Sir William Dugdale, John Selden, and Patrick Young [S7, S15, and S20] and transcribing Old English manuscripts belonging to Sir Robert Cotton [S5 above]. He compiled a new Latin–Old English glossary, an edition and dictionary of the Gothic Gospels, and a monumental etymological English dictionary, published posthumously in 1743. Finally in 1676 the peripatetic Junius settled in Oxford, to which university he bequeathed his Old English manuscripts and other volumes pertaining to Germanic studies. Among these were

1978); Stanley G. Gillam, 'Thomas Hearne's Library', *Bodleian Library Record*, 12 (1985–88), 52–64; Theodorus H. B. M. Harmsen, *Antiquarianism in the Augustan Age: Thomas Hearne, 1678–1735* (Oxford, 2000); Harmsen, 'Letters of Learning: A Selection from the Correspondence of Thomas Hearne and Thomas Smith, 1703–1710', *Lias*, 24 (1997), 37–66; Harmsen, 'High-Principled Antiquarian Publishing: The Correspondence of Thomas Hearne (1678–1735) and Thomas Smith (1638–1710)', *Lias*, 23 (1996), 69–98; Harmsen, 'Bodleian Imbroglios, Politics and Personalities, 1701–1716: Thomas Hearne, Arthur Charlett and John Hudson', *Neophilologus*, 82 (1998), 149–68; *The Remains of Thomas Hearne: Reliquiae Hearnianae, Being Extracts from his MS Diaries*, ed. by T. Hearne, Philip Bliss, and J. Buchanan-Brown (Carbondale, 1967); Frans J. M. Korsten, 'Thomas Hearne: The Man and his Library', in *Order and Connexion: Studies in Bibliography and Book History; Selected Papers from the Munby Seminar, Cambridge, July 1994*, ed. by R. C. Alston (Cambridge, 1997), pp. 49–75; Ian G. Philip, 'Thomas Hearne as a Publisher', *Bodleian Library Record*, 3 (1951), 146–55; Kathryn Sutherland, 'Byrhtnoth's Eighteenth-Century Context', in *The Battle of Maldon AD 991*, ed. by Donald Scragg (Oxford, 1991), pp. 183–95; and *ODNB*, XXVI, 156–60.

a number of manuscripts containing Anglo-Saxon homiliaries: Oxford, Bodleian Library, MSS Hatton 113 (formerly Junius 99) + Hatton 114 (formerly Junius 22) [App 1.1.12, 1.3.7, and 3.4], a two-volume homiletic collection that likely forms a continuation of the ecclesiastical material in Oxford, Bodleian Library, MS Junius 121; MS Hatton 115 (formerly Junius 23) + Kansas, Kenneth Spencer Research Library, MS Pryce C2:2 [App 3.5]; MS Hatton 116 (formerly Junius 24) [App 1.3.8]; and MSS Junius 85 + Junius 86 [App 2.7]. Hatton 113 + 114, Hatton 115, and Hatton 116 had been given to the Bodleian in 1675 by Christopher, first Viscount Hatton [S10 above]; the Library subsequently lent these volumes to Thomas Marshall [S13 below], who lent them to Junius, who left them again to the Bodleian on his death. Junius 85 + Junius 86 were owned by Voss, as attested by a note in Oxford, Bodleian Library, MS Junius 45, fol. 9^r; they were given by Voss along with other manuscripts to Junius, who in turn bequeathed them to the Bodleian.[48]

[S12] Le Neve, Sir William (bap. 1592, d. 1661), herald and genealogist; Mowbray Herald-Extraordinary from 1624; Herald of York from 1625; Norroy King of Arms from 1634; Knight from 1634; and Clarenceux King of Arms, 1635–46. Baptized William Neve after his father (d. 1609), William displayed from an early age an interest in heraldry that led him to assume the surname Le Neve and to pursue armigerous rights, which he received in 1627. A series of appointments as herald promoted him in 1635 to Clarenceux King of Arms, one of the three chief offices in the College of Arms which presided over and arbitrated matters of ceremony in the kingdom. In this role he faced opposition by Sir John Borough, Garter King of Arms; having been displaced by act of parliament during the Civil War for his loyalty to the crown, moreover, he was prevented from returning to his

---

[48] See further *Franciscus Junius: The Literature of Classical Art*, ed. by Keith Aldrich, Philipp Fehl, and Raina Fehl, 2 vols (Berkeley, 1991); Peter S. Baker, 'Time for a Revival of Old English Types', *OEN*, 27 (1993), B1–B3; *Franciscus Junius F. F. and his Circle*, ed. by R. H. Bremmer (Amsterdam, 1998); P. H. Breuker, 'On the Course of Franciscus Junius' Germanic Studies, with Special Reference to Frisian', *Amsterdamer Beiträge zur älteren Germanistik*, 31 (1990), 42–68; Merrel D. Clubb, 'Junius, Marshall, Madden, Thorpe – and Harvard', in *Studies in Language and Literature in Honour of Margaret Schlauch*, ed. by Mieczyslaw Brahmer and others (Warsaw, 1966; repr. New York, 1971), pp. 55–70; Kees (Cornelis) Dekker, *The Origins of Old Germanic Studies in the Low Countries* (Boston, 1999); Peter J. Lucas, 'The Metrical Epilogue to the Alfredian Pastoral Care: A Postscript from Junius', *ASE*, 24 (1995), 43–50; B. J. Timmer, 'Junius' Stay in Friesland', *Neophilologus*, 41 (1957), 141–44; *'For My Worthy Friend Mr Franciscus Junius': An Edition of the Complete Correspondence of Francis Junius F. F. (1591–1677)*, ed. by Sophie Van Romburgh (Leiden, 2004); and *ODNB*, XXX, 834–35.

duties after the Restoration, having been judged in 1658 and 1661 to be insane. Le Neve's researches into the arms of medieval families were advanced by his acquisition of the library of Sir William Dethick and by access to the library of Sir Thomas Cotton [S6 above]. Two manuscripts containing Anglo-Saxon homiliaries loaned to Le Neve by Cotton in 1641 were London, British Library, Cotton MS Vitellius C. V [App 1.1.7] and London, British Library, Cotton MS Faustina A. IX [App 1.2.6].[49]

[S13] Marshall, Thomas (1621–85), dean of Gloucester and philologist; Fellow of Lincoln College, Oxford, from 1668; Rector of Lincoln from 1672; Royal Chaplain from 1680; Rector of Bladon from 1680 to 1682; and Dean of Gloucester from 1681. The son of an illiterate blacksmith, Marshall attended Lincoln College, Oxford, as an undergraduate from 1640 to 1645 and went on to be elected fellow of the college and to receive his DD *in absentia* in 1668 and 1669. In the interim, his knowledge of ancient languages grew to be considerable. Having moved to Holland to become chaplain of the Company of Merchant Adventurers in 1650, he stayed there until returning to England in 1672. In Holland, he worked with Francis Junius and his nephew Isaac Voss [S11 above and S19 below], producing for Junius an edition of the Anglo-Saxon Gospels with commentary and facing Gothic translation, published in 1665, and assisting Junius in developing matrices for Old English type. He began work on an Old English and Gothic grammar, studied Old Frisian law and Icelandic, and collected material for editions of the Gospels in Coptic and Arabic, among others. In the course of his work, he also borrowed certain volumes containing Anglo-Saxon homiliaries from the Bodleian: Oxford, Bodleian Library, MSS Hatton 113 (formerly Junius 99) + Hatton 114 (formerly Junius 22) [App 1.1.12, 1.3.7, and 3.4]; perhaps along with MS Hatton 115 (formerly Junius 23) + Kansas, Kenneth Spencer Research Library, MS Pryce C2:2 [App 3.5] and MS Hatton 116 (formerly Junius 24) [App 1.3.8]. Hatton 113 + 114, Hatton 115, and Hatton 116 had been given to the Bodleian in 1675 by Christopher, first Viscount Hatton [S10 above]; after borrowing these volumes from the Bodleian, Marshall lent them to Junius, who left them again to the Bodleian on his death.[50]

---

[49] On Le Neve, see Peter Le Neve-Foster, *The Le Neves of Norfolk: A Family History* (privately printed, Sudbury, 1969); Anthony R. Wagner, *Heralds of England: A History of the Office and College of Arms* (London, 1967); and *ODNB*, XXXIII, 343–44.

[50] Marshall figures in the studies of Clubb, 'Junius, Marshall, Madden, Thorpe – and Harvard'; Kees Dekker, 'The Old Frisian Studies of Jan van Vliet (1622–1666) and Thomas

[S14] Pepys, Samuel (1633–1703), naval administrator and diarist; Member of the naval Corporation of Trinity House (Younger Brother from 1662, Elder Brother from 1672, and Master, 1676–89); Fellow of the Royal Society from 1665 and President, 1684–86; Member of Parliament for Castle Rising, Norfolk, 1673, and for Harwich, 1679 and 1685–88; Secretary to the Admiralty Commission, 1673–79; and Secretary for the Affairs of the Admiralty, 1684–88. After taking his BA and MA from Cambridge in 1654 and 1660, having spent most of his time at Magdalene College, which would ultimately receive his library, Pepys advanced in the navy bureaucracy through the patronage of his cousin Edward Mountagu, later Earl of Sandwich. In 1660, he became clerk of the acts at the Navy Board, dealing with provisions and personnel. In 1673, when Charles II replaced the Lord High Admiral with an Admiralty commission, he became its secretary, drafting navy regulations and obtaining funds to build new ships. Resigning his post in 1679 after being wrongfully charged with passing naval secrets to the French, he was named secretary to the Admiralty in 1684 when Charles disbanded the commission and himself acted as Admiral. His scholarly interests led him to be elected fellow and then president of the Royal Society, and his extensive library of manuscripts and books — numbering over three thousand by his death — brought him into contact with such antiquarians as Humphrey Wanley (1672–1726). Pepys is chiefly remembered, however, for the private diary he kept from 1660 to 1669, which serves as a valuable eyewitness to such events as the Second Dutch War (1665–67), the Great Plague of London (1665), and the Great Fire of London (1666). Pepys is associated with one homiliary fragment: London, British Library, Harley MS 5915, fol. 13 + Cambridge, Magdalene College, MS Pepys 2981, no. 16 [App 1.1.8]. While Harley 5915 was one of several binding scraps collected as specimens by John Bagford [S1 above], Pepys 2981 forms Specimen 16 of volume I of Pepys's 'Calligraphical Collection'; pasted into the volume, only the recto can now be read.[51]

Marshall (1621–1685)', in *Approaches to Old Frisian Philology*, ed. by R. H. Bremmer, T. S. B. Johnston, and O. Vries (Amsterdam, 1998), pp. 113–38; Alastair Hamilton, 'The English Interest in the Arabic-speaking Christians', in *The 'Arabick' Interest of the Natural Philosophers in Seventeenth-Century England*, ed. by G. A. Russell (Leiden, 1994), pp. 30–53; Horace Hart, *Notes on a Century of Typography at the University Press, Oxford 1693–1794: With Annotations and Appendixes by Horace Hart* (Oxford, 1900); G. J. Toomer, *Eastern Wisdome and Learning: The Study of Arabic in Seventeenth-Century England* (Oxford, 1996); and *ODNB*, XXXVI, 870–71.

[51] Further studies of Pepys's life and works include *Particular Friends: The Correspondence of Samuel Pepys and John Evelyn*, ed. by Guy de la Bédoyère (Woodbridge, 1997); J. D. Davies, 'Pepys and the Admiralty Commission of 1679–84', *Historical Research*, 62 (1989), 34–53; *Cata-*

[S15] Selden, John (1584–1654), jurist, politician, and legal antiquary; Member of Parliament for Lancaster, 1623 or 1624, for Great Bedwyn, Wiltshire, 1626, for Ludgershall, Wiltshire, 1628, and for Oxford University, 1640; Bencher of the Inner Temple from 1632; and Keeper of Records in the Tower of London from 1643. Admitted to Clifford's Inn in 1602 and the Inner Temple in 1603, Selden was called to the bar in 1612 and worked thereafter as a London barrister. It was as a scholar, however, that Selden left his mark on history. A polymath versed in at least fourteen languages, he was keenly interested in legal history, and was aided in this regard by the library of his early patron, Sir Robert Cotton [S5 above]. His *Iani Anglorum facies altera* (London, 1610) offered a detailed study of Anglo-Saxon law, underscoring continuities between Anglo-Saxon and Norman governance. *Analecton Anglobrittanicon* (London, 1615), dedicated to Cotton, considered Briton, Anglo-Saxon, and early Norman rule. His critical edition of Eadmer's *Historia nouorum*, tracing the history of England from the Conquest to 1122, echoed the work of William Lambarde's *Archaionomia* [T8 above]. Throughout, he emphasized the need to rely on primary documents to approach an accurate understanding of the past. His research influenced his political theory, which viewed England from early times as a mixed monarchy in which the nobility and commons as well as the monarch shaped the law of the state. His strong opposition of royal infringement on commoners' rights in time of crisis led to incarceration from 1629 to 1634; access to his books, however, permitted further investigation into the Anglo-Saxon and Norman periods. The next decades saw Selden engaged among other matters in Judaic studies, reflecting on such issues as the fundamental moral duties of human beings, the Hebrew calendar, and marriage and divorce. From 1643 on, he played a key role in the debates of the Westminster assembly regarding the reform of the Church of England, drawing on his wide learning to examine such subjects as excommunication and the translation of scripture. In *Fleta* (London, 1647), he returned to English legal history, comparing Roman and Anglo-Saxon law codes and arguing for the strong influence of both on Norman England. It was in 1641, however, that his research brought him into contact with a manuscript

logue of the Pepys Library at Magdalene College, Cambridge, ed. by Robert C. Latham, 8 vols (Woodbridge, 1978–94); *Samuel Pepys and the Second Dutch War: Pepys's Navy White Book and Brooke House Papers*, ed. by Robert C. Latham, W. Matthews, and C. Knighton, Navy Records Society, 133 (London, 1995); Richard Ollard, *Pepys: A Biography* (London, 1974; repr. 1991); and *ODNB*, XLIII, 644–52.

containing an Anglo-Saxon homiliary: London, British Library, Cotton MS Vitellius D. XVII [App 2.5], loaned to Selden by Sir Thomas Cotton [S6 above].[52] [S16] Spelman, Sir Henry (1563/64–1641), antiquary and legal historian; Knight from 1604; Sheriff of Norfolk, 1604–06; Justice of the Peace for Norfolk, *c.* 1604–16; and Member of Parliament for Worcester, 1625. Not to be confused with his father, Henry Spelman (d. 1581). A student at Trinity College, Cambridge from 1580 to 1583 and Lincoln's Inn from 1586 to 1598, while at the latter, disliking his legal studies, Spelman helped to found the Society of Antiquaries. In consequence, his circle of acquaintances in London came to include other like-minded scholars such as John Selden [S15 above] and Sir Robert Cotton [S5 above], whose library he consulted. He delivered papers on numismatics, completed a study of Anglo-Saxon and Latin legal and ecclesiastical terms (*Archaeologus*, published in 1626), examined the Norman origins of feudalism (*Codex legum ueterum*, finished in 1627), and documented the history of British Church councils from Anglo-Saxon times (*Concilia, decreta, leges, constitutions, in re ecclesiarum orbis Britannici*, 2 vols (London, 1639–64)). From 1621 to around 1637, moreover, he participated heavily in a commission appointed by James I to investigate the possible abuse of fees levied by courts of justice. In 1640, he endowed the chair in Anglo-Saxon at the University of Cambridge, first held by Abraham Whelock [S18 below]. It was on Spelman's behalf that Whelock transcribed legal and confessional texts from pp. 97–101 and 114–25 in Cambridge, Corpus Christi College, MS 201 [App 3.2] into London, British Library, Additional MS 35333, fols

---

[52] For more on Selden, see Anonymous, 'Selden Correspondence', *Bodleian Library Record*, 2 (1943), 73–74; D. M. Barratt, 'The Library of John Selden and its Later History', *Bodleian Library Record*, 3 (1951), 128–42, 208–12, and 256–73; David S. Berkowitz, *John Selden's Formative Years: Politics and Society in Early Seventeenth-Century England* (London, 1988); Paul Christianson, *Discourse on History, Law, and Governance in the Public Career of John Selden, 1610–1635* (Toronto, 1996); Mordechai Feingold, 'John Selden and the Nature of Seventeenth-Century Science', in *In the Presence of the Past: Essays in Honour of Frank Manuel*, ed. by R. T. Bienvenu and M. Feingold (Dordrecht, 1991), pp. 55–78; Parry, *Trophies of Time*; Alfred L. Rowse, *Four Caroline Portraits: Thomas Hobbes, Henry Marten, Hugh Peters, John Selden* (London, 1993); Johann P. Sommerville, 'John Selden, the Law of Nature, and the Origins of Government', *Historical Journal*, 27 (1984), 437–47; Richard Tuck, '"The Ancient Law of Freedom": John Selden and the Civil War', in *Reactions to the English Civil War, 1642–1649*, ed. by J. Morrill (London, 1982), pp. 137–61; Tuck, *Philosophy and Government, 1572–1651* (Cambridge, 1993); and *ODNB*, XLIX, 694–705.

45–69, which served as the basis for entries in Spelman's *Concilia* and in Whelock's own re-edition of William Lambarde's *Archaionomia* [T8 above].[53]

[S17] Theyer, John (bap. 1598, d. 1673), antiquary. A practitioner of law in London and later part of Charles I's army at Oxford, Theyer came under the censure of parliament after his conversion to Catholicism following his publication in 1643 of *Aerio-mastix*, a defence of episcopal Church governance. Theyer is primarily known to history for his collection of some eight hundred manuscripts, many inherited from his grandmother's brother, Richard Hart, last Abbot of Llanthony Priory, Glouchestershire. On Theyer's death, the collection passed to his grandson, Charles Theyer (b. 1651), and thence, after Charles's unsuccessful attempts to present it to Oxford University, to the London bookseller Robert Scott. After a partial catalogue of the manuscripts had been compiled in 1678 (now London, British Library, Royal Appendix 70), 312 of them were purchased by Charles II. One such, London, British Library, Royal MS 8. C. vii [App 1.3.6], contains on fols 1 and 2 the fragmented remains of a possible homiliary containing saints' lives by Ælfric.[54]

[S18] Whelock [or Wheelocke], Abraham (*c.* 1593–1653), linguist and librarian; Exeter Fellow of Clare College, Cambridge, 1619–32; Vicar of the Church of Holy Sepulchre, Cambridge, 1622–42; Librarian of Cambridge University Library, 1629–53; first Professor of Arabic at Cambridge from 1632; and first Professor of Anglo-Saxon at Cambridge from 1639. After taking his BA and MA from Cambridge in 1615 and 1618, and as a fellow of Clare College from 1619, Whelock built on his knowledge of Hebrew by studying Arabic and other Middle Eastern languages. His aim in such study was at least twofold: to aid the work of Christian missionaries in the Middle East, and to gain insight into the Eastern roots of

---

[53] Spelman is considered in such studies as Sr Mary Joan Cook, 'Developing Techniques in Anglo-Saxon Scholarship in the Seventeenth Century, as they Appear in the "Dictionarium Saxonico-Latino-Anglicum" of William Somner' (unpublished doctoral thesis, University of Toronto, 1962); Cook, 'Minsheu's Guide into the Tongues and Somner's *Dictionarium*', *Mediaeval Studies*, 24 (1962), 375–77; Cronne, 'Study and Use of Charters'; Giese, 'Anonymous Seventeenth-Century Bodleian Manuscript Dictionary'; Angelika Lutz, 'Zur Entstehungsgeschichte von William Somners Dictionarium-Saxonico-Latino-Anglicum', *Anglia*, 106 (1988), 1–25; Parry, *Trophies of Time*; Woolf, *Idea of History in Early Stuart England*; Yerkes, 'Dugdale's *Dictionary* and Somner's *Dictionarium*'; and *ODNB*, LI, 791–93.

[54] On Theyer, see I. Gray, 'John Theyer, 1598–1673', *Antiquaries of Gloucestershire and Bristol, Bristol and Gloucestershire Archaeological Society Records Section*, 12 (1981), 43–44; and *ODNB*, LIV, 240–41.

Christianity prior to the influence of Rome. The latter concern likewise fuelled Whelock's interest in Anglo-Saxon England, that is, in early English doctrine uncorrupted (as he thought) by the Catholic Church. So competent in these languages did he become, and so persuasive a proponent of this vision of their importance, that he secured funding for the establishment first for a professorship of Arabic in 1632 and then for a professorship of Anglo-Saxon in 1639, the inaugural terms of which posts he himself served. As university librarian from 1629, moreover, his access to manuscripts furthered both his research and that of other antiquarians who consulted him. One such scholar was Sir Henry Spelman [S16 above], whose pursuit of Anglo-Saxon material for his *Concilia* precipitated Whelock's own study of Old English. It was Spelman who ultimately sponsored the Cambridge chair in Anglo-Saxon, arguably shifting the centre of such study thereby from the library of Sir Robert Cotton [S5 above], which had been closed by royal decree in 1629 after being viewed as a repository of dangerous political precedent. Among the works edited and published by Whelock as professor were the Old English translation of Bede's *Historia ecclesiastica* and selected versions of the *Anglo-Saxon Chronicle*, as well as a reissue of William Lambarde's 1568 *Archaionomia* [T8 above]. He died leaving unfinished an Old English dictionary and grammar.

Whelock was associated with seven manuscripts containing Old English homiliaries. To five he provided a topical index on flyleaves: Cambridge, Corpus Christi College, MS 162 [App 1.2.2]; MS 188 [App 1.1.3]; MS 201 [App 3.2]; MSS 419 + 421, pp. 1 and 2 [App 3.3]; and Cambridge, University Library, MS Gg. 3. 28 [App 1.1.1]. CCCC 162 Whelock used to supply the missing text of *CH* I.40 in CUL Gg. 3. 28. CCCC 188 Whelock annotated and used to supply the missing text of *CH* I.30 in CUL Gg. 3. 28. CCCC 201 Whelock annotated and entered his partial topical index in 1644, and on Spelman's behalf transcribed the legal and confessional texts from pp. 97–101 and 114–25 into London, British Library, Additional MS 35333, fols 45–69, which served as the basis for entries in Spelman's *Concilia* and in Whelock's re-edition of Lambarde's *Archaionomia*. CCCC 419 Whelock annotated. In CUL Gg. 3. 28 he entered the missing text of *CH* I.30 from CCCC 188, p. 318, and of *CH* I.40 from CCCC 162, pp. 553–63, on paper supply leaves. Cambridge, University Library, MS Ii. 1. 33 [App 2.1] Whelock consulted, referring to it as 'hom. 51' in his 1643 edition of the Old

English Bede. Cambridge, University Library, MS Ii. 4. 6 [App 1.2.1] he consulted in 1643, adding thereafter an index to the volume.[55]

[S18B] [Willis, Browne (1682–1760), antiquary; Member of Parliament for Buckingham, 1705–08. Though a student of law at the Inner Temple and for some years a politician, Willis's early and lasting interests were antiquarian in nature. Travelling extensively through England and Wales, he published multiple studies of cathedrals, examining medieval as well as classical architecture, an unusual focus for the period. In the process, he emphasized the importance of primary evidence, as had a previous student of cathedrals, Sir William Dugdale [S7 above]. He also showed a concern for their preservation, successfully helping to revive the Society of Antiquaries in 1717 to this end. His relationships with his colleagues were not always tranquil, however: eccentric in manner and appearance, his character and scholarship drew occasional criticism even from friends such as Thomas Hearne [S10B above]. It was to Hearne, however, that Browne gave a leaf from London, British Library, Cotton MS Otho B. X that had found its way into the hands of Willis's son, a 'commoner' of Christ Church, Oxford on 15 November, three weeks after the 1731 Ashburnham House fire; the leaf is now Oxford, Bodleian Library, MS Rawlinson Q. e. 20 [App 2.3].[56]

[S19] Voss [Vossius], Isaac (1618–89), scholar; Historian to the Provinces of Holland and Zeeland, 1646–70; Tutor of Greek to Queen Christina of Sweden, 1648–50; Royal [Swedish] Librarian, 1650–52; and Prebendary of Windsor Chapel from 1673. Born in Leiden, the Netherlands, Voss was the son of the sister

---

[55] Further studies of Whelock include Angelika Lutz, 'The Study of the Anglo-Saxon Chronicle in the Seventeenth Century and the Establishment of Old English Studies in the Universities', in *The Recovery of Old English: Anglo-Saxon Studies in the Sixteenth and Seventeenth Centuries*, ed. by Timothy Graham (Kalamazoo, 2000), pp. 1–82; Michael Murphy, 'Abraham Wheloc's edition of Bede's *History* in Old English', *Studia Neophilologica*, 39 (1967), 46–59; Michael Murphy and Edward Barrett, 'Abraham Wheelock, Arabist and Saxonist', *Biography*, 8 (1985), 163–85; J. C. T. Oates, *Cambridge University Library: A History from the Beginnings to the Copyright Act of Queen Anne* (Cambridge, 1986); Toomer, *Eastern Wisedome and Learning*; and *ODNB*, LVIII, 444–47.

[56] Willis is treated for example in Joan Evans, *A History of the Society of Antiquaries* (London, 1956); A. S. Napier, 'A Fragment of Ælfric's *Lives of Saints*', *Modern Language Notes*, 2 (1887), 189–90; Andrew Prescott, '"Their Present Miserable State of Cremation": The Restoration of the Cotton Library', in *Sir Robert Cotton as Collector*, ed. by Wright, pp. 391–454; Rosemary Sweet, *The Writing of Urban Histories in Eighteenth-Century England* (Oxford, 1997), pp. 40–43 and 59; and *ODNB*, LIX, 372–75.

of Francis Junius [S11 above]. Much of Voss's early career he spent travelling and copying manuscripts of classical texts in European libraries. In 1641 he went to England, where Junius was librarian of Thomas Howard, Earl of Arundel; there he met, among others, royal librarian Patrick Young [S20 below]. The next few years saw him in France and Italy before returning in 1644 to his parents' home in the Netherlands. In 1646 he succeeded his elder brother as historian to Holland and Zeeland, managing to write nothing on the subject during his twenty-four years in office. Instead, over the next few decades he published studies of such diverse matters as biblical chronology, the nature of tides, and the Sibylline Oracles. In 1648, he was invited to the court of Christina of Sweden (1626–89), becoming thereafter her Greek tutor and then librarian. In the latter post, he augmented the royal holdings considerably, first by selling Sweden his father's ample library and then supplementing it with volumes from his own collection and others acquired elsewhere. Contention with another scholar at Christina's court, Claude Saumaise, exiled him from the court from 1652 to 1653; thereafter, though reconciled, Voss left the Queen's service to move to The Hague, living with Junius and his mother from 1655. When in 1670 the states of Holland finally refused to pay the salary of their less-than-prolific historian, he returned to England under the patronage of John Pearson, master of Trinity College, Cambridge. The same year, he was created Doctor of Civil Law at Oxford. After Voss's death, Oxford nearly acquired his library of some 762 manuscripts, but found itself outbid by Leiden University. The Bodleian did, however, manage to purchase part of his collection in 1805, including a tenth-century Insular Latin psalter. As attested by Oxford, Bodleian Library, MS Junius 45, fol. 9[r], one two-volume homiliary owned by Voss was Oxford, Bodleian Library, MSS Junius 85 + Junius 86 [App 2.7]; these he gave along with other manuscripts to his uncle Junius, whose collection the Bodleian acquired in 1678.[57]

[S20] Young [Junius], Patrick (1584–1652), librarian and scholar; Royal Librarian, c.?1609–49; Prebend of Chester Cathedral from 1613; Burgess of Dundee from 1618; Prebend and Treasurer of St Paul's Cathedral, 1621–52; and Rector of Hayes, Middlesex, 1623–47. The son of Sir Peter Young (1544–1628), tutor to James VI of Scotland, Young was well positioned for a promising early career.

---

[57] On Voss, see Astrid C. Balsem, 'Libri omissi' italiani del cinquecento provenienti dalla biblioteca di Isaac Vossius ora nella biblioteca della Rijksuniversiteit di Leida (Leiden, 1994); F. F. Blok, Isaac Vossius and his Circle: His Life Until his Farewell to Queen Christina of Sweden, 1618–1655 (Groningen, 2000); Blok, Contributions to the History of Isaac Vossius's library (Amsterdam, 1974); and ODNB, LVI, 602–07.

Having served first as librarian to Bishop George Lloyd of Chester, he became chaplain at Oxford of All Souls College after 1605. A distinguished scholar in his own right, Young was marked by his proficiency in Greek, working with early Greek patristic writers and the Septuagint Codex Alexandrinus, among other matters. It was for his work on libraries, however, that to history he would chiefly be known. As Royal Librarian, he was given the charge of the reorganizing (if not refounding) of the Royal Library. He systematically catalogued the Crown's various collections and from 1609 to 1610 oversaw the construction of a new library at St James's Palace. In 1622, by royal order, he undertook to inventory manuscripts and early records in cathedrals throughout the kingdom, having select copies made for the Royal Library in the process. Itemizations of other collections followed, such as the Barocci collection at Oxford's Bodleian Library. It is in the catalogue of manuscripts in Worcester Cathedral Library he made in 1622–23, however, that an Anglo-Saxon homiliary appears: Oxford, Bodleian Library, MS Hatton 116 [App 1.3.8].[58]

---

[58] Additional treatments of Young include N. R. Ker, 'Salisbury Cathedral Manuscripts and Patrick Young's Catalogue', *Wiltshire Archaeological and Natural History Magazine*, 53 (1949–50), 153–83; Ker, 'Patrick Young's Catalogue of the Manuscripts of Lichfield Cathedral', *Mediaeval and Renaissance Studies*, 2 (1950), 151–68; and *ODNB*, LX, 929–31.

ANGLO-SAXON HOMILIARIES AS DESIGNATED BY KER

In the first, topical index to N. R. Ker's *Catalogue of Manuscripts Containing Anglo-Saxon*, Ker provides a list of manuscripts which he designates as homiliaries. In the absence of any categorical definition of the term — the minimum number of items required to constitute a homiletic collection, the precise qualities requisite to call a piece 'homiletic', and so on — this list provides a useful framework for an introductory survey of such manuscripts. It also offers a method for organization: Ker groups homiliaries into (1) ordered collections for the whole or for part of a year, distinguishing further between (1a) *temporale* and *sanctorale*,[1] (1b) *temporale* only, and (1c) *sanctorale* only; (2) collections containing items of *temporale* or *sanctorale* in disorder; and (3) collections for general occasions (*Catalogue*, p. 527).

While the categories are conceptually helpful and are employed here, they are also sometimes reductive, inasmuch as Anglo-Saxon collections are not always known to reflect clear logical lines. In Cambridge, Corpus Christi College, MS 162, Part I, pp. 1–138 and 161–564, for example (1.2.2 below), Ker singles out pp. 109–563 as a 'homiliary' of *temporale* pieces. While the set indeed consists of anonymous and Ælfrician homilies for Sundays and non-saints' feasts for a portion of the liturgical year, it is followed in CCCC 162 by an anonymous homily in a hand nearly contemporary with the original and preceded by eight homilies for general occasions unaccounted for by Ker in his reckoning of homiliaries. Even were the items in pp. 109–563 derived originally from a self-contained set, therefore, this

---

[1] That is, pieces for Sundays and moveable non-saints' feasts linked to Easter (*temporale*) versus feasts celebrated on set days in the calendar year (*sanctorale*); see the further definitions given in note 1 of Loredana Teresi's 'Ælfric's or Not? The Making of a *Temporale* Collection in Late Anglo-Saxon England', in this volume.

'homiliary' is now a theoretical construct rather than an independent entity, a subset of a larger textual assembly. The fact that the volume was augmented in the sixteenth century with twenty-two pages taken from yet another Anglo-Saxon homiliary (3.1 below) only serves to complicate the picture: CCCC 162 as we have it is not a homiliary per se, but housing for a *temporale* collection surrounded by assorted sermons and supplemented by part of a homiliary for general occasions.

The categories offered by Ker likewise do not account well for collections that include homilies both for specified and for general occasions, whether 'ordered' or not. A number of manuscripts might fall into this 'miscellaneous' camp: London, British Library, Cotton MS Cleopatra B. XIII (Ker no. 144), cross-referenced by Joscelyn to CCCC 198 (1.1.4 below); London, British Library, Cotton MS Tiberius A. III, fols 2–173 (Ker no. 186); and London, Lambeth Palace Library, MS 487 (not in Ker) and MS 489 (Ker no. 283). There is also the episcopal collection of material (including homilies) prepared by Wulfstan for export to Denmark: Copenhagen, Kongelige Bibliotek, Gl. Kgl. Sam. MS 1595. Others remain as tantalizing possibilities, such as London, British Library, Cotton MS Otho B. X, fols 29–30 (Ker no. 178) — two homilies that alone survive from a homiliary, now lost, from which they were extracted and inserted into Cotton Otho B. X (2.3 below), perhaps by John Joscelyn. In most cases, such possibilities must remain avenues for future scholarly exploration. One manuscript, however, particularly merits inclusion here: Cambridge, Corpus Christi College, MS 421, pp. 99–208 and 227–354 (with additions at pp. 3–98 and 209–24) (4.1 below). Of the ten volumes explicitly designated Anglo-Saxon homiliaries by that most (in)famous early aficionado of Old English, Matthew Parker, it is the only one not to be treated as such by Ker. In short, while the practical value of Ker's delineations is indisputable, it will come as no surprise to students of manuscripts that these categories should be viewed with caution and that their boundaries are rarely neat.[2]

1. Ordered collections for the whole or for part of a year

1.1. Temporale and Sanctorale

1.1.1. Cambridge, University Library, MS Gg. 3. 28 (s. x^{ex}/xi^{in}, provenance Durham prob. by s. xii (Godden, p. xliii))

---

[2] A fuller account of these homiliaries, noting homiletic and additional contents, their relationship to other manuscripts, and their post-Dissolution use, is forthcoming by Kleist.

Summary: The only surviving copy of Ælfric's *Catholic Homilies* containing the Latin and Old English prefaces to both series, as well as the *Ammonitio*, *Explicit*, and *Oratio* from the Second Series, CUL Gg. 3. 28 is also the only complete copy of the Second Series.

Described by: Ker no. 15; Gneuss no. 11; Hardwick and Luard, III, 71–82; Clemoes, p. 24; Godden, p. xliii; Pope, I, 34–35; and Kenneth Sisam, pp. 165–71. CUL Gg. 3. 28 serves as the base manuscript for Thorpe's edition of the *Catholic Homilies* (1844–46) and Clemoes's edition of the First Series prefaces and supplements to *CH* I.15, 20, 23, and 24.

1.1.2. Cambridge, Corpus Christi College, MS 178, Part I, pp. 164–270 (s. xi[1] or xi[med],[3] provenance Worcester by s. xi) [see also 3.1 below]

Summary: The second of two books of homilies by Ælfric in CCCC 178 and CCCC 162, pp. 139–60, the first book being for general occasions and the second for principal festivals from Christmas to Pentecost.

Described by: Ker no. 41A.20–32; Gneuss no. 54; James, *Corpus Christi*, I, 414–17; Budny, I, 548–51 (in a discussion of CCCC 178, Part II (fols 287[r]–458[r]; Ker no. 41B.1–2)); Clemoes, pp. 37–40; Godden, pp. lxviii–lxx; and Pope, I, 62–67.

1.1.3. Cambridge, Corpus Christi College, MS 188 (s. xi[1])

Summary: A complete copy of Ælfric's First Series of *Catholic Homilies*, with additions.

Described by: Ker no. 43; Gneuss no. 58; Budny, I, 571–75; James, *Corpus Christi*, I, 445–48; Clemoes, pp. 36–37; Pope, I, 59–62; and Kenneth Sisam, pp. 175–78.

1.1.4. Cambridge, Corpus Christi College, MS 198, fols 1[r]–247[v] (s. xi[1], south-east England; provenance Worcester), fols 150[r]–159[r] and 218[r]–247[r] being 'nearly contemporary' interpolations into the original collection (Ker, *Catalogue*, pp. 76 and 79) [see also 1.3.1 below]

Summary: An orderly early eleventh-century collection primarily of entries from Ælfric's *Catholic Homilies*.

Described by: Ker, *Catalogue*, pp. liii–liv and no. 48.1–43 and 44–51; Gneuss no. 64; Budny, I, 557–69; James, *Corpus Christi*, I, 475–81; Clemoes, pp. 10–13; Godden, pp. xxviii–xxxi; Pope, I, 20–22; and Scragg, p. xxviii.

1.1.5. Cambridge, Corpus Christi College, MS 367, Part II, fols 3[r]–6[v] and 11[r]–29[r] (s. xii)

---

[3] Pope, I, 62, dates the two main hands 'only a little before the middle of the century'.

Summary: Designated a possible homiliary by Ker (*Catalogue*, p. 527), fragments of six quires survive of this manuscript, primarily containing Ælfrician material.

Described by: Ker no. 63; Gneuss no. 100; James, *Corpus Christi*, II, 199–204; Clemoes, pp. 50–52; Godden, pp. lvi–lvii; and Scragg, p. xxxvii. Not in Budny.

1.1.6. The Hague, Koninklijke Bibliotheek, MS 133. D. 22 (21) + Copenhagen, Rigsarkivet, Aftagne pergamentfragmenter 637–64, 669–71, and 674–98 (s. xi¹)

Summary: The Dutch manuscript preserves fragments of three Ælfrician homilies, while parts of six more appear in the Copenhagen binding strips. Despite its fragmentary nature, Ker counts the manuscript as a possible homiliary (*Catalogue*, p. 527) because the sermons found here elsewhere appear consecutively only in the four complete copies of Ælfric's First Series of *Catholic Homilies*: CUL Gg. 3. 28 [1.1.1 above], CCCC 188 [1.1.3 above], Cotton Vitellius C. V [1.1.7 below], and Royal 7. C. XII [1.1.9 below].

Described by: Ker no. 118; Gneuss no. 830; Fausbøll, *Fifty-Six Ælfric Fragments* and 'More Ælfric Fragments'; and Clemoes, pp. 56–59.

1.1.7. London, British Library, Cotton MS Vitellius C. V (s. x/xi and xi¹, southwest England)

Summary: A collection of Ælfric's First Series of *Catholic Homilies*, with additions. Vitellius C. V consisted initially of a now-imperfect set of First Series homilies from *c.* 1000; to this set was appended in a nearly contemporary hand Ælfric's first four homilies for the Fridays in Lent and at least two other texts, now lost. In the first half of the eleventh century, another scribe inserted a series of seventeen homilies and two interpolations throughout the volume at the appropriate points for the liturgical year. See Clemoes, pp. 19–20, and Pope, I, 26–28.

Described by: Ker no. 220; Gneuss no. 403; Planta, p. 424; Wanley, p. 208; Clemoes, pp. 18–21; Godden, pp. lxv–lxvi; Pope, I, 26–34; and Tite, p. 163.

1.1.8. London, British Library, Harley MS 5915, fol. 13 + Cambridge, Magdalene College, MS Pepys 2981, no. 16 (s. xi^in (Gneuss s. xi^med))

Summary: Designated a possible homiliary by Ker (*Catalogue*, p. 527), the fragments preserve parts of two Ælfrician First Series homilies.

Described by: Ker no. 243; Gneuss no. 440.5; *Catalogue of the Harleian Manuscripts*, III, 308 (single entry for Harley 5914–5939); and Clemoes, pp. 63–64.

1.1.9. London, British Library, Royal MS 7. C. XII, fols 4–218 (s. x^ex, Cerne?)

Summary: The base manuscript for Clemoes's edition, Royal 7. C. XII constitutes the unique witness to the earliest known stage of Ælfric's First Series of *Catholic Homilies*, with notes in Ælfric's own hand.

Described by: Ker no. 257; Gneuss no. 472; Clemoes, p. 1; Eliason and Clemoes, pp. 28–35; Warner and Gilson, I, 180–81; and Kenneth Sisam, pp. 171–75. Standard edn: Clemoes (1997); facsimile edn by Eliason and Clemoes (1965).

1.1.10. Oxford, Bodleian Library, MSS Bodley 340 + Bodley 342 (2404–05) (s. xi^{in}; provenance Rochester)

Summary: An early eleventh-century homiliary arranged in two volumes according to the liturgical year, with the vast majority of sermons being taken from Ælfric's *Catholic Homilies.*

Described by: Ker no. 309; Gneuss no. 569; Madan and others, II.1, 351–52; Clemoes, pp. 7–10; Godden, pp. xxv–xxviii; Scragg, p. xxvii; Pope, I, 20; and Kenneth Sisam, pp. 148–98.

1.1.11. Oxford, Bodleian Library, MS Bodley 343 (2406), fols 65^r–128^{v4} (s. xii^2) [see also 2.6 below]

Summary: A collection of two anonymous and some twenty-nine Ælfrician homilies, loosely ranging from Advent to the Common of the Saints. Set apart from the larger, surrounding collection of unordered homilies by blank space before and after this section of the manuscript.

Described by: Ker no. 310.32–64; Madan and others, II.1, 352–53; Wanley, p. 15; Irvine, pp. xviii–liv; Conti, pp. 28–57; Clemoes, pp. 1–5; Godden, pp. xxxvii–xl; Pope, I, 14–18; Bethurum, p. 5; and Scragg, p. xxx. Not in Gneuss.

1.1.12. Oxford, Bodleian Library, MS Hatton 113 (5210; formerly Junius 99), fols 115^v–144^v (s. xi^2 (1064 x 1083), Worcester) + MS Hatton 114 (5134; formerly Junius 22), fols 9^r–140^r (s. xi^2 (1064 x 1083), Worcester) [see 1.3.7 and 3.4 below]

Summary: An ordered collection of homilies, primarily by Ælfric, spanning the period Christmas to Pentecost.

Described by: Ker no. 331.33–58; Gneuss nos 637–38; Madan and others, II.2, 967–68; Wanley, p. 26; Clemoes, pp. 41–45; Godden, pp. li–liv; Pope, I, 70–77; Bethurum, p. 4; and Scragg, p. xxxii. For Oxford, Bodleian Library, MS Junius 121, the volume of ecclesiastical material to which Hatton 113 + 114 likely form a continuation, see Ker no. 338.

---

[4] While Ker's index of homiliaries (*Catalogue*, p. 527) groups no. 310.64, the anonymous homily on the *Visio Pauli*, with no. 310.1–31 and 64–84 (2.6 below), this is likely an oversight: in his introduction to Bodley 343, Ker associates the homily with the preceding block of texts, arranged loosely according to the liturgical calendar and set apart before and after with blank spaces in the manuscript (p. 368); Clemoes (pp. 3–4) likewise classes no. 310.32–64 as a unit (his 'Be').

1.1.13. Princeton, Princeton University Library, W. H. Scheide Collection, MS 71 (s. x/xi)

Summary: The Blickling Homilies, eighteen sermons for Sundays and saints' days largely following the order of the liturgical year, beginning and ending imperfectly.

Described by: Ker no. 382; Gneuss no. 905; Scragg, pp. xxv–xxvi; and Scragg, 'Blickling Manuscript', pp. 299–304. Standard edn: Morris (1874–78; repr. 1967) (Kelly (2003) being inadequate); facsimile edn by Willard (1960).

1.2. Temporale only

1.2.1. Cambridge, University Library, MS Ii. 4. 6, fols 22^r–289^v (s. xi^{med}, New Minster, Winchester; provenance Tavistock?)

Summary: Homilies for Sundays and non-saints' festivals from Septuagesima to the First Sunday after Pentecost.

Described by: Ker no. 21.4–35; Gneuss no. 18; Hardwick and Luard, III, 442–46; Clemoes, pp. 28–30; Godden, pp. xlv–xlvii; Pope, I, 39–48; and Scragg, pp. xxxv–xxxvi.

1.2.2. Cambridge, Corpus Christi College, MS 162, Part I, pp. 1–138 and 161–564 (s. xi^{in}, south-east England (probably Canterbury or Rochester, perhaps St Augustine's Abbey, Canterbury; Budny, I, 463)), pp. 109–563 [see also 3.1 below]

Summary: A set of ten anonymous and thirty-two Ælfrician homilies for Sundays and non-saints' festivals from the Second Sunday after Epiphany to the Second Sunday in Advent.

Described by: Ker no. 38.9–54; Gneuss no. 50; Budny, I, 463–73; James, *Corpus Christi*, I, 363–68; Clemoes, pp. 13–16; Godden, pp. xxxi–xxxiii; Pope, I, 22–24; and Scragg, pp. xxviii–xxix.

1.2.3. Cambridge, Corpus Christi College, MS 302 (s. xi/xii)

Summary: A set of homilies for Sundays and non-saints' festivals for the First Sunday in Advent to Wednesday in Rogationtide, six anonymous, one by Wulfstan, and some twenty-six by Ælfric.

Described by: Ker no. 56; Gneuss no. 86; James, *Corpus Christi*, II, 92–94; Wanley, p. 128; Clemoes, p. 33; Godden, pp. l–li; Pope, I, 51–52; Bethurum, p. 4; and Scragg, pp. xxx–xxxi. Not in Budny.

1.2.4. Cambridge, Corpus Christi College, MS 303 (s. xii^1), pp. 1–75 and 211–90 [see also 1.3.2 below]

Summary: A collection of five anonymous and some twenty-nine Ælfrician pieces for Sundays and non-saints' festivals from the Second Sunday after Epiphany to Easter and from Rogationtide to the Twenty-First Sunday after Pentecost.

Described by: Ker no. 57.1–17 and 42–61; James, *Corpus Christi*, II, 95–100; Clemoes, pp. 5–7; Godden, pp. xxxiii–xxxvii; Pope, I, 18–20; and Scragg, p. xxix. Not in Gneuss or Budny.

1.2.5. Cambridge, Trinity College, MS B. 15. 34 (369) (s. xi^{med}, prob. Christ Church, Canterbury)

Summary: A set of some twenty-seven homilies by Ælfric for Sundays and non-saints' festivals for Easter to the Eleventh Sunday after Pentecost, ending imperfectly.

Described by: Ker no. 86; Gneuss no. 177; Clemoes, pp. 45–46; Godden, pp. lxx–lxxi; Pope, I, 77–80; James, *Trinity College*, I, 500–02; and Keynes, pp. 34–35.

1.2.6. London, British Library, Cotton MS Faustina A. IX (s. xii^{1})

Summary: A set of some six anonymous and twenty-nine Ælfrician homilies for Sundays and non-saints' festivals for the Second Sunday after Epiphany to Pentecost, beginning imperfectly.

Described by: Ker no. 153; Planta, p. 604; Wanley, p. 199; Clemoes, pp. 30–33; Godden, pp. xlvii–l; Pope, I, 48–51; Scragg, p. xxx; and Tite, p. 219. Not in Gneuss.

1.3. Sanctorale only

1.3.1. Cambridge, Corpus Christi College, MS 198, fols 328^r–366^r and 378^r–385^r (s. xi^{1}, south-east England; provenance Worcester) [see also 1.1.4 above]

Summary: Six sermons, mostly Ælfrician, for saints' days in August, September, November, being nearly contemporary additions to the preceding set of *temporale* [1.1.4 above].

Described by: Ker no. 48.52–57; see also 1.1.4 above.

1.3.2. Cambridge, Corpus Christi College, MS 303 (s. xii^{1}), pp. 76–202 [see also 1.2.4 above]

Summary: A collection of five anonymous and some fifteen Ælfrician pieces for saints' days for the period 3 May to 6 December and for the Common of Saints.

Described by: Ker no. 57.18–39; see also 1.2.4 above.

1.3.3. New Haven, Yale University Library, Osborn Collection, fragment + Oxford, Bodleian Library, MS Eng. th. c. 74 + Cambridge, Queens' College, MS Horne 75 + Bloomington, Indiana University, Lilly Library, MS Poole 10 (s. xi^{in})

> Summary: Designated a possible homiliary by Ker (*Catalogue*, p. 527), these fragments appear to constitute the remnants of a complete set of Ælfrician *Lives of Saints*, preceded or followed by a selection of items from Ælfric's *Catholic Homilies* (Clemoes, p. 55).
>
> Described by: Ker no. 81 (for Horne 75); Ker, 'Supplement', p. 123; Gneuss no. 146; Clemoes, pp. 54–55; Collins and Clemoes. Not in James, *Queen's College*.

1.3.4. Gloucester, Cathedral Library, MS 35 (s. xi^1; provenance Gloucester all fragments)

> Summary: Designated a possible homiliary by Ker (*Catalogue*, p. 527), these fragments preserve parts of three Ælfrician homilies and two anonymous texts.
>
> Described by: Ker no. 117, Gneuss no. 262, Eward, p. 5, Clemoes, pp. 55–56, and Godden, p. lvii.

1.3.5. London, British Library, Cotton MS Julius E. VII (s. xi^{in}, southern England; provenance Bury St Edmunds)

> Summary: The base manuscript for Skeat's edition of Ælfric's *Lives of Saints*, Cotton Julius E. VII provides sermons for saints' days for the whole of the liturgical year, beginning at Christmas.
>
> Described by: Ker no. 162; Gneuss no. 339; Planta, p. 18; and Wanley, p. 186.

1.3.6. London, British Library, Royal MS 8. C. VII, fols 1 and 2 (s. xi^{in})

> Summary: Designated a possible homiliary by Ker (*Catalogue*, p. 527), these fragments of a bifolium preserve sections of Ælfric's lives of Agnes and Agatha.
>
> Described by: Ker no. 260; Gneuss no. 476; and Warner and Gilson, I, 234–36.

1.3.7. Oxford, Bodleian Library, MS Hatton 114 (5134; formerly Junius 22), fols 147^v–200^r and 201^r–230^r (s. xi^2 (1064 x 1083), Worcester) [see 1.1.12 above and 3.4 below]

> Summary: A collection of sermons for saints' days from 1 May to 1 November, nearly all from Ælfric's *Catholic Homilies*.
>
> Described by: Ker no. 331.60–69 and 72–75; see also 1.1.12 above.

1.3.8. Oxford, Bodleian Library, MS Hatton 116 (5136; formerly Junius 24), pp. 18–239 and 279–90 (s. xii^1) [see 3.6 below]

> Summary: A collection of a dozen Ælfrician homilies for saints' days spanning the period 24 June to 30 November.
>
> Described by: Ker no. 333.2–15; Madan and others, II.2, 969; Clemoes, pp. 40–41; and Pope, I, 67–70. Not in Gneuss.

2. Collections containing items of Temporale or of Sanctorale in disorder

2.1. Cambridge, University Library, MS Ii. 1. 33 (s. xii²)
Summary: Primarily a passional (Ker, *Catalogue*, p. 23) comprised of selections from Ælfric's *Catholic Homilies* and *Lives of Saints* augmented by several anonymous texts.
Described by: Ker no. 18; Hardwick and Luard, III, 358–63; Clemoes, pp. 25–28; Godden, pp. xliii–xlv; Pope, I, 35–39; and Scragg, p. xxxv. Not in Gneuss.
2.2. Cambridge, Jesus College, MS 15 (Q. A. 15), fols i–x and 1–10 (binding leaves) (s. xi¹; provenance Durham)
Summary: Fragments of five homilies by Ælfric. A palimpsest, with the text largely erased and replaced with thirteenth- and fourteenth-century texts, the leaves were trimmed and used in the medieval binding of a thirteenth-century copy of Peter Lombard's *Sententiae*.
Described by: Ker no. 74; Gneuss no. 122; James, *Jesus College*, p. 14; Clemoes, pp. 53–54; Godden, pp. lxxiii–lxxiv; Pope, I, 88–91.
2.3. London, British Library, Cotton MS Otho B. X, fols 1–28, 31–50, 52–54,[5] 56–57, 59–60, 65, and 67, and Oxford, Bodleian Library, MS Rawlinson Q. e. 20 (15606) (s. xi¹)
Summary: A collection of Ælfrician saints' lives augmented by anonymous works and one homily by Wulfstan.
Described by: Ker no. 177A; Gneuss no. 355; Planta, p. 365; Wanley, p. 190; Madan and others, III, 445; Clemoes, pp. 60–61; Godden, pp. lvii–lviii; and Tite, p. 151.
2.4. London, British Library, Cotton MS Vespasian D. XIV, fols 4–169 (s. xii^med)
Summary: A collection of anonymous and Ælfrician theological works, the latter taken largely from the *Catholic Homilies*.
Described by: Ker no. 209; Planta, pp. 476–77; Wanley, p. 202; Clemoes, pp. 16–18; Godden, pp. xl–xlii; Pope, I, 24–26; and Tite, p. 183. Not in Gneuss.
2.5. London, British Library, Cotton MS Vitellius D. XVII, fols 4–92 (formerly fols '23–234') (s. xi^med)

---

[5] Where Ker tentatively includes fol. 54 in this collection, a more recent discussion of fols 52 and 54 by Stuart Lee identifies them as fragments related to Ælfric's *Lives of Saints* (*LS* I.2, I.5 and II.33 (the last not written by Ælfric)), and reconstructs them using the relevant passages from Skeat; see S. D. Lee, 'Two Fragments from Cotton MS. Otho B. X', *British Library Journal*, 17 (1991), 83–87.

Summary: A *sanctorale* collection drawing almost entirely on Ælfric's *Catholic Homilies* and *Lives of Saints*.

Described by: Ker no. 222; Planta, p. 428; Wanley, p. 206; Clemoes, pp. 61–63; Godden, pp. lviii–lix; and Tite, p. 167. Not in Gneuss.

2.6. Oxford, Bodleian Library, MS Bodley 343 (2406), fols vi^r–64^r and 129^r–70^r (s. xii^2) [see 1.1.11 above]

Summary: An unordered collection of homilies, eight anonymous, thirty-five by Ælfric, and three by Wulfstan, with some additional theological texts interspersed. The collection surrounds a set of some thirty-one homilies ordered from Advent to the Common of the Saints [1.1.11 above], set apart in the manuscript with blank space at the set's beginning and end.

Described by: Ker no. 310.1–31 and 65–84; see also 1.1.11 above.

2.7. Oxford, Bodleian Library, MSS Junius 85 + Junius 86 (5196–97) (s. xi^{med}, south-east England)

Summary: Fragments of a collection of homilies, now comprising half-a-dozen anonymous works and a homily by Ælfric. Divided into two volumes at fol. 35 in the post-medieval period.

Described by: Ker no. 336; Gneuss no. 642; Godden, pp. lix–lx; and Scragg, p. xxv.

2.8. Vercelli, Biblioteca Capitolare, MS CXVII (s. x^2, south-east England (St Augustine's, Canterbury? Rochester?))

Summary: The Vercelli Book, an original collection of homilies compiled from a variety of exemplars and interspersed with works of Old English verse.

Described by: Ker no. 394; Gneuss no. 941; Scragg, pp. xxiii–xxv. Standard edn: Scragg (1992); facsimile edn by Celia Sisam (1976).

3. Collections for general occasions

3.1. Cambridge, Corpus Christi College, MS 178, Part I, pp. 1–163 + Cambridge, Corpus Christi College, MS 162, Part II, pp. 139–60 (s. xi^1 or xi^{med}, provenance Worcester by s. xi) [see also 1.1.2 and 1.2.2 above]

Summary: The first of two books of homilies, nearly all by Ælfric, in CCCC 178 and 162, pp. 139–60, the first book being for general occasions and the second for principal festivals from Christmas to Pentecost.

Described by: Ker no. 41A.1–18; see also 1.1.2 above.

3.2. Cambridge, Corpus Christi College, MS 201, Part I, Section B, pp. 8–160 and 167–76 (s. xi^{med}, Winchester, New Minster?)

Summary: This 'handbook for both ecclesiastical and secular life' (Budny, I, 475) comprises a collection of legal, monastic, and homiletic texts, many of them associated with Wulfstan, Bishop of London (996–1002), Bishop of Worcester (1002–16), and Archbishop of York (1002–23). The manuscript forms, in fact, the principal source of Napier's edition of Wulfstan's sermons (though cf. 3.4 below).

Described by: Ker no. 49B.1–58; Gneuss no. 65.5; Budny, I, 475–86; James, *Corpus Christi*, I, 485–91; Wanley, p. 137; Bethurum, pp. 2–3; and Scragg, p. xxxvi.

3.3. Cambridge, Corpus Christi College, MS 419 + Cambridge, Corpus Christi College, MS 421, pp. 1 and 2 (s. xi[1], south-east England?; provenance Exeter)

Summary: 'A handy and rather attractive portable copy of homilies on divers subjects', either anonymous or by Wulfstan and Ælfric (Budny, I, 526).

Described by: Ker no. 68 (and p. xli); Gneuss no. 108; Budny, I, 525–33; James, *Corpus Christi*, II, 311 and 313; Wanley, pp. 131–32; Clemoes, pp. 46–48; Godden, pp. lxxi–lxxii; Pope, I, 80–83; Bethurum, pp. 1–2; and Scragg, p. xxxii.

3.4. Oxford, Bodleian Library, MS Hatton 113 (5210; formerly Junius 99), fols 1[r]–102[v] (s. xi[2] (1064 x 1083), Worcester) [see 1.1.12 and 1.3.7 above]

Summary: A collection of homilies primarily by Wulfstan, the first thirty of which are printed by Napier in the order found here (cf. 3.2 above).

Described by: Ker no. 331.1–31; see also 1.1.12 above.

3.5. Oxford, Bodleian Library, MS Hatton 115 (5135; formerly Junius 23) + Kansas, Kenneth Spencer Research Library, MS Pryce C2:2 (formerly Y 104) (s. xi[2], xii[med])

Summary: A compilation of some thirty homiletic works by Ælfric, along with four anonymous texts and part of a homily by Wulfstan; the final three items are on two twelfth-century quires.

Described by: Hatton 115: Ker no. 332; Ker, 'Supplement', pp. 124–25; Gneuss no. 639; Madan and others, II.2, 968–69; and Scragg, pp. xxxi (describing fols 140–47 / Ker no. 332.34) and xxxvi (describing fols 148–55). Pryce C2:2: Colgrave and Hyde; Collins, pp. 50–51 and plate 7. Both manuscripts: Clemoes, pp. 33–36; Godden, pp. lxvi–lxviii; and Pope, I, 53–59.

3.6. Oxford, Bodleian Library, MS Hatton 116 (5136; formerly Junius 24), pp. 253–78 and 290–395 (s. xii[1]) [see 1.3.8 above]

Summary: A collection of some eleven homiletic works, all but one by Ælfric.

Described by: Ker no. 333.16–26; see also 1.3.8 above.

4. Collections for specified and general occasions

4.1. Cambridge, Corpus Christi College, MS 421, pp. 99–208 and 227–354 (s. xi[1], south-east England?), with additions at pp. 3–98 and 209–24 (s. xi[3/4], Exeter) [pp. 225–26 are blank; see also 3.3 above]

Summary: A collection of seven homilies by Ælfric and Wulfstan, supplemented by another eight anonymous and Ælfrician homilies. The original set contains both selections for the Proper of the Season (*temporale* pieces, as for Pentecost) and the Common of the Saints (material appropriate for various saints' days, such as martyrs or virgins) and general addresses; the supplementary material contains both *temporale* pieces and sermons for unspecified dates. Described by: Ker no. 69; Gneuss no. 109; Clemoes, pp. 47–48; Pope, I, 81; and Bethurum, p. 1.

Works Cited

A Catalogue of the Harleian Manuscripts in the British Museum, 4 vols (London, 1808–12 (vol. III, 1808))

Bethurum = *The Homilies of Wulfstan*, ed. by Dorothy Bethurum (Oxford, 1957)

Budny, Mildred, *Insular, Anglo-Saxon, and Early Anglo-Norman Manuscript Art at Corpus Christi College, Cambridge: An Illustrated Catalogue*, 2 vols (Kalamazoo, 1997)

Clemoes = *Ælfric's Catholic Homilies: The First Series, Text*, ed. by Peter Clemoes, EETS: SS, 17 (Oxford, 1997)

Colgrave, B., and A. Hyde, 'Two Recently Discovered Leaves from Old English Manuscripts', *Speculum*, 37 (1962), 60–78

Collins, Rowland L., *Anglo-Saxon Vernacular Manuscripts in America* (New York 1976)

Collins, Rowland L., and Peter Clemoes, 'The Common Origin of Ælfric Fragments at New Haven, Oxford, Cambridge, and Bloomington', in *Old English Studies in Honour of John C. Pope*, ed. by Robert B. Burlin and Edward B. Irving, Jr (Toronto, 1974), pp. 285–326

Conti, Aidan, 'Preaching Scripture and Apocrypha: A Previously Unidentified Homiliary in an Old English Manuscript, Oxford, Bodleian Library, MS Bodley 343' (unpublished doctoral thesis, University of Toronto, 2004)

Eliason and Clemoes = *Ælfric's First Series of Catholic Homilies, British Museum Royal 7 C. xii, fols 4–218*, ed. by Norman Eliason and Peter Clemoes, EEMF, 13 (Copenhagen, 1965)

Eward, Suzanne Mary, *A Catalogue of Gloucester Cathedral Library* (Gloucester, 1972)

Fausbøll, Else, *Fifty-Six Ælfric Fragments: The Newly-Found Copenhagen Fragments of Ælfric's 'Catholic Homilies' with Facsimiles*, Publications of the Department of English, University of Copenhagen, 14 (Copenhagen, 1986)

——— , 'More Ælfric Fragments', *ES*, 76 (1995), 302–06

Godden = *Ælfric's Catholic Homilies: The Second Series, Text*, ed. by Malcolm Godden, EETS: SS, 5 (London, 1979)

Gneuss, Helmut, *Handlist of Anglo-Saxon Manuscripts: A List of Manuscripts and Manuscript Fragments Written or Owned in England up to 1100*, MRTS, 241 (Tempe, 2001)

Hardwick, C., and Henry Richards Luard, *A Catalogue of the Manuscripts Preserved in the Library of the University of Cambridge*, 6 vols (Cambridge, 1856–67 (vol. III, 1858))

Irvine = *Old English Homilies from MS Bodley 343*, ed. by Susan Irvine, EETS: OS, 302 (Oxford, 1993)

James, Montague Rhodes, *A Descriptive Catalogue of the Manuscripts in the Library of Jesus College, Cambridge* (London, 1895)

———, *A Descriptive Catalogue of the Manuscripts in the Library of Corpus Christi College, Cambridge*, 2 vols (Cambridge, 1912)

———, *A Descriptive Catalogue of the Western Manuscripts in the Library of Queen's College, Cambridge* (Cambridge, 1900)

———, *The Western Manuscripts in the Library of Trinity College, Cambridge: A Descriptive Catalogue*, 4 vols (Cambridge, 1900)

Keynes, Simon, *Anglo-Saxon Manuscripts and Other Items of Related Interest in the Library of Trinity College, Cambridge*, OEN Subsidia, 18 (Binghamton, 1992)

Kelly = *The Blickling Homilies: Edition and Translation*, ed. and trans. by Richard J. Kelly (London, 2003)

Ker, N. R., *Catalogue of Manuscripts Containing Anglo-Saxon* (Oxford, 1957)

———, 'A Supplement to *Catalogue of Manuscripts Containing Anglo-Saxon*', *ASE*, 5 (1976), 121–31

Madan, Falconer, H. H. E. Craster, and N. Denholm-Young, *A Summary Catalogue of Western Manuscripts in the Bodleian Library at Oxford*, 7 vols in 8 [vol. II in 2 parts] (Oxford, 1895–1953; repr. with corrections in vols I and VII, Munich, 1980 (vol. II.1, 1922; vol. II.2, 1937; vol. III, 1895))

Morris = *The Blickling Homilies of the Tenth Century*, ed. by Richard Morris, EETS: OS, 58, 63, 73 (London, 1874–80; repr. as one volume, 1967)

Planta, J., *A Catalogue of the Manuscripts in the Cottonian Library Deposited in the British Museum* (London, 1802)

Pope = *Homilies of Ælfric: A Supplementary Collection*, ed. by John C. Pope, EETS: OS, 259 and 260 (London, 1967–68)

Scragg, D. G., 'The Homilies of the Blickling Manuscript', in *Learning and Literature in Anglo-Saxon England: Studies Presented to Peter Clemoes on the Occasion of his Sixty-fifth Birthday*, ed. by Michael Lapidge and Helmut Gneuss (Cambridge, 1985), pp. 299–316

Scragg = *The Vercelli Homilies and Related Texts*, ed. by D. G. Scragg, EETS: OS, 300 (Oxford, 1992)

Sisam, Kenneth, *Studies in the History of Old English Literature* (Oxford, 1953; repr. 1998)

Thorpe = *The Homilies of the Anglo-Saxon Church: The First Part, Containing the Sermones catholici or Homilies of Ælfric*, ed. by Benjamin Thorpe, 2 vols (London, 1844–46)

Tite, Colin G. C., *The Early Records of Sir Robert Cotton's Library: Formation, Cataloguing, Use* (London, 2003)

The Vercelli Book: A Late Tenth-Century Manuscript Containing Prose and Verse (Vercelli Biblioteca Capitolare CXVII), ed. by Celia Sisam, EEMF, 19 (Copenhagen, 1976)

Wanley, Humphrey, *Librorum ueterum septentrionalium* [...] *Catalogus Historico-Criticus*, vol.
    II of George Hickes, *Linguarum ueterum septentrionalium Thesaurus Grammatico-Criticus
    et Archaeologicus* (Oxford, 1705)

Warner, George F., and Julius P. Gilson, *Catalogue of Western Manuscripts in the Old Royal and
    King's Collections*, 4 vols (London, 1921)

Willard = *The Blickling Homilies: The John H. Scheide Library, Titusville, Pennsylvania*, ed. by
    Rudolph Willard, EEMF, 10 (Copenhagen, 1960)

INDEX

Note: where terms occur on a page in both the main text and footnotes, only the page is cited (e.g. '369', not '369, 369 n.20').[1]

---

[1] The editor gratefully acknowledges the invaluable service of the following in the final stage of indexing: Brian Baird, Hayden Butler, Krista Daniel, Michelle Davis, Douglas Fisher, Benjamin Flemming, Andrew Honore, Jaime Knowles, Julianna Nass, Zachary Price, and Rob Schannep.

STUDIES IN THE EARLY MIDDLE AGES

All volumes in this series are evaluated by an Editorial Board, strictly on academic grounds, based on reports prepared by referees who have been commissioned by virtue of their specialism in the appropriate field. The Board ensures that the screening is done independently and without conflicts of interest. The definitive texts supplied by authors are also subject to review by the Board before being approved for publication. Further, the volumes are copyedited to conform to the publisher's stylebook and to the best international academic standards in the field.

Titles in Series